ISBN 978-1-333-00846-8
PIBN 10449243

REPORT

OF THE

CENTENARY CONFERENCE

ON

THE PROTESTANT MISSIONS

OF

THE WORLD,

HELD IN

EXETER HALL (JUNE 9TH—19TH),

LONDON,

1888.

EDITED BY

THE REV. JAMES JOHNSTON, F.S.S.,

Secretary of the Conference;

AUTHOR OF

"A CENTURY OF CHRISTIAN PROGRESS," "OUR EDUCATIONAL POLICY IN INDIA;"
"ABSTRACT AND ANALYSIS OF VICE-REGAL COMMISSION ON EDUCATION,"
ETC., ETC., ETC.

VOL. II.

LONDON: JAMES NISBET & CO., 21, BERNERS STREET, W.
1889.

CONTENTS OF VOL. II.

PART IV.

MEETINGS OF MEMBERS IN SECTION.

PART IV.

MEETINGS OF MEMBERS IN SECTION.

CONTENTS.

MEETINGS OF MEMBERS
IN SECTION.

FIRST SESSION.

MISSIONARY METHODS.

(1) *THE AGENTS.*

(*a*) The Missionaries—their qualifications, mental and spiritual.

(*b*) Their training—should there be special training for Missionary service in addition to general education? If so, what should be its usual character? Should a knowledge of medicine be made a necessary branch of preparatory study?

(*c*) Should Missionaries be required to give evidence of their having acquired an adequate knowledge of a native language before being finally fixed in their appointment; and before marriage, now that the facilities of travel are so changed?

(*d*) Are special Missionary Professorships or Lectureships in colleges and theological seminaries in Christian lands desirable?

(Monday morning, June 11th, in the Lower Hall.)

Sir Rivers Thompson, K.C.S.I., C.I.E., in the chair.
Acting Secretary, **Rev. William Stevenson, M.A.**

Rev. Dr. Welch offered prayer.

The Chairman: Ladies and gentlemen,—I am aware that on Saturday last a public reception was accorded by Lord Aberdeen, the President of this Conference, to those who have come from afar to join us in these meetings; but I cannot forbear, in taking the chair this morning at the first select meeting of our Conference, from giving a cordial expression of greeting and welcome to Words of those who have come from distant lands as the representatives of distant Missionary Societies to join us in this great work. I feel, and I am sure I express the feeling of all who are here present, that however great the distances that may have separated us, or however different the nationalities that may affect us, we are all here **in the bond of one common spirit, in one common cause, to serve**

one common Master, and to carry out the commission of His parting words to those who should follow Him in all things.

My own sphere of connection with the Missionary enterprise— not as a Missionary exactly—though as far as I can recollect my service in India, I can recall with pleasure my interest in the development and working of Missions throughout that vast continent, my own connection with Missionary enterprise has been in that great **Recollections of** eastern dependency of our Sovereign; and I look back **Indian Missions.** with gratification to the fact that in many places of that vast continent in the North-west Provinces, and especially in Burmah, the work of Missions was chiefly carried on by Missionaries from Germany and America. I am present to-day rather as a listener and a learner than as an instructor in the special subjects of our Conference, and I will not detain you, at least at present, with any further words upon this subject. I will now call upon Mr. Barlow to read the first Paper.

PAPER.

1.—By the Rev. W. H. BARLOW, B.D. (Islington).

In addressing myself to such a subject as this, and in compressing my thoughts into an address of twenty minutes' length, there is much that must be taken for granted. For example, I do not refer **Truths and facts** to the cases of those who offer themselves for Missionary **assumed.** work as ordained labourers, or as men already equipped, educationally, for foreign service, because the *training* of such agents is not in question. And in regard to those candidates for Missionary enterprise whose position I am about to examine—these points must be considered as settled, viz., that they are themselves partakers of Divine grace, men of a holy life, of clear views as to the doctrines they hold and will be called upon to teach, of vigorous health, of energy and determination of character, aglow with love to souls, and able to show proof of activity and zeal in Christian work at home.

My subject is the training of men of the class so defined. It will be remembered that I speak as an attached member of the Church of England, but with a real and ever-deepening brotherly regard for the members of every Protestant and Evangelical institution, whose end and aim are to preach the simple Gospel of our Lord Jesus Christ.

I. The first point that I would press is the constant and thorough study of the Holy Scriptures. They are the sword of the Spirit, the first and great weapon on which the Christian warrior has to rely. Whatever other books he may or may not know, he must know this. It will be the beginning and end of all his teaching. Knowledge he **Study of** must have, sooner or later, of the systems of religion, **Scripture.** so called, which it will be his duty to attack and overthrow. But unless he possess a full, clear knowledge of the Word of God, the antidote to error will not be supplied by him as it ought to be.

In teaching others, it will not suffice to be negative and destructive; he must be positive and constructive also. He will invite the attention of those amongst whom he may dwell to this one Book, to the exclusion (at least in the first instance) of almost every other. Without the Bible in his hands, in his head, and in his heart, he would not be fitted to go at all. His appeal must be to it from day to day—to its authority, its disclosures of Divine truth, its invitations, its warnings, its hopes, its consolations. He should know it from cover to cover,—better, if it be possible, than the evangelist and pastor at home.

II. But there is a danger lest this constant handling of the Word of God and the growing knowledge of its contents should become in any degree professional. To avoid this unhappy result, the student must cultivate the habit of devout and humble and reverential study of the Word for its own sake, and for *Danger of professional study.* his own profit. To know the Bible for the good of others is one thing; to pore over it, and pray over it, as our own guide to life and peace is another. Therefore the habit of prayer both general (in regard to the Christian life), and particular (in regard to the opening of the Scriptures to the heart by the power of the Holy Spirit) should be diligently maintained. Time should be set apart each day for prayer,—public, social, and private. Every college lecture should be commenced with prayer. The atmosphere which a Missionary student breathes should be one of prayer. Men of prayer should alone be placed in authority; men of prayer should alone be teachers of God's blessed truth.

The dangers of a merely critical, or historical, or intellectual study should be pointed out. The end for which all reading of the Divine word is undertaken,—viz., "that the man of God may be perfect, thoroughly furnished unto all good works," should be constantly enforced. Only thus, as I conceive, can a real and lasting spiritual benefit be secured.

III. I plead, in the third place, for a critical study of at least Latin and Greek; and Hebrew should, if possible, be added. On many grounds a knowledge of the languages selected is most desirable. No one can be an accurate and accomplished theologian *Importance of* without them. No one can be an exact teacher of others *Latin, Greek,* without them. No one can attempt to translate the *and Hebrew.* Scriptures into other tongues—a most noble office—without them. And further, the study thus inculcated serves as an admirable test of capacity. For if a man cannot acquire a fair knowledge of the languages specified, with all the help of good grammars, dictionaries, and teachers, which may now be provided at home; what probability is there that he will be able to express himself in other forms of speech, when he has to fit himself for the task under very different surroundings of books and instructors?

Now and again a student has asked me why he should spend time over this or that department of classical work, inquiring of what use it was likely to be to him in the Mission-field. The answer is obvious. The direct use of the knowledge in question might be small ; but the indirect benefit arising from a habit of patient thought, investigation, and judgment, could not fail to be great.

Thus the effort made within college walls is not only essentially useful in regard to the acquisition of precise knowledge of the originals of the Word of God, but it becomes a touchstone of character and of power, whereby it is seen whether or not there is likely to be proficiency in learning, speaking, and writing difficult modern tongues.

IV. Concurrently with efforts in the direction just indicated, I strongly recommend the theory and practice of vocal music. Many countries to which Missionaries go have only *spoken* languages. The strangers find nothing reduced to writing. And whether they have to deal with districts where there is civilisation and a literature, or with those rude and barbarous races which have none, this is matter of common experience, that living tongues are best learned by those who go out with a well-trained ear. It might be a piece of playful exaggeration—but if so, it was one under which lay a great truth—when a former student wrote to me from China that it was rather dull work to pass his day saying " Ting, Tang," in a hundred different tones. My satisfaction, when I read this, was that he had been taught whilst in England to mark such distinctions. For if a man has not been disciplined to separate sound from sound, and tone from tone, at what a real disadvantage will he be placed when he comes to deal with a spoken language, where so much depends on catching the meaning of a speaker from the intonations of his voice. Confusion of sound leads to confusion of word and of idea. Failure, more or less real, is sure to follow.

Value of vocal music.

V. I beg earnestly to recommend a thorough study of the outlines of Church history. Human nature has been one and the same in all past ages, and will continue to be the same to the end. Satan adapts his temptations to each age and class with marvellous dexterity. But the conditions of Missionary work, and of the founding and developing of native Churches, repeat themselves constantly. And he who has watched the rise of false doctrine and heresies in one age, who has traced their causes, and observed their decline or removal, will be better armed for the work of his own. He will not be surprised or dejected at the appearance of tares among the wheat. From the experience of the past he will know, in some measure, what to hope for and what to fear in the present and future.

Church history a necessity.

VI. Closely connected with Church history is the question of doctrine. Speaking from the point of view of a member of the Church of England, I attach great importance to the study of the Articles, the Prayer Book, and the Homilies. Members of other denominations will necessarily regard with great respect the formularies of worship and the statements of Christian doctrine, that are in force amongst themselves. All these should be mastered from the man's own standing ground, and for his own benefit. My experience is that a diligent investigation of the ecclesiastical position which a Christian man or Christian

Study of theology.

teacher holds, does not lead him to intolerance towards others, but rather the reverse. The more carefully he inquires into doctrine as enshrined in documents with which he is textually familiar, the more ready he is to see the same points from other sides. Not, however, in such a way as weakly to surrender his own views, but so as to be able to state them with clearness to those who may differ from him.

Added to this, I earnestly commend the reading and analysing, with patient care, the works of recognised and standard divines, *e.g.*, our Hooker, Jewel, Butler, Pearson, and Paley. We have in our libraries a storehouse of works on theology, for which any nation and any Church may well be thankful. And even an introduction to these masterpieces may be of the greatest benefit to those who are to be sooner or later the leaders and guides of infant Churches in the things of God.

VII. Mingled with these heavier books and severer studies should be the biographies of eminent servants of God,—His Missionary workers in particular. A young subaltern, anxious to rise in his profession, studies the art of war in the lives of great commanders. **Reading of biographies.** A young musician, or medical student, or scientist, inquires into the lives and training, the failure and success, of those who have preceded him in the walk of life which he has chosen as his own. So should the future Missionary ever have in hand, perusing and reperusing them, the biographies of representative men in various ages of the Church of Christ. As far as possible, also, he should be informed of the present state of Missionary enterprise over the whole world. Brief pictures should be set before him, from time to time—and perhaps he may not be able at this stage to pursue the subject further—of the work going on outside the pale of that particular organisation to which he is attached. God spake πολυμερῶς καὶ πολυτρόπως in times past. And He does so still.

VIII. I hope to carry my hearers with me when I urge the advantage of instruction in the elements of surgery and medicine. I say the elements; for if a student is to make such advance as to be legally **The elements of surgery and medicine.** qualified to practise, then the time required (some four or five years) is too long, if, at least, the points already dwelt upon are to be enforced.

But a knowledge of the first principles of the healing art may be acquired, under good teaching, and with the experience which many hospitals will afford to Missionary students, in a couple of years. And the contrast between one who has such an elementary training as this, and one who has none at all, the difference in calmness and nerve as respects himself, and the difference in usefulness in regard to others, when sickness or accident may have arisen, is immense. It needs to be witnessed to be fully understood.

IX. Once more, I would urge the benefit of some kind of manual training. There are many opportunities for this kind of preparation—be it gardening, carpentry, printing, or the like. Anything that makes a man ready in an emergency, not with head only, but with hand **Manual training.** also, that gives him fertility of resource, self-reliance, power to grapple with difficulties—this must be a real benefit. We want, in the foreign field as in the home field, neither clumsy brains nor clumsy fingers. There is room in God's household for those whose spirit, mind, and body are alike trained, and that to the utmost point of perfection, for the work to be done.

It may be said that the chief points set forth above apply almost as truly and fully to the pastor at home as to the Missionary abroad. This may well be so; for what fits a man most thoroughly for work in England will fit him most completely for work anywhere else.

In conclusion, may I plead for as adequate and comprehensive a *Let training be* training as possible for Missionary candidates? For *comprehensive.* more than thirty years I have watched closely the career of men who have gone out to do this noble work. There are, of course, exceptions to every rule. But I am bound to say that, so far as my observation goes, those who have served most faithfully and remained at their posts most loyally, and rendered most conspicuous service in the vineyard of the Lord Jesus Christ abroad, are the men who went forth most thoroughly equipped by previous training for the enterprise to which they were called.

PAPER.

2.—BY THE REV. H. GRATTAN GUINNESS.

We have in this year 1888 reached an important crisis in Missions. A hundred years of Missionary labour lie behind us, and we gather at this International Convention from east, west, north, and south, to study its records, and to learn its lessons, that we may start with fresh knowledge, and renewed energy, for our still unreached goal—the evangelisation of the world.

We gather here to-day at the outset of this Convention, to consider the *qualifications* and *training* necessary for Missionaries. *Four questions* Four points are raised for discussion—the first as to *raised, two* mental and spiritual *qualifications;* the second as to *treated of.* special *training at home;* a third as to *training in the field;* and a fourth as to the advisability of establishing *Missionary lectureships* in our colleges. I take up here the first two of these points—the *testing* of candidates to ascertain their suitability for the work, and their *training* after acceptance, and before being sent out.

And firstly, as to the *qualifications* required. A Missionary is an ambassador for Christ to the heathen—or to any non-Christian people. It is of necessity, therefore, that he be a true Christian— an anointed man, one called of God to the ministry of the Gospel, and sent forth by Him. The Church cannot create such labourers; only He who made the world can make a true Missionary. No training can manufacture him—no human ordination can fit him for his work.

In considering the application of a candidate therefore, the question to be settled, is not, Can he be made into a Missionary? but, Has God called *Qualifications* him to be such? Have the necessary qualifications been be- *and* stowed? Only where this is the case can the training be of *disqualifications.* any use. If a man or a woman is to become a true and useful Missionary, there must first be not only genuine conversion, and sincere personal piety, but whole hearted self-consecration to the work of God, and a call to His holy service; including a strong inward sense of vocation, together with providential indications and adaptations. There must be mental and physical fitness for foreign service, and above all *the Spirit of Christ*, for no matter what other qualifications a man may have, he will never be a Missionary unless he is filled with Christ-like compassion for the lost, and with a burning desire to seek and save them. This should be the ruling feature of his character. With this almost any special talents may be utilised in Missionary service; without it, even the most brilliant are useless. If the heart be intensely set on the salvation of the perishing, love will teach ingenuity, and lead to painstaking and perseverance. Love will overcome all obstacles, and accomplish its object. The love of souls, the longing for their salvation, is one of the leading qualifications that should be looked for. But even the presence of this does not make testing needless, for there may co-exist with it physical, mental, or moral disqualifications.

On the other hand it should be noted that there are defects of a different character, which constitute no real disqualification, because training may, to a great extent, remedy them. Ignorance, lack of habits of study, or of experience, narrow-mindedness arising from want of intercourse with various classes of men, awkwardness of manner, and many and similar faults, indicate only a candidate's need of education and training, and should not stamp him as ineligible.

Secondly, we turn to the subject of the TRAINING of accepted candidates. The question stands in the prospectus, "Should there be special training for Missionary service in addition to general education?" The answer is, *Undoubtedly*. God always trains His instruments. Every true Missionary must be specially trained for his work, though not all in our schools. God has His own schools. They are very various, and some of them strange and severe. Moses was trained to be the deliverer and lawgiver of Israel, in Training of the courts and schools of Egypt, and in the mountain Missionaries. solitudes of Midian, for eighty years. David was trained to be king over Israel by years of spiritual experience, and by many dangers and toils. Daniel was trained for his wonderful prophetic office by his education and career in Babylon. Any training that we can give to a volunteer for Missionary work will form at best but a small part of a greater and more effectual training which God Himself bestows. We can do something to help, though not much. Let us see to it that what we do be done in harmony with that which is done by the great Master. Our Lord Himself carefully trained His Apostles for the great work He committed to them— the evangelisation of the world. His example is full of instruction for us.

Christ gave His disciples a threefold training—*theoretical, moral,* and *practical*. This was one of the principal works which He accomplished in the world. He prepared the instruments, He trained the men who should afterwards evangelise it. He chose them, called Theoretical, them, kept them, taught them, prayed with them and for moral, practical. them, impressed His Spirit upon them, breathed it into them : He corrected them, expanded their minds, exalted their conceptions, and purified their motives and purposes. Before He sent them forth into the world He kept them for over three years with Himself, during which He set before them His own glorious and sacred example. What a development of soul! What a training for service! "Follow Me," He said, "and I will make you to become fishers of men." "Take up your cross and follow Me." "Learn of Me." "Abide in Me."

Besides this He imparted to them priceless *instructions*. He taught them the nature of His Divine kingdom, His own personal character and claims, the nature of true holiness, the simplicity, spirituality and power of prayer, the excellence of humility, the essential duty and blessed results of self-sacrifice, the sin of hypocrisy and formality, the spirituality of worship, and the supremacy of the Word of God over all human traditions.

Hence it is evident that the development of *spiritual life* is the great thing to be aimed at in Missionary training. Woe to the Church if she neglects *this*, or gives it a secondary place! Her messengers will be of little use, for unspiritual agents can never accomplish spiritual work.

The calling, qualifying, and directing of the labourers thus commenced by our Lord was afterwards continued by the Holy Ghost through the Church. He sent forth Missionaries unto the Gentiles. The Apostolic Church acted directly under the Spirit's guidance. "As they ministered to the Lord and fasted, the Holy Ghost said, Separate Me Barnabas and Saul for the work whereunto I have called them." Then the Church fasted, prayed, laid their hands on those men and sent them away. That is *they* set apart and sent out those whom *God* had qualified and called. The Lord was with these Missionaries, and wrought glorious things through their instrumentality.

The Spirit's training.

We cannot improve on this example of the primitive Church. The Acts of the Apostles form the best guide-book for Missionary Societies and Missionaries. The impulse and the energy must always come from Heaven. Successful Missionaries are God-appointed men. We must pray for such; watch and wait for them; welcome them and utilise them as they are given. Yes, for the thousands of workers still needed in the Mission-field we must first of all *pray*—pray as Elijah prayed for the rain, fervently, effectually, incessantly till the prayer is answered; pray as the Church prayed for the promised Spirit before Pentecost.

Next, perhaps, in value to spirituality may be ranked *evangelistic gift and ability*. How is this to be developed? In the same way that skill in any other line is imparted—by instruction and practice. The preparation for all ordinary work consists in the actual doing of it, not merely gaining a theoretical knowledge of how it ought to be done. East London, for instance, with its vast and varied population, is an admirable training ground for Missionary students. It was this fact which led us, many years ago, to plant there our *Institute for Home and Foreign Missions*, from which, during the last fifteen years, many hundreds of Missionaries have gone forth. We have more than a million of the working classes in this quarter.

The value of *open-air preaching* as a preparation for Missionary work is exceedingly great. It cultivates aggressiveness, boldness, simplicity, directness, and earnestness of style, an extemporaneous delivery, and an interesting and striking manner of presenting Divine truths. The open-air preacher must first gather his congregation, and then hold it in spite of surrounding distractions, with nothing but the Open-air preaching. simple power of his words. He must suit his style to the roughest and shrewdest of his auditors. He must promptly meet objections, answer questions, and quiet disturbances, as he seeks to win an entrance for unwelcome truths in the hearts and minds of neglectors and rejectors of the Word of God. He has to face opposition, and endure at times contempt and shame for the Master's sake. It is not easy work, and there is nothing in it to foster conceit or gratify self-esteem. It is really hard, self-denying service, more analogous to that which would be required of a Missionary in the streets of India or China, than almost any other form of Gospel labour.

In addition to such experiences a Missionary needs of course *knowledge of various kinds*. Education of the mind *has its place*—though it be not the first place. The higher the mental qualifications of a man or woman (other things being equal) the better. But here it should be clearly stated that the nature of the case indicates that only a certain proportion of Missionary workers require what we call a thorough education. On the other hand, to send out ignorant and untrained men to undertake Missionary work were clearly folly. " Let such first be proved," is a dictate of common sense as well as a precept of Scripture. Paul said to Timothy as regards the truths of the Gospel which he had taught him, " The same commit thou to faithful men who shall be able to teach others also." Of all men a Missionary should be a man of general intelligence and fertile resources. Without a measure of cultivation it is impossible that he should be this. Knowledge is power, and Missionaries as a class should know something of everything. A Missionary Needful knowledge. has to travel, and should understand *geography*. He *may* perhaps have to build his *house*, to make his own *furniture*, to till or direct the tillage of his *garden*, the cooking of his *food*, to work the printing *press*, etc., etc. Knowledge even on such matters will therefore be valuable to him. He may be situated far from any skilled *physician*, and ought therefore to have at least some elementary knowledge of anatomy and physiology and of the use of simple surgical and medical aids. The more *grammatical* knowledge he has the better, for he will have to learn and use a foreign tongue, and possibly to translate into it the Word of God. ·He ought to know enough of *nature* to appreciate the works of God, and enough of *history* to perceive the background of Bible facts. As he has to teach Christianity, he should know something of the history of its planting, its early sufferings and triumphs, the origin and progress of existing apostacies, and the story of the Reformation. He should also be acquainted to some extent with the history of Modern Missions, including the lives of eminent Missionaries. But above all, he ought to be well acquainted with the Bible. That Book will have to be the companion of his loneliness, the guide of his perplexity, the support of his life, the instrument of his labours. It should be the chief subject of his study. His mind should be familiarised with the sacred text, with the evidences of its inspiration, and with the varied doctrinal and practical truths which it reveals. He needs to be rooted and built up in Christ, and established in the faith, and the aim should be to give him a firm grasp of the teachings of Scripture, and instruction, as far as possible, in the whole counsel of God.

It is the desire of this Conference that those who take part should contribute to the general stock the results of their experience, suggesting for the consideration of their brethren the chief practical conclusions to which they have been led. I may mention, then, that guided by the principles indicated in this paper, we founded, fifteen years *Experience of the Institute.* ago, in East London, an Institution for training and helping into the foreign field young men who desired to be Missionaries. We subsequently added a country branch of the Institute, and later on a Training Home for Deaconesses. During these fifteen years we have dealt with more than three thousand volunteers for Missionary work, have received on probation between eight and nine hundred, have trained and sent out five hundred Missionaries, and have now about a hundred students in the Institute. Our plan is to give the students, where they require it, preliminary secular instruction in the country branch, and then practical training in East London, including Missionary, Evangelistic, Linguistic and Medical departments. All our students receive from a qualified medical man the training of the ambulance corps, the results being tested by a public examination. The deaconesses, in certain instances, are sent for three months to live in hospitals, where maternity cases are treated. Students going to Africa receive instruction in the treatment of tropical fevers, and where there has been special fitness we have given students the advantage of a four years' medical course in the London Hospital. In almost every case these have become qualified medical men, and are now in the Mission-field. The time spent by students in the Institute has varied according to their age and needs. Our system has been an elastic one. We have tried to give to each the help he or she was capable of receiving, and to introduce each to the sphere in which we saw they could best do good Gospel service.

The results have not disappointed us. We have received men of all nationalities and all classes, as well as of all Evangelical denominations. We have trained them for all countries, and former students are now working in connection with between twenty and thirty Societies and Organisations, while many of them have founded new and independent Missions. As a rule they have done well, and given much satisfaction in the Missions they have joined. There are exceptions. Every rule has such, but we thank God on remembrance of the great majority of them.

Allow me, in conclusion, to summarise what I have said, and to emphasise certain points.

First, we agree most thoroughly with our highly esteemed and respected friend, Dr. Pierson, in his published opinion that "if we would largely increase the Missionary force we must in some way lessen the time and cost of preparing the average workman. . . . A most formidable barrier to the work of evangelisation is that, even where both men and money may be obtained it takes too long a time *Summary of Paper.* and too costly a culture to train the average workman; and this one obstacle often overtops all others, and is practically unsurmountable. . . . There ought to be a change in our ecclesiastical tactics; our system of training for the Mission-field must be more flexible, and more economical of time and money, or we cannot send workmen into the great world-field in adequate numbers."

Without any rigidly uniform system of training we must encourage every willing soul to do the work for which he or she is best fitted, and endeavour further to fit each for their proposed sphere of labour, and we must shorten and simplify the course of training.

Secondly, no candidates whatever should be accepted for training save spiritually-minded men and women, possessed of good health, good common sense, devotedness to God's service, and a Divinely indicated call to the work.

Thirdly, such persons should be thoroughly tested, and carefully trained. Their training should be adapted to develop the unworldly spiritual character which Missionary work requires. It should always be adapted to the individual case. All Missionary students should be trained in laborious and self-denying habits, and exercised in evangelistic work among our own lapsed masses, especially open-air preaching.

Lastly, every Missionary student should be furnished with the practical instructions of the Ambulance Corps, as to how to deal with the accident cases; while those who are preparing for labour in Central Africa and other parts of the world, where no qualified medical aid is to be had, should receive, in addition to other teaching, special medical instruction of an elementary and practical nature, and in those instances where there is marked aptitude and desire for it, the Missionary student should have the advantage of a full medical course.

DISCUSSION.

Rev. A. Merensky (Superintendent, Berlin Missionary Society): Brethren and sisters,—I have very little to say on the subject before us, because what I wanted to say has been stated in such an able way by the readers of the Papers. I have only to express my thanks that this very important subject has been brought before this Missionary Conference. Great stress has been laid upon the want of men and upon the want of money, but I believe that if the Lord would grant us the men the money would be forthcoming, and I believe that we shall not obtain the men who are fully up to the work if we do not follow the commandment of our Lord Jesus Christ when He said, "Pray the Lord of the harvest that He may send forth labourers into His harvest." If we bring this matter before Him in prayer, with all our power, the Lord will give us fit men for the purpose.

I beg to state that the leading German Societies have adopted Educated men. the principles mentioned by Mr. Barlow.

Rev. Arthur T. Pierson, D.D. (Philadelphia, U.S.A.): Mr. Chairman, and friends,—It was at Mr. Guinness's personal request that I consented to say a few words at this stage of the Conference upon this most interesting and vital topic. I have been placed in circumstances which have compelled me to give a great deal of time and study to the subject of the training of Ministerial and Missionary candidates, and I have a very deep and profound conviction that there are some radical errors that lie at the basis of our whole system of Missionary training.   I want especially to say that I believe that a prolonged course of merely literary and intel-

Mere study deadening. lectual culture is in most cases fatal to a thoroughly spiritual and evangelistic career; that the separation of a student from practical contact with human souls in direct spiritual work prepares him to go through the rest of his life with a chronic or at least intermittent chill, and if the chill happens to be accompanied with any fever alternating with it, it is only the fever of an intellectual enthusiasm, which has little or none of the glow of the Holy Spirit; that the effect of the college and even of theological Ministerial training is oftentimes simply to stimulate a worldly type of ambition, which sends men into the Christian field of Missionary or of Ministerial labour, ambitious to produce highly intellectual and elaborate literary essays which have little or none either of Gospel truth or of the aroma of the Gospel.   Therefore I wish to emphasise with all the intensity of conviction that which Mr. Guinness so admir-

Study and work. ably presented this morning, that there should be, together with intellectual training and college or seminary life, personal contact with the lost.   If a man is not ready to preach the Gospel anywhere, he is fit to preach it nowhere; and the reason why I would send men down into contact with the lowest classes is, that if they can reach the lowest they can reach the highest; but it does not always follow that if they can reach the highest they can reach the lowest.

Daniel Webster is said to have affirmed that there is always room at the top.   I venture to join issue with my distinguished American fellow-countryman by saying that that is the very place where there is not any room.   Society is a pyramidal structure, and there is room for only one stone at the top, but there is plenty of room at the bottom.   The broad basis of the pyramid of society is that to which we must first of all diligently, carefully, and prayerfully look.   If that be not a sound and well laid basis the whole pyramid of society is in danger of sinking and being destroyed.   Therefore I say that to send a man down to work

In the slums. in the slums among the outcast classes will test his consecration; it will test whether he is after souls, or after salaries and places and positions of emolument and of honour and distinction.   If a man can reach the lowest classes in our great cities successfully, so far as that test can be applied, he can reach that class in any community in which God may place him.

I would also emphasise open-air preaching.   I have never heard so much said as I think ought to be said in favour of extemporaneous modes of presenting the Gospel.   The fact is, dear friends, that you may put in an essay form a great deal that seems profound only because it is muddy.   If you

Open-air preaching. are obliged to speak without notes and extemporaneously, your train of thoughts must be so carefully laid out as that it can be correctly and distinctly preserved in your own memory, and in that case it will be likely to be plain enough and simple enough to be remembered by your audience.   But that which you may reduce to writing, or which a man may read from paper, may be neither very intelligible to himself nor to anybody that hears him.   Then again I wish to say—and I think every word ought to be weighed, and as far as possible we ought to speak very briefly on these topics—I believe that if a man is a thoroughly consecrated man it will go far to supply to some extent even the original lack of common sense; for we are told that we ^Consecration and love.^ shall have from the Holy Ghost the spirit of power and of love and of a sound mind. Brethren, there is no genius in the world that is equal to the genius of love; there is nothing that is so inventive; nothing that is so fertile; nothing that has such grand conceptions and inceptions of all noble spiritual work for Christ. I believe we ought to emphasise with Missionary candidates, what our blessed Lord said—" If any man will come after Me, let him deny himself, and take up his cross and follow Me." We have a kind of familiar and informal way of saying that life is full of daily crosses; but there is no Scripture for any such perversion of that phrase of Christ's. There is only one cross, and that is the cross of voluntary self-martyrdom, and he who is to become a winner of souls must take up once for all, and daily carry after Christ, that cross on which he is crucified unto the world and the world unto him.

Rev. W. McGregor (English Presbyterian Mission, Amoy): Mr. Chairman, and Christian friends,—I think there is entire unanimity in this meeting with regard to everything that has been said both by the readers of the papers and by the speakers as to the spiritual qualifications of those who should engage in Mission work. Experience ^Spiritual qualifications.^ in the Mission-field soon teaches anyone that it is no use to send there a man who himself has not yet fully learned what Gospel it is he is to preach to the heathen. He must himself have felt the power of the Spirit of God in his own heart: he must himself have known what it is to have sin forgiven, if he is to preach a Saviour or Redeemer to the heathen in China or anywhere else. With regard then to the spiritual qualifications of men we are all agreed.

With reference also to the value and the exceeding importance of practical training in work at home and in public speaking in the open air, I think all Missionaries will agree with what has been said. I feel, however, that mental training, mental culture, is of great importance. I believe that the Church at home ought to be taught and ought to know that she is not to rest satisfied with offering for Christ's work in the Mission-field that which she is not prepared to employ ^Intellectual qualifications.^ at home. The example of Christ, of the Apostles, and of the Early Church has been referred to. It is not unusual to speak of the Apostles as uneducated fishermen; but we have been reminded to-day that they were not uneducated; they themselves were trained by our Lord apart from what education they had before; and I think it would argue some hardihood in anyone to stand up and say that the writer of the Gospel of John was an illiterate and uneducated man. And apart from this, who was it that was sent to be the Apostle to the heathen? ^The Apostles.^ When God himself chose from the Apostles a man who was to be specially set apart to labour among the heathen, He did not choose any of those original Apostles who lived and laboured with our Saviour; their work lay chiefly among their own countrymen, and the man who was chosen to go forth into Heathendom, and there carry the message of salvation, to those who knew nothing of God, or Christ, was a man who had all the learning that Judaism could give him added to the culture that Greece could supply. The Apostle Paul was not an illiterate man, and I feel that for us here met together to say anything that might imply that the Church had discharged her duty to Christ, when she had sent forth those who were scarcely qualified to serve her best purposes at home, would be to make a very great mistake indeed.

With regard to labour in heathen lands, let me say it is not an easy matter to preach the Gospel to a heathen audience in such a way as to secure their attention, to make them really understand what you are aiming at, *Preaching to heathen difficult.* and carry home a conviction of the truths you wish to preach. To stand up in a crowd here in London, a chance crowd, gathered from all quarters, and to preach the Gospel effectively, so as to secure their attention, and to carry home the truths to their hearts, is not an easy matter; but it is still more difficult in a heathen land. You have there a people who do not understand the language you speak—I mean that the truths you speak of, are so entirely new to them that they invariably attach other senses than the correct one, to that which you are saying, and therefore it needs a man with adaptability —with great ability to realise the intellectual position of the people to whom he is speaking—to accommodate himself to them, and to realise in every way what *Training as a rule needed.* effect the words he is using will produce. Although an uneducated man, without much literary training, if he is a man of superior ability, and has the grace of God in his heart, may, under such circumstances, discharge his duty fully and effectually, yet *cæteris paribus* it is to be expected that the man who has had some literary training will, under such circumstances, be better fitted to adapt himself to the condition of those among whom he is placed. And I think that the experience of those who have laboured in heathen lands will go with me, when I say, that they have in their own observation seen that this is so—that the men who have had more of the preliminary training have greater versatility and adaptability in their intercourse with those with whom they come in contact in heathen lands.

But the thing that I feel in my heart most strongly is that which I have already alluded to, that for us as a Mission Conference, met together to speak of the work among the heathen and the men to be sent thither, to *Missionaries to be equal to Ministers.* say anything that should lead the Church of Christ to suppose that she has discharged her duty to Christ by sending forth men less qualified to preach the Gospel than those she employs to preach the Gospel to congregations at home, would be to make a very great mistake. It has been said that the great difficulty is the fewness of the Missionaries we have to send. With all this I fully agree, but our duty is not on that account to lower the qualifications of the men who are to be sent. We are to seek to rouse the Church of Christ to realise the claim that Christ has upon His Church to send forth her best men, and to send them forth in large numbers. Christ gave Himself for the Church, and died for our salvation; shall we deny Him the best we have to offer?

Rev. J. Hudson Taylor, of the China Inland Mission (after a short prayer): I fully believe, my Christian friends, in the words of the last speaker, that we must not lower the standard of Missionary service. I think we want to raise it immensely. I believe in the Holy Ghost, and in the power of the Holy Ghost. We have been too much satisfied with men who have not had to a large degree the power of the Holy Ghost. I speak for myself. Many years I spent in spiritual work in China, in which I was oftener hungry *The Spirit's power and prayer.* than well fed, oftener thirsty than overflowing. We want a higher standard of Holy Ghost power in all our Missionary servants if they are to do the work of the Church effectually. Then again, we want to have more belief in the power of prayer. We have been reminded of this again and again. Let us go to the right quarter for our Missionaries. Not to the plough or to the anvil, not to the university or the forum, but to the great Head of the Church. "Pray ye therefore the Lord of the harvest that He will thrust forth labourers into His harvest;" and depend upon it He will select the right men and the right women. He knows where they are, and who they are, and it is at the peril of the Church if she refuse them. And we must not spoil them when we have got them. I have sometimes taken a piece of chalk pencil, and have thought that I would improve the point, and have tried to do it, at the expense of breaking the chalk off. There are many spoiled by training; the training was not training that helped them, but training that injured them. I have met with many Missionaries, and that not merely in one land, who have regretted the loss of fervour and zeal that they experienced during their academic course. We must not despise academic training. Thank God we have in **Spoiled or improved by training.** the China Inland Mission some noble men who have not been spoilt, but improved by it; but I do think we want to take into account that *all* are not improved by it.

When the Holy Spirit comes down upon a man and gives him a sense of His call, we want to set ourselves to ascertain, "Is it a real call?" This should be the first point. Mr. Guinness has spoken of some of the disqualifications for Missionary service. I do not believe that those who are called have these disqualifications. I should rather think that their having these disqualifications was evidence of a want of call. If there is evidence of the call we have very few other questions to ask. Let me say briefly that the world is just where it was when the Lord Jesus Christ gave His command. Missionary work is not one whit harder now than it was then, and not one whit easier now than it was then. The Holy Ghost's power sufficed then, and nothing else will suffice now. Nothing more is needed, and if the Lord Jesus should call by His Spirit the most illiterate man and send that illiterate man forth, He can do a mighty work by him, perhaps because he is illiterate, and God Himself will have the glory. God will not give His glory to another, and we must take care that we do not do anything that will rob God of His glory.

And when we have found men who are really called of God, let us see that they give evidence of the call at home. We do not put down, in our selection of candidates for China, any particular level of education or ability **Divine call, evidence of.** that men must have, but we do look out and see that they are men whom the Holy Spirit has used in soul winning. A voyage across the Indian or Pacific Ocean will not make a man a soul winner. If God has used him for soul winning at home, my experience is, that He will be a soul winner abroad, and that if He has not used him at home, He will *not* use him abroad. Therefore it is so important to have proof of the call in the work that has been done at home.

One word with regard to the Medical qualifications. Twenty years ago my own opinion was very much what has been expressed here, that all Missionaries should have a limited measure of Medical training. I have now come to the opposite opinion. I think it is a profound mistake to give a person just a smattering of Medical knowledge. I have seen many good Missionaries spoiled, and very few really benefited **Medical training to be thorough.** by it. Let us have Medical Missionaries. God will lay His band upon them when they are fully qualified, if you will ask Him. You will not have the expense of training them; God will train them, and give you plenty of them, if you will only have them, and put them in the right position.   God will answer your prayer with regard to Medical Missionaries, but let us not spoil a good evangelist by making a poor doctor of him.   There are others who wish to speak, and I will only say that I would with all my heart seek to impress upon our dear friends present the supreme importance of having the guidance of the Holy Spirit as to the selection of the workers; and when the Holy Ghost gives the call, again I say, it is at our peril if we refuse the men or spoil them.

Rev. G. E. Post, M.D. (Syrian Protestant College, Beyrout): As a Medical Missionary of twenty-five years standing I want to give my emphatic confirmation to the last sentiment with regard to Medical men.   I am opposed
No "quacks."   *toto cœlo* to sending quacks to a Mission-field.   We want either well-educated Missionaries, or else men that make no pretence to know anything of medicine.   I have seen the evil of it.   I have studied the question for twenty-five years, and I say again send us intelligent Medical men, or else send us men that make no pretence to Medical science, and have no intention of carrying out Medical practice.   There was one remark made by a previous speaker to which I must take exception from the practical standpoint.   If I understood him rightly he said that the qualification of music is an aid to acquiring a foreign language.   I can only appeal to my personal experience.   I cannot sing a note, but I delivered a lecture in the Arabic language after being five months in the country, and I preached an extempore sermon at the end of nine months.

With regard to the general question of qualification, I am on both sides of that question.   I am quite prepared to defend to the last all the positions taken up here.   I believe we want men of the grade of city
Want men of all grades.   Missionaries, and street preachers; I believe we want farmers and blacksmiths; I believe we want men who are simple practical printers, and who carry out a knowledge of type-setting, type-casting, cutting on wood and steel and copper, and electrotyping, and along with these things the Spirit of Christ.   For every man who enters Missionary work, must be imbued with the Spirit of Christ.

I believe we want men who will engage in translating, but I differ from the sentiment uttered here that every Missionary should sooner or later expect to be
Abroad as at home.   a translator.   I believe it is a waste of time and talent to expect that; just as it would be a waste in this land.   We do not expect everybody here to be a Greek and Hebrew scholar; we do not want every Minister here to be a good translator of the Scriptures; we do not expect him to understand every intricacy of Biblical geography and archæology.   There are some whose gifts are simply evangelistic; there are some whose gifts lie in translating; there are some teachers and some preachers, and some who have the gifts of healing.   We want them all.   We want to fill the Mission world with just such candidates as you want in the Church at home.   There is room for them all.   No man can say, "I have no call because I am not an effective street preacher."   No man can say, "I have no call because I am not an effective extempore speaker."   No man can say, "I have not a call because I am not a speaker at all."   He can go with his deft fingers and place the type in order and do a work in printing which shall perhaps be greater than that of the greatest of living preachers.

I want this one thought to be imprinted upon the minds of my brethren and sisters here, that there is room in the Mission-field for every talent, so that it be consecrated by the Spirit of prayer and by the inspiration of the Holy Ghost.

Rev. H. Grattan Guinness: I wish to utter just a simple sentence by way of explanation. It has been our privilege to send out at least one hundred Missionaries to Africa. Some of these have gone into the centre of that great country, one thousand three hundred miles from the coast. These Missionaries had *nolens volens* to practise medicine to some extent; that is to say they had to give certain remedies in cases of fever, and to take them too, and to attend to certain simple surgical cases. For example, Captain Hoare who is connected with the London Missionary Society, and who was trained in our Institute, had on one occasion even to perform amputation to save life, and he had to do it with a penknife. It was an amputation of the arm, and was successful. Now in order to help these Missionaries—I am referring not to China, but to Africa,—it is our practice, and we found it very useful, to give to every one of our students, first of all, special instruction in connection with the Ambulance Corps, which is a very simple thing and a thing that every one would be the better for. Then we give special instruction to our women Missionaries. We send them to hospitals for training in treating maternity cases. Many of them, in times of Nature's trial, their own or others, may be in isolated positions, far away from Medical help. Then we give full Medical instruction to certain Missionaries—a complete Medical course.

[margin: Adapt training to circumstances:]

Rev. L. Dahle (Secretary, Norwegian Missionary Society): I must begin by asking your forbearance, since I am at a disadvantage in speaking in a foreign tongue. The subject we are discussing is the qualifications of Missionaries for their work. The subject seems to me to fall under three heads. There are some qualifications that I would call natural; others that are qualifications of grace; and a third class consist of qualifications to be acquired by study.

[margin: Natural and acquired qualifications.]

As to the FIRST class, I think we have to lay a good deal of stress on these qualifications of nature. Under this class I would reckon a good strong frame—a good physical condition of life. It is no use sending out men that you have to send home again next year. It is no use sending out men for whom you have to send a nurse or a Medical man to attend them by the next mail. We want men who can rough it, men who can stand years of work in a tropical country.

Having been a Missionary myself continuously for eighteen years without going home, in a country like Madagascar, I have had some experience on this point, But not only do we want this class of men ; we go in for men of energy. Learning is a most useful thing, but energy is quite as useful, and quite as necessary for a Missionary. I have seen men sent out to Mission work, very pious men, and when you saw them you thought you saw living saints. But they were not successful. You cannot go with folded hands through a heathen country as a Missionary, and only look up towards heaven. You will have to look round about you sometimes, and have tact and common-sense at your fingers' ends, or you will be worth nothing. A very important thing in a Missionary is that he should have the ability to attract people, and not frighten them. That is a special gift that cannot be acquired if you have not got it by nature. You see it sometimes when a man goes into a house where there are a lot of children. They will go to one man and not to others. They will feel attracted by one man and not by others. You cannot tell exactly what the special feature is in the man who attracts them—but so it is, they are attracted by one more than by the other Now the Missionary ought to be, above all, an attractive man to the natives.

[margin: Saints without energy.]

[margin: Attractive power.]

Then if we turn to the SECOND class of gifts, the gifts of grace, I
think we all agree that if a man has not got the Spirit from above,
the unction from the living God, if he has not felt in his own
Gifts of   heart that burning love to God that makes him willing to
grace.   sacrifice himself entirely for the sake of God, he ought never to
leave his native shore, and go abroad as a Missionary.

As to the THIRD class, I am glad to find my opinions stated in the first
paper read to us this morning, at least in all the essential points, and also
by some of the later speakers. But there are some few points on which I
differ a little from them. There is no doubt that the Apostles were sent
                out with a training which we should not call very perfect from
Apostles and   our college standpoint, but then they had quite a different
their Mission. Teacher from the teachers we have in our colleges—with
all respect for those learned men. And not only that, but they had
the Spirit of Pentecost in a fuller manner, different in degree from what
we can expect now, and different in kind, although it is the same. They
had not to go to foreign lands and learn a foreign tongue. They had to
work within the Greek and Roman world. They lived in that world,
and they knew a great deal beforehand what we now have to acquire
by study.

Finally, they were sent out as Apostles; those whom we can now send
out are only Evangelists. With regard to the curriculum of education, I
agree generally with the first speaker, but let me say that I would not lay so
much stress on the knowledge of the ancient languages. This is no doubt a
                very useful thing. I shall always be thankful to God for the
Uneducated   little smattering I have had of these languages. I have never
Missionaries.   found the knowledge to be too much in the Mission-field. You
always feel that you want much more than you have got; but still I have
known Missionaries who have never seen a Greek, Latin, or Hebrew
Grammar, and yet I know a case in one station where there are four
or five thousand Christians, and a large number of school children, all the
result of men of that character. That proves that it is not quite necessary
under all circumstances to have a knowledge of the ancient languages. It
depends on the position you intend to give a man in the Mission-field.
There is a German proverb to the effect, that you want all kinds of nets for
                all kinds of fish, and I believe that is true. If you were going
Adapt men   to place a man in a situation as a college tutor, or if you were
to their work. going to send him to take part in the translation of the Bible
into a foreign tongue, or if you sent him out to fight with Mohammedans
or Jews or learned Brahmans, then he would certainly want a fair amount
of knowledge; but if he is to work as an ordinary Missionary, among what
the Germans would call the Naturvölker—people whose minds are like a
tabula rasa on which nothing is written—he can do fairly well with a
smaller amount of knowledge.

Rev. J. Murray Mitchell, LL.D. (Free Church of Scotland): I venture
to think there is no essential difference on any important question that
has this day been brought forward. I certainly quite agree with every
word that has been said so fervently by my friend Dr. Pierson and many
others, in regard to the spiritual qualifications of Missionaries. Unless
those spiritual qualifications exist, the man is not called of God to be a
Missionary; and we ought to see, as far as human beings can judge, that a

man is a Spirit-taught man. That must be regarded as absolutely essential. By all means, test Missionaries by bringing them into contact with home work. We heartily concede that many a devoted man has gone forth without any college training, who has done noble work for God. It is the same abroad as it is at home. Multitudes are labouring with **Devoted but uneducated.** heart and soul in the home field, who have never been at college; but, being taught by the Spirit of God, they are largely blessed. I think the qualifications for Missionaries abroad are very much the same as those that are necessary for Ministers and workers at home. I cannot draw a distinction.

But that being granted most heartily and fully, I think that, when we can get a man with mental training, there is a higher work that he is qualified to do in the foreign field. I cannot forget that Moses, " learned in all the wisdom of the Egyptians," was employed by God to do the mighty **Educated and devoted.** work committed to him. When I name Paul—to whom reference has been made—Luther, Melanchthon, Calvin, Knox, Whitefield, Wesley, am I not mentioning the noblest names that are contained in the history of the Church? But every one of them was a man of high education. And I remember, too, that John Wesley lays it down, that his preachers should be thoroughly trained in logic. He was himself thoroughly trained in logic, and I venture to say that his preaching told more in consequence of that than it would have told if he had not been versed in logic, and had consequently reasoned badly.

Now let it be remembered that in such a land as India (I speak of the field which I know best) we have men of all grades of society, from savages up to men of the acutest intellects and the highest civilisation. **Variety of work in India.** Therefore we require various classes of men to deal with them. I would not send a man, however earnest, however devoted, who had received no mental training, to argue with a Mohammedan Maulavi, or a highly-trained Brahman. I should think that I was doing injustice to the cause of truth. It would be like sending a man into the battlefield without his armour.

Then be it remembered that the translation of the Word of God is a most important, but a most difficult work. I have been engaged in it; and no work ever tried my head more than that of getting the very best expressions supplied by the native language for the truths **Translation of Scriptures and writing books.** which the Spirit of God has given in the Word. Are you then to send out men who have no mental training to do that work? God forbid, I say. Then, books are to be written. I have myself written not a few, and I believe if I had not gone to college I could not have written so many; at all events, they would not have been fitted to do the good that I trust they are doing. Therefore, dear friends, we can all agree that there are different positions in the heathen field, for which different intellectual qualifications are required. Spiritual qualifications are absolutely essential in every case; but in many cases—I do not say in all—college training, thorough, and the highest available, is also to be sought.

Mr. Frederick Freeman: I should like to ask one question. Dr. Pierson and Mr. Guinness have both stated the need of getting men into the field without delay and without cost. I am engaged in business, and I know many labourers who are earning their living in mercantile pursuits, and labouring in the Gospel in the open air at the East End and elsewhere, who would long to be fishers of men in foreign lands, but they do feel that it would be a blessed thing if they could abide in their calling and labour in the Gospel too. When one goes fishing one does not like to go where there is a rod at every yard of the stream, but one prefers to go to the preserved portions. Just one word about training. When I was brought to the Lord, a quarter of a century ago, my first thought, after I knew that my sins were forgiven,—the first phrase of Scripture that came to me, within half an hour, was this, "The earth shall be filled with the knowledge of the Lord, as the waters cover the sea." That was more than a quarter of a century ago. I was in a merchant's office when I was brought to the Lord. I afterwards went to Oxford, and I learned a good many things and took a degree, and four years in Oxford knocked out all thought of labouring in the Mission-field. It has taken ten or twenty years of street preaching to bring the desire back again.

Trade and Mission work.

I know that in tropical climates like India and China, it is impossible to labour in your calling unless you are a specialist; labour is so cheap. But this is not the case in many countries, like South America for example. I am thinking now especially of Roman Catholicism—of that land of Roman superstition—and I say that a man who is a printer, or a railway engineer, or a bank clerk, and who is living for Christ in the midst of a Roman Catholic people, will find that the grace of God is not limited to the priesthood. Let me only throw out this one thought. You know that three hundred years ago to-day the Spanish Armada was crossing the Bay of Biscay, delayed by contrary winds, while England was gathering together and asking God to deliver us. Do we not remember that circumstance?

Grace not limited to priesthood.

Now, dear friends, we are in danger to-day of a far greater invasion of Roman Catholicism and Ritualism—a far more desperate invasion than that was. The end of the Spanish Armada was that England went into the new world and won it from the Spaniards. Now let us carry the Gospel of the Lord Jesus into this new world which is to this very day under the superstition of Rome.

Rev. E. W. Syle, D.D. (American Church Missionary Society, from Japan): One of the prominent features of these meetings is that they are Conferences, and that we compare notes. All that I have to contribute this morning will be one or two remarks in confirmation of some things that have been said by others. It is noteworthy that when the Gospel is sent to a people who have a literature and training, and philosophy, and various systems of false religion,—it is noteworthy that among them the early heresies develop themselves in their early order. First there is Arianism, and then Sabellianism. I shall not go into the reason of the case. Now that great doctrine of the Trinity does challenge the thoughts of men,—the pride of intellect and so on. I think this will be found to be the fact with regard to India; I know it is with regard to China and also Japan. Now I would suggest that part of the knowledge which every Missionary should have, who has any intellectual training given to him, is the early history of what has taken place in the Church and in the world from the beginning. Thus he would be forewarned and forearmed. I remember a Missionary coming to a meeting with the rest of us, and telling us that his Chinese teacher had said a beautiful thing, namely, that the Father was the great God manifesting Himself in one way, the Son manifesting Himself in another, and the Spirit in another. That dear good Missionary did not know that that was Sabellianism; but he ought to have known it, and he

Heresies in foreign fields.

Need of knowledge of Church history.

would have known it if he had had a training in the history of the Church from the beginning.

Then there is another point which I must emphasise, the terrible calamity (there is no other word for it) of sending out a Missionary who has to be sent home again. The lack of certification before sending out a Missionary is one of the most deplorable things in the past history of our Missionary experience. The Missionary goes out, he labours awhile and he finds himself mistaken; his heart fails him, and, after lingering a little while to see whether he can recover himself or not, returns home. There has been a loss of a year of time and a year of expense. After coming and staying, he returns home an unhappy and dissatisfied man. He does not like to blame himself, he generally blames the Society. What the heathen think of him you can guess. They cannot understand it. I have said this only for the purpose of emphasising the great importance of certifying ourselves that those whom we assist to go forth are indeed those whom the Lord hath called. *Looking back from the plough.*

Then allow me to emphasise one other fact. We want all kinds of character in the Mission-field—Christian character; and we want all kinds of talent—sanctified talent. We want the leader: what would the China Inland Mission have been without Mr. Taylor? We want the translator: what would the Chinese Bible have been without Dr. Morrison? We want the pioneer of schools: what would the education of India have been without Dr. Duff? We want the Christian teacher; we want the Christian nurse; we want the colporteur; we want every man to whom God has given his talent, whether it be one, or two, or five, or ten, to exercise his gift and be content with it. There is trouble, dear friends, and the trouble is this, that men are not content with the gifts which God has given them. I knew one Missionary who would have made an excellent colporteur; he had active habits, he could learn a few words in the native language, and when he sold a Bible or a tract he could commend it, though it might be with a very imperfect pronunciation and with none of that musical tone which the Chinese language requires. But that was not enough for him; he must have his own school and his own hospital, and this, that, and the other; he must be a full-blown Missionary in every respect—in other words, a private in the army but with all the privileges of a general. *Content to use the gifts bestowed.*

Now, while we want men of all characters, we want men who are able to meet with and deal with the minds of acute and learned natives. We want men of training in logic, to which reference has been made, and training in the previous history of the operations of the human mind, so that, as has been remarked, when they return they may not be ashamed. One word more, dear friends. I see before me an ornamentation—it is the chrysanthemum of Japan. We have borrowed many artistic things from Japan, things that are now accepted on all hands. I must not branch out into this subject, which is one of significance; but bear in mind that at this moment Japan is like a nation born in a day, demanding a religion, because they have found that even a morality without a religion has no basis that will stand. *Need of basis for morality.*

Rev. C. H. Bell, D.D. (Cumberland Presbyterian Church Board of Missions, U.S.A.): I merely wish to emphasise one point with regard to the last item in our morning's programme: "Are Special Missionary Lectureships in schools and theological seminaries in Christian lands desirable?" I wish to say, I would have a Professorship, not a mere Lectureship. Let there be men appointed to our colleges, filled with the spirit of Missions; let them instruct the youth, and then select the best men in our seminaries and send them *Professorship of Missions.*

abroad; that is, of course, if the Holy Spirit has called them. We want our best men in the foreign field. In America the call comes to us even from the Western border, "Send us your best men; keep your poor brethren at home, but send your strongest and most powerful workers to the foreign field."

Rev. J. A. Taylor (Baptist Foreign Missionary Convention of the United States): Mr. Chairman, ladies, and gentlemen,—It affords me no ordinary pleasure to stand in this august body and say a word in the interests of the spread of the Redeemer's kingdom in the world.

I should not attempt to intrude upon you with any thought of mine, were it not for the fact that I represent a denomination or a people in this Conference who until recent years have appealed to historians in vain for a place in their records, and have had to rely on the recording angel for a place in the Book of Remembrance. As a coloured Baptist of the United States, I am here to represent the coloured Baptist Foreign Convention. They did not send me here because they thought I was able to give any instruction, but to receive information. After God had so wonderfully blessed us, we have begun to feel that He had preserved us and bestowed His mercy upon us, that we might be instruments in His hands of developing that grand country of Africa.

A coloured pastor.

I now come to the subject of discussion—Missionary methods and Missionaries, their qualifications, mental and spiritual. I have been very much impressed with one or two sentences uttered by the first speaker, Mr. Barlow, who spoke of having Missionaries trained in one or more branches of industry. We have opened a Mission Station in West Central Africa. We have been labouring among the people there for about eight years. We have made mistakes, like all other young Missionary Societies. But as regards the idea advanced by Mr. Guinness, we are thoroughly satisfied that the first thing necessary is a call of God and a consecration to Missionary work. Without that, we feel that nothing added by intellectual training will ever make a man fit to labour among the heathen people. We are not satisfied with requiring the intellectual qualifications. These are the things that I have been sent to gain information about at this Conference, with its varied experience, that I may be enabled to carry it back to our young organisation, which is beginning to add its little drop to the great ocean of Missionary work, that it may be an humble instrument in the hand of God of bringing that long neglected people out of darkness into light and from the power of Satan unto God.

Qualifications desired.

Rev. James Calvert (Wesleyan Missionary Society, from Fiji Islands): I was greatly gratified in hearing a Medical Missionary who has been in the work for a long time commend this full qualification for that important work. But I happen somehow or other to have had a different experience from his, and I thought that variety might be helpful to us.

I was much surprised to hear Mr. Hudson Taylor, a man of such vast experience, carrying on such an extraordinary work, seeming to pooh-pooh a trifling Medical knowledge; and then I was afraid that some might be sitting down under the terrifying epithet of "quacks" that was given to those who had not much knowledge. I thought that must mean myself. More than fifty years ago, when I was designated in London for a Foreign Mission, I thought it well to get a little smattering of Medical knowledge. That was all that I could possibly gain, but I resolved to get as much as I could, and I begged a practical surgeon to be kind enough to come to my study

A little Medical knowledge useful.

where I had asked other students who were designated for Mission work to join me, to give us some plain practical instructions with reference to disease and medicine. He did so ; and we obtained knowledge and a supply of medicines, books, tooth-drawing instruments, and other things, which were invaluable.

We went abroad to a field where there was no Medical man within twelve hundred miles, and we were sometimes compelled to act whether we knew or not ; and we found that this small smattering of information that we had gained in no technical way, but just in a practical form, was of the utmost advantage to us. Of course many a time we had to guess, but better men than we have to guess a good deal, and I am thankful to say that we often guessed right. God blessed us in our Medical department; and I hope that all Missionaries who go where there is no doctor at all will get as much knowledge as they possibly can.

Rev. T. W. Drury (Principal of the Church Missionary College, Islington) : I think that one point on which we must be all agreed this morning, is that a Foreign Missionary must be pretty well an all round man. If we can manage to get our Missionary students to come up to all the requirements of this platform, we shall do very well indeed. But that is just where we are apt to make a mistake. I do not for a moment think that any Missionary Society has aimed too high in the education and training of its candidates. I will not give way *Aim high.* on that point one jot or tittle. But I think that we may make the mistake of attempting to apply that training to each and every case.

I think the practical suggestion with regard to that point is this, that all who are placed under training for Missionary work ought to be prepared, wherever they are being trained, to go out at any time for whatever work they may seem to be best fitted. When one enters into training in a college, it should not be with a certainty that he is to go on to the conclusion of the regular training course ; but he should be ready to go forth at such a time, and to such work, as those who have experience in training him *Ready at any* think best. I want to refer to one point in particular. We have *stage.* heard this morning hints thrown out,—and I am sure they are hints that must have touched the heart of many here,—with regard to those who are being trained for Missionary work ; I mean that the studies to which we put our young men have a decided tendency to deaden their spiritual life, and unfit them to go out as hearty, enthusiastic workers for Christ to the heathen. I want to speak to that point. I do not for a moment deny, and I have had some experience in this matter, that there is a danger. But I wonder in what position you can place a young man where there will not be that danger. If you send out young men night after night to preach to crowds in London, you place those young men in very great danger with regard to their spiritual life, especially if you send them out unfitted and untrained for it, teaching others when they need a great deal more teaching themselves. I am not speaking against that for a moment, but I am asking where can you put a young man in these days without placing him in great danger? I have seen a great deal of this deadening process. I acknowledge it. But what I say is this : that those who are engaged in the training of these young men must not be disheartened, and must not give in. It need not be so. We need not lower the training which we give our men. We need not take them away from their studies, and send them out in a half-trained condition, simply because in some cases the training seems to have that effect. May I tell you what a student of mine said to me? I said to him : "How is it that the work has been done?" And he answered : "By prayer and pains." He said *By prayer and* that he had found sometimes when sitting at his work that he was *pains.* not holding that communion with his God that he desired to hold, that then he would stop and kneel down and hold communion with God, and then go to work again, perhaps at a Hebrew grammar or some stiff work of another kind. "Thus," he said, "I regained my communion with God, and went on, and was refreshed in my work."

I believe there are two safeguards. First, a very great care as to the devotional life of the college; and, secondly, keeping the students in touch
The safeguards. with outside work. If these two things are carefully guarded, and if the danger is put before the students, I believe that the very danger we anticipate may be turned into a vantage ground, and may be a means of drawing our students nearer to God by making them feel their weakness in this respect, and thus making the very hardest study a means of blessing.

Lastly, our training is not only training, but it is testing. We have been speaking as though the training were merely training for work. Is it not far better, as I have heard it said, to burst a gun at Birmingham than to burst it out on the Afghan frontier? Of course it is. And you may depend upon it that those men who are in the field, and are saying:
A testing time. "My college studies and my college training deadened my spiritual life, and drove all the Missionary spirit out of me," are the men who had not stood the test. [*A voice:* "They should have stayed at home."] Precisely. In this very trial we have a good way of testing whether they have real spiritual power to remain and stand firm to the end.

Rev. Dr. Syle closed with prayer.

MEETINGS OF MEMBERS
IN SECTION.

MISSIONARY METHODS.

(2) MODES OF WORKING.

(a) The position of Foreign Missionaries as the chief agents in evangelistic and school work in heathen countries, and as the leaders and trainers of natives.

(b) The relation of itinerant to settled Missions.

(Monday afternoon, June 11th, in the Annexe.)

Chairman, Rev. John Stoughton, D.D.
Acting Secretary, Mr. B. Broomhall.

Rev. J. F. Gulick offered prayer.

The Chairman: My Christian friends,—It gives me very great pleasure to meet you this afternoon. I think this Conference is likely to be productive of very great and important results ; but very much will depend upon the manner in which these sectional meetings are conducted.

Looking at the Conference as a whole, it appears to me that there are two great objects which we have in view. The first is to stimulate Missionary feeling, and the second is to make practical observations as to the mode in which the work is to be carried on. I think we may compare the former, the production of Missionary feeling, to getting up the steam, and the sectional meetings, I apprehend, may be regarded as intended to improve the organisation, or the machinery, as much as possible. During the many years that our Societies have been at work, a great deal of information has been gained as to the best mode of dealing with those whose spiritual welfare we are seeking to accomplish. I see a variety of subjects which are specified for consideration at these meetings; and with very great propriety the meetings to-day have reference to Missionary methods as they regard agents, and Missionary methods as they regard modes of working. I cannot say that I have ever had any practical knowledge of the working of Missions, but I spent, some years ago, a little time in Syria, and there I was brought into contact School work. with American brethren who are seeking the evangelisation of those who have been brought up in the religion of Mohammed, and I found how very much importance the brethren attached to schools; and I gathered from the opportunities I had of questioning my dragoman, who went with me through the desert, that the schools were indirectly the means of conveying Christian knowledge to the parents of the children; for the man told me that after his boys had been to school at Cairo morning and afternoon, when he came home he heard from them a great deal about the New Testament, and so he had picked up an amount of information at which I was very much surprised.

Then, again, I thought, when I was at Damascus, "Now, if I were a Missionary, what should I do here?" I walked into the bazaars and saw vast multitudes of people, and I felt what a difficulty it must be to preach to these people, and how important it is to get hold of the children, and to train them up in the elements of Christian truth. So I am very glad that these two things are to be brought together, and that they are to be considered this afternoon in relation to each other. I hope they will be very seriously considered, and I hope I shall be forgiven for throwing out this practical observation,—that as this morning a good deal no doubt has been said with regard to agents, we had better not enter into any questions with regard to agents, but confine ourselves strictly to this matter of the modes of working.

There are to be three Papers read,—one by the Rev. Dr. Schreiber, the second by the Rev. J. Hudson Taylor, and the third by the Rev. J. Hesse. I will now call upon Dr. Schreiber to read his Paper on "The influence of German colonisation on Missions."

[NOTE.—Dr. Schreiber's able and interesting paper, instead of dealing with the "modes of working" by Missionary Societies under the new conditions of German colonisation in heathen lands, took a wider sweep, outside the lines laid down for discussion in this section. We have therefore taken the liberty of placing it under the head of "The Relations of Commerce and Diplomacy to Missions," where it would have been placed at first if there had been time and opportunity for the distinguished Author to confer with the Committee or Secretary beforehand. This will prevent the interruption of the continuity of the discussion, and preserve a valuable paper for our pages.—EDITOR.]

The Chairman: The second Paper is to be read by our friend, the Rev. Hudson Taylor.

PAPER.

2. BY THE REV. J. HUDSON TAYLOR (China Inland Mission).

The relation of itinerant to settled Missionary work.

The relation of itinerant to settled Missionary work is a subject in which I have long taken the deepest interest. It was first suggested to me in 1848 by the publication of the accounts of Gützlaff's Missionary Union by the Secretaries of the Chinese Evangelisation Society. This Society, which sent me out to China in 1853, had, from the commencement, strongly advocated the fullest development of itinerant work. The early itinerations in China of Medhurst, Milne, and Edkins, of the London Missionary Society, and yet more especially of my revered friend, the late Rev. William Burns,—with whom I personally itinerated in 1855-6 in Kiang-su, Cheh-kiang, and the Swatow district of Kwang-tung,—gradually deepened my interest in the subject, and my sense of its importance. Indeed, the views impressed upon me by Mr. Burns, who had laboured as an evangelist in Scotland, England, and Canada, before going out, and whose life in China had been that of an itinerant evangelist, have moulded the whole of my subsequent life, and been largely influential in the formation and course of action of the China Inland Mission. I have therefore, with much pleasure, accepted the invitation to write on this interesting and important topic. *[marginal note: Itinerant missionaries.]*

I. To prevent misconception, it may be well, at the very outset, to notice that our subject is the *relation* of itinerant to settled Missionary work ; it is not itinerant *versus* settled Missionary work. Both are essential and important, and, so far from being antagonistic, are mutually dependent on each other. That we cannot do without Missionary stations is too obvious to require demonstration. When Missionaries commence work in a country their first need is of a home in which to acquire the language ; and in which subsequently to translate the Word of God, and to prepare suitable tracts, as well as to preach the Gospel to those immediately around them. And when a useful amount of Christian literature has been prepared, the station is equally necessary as a basis from which to evangelise the surrounding district, and to develop and extend local work. In many countries itinerations can only be carried on during part of the year; the station, to which the Missionary may retire, and in which he may labour for other parts of the year, becomes as essential for the itinerant Missionary as for those who are wholly engaged in localised work. The fullest development of medical work, and much educational work, can only be carried on in settled stations, so that the importance and necessity of such *primary* stations, which are the very foundation of all Missionary work, needs no further demonstration. *[marginal note: Stationary and itinerant necessary.]*

But not only are stations the necessary basis for further work, but, as the work extends, the multiplication of stations becomes essential. The whole country has to be evangelised, and when the itinerant Missionary reaches regions really remote, there is a great loss of time and expense in returning to a distant station for supplies and recuperation. When, in the China Inland Mission, we first commenced itinerant work in Shan-si, Shen-si, Kan-suh, Si-chuen, and Yun-nan, our Missionaries had to return, from time to time, to Hankow for supplies, involving an absence of three to six months from the provinces in question. Thus the need of secondary stations in these provinces became very urgent. In China, the itineration which has created the necessity for opening these secondary stations, has proved the best means of securing them.

Itinerant prepares for stationary Missions.

We attempted, twenty-two years ago, without previous itineration, to open stations as convenient centres for future evangelistic work; but these efforts frequently resulted in opposition, or even riots, arising from the superstitious fears of the people, and the hostility of the *literati*. We then reversed the process, notwithstanding that it involved much difficulty and labour. We first itinerated through large and remote districts, and, seeking the guidance of God, selected suitable points for future head-quarters. These places were visited frequently, friends were made, and we became well-known before attempting a settlement, which then was usually accomplished with little difficulty, and without subsequent cause for regret. The stations thus formed were both the outcome of preliminary itinerations and the prelude to more thorough and systematic work in the provinces in question.

The foregoing considerations show the necessity for both itinerant and settled Missionary work. The settled work affords opportunity for the evangelisation of the station and its environs, and is a basis for work in the surrounding region; it is also the starting point for longer journeys. On the other hand, the itinerant work utilises the books prepared at the station, affords scope for the Missionaries trained there, and directly carries the Gospel amongst the masses scattered over large areas.

II. We have seen the importance of work in settled stations : let us now turn our attention to itinerant work, and it will be seen that its importance can scarcely be exaggerated. The Gospel is for the *whole world*. Scripture and experience alike prove this. The Apostle John wrote, "We know that we are of God, and that the *whole world* lieth in the evil one." The LORD JESUS CHRIST came and lived and died that He might "destroy the works of the devil," who had enslaved the *whole world*. "God so loved *the world*"—the *whole world*—"that He gave His only-begotten Son." JESUS CHRIST became the propitiation for our sins, "and not for ours only, but also for the *whole world*." Before His ascension He commanded His disciples to go into " *all the world* and preach the Gospel to *every creature*."

Arguments for itinerant work.

In seeking to make the Gospel known, what was the example of our Lord and of His disciples? During His personal ministry on earth, our Saviour worked throughout the *whole land* to which He was sent. When His ministry had been successful, and "the multitude sought after Him . . . and would have stayed Him, that He should not go from them," He refused to remain, saying, "I must preach the good tidings of the kingdom of God to other cities also, for therefore was I sent." The Apostle Peter, to whom was committed the Gospel of the Circumcision, itinerated much, leading about a sister, a wife; and he wrote his letters to the dispersed elect of *many regions.* The Apostle Paul, to whom was committed the evangelisation of the Gentiles, spent his *whole life* in itinerant work : he employed the beloved Timothy in *visits* to set in order things that were wanting in many Churches ; and sent Titus to Crete to arrange matters and appoint elders, not in one place, but in *every city.*

The rapid diffusion of the Gospel in ancient times was mainly through the labours of itinerant evangelists. In modern times, the Methodist denomination, which has sought to make all its Ministers itinerants, has had the most rapid and remarkable growth. In America, within the memory of one person's life, Methodists have grown from a few thousands to as many millions. Even at home, men like the American evangelists, Moody, Sankey, and others, have been marvellously honoured and blessed ; and Evangelistic Missions are recognised now as a power in all our Evangelical Churches on both sides of the Atlantic.

If the importance of itinerant and evangelistic work at home is self-evident, from the fact that even in *Christian* lands the vast majority of the population *will* not, and *do* not, attend the ordinary services of our Churches, how much more is it so when we turn to Roman Catholic lands, to those in which the Greek Church prevails, and to Mohammedan and heathen lands ! Here the mass of the unsaved can by no possibility be reached in any other way.

There is unfortunately a very paralysing doubt in some minds as to the necessity, or even advisability, of preaching the Gospel to these classes. There are those who are kinder and wiser than CHRIST, forsooth, who commanded that to *every creature* His Gospel should be preached. They know more about the state of the heathen than did the Apostle Paul, who wrote under the inspiration of the HOLY GHOST. "They that sin without law perish without law." Nay, there are those who are not afraid to contradict "the revelation of JESUS CHRIST, which GOD gave unto Him, to show unto His servants;" in which He solemnly affirms Objections
answered. "I am the Alpha and the Omega, the Beginning and the End; . . . the fearful, and unbelieving, and abominable, and murderers, and fornicators, and sorcerers, and idolaters, and all liars—their part shall be in the lake that burneth with fire and brimstone, which is the second death." Such being the state of the unsaved of India, Africa, and China, and of every unevangelised people in the whole earth, do not their urgent needs claim from us that with agonising eagerness we should hasten to proclaim everywhere the message through which alone deliverance can be found ! Oh, that the Spirit might be so poured out from on high, that from our home pulpits many ministers might be constrained to leave their surfeited congregations ; that in the foreign field many Missionaries might be impelled to leave to the care of resident natives, schools and chapels, among those who have already heard the Gospel, alike to emphasise by obedience the reality of the Gospel, and to preach it *everywhere* until not an unevangelised village remains ! It is not sufficient to be doing a work good in itself, while the MASTER'S great commission is unfulfilled ; and that commission is, " Preach the Gospel to *every creature.*" And yet we all know that three-quarters of the world's population have never had it offered to them ! What CHRIST commanded eighteen hundred years ago, and what the needs of the world now demand, is *itinerant* work. The Gospel is for all; all need the Gospel, and few as yet have had it. The unevangelised now living have but a few years to live ; and the immediate and urgent necessity of the world is earnest, widespread, itinerant evangelisation.

III. How then should our work be conducted so as to secure in the shortest time the fullest carrying out of our Lord's command?

We may assume that in most cases a Mission is commenced with comparatively few labourers, and that, as the work develops, a larger number of foreign workers, together with an increasing band of native Christians, will be available for its extension. The carrying on of widespread evangelisation will not be found to seriously retard the work at the local centre, while it will prepare a large district for the more thorough evangelisation that will in the course of time become practicable. A little consideration will suffice to show this.

It is well known that in most cases, even where the whole strength has been devoted to working a single station, years have elapsed before many converts were gathered. Confidence in the Missionary is of slow growth, superstitious fears do not die out at once. The debased and materialised minds of idolaters do not readily grasp the thought of one living, personal GOD, and of our responsibility to do His will and to obey His law. Yet these thoughts have to be apprehended before any true sense of sin is felt, and true repentance can take place ; while without conviction of sin the offer of a SAVIOUR will be unappreciated.

How best to itinerate.

It is granted that there are a few persons everywhere who are remarkably prepared by the HOLY SPIRIT for the Gospel, and who will readily accept the offered SAVIOUR ; but such cases are the exception. Therefore, while the truths preached at the station are slowly permeating the minds of the people there, the widespread evangelisation of the more important centres of population around may be carried on with great advantage.

It is most desirable that the itineration be systematic, and that these centres be visited again and again. Short visits are best at first, but longer and more frequent ones will become desirable as time progresses. Meanwhile the number of workers, native and foreign, will probably be increasing, and the districts to be visited may be sub-divided with advantage ; rendering it possible to reach smaller towns and villages, and perhaps to increase the number of stations occupied. Still, each newly-opened station should be looked upon as a centre for the fuller evangelisation of circumjacent regions ; and converts should be urged, from the commencement, to labour as voluntary and unpaid helpers, as do so many lay workers at home. The Missionary should carefully avoid subsiding into the Pastor and the Paymaster : his is a higher and distinct vocation. But he should afford all possible countenance and instruction to such native Christians as give promise of teaching power and pastoral gift. Itinerant work thus carried on will enhance the importance and value of central stations, for the production of Christian literature and the instruction of inquirers. Where itineration is only practicable at certain seasons of the year, the books and tracts circulated on the journeys should contain information as to the locale of the Missionary, and an invitation to those interested to visit him at stated times for fuller instruction. Many from a distance will avail themselves of this opportunity, while those nearer home will at such times be specially helped. When I was in China, a valued friend—the Rev. J. L. Nevius, D.D., of the American Presbyterian Mission, Che-foo—was accustomed to spend the two hottest months of summer, and the two coldest months of winter, at home. During his four months' itineration, he would invite those specially interested to spend a month with him at his home, where he entertained them simply, and daily instructed them in Christian doctrine. Men would come one hundred or one hundred and fifty miles at their own expense, and then return, to pass on to their own neighbours that which they had themselves learned. When the first month's contingent of visitors left, the second month's arrived; and when they in their turn went home, Dr. Nevius would set out for another four months' tour. In course of time, *scores* of self-supporting village churches were formed, superintended, and helped by Dr. Nevius, and only two paid native helpers, who were really itinerating Missionaries like the Doctor himself. Were work more frequently conducted on these lines, whole countries might be rapidly evangelised.

Dr. Nevius.

Missionaries who have some knowledge of medicine may do much good and win golden opinions while on journeys, and will be successors of the Apostles, who were commissioned to preach and to heal. While Medical Missionaries are comparatively few, most of them will be needed in the stations to carry on hospital work, and to such hospitals the more serious cases met with on Missionary journeys will frequently be sent. But though the Medical Missionary may not himself be able to itinerate, he may forward the work by facilitating the absence of other Missionaries from headquarters.

Medical itinerants.

To the question, "How far can woman's work be itinerant?" I can best reply by reference to the field with which I am most familiar. When travelling with my wife in China, her opportunities for work among the women have not been fewer or less valuable than my own amongst the men. Not to refer to members of the China Inland Mission, the writings of the late Mrs. Dr. Williamson, of the Scottish United Presbyterian Mission, of Miss Fielde, of the American Baptist Mission, and the reports of Miss Ricketts, of the English Presbyterian Mission, are well known. In the China Inland Mission the married ladies frequently take journeys of one or two thousand miles, when on their way to or from distant stations, and find daily opportunities of labouring amongst their own sex. We have a number of inland stations in which the only foreign workers are ladies, residing with married Christian helpers. Long evangelistic journeys of the greatest value are from time to time undertaken by our single Missionary sisters. Besides the fifty-six wives of our Missionaries, who nearly all of them continue to be Missionary workers, as they were before marriage, we have ninety-five single ladies, working in thirteen of the eighteen provinces. Several of them have done itinerant work in Hu-nan,

Female itinerants.

a fourteenth province. So that we speak on this subject with some experience.

In conclusion, while we would not undervalue stationary work, we ask, Is there not a danger of devoting an undue proportion of strength to it? Scripture, as we have seen, is full of instances of itinerant work, and the words of the great commission directly suggest it; but is it not remarkable how very little is said, or even suggested, in the New Testament, about localised work?

As climate, family, and other circumstances preclude the possibility of stationary work being neglected, do we not need all the more earnestly to stimulate Missionary workers to give as much as possible of their time to that branch which is more in danger of being neglected, and without which nine-tenths of the heathen can never hear the Gospel at all? Few can be familiar with the history of Missions without coming to the conclusion that serious mistakes, leading to the neglect of evangelistic and itinerant work, have been made in the past, from which we should carefully guard in the future.

Itinerant work needs stimulating.

Auxiliary works must not be allowed to become substitutes for that which is primary. " Preach the Gospel "—" Preach the Gospel to *every creature* "—is the clear command of the Master. Literary work is valuable, but it must *not* take the place of preaching; educational work is useful, but the minister of CHRIST must *not* become a mere schoolmaster; even medical work must be a means of bringing souls under the influence of the Gospel, and not a substitute for it. Localised work *may* be essential, itinerant work is absolutely *imperative*, and both must be mainly evangelistic. CHRIST commands us to *preach*, the Apostles enjoin us to *preach*, the needs of dying men implore us to *preach*,—to preach everywhere and to every one. Our wisdom, our happiness, and our success, all lie in obedience.

The Chairman: I suppose that any remarks had better be reserved until the three Papers have been read. The next Paper is to be read by the Rev. J. Hesse.

PAPER.

3. BY THE REV. J. HESSE (of Calw, Würtemberg).

The little I have to say on the subject before us will best be said when I arrange it under three heads : (1) The Missionary as an agent of the Home Church; (2) his place among his colleagues; and (3) his position as leader and trainer of his native brethren.

I. The true position of the Missionary with regard to the Home Church has unfortunately become obscured, partly by the deplorable prevalence of sectarianism among us, partly by the thoughtlessness and ambition of men.

The Missionary a representative.

A Missionary, it is true, is an ambassador of Christ, inwardly called and endowed by the Spirit to assist in spreading the kingdom of God (not to proselytise for any particular Church or party); but, let us remember, *he is not an Apostle, i.e.*, a person sent *direct* by Christ, receiving his instructions from above, and subject to no human authority whatever. On the contrary, he is a responsible agent of the Church or Society which has sent him out, supported by their gifts and prayers, directed by their instructions, and controlled by their supervision. I know there are private individuals who have gone out on their own responsibility, and if they are at all like a Norris Groves, Dr. Kalley, Louisa Anstey, or Frederick Arnot, they may do excellent work as pioneers to the regular army, and their irregularities may be excused by the divided state of Christendom in general, and by the inelasticity of Missionary Committees in particular. But the exigencies of practical work as well as the failings of human nature certainly make it desirable that, in order to secure economy and avoid imposture, every Missionary should take his position as an humble servant of that particular Church or Society with which he can best agree. *The place of independent Missionaries.*

Is it not a humiliating fact that, apparently, there is so much zeal without knowledge, and, perhaps, on the other hand, so much knowledge without zeal? Is it not a pity that so much time and talent are all but wasted in erratic exertions of men and women who boldly assume that they pre-eminently do an apostolic work? And is it not a pity, too, that some of the best organised and most carefully managed Societies seem rather to repel than to attract many whose singleness of purpose cannot be denied? Let us pray the Lord so to bless this our united Conference, that a more universal and a more complete combination of wisdom and zeal, of enthusiasm and discretion, may be the abiding result. *Pray for unity of purpose.*

Well, then, if I have correctly described the legitimate position of a Missionary, it follows that the best thing he can do is to study, and to obey his instructions as laid down, not only in the formal rules and regulations, but also in the history of his Society and of his particular district and stations. If he does this it will profit him more than if he breaks his head to find out the best modes of working for himself. After a century of Protestant Missions we ought to have learned some lessons and acquired some settled habits as well as convictions. Young Missionaries should not make light of such honoured traditions, but rather fall in with them. It is astonishing to what an amount of trouble and experiment most people will expose themselves, rather than patiently go on with the work entrusted to them.

II. And this brings me to the second point—the position of the Missionary with regard to his co-workers. Of course he will not stand alone. To appoint a single man to a dangerous post, to let him die or break down, then to hunt for a successor, and, after a delay of months, to send him out

—such things, let us hope, do not happen nowadays. As a rule there

Mutual relation of Missionaries. must be two men, at least, to every station; and each station must have its conference, where the work is divided among the labourers, where difficulties may be adjusted and united prayer is offered. And again, several stations together will form one district, and every district will have its conference. In this way every detail of work as well as the general interests of a whole province will be taken into account, everybody will know what his business is, the home committee will be kept informed of everything, confusion will be avoided and order maintained. But in these conferences or local committees—or whatever they may be called—not every young brother ought to have a vote. Let him first pass an examination in the language and make himself acquainted with the whole work of the station, then, after a year or two of apprenticeship, let him have a share in the management of affairs. Nor should all Missionaries be equal, without any distinction between senior and junior, between leader and led. Some think that ordination at least should confer equality in every respect. But even among those who lay great stress on the equality of ministers (nay, even among those who would acknowledge no ministers on the ground of the universal priesthood of believers), practically some act as bishops and leaders, while

Equality impossible. others take a more humble place. Let every man have his own office for which he is best adapted, and above all, let there be a well understood *division of labour*. In the Basle Mission this is carried almost to an extreme. Special men are appointed for almost everything, as for the management of money matters, for building, for the administration of landed property, for literary work, for the schools, for the pastoral care of churches, for itinerating, etc. Besides, there are chairmen of station and district conferences, a general superintendent, an inspector of schools, and a general treasurer, who are from time to time deputed by the home committee to make a tour of inspection from station to station, and then to report as to the efficiency of every branch of work.

Two things are expected from every brother, be he lay or clerical, namely—(a), that he learn the language, and in some measure take a part in the actual proclamation of the Gospel (not only in the meetings of Christians but also before the non-Christians); and (b), that at a moment's

Rules of Basle Mission. notice he be ready to take the work of any brother who may have fallen at his post or otherwise been laid aside. In this way the solidarity and continuity of the whole work is maintained, and great prominence is given to the oral proclamation of the Gospel in the vernacular by every member of the Mission.

III. In the third place we have to consider the position of the Missionary as leader and trainer of the natives. And here let us at once dismiss the notion that every Missionary is a born leader of men. He may be, and he must be, an example to all by faithfulness in small things and by unselfish continuance in well-doing; but few Missionaries only will be able to exert anything like the influence of a Rhenius, a Duff, a Hebich, a

All men not born to lead. Patteson, a Mackay, or a Chalmers. The large majority will have to content themselves with a very modest share in this work where it is so easy to do more harm than good. Yet, I think, every Missionary should make it his aim, so to win and influence at least one native brother that he may, after his own removal from the field, leave behind some mark and impress of his character in the person of such a disciple, as Paul had his Timothy and Boniface had his Lullus. As to the training of native helpers and the leading of the native Church in a technical sense, they are subjects that will be treated by other speakers. I will only venture to add a few general rules, by which in all cases the personal intercourse between the Missionary and his native assistants should be regulated.

(*a*) *Never ask them to do what you would not do yourself.*

" Leading and training " does not mean driving but drawing. Bishop Patteson himself cleaning his shoes, dusting his rooms, boiling some soup for an invalid ; Mr. Kirk, in Pithoragarh, with his own hands carrying to the grave the dead body of a leper; Mr. W. Martin of Ashapura, riding a distance to fetch water in one of **Respect native helpers.** his boots and giving it to a dying stranger by the wayside ; Hebich of Cannanore, jumping into a well after a boy and saving his life—such acts are seeds.

In some Missions the Catechists are all but personal servants of the Missionary, to relieve him of everything below his dignity, or contrary to his tastes. And even where this is not the case, we are too apt to speak of *my* Catechist, *my* Bible woman, and the like, as if they belonged to us. A dismissed Catechist in Malabar some time ago started an opposition periodical, and in one of the first issues published a sarcastic article on the question, Who is the true Agnani ? this being the term by which the heathen are spoken of among Indian Christians, meaning the ignorant. But he applied it to a Catechist, who never knows what his real business or calling is, he being to-day deputed by the Missionary to superintend some station building, and to-morrow to arrange the Missionary's library, and once on a Sunday to preach for him, etc., etc. Such caricatures may at least show us the direction in which our shortcomings and our native brethren's difficulties lie.

(*b*) *Do not be ashamed to learn from them. Teachers must be learners.*

If we wish the natives to follow us, we must show them that we too are willing to follow them in every particular in which they can be a model to us. Make it a habit to have your sermons and other speeches criticised by your native assistants, not only as to pronunciation and idiom, but also as to choice of illustrations, adaptation to the people and **Learn from them.** circumstances. Listen carefully to how they preach and teach. You will find much to imitate. True Missionaries quite involuntarily become influenced by their surroundings, so that in some cases it is easy to distinguish a brother who has laboured in China from one whose work has been in India or Africa, or in a Mohammedan country, by his very appearance, his way of speaking, of thinking. Woe to him, who remains *semper idem* as to national peculiarities and home prejudices ! It is much safer for us, in a certain sense and in a certain degree, to become Hinduised, or even Chinesised or Africanised, rather than to Europeanise and Americanise the natives. Why not adopt what is good and reasonable even in their diet, dress, and other habits ?

And then, in regard to cases of discipline, settling of disputes, and other matters requiring not only Christian tact, but a minute acquaintance with national, local, and personal affairs, customs, and the like, let us never neglect to consult our native fellow-labourers before committing ourselves in any way.

(*c*) *Our intercourse with them must not be restricted to business matters.*

There must be free brotherly communion, and some social intercourse as well. This will draw out their hearts as nothing else, not even, in many cases, united prayer will do. **Use their language.**

And here I take it for granted that the Missionary will not converse with his native brethren in any other language but their own. If he does, he will always remain a stranger to them, and they to him.

All this, it is true, cannot be done without a genuine love to, and a certain admiration for, the natives as such. By genuine love, I do not mean Christian charity, but natural affection. It has both grieved and shocked me to read in the report of an American Society a statement to the effect, that "there is nothing in the character of the African which could draw our hearts toward him, but compassion ought to move us to do something for him." I have always found that the noblest Missionaries, even African Missionaries, were filled with admiration for some one or more good qualities in their respective charges, and with a considerable degree of enthusiasm for them even from a natural point of view—(Zimmermann, Livingstone, O'Flaherty, General Gordon, etc.); and I would ask, Is it possible to have mastered any one language without admiring it, and without feeling drawn to the people who produced it and who use it?

The Moravian Solomon Schuman in 1749 wrote : "To me no tongue on earth sounds sweeter than the Arawak ; and when I find a new word to express

Sympathy in
details. some feature of the Lord and His work, I rejoice infinitely more than if I had found a lump of gold." Then he speaks of fearful disappointments and bitter experiences with the natives, and adds : " Knowing, however, that probably nobody has ever caused more trouble to our dear Lord than myself, I can submit to all this, and love them all the same right heartily."

That is the right spirit. And that will do more to win and inspire the natives than even the otherwise commendable "muscular Christianity" of the first Bishop of New Zealand, or the founder of self-supporting Missions in Africa.

(d) *Let us avoid technicalities* of theological and denominational phraseology in our conversation with the natives, and rather aim at Biblical simplicity in everything we say. "Triune" is a grand expression, but when you have once heard a native Christian pray to the triune Jesus, you ask yourself, if it were not better to restrict its use to the theological hall ; and of Zion it may be true that the Lord loveth its gates more than all the dwellings of Jacob ; but to hear a Chinese or a negro Methodist continually speak of "our Zion" has a sickening effect. Nothing is easier than to make our native friends surpass ourselves in denominational zeal, but nothing is more unprofitable. Let us beware of it !

(e) My last rule is : *Be true, absolutely true and honest.* There is too much of sham and show, of mannerism and making in religion, nay, of hypocrisy and

Practise what
you preach. cant, even in Evangelical Missionaries. Gossip in India will have it that there are Missionaries who, in public, profess total abstinence, and at home consume quantities of beer and wine "under medical advice"—and I am not prepared to deny the charge.

Europeans everywhere, and natives as well, have an impression that Missionaries are not exactly those self-denying beings they are often assumed to be in Missionary literature. But how can we expect our converts to lead a self-sacrificing life, "unless our own self-sacrifice is plain enough to be discerned by them?" (G. Bowen, in *Bombay Guardian*, December 3, 1887.) Here is what one of them has to say on the subject : "The European mind, from the climatic influences under which it was moulded, is intent upon *having* things, to give it numerous comforts. I do not like to deny these to it. But my evil tendencies are running rapidly in the course of imitation of European manners, and I have really begun to feel the *want* of things which my European friends and acquaintances think it right to have for themselves. I have become so well versed in the art of imitation that I have lost the faculty of perceiving the 'thus far and no further.'" "The lesson we learn now is the lesson of securing as many comforts as are within our reach, and as many European fashions in costume as we may happen to know of." (Govind N. Kane, in *Bombay Guardian*, 1887, p. 775.)

Oh, for more men like George Bowen, of Bombay, and for less like the young brother who wrote from Africa : "I do not care for the goods of this world, if I have only enough *to make me comfortable!*" It is true some people think nobody in the world has a greater right to travel first-class by land and sea than the children of God, but I doubt if these persons would enjoy meeting a native catechist in a first-class car. **More simplicity of living.**

Part of the truth we owe our native brethren must consist in confessing our faults before them and asking their forgiveness when we have lost our temper, or otherwise sinned against them. Confession has a power and a promise. Beloved brethren, is it out of place in an august assembly like this to make mention of our shortcomings? I think not. If we wish to have Him on our side, without whom nothing is strong, nothing is holy, we must have a contrite heart and a broken spirit. And although we ought at all times humbly to acknowledge our sins before God, yet ought we most chiefly so to do, when we assemble and meet together in a Conference like this.

O Lord, have mercy upon us, and deal not with us after our sins! From all blindness of heart, from pride, vainglory and hypocrisy; from envy, hatred and malice, and all uncharitableness,

Good Lord, deliver us!

The Chairman: Now we are to have, I hope, some remarks upon these Papers. I think it is very important that some gentlemen should be able to make some suggestions as to what they understand by the relation of the one kind of work to the other, and how they may be amalgamated—how there may be, as it were, more mutual understanding and co-operation. That, I think, is of immense importance. I very largely sympathise with our friend, who has taken a very great interest in the Inland Mission, but at the same time I look to the Societies with which I have been identified, and I want to see some method in which we might co-operate more than we do. That, I think, is a subject which is very proper for discussion. I have two names of gentlemen who wish to take part in the discussion, and I shall be happy to receive other names if gentlemen will send in their cards. I have first to call upon the Rev. Robert Rust Meadows. **Importance of co-operation.**

DISCUSSION.

Rev. R. Rust Meadows (C.M.S.): My Christian friends,—The only reason I venture to stand up before you is because I have been an itinerant Missionary, and also a stationary Missionary. I have been an itinerant Missionary four or five years, and a settled Missionary for eighteen years. As the subject of itineration is a very prominent one here at this meeting, I want to tell you, in as few words as I possibly can, the method which we pursued, and then to show you how our itineration acted upon the native Church, and how each acted and re-acted upon the other. First of all, I want to tell you our methods. There were three of us—three English Missionaries—and we were three University men—Cambridge men: we lived in the north of Tinnevelly, and had a district that was about fourteen hundred square miles in extent. We purposely made it so small in order that we might be able to **Itineration.** **The methods.**

go backwards and forwards all through, again and again, and this district of about fourteen hundred square miles contained about fourteen hundred villages and towns, and a population of a little more than 270,000 people. We lived in our tents all the year round, though it was very hot indeed at some times of the year. Each of us had his own tent, and each tent was pitched at a distance of eight or ten miles from the other.

We had each to help us a native brother, and these native brethren, too, had their own tents, and they also had their tents ten miles perhaps apart from each other. We always met together once a fortnight in order to confer and to pray together. We stayed at a place a week, and every morning and every evening we got on our horses and rode to a village, and preached in the street to anybody whom we could meet with. Our tents were easily removed from one place to another. Having no fixed home, we used to stop in any native town or village, in what is usually called the "Rest House;" and the fact of our being in the "Rest House," sitting there and eating there, and our faces being white, always brought in a great number of the villagers, who came in merely from curiosity. Then we used also to have to help us, not only our native preachers, who were highly educated men, and spoke English perfectly, but a number of native catechists, brought from the south of Tinnevelly and from the native Christian Churches.

Adjustment of districts.

Helpers.

What I want principally to show you is, how the one branch of work reacted upon the other. We noticed that the native Church down in South Tinnevelly, a very large Church indeed, was not very decidedly a Missionary Church, and we thought it ought to be, and so went down periodically to the South of Tinnevelly to hold Missionary meetings, the object being to stir up the native Churches to care for the heathen about them. At these meetings the question was put to the native Church, "Ought you not to be an evangelising Church, and will you not undertake to send to North Tinnevelly, to the heathen there, to itinerate with the itinerating Missionaries and native Catechists from the various villages?" The native Christians subscribed the money necessary for the support of these native Catechists while they were with us. The native Catechists stayed with us for a month at a time, going about with us and preaching with us, and then they returned to their own congregations, and told them what they had seen in the heathen part of Tinnevelly.

Stimulating a Missionary spirit.

This method acted very beneficially indeed, in producing a feeling of responsibility towards the heathen in the minds of native Christians. Coming back again to our itinerating; we used often to meet for prayer. If I was with two or three Catechists, for instance, we always met together, first of all to pray before we went out to preach; sometimes we would go two together, and sometimes we would go alone; one to one place and one to another. When we came back we all sat down and heard the several reports, and then we would kneel down and ask God to give the blessing upon what we had said. The result of all this, it seems to me, has been very beneficial as regards the Tinnevelly Church.

Evangelists' mutual Conference.

The Tinnevelly Church is now very distinctly a Missionary Church. It has sent Missionaries—I mean, native Catechists—to a good many parts where they have had to learn another language. The Tinnevelly Christians going to the North, or Telugu country, have been obliged to learn another language; and Tinnevelly native Catechists have also gone, and are constantly going, over the water to Ceylon,

A Missionary Church.

in order to be preachers there; and Tinnevelly Catechists have also gone as far as the Island of Mauritius that they might preach there. We visited the fourteen hundred towns and villages over and over again. We used to visit every one of these villages at least twice *Villages visited.* in the year, and many of them a great many more times *Churches formed.* than that. The result was that a great deal of Christian knowledge permeated the whole of that district. But further than that there were a few native Christian congregations scattered abroad here and there. They were elevated by our influence, and in time in that entire district so many congregations were formed that we were able to make it a Station Mission; and then we built our bungalow, and there I spent my last eighteen years of Missionary life, superintending the whole of the district, itinerating still, but itinerating more particularly amongst the Christian congregations, and at the same time carrying out an organisation for preaching, if possible, in every one of the fourteen hundred villages. This is the experience of one itinerating Missionary, and I hope it may help to guide others in their work.

Mr. John Archibald (National Bible Society of Scotland, from Hankow): Mr. Chairman, and dear friends,—The fact that the last twelve years of my life have been spent in itinerant work must be my excuse for addressing you. Those twelve years have been spent in China. As an itinerating Missionary in the service of the National Bible Society of Scotland it has been my privilege to see perhaps more Mission stations and more methods of working than ordinary Missionaries are permitted to see, as we are now in one province, now in another. I have thus travelled over many of the Provinces of China, and I will tell you a discovery I made.

Shortly after I went out to China I began to read up all the literature that the Missionaries had written about their work, and I made this discovery: That Missionaries are apt to look at their work as a question of one kind *versus* another kind; and in the paper which Mr. Taylor read to us he laid special stress on the fact that it is not a ques- *Varied work not antagonistic.* tion of itineration *versus* settled work, but a question of the interdependence of one kind of work upon another. Sometimes Missionaries appear to think that one kind of work is opposed to another. Thus I find a statement made by one good brother that the preaching of the Gospel is the greatest hindrance to the cause of Christianity; another brother condemns Medical Missions; another is opposed to circulating the Word of God, and so on.

Then I made this discovery, that the men were better than their theories. You would go and you would find that the brother who did not believe in the preaching of the Gospel, preaching it as hard as he could; and the brother who did not believe in circulating the Word of God and Christian tracts, was circulating his own which were really very good; and you would find that after all, although they held different theories, the fact was that in practice they pretty nearly approximated. Now if you consider the matter *Theories differ but practice the same.* of the different Missions, you will find the very same thing. I do not believe, from what I have seen in China, that any one man can claim to have the monopoly either of stationary work or of itinerating work: for each man who is an itinerating Missionary, also carries on stationary work. Go right from the north to the south of China, and from the east to the west, and you will find the Missionary now visiting in his district, and going through his stations, and now at home looking after the churches; and that is the way in which the work is carried on.

I have risen chiefly to make one remark, and it is this. A good deal of the literature and a great number of the people that I have come in contact with have given me the idea that the impression prevails that there is some royal road, some patent plan for converting the heathen world, and it is to be found in the direction of itinerating round and round the country as rapidly as you can. I would not wish to speak ill of the work in which my fellow labourers have been engaged, only I wish to tell you there is no such royal road.

No royal road to convert heathen.

This itineration is important work, but it is not the whole of the work. I will tell you how I work, and then you will see. I go out into the country. When I go into a new village or town in China, the whole population turns out *en masse* to see the stranger. They call him the foreign devil and even worse names. We preach the Gospel to them, we circulate the Word of God and other Christian books as largely as we can, and we go away. That city is not converted, not by any means. When you go back again the second time you find that a certain impression has been created. You find that the great mass of the people have penetrated your object. They know you have been there as the teacher of a religion which they do not want, and therefore a great number of them are indifferent. You find others of them hostile, but you will find quite a number who are deeply interested, who have taken in what they have heard and are willing to learn more. This number may be increased, and as you continue to teach them, the number will grow, and by-and-by you will have your converts. But if you merely go from city to city without forming centres, you will have no converts; but if you can carry on the stationary work as the other work opens out the way for it, and you can get your people gathered together, your work spreads, and in that way the whole field will be overtaken.

Itineration not enough.

Repeated visits necessary.

Now, friends, that is the work that is being carried on pretty generally by all the Missions in China. We have a splendid field there, and the work is going on gloriously, and if you would only give us more men and more money, I believe you would soon see wonderful things done in that ancient Empire.

Rev. John Ross (United Presbyterian Mission, Manchuria): Mr. Chairman, Christian friends,—It affords me very great pleasure, and I esteem it a high honour to be present at this great series of meetings. In order to be present at them I rushed through Japan, and came, without staying more than two or three days, through Canada and the States. This series of meetings should give an impulse to Mission work all over the world, such as it has not had since the time of the Apostles.

Now, regarding this point of itineration, I do not know that absolutely there is any great difference of opinion among Missionaries as to the value of itineration. I began my life-work in the north of China as an itinerant, simply because I was not fit to carry on the work of a settled station. By-and-by I settled down to steady work, and I found it was the only way, so far as I could then see, to be successful. There is one Missionary, who has been referred to already by a gentleman whose name is very prominent both in this country and in China, in connection with Foreign Missions, that is the name of Dr. Nevius, of Che-foo. I was very much interested in the account of his Missions which I had from his own lips a year

Began itinerating.

successful.

Dr. Nevius' experience.

ago. He went out to China many years ago. For fifteen years he laboured, itinerating for six or eight months of the year over a certain district. Out of that district, and a very large district it was, he has never had a single convert. But at the end of the *No convert for fifteen years.* fifteen years there was a movement begun by the conversion of one man to Christianity in quite another district. The movement spread from that man's village northward to the gulf of Pe-Che-Lee, and southward to the shore of Hoang-hai, so that he has now a line of stations from north to south at right angles to the direction in which he began the work originally, with over eleven hundred members in them.

Now how was that? It was exactly by carrying out the line of work which we have ourselves adopted in our northerly province, that of Manchuria. Fifteen years ago I went out to that province where no one was labouring *Experience in Manchuria.* at the time. As I have said I began by itinerating and gradually acquiring the language. There were three converts within the first year. These I instructed and sent them out to do itinerating work. We have now Christians in something like forty or fifty villages, and in very many of the large cities. There are somewhere about a thousand *Converts itinerate.* who have been baptised. Now I would like to mention this, that of this thousand, and of several other thousands who are believers though unbaptised, those who have been converted under the direct influence of the Foreign Missionary will not count up more than a dozen. The rest have been all drawn in through the influence of these few men who were converted by the agency of the Foreign Missionary.

Now this touches what I would like earnestly to impress upon this meeting, viz., the absolute necessity of training the natives to carry on Christian work in their own land. It would be impossible for all the Churches in Europe and America combined to send a sufficient number of Missionaries even into that one land of China. It is impossible, nay further, I consider it is undesirable. What I am *Result of experience.* inclined to recommend as the result of my experience is this : let all the various Missionary Societies pick out, not as many men as they can find, but pick out a few, choice in all respects, spiritually, mentally, intellectually, physically. There is no time at my disposal to enter as I would like to on this subject,—but let *Train native workers.* there be a few choice men, let those train the natives, and the natives will do the work. It seems to me that is the only way you can get the work properly done.

Now regarding itinerancy. We have set a few native converts, well-instructed men, in native cities, at distances varying from thirty to forty or fifty miles from each other, to preach the Gospel. They were previously well trained. These men we visit ; we itinerate amongst these cities where there are Christians, where there is a certain amount of Christian instruction ; and what with the work in the city, *Missionaries to superintend.* and of training these men to send them out, and then once or twice or three times a year visiting them to gather in the fruits of their labours, we find our hands quite full. We could not, even if we thought it was proper, do more itinerancy than this. We may run from city to city and merely preach once or twice ; but that is not what we desire. We want the heathen to be converted, and in order that they may be converted they must be in contact with Christianity for some time ; and that touches the question of the relationship of the station to itinerancy. Train the natives. Train them as fully and as thoroughly and make them as able preachers as you can. Send them out to itinerate; superintend them; go after them; itinerate in that way. It seems to me that this is the only way in which you can bring the settled work and the itinerating work into harmonious and effective co-operation.

Rev. L. Dahle (Secretary, Norwegian Missionary Society): The subject upon which I wish to speak is the method of Mission preaching and teaching, a subject scarcely touched upon up to this time; but I do not see how I can deal with the subject, because I have arranged a discourse systematically, and time will not admit of my going through with it, but I can give you the headings.

My first question is—Is there a Missionary method of preaching and *Is there a special method?* teaching, or is there not? Is there a method, or is there not—a special Missionary method, I mean?

The Chairman: There may be several.

Rev. L. Dahle: Yes; but I mean, Can the Missionary do the same as the preacher of Christianity at home, simply go and preach on the lessons for the day, for instance, if it is on Sunday, or take any Mission books, or do anything so as to bring, or try to bring, his teaching and preaching under methodical rules? That is my first question.

The second would be—If there is such a special method,—I mean for Missionary preaching and teaching,—wherein would it consist? And I would say there should be two things that should characterise it as Missionary teaching and preaching in contradistinction to ordinary teaching and preaching; that would be the starting point of the manner of elucidating and illustrating the matter. Now as to the starting point. *Two modes.* There are two different modes, as far as I know, of doing it. Some begin with natural theology, and make that a bridge over to revealed religion; and some plunge *in medias res*, and go into revealed religion at once.

As a subject for discussion, I will give you the heads of my Paper, and perhaps others may take up the discussion afterwards. If we make natural theology the starting point, there would be two ways of doing that even. You might either *Natural and* take up the cosmological way; you may point to the whole creation *revealed* and lead them to think of God through His work, and make that a *religion.* starting point. You may point to the conscience of the human heart and the consciousness of sin, and to all the misery in this world and the fear of death and of condemnation, and try to lead them to think of the Supreme Judge. If we now come to the revealed religion, there would be many ways of dealing with it from that point of view; and if you have bridged your way through the natural religion, you might even begin with texts stating the commission you have got from God to go out and preach the Gospel of the grace of God as given by Christ to His disciples. That would be one way. Another way would be to begin to explain to them such a Gospel text as "God so loved the world, that He gave His only-begotten Son, that whosoever believeth on Him should not perish, but have everlasting life."

Mr. George Saunders, C.B., M.D. (Medical Missionary Association, London): Mr. Chairman, and dear friends,—Mr. Hudson Taylor referred to fixed Hos- *Itinerant and* pital Missions, and I think thereby implied that he did not com- *stationary* prehend also itinerating. I would only wish to observe that *doctors.* a fixed hospital has this great advantage, that patients come from a distance to be healed, and thereby they receive the Gospel. A

Missionary, of course, has to go to the people—mark the difference!—they have to go to the people, and speak to them about their souls. What I rise particularly for is this, to emphasise the immense importance and advantage of Medical Missions.

The Chairman : I see that to-morrow one of the topics will be Medical Missions, and the comparative value, for Mission purposes, of hospital, dispensary, and itinerant Medical Mission work. I hope you will be good enough to come and speak upon that to-morrow.

Rev. J. Hesse : As to the relation of itinerant to settled Missions, the one must supplement the other, and both must be conducted so as to fit in with each other. There have been enthusiasts of the settled Mission or station system, who went so far as to say, they had never heard of a well running after thirsty people, but only of thirsty people running after a well, and who tried hard to make their station, and, I suppose, themselves, such an attraction to the surrounding heathen, as to render itineration unnecessary—without any success! And there have been itinerating Missions as, *e.g.,* that fantastical China Association of Dr. Gützlaff's, where there was no attempt at forming regular congregations and conducting common worship, but everything on the move, nominally, throughout the eighteen provinces, and which ended as a grand system of imposture, as far as the natives were concerned. Here, too, systematic, well-planned, and patiently-performed work is the one thing needful ; not well-meant, crude attempts at blowing down the walls of Jericho with a flourish of trumpets.

1. No settled Mission is complete without thorough provision being made for a regular and systematic itinerancy, and no itinerant Mission can be of much use, unless it be connected with some fixed station, where Divine service is statedly carried on, and where inquirers can be prepared for baptism.

2. Every Mission station ought to have one Missionary, and one or more native evangelists, whose one chief work is travelling about and preaching the Gospel in every village, nay ! at every house door in the district.

3. Every station should be provided with a minute map of the neighbourhood, and a list of all the villages, hamlets, temples, etc., in it, with distances, number of inhabitants, facilities for lodging or camping, etc.

4. Every evangelist should keep a record, not only of the places visited by him, but also, as far as possible, of the names and characters of the persons with whom he has come into closer contact, either in a friendly or in an unfriendly way, this record, or book of addresses, being the property of the station, and serving as a directory for all present or future workers.

5. He may also note the titles of tracts distributed in the various places visited, to be able, on another visit, to inquire after the

contents, if read or not, and also to avoid flooding one place with the same books over and over again.

6. In like manner he may note the texts and subjects on which he has spoken, in this or in that particular place, to avoid repetition and to make reference to what has previously been said possible.

7. Educational Missionaries should keep lists of their former pupils, with full particulars as to their whereabouts, by personal visits, by correspondence, or through their evangelistic colleagues, to keep them under the influence of the Gospel. Every old Mission pupil must be utilised as a connecting link between his people and the Mission.

8. Native Church members, living on the station, may be encouraged from time to time, as their private business permits, to accompany the preachers, in order to add their testimony to theirs. It may not be expedient, however, to pay them their travelling expenses, as is done in some Missions.

9. The heathen must be invited to come to the station to see how Christians worship and live. If they can be present at a baptismal service it will help to dispel prejudices.

10. Every book and tract distributed should have on its title page, or somewhere else, an intimation as to where and how further instruction can be obtained (name of station, etc.).

11. As often as the evangelists start on a journey they should be commended to the grace of God in a short service at church, and continual intercession should be made on their behalf by the congregation.

12. From time to time they may—also in church—give an account of their experiences, so that the whole congregation may be kept in contact and sympathy with the work among the non-Christians.

13. If the Station schools will, from time to time, march out with the preachers, and help in the singing, it will make a good impression, and refresh boys as well as teachers.

Rev. J. Hudson Taylor: I wanted just to make a remark to prevent misconception. In the first place, I think, perhaps, our dear Chairman has no idea how very closely the old Missions and the new ones are connected together.

The Chairman: To be sure I have.

Rev. J. Hudson Taylor: The very legs we stand upon are the old Missions. There is one topic upon which I should like to say a word or two, and that is the question of converts. I could give you twenty instances of converts in twenty minutes, but as I cannot ask for that I will only give you one. My friend, Stanley Smith, after he Examples of itinerating work. had been for seven months in China, thought he would give himself a vacation to go and see a friend who was distant from him three days' journey. Half way across he came to a city of which he had never heard before, and in which no evangelistic work had been done. While the mules were eating their dinner he went out to preach the Gospel, and it was not with him any question as to Missionary methods, but he said, "You all know what you ought to be; why are not you what you ought to be? You all know what you ought to do: why do not you do what you ought to do? Is it not just this, that you like to do the thing that you know to be wrong rather than to do the thing you know to be right? Now I have not come to talk to you about philosophy, but to tell you about a living Saviour who is willing to forgive all your sins if you will only go to Him." A young Chinaman was passing by, a learned man, a B.A. of his university. He heard these words, and said, "If there is a Saviour like that there is not a man in this world who does not want Him." He accepted Him there and then, and after a short time he came to my friend to learn more about Christianity. A question was afterwards put to him by a native Christian, "What have you done for Christ since you believed?" "Oh!" he said, "I am a learner." "Well," said his questioner, "I have another question to ask you: when you light a candle, do you light it to make the candle more comfortable?" "Certainly not," he said, "in order that it may give light." "When it is half burnt down do you expect that it will first become useful?" "No; as soon as I light it." "Very well," he said, "go thou and do likewise; begin at once." Shortly after that there were fifty native Christians in the town as the result of that man's work. I think this will show you that itinerating Missions are not chimerical, and if I had more time I could give you more instances of it. Let us hope that when a Missionary goes forth to do God's work, he will have just as good success as the Apostle Paul.

Sudden conversion and wonderful results.

The Chairman: Has anybody suggested that itinerant Missions are chimerical?

Rev. J. Hudson Taylor: I do not want the idea to go forth.

The Chairman: I do not suppose the idea is in anybody's mind. You only raise a spirit of antagonism by saying that.

Rev. J. Hudson Taylor: But, my dear sir, this is the remark which I replied to. Dr. Nevius is said to have itinerated fifteen years, if I understood rightly, without fruit. He did not tell me so. I think it is a mistake; but I will not say it may not be so. But if it be so, on the other hand there are others who have gained converts in less than fifteen months.

Rev. F. E. Wigram offered prayer, and

The Chairman pronounced the Benediction.

MEETINGS OF MEMBERS
IN SECTION.

MISSIONARY METHODS.

(3) *DEALING WITH SOCIAL CUSTOMS.*

The relation of the Missionary to national, religious, and social customs, such as (a) caste, (b) slavery, (c) polygamy, (d) Indian marriage law, etc.

(Tuesday morning, June 12th, in the Lower Hall.)

Albert Spicer, Esq., in the chair.
Acting Secretary, **Rev. W. Stevenson, M.A.**

Rev. Professor Aiken, D.D. (Princeton, U.S.A.), offered prayer.

The Chairman: My Christian friends,—As I look round at this gathering this morning, and think of the many friends present who have seen years of service in the Mission-field, I confess I realise even more keenly than I have done in the thought of this meeting, the responsibility of presiding. I hold that the Chairman of a meeting like this is not called upon to traverse the whole ground which is to be occupied by those who have come to read Papers on the different subjects allotted to them. At the same time I think the Chairman is very largely responsible for giving the key-note to the after discussion, and for what we may look forward to as the happy result of a Conference like this. Our Conference this morning refers to the relations of the Christian Missionary to national, religious, and social customs, the aim being to turn to account the experience of the past for the improvement of the methods of Missionary enterprise in the foreign field. I should simply like to ask this question: "What are the essentials to a successful Conference on such very difficult subjects as those which are to be placed before us this morning?"

Need I say, in the first place, that if this Conference is to be really useful, each one of us must realise the presence of our Master. We have asked His presence; we have come together in His name, and is there any one here who doubts that He is here to lead our thoughts, to guide us and to teach us? May every word that is uttered this morning be in harmony with His Divine will!

The next essential, I take it, for a successful Conference is that there should be honest and brotherly outspokenness. There is great need for this. Perhaps I feel the importance of it more than many, looking from a different standpoint to that of some here this morning. I am not a Missionary, but I have had the privilege of seeing a great deal of Missionary work. I have had the pleasure of seeing all the different stations, connected with the London Missionary Society in India, and also those in connection with the Samoan Islands in the South Seas, and I have also had the privilege of seeing many of the stations of other Missionary Societies. In all the other stations, to say nothing of our own, we were always heartily welcomed, and we were made to feel that however high—God grant that they may soon be lowered!—may be the barriers that divide Christian men in the old country, Christians of different denominations in foreign lands do sympathise very heartily with one another; and that to a very large extent, although not altogether as completely as we might wish, we are working hand to hand, and trying to avoid the difficulties of overlapping one another's work. But I often used to feel in these visits, when statements were made to me as to the right rules and plans to be adopted, that there was a very great difference of opinion amongst many good and earnest Christian Missionaries as regards the lines of policy that had thus been laid down.

Honest outspokenness.

Sympathy among Missionaries.

I venture to think that if we look a little further, we shall see that many a Missionary and many a book designed to excite interest and sympathy with the Missionary cause published in this and other lands, loses a certain amount of power because we do not sufficiently deal with the difficulties of Mission work. We are made to feel in such books, especially those of us who know something of the work, that there is something kept back; and the public is beginning to discriminate on the subject. When everything is put *couleur de rose*, it does not have the same weight as it would have if we dealt a little more courageously with the difficulties that meet us on every hand. Since those journeys, I have read many reports of Missionary Conferences; and how often have I closed the books giving accounts of those Conferences with the feeling, "Here again is the same evil—the brethren have kept back in their Conferences many of those things which are creating heart-burnings and anxieties." Christian friends, these things ought not to be. We have a chance, in a meeting like this, composed of members only, of looking at some of these questions face to face.

Difficulties not faced.

We are also given from time to time the criticisms of travellers, men who are before the Christian public in this country as loyal supporters of the Christian cause, who pay visits of twenty-four hours to stations where Christian Missionaries have

Travellers' criticisms.

been at work for years, and who give us as the result of their twenty-four hours' visit very definite opinions with regard to the weaknesses and the strength of such Missions. Gentlemen, I think that we have, perhaps, ourselves to thank for some of these things, because we are not sufficiently outspoken in our conferences and discussions.

But again, if this Conference is to be a real success, whilst we express our own ideas and the opinions that we have formed,—some of us after many years of careful study and experience,—we must, with God's help, keep our minds open to learn from others. This is not so easy, even in a Christian assembly, as some might imagine. The Missionary work is being carried on to-day in the full Missions not glare of public light. Missionaries are not now isolated now isolated. in a way that was comparatively common many years ago. Then again, we must remember that many of our Missionaries are working in countries by the side of white men, men of different nationalities, some of them sympathising heartily with Christian effort, and able to give testimony to the English public—if they would but see it and understand it—of the way in which they, living on the spot, think of and treat Christian effort. But this is not always the case, for we know, too, that living side by side with the Christian Missionary are men whose lives are antagonistic to the principles of Christian faith ; who recognise it, and who look upon the Missionary as a standing protest against the lives that they are leading. Is it a wonder that these men are only too glad to catch at any weakness to disparage Christian work? They are only too glad of the opportunity. Friends, we have no need to be ashamed of our Christian work and of our Christian Missions ; we have no need to be ashamed of the difficulties that are troubling us in the conduct of that work.

It is at the second stage of Missionary enterprise that you enter upon the period when the position of the Church has to be looked Social problems. at with regard to these great social problems which are to engage our attention this morning, such as caste, polygamy, and slavery. I have no doubt that some at any rate— I do not say in this hall, but outside it—connected with Missions think that there can be no difference of opinion with regard to all these different subjects. You will hear this morning whether there is any difference of opinion. And I ask you to look at the questions that will be brought before you in a kindly and Christian spirit ; I ask you to look at them with honest and outspoken brotherliness ; I ask you to look at them with receptive minds, willing, not only to give the information which is in your heart to give, but ready also to learn from your Christian brother. The Importance of importance of such gatherings cannot be over-estimated. this Conference. And whilst we think of our own circle, let us this morning, as we carry on this Conference, think of many an anxious and weary one in distant parts of the Mission-field, not with us in body but with us in spirit—men who are troubled about some of these questions, and who are looking to your concerted wisdom this morning to try and find more light. May this Conference be very happy in its results, happy all through the different discussions, and be blessed in enabling us to go out with stronger convictions to do our Master's work, and try and extend His knowledge even unto the uttermost parts of the earth!

PAPER.

1. By the Rev. D. J. East (President of Calabar College, Kingston, Jamaica). Read in part by Dr. Underhill.

[Although Slavery was one of the subjects on the programme, and the effect of its introduction into a Christian country, and of emancipation, in getting rid of the social customs which the slaves brought from Africa, might have formed the *Paper why omitted.* subject of interesting and profitable discussion; yet the question of polygamy so completely occupied the thoughts and time of the meeting, that the Paper, though of acknowledged merit, was felt to be out of place. Its intrinsic value is such that we take the liberty of printing as much of it as space will admit of, as an Appendix to the discussion on "Organisation and Government of Native Churches, No. 2: the Training of Workers;" under which heading it would have been inserted had the Papers on that subject not been already too numerous.—EDITOR.]

PAPER.

2. By the Rev. W. Holm (President, Danish Evangelical Missionary Society).

The relation of the Mission-Church to Polygamy.

When called upon to read a Paper before this select audience, I chose as my subject the question—how the Mission-Church is to deal with such polygamists as wish to be baptised. I know perfectly well, that this question has been discussed here in England by many distinguished and able men, and that probably, within a short time, it will be deliberated upon by the highest authorities in the Church of England at the Pan-Anglican Synod. I will therefore begin by saying that I do not at all believe *Difficult* myself in possession of so much learning and ability *question.* that I shall be able to contribute to the solution of this problem in any conclusive way. Besides, it is doubtful, whether any one of those who have taken part in the discussions which have been held on this question, has been convinced by his opponents that he is in the wrong; and these discussions have, perhaps, with many readers, left the impression that both parties were right.

I do not suppose that I shall be able to set anything before you which has not formerly been done, by throwing a quite new light upon the question. I am so far from thinking myself capable of giving a perfect solution of the problem, that I am rather convinced that it cannot be fully solved. As far as I can see,

Solution doubtful. we are here placed before a set of conflicting duties which has not its cause in the want of discernment in those who discuss this question, but is inherent in the state of things we discuss. In whatever way we try to solve this problem, we shall not be able to attain, that our solution will be so just, that injustice is not done somewhere.

When, nevertheless, I chose this subject, it was because the programme of this Conference puts as the first of the ends aimed at " To turn to account the experience of the past, for the improvement of the methods of Missionary enterprise in the foreign fields." In accordance with this I will simply set forth what the Missionary Society I have the honour to represent, has decided in regard to this problem, and by what reasons it has been led to this decision.

It is only a few years since this question was placed before our Home Committee, when one of our Missionaries in South Arcot, East India, reported that a man with two wives wished to be baptised; and he now asked whether this might be done, in spite of the said bigamy.

Arguments for baptising Polygamists. On this question being discussed in the Committee, opinion proved to be different. Some members asserted that the ancient Church had, no doubt, regarded polygamy in the same light as it regarded slavery. Polygamy was tolerated by those who had entered into it before their baptism, just as slavery was tolerated. It was acknowledged that neither agreed with true Christian life; but it was relied upon that these remains from ante-Christian time would gradually disappear, conquered by the spirit of the Church, leavening the community as the leaven leavened the dough. And so it came to pass, polygamy disappeared, and monogamy prevailed in the Christian community. *We* ought to do as was done by the ancient Church, viz., baptise those polygamists, who, in other respects, were fit to receive baptism, while we, of course, could never allow baptised Christians to enter into matrimony with more than one wife. When, in this way, we only tolerated a connection originating in the former ignorance, whilst maintaining, at the same time, that only monogamy was justified by Christian morals, polygamy would gradually disappear. If we would not do so, if we would deny baptism to polygamists, and force them, as a condition of their baptism, to discard those wives,—they had more than one,—we should only drive

Arguments of Missionaries confirming. out one devil by another. We should, by that proceeding, force the man to do wrong to her, or those, he dismissed against their will ; they being, the one as well as the other, his wives, with the same rights. Also, from our

Missionaries we received statements to the same effect. It was pointed out that polygamy among the Hindus was only an exception, not the rule; it generally only took place when a wife had no issue; it might then happen that her husband took another wife in order to get children, which, it is known, is a thing of very great importance to the Hindus. If he had to divorce one of these wives which should it be? It would seem to be most in accordance with the general idea of monogamy, if he retained the wife he had married first; but if he had children by the second, how could he send her away then? Would he not commit a double sin, both against her and against the children? How much would she suffer, if he retained the children, who would thus become motherless; and if he allowed her to keep them, they would become fatherless! It was far from being only rich people who had more than one wife, among poorer people bigamy also took place. Suppose a poor man divorced one of his wives, and sent her away, together with her children, he would give both her and them up to physical and moral misery and evil. And even if he had the means to provide for their subsistence, the state of such a woman would be very deplorable; she would not be able to marry again, and would probably fall a victim to the worst of vices.

Other members of our Committee maintained that the usage of the ancient Church had certainly not been as asserted. In the New Testament there was no trace of polygamy Arguments against baptising. having existed within the Church;—1 Tim. iii. 2, 12, and Tit. i. 6 do not say so. 1 Tim. v. 9 was sufficient to show that the words, "One husband of one wife," in the quoted texts, are not said in contrast to those who had several wives at one time, but to those who had married consecutively more than once. Though there were many illicit connections in the Græco-Roman community, there was no polygamy to be found, so the problem did possibly not exist at all in the Apostolic time. Besides, it could not be shown that polygamists had been baptised at all in the ancient Church. But, at all events, the monogamic matrimony must now, most decidedly, be maintained, as being the only one in harmony with Christian faith and Christian life, the only one justified by the Lord's Word and Spirit. And how should we be able to maintain this, if by baptism we admitted polygamists, with or without their two or more wives, into the Church? It would be nearly impossible to make it clear to the new Christians in the Mission-Church, that polygamy, which was sin when entered upon by baptised people, nay, a sin so great that it would lead to the excommunication of those who made themselves guilty of it, could be permitted to those who had Effect of toleration abroad. entered into it before their baptism, and that they could continue in it without losing their privileges as members of the Church. Not only the new Christians in foreign countries, also

many Christians at home would not be able to understand this.
They would be offended by it, look upon it as a
At home. transgression of the law of Christ, and turn away from
a Mission tolerating such things. It would appear to them as if
the Mission associated with those at home, who, while proclaiming
free thought, also proclaim what they call "free love," teaching
that a man is not to be tied to one wife, nor a woman to one
husband, but that they may connect themselves with whatever
number such a love might connect them with. At a time when
so much is done in Christendom to violate the bonds of matrimony,
the Mission should carefully avoid everything apparently pointing in
the same direction.

Although this view prevailed in the Committee, it was acknowledged that, when polygamists, in order to be baptised, dismissed
the wives—they had more than one—without the voluntary
consent of the said wives, a real sin was committed; and how
a sin could be atoned for by a new sin the Committee could not
see. The result arrived at was therefore this, *that a polygamist
cannot be baptised, but must remain in the state of a catechumen.*
Conclusion He can only be looked upon as an adherent, not as a full
arrived at. member of the Church, and he must necessarily be
excluded from all privileges to which only baptised people can be
admitted. As he has no part in the Lord's sacraments so he cannot
be admitted into any Church office. In this state he must remain,
until the Lord some way or other releases him from the hindrances
to his baptism, either by the death of those wives he had,—more than
one—or by his wives coming to the faith themselves, so that they,
understanding that polygamy is a sinful relation, decide upon dis-
solving the polygamic connections in the best way possible, or by
his own death; on his death-bed he may receive baptism, when he
asks for it. According to this decision of the Committee, polygamists
will not only not be induced to remove the hindrance for their
baptism by divorcing one or more wives, but it would even not be
approved of if they did so. One sin cannot more than the other give
them access to the community of the Lord and the Church.

By this solution of the problem I am persuaded that we must
abide as the best we have been able to find, although I am fully
aware it cannot be called perfect. It may be objected that such a
half measure as a permanent catechumenate cannot be in accordance
with His will who says, "He that is not with Me is against Me," and
that it may become a very heavy burden to a man who has become
anxiously concerned about his salvation, and therefore claims
baptism. It is said to him, as the Apostle Peter said to those who
A convert's asked, "What shall I do to be saved?" "Repent, and
perplexities. be baptised every one of you in the name of Jesus Christ
for the remission of sins;" and at the same time he is not allowed to
act up to this word. He is told that Christ says, "He that believes
and is baptised shall be saved," and at the same time he is denied

one of these means of grace, and that from a cause which seems also to make him unfit for partaking in the other. It may be said to be inconceivable to such a man, that it is said to him, "You cannot be baptised, because you are keeping up a sinful connection, nor can we claim or advise you to break this connection; and if you did it yourself we would not receive you." History can be cited against us; it is surely without example from the history of ancient Missions, that it has been demanded of anybody to remain a catechumen, and continue standing at the door of the kingdom of God, without being allowed to enter it, while on the other hand many have themselves been satisfied by remaining in this state, and that from many different reasons, as when they believed that the baptism on the death-bed would give them a sure access into heaven, because they would then not be exposed to the danger of breaking the covenant of baptism, or as our Scandinavian ancestors who accepted the rite of being marked with the sign of the cross *prima signatio*, Prima signatio. either in superstition that they might thus secure for themselves the protection of the God of the Christians, while they lived in Christian countries, or because they could then be sure of being treated friendly by the Christians in foreign lands, while they had not, by doing this, renounced the heathenism of their home country in such a way that they could not, when returned, live with their countrymen as brethren and partake together with them in their heathen festivals.

In spite of all this, I am sure, that the decision we have come to is the best possible. As far as I can see we cannot allow the polygamist to be baptised if he retains more than one wife after the baptism; for by this sacrament we are clad in Christ that we should live a new life in Him. How then can he be baptised who in receiving baptism will reserve to himself to remain without Christ in one part of his life, in which he will remain in the old life derived from heathenism? What formerly might be looked upon as something excusable, as something belonging to what God in His long-suffering tolerates in the times of ignorance (Acts xvii. 30; Rom. iii. 25), that becomes real sin to the baptised. And if such a man will earnestly try to live according to the covenant of baptism, how then can he be at any time feel satisfied with his polygamy? But on the other side it is my conviction that we dare not say Polygamy not that the compact he has concluded with his wives is quite adultery. analogous with many other contracts he may have made while being a heathen, and which must be said to be repealed by the new light which shows him that they are in themselves sinful, so that he ought not to keep them. Was the polygamic matrimony, as contracted by heathens, against all morals to such a degree that he who lived in it committed adultery, because his living together with several wives was a breach of his compact with the first one, then the compact with the others would have to be broken as a matter of conscience? But I do not think that the polygamic matrimony can be looked upon in that light.   Although such a matrimony is very much contrary to God's idea of the matrimonial relations between man and woman, wherefore it can never be blessed by the Church of Christ nor acknowledged by it; it is nevertheless contracted as a real matrimony in which each of the wives has the same privileges. The position in the times of the Old Testament is an evidence for this.   Even if the law given by Moses has not expressly declared polygamy to be lawful, yet it has never declared it to be against the law, although it was a well-known fact in Israel.   As far as I know the only text quoted as containing a declaration against polygamy is Leviticus xxi. 13, where it is said that "the high priest shall take a wife in her state of virginity;" but even if this "*a* wife" is to be understood as the same as *one* wife, this commandment could only have reference to the high priest.   Certainly in Deut. xvii. 17, the king was forbidden to take to himself many wives, but from reasons that do not appear to be of a moral nature; and how many wives had not David; and the Lord did not disapprove of it!   He says Himself through Nathan the prophet (2 Sam. xii. 8): "I gave thee thy master's wives into thy bosom!"   And he, whom God blesses amongst his children more than all the rest,—he who, according to the will of God, becomes the king of Israel after him, and to whom He gives what He denied to David—the permission to build a house to His name; is Solomon the son of Bathsheba.   When *he* is thus accepted, while her firstborn son, begotten by David, must die,—is this not an evidence that to the Lord he is a legitimate son, while the first one is looked upon as born in adultery?   Is polygamy thus acknowledged as a real marriage in the Old Testament; should it not then be worthy of the name of matrimony amongst the Gentiles who have much less understanding of what is the will of God, than such a man as David had,—he who spoke moved by the Holy Ghost?   But is not then the contract, which in heathenism has connected one man with more than one wife, also such an one that it cannot be broken by one polygamist against the wish of the other without sin?   It must be a sin so much the more, as many times not only the happiness but also the existence of the divorced wife is at stake, so that she sinks into misery on account of this breach of contract.   It must therefore be called a great sin when such a breach is made; and when it shall be the condition for a man's being baptised, do we then not say: "Let us do evil, that good may come," as some slanderously reported and affirmed that the Apostle Paul said?   But of these he says: "Their damnation is just" (Rom. iii. 8).

The permanent catechumenate may certainly become a heavy burden to him who is put in that position; but that is an evil common to all consequences of past sins, and not only the sins of the man himself, but those of his ancestors, of his people.   Nothing else can be said to him who is sighing under the weight of such a burden, than, You must endure

[margin note: Old Testament practice and teaching.]

[margin note: Position as catechumens a chastisement.]

it,—bow down under the burden, that it may be to you what God
wants it to be, namely, a beneficial chastisement by which God will
bring you up for Himself!

But even if we cannot exempt him from this chastisement, as
long as the Lord wants it to last, we can do what is in our power
to lighten the burden to him.   Not only may we cheer him by such
words of consolation as Hebrews xii. 11 : " No chastening for
the present seemeth to be joyous, but grievous ; nevertheless afterwards it yieldeth the peaceable fruit of righteousness unto them
which are exercised thereby." But we may also give him a sign,
that he is not only not despised by the Church, but is looked upon
with heartfelt sympathy, and that we would like to count him right
out amongst our own. We may give him as much blessing from
the Lord, as we can, without sinning against His ordinances, that
so he may be strengthened to remain faithful, also to remain
quiet and wait for the salvation of the Lord. This is done when
he is received among the catechumens by a solemn rite. This idea
struck one of our Missionaries. He remembered how many Scan-
dinavians had caused themselves to be marked with the sign of the
cross in the times of old. He then performed such a rite with a
man who, being a bigamist, could not be baptised. The Committee
could not approve of the manner in which he performed this rite,
but they approved of the idea, and they will edite a ritual for this
act. It must be said that the man mentioned has afterwards often
asked whether he could not be baptised, as he longed for baptism,
but on the other hand, we hear that he has derived blessing from
what is given him by the relation in which he stands to the congregation ; he lives in several ways a new life, and in the Church he
is one of the best singers. When a Possari he had often accompanied
himself on the "udukkei" (a small hand drum, used in the Tamil
country) to songs about the idols, now he sings Christian hymns to
the praise of God.

Finally, only this. It has been said in defence of the baptism
of polygamists, that by this the Mission would make great progress.
Many, especially in Africa, who now keep away would Gaining converts
come to baptism. But let it never be the aim of the no reason for
Evangelical Mission to have a large number of baptised toleration.
people to make a show with. Let it always remain its single aim
to gain souls for the Lord. This we can only do by preaching the
truth in Christ, and remaining in it ourselves. If we depart from
this in order to adorn ourselves with large numbers; if many
baptisms, independent of all other things, are sufficient to recommend a certain method of Mission work, then we are sliding down
an incline on which we shall only sink deeper and deeper down,
until we come so far down, that we cannot rise any more. Let us
remember to what consequences such accommodation brought
Nobili and his successors, and say, *vestigia terrent.*

PAPER.

3. BY THE REV. M. E. STRIEBY, D.D. (Corresponding Secretary of the American Freedman's Association). Read in part by the REV. DR. BEARD.

[This Paper on a subject of great importance is one of a very few that got out of its proper place. It was approved by the Committee in New York, and is of such sterling merit, that to have left it out in the Conference would have been a real loss, and to leave it out of the Report would be a grave omission. To avoid breaking the continuity of the discussion at this meeting, which dealt with the subdivisions on *Slavery*, on lines different from those of the Paper, we shall take the liberty of inserting it as an Appendix to the Session on "Organisation and Government of Native Churches." The division (a) "The Best Method of Training Native Workers" is quite germane to the subject and treatment of the Paper. Dr. Strieby shows the great purposes of Providence in converting and training a large body of the liberated slaves of African origin now in America, fitted by the constitution, and education, and character to be the great workers in grand schemes for the enlightenment of the "dark continent."—ED.]

DISCUSSION.

Sir Thomas Fowell Buxton, Bart. (Treasurer; C.M.S.): I did not at all expect to be called upon at this early period of the meeting, but I Introduction of think that I shall make the most concise and economical use of European the few minutes at my disposal if I venture, first, to express customs. an opinion and then give my illustrations of it. It has happened to me lately, during the winter, to be in India, and my illustrations will be chiefly drawn from that country. Let me say that I have arrived at the opinion that in India and elsewhere, according to what I have heard in years past, there has been far too great a readiness on the part of European Missionaries to insist upon the teaching of European customs. I believe that the tendency is much less now than it was forty or fifty years ago; nevertheless, I believe there is far too much of it, and I hope that the discussion this morning will do something to remove what may remain of that which I believe to be an evil tendency.

Let me ask you to think of the customs as to buildings. I have in my mind large churches in Cawnpore, built by the Government, and at Buildings too Allahabad, built by a sort of trust, half episcopal and half European. official; also different churches in Bengal, built by those who represented the Church Missionary Society. Having seen those buildings, my impression is that they were not the most suitable to the climate or the people, and that they would not have been built had they consulted the feelings and the tendency of the native mind, rather than our own impressions. My belief is that the churches, especially in Bengal, which were built by gentlemen who have done most noble work

which we ought always to acknowledge,—work done by men who by
nationality were Germans, and Missionaries of the Church Missionary
Society,—my belief, is that they had too much in their minds as an object
to accomplish the reproduction in some Bengal village of the scenes which
they left behind them, it might be in the north of Germany or in
England.

Perhaps the most suitable church that I saw in India, for a native
church, was at Peshawur. I was told by the Chief Commissioner there,
and other Europeans, how successful a church it was, and
the history of it was this. The European officials, engineers ^{A native church.}
and others, had recommended a certain building; the natives being there
of a somewhat stronger backed disposition than elsewhere said, "We will
have none of your suggestions, but we will build such churches as we
please;" and they built an exceedingly graceful and pretty church, and, in
reference to the seats and arrangements, they were far more suitable than
those in any church that I saw. Then, as to the matters of dress, I do
hope we shall at all events avoid one danger, that we shall impress upon
our agents all over the world the danger of leading those under their
instruction to suppose that matters of dress are matters of religion.

Mr. R. N. Cust, LL.D.: My remarks this morning shall be upon the
subject of polygamy. Marriage is the type of the union of Christ with
His Church, and the relation of the sexes is the touchstone of ^{Polygamists not to be baptised.}
the purity of the Church. If once you allow polygamy in a
Church, away with its purity. It is no empty threat, or no
empty fear, that African Churches are trying to introduce polygamy. We
must cut at the root of the tree, and permit no polygamists to be baptised
under any circumstances. If you allow it, how can the preacher condemn
the practice, when in the seat below the pulpit there sits a man with three
or four wives, and perhaps three or four new-born babes? You must
forbid it absolutely and entirely.

Then, as to the second alternative, shall we call a man to commit
a second sin in order to wipe out a first sin? Shall we call him to put
away innocent women to whom he has been married from
childhood or youth, with their children, and drive them into ^{Danger to discarded wives.}
other sins by living with other men? God forbid. The
second alternative of putting away the wives must not be entertained for
a moment.

Then there is a third course. What is that? Admit such a man
as a catechumen: baptise his wives, two or three innocent women: they
are wives of one husband: baptise his children; but tell him,
"You have placed yourself in such a situation, that you cannot ^{A third course.}
be admitted into the Church of Christ. We leave your future state to
One who cannot do wrong, but we will not have the young Churches
of Christ defiled by the admission of one who is a polygamist." This
is the practice of one great Church in East Africa, the Universities'
Mission, and I think it is the right practice; indeed, I see no other course.
Any other course will lead you into more deplorable inconsistency. In
the West African Churches, we hear, in our last reports of the Church
Missionary Society, of other habits which they wish to introduce. They
wish to be allowed to marry the widows of their elder brothers according to
the law of Leviticus, a custom that prevails in Northern India amongst the

Sikhs. And I see in one report that they wish to practise polyandry, one woman with several husbands. Once depart from the Word of our Lord, "They twain shall be one flesh," "Male and female created He them," and you are led into wondrous inconsistencies.

Rev. A. Merensky (Superintendent, Berlin Missionary Society): Brothers and sisters,—I must ask your forbearance because I am not well versed in the English language. But if it is not possible for me to bring pleasing words before you, I hope I shall be able to tell you some encouraging facts with regard to Missionary work and the treatment of polygamy in Africa. In Africa the treatment of polygamy is a burning question. Polygamy is the greatest obstacle to the spread of Christianity among the African tribes, and very often younger brothers coming to the new countries and the fresh tribes are perhaps inclined to have too little courage with regard to this great obstacle. It is like a mountain before us, but we know that even mountains may be removed by the power of Christian faith; and so it is with polygamy in Africa. I have baptised in South Africa very many who were polygamists before their conversion. I have lived for more than twenty years among the tribes of the interior and Transvaal, and I have had to deal with this question. I am glad to say that on this subject there is almost complete unanimity between all the Missionary Societies of South Africa, and the system of toleration in regard to polygamy is, as far as I know, entirely done away with.

Customs of Berlin Missions.

Where the Spirit of God is working upon the hearts of the natives I cannot see that there is any difficulty in treating this question. When a polygamist came to us asking to be received into instruction, he often asked, "How about the women?" And I said, "Do not trouble yourself about that; come and hear the Word of God. You have no power in yourself to deal with this question before you are a really converted man, a true follower, willing to follow Christ; you must follow Christ, and I will instruct you if you come." Month after month passed by, and when the time for baptism arrived we selected some of those who were perhaps ready for it; then most of them came and said, "This matter is regulated already; it is all right; I have given my wives back to their parents." We have not tried to press that upon such men; but it has been simply the effect of other Christians upon them, and the effect of the Word of God. Therefore we have found that the question was not so difficult as we thought before. Very often those native "wives" are young girls five or six years old, and when they are sent back their parents receive them with joy, because they think they can sell them again and get more cattle for them.

There are also some other difficulties connected with this subject, and one of those difficulties is, How are we to deal with the women? which wife must be kept by the man? We have never tried to find out which was the first wife, because such vexed questions would arise which are very difficult to decide. I always said to the man in such a case, "Take the wife whom you love, and the wife you believe you can live with as a Christian,—who is ready to accept Christianity." With regard to the wives of polygamists, we never tried to separate them from their husbands, because it was against the law of our people, and we did not believe it was our duty to interfere with that law; but we have had the result that polygamy, by the Word of God, has been conquered and has disappeared.

Difficulty about the wives.

Rev. J. A. Lefevre, D.D. (Foreign Missions of the Presbyterian Church in the United States): I wish to speak for a single moment on the subject of polygamy. I wish to do so because, having been Chairman of the Board of Foreign Missions of that grand, though young, Southern Presbyterian Church in the United States, I have been compelled to fight some battles upon this point. The question has come up in our Board, and it .is of the highest importance to have some clear principle in our minds, for, if it does not solve all the difficulties of detail, it will certainly solve the great difficulties that appear to be practical, and that press upon the consciences of the Lord's people.

In fighting this battle, I have always raised the question, Are these polygamists married at all? Are they married in the only sense in which, as a Church of Jesus Christ, we have a right to deal with the question. Is it not of the very essence of marriage that two shall pledge themselves to each other to cleave to each other and forsake all others? Is not that the essence of Christian marriage as it was promulgated in the Garden of Eden in the days of man's innocence? No institution has survived with less damage the ruins of the fall. The principle was re-expounded by the Lord Jesus Christ when the question came before Him. Now the question is, Did the man whom you call a polygamist enter into a covenant with any woman to cleave to her alone and forsake all others, which is of the essence of Christian marriage? Did that first wife whom he married understand him to come under that obligation to her? No. And I have uniformly taken the ground that in such a case there was no marriage at all, that these people are living in a system of sin, or call it what you please.

As to the toleration of sin, I am not troubled about that question. The Scriptures of God and the words of Jesus Christ are enough for me. "For the hardness of your hearts" God allowed it. Whatever that may mean, I am not shocked at the principles that God overrules and regulates the sins of men, the sins of the world, and the sins of devils. What do we see God do in daily providence? What do we see Him do in our own history? I would require a man who has been living in what is called polygamy to separate himself fully, as far as that special relationship is concerned, from all those to whom he formerly sustained that relationship; but at the same time, while he is bound to give up his civil rights in the community, he cannot shirk his duties. He must take care of his wives; he must support them; he must protect them from sinking into sin or temptation or want, according to his ability; and then, if he afterwards chooses to enter into the holy covenant of matrimony, whether with one of his former wives or another, he may be allowed to do so.

Rev. James Thomas (B.F.B.S., formerly of Shanghai): I wish to say one or two words upon the subject of polygamy. It is a very great subject, and we have heard enough to make us all acquainted with this fact, that it is troubling Christian Missionaries all over the world. Our treatment of it will leave an impress upon the very name of Christianity throughout the world. If we deal with it unwisely, the heathen people will have a conception of Christianity that I venture to think is not true or right. I will deal with it only as it came before me in China. Polygamy prevails there, as everyone acquainted with the social condition of China very well knows.

How shall we deal with this question? We have listened to some very startling things to-day. They are amazing even to me. Surely, what has been said cannot go forth from this Conference endorsed by the sentiment of those who are here representing Christian Churches. The matter, I know, is a very difficult one, and it would ill become me to speak one word in a spirit of dogmatism; but, is it possible that any Christian Missionary can dare to say, in the name of Jesus Christ, " Take from your wives the one that you love best ?" The paper read first shows how very great the difficulties are. Let me set two

A case at Shanghai. very brief pictures before you,—one from Shanghai and the other from a southern port. They are matters of fact. In the one case, a Christian Missionary had to deal with a man who, having heard casually of the Gospel of Christ, and being the husband of many wives, was led in faith to trust himself as a sinner to the Lord Jesus Christ as his Saviour. The Missionary insisted that he should put away all his wives, except the one he married first. There were children by them all, except the first. There was nothing before these women but a life of sin and shame. Can that be done in the name of the Lord Jesus Christ and of His Church ? Another case was this, showing the straits Christian men are put to when they find themselves in this difficulty. A number of men who had several wives were baptised, and from the Christian community the Christian Missionary selected a number of unmarried men to marry the many wives of those whom he had baptised. They were all of the fellowship of that one Church. Now I want to ask if that is to be done in the name of Jesus Christ ? Surely, it is possible

St. Paul's dictum. to act upon the principle and the mode of treatment of the early Church, when St. Paul said : See to it, that a bishop and a deacon be "the husband of one wife." I know that the Greek Church makes nonsense of that passage, and many other Churches deal strangely with it. To me it presents this simple solution. There were Jews who were poly-gamists—for have we forgotten that polygamy existed in the Church of God among the Jews ?—and there were heathen men who had married many wives; and the simple explanation appears to me to be this : " Timothy—Titus—see to it, that whoever be your bishop or your deacon that he be a monagamist, a husband of one wife, in order that the purity of the Church may be maintained."

Rev. John Ross (United Presbyterian Mission, Manchuria) : Mr. Chair-man, Christian friends,—I have risen to say a word upon this same subject of polygamy, and I should like to raise it to a higher platform than that which it has been placed upon. I do not wish to consider it as

Not an isolated nor simple question. an isolated question. There is that other question that has already been spoken of, For what purpose is Christianity going into heathen lands ? Are we going into heathen lands in order to root up everthing that differs from our opinions and practice, even to our very clothing ? Are we not rather to go into heathen lands to plant Christian principles, and give higher principles of life than they have ever had before ? not to wrench up all old customs, but gradually to raise them and allow those principles to grow, as they grew in the early Church, and to become gradually assimilated by the people who have learned them ? Let us uproot every vice, every practice, that is in any way inconsistent with holiness.

In regard to polygamy, I am not sure that the question is quite so simple as some of the previous speakers would have us understand. I have not myself baptised any polygamists, and yet, if a polygamist came to me for baptism, I should hesitate very long before saying to him, either " I cannot admit you into Christian fellowship, though you are a believer," or " You must divorce one or other of those women whom you have been living with as wives." One gentleman, to my amazement, spoke of marriage, other than Christian marriage, as only a form of marriage. What about Jacob ? Was he not a godly man, and yet he had two wives. Perhaps it would have been better if he had had only one —he might have been more comfortable, but that is not the point.

One wife, a happier life. I know several polygamists, and I have no doubt that if they had been wise they would have contented themselves with one wife,— certainly their families have not been more peaceful or happy. But I say that is not the point. The point is this : here are two or three women who have been married to one man ; is he to cast off two of these wives? It seems to me that the solution of the question lies in what the reader of the paper on this subject stated. I was greatly pleased with the manner in which he put the practical issues before us, but I was sorry at what I considered his lame conclusion. It seems to me that the only practical solution is that which he pointed out. Let those who are truly believers be baptised, if The solution. they are polygamists ; but make very short work of a Christian who takes a second wife. In that way you can soon root out polygamy. With regard to the passage quoted by a previous speaker, I must say that I have not much sympathy with some of the interpretations that have been given of it. Logically, it seems to me to be this, that a bishop must be the husband of *one* wife. Well, it seems to me either that Paul was himself guilty of a breach of that law, or else some of the interpretations that have been given are not correct. It seems to me to signify that he must be the husband of not more than one wife.

Rev. Professor T. Smith, D.D. (Free Church College, Edinburgh, formerly of Calcutta): What I was anxious to say has been said to a very considerable extent by the last two speakers. When my friend Dr. Cust was speaking so very strongly about his view on the matter I felt that it would be a want of courage on my part not to state the other view, which I strongly hold and have held all the time I was a Missionary, and ever since,—the view that we have no right to exclude polygamists, and certainly no right to require of them to abandon their Is it right to wives ; and least of all can I admit, with the reader of one of exclude the Papers, that we should keep them waiting as catechumens Polygamists? for an indefinite period, making their admission to the Church dependent upon the death of some unfortunate woman. I greatly admired the way in which Mr. Holm stated the matter. I admired his honesty and straightforwardness ; but it did seem to me a strange thing that so sensible a man as he evidently is, and so sensible a Society as I know his Society to be, should come to such a conclusion.

I endorse all that Dr. Cust said with regard to polygamy getting into the Church. It never can get into the Church, because it is an impossibility that any Christian can desire to be married to two wives, and it is an impossibility that any Christian minister can marry a man to two wives. The Apostle has put a brand upon bigamy and polygamy by preventing a polygamist from Exclusion from holding any office in the Christian Church ; but I think that very office. prohibition implies that there were men otherwise eligible—that is, that they could be members of the Church, but were debarred from holding office in the Church by that brand being put upon them, for what was verily a sin against even the light of nature. Our American friend told us that he was willing that a polygamist who had discarded all his wives should marry any other woman. I must say it appears to me, with all deference and humility, that that would be directly violating the command of our Lord : Sin of putting "He that putteth away his wife save for fornication, and mar- away. rieth another, committeth adultery." They are his wives. But our friend says that these marriages are not marriages at all in a Christian sense. Would he say that the marriages of ungodly men before they are converted are strictly Christian marriages ? Yet he does not think that they are void when such a man becomes a Christian. These were real marriages—real in the sight of man, and I believe real, however imperfect and sinful, in the sight of God, and I maintain that our friend had no right to marry such a man to another woman.

Rev. W. McGregor (English Presbyterian Mission, Amoy): I should also like to say a few words upon this question of polygamy. When our Lord reminded the Jews of the original institution of marriage, I believe He laid down a rule which is to be the rule of the Christian Church in all ages. If we are to admit Christian polygamy, I do not see how we are to exclude Admit Polygamy, Christian polyandry. With regard to the question of different Polyandry rules for those who are already married, my experience in the must follow. Missionary field has led me to think that in what we do we must carry with us the consciences of our Christian converts; and I am persuaded that if we have one rule for this member and another for that member, we shall not carry their consciences with us.

With regard to the case of China, which I know best, I was very much amazed to hear a gentleman who has been in China saying that all the women whom a Chinaman has in his household are equally wives. The Chinese recognise simply one woman as the real wife—one woman as the mistress of the household; there is a second wife who has quite a different position Only one real subordinate to her. All the others are simply concubines, bought wife in China. for so much money, and they do not hold the position of wives at all. The children, whether they are of the secondary wife or of the concubines, do not address their real mother as mother in their own family; they address the mistress of the household as mother; they are all considered children of the mistress of the household, who is considered to be the real wife. Consequently I do not think it is doing anything in the way of breaking up a Chinese family, when we insist if a man is to be received into the Christian Church, The rule. that he shall make provision for these other women belonging to his household, and that he shall regard his real wife, the mistress of the household, as his wife, and live with her as his wife. We have had several cases of men who have been long kept in the position of catechumens, not being received into the Church simply on account of these women in the family. We have had cases of men making provision for these women, and being ultimately received into the Church. In one case we have a native minister, a most valuable man in connection with the Mission, who is the son of such a family. I do not believe that he would have been in the position of an ordained Christian minister to-day if we had received the father into the Church while he had a number of women in his harem.

Rev. James Calvert (Wesleyan Missionary Society, from Fiji Islands): This is an extremely difficult question in lands where polygamy prevails. We commenced in a straightforward way by telling the people that they must have only one wife, and that one must be one of those with whom they have been united. Difficulty in such cases was lessened. As has been just Conscience intimated, the conscience of the Christian people has confirmed against that decision; and not only so, but the heathen mind felt that it Polygamy. was a right decision. I remember a chief saying to King Thakombau, "This religion is all very well, but a chief can only have one wife!" "You fool," said the king; "that is God's ordination, and it must be right." This man at the time had eighty wives. I never knew a single instance in which a polygamist who continued in that state, made any progress in religion. I do not believe that I ever knew one of the many whom we have had in that state being really converted to God. Polygamy People submitted cheerfully, when they wanted to be right hinders progress. with God, to abandon all their wives except one. We have found that work remarkably well. I am sorry that the discussion seems to carry us about hither and thither; but I believe if we put our foot firmly down upon this, that a man can only have one wife to approve himself in the sight of God, God will work with us, and matters will be carried on successfully.

Rev. John Hesse (Würtemberg): As an old Indian Missionary I am sorry that the question of caste has not yet been mentioned. Caste is as great an abomination as polygamy. Fancy a number of men clubbing together and making a law for themselves that they will never eat nor drink with any other man not belonging to their society; that they will never shake hands with anyone else; never touch anyone else, even when sick or dying. People say that *The caste question.* caste is connected with racial differences and with the division of labour. That is all right; it has been connected with these things, but the essence of caste, against which we fight as Christian Missionaries, is this, that the caste man makes it a rule for himself and for all his caste people never to get into touch with people who do not belong to their caste; and that is essentially unchristian. It has unfortunately become rather out of fashion to protest against caste nowadays. There are several great Missionary Societies who are a little lax in this respect, but I have found in India and by study that those Missions which make it a point that caste be broken before baptism are not only right in principle, but most successful in practice. Once a converted Brahman in Southern India *A Brahman convert* came to a church where caste was kept, and at the door he was *disgusted.* asked, "What caste do you belong to? because there are different mats; one for the Sudras, one for the Pariahs, and one for the Brahmans." The man turned away disgusted, and said, "I do not want a seat on your mats." There have been cases where catechists and evangelists who have been Pariahs were turned away by the Sudra Christians! That shame ought not to be. I want to impress upon the Conference that caste must be formally done away with before baptism is administered.

Rev. G. Smith (English Presbyterian Mission, Swatow, China): I want to say a word as to the subject of polygamy that has been so much spoken of. The subject is so important, having to do with the family, and thus having so much to do with the purity and perfectness of religion, that it warrants all the attention we can give to it in the time allotted. A good deal has already been said upon this *The fundamental law.* subject, and I will only refer to one or two points. God's ordinance is that *two* should be one flesh; not three, not more than two, but two, are to become one flesh. This is the fundamental law of human society. Christ tells us to go back to what was at the beginning, and He evidently means to lay it down for the regulation of His Church in all time to go back to the original law. There is more grace now than there was under the old dispensation, and so a higher standard of attainment is required. Thus, much that was permitted under the former is not tolerated under the present dispensation.

Then there is another thing that we must remember. A great deal has been said about the hardship arising from a man who has more wives than one putting some of them away. But there are many hard things to do in Christianity. A man is required to give up his life if need be in order to be a Christian; he is required to pluck out his right eye, and cut off his right hand, and cut off his right foot. This is the law of Christ. A great deal *Christianity demands self-denial.* that is sentimental may be said against it; but that is the law of Scripture. Then we are to remember another thing. When Christ calls us to do anything He always gives grace to do it; there is grace for whatever we are called to do, and to do right wrongs no man. A right thing done in a Christian way has no bad results. A passage has been quoted about a bishop being the husband of one wife, and it was quoted as implying that there might be polygamy in the Christian Church. Now I wish another passage to be taken and kept side by side with it. It is the converse of it : The woman is to be the wife of one husband. Does that imply polyandry? Are you prepared to receive as a member of the Church a woman who has several husbands? I say it is impurity, and I do not suppose that there is a Christian minister who would allow it. But it is only the converse to the other.

Rev. B. La Trobe (Secretary of the Moravian Missions) : I feel it my duty to give to the Conference the result of the Decennial Synods The Moravian rule. of the Church which I represent, the Moravian, which has had to deal with this question for more than one hundred years. The following is the resolution passed at the General Synod of 1879 :—

" Baptism of Polygamists and Polyandrists.

" Polygamy and polyandry are opposed to the idea of Christian marriage.

" It is, therefore, the duty of our Missionaries to bear a decided testimony against these heathenish customs. While it can on no account be permitted that baptised persons form such connections, the Synod was conscious that there might be cases in which it would lead to yet greater sin if a heathen before his baptism were obliged to dismiss all his wives but one, and therefore resolved :—

" That in exceptional cases, and only in such, polygamists may be admitted to holy baptism, but polyandrists in no case. These exceptions are to be considered and determined upon by the Mission Conference of the district in which such cases occur.

" It is a matter of course that a baptised man living in polygamy cannot be appointed to office in the Church."—Page 117 of Results of General Synod of the Brethren's Unity (Moravian Church), held at Herrnhut in 1879.

That is the result of our experience from different parts of the world amongst the Esquimos, Indians, Africans, and others whom I might mention.

Rev. James Scott (Free Church of Scotland Zulu Mission) : I have spoken very little at public meetings, except in the Zulu language, for the last ten years, and I hope, therefore, that you will excuse me Personal experience. if I am not quite at home in my own tongue. I rise to speak on the question of polygamy, and I doubt if there is any one here to whom that is such a burning question as it is to me. I have at this moment dozens and scores of polygamists waiting to be admitted to my Church, and it is a very serious question what we are to do with them. I could, if time allowed, speak very strongly for half an hour on either side of the question. I have to do with it every day of my life.

As I have said, there are dozens and scores of polygamists wishing to be baptised, and I scarcely know what to do in the matter. I was delighted to hear some of our brethren speak for freedom. I was delighted to hear Among the Zulus. the remarks of Dr. Smith and of the Rev. John Ross from China, because I believe that in some cases we must and ought to accept polygamists. We ought not, of course, to allow polygamy to be rooted in the Christian Church. Amongst the Zulus in South Africa, we have grey-headed old men with their grey-headed old wives coming and asking to be baptised into the Church of Christ, and are we to say to these men, " Send those old women and your children away "? Let me mention one case that happened several years ago. Far away from any white men, a man with two wives came forward for baptism. What was to be done ? They knew the custom of the Missionaries ; they knew that the Missionaries had laid down a strict rule that no polygamists were to be baptised, and all the Societies had agreed upon that; but I had felt in my own mind for a considerable time that there were cases in which that was a wrong thing to lay down as a hard and fast rule. This Sabbath morning, amongst thirty or forty others, came one man, as to whose Christianity I had no doubt; he had testified at public meetings, and had spoken nobly for Christ, and he came with his two wives for baptism. I said to him, "What is to be done?" "Oh," said the man, "I will release one of the women to return to her father's house; but as I am a Christian now, she must not take those children of mine to be brought up in that heathen kraal." "I will go," *The children a difficulty.* says the woman; "but I must have the children; I cannot leave my children, I must take them." Let me tell you, ladies and gentlemen, I should not have known what to do that morning but for the fact that my wife was by my side, and she knew that my views were not so strict as the views of some other people, and she said, "Carry out your own views and baptise them, and then leave the question to themselves."

Rev. E. E. Jenkins (Secretary, Wesleyan Missionary Society): I wish to say a word about the Indian marriage curse. I am very thankful that so many speakers, and some of them practical speakers, have addressed the audience on the most difficult subject of polygamy, *The Indian* with which I have been familiar for many years. I wish I were *Marriage Law.* as familiar with the solution of it as with the problem. But I hope that the Conference will speak out in no uncertain tones on the Indian marriage question. We have been preaching against marriage usages. I preached against them for eighteen years, and my successors, and the honoured ministers of other Societies have preached against it; and now, thank God, the Hindu youths themselves are denouncing them. These young men have been educated in the English language, and when you teach a man English you not only teach him to read our books, but you put English ideas into his mind, and you put before him the examples of Englishmen, and the history of great and free nations. The fact is, that you make such a student, in a very important respect, a new man. Now these men are with us, and they say that this infamous marriage system must come to an end.

I wish the Government would act; I mean the Government of India. I wish they would listen to the constant appeals presented to them, not from Missionary Conferences only, but from the people themselves. Of course a great social movement like this cannot be attempted by *Widows eight* Government until they see that the people are prepared for it. *years old.* How many widows do you think there are in India? Twenty millions. Now there is hope for a widow in this country, they tell me, but there is no hope for a widow yonder. And the poor little girl who happens to be betrothed at the age of two to a youth at the age of eight, if he dies, will be left a widow, and a widow for life! The enormity of this system has become more and more apparent to the intelligence of India. Oh, if our Queen, the Empress of India, had placed before her a short measure, setting free the vast sisterhood of India from this bondage, and if she would put her well-known signature at the bottom of it—they may talk about the glories of her Jubilee, but I venture to say that a measure of that kind would shed a far more shining and enduring lustre upon Queen Victoria's reign than anything that has ever been done before.

Rev. Professor Lindsay, D.D. (Free Church College, Glasgow): Allow me to say one or two words on this subject. I am one of those who have come here not to give light, but to get it. These questions are constantly being referred to Home Committees, and two of them have been referred to the Home Committee of my Church, of which I am Chairman. The two questions that have been discussed most are the questions of caste and of polygamy, the one offending against the brotherhood of mankind, and the other offending against the Christian elevation of woman. I think that the discussion of this day has shown us that polygamy is not a question that can be very easily settled by people sitting in council at home. It is a question which has very many sides, and those sides are as manifold as the various nations among which we preach Christ. The China Missionaries almost all go together, African Missionaries go together, and Indian Missionaries go together, and none of them have suggested a common rule; nor has it always been remembered that polygamy affects women and children as well as men. The lesson that we have been taught to-day is that we Christians at home must remember that our Missionaries, who in our stead are preaching Christ to the heathen, have difficulties to contend with, practical difficulties, in this matter, that we at home cannot estimate, and therefore we must do something like that which has been done by the Moravian Brethren. I admire the wisdom of the Moravian decision. The Moravian Church is, I believe, the most honoured Missionary Church in the world, and the decision it has come to is the decision that I think almost every Missionary Society might very well adopt as a general principle to guide Missionaries, then they must leave the matter, not to a single Missionary, nor even to a single Missionary's wife,— though I think the wife is better able to discuss the matter in all its bearings than the husband—but to the general council of Missionaries within that Mission district.

Polygamy a many-sided question.

To be left to Missionaries.

In general councils.

Rev. William Clark, M.A., of Barrhead, Glasgow (United Presbyterian Church of Scotland): I do not think I should have ventured to address the Conference but for a remark made by one of the speakers—a German brother labouring in Africa—to the effect that there was almost unanimity amongst Missionaries in South Africa on this question. The Church to which I have the pleasure of belonging differs in its practice on this matter from the Church represented by that Missionary. The United Presbyterian Church, which has Missionaries in China, in Japan, in Jamaica, in Kalabar, in Kaffraria, and in India, is said to be the largest giving Church for Missions in proportion to the number of its members of any Church in the world, except the Moravian, and this circumstance will give us some claim to be heard on such a subject as this.

Experience of an old Mission.

Our Missionaries in South Kaffraria act in this way. If a polygamist, in regard to whom they have hopeful evidence that he has been converted, wishes to be baptised, he is instructed that the first wife is his rightful wife and that the others must go. I understand that there are some Churches in South Africa that say rather to such a candidate for baptism: "One of your wives you must take as your wife, the one that you love best." Our Church allows no such liberty of choice; we say, "The one you married first is your real wife in the sight of the Lord, whatever consequences may be feared; you are pretty safe in keeping the rule, 'They twain shall be one flesh.'" The example of Jacob has been referred to by one of the speakers; but we are

First wife only recognised.

under New Testament law, and, as another speaker pointed out, "there is more grace in this dispensation than there was in the former."

Allusion has been made to the two passages of Scripture in which it is laid down as one of the qualifications of a bishop that he be the husband of one wife, and to an inference which is often drawn from this expression. I have heard no Scriptural argument used in favour of what is called freedom, except this doubtful inference. I have lectured through the two passages referred to, and after reading all I could lay my hands upon bearing upon their exposition, I have not been able to see evidence of the actual admission of polygamists to membership in the Apostolic Church. We cannot make a controverted question in Church history as to the usage of early times a rule to determine our course in South Africa and else-where in these days, so long especially as we have the plain enactment, "They twain shall be one flesh." Mr. Smith of Swatow has expressed most of the views I thought of defending. Let me only advert in conclusion to the desire which it seems is being expressed in some instances by the heathen themselves for an improvement of the law, and the forcible putting down of this evil system of polygamy. Is the Church going to lag behind? Can you get the Government to improve *Higher aspirations not to be discouraged.* its legislation, so long as the Church is found countenancing the evil by admitting polygamists to baptism and Church membership? I was glad to hear my friend Mr. Ross, while rather more free in his views than I should be inclined to be, declare that he had never admitted any polygamists to the membership of the Christian Church.

ADJOURNED DISCUSSION

ON

MISSIONARY METHODS—(3) DEALING WITH SOCIAL CUSTOMS.*

(*Friday evening, June 15th, in the Lower Hall.*)

Dean Vahl (Denmark) in the chair.

Bishop Crowther offered prayer.

The Chairman: This meeting is to be a continuation of the meeting which was held here on Tuesday morning, on the relation of the Missionary to social customs, such as caste, slavery, polygamy, Indian marriage law, etc. I should like, before I call upon any gentleman to speak, to make some observations about polygamy. It is necessary that we should arrive at right conclusions and make right distinctions in regard to these grave subjects. It seems to me that it is absolutely necessary to make a distinction between polygamy and concubinage. It has been asked, "Why has not Christ forbidden *Polygamy and concubinage distinct.* polygamy?" and "Why is polygamy not forbidden in the New Testament?" For myself I do not believe that polygamy existed at all in the Hebrew and the great Latin world, at the time of Christ and the

---

* This meeting contains a large amount of repetition. But as it is a question which requires much and varied experience for its solution, we have not limited the expressions of opinion or statement of facts, but have given all in small type.—EDITOR.

Apostles. Herod Antipas. it is true, had two wives, but he divorced his first wife, and lived only with one. It was the same in the great Roman world. I have never seen anything in the classics to lead us to believe that polygamy existed at that time. There was very great licentiousness, and there was concubinage. A man had a wife.—but, though he lived with many others, he had but one wife.

We heard on Tuesday that the same custom prevailed in China, and that a man has only one wife, although he lives with many others; but only the first is considered to be his real wife, the others being looked upon as concubines. If this is really the case, then we can see why polygamy is not forbidden in the New Testament. But when we look to St. Paul, who says a bishop shall have but one wife, the conclusion is drawn that, although it was permitted that men who lived in polygamy should retain their wives, it was forbidden that a man who held a prominent position in the Church should have more than one wife. The conclusion, I think, is not right at all ; because, when we look to 1 Timothy v. 9, it is said, " Let not a widow be taken into the number under threescore years old, having been the wife of one man." From this it cannot be concluded that it was allowed to other women to live in polyandry. Then there is another distinction that should be made. It has been said, " What shall a man do when he has more than one wife ? Shall he give them up to a life of sin or beggary, when baptised on condition that he must have only one wife ; shall he leave the children of the other wives to destitution ?" I do not think that is right. If a man in our country has a wife, and lives a profligate life, and has children by another woman, what has he to do when he is converted ? Shall he put her aside and give her up to an evil life, or to beggary, and shall he put his children away? I think that is not right. He should support these unhappy women and his children until they get a livelihood in another and brighter way. I think the same should be demanded from a man who has more than one wife if he is to be baptised. It seems to me that the proper way would be that a man who has more than one wife should support the other wives and children, if there are any, until provision can be made for them in a satisfactory way. After these remarks I will ask for a discussion upon this most difficult question.

The Scriptural argument, a wrong conclusion.

Support of discarded wives.

Rev. James Scott: Mr. Chairman,—I said before, at the meeting of which this is a continuation, that this is a difficult question with which to deal. In the Mission-field from which I come it is a burning question, and is causing great difficulty to many Missionaries and great difficulty to myself. I am thankful that the Chairman has so clearly put before us the difference between polygamy and concubinage. There is no difficulty as to the course to be taken in the one case, but there is difficulty in the other. Now this question has been before us in our Natal Missionary Conferences for a good many years. I brought the matter up there, and at first I stood alone—I believe entirely alone. But I am glad to say I am not now entirely alone in my view of the subject in this large Missionary Conference.

I will state shortly the positions taken up in the Natal Mission-field. First, no marriage at all amongst the Zulu-Kaffirs. Therefore if a man had fifty wives and he became a Christian, he was at liberty to reject all those wives and marry any one he chose. If I could accept that all my difficulties would vanish, but the difficulty of accepting such a thing is very great. Where do we put Jacob, and David, a man after God's own heart, in such a case ? The second position is that very commonly taken up by the Missionaries: marriage is between one man and one woman ; therefore when a polygamist and his wives are converted he must take one wife—one of those wives as his real wife. A great difficulty exists, however, as to which one he is to take ; and it was my seeing the Missionaries' action upon that point, during the period when I was still a commercial man among the natives in Kaffirland, that set me thinking;

Zulu-Kaffirs.

and I have been thinking these last twenty years, and I have come to hold a different opinion from that of the majority.

At the time I am speaking of, a Missionary allowed a chief to take which wife he liked to choose, and he took the youngest. This is a very difficult Which wife question, as to which wife should be taken. Amongst the Zulus it to be chosen? is a fact that a man's first wife is not his own choice. Wives are bought and sold for—say, twenty head of cattle ; and if a young man's father is wealthy, he is presented by his father with a wife. He has that wife with the full knowledge that if he has twenty more head of cattle he will have a wife of his own choice, and if he has still more cattle he can have a third wife, or a fourth, or a fifth—as many as he chooses. Now, as to which of those women should be his real wife, whether the first or the second, is a very difficult question to determine. The third position is that of those who maintain that the Zulu-Kaffir marriages are exactly on the same footing as Old Testament marriages, and when a polygamist and his wives are converted, there should be no breaking up of the Breaking up family, but they should all be accepted as one. My friends, this the family. last-mentioned view is the view I have come to consider to be the right view. Remember, there is not one in this house who would stand up against polygamy in the Christian Church more than I would. I have, I know, been misrepresented on that question, and I will now tell you that I would fight against it and turn out of membership any member who sought to take a second wife. I have been fighting this question alone as regards Missionaries, but I Opinion of Christian Colonists. have on my side the whole body of the lay Christian young men who understand the question, having grown up among the Zulus, so I am not afraid as to how the question will go in the future.

Now, I will bring forward a few difficulties that there are in this matter. First, if we accept into the Church old polygamists with their wives, young men will hang back and keep out of the Church until they have the two or three wives that they may want. They will say, "You have accepted that old man and his wives, and you must accept me also." That is a very grave difficulty. It is no trifling thing. Then if we accept on our communion roll a man with one or two wives, why turn out the man who takes a second wife? All these things are serious ones to contemplate. But these difficulties, I consider, can only be put against the difficulties which can be brought forward on the other side. The refusal to receive polygamists into the Church of Christ is a great hindrance to the Gospel amongst the Zulus. It is Hindrance to not because a man is a Christian that he will not make any sacrifice Gospel. that is necessary. It is that the old men will not listen. Again and again they have said to my evangelists, "I will rather go to hell with my wives and children than to heaven without them." It is a very serious thing for us to drive a man to such a position as that—that they will not listen to the Gospel, because they know the usual course is that they must part from their wives and children.

But these are merely secondary questions. We must look to whether it is right or wrong, and consider what our Head and Master, the Lord Jesus Christ, thinks of the matter—and I will take up this verse, "Whosoever putteth away his wife and marrieth another committeth adultery." But I think, when we bring forward that text, we must not forget that our Lord Jesus Christ was speaking to a nation where polygamy was allowed ; and What does the if that was so then the verse cuts another away, because if those Master say? women are the wives of that man we are forcing him and them to commit sin in putting them away.

Rev. D. D. Young (Free Church of Scotland Mission, North Kaffirland) : Mr. Chairman, Christian friends,—During this Conference I have been silent because I came here with the object of learning, and my only reason for speaking to-night is that, like the speaker who has just preceded me, my work has been in a country where this question is a burning How led to question. I am labouring in South Africa, and I have been there present views. for twelve years. During the first five years I laboured in an institution ; and from my own experience I know that there are many in the field labouring who have not been brought face to face with this great question. While I was labouring at that institution I did not have this question brought before me, but when I went into the midst of heathenism, and laboured amongst the people as I am doing now, I was led again and again to think seriously of this question. And my own conclusion is very much the conclusion of the former speaker. The best way I think that I can bring the question before you is by narrating one or two cases that came under my own observation.

I have at present in my Missionary district a man grown up in heathenism who holds a prominent position. He is chief of a tribe and has three wives, and has practically accepted Christianity. He has gone so far as to fall upon his knees and to ask God to forgive his sins and to accept him and make him His own child. The only reason that hinders him from coming out *A converted chief's difficulty.* boldly is that his three wives are middle-aged, and all have families, and he is brought face to face with this question, " If I join the Church and become baptised I will have, according to the rule of the Church, to put away two of my wives ; " and of course he feels his position. It is very hard for him to put them on one side, but I think it is harder still for the two women who would be put away. The wives at present have a social status, they are recognised as the wives of that man, but if they are put away there is no chance of their being married again, for I have not heard of one who has been put away being accepted by another husband and thus being provided for. But the question not only affects the husband, and not only the wife, but I think in a very special manner it affects the children of those wives.

I have in my Mission district a very worthy elder. In his heathen days he had three wives, and when he became converted he put away two of the wives and remained with the first. But he had children by the other wives ; and, while one of these other wives is dead, the second is now a *Children without a father's care.* Christian, and her children are Christians, but they are without the fatherly care and fatherly attention ; and there is great danger of these Christians wandering away, because we all know what it is for a young man to live in his father's house and have fatherly care shown him day by day.

Although I have spoken as I have done—and I might say a great deal more yet—I recognise the difficulty of this matter. It is a most serious question— a question that calls not so much for discussion as quiet persevering prayer to the Lord that He might show us the way in this matter. And it is also difficult in this way, that we have an established practice. I think the concensus of the older men in the Mission is in favour of the practice that we *Much prayer needed for guidance.* already have. It is against polygamy. I think so, from all my intercourse with the Missionaries. Of course, experience teaches many lessons, and we have to think over the past again and again, and gather lessons from new experience to deal with the subject. But since we have an established practice I recognise the difficulty of the matter, and I therefore entreat all that love the name of the Lord Jesus Christ, that they will make this a matter of prayer. There is another thing I think we ought to do, and with this I will close. I think it is a question that ought to be sent down and discussed in all our native Churches. It is a question I think that for myself I should like to see taken up and discussed by the native brethren, like our good father on the platform here, who can look at this question from an entirely different point of view to us in England. I should like to hear his opinion on the subject.

Bishop Crowther, D.D. (C.M.S., of the Niger) : Mr. Chairman, ladies, and gentlemen,—The matter before this meeting is one of very great importance, and it is one which ought to be looked at and judged from a *An octogenarian's views.* Scriptural point of view. If we go to consult the feelings of this tribe and that tribe of this or that nation and leave the Word of God behind we shall err. We may as well save all the people who are worshipping imaginary gods instead of the one only true God. My opinion, and the opinion of the women in my own country, is that polygamy is a misery to mankind. You consult men's feelings, but you do not consult the women's. Now I will just give you some information about the state of things in Africa where I come from. Whoever has witnessed this life of polygamy would never venture to support or commend its being continued at all. It is an evil. Supposing a man gets married to one wife, and then he marries another, and another, until he has five, seven, or ten wives. When he becomes converted he is received only with one wife, but the others must be put away. And we have witnessed in the heart of the country, where we Missionaries go, that where there are illegitimate children born there is a great deal of heart-burning between the husband and the women. This is a fact. And why? Man was not made to have so many wives in the house. If you understood the secret of the thing you would never advocate a man having more than one wife.

Difficulties in facts.

Another thing I must tell you is this: As a matter of fact the wives of these polygamists are not fed by their husbands. The women have to provide for themselves. You have only to go to New Calabar to find these poor women, the wives of chiefs—these polygamists—being obliged to take axes and go into the forests either to cut wood or to make a fence; to cut bamboo poles, to thatch houses, while others again—I am talking of the women—have to go out in their canoes to fish, and one or two may have a little baby on their backs. They have to paddle out and catch fish to support themselves and their husbands. Now, is such a state of things as that to be advocated? My dear friends, I am just telling you all this that you may see what is the state of things. Well, under the circumstances I have mentioned, the wives of polygamists, having children, are not fed by the husbands, neither are the children. The children are not taken care of by the husband at all.

How provide for wives?

Before I sit down, I would ask whether, if the husband dies, you think these women live ever afterwards in misery. No; before many months you find each of them will get a husband.

A Member: May I, for the information of this Conference, be permitted to ask Bishop Crowther a very important question?

The Chairman: Yes.

The Member: Will you tell us, please, whether, in the case of a native chief having more than one wife, having married them as a heathen, if he becomes a Christian, would you compel him to put aside all but the one wife before he is baptised? and whether, on the other hand, when one of the wives becomes a Christian first, you would baptise and receive into the fellowship of the Church such a woman, she being the wife of a heathen husband, and being one of many wives?

Difficult question.

Bishop Crowther: We do not scruple about this. If a chief with two or three wives were to come we should say, "If you wish to be baptised you must put your wives away;" and if he did not we should not baptise them. If there were to be a hundred women come to us, being the wives of one man, we should baptise the women, because we should know that they had no choice in regard to marriage; we should know that they were drawn into it, and that they could not help it. It is not their choice, so we should baptise them.

At the request of the Chairman the meeting engaged in prayer.

Rev. J. Hudson Taylor (China Inland Mission): Dear brethren,—There is no subject before us which requires to be approached in a more prayerful spirit than this, and I am exceedingly thankful that our Chairman has called for prayer. I went out to China some thirty-four years ago, holding very strongly the view

that I suppose most hold, namely, that every man having more than one wife, if
converted, must be prepared to put them aside. I saw before I had
been out there very long an instance in which a man was converted
who had two wives. He desired to be admitted to the Church, and
he was told that in order to be admitted he must put one of his wives away.
"Well," he said, "may I take my choice, because my second wife is the mother of
my children, and my first wife has no children?" He was told by the Missionaries
in charge, "No, you have no choice in the matter; the woman you first married
is your wife, and your only wife. You never have been married to the other
woman; these children are illegitimate, and you have no right to keep her or to
keep them." Well, he was in great trouble and perplexity and did
not know what to do. His own feeling was, I believe, more correct
than the advice he got from his Missionary friends. However, at last, feeling
that these good men, who had come so far and had brought knowledge of Christ
and salvation, must be right, he put away his wife and children, and condemned them practically to a life of disgrace. They were disowned. Can you
wonder that this woman had a bitter hatred of Christ and Christianity? She
said, "If this is the system of Christianity, it is not from heaven." I believe she
was right; it was not the right system, and it was not from heaven. Finally,
the man was so distressed when he saw his wife and children put away that he
gave up his profession and went back to her. I believe, dear friends, that here
a profound mistake was made.

I have read and studied the Word of God on that subject, and I was pleased
to see in a pamphlet the other evening the very conclusion that I
and many others have been led to express here. This pamphlet is
a brief examination of the Old and New Testament Scriptures on
marriage, polygamy, and concubinage. There is one sentence in it which gives
you briefly the conclusion that we were led to in considering this matter:—
"Thousands of persons were speedily converted when the Holy Ghost came down,
and were received as members; but there is no proof that before they were
received any inquiry was made as to their previous family arrangements, or that
any who were found to be the husbands of more than one wife, were constrained
to retain only one and to put the others away. Nevertheless," says the author,
"without violence or harshness to those who had previously been entangled with
the sins of polygamy, its speedy extirpation was made." The effect of study of
the Old Testament will lead us to believe that polygamy is a great evil, and the
New Testament is most pronounced, that the will of God is that one husband
shall only marry one wife. But when a husband has married more than one wife
before he knows that law, what is to be done? There is the question. In China,
as a rule, a man marries a second wife because there are no children
by the first wife, and it is thought to be the duty of the people, at
any cost, to secure legitimate posterity. These women are lawfully
married. They could not but be married; they have no voice in the matter.
But if they are put away they are put into a false position, and very few of them
will be able to live respectable lives, while they and their children will be greatly
lowered in the estimation of all around them. Are we to make the children
illegitimate, and let them go with the wives who are put aside, or are we to say
that the husband must keep the children and train them? I hold that there is
no lawful cause to put away a wife except that of adultery.

So strongly do I feel on this question that if a man were to come and say, "I
am married to two wives; I am prepared to put one away; I will turn her out;
I want you to receive me and baptise me," I should tell him I could not do
it under the circumstances. This matter is one for much prayerful consideration. Might I suggest that, possibly, in different countries the
question must be dealt with in different ways? I think perhaps we
have been talking sometimes in a general sweeping way, forgetful
that there may be very great differences in our circumstances. For
instance, perhaps those who hold views of one kind about education are quite
right with regard to the country with which they are familiar, yet their par-

Marginal notes:
Reason for change of view:
A painful case.
Study of Scripture.
The case in China.
Varying conditions in different lands.

ticular line of action might become quite unnecessary in regard to another country. So possibly the polygamy of Africa may be different from the polygamy of China. I hold that holy men must have latitude, and seeking God's guidance do the best they can.

Mr. W. C. Bailey (Secretary, Mission to Lepers in India): Would those gentlemen who advocate the putting away of all wives but one kindly tell us, first, What would they do with the remaining wives? Second, so far as their experience has gone, What is the usual fate of those women who are put away? Third, When a woman who has children is put away, to whom do the children go?

Rev. C. H. V. Gollmer (C.M.S., from Lagos, West Africa): I think I must leave these questions for a more experienced Missionary than myself to answer. We have heard already from one of the speakers that there has been, up till now, a recognised rule that in most countries polygamists have not been admitted by baptism into the Church; and we must have a very good reason indeed, it seems to me, for altering that rule. We ourselves, as Christians, thank God, are growing more and more into the light of His truth, and enjoying more the privileges of the Gospel than some of our forefathers did, and we want to bring these blessings to the native Churches. *We desire a higher standard.* We want to preach a full Gospel and not half a Gospel. If we bring polygamy into our Churches we shall never get rid of it. I will just say this, that although I have not had much experience myself, I have the great privilege and honour of being a son of a Missionary who was associated with Bishop Crowther many years ago, and I know something of his experience and difficulties.

It has already been said that this subject is of vital interest to the religious life of native Christians, and should be discussed in all the native Churches. I can inform you that this important subject has been already *Opinions of native Church.* discussed at a Diocesan Conference at Lagos, on the West Coast of Africa. Thirty-five years ago Lagos was one of the great slave marts in Africa. Twelve months ago there was this Conference held to consider certain questions which affected the well-being of the African Church connected with the Church of England especially; and I would like to read to you a few extracts from one of the addresses by a native gentleman, a Christian communicant of our Church, showing you a native view of the subject, and also the conclusion that was come to; and I will read the very important document which is to be presented to the Archbishop of Canterbury, and which, it seems to me, is an answer to Bishop Colenso. They do not want to have anything to do with polygamy in that part of West Africa. This gentleman says, first of all, that he believes, and many other people in the Yoruba country believe also, that originally polygamy was not the custom; and Bishop Crowther, I think, will bear me out in that statement. It was introduced by the Mohammedans.

[The quotation was too long for insertion, but the following is a copy of the memorial to the Archbishop of Canterbury:—

"Memorial from the Yoruba Division of the Diocese of Sierra Leone, W. Africa.
"To His Grace the Lord Archbishop of Canterbury.
"May it please your Grace,—
"We, the Bishop of Sierra Leone, English and African Missionaries of the Church of England, engaged in Church Missionary Society work in the Yoruba country in Western Africa, and Pastors of native Churches, desire to approach your Grace, and to record our firm and sincere convictions, grounded on practical experience of work in this country, on the subject of polygamy.
"We have heard that this question is being debated in the Mother Church, and we are hopeful that it will receive its due attention at the approaching

Conference of Bishops, but we feel constrained at once to express our view of the matter.

"We consider that we are in the very best part of the world to see the evil of this system; we are well and painfully aware of its complications, and we clearly see how it hinders our efforts in the matter of evangelisation.

"Polygamy is to this part of the world what ancient heathen systems of belief are in India and China. It forms the principal barrier in our way. We believe that to remove it, however, in the way that some would suggest, would be to remove all test of sincerity and whole-heartedness in embracing the Christian faith, and thus lead to the admission of a very weak and heterogeneous body of converts; and we are certain that the effect of any—the least—compromise in the view hitherto maintained of the Christian marriage-tie, would be a great blow to Christian morality in these parts.

"We respectfully request our ecclesiastical leaders to give forth a united utterance on this subject, as soon as may be, for we are of opinion that for it to be treated as an open question is in itself a weakness to the Church, and an additional difficulty to us in our very arduous efforts for Christian purity in this part of Africa.

"We, who sign this memorial, are in Conference assembled at Lagos, in the Southern Division of the Diocese of Sierra Leone, a Conference convened by the Bishop to consider this and other matters, and we are present as representatives, lay and clerical, from various parts of this Yoruba country.

"We are, your Grace's humble Servants in Jesus Christ,

(Signed)   "ERNEST GRAHAM, Bishop of Sierra Leone.
"JAMES HAMILTON, Archdeacon of Lagos."
&c., &c., &c., &c. ·

Here follow the names of eighteen clergy, of whom four are European and fourteen African, also the names of the twenty-five lay members of the Conference.]

Rev. James Calvert: My dear friends,—It was stated the other day that the members of all the Missionary Societies were of one mind. That is altogether incorrect. I think we should act wisely if we resorted to common sense in the matter, because polygamy is so manifestly an evil that it ought *Cannot tamper with polygamy.* to be grappled with, overcome, and put aside, like all other abominations that exist. We cannot tamper with this polygamy. I have never known any individual get on in the least in his religion who refused to abandon every wife but one. I have found that the natives have a conscience, and they feel that it is wrong in the sight of Him who made them,—one man and one woman at the beginning,—and it is manifestly an impropriety that they have been led into; and that they have transgressed against God and lived in darkness. The native Christians are generally enabled to give up all their wives but one. It is true that some of them would like to give up the entire lot, and have another woman altogether, but that we have objected to.

With regard to the question of a man keeping to the first wife and leaving all the others, he is no more married to the first than he is to the other women. He never takes any of them saying that they would live together "till death did them part." He takes one and then another. But the question is, *Equally married to all the wives.* What shall be done with the remaining wives? When the King was converted he chose one and was married to her, and was faithful to her for twenty-nine years. What became of all the rest of the women? it may be asked. They were married to the persons who ought to have had them years before. These women afterwards turned out to be good wives, and their husbands were industrious and took care of them. With regard to the children, the women generally had them. The chief had had many wives, but kept only the one he was married to and all their children. I believe that if we talk this over, and are determined to stick to the Scriptures and to common-sense, we shall find that polygamy will vanish as all other sins vanish,

Rev. Francis H. James (B.M.S., from China): First of all let me say that none of us advocate polygamy. It does seem impossible to make some things clear, especially if people do not wish to see *Wives in China* them. Now, not in every case do the wives earn the food for *do not earn* their husbands. They do not in China. It has been denied by *living.* Chinese Missionaries that these women are wives.

Let me give you some facts. In the imperial temples of China, on the . tablet by which the Emperor is worshipped, you will find mentioned the Empress and all the concubines. They are something more than concubines, and they cannot lightly be put away. If they are discarded they are taken and kept in a special part of the palace for the rest of their lives. They can never, however, become the wives of another. The common word for " lady " in China is " taitai," and the first wife is called the " taitai." The second is called " e-tai-tai," which similarity of designation is another proof that these women are something more than concubines, that they are in fact wives. The Chinese conscience does not look upon them as concubines, but as women in a far more honourable position.

Again, it is sometimes assumed that we do not want to keep to the Scripture. We do keep to it. It is an unfair thing to assume that those who take the other side of the question are wishing to depart from the Scripture. We have no wish to do anything of the kind. I think a common-sense interpretation of the Scripture, as stated by Mr. Hudson Taylor, is certainly on our side. We do not want to go back to rules made *Interpretation* forty or fifty years ago. We want the teaching of Scripture in its *of Scripture.* clearest passages, and when we have that we are safe. It has been said that we must not appeal to feelings. There are feelings and feelings. There are feelings we do not wish to consider or countenance ; but I maintain that we have a right to listen to the feelings of justice, mercy, and compassion, and we are wrong if we do not go according to them. I believe that in the sight of our Lord and Saviour Jesus Christ, and in the sight of God, those who are in the position of my opponents to-night are wrong, and I hope the day will come soon when they will heartily repent and change their way of dealing with this matter.

Rev. Paulus Kammerer (Basle Missionary Society, from China): All I wanted to say has been said by Mr. Taylor and the previous speaker about this question. I only want to add that the Basle Mission has settled this question in this way : We admit polygamists to the congrega- *Custom of* tions, but not to any official post. We never allow anything like *Basle Mission.* that, and I think there is nothing in the Scripture against this method. The Basle Mission has experience in Africa, India, and China, and this has been the conclusion of all the experience met with in these three fields ; but I believe there is a great difference between polygamy in Africa and in China. I have discussed this question with my fellow brethren from Africa.

I heard from them that a negro wife is quite content when she has one child by her husband, to leave the husband with her child, and earn her livelihood. This was what was told me by an African Missionary, but I am very sorry that such a length of time is devoted to this question, for there are many others which should have been discussed in this Conference ; one for instance being the betrothal of infants in China, which is a very important question. *On betrothal* I believe this question has been neglected too much by some Mission- *of infants.* aries in China. The Basle Mission had very much difficulty discussing this question, the Missionaries not being unanimous. I will ask some of the Chinese Missionaries who may speak after me, to give us their opinions upon this question. We have always to bear in mind the various customs of various nations. We have difficulty in dealing with them, and we are not to look to see whether they are connected with idolatry or not ; and the betrothal of infants is, I believe, connected with idolatry, because it rules in their ancestral worship ; so we ought to be very careful as to allowing the betrothal of infants to any who are connected with our Churches, because much mischief might accrue. I would ask you to give us some information about this matter.

A **Member** : I should like to make a few remarks, and I would say that my reason for asking to be permitted to speak was not that I wished to say anything about polygamy, but about slavery. I was the very man, I believe, who suggested that we should have a meeting to continue this discussion and to extend the subject to slavery. The petition was sent in at my suggestion, but the subject of slavery, curiously enough, is left out. With regard to polygamy I will only take this opportunity of stating that the practice of our Norwegian Missionary Society has been the same as that of the Berlin Society, as stated by the Rev. Mr. Merensky, and further explained by his friend here this evening.

Custom of Norwegian Society.

Rev. Professor T. Smith, D.D. : I will say first of all that I am exceedingly glad that the right reverend father behind me (Bishop Crowther) has made a speech on this subject. I can freely argue with his speech, but I hope I shall say nothing which will appear to be inconsistent with the very profound respect which I and others have for him, as one who has been and is greatly admired and loved. I think his views on this subject are utterly wrong. First of all he takes it for granted that in some way or other we have less hatred and less sense of the evil of polygamy than he has. I venture to say there is not one member of this Conference who does not as thoroughly detest and abhor polygamy, and is not as certain of the perfect evil of it as the right reverend father himself. He seems to assume that we have to require of our professed converts the renunciation of all sins except this one sin, which we are to allow them to retain.

All feel the evils of polygamy.

I can scarcely deny that some who spoke on my side of the question may have given something like a countenance to this, but certainly that is not my view of the matter. I myself would not baptise a man or admit him to baptism who did not confess his sin of polygamy as a sin committed against nature—and against the light of nature which he possessed, although he had not the light of the Gospel—and if I baptised him it would be with the understanding that I should debar him for ever from holding any office in the Christian Church. I would say, "You renounce idolatry and all the sinful habits you have formed ; but you are bound to retain the *obligations* which you had incurred as a heathen man ; you came under obligation to these women, and these obligations you must fulfil ; they are an evil you have brought upon yourself by your sin." Polygamy is an evil, an unspeakable evil, and that evil he must bear on account of his sin, just as the drunkard must bear the evil he brought upon himself through drunkenness. I cannot release him by conniving at an injustice. I should hold him to be bound to do his duty towards those women, and if he refused to do this and put them all away but one, or if he put every one away, I say he would commit sin against God, and bring scandal upon the Christian name.

Husband's obligation to all alike.

Dr. Robert Pringle (of the Bengal Army) : Mr. Chairman, and Christian friends,—You have had the ministerial view of the case, and now I will take it up from the professional point of view—at least, I will deal with the subject according to my professional knowledge. Mohammedanism has permeated the whole of the East. One gentleman alluded to it just now, and I may say that Mohammedanism will rule the whole world by getting the bridle rein of sensuality.

Polygamy is the custom of Eastern countries, and I say that if we are going to ask these men to give up all but one wife when they come into the Church, it is not to be a question of whether it is to be the one by whom they have had children. I put that on one side. That is not the point. I say it is the question as to whom they were first married, that woman is the man's wife, and every one else is not his wife, and these people know as well as we do that this is right in the sight of God.

Rev. G. Smith (English Presbyterian Mission, Swatow, China) : I have been a Missionary for fully thirty years, and the Church with which I am connected consists of Chinese converts and communicants, the latter numbering three thousand five hundred odd, and with another Church united with us, more than four thousand communicants. Large experience of E.P. Mission in China. Well, during all these years the uniform practice of this Church has been to exclude polygamists, and this has helped to maintain the purity of the Church, and is no barrier to the conversion of the Chinese. I must explain about the Chinaman and his wives. There are what are called wives, and also concubines, and it is the ambition of a Chinese mandarin to have a wife from each of the eighteen provinces in China, and as many concubines as he can afford to support. Polygamy is very common among the higher circles, but I venture to say from my own experience that a man who indulges in polygamy goes against the conscience of the Chinese. I have had it pointed out that a man, when he became wealthy and took a second wife, while he was rising in the scale of wealth was falling in the scale of morality. I believe that we have the conscience of the people on our side when we oppose polygamy.

It is laid down by Christ, as the law of His Church, that we are to return to the original law given in the beginning ; and, I hold that it is most important for the future of the Church of Christ, that its foundation be laid on social purity. There may be what appears to be severity at first. When Peter said, "Far be it from Thee to do such a thing," the Master answered, "Thou savourest not the things that be of God, but of man." I have no sympathy with the appeals to the love of God to sanction polygamy. I believe such appeals to be an utter misrepresentation of the meaning of Scripture. God is a holy God, as well as a God of love. I was deeply grieved to hear the sentiments expressed by a man holding such a position as Mr. Hudson Taylor. When he told us the story about the woman who was put away by her husband, and then suffered all the hardships that she did, I cannot but say that, as far as I can judge, the case was mismanaged.

Let it be always remembered that in China there is not the slightest difficulty for a woman to get a husband ; the great difficulty is for a man to get a wife ; and if a woman is put away, she can get a dozen men to choose from, if she wish, without trouble. So that it is not a fair representation of the thing to say, "She is an outcast when put away." Re-marriage easy in China. Her former husband is still bound to care for her welfare." Now, coming to another point, we have heard from Africa (Bishop Crowther), we have heard from the Fiji Islands, and from other places how the work has been done. Polygamy has been banished from the Church in these parts and elsewhere, and the Church is flourishing, and that shows that it is practicable. It has been found to be successful, for the Church becomes prosperous.

Rev. John Mackenzie (L.M.S., from Bechuanaland) : I will speak to you about a part of Africa that has not been alluded to this evening—Bechuanaland and Basutoland. The native custom there has always been, amongst the great majority of the people, for one man to have but one wife. Bechuanaland custom. Polygamy is like a man who purchases a carriage ; it is an indication of rising in society. According to a man's rising in society so is the number of his wives.

When a man takes a second wife, and then a third, he at once makes provision for each one of these women. In the case of a wealthy man, he gives them cattle and servants, and surrounds each of them with all that makes a separate establishment. We have unfortunately called all those people wives, bringing down that beautiful English word. They Provision for smaller wives. themselves consider that there is only one wife, and the others do not occupy her position. The custom was that while a wealthy man had a

...... of them, he had only one wife, concerning whose children no provision ...... to be made. Her children were the heirs at law; and the man did not ...... provision for them in the sense in which he made provision for the others. When he died, if he had not made provision for the issue of the smaller wives, of course they would get nothing; so that the social standing of these women ...... for itself.

It is now a great many years since Christianity went into Bechuanaland, borne by Robert Moffat, followed by Livingstone, and by others who passed through those difficulties in their time. There is now a Christian influence

Experience of the Church of Moffat and Livingstone. in that part of the world; and if any one were to bring the new doctrine there he would have no chance whatever, on account of the public opinion of the country already created. The course to pursue has already been decided there, where Christianity has been so long established. A friendly settlement is always made as regards the children, and also as regards the women. They do not lose caste, and certainly the children do not, because according to the heathen arrangement they belong to the father, and are as dignified after the man becomes a Christian as they were before. Polygamists showing interest in Christianity should be helped in every way, and treated with consideration and patience. But their place was the catechumen's class; the water of baptism did not belong to them.

A Member: But do they keep the provision that he makes for them?

Rev. J. Mackenzie: They do; and when the man dies they are surrounded by the property he has left to the woman, their mother, and it is theirs. And I may say, with reference to this matter, no practical difficulty ever occurred in my own experience, now extending over some twenty-eight years.

Rev. John Hewlett (L.M.S., from Benares): Mr. Chairman,—It seems evident from the speeches that have been made by our African brethren that the difficulties they have experienced in dealing with this question are different from those met with in India and China. After a great deal of serious, painful, and prayerful thought, I have come to the conclusion that under certain circumstances it is not required that a man, who has more wives than one, should, before embracing Christianity, put away all his wives except one.

Now the question in India is narrowed down very much. The Christian Marriage Act prevents polygamy after embracing Christianity. Then again

The question narrowed in India. there is no question about concubinage. No one, of course, would wish to baptise a man that kept a concubine, a woman whose legal status as wife was not acknowledged. But there are cases of the following kind in India. A man who has one wife and no children often takes an additional wife with the hope of having children by her. That is looked upon as a respectable thing in India. It is quite legal. The Indian conscience does not revolt against it. On the other hand, it is regarded as perfectly honourable. But it does sometimes happen that a man who has two wives becomes convinced of the truth of Christianity, and wishes to be baptised. Some Missionaries would tell him that he cannot be baptised unless he puts away his second wife, although she may have had children by him.

The rights of wives. Other Missionaries would take the opposite view, and I have been compelled to take that view. I feel that the woman has rights as much as the man. A good deal of the discussion here this evening has assumed that it is only the husband who has rights, and that his advantages only should be considered. But as all his wives, who married him in good faith, according to the law and sentiment of the country, have they not rights as much as he? They did no wrong, according to their light, in marrying. In fact—in India they have no choice in the matter—marriage is arranged for them by their parents.

Children's rights. As to the children, the husband could keep them, I suppose, but then they would be deprived of the mother's love and care. Have they no rights? I believe that their putting away of the wife under these circumstances is revolting to all our best feelings; and if so, are not they revolting to the feelings of the God of love? Well, such a man sometimes really embraces Christianity. But it has been asked, "Would you not only baptise such a man, but also receive him into Church fellowship?" Yes, as our dear friend Dr. Smith says, but I would not give him any office in the Church, because he should suffer in consequence of having erred, though in ignorance.

There is another point: It has been asked, but not answered, "Would you admit all the wives of such a man into Church fellowship?" To that I say, Yes. If I had reason to believe that all the wives were truly converted, I would admit them into Church fellowship.

Rev. J. A. Taylor (Baptist Foreign Missionary Convention of U.S.A.): I regret very much to have heard some of the statements that have been made by gentlemen who are so old in Missionary work. It places me, in my opinion, in a very awkward position, but I have a very firm decision on this question. I think if we kept pace with the New Testament Scripture we should have no difficulty in finding how to decide this question. Let the teaching of the Son of God be our guide, and we shall always keep right. I fear that sometimes we let our zeal run away with our best judgment in this matter.

The very first difficulty that met our Society, some eight years ago, when they opened the Mission Station in West Central Africa was this very question, as to whether we should admit polygamists into our Churches. Having suffered to a great extent in the United States from the allowance of this kind of thing we met, and decided emphatically, "No; the Gospel of Jesus Christ did not allow polygamy in His Church." *Decision of Baptists, U.S.A. (coloured).* And I feel so to-day, and whatever you may decide for India or Africa, I am here to appeal to you in the interests of millions of coloured people in America who have a deep interest in the evangelisation of Africa. I say for God's sake do not make such a provision for Africa as to allow polygamists into the Church. We do not want it. The Africans themselves do not want it.

Our principle of Missionary work is based on this, that it is better to have a few firm Christians with clean moral principles, who will hold up the light of the Gospel of the Son of God, than to have a multitude who have sin mixed up in them. Let me tell you that if we want to convert the world to Christ, if we want a Church that will shine out "as clear as the sun and as fair as the moon, and be as terrible as an army with banners," against *Call for a pure Church.* every sin, that Church must be purged from sin, and polygamy is one of the worst and most demoralising of sins. May I ask that whatever you may decide for India or for China, do not make any provision for Africa, that dear old country which I love, to admit polygamists into the Church of Jesus Christ.

Mr. Edward Whitwell (Kendal): I just wish to say a few words as a Christian outside Missionary work. We are told by the Apostle that if a man is married to an unconverted woman he is not to put her away. Now we all know that it is a sin for a Christian to marry an unconverted woman, but when in ignorance they are married, and the man subsequently becomes converted, he is not to put his wife away; therefore I argue that *Sin of ignorance.* the same principle will apply to the cases mentioned by our dear brethren from China. They married two wives in their ignorance—before they were converted. Just the same then as this unconverted man and woman were married, now that he becomes converted the converted man is to continue living with the unconverted woman and not put her away. I think the argument applies.

The meeting concluded with prayer by the **Rev. H. Grattan Guinness.**

MEETINGS OF MEMBERS
IN SECTION.

MISSIONARY METHODS.

(4) *DEALING WITH FORMS OF RELIGIOUS BELIEF.*

Adaptation of methods to different forms of religious thought, (a) Unreformed Churches, (b) Ancestral .Religion (Confucianism), (c) Mohammedanism, (d) Brahmanism, (e) Buddhism, (f) Fetish worship.

(*Tuesday afternoon, June 12th, in the Annexe.*)

Chairman, **J. Bevan Braithwaite, Esq**
Acting Secretary, **Mr. B. Broomhall.**

Major-General Haig offered prayer.

The Chairman: Ladies and gentlemen,—I have felt it to be a great privilege to have any part, however small, in a Conference of this kind. The subjects presented to us are so vast that we might be in danger of being led away into too discursive a discussion, and I have been exceedingly anxious that we should keep to that which is really practical and serviceable to the great cause for which we are met here.

Vastness of subjects.

I have thought that in the few words I venture to address to this meeting, I could not hold up a better model for Missionary effort than the Apostle divinely called and raised up for us Gentiles. In his character and in his work we may see very much that is practically applicable to our present duty even in this age of the world ; his call, his dedication, keeping to one thing,—"This one thing I do, forgetting the things that are behind, and reaching forth to those that are before—I press toward the mark,"—and his sympathy for souls. His great motto was, "God forbid that I should glory save in the Cross of our Lord Jesus Christ, by whom the world is crucified unto me and I unto the world." The same Holy Spirit that taught him to follow in the footsteps of the same adorable Redeemer,

The Missionary model.

His motto.

will bring us in the power of the same faith, to share in the same blessed victory. Let this be the motto which we take up afresh even at this hour, as we each make it an hour of renewed consecration to our Lord and Master, " God forbid that I should glory, save in the Cross of our Lord Jesus Christ, by whom the world is crucified unto me and I unto the world. There are two Papers to be read this afternoon. The first will be read by the Rev. R. S. Ashton, B.A.

Our motto.

PAPER.

1. By the Rev. R. S. Ashton, B.A. (Secretary, Evangelical Continental Society).

The best method of evangelisation in Romish lands.

The end sought by the discussion of the subject is, I presume, a practical one. Evangelisation is the presentation and enforcement of the Gospel and its claims. And the question is not, should this object be aimed at by the circulation of the Scriptures and religious literature, *or* by preaching and visitation. In every country all such, and perhaps other, methods will be adopted, and in such ways and proportions as are determined by the condition of the countries and of their peoples, their state of enlightenment, and the kinds of Mission work rendered possible by the laws or by the rulers.

The question is this, How can the Gospel be most suitably presented, with a view to its ready and hearty acceptance, to people brought up amid the errors of Rome, and in complete ignorance of the real teaching of the Scriptures. In other words, How is the Gospel message to be adapted to the peculiar needs of Romanists?

The question to be answered.

In proceeding to study this question it will be well to inquire whether the Apostles and first preachers of the Gospel adapted their methods to the peculiar condition of people whom they addressed. Their audiences were very various—Jews and proselytes of Jewish religion; Athenians with their philosophical habits; Corinthians, the devotees of sensual pleasure; Romans, energetic and imperious; Egyptians, lovers of mystic rites; and also the less civilised or even barbarous peoples of Libya and of the British Islands. Then, too, the men themselves differed in temperament and in intellectual power. There were in the Apostolic band a Peter and a Paul, a John and a James, and among the first preachers an Apollos and a Timothy. Their mode of preaching would, of course, depend on the bent of their mind, and we may presume also on the intellectual and spiritual condition of the audiences to be addressed. The reports of Paul's preaching in the course of his Missionary journeys, brief and summary as they are, tend to confirm this presumption. Certainly, his sermons did not always follow the same method. The discourse delivered in the synagogue at Antioch in Pisidia contrasts with that on Mars' Hill. In Thessalonica on three successive Sabbath days Paul reasoned out of the Scriptures respecting Christ, in order to show that Jesus of Nazareth was none other than this Christ; while before Agrippa he set forth his own conversion and call to the great work of preaching the Gospel. Adaptation was surely one element in the success of his preaching.

Guided by this example we may safely conclude that the preacher's or evangelist's duty is to study the position of his hearers in relation to the truths of Christianity. He will not think *Adaptation, our duty.* that an address adapted to people surrounded from childhood with more or less of Christian notions and influences would suit an audience of Hindus in some region of the great Indian Peninsula where the Missionary had never before been seen. The needs of the human heart are the same in each case, but the first thing to be done is to awaken the consciousness of these needs, and while appeals to forgotten truths might be efficacious in the case of the dwellers in some East End slum, they would sound as strange and unintelligible jargon in the ears of an utterly heathen and idolatrous people. Similarly, a Protestant addressing a Roman Catholic audience must remember that his hearers are more or less acquainted with Christian names, and even with some Christian truths, but that they connect therewith ideas and notions derived from the false light in which they have been taught to view them. The Protestant evangelist must, therefore, endeavour through study of Romanism, and through intercourse with Romanists, to enter into and thoroughly understand the way in which Christianity—or as much of it as is taught by Rome—is understood by Romanists.

One idea, indeed the dominant idea, inculcated by the Papal Church, is man's need of salvation—an idea underlying all the teachings of Christianity—"Christ Jesus came into the world to save sinners." On this point Catholics and Protestants are at one. But divergence arises the moment the meaning and necessity and methods of this salvation are examined. A deliverance is needed—on this all are agreed. *Roman Catholic views of sin.* When, however, the nature of the deliverance is inquired into, it is at once seen how widely different are the teachings of Romanism and Scripture on this subject. Rome speaks of three kinds of sin, *original, mortal,* and *venial,* and thereby promotes its own end—the making the Church's intervention indispensable for the salvation of men; at the same time it thereby lessens the heinousness of sin in general, and lulls the conscience of the sinner. This may be gathered from the Church's own statements respecting the different kinds of sin.

"The guilt and stain of *original* sin"—that is, Adam's sin and guilt, become morally our own, because of our connection with Adam, the head of the race—"are entirely washed away by the Sacrament of Holy Baptism." Once baptised, therefore, there is no need to be troubled on the score of original sin. There remains *actual sin,* which may be either *venial* or *mortal.*

"Venial sin is a slight infringement of the law, or it may be in some cases a great violation of the law, but rendered slight in the person who

commits it through his want of sufficient knowledge, deliberation, or freedom." "It is not abandoning God for a creature, but it is in some degree
dallying with created objects, whilst still adhering to God.
It is a sin which, though heinous in itself, does not so ^{Results of these distinctions.}
grievously offend God as mortal sin does." "It causes a
stain of guilt in the soul, of which we can *easily obtain pardon*"—hence
its name *venial*. "*Mortal* sin is beyond comparison more dreadful
than venial sin." "It is a dethroning of God from one's heart."
"It causes the death of the soul." This distinction between venial and
mortal sins is the open door for the entrance of casuistry, a principle
innate in the corrupt human heart, and which the Romish Church
has marvellously developed and strengthened, and that too in face of the
condemnation pronounced upon it by Christ, when dealing with the
Pharisees of His time. We may add that so-called Christian morality
has been made, by writers of the Romish Church, "to sanction what human
morality and the conscience by itself never sanctioned. The most vicious
of men will never say openly or in the shape of maxims, what Romish
theologians have dared to say about robbery, lying, adultery, and murder."
(*Rome et le Vrai, Bungener.*)

The natural consequence of all this trifling with sin has been to deaden
the moral sense, to make almost every kind of sin appear venial, and to
confine the area of real sin within the limits of the Church and its decrees.
One of the first duties, therefore, of an evangelist working among Roman
Catholics is to try and set sin in its true light, by revealing the
casuistry of the Church on the subject, and by bringing the ^{The truth to be presented.}
light that shines from the Cross of Christ to bear directly on
the conscience of his hearers. He must seek to re-awaken the sense of sin.
However beautifully and faithfully the Gospel may be preached, it will
have but little power over hearts not made conscious of their need of the
salvation it offers. The complaint is often made by workers in Romish
countries that they seldom or ever meet with persons bowed down with a
feeling of their sin. The question addressed to Paul by the heathen
gaoler, is not heard by them,—"What must I do to be saved?" Until,
then, they have been able to set sin in its true light as in all its forms a
transgression of the law of a holy God, for which the sinner is himself
responsible, their proclamation of a Saviour is likely to be a comparative
failure.

Further, the doctrine is carefully and constantly insisted on by the
Romish Church, and has taken general possession of the minds of its professed members that the work of saving men devolves on the
Church, that the priest is the indispensable agent or channel ^{R.C. views of salvation.}
through whom the blessings, over which the Church has
exclusive power, can be imparted to men; also that the observance of the
sacraments prescribed by the Church, and performed by the priest, is the
only means by which they can be made partakers of salvation. In confirmation of the last of these three points, let me say that in a popular
exposition of Catholic belief intended for the special use of Protestants,
and from the pages of which I have already quoted, there is a chapter
entitled, "How Christ's redemption is applied to man, that they may be
justified and sanctified." It is a singular and startling fact that this
chapter is the shortest in the book—not filling one page—and that the
whole gist of it is contained in the last paragraph, which is as follows:

"The direct means instituted by Christ Himself for applying His infinite merits to the souls of men, are the holy sacraments, which are so many channels instituted by Jesus Christ to convey to men His grace, purchased for us at the price of His most precious blood, 'You shall draw water with joy out of the Saviour's fountains'" (Isa. xii. 3).

Romanism is thus clearly shown to be a purely sacramental religion, and the evangelist who wishes to lead Romanists to a participation of the blessings of the Gospel, must keep this fact in mind. He

Sacramental system to be met. must seek to undermine this sacramental notion, so fatal to all true appreciation of Christ. He must show from Scripture that salvation does not come as the result of a slavish discharge of certain supposed religious duties. The performance of work must be supplanted by faith and obedience. Men must be taught that through Christ they have free access to God, that Christianity knows nothing of the manifold barriers erected by priests in every age to prevent men from thinking that they can speak to their Father above. The heaven and the Christ, which Catholicism represents as so far removed beyond the ken of ordinary men, must be shown to be within reach of the greatest sinner and the humblest believer. Christ must be proclaimed as the great High Priest and only Intercessor, so tender and gracious that He readily welcomes all who approach Him. "Him that cometh unto Me I will in no wise cast out." He must be set forth as nearer to men now than in the days of His earthly life; as still Jesus of Nazareth, the Brother and Helper of man, though seated at the right hand of the Majesty on high; as the Lamb of God whose one sacrifice is sufficient to meet all needs, because offered to take away all sins; and as the Mediator through whom salvation is imparted to all who accept Him. The evangelist in Romish countries must insist on the absolutely free nature of the Gospel, its direct message to every one, and its promise not only of forgiveness, but also of *eternal life*.

This last point is of great importance. Popery has much to say about holiness, but it has always gone on the assumption that only a small section of the human race can attain to it, or at least to any high

Views of holiness. degree of sainthood. Its saints, too, are men and women whose virtues have been the result of a perpetual practice of certain prescribed rules, rather than the outgrowth of a sure and eternal life imparted to the soul through faith in Christ. The Romish Church has always upheld the notion of an aristocracy in piety to which the great mass of men cannot lay claim. It must be the business of the preacher of Christ to show that there is no aristocracy in Christianity, that the holiness and perfection to which the Saviour urges His disciples is one quite within the reach of all, and should be sought by all. The fictitious piety with which Romanists are so familiar, and which has too often been but a cloak to cover hideous vice must be exposed, its hollowness and worthlessness made evident, and it must be shown that through the grace of God, and by the power of His Spirit men may become new creatures in Christ Jesus, and may live a life beautiful for its purity, and rich in its power of usefulness.

In one word, the duty of the evangelist who has to labour among the victims of priestcraft, and among a people educated in the idea that

Present objective Gospel. "Catholicism dispenses man from keeping a personal conscience, and devolves on the priest the care of his salvation," is to dwell especially on the objective side of Christianity, presenting the Saviour as ready to welcome with open arms every penitent sinner and to make him partaker of His own nature. Dispensing as far as possible with theological terms and distinctions, he must try and unfold the Gospel as a message of life, sent direct to every man, and urging him at once, and without any intermediary, to welcome the grace of God, and to submit to the redeeming, sanctifying power of the Lord Jesus Christ, and so to realise the blessedness of one who is reconciled to God, and can with all freedom and in all the fulness of the term, say, that God is His Father.

Passing now from the consideration of the mode of evangelisation, allow me to make a few remarks on the slow progress of Missions in Roman Catholic lands. I say *slow progress*, because after twenty or thirty years of labour in Italy, for example, one might have expected to see Evangelical Christianity more deeply rooted in the country than it seems to be at the present time.

First of all, it should be borne in mind that the acceptance of Bible-teaching, followed by the open confession of Christ ordinarily entails in Popish countries suffering and loss. It seems to be a rule of society, even in France, and acted on even by Freethinkers, Consequences of conversions. and by the more worldly and rationalistic section of the Protestant community, that a man must not change his religion. To do so is to incur an amount of obloquy, which nothing but a real conviction of the truth, and a strong faith in Christ can enable him to bear.

Again, has not the work of evangelisation been often impeded by over-haste in founding Churches? The fact that a few people have listened with apparent pleasure to a preacher who has denounced the Over-haste in founding Churches. errors of Romish teaching, and proclaimed that true liberty is to be found only in Christ, has often been deemed sufficient reason for organising them into a Church and treating them as a body of persons fully qualified to represent and promote the kingdom of Christ around them. And yet, perhaps, not one of them has been truly converted to Christ, or formed any true conception of what the Christian life and the kingdom of God really are.

But over-haste in forming Churches has not been the only mistake committed. The method of their formation has often been, to say the least, prejudicial to their growth. Why should not evangelisation be carried on far and wide, the Gospel earnestly proclaimed, Methods of formation. and men and women brought to the saving knowledge of Christ? And then, and not till then, let these converts be encouraged to form themselves into Christian Societies or Churches for the purpose of mutual edification, and the promotion of the kingdom of God. Churches composed of persons whose Christianity is a negation of Rome and its doctrines, rather than an acceptance of Christianity, or which are entirely dependent on foreign gold for existence, may figure well in the reports of Societies, but they have in them no element of vitality or spiritual power.

Another reason of the slow advance of Gospel truth in Romish lands has often been the unsuitable character of the preacher.

1. He has employed wrong methods in presenting the truth. In some cases the staple of his discourses has been the exposure of the errors of Rome, with very little direct exposition of the cardinal truths of Christianity. Such preaching has enkindled animosity to- Unsuitable agents. wards the Pope and his teachings, but not won souls for Christ! Men have learnt to hate error, but not to love the truth. Catholic superstitions have been denounced, but the good news of salvation has not been

pressed upon men, nor their consciences aroused to feel their need of it. Christian morality has been taught, but the heart has not been prepared for its acceptance. There has been an attempt to build up the Christian edifice, but without sufficient care in first of all preparing and laying its foundations. The Apostle's warning has been overlooked : " Neither is circumcision anything," says he, " nor uncircumcision, but a new creature " (Gal. vi. 15).

Again teachers, born and trained amid Protestant surroundings, and accustomed to Protestant views of truth and Protestant modes of speech, have often failed to place themselves in the position of Romanists and to understand the meaning they attach to Christian terms. They have talked as Protestants to Protestants, and consequently their teaching has been misunderstood. They have lacked the spirit or the power of adaptation.

2. This suggests another reason of the comparative failure of Continental Missions. Men have been appointed as evangelists without any previous training. Good men, perhaps, they have tried to teach others, when destitute themselves of anything like a competent knowledge of the truth of Christ. Their glibness of speech has misled them and others into supposing that they were able to preach. And to this must be added the remark that Societies, anxious to push forward the work, but unable to find fitly trained men, have engaged these ready speakers and self-confident evangelists, rather than allow the doors opening before them to be closed. And in this way, it is to be feared, they have done irreparable injury to the cause they wished to advancce. A little work well done is surely better than large undertakings carried on by inefficient workmen.

3. But worse than the untrained, though perhaps well meaning and pious labourers, are the men who have taken up the preacher's calling, as others have become lawyers and doctors, simply with the idea of obtaining a livelihood.

Such agents may be able exponents of the doctrine, they may render the services of the Church with correctness and beauty, their words may even glow with an eloquence that captivates the hearers and awakens admiration for the truth, but being destitute of living faith, having none of the unction of God's spirit, not being living examples of the power and blessedness of the truths they advance, their ministry has no converting, uplifting power. It is not such labourers that God thrusts into His vineyard, and the vineyard suffers from their presence in it.   .

Men of God, baptised with His Spirit, full of faith in His Son Jesus Christ, men possessed withal of the power of adaptation, and trained to
Conclusion.   understand the peculiar needs of Roman Catholics, such are
the men that are required in Continental countries, and by such and such only will those countries be really evangelised.

The Chairman : I think we must all have felt that there is much to instruct us in what we have heard. The Rev. G. M. Cobban will now read a Paper.

[We regret that we cannot give Mr. Cobban's Paper, as it has been sent for publication to some periodical, and no manuscript or copy has been sent us. The following brief abstract has been forwarded by the writer.—ED.]

Christianity in relation to Hinduism.

2. Rev. G. Mackenzie Cobban (Wesleyan Missionary Society, from Madras) read a Paper on the above subject, the gist of which was to show that the method of the Missionary must be discriminating and intelligent. Everything non-Christian is not of the devil. God and spiritual truth are not shut up in the Hebrew and Christian sacred books; they are outside these as well as inside. Every intelligent Missionary knew that this was true of the Aryan and non-Aryan literature of India which contained many spiritual truths with which Christianity has affinity. These might be a surprise to the Missionary, still he must bow to facts and give to them a cordial recognition. He must not minimise them. What does it matter whether men learn to hate idolatry by the teaching of a Hindu poet, or whether by the teaching of a Hebrew sage? We were not yet able to deal with the question of "origin," of how all the truth came to India which we find there. But all were agreed that every fragment of spiritual truth came from God. Apart from the Brahmanical section of the Indian people and those castes whose are the privileges of the Aryan faith, there were one hundred and seventy-five millions denominated Hindus, for whom the Aryan priesthood and faith could do nothing. These presented a magnificent field for Christian Missionary work. In South India, the Sivites are divided into Vedantists and Siddhantists, who are non-dualists and dualists. The dualists professedly hold the tenets of the Agama philosophy. There are dissenters who have flung off Brahmanical authority, consisting of a large section of the people The Vaishnavas represent three schools, the two principal being the Sri and Mâdhva Vaishnavas. The Saktis have a large following. Besides all, there are the worshippers of the ruder deities, and the aborigines. The audience to which Christianity made its appeal was a varied one.

With regard to the truths known in India, these would be used by the wise Missionary as allies. And since there was in embryo among the Hindus a doctrine of Christ, this especially should be used. Christianity had suffered greatly from a narrow and imperfect representation, and had been in consequence grievously misunderstood by the better classes of the people. The narrowness of some Missionary fathers, who insisted on beef eating as a badge of Christian discipleship, had greatly increased the difficulties of the modern Missionary. Christianity must be presented more intelligently and with greater sympathy with the truths as well as with the men of India.

The Acting Secretary: I can only say that if I were prepared to concede as much as our friend does, I should not be prepared to leave home and country to preach the Gospel anywhere. Owing to the absence of writers of Papers on Confucianism and other subjects, two friends in the room have kindly offered to speak, namely, the Rev. George Piercy, for many years a Missionary in China, and Mr. Samuel Clarke, from Western China.

DISCUSSION.

Rev. George Piercy (Wesleyan Missionary Society, from Canton): Mr. Chairman, dear friends,—I have only ten minutes, and I have a greater difficulty than that. I was not warned to speak on this subject until a few minutes before the gathering; but I want to make the most of my opportunity with your kind help. The first point is as to ancestral worship in China. Here it is said, "Ancestral Worship: Confucianism." Now, these three words will help me, and they will help you, perhaps. Please **Confucianism** understand at the outset that Confucianism is very much **not ancestral** broader than ancestral worship. Anybody here that wants to **worship only.** study Confucianism had better immediately buy Professor Legge's translation of the Chinese classics and study them, or put themselves under his tuition, which will be still better.

Now a few words as to ancestral worship in China. You all probably know that in China we have three forms of religion,—Confucianism, Buddhism, and Taoism. I have nothing to do with the two latter. I have nothing much to do with Confucianism, except on this one point **Ancestral wor-** of ancestral worship. Ancestral worship is dearer to the hearts **ship the worship** of the Chinese than any other kind of worhip. They worship **of China.** Buddha, they worship idols of many kinds, but they say that the idols belong to everybody, but their ancestors are their own, therefore they worship them. Ancestral worship in China pervades the whole land. There is no heresy in China with regard to this point of worship. Now, an ancestor who is worhipped is a dead ancestor of course. He is in the spirit world. It is the spirit of the dead ancestor that is worshipped. Then you must understand that the Chinese take the spirit of a man to consist of three; or, if you like it better, that the spirit is in three parts—three spirits, I would say, in one. The spirit having passed away may be instantly worshipped, worshipped, as I have said, by offerings, and by reverential postures of the body, and by the soul of the worshipper also **Much money** pledging itself to come into harmony with the teachings of **spent on it.** the dead ancestor, and of the generations gone by. This is also carried out at the graves, and before the ancestral tablets in every house. This form of worship is universal in China, and sometimes a great deal of money is expended upon it.

This kind of worship is probably the most earnest form of religious belief that obtains in China. It is universal. It reaches to the highest, and it goes **Universal.** down to the very lowest. I remember I once asked an old and venerable-looking man, " Do you worship idols ? " " No," he said, " I do not." But you come nearer and nearer still. Then he will admit that his family does; he must admit that there are the ancestral tablets in the ancestral hall ; he must admit that the family worships at the tombs ; he must admit that this peculiar form of worship is very active, and that he is more or less identified with it.

We have this ancestral worship, and anybody here can see at once that any **An argument** Christian Missionary has very solid ground in Chinese thought, and **for a future** in Chinese practice, and in Chinese feeling to say, " The dead do **state.** not pass into absolute non-existence. If they do, why do you worship them ? Why go right and left, here and there, and worship your ancestors ? " And so we have in this recognised fact of the worship of ancestry, the belief in the spirit of the ancestor existing, good ground for appealing to them as to the existence of other spirits, and of the great Eternal Spirit.

Mr. Samuel Clarke (China Inland Mission) : The Chinese have a saying that of all virtues filial piety is the greatest and most praiseworthy. Now, Chinese notions of filial piety are very stereotyped, and among their notions of the obligations pertaining to filial piety is the duty of sacrificing to ancestors. Chinese opinions in reference to another world, and with reference to the soul of man after death, are very cloudy and obscure; but they do have some sort of faith that the soul in some state or another does exist after death. Moreover, they believe ^Chinese belief in immortality. that these sacrifices which they offer to their ancestors do ensure, in some way or another that they will not undertake to explain, that the souls of the deceased will be the better for these sacrifices. A Chinaman as a rule is very willing to promise not to worship idols, not to call in Buddhist priests to offer prayers for him after his death; but the last thing he will promise is that he will not offer the usual sacrifices at the graves of his ancestors. And I am present to say that I do not think there is any difference of opinion among Protestant Missionaries in China about the treatment of this subject. We are all agreed that a Chinese Christian must not be allowed to worship his ancestors.

It is objected by some that the Chinese do not worship their ancestors, that these things are only civil rites, which do not mean anything at all. But, now, what is it that the Chinese do? At the graves of their ancestors, ^Is it worship? and at the ancestral tablets, and in the ancestral temple they prostrate themselves, they invoke the spirits of their ancestors, they offer sacrifices, and they burn incense. Now, if that does not amount to worship I cannot understand what worship is.

We have very little to say against the Chinese notions of morality. These notions, I venture to say, are the highest notions to be found anywhere apart from Christianity; and as Christian Missionaries we do not say one ^Chinese notions of morality, high. word against Confucius as a teacher, or against the ancient sages of China. We tell the Chinese that the doctrines the sages taught them in reference to morality were very good, and we find fault with the Chinese because they do not practise what these sages taught. As Christian Missionaries I think that in the Chinese classical books we can very ^But practice, low. easily show the Chinese, perhaps much more easily than Indian Missionaries can in India, that there is one God, that this God is a person, that this God owns all things, and rules over all. Moreover, from Chinese classical books I think we can very well prove to the Chinese that they are sinners and ought to receive punishment. Missionaries going out to China should try to get some correct notions of what the Chinese really believe. We sympathise with the speaker who said that a Christian Missionary ought to know, or try to know, what his hearers think, and I believe Christian Missionaries in China, all of them, do more or less attempt to understand what a Chinaman thinks.

Rev. C. H. Rappard (St. Chrischona Missionary Society, Basle): I would only say a few words on the subject of how to deal with members of unreformed Churches. I have had a little experience of that. I think the first thing is that we who belong to reformed Churches should be reformed, renewed, and sanctified people; that will make a great impression upon members of the Roman Catholic Church to which ^How to deal with Roman Catholicism. I especially refer. We have in our training college near Basle a certain number of young men, and also in the Mission-field, a number of old men and very good evangelists, who came from Austria, and who were Roman Catholics before. One of them came to Switzerland as an artisan, an ignorant man. He was received into a family in the Canton of Berne; they were very pious people. When he was there they had family worship. The father read the Bible and afterwards he prayed, and the young man was quite astonished, and there he learned to know what Christianity really is. He became a converted man. He presented himself to us, we have received him, and he is now a successful preacher of the Gospel.

In some parts of Switzerland where there are many Roman Catholics, we had meetings for evangelisation for a whole week; and we told those who came to invite their Roman Catholic neighbours. They came and listened, *Meetings for Romanists.* and they saw how the Christians rejoiced in the free grace of their Lord Jesus Christ; and many have been brought to a living faith in Jesus. And then I think it is a very good thing to bring them the written Word of God, through men who love the Word of God, because they have themselves found in the Bible the living Person of the Book, our Lord Jesus Christ.

Rev. J. Kennedy (L.M.S., late of Benares): At the commencement, sir, of your address, you very properly referred us to the example of the Apostle Paul, the Apostle to the Gentiles. For nearly forty years I have *Forty years' experience.* been in the midst of Hindu idolatry and darkness, and I think I know pretty nearly what they think from what I have learned. I may just say this: I have done my very best—I may say that in the sight of God—to know what Hinduism is in all its aspects. I have read their books, and I have arrived at very different conclusions from those of our friend here. I have arrived at this conclusion, that *Conclusion arrived at.* while undoubtedly God has been speaking to them in various ways, they have not been learning; and until we can take to them the Gospel we cannot expect to find among them anything like those views of God which we should wish to find. They have a need of something direct from Heaven, to teach them the lessons which they can never, never learn themselves. Far be it from me to speak against them. There are some whom I have cause to look upon with deep affection, and I have received much kindness from them; but it is only the Word of the living God that can bring them to the living God through Jesus Christ.

Rev. John Hewlett (L.M.S., from Benares): I have had the privilege of spending nearly twenty-seven years as an Indian Missionary, a great deal of the time in Benares, and I feel bound to rise and do what I can to set right these apparently conflicting views about Hinduism and the Gospel. I believe that if the brethren, who have uttered sentiments to which we have listened, could see the matter from the same standpoint, and know *Different views not conflicting.* each other's views well, they would not have differed as they have done. I did not understand Mr. Cobban to say in the least that there was anything in Hinduism which could take the place of Christianity; that, for example, there was anything in Hinduism which could take the place of the atonement of Christ or the work of the Holy Spirit in the heart; but if I understood him aright, he meant that in Hinduism there is an immense variety, from what is basest, on the one hand, to a good deal that looks very fine on the other.

Hinduism is a vast system variously developed, aiming at meeting every phase of the soul's longings, every want of human nature. For nearly *Hinduism.* thirty centuries, the leading spirits among the Hindus have been brooding over problems of life and death, of God and the universe; and I believe that if we condemn Hinduism as a whole, and say it is nothing but a religion of the devil, we err, we say what is wrong. I believe that many of the Hindus have earnestly groped in the dark, without a ray of the great revelation to guide them, after *Its inability to satisfy.* something that would satisfy the deepest longings of their souls. I do not say that they have attained to that which can purify and save the soul. I believe they have not; but I believe they have been most sincere. This is what I understood Mr. Cobban to mean; and I believe if he had been allowed to finish his Paper, he would have shown that this was his meaning; and I am persuaded that in dealing with the Hindus, we are wrong in condemning everything they say and everything they believe, and that it is our duty to try to find out what they really believe, and what appears good and true in their system. And we must admit that there are some grains of truth and some grains of goodness in their system, and we should make these the basis of our reasoning with them about Christianity.

Then again with regard to much we cannot call true, I think it is our duty to try to understand it. Now, for example, their highest belief is pantheism: a belief in a Supreme Being of some kind. I think it is our wisdom to make that the basis of our talking to them about Chris- **Belief in a Supreme Being.** tianity. We can agree with them at least as to God's omnipresence, point out what is wrong in their belief, and tell them what is the real truth about God's omnipresence, God's pervading all things and upholding all things. Again, when the Hindus speak of their absorption into the Deity, we can correct that and tell them what the Christian doctrine of the union with the Deity really is, and then we can gradually come down to point out the errors of some of the less sublime aspects of Hinduism.

I will just say this in conclusion: I believe with the Hindus there are some really earnest and sincere aspirations. I have in conversation with many of the Pundits in the Schools of Philosophy in Benares, and with the Monks in the Monasteries, found men who seemed to be most **Sincere seekers after truth.** sincere, and I tried to lay hold of their beliefs, and make them the basis of my talking to them about Christianity. I have thus sought to commend Christianity to them. I believe many have been led to love Christ. They have felt there was something very beautiful in His Gospel, and I trust I shall find some of them hereafter at His right hand.

Mr. David McLaren, J.P. (Putney): I certainly regret, with, I am sure, the whole of this audience, that the second Paper which was read was not read to the end. I earnestly hope that there was something in the **Objections.** latter part of it which might have relieved the anxieties of not a few who heard that Paper. I do not wish to say a single word now in condemnation of it. I only wish to suggest that there are a few questions which I shall be very glad if the reader of the Paper has an opportunity of answering here, but which, if not answered here, I daresay will be answered by him, or some of his friends elsewhere. I just took note of such expressions as "spiritual truth," which frequently occurs in that Paper, and it is referring to the spiritual truth which **"Spiritual truth."** was to be found in the books of the Hindu philosophers. I should just like to ask if this is the spiritual truth proved there?—"there is one God and one Mediator between God and man, the Man Christ Jesus." Is that to be found there?

But instead of preaching the true salvation: "There is none other name under heaven given among men whereby we must be saved," but the name of the Lord Jesus,—instead of preaching salvation by the blood of Christ, I have seen it stated, we must keep that back from some of the Hindus.

Principal Brown: That was not said this afternoon.

Mr. McLaren: I should like to know whether those who follow that school of thought, which they call "the liberal school," preach judgment by the man "whom He hath ordained." These are the questions I should like to have answered in all honesty; and I will just say this **Views of future judgment.** in conclusion: I sometimes think our friends forget what was the special thanksgiving of our Lord: "I thank Thee, O Father! that Thou hast hid these things from the wise and prudent, and hast revealed them unto babes."

The Chairman: We have had the example of the Apostle Paul set before us, and I think we may rest upon his example. "God forbid that I should glory, save in the Cross of our Lord Jesus Christ." Now I will call upon Dr. Junor, to address the meeting.

Rev. K. F. Junor, M.D. (Formosa): This subject is a very interesting one to me, the method of dealing with the religions of the East. I think we go very much to the East, thinking that this Christianity **Christianity not ours, but for all.** of ours is for us, and that it is ours, manufactured by us to order. We are resting too much under that opinion, and at the same time I think we introduce too much of our personality in preaching the Gospel to these heathen nations. It seems to me that we could do very much better, not by attacking, but by supplanting. Now in China there are many things as has been observed with regard to India, many things which we can find like hooks upon which we can hang truth. The gods of China are not mentioned in the classical books of China. That is one nail driven into the coffin of idolatry. I say there are not any of the gods which are this day worshipped in China mentioned in the Chinese classical books. Tell a Chinaman that; he does not know it. Only a few learned men know it. If you go to a Chinaman, or to any countryman different from yours, and give him the impression that it is some religion of yours, it sets up his opposition at once.

Christianity is from the East. It is not ours. We are simply transmitters of it, and we are to fill our hearers with that impression that we are simple **Our religion from the East.** messengers of God, sent forth to preach something that we ourselves have received; not that we have found that it has been good, or simply to proclaim that we have known the comfort of it; but as messengers of God to teach them the truth. They are seeking after truth, just as we are. I believe we make a mistake, Christian brethren, in presuming that the value of Christ's sacrifice is confined to you and me. Who is it that knows God's purpose? Did Christ die for the world or not? Yes. May not God be dealing with these heathen nations through Christ Jesus? May they not be saved through Christ Jesus—those who believe in Him? I do not believe that *the heathen* are saved, observe. That is not what I am saying; but I say that we do not know God's purpose in Christ. I have no doubt that other Missionaries have met men in India and other lands who have been seeking after God, who have no ancestral worship and no idolatry whatever. They are blindly seeking in the dark, and they will gladly hear the truth if you will point it out to them. Why should we deny them the privilege of finding Christ through God, as well as God through Christ?

Brethren, we must go to these people and take their religion, not in the spirit of opposition, but taking the things that are good in it, and pointing **Good in false religions.** out to them better things that may be substituted; and many of them have already the belief in the one God. I believe that the old religion of China was the belief in and worship of one God, and not the idolatry that we have to-day. I tell them that "we are going back"—that is what I used to do—"going back to the old forms of worship in which your forefathers, your ancestors, whom you so revere, once worshipped." I believe that to be the case. I wish we could but get them to worship the true God. There are many men, it seems to me, who are now seeking after the true God, and if we go to them, in the fulness of the Gospel of Jesus Christ, we shall have great power with it if we tell them that it is by faith that He is to be found.

All idolaters are on the same level. There is no distinction between men who offer offerings to idols. It does not matter what the character of the idolater is, the offering is acceptable; and if you tell that to a Chinaman he sees the force of it at once; and he sees also that the richer man can offer the better gift. But when we tell them that *All on same level.* in Christ Jesus we are all sinners, and that we are only saved through Jesus Christ, and tell what He has done for us; then we appeal to their common sense as well as to their best instincts, and we shall do more for them than by attacking the religious system that we find existent there. Every man should try and understand, as has been said just now, how they think and how they feel: you can do nothing unless you do that; just as a minister here must go to his people and understand how they think and feel, and then he can preach to them. So among the heathen we must understand what they want; and they do, brethren, want the Gospel: they want to serve God just as truly as we do. They have their bad and good just as well as we have; but we can by the grace of God, through His glorious truth which is in Christ Jesus, lead them to see and feel that they need something outside of themselves, and that that is to be found in Christ, God's representative in the flesh.

The Chairman: I have great pleasure in introducing our venerable friend, Dr. Brown, Principal of the Free Church College, Aberdeen.

Rev. Principal Brown, D.D. (Aberdeen): Mr. Chairman,—I should not have thought of addressing the meeting at all this afternoon but for the Paper of Mr. Cobban. I agree with those who wish that they had heard the whole of it, because I should not like to do injustice to what he intended to impress upon us, for to tell you the truth, the impression which left itself upon my mind, after he had finished that portion of his Paper which he read, was this: That there is a great deal of *Injustice done to the Paper.* genuine religion outside of Christianity, but that Christianity is the perfection of the thing, and that they would be far better to be Christians. Now, I can hardly think that he believes what is surely very far from being correct.

The question is not how many good beliefs these people have, for there are elements of true religion all over the world which require only to be developed in order to show that there is a spark of truth in them. But what I want to know is, Is there anything saving, *Insufficiency of false religions.* anything quickening, anything elevating, anything purifying outside of Christianity? My friend Mr. Swanson, who has been speaking with great power to-day and has known China for nearly thirty years, once said to me, Say what men will, nothing lifts humanity out of the dregs and dirt into which it has been plunged in heathen lands, but the Gospel of Christ; there may certainly be a great many elements of truth, but because they want that which is saving and quickening in it, they do nothing whatever to accomplish the great object that God has in view: there is no salvation for the human soul in them.

I may tell you that my precious friend Dr. Duncan, who is known to some here as one of the most learned men in his day, was once asked, "What do you think of the condition of the heathen outside of Christianity?" "Ask a converted heathen what he thinks of the state he was in *Dr. Duncan's views.* when he was an unconverted heathen, and I leave the question there."

In the first ages there were those who thought by philosophy to bring people

to Christ, and there was Neo-Platonism, and Plotinus went into such elevated
regions of spirituality that you would almost say that that was
surely as good as Christianity. But did any one of them become
Christians? Look at any of those systems which seem to approximate to
Christianity. They come very near to it, but they never reach it. But go
to them with Christ, with the precious blood of the Lamb, and tell them that
is the way by which alone sin can be taken away, and you touch
their hearts. You may say they do not understand what sin means.
Well, I believe it; they do not; but there is a conscience within
them, there is that within every one of them which, if you tell them the right
thing, will be touched, and I believe that has been abundantly testified. Bring
the simple Gospel to them and we elevate their intellectual character and bring
them to a luminous understanding of the very thing about which
you say they know nothing. What did the Apostle Paul do? I
think his experience will teach us. He went to Athens. He took
the method of our friends, that is to say, he appealed to them
by common principles, principles common to them both, and he took a glorious
text, and you may say a very ingenious text,—" The unknown God." Well, he
delivered a grand lecture, and what was the fruit of it? Why, we are told:
"So Paul departed from among them. Howbeit certain men clave unto him,
and believed: among the which was Dionysius the Areopagite, and a woman
named Damaris, and others with them." Very well, he went away; and where
did he go? To Corinth. A very short distance it was, and he said he was among
them in weakness and in fear and in much trembling. Why so? Because he
had failed. He thought he would make a great impression upon these people by
appealing to what was common to them, and he produced no effect. When he
went to Corinth, he determined to know nothing but Jesus Christ and Him
crucified, and we know the result.

Neo-Platonists.

Christ touches the heart.

St. Paul's experience at Athens.

Rev. John Ross (United Presbyterian Mission, Manchuria): Mr.
Chairman, and Christian friends,—Duties in another part of the building
have prevented my being here to hear all the Papers, but I was particularly
struck with, and very much interested in, what I have heard of the Paper
on which so much discussion has taken place. I do not know
that I heard anything that was objectionable, but it seems to
me from what I did hear that if the opinions of the various
speakers could be sifted out, there would be found no essential difference.
It seems to me, that the position of the Paper was this: that all moral
truth is important whether it be much or little. I do not think that the
writer of the Paper wished, as I in my Mission work do not wish, to see
mere moral truth substituted for Christianity. I know that in the various
heathen systems there is some truth. We do not in this little island of
the sea embrace all the wisdom of the world, nor all the thinking of the
world; and we must, when we go into other lands, either oppose or utilise as
auxiliaries the truths that are there. In order to know what
truth there is we must examine. It seems to me the writer
of the Paper does that, and that has been my own practice.
We must examine the various systems with which we come into contact;
and what am I as a Missionary to do with these? Are we to spurn all
the systems *in toto*, because nine-tenths of them are false; or are we to
utilise the tithe of truth, and say: "Now, here we agree: here we
Christians and you heathen agree; but this won't save you; we have come
here with a higher truth, with another truth, with a totally different truth,
a soul-saving truth, which you have not here." It seems to me, the position of the Paper was that, and that is exactly the standpoint I occupy
with regard to Confucianism

Views of Mr. Cobban's Paper.

Examine all systems fairly.

Now, Confucianism in China is a moral system; it is not a religious system; we have no business to call it so; it is as much a moral system as that of Socrates or Plato, and worthy of being named alongside of anything that was ever concocted by human brains outside of Christianity. I come *Confucianism a system of morals.* before the Chinese, and perhaps my text is a sentence from Confucius; and I say, "Do you observe this?" No. Then I say to them, "We have brought you something else." "We have come with something which will enable you to observe the truths you know,—at present they are a dead body,—we have come here with the living soul and spirit of Christianity, which will make that dead body of yours a living body, from which living, vital Christianity will shine forth, and act in your national life, in your family life, and in your individual life." That is the position I take up. I am sorry the time is so short that I cannot fully explain myself; but it seems to me there is not really such a great disparity of opinion at bottom if we could but quietly compare our views together.

With regard to ancestral worship, let me say one word. In connection with this phrase I do not like the word worship. I am one of those Missionaries who do not admit any person into the Christian Church except on renunciation of this ancestral ritual, as I would prefer to call it. *Ancestral ritual not worship.* Worship, I imagine, always implies prayer; in connection with what is called ancestral worship there is no prayer. There is burning of incense, there is offering of fruits and flowers, and there is bowing to the ground; but there is no prayer, either to the deceased spirit, or for the deceased spirit. We ourselves like to go to the graves of our deceased friends, and we desire to see them clean and neat. We go there with crowns of flowers, and with garlands, and they are laid there. I do not dislike the foundation of this ritual in China, which is that same filial spirit which prompts a son or a daughter to go to the grave of a father and mother in this country and keep it in order. Let us not destroy that spirit; but let us eliminate all that is non-Christian from the practice which has grown out of it.

The Acting Secretary: Our time is so far gone (in fact, we have exceeded the time allowed for this meeting), that we cannot call upon any more of the speakers whose names have been sent *Mr. Cobban may reply.* up; but if it be the will of the meeting to hear Mr. Cobban for two or three minutes, we cannot refuse that.

Rev. G. M. Cobban: I thank you, Mr. Chairman, and I thank the meeting for this opportunity of saying just a word. My object in the Paper, part of which I read, was to urge this: That a Christian Missionary going into the midst of people of another faith to preach our Gospel to them, should know those people, and know what they are *Missionaries should know the people.* thinking. That was the first point. Men going with the foregone conclusion, like my adviser to whom I referred, that all Hinduism and all Buddhism is of the devil, will never take the trouble to know. That was what I wished to emphasise. Next, I wish to bear witness—I speak as a witness of what I know,—to the fact that in Hinduism —I was not speaking of the idolatrous section of it, or of the priestly section of it, but of the other section—there is a great deal of truth, of spiritual truth—to repeat the word. As to where it came *All spiritual truth from God.* from, and how it came, I have nothing to say now. All spiritual truth is from Him; that is my conviction. And when I meet spiritual truth yonder, either on the lips of a Hindu or in a Hindu book, I say this has come from God, and I rejoice.

As to the extent of the spiritual truth, I will give you an illustration.

A little poem in my carpet bag, says: "Why should Grace take the human form to save us. If Grace be in the heart, is not that enough?"

And the poet's answer is: "Just as the hunter takes a deer, **The idea of an incarnation.** and exhibits it, that he may catch a deer; just as the fowler takes a bird of that class which he wishes to catch; just so Grace, wanting to catch man, took the form of a man." Now the fact which this brings out is this: that among the Hindus there is a doctrine of God manifest in a human form, something like the Theophanies of the Old Testament; and how easy it is for a Missionary to preach Christ to a people who believe as far as that!

Take another point, spiritual worship. Here in another poem I find the poet exhorting the people. "You are going to worship, are you not? and you have brought flowers from your garden, and you are going to offer them, but that idol is not God, and these are not the right flowers. **Heart worship taught.** God is a spirit. God wants a flower; but the flower that He wants is the flower that grows in the garden of the heart, the flower of love. That is the flower you must bring." Very true. Very true. I do not believe that came from beneath, you know. But these are only specimens. Why, I tell you I have met with expressions of truth yonder in those heathen books that have surprised me, but they have also delighted me, because they have given me the conviction that God has been in this country before I came. The Spirit of God has been speaking somehow, whether by fragments of prophecy or revelation I cannot tell, and I do not care.

But the great fact is this: that all the religious truth that is in India has come from God, and that Christianity finds there a line of approach to the Hindu heart by these truths which are already there. **No substitute for Christianity.** Do not imagine that I was going to run my Paper to this conclusion: that they have quite enough yonder without Christianity. God forbid. No; I am a Scotchman. No; there can be no substitute for Christianity, and no substitute for, as there is no rival to, Christ. No; India must have Christ; but I venture to say that any one who knows even the little that I know about Hindus, will preach Christ with more zeal and with greater joy, than if he were preaching in the dark, not knowing how much of truth there is amongst the people out there. I do not believe **Christianity not to be modified.** in a modified Christianity, nor do I believe in any compromise between Christianity and other religious systems. Christianity stands alone; and after we have made allowance for all the truth outside Christianity, Christianity is without a peer. There is no doubt about that. But if I find spiritual truth there, the same kind of truth as I find in Christianity, am I to call it brass when outside, and gold when it is inside Christianity? No; I won't. It is not honest.

The **Chairman**: I suppose we must now bring this very interesting meeting to a conclusion.

Rev. E. O. Williams closed with prayer.

ADJOURNED DISCUSSION

ON

MISSIONARY METHODS—(4) DEALING WITH FORMS OF RELIGIOUS BELIEF.

(*Thursday evening, June 14th, in the Annexe.*)

Bishop A. W. Wilson, D.D. (U.S.A.), in the chair.

[It is not thought necessary to give a full report of this meeting. The attendance was so small as to make it doubtful whether the discussion should be begun, and led to its being brought to an early close. The speeches were well worthy of a place in our report, but being chiefly from delegates who had not attended the meeting of *Reasons for short report.* which this was an adjournment they naturally travelled over the same ground. The following is a brief abstract.—ED.]

Rev. G. Owen (L.M.S., from Pekin) gave an interesting and elaborate account of the character, origin, and history of ancestral worship in China, and dwelt on those aspects of the customs observed in connection with it which are not idolatrous, and advocated the tolerance of certain modified forms of observance of them by Christian converts.

He showed how the customs were "based on filial piety," and *Ancestral worship.* that filial piety was the basis of Chinese government and morality, and the sudden and entire abandonment of them was apt to react on the fundamental principles of reverence and filial love, and to lead to the neglect of the great law, "Thou shalt honour thy father and thy mother." He thought that for example once a year the converts might take part in the great *ching ming* festival at the period *A suggestion.* corresponding to the Jewish Passover, when the Chinese went out to sweep the tombs, and hang strings of paper money for the use of the departed spirits, the Christians might attend to the graves of their ancestors, and strew flowers on the tombs, but must be absolutely forbidden to make offerings of money, food, and such like. They might also keep a register of their ancestors, like a family pedigree in Western lands, instead, of the present tablets.

Mr. Owen observed that there was no great difficulty in getting real converts to give up heathen customs, in fact they are apt *Converts* to go too far; and the Roman Catholics who made a half-way *abandon* house for their converts did not gain thereby. *customs.*

Rev. J. Ross referred to the testimony of one of the advisers of the father of the King of Corea, who had studied Christian books, when a prisoner in China, and who had become quite friendly toward Christian Missions, to which he had formerly been much opposed. This adviser told one of Mr. Ross's teachers that the king's father had stated that if the people were allowed to observe these old ancestral customs he believed, all Corea might become Christian in three years.

Rev. W. S. Swanson (English Presbyterian Mission, Amoy) advocated a different policy, more in harmony with the " root and branch " methods of the Puritans, while he condemned interference with customs which were not sinful in themselves, or connected with idolatry, such as binding the feet of girls. These old customs were best removed by the New Testament method of laying down principles which undermined or supplanted them than by positive laws or external authority, as in the case of slavery in the early days of the Christian Church.

" Root and branch" methods.

Rev. George Piercy asked Mr. Swanson whether the Churches in the region of Amoy allowed the Christians to perform any ceremonies in connection with ancestral worship or ancestral ritual, by whatever name it might be called ; to which Mr. Swanson gave an emphatic " No ; it would not be allowed for a single moment by any native office-bearer. They know what it means."

General testimony.

Mr. Piercy then asked whether the answer would be given for other parts of China, to which the answers were—

From Mr. Owen : Yes ; from Pekin.

Mr. Clarke : Yes ; from Chen-tu.

As the question as to the best way of preaching the Gospel to the heathen, which led to the adjournment of the discussion, had not been taken up, it was thought best to close the meeting.

MEETINGS OF MEMBERS IN SECTION.

FIFTH SESSION.

MEDICAL MISSIONS.

(1) *THE AGENTS.*

(a) The place and power of Medical Missions.
(b) The relation of the doctor to the Mission and to Mission work.
(c) Ordained and unordained Medical Missionaries.
(d) Training of native Medical Students. Should it be confined to those who are designed for Mission work?

(*Monday morning, June 11th, in the Annexe.*)

R. A. Macfie, Esq., in the chair.
Acting Secretary, Mr. J. L. Maxwell, M.D.

Prayer was offered by Dr. Andrew Jukes.

The Chairman said : I have been asked to take the chair, presumably because I am a survivor of the Conference at Liverpool in 1860. The memory of that enjoyable occasion recalls to mind, among the worthies passed away, its warm participants, Lord Shaftesbury, Sir Herbert Edwardes, the genial chairman General Alexander, the organising energy of Mr. Carre Tucker, the consecrated talents of Dr. Mullens, who, a model secretary, fell on the African field which he went to survey. These, though we met in Lancashire, may be regarded as citizens of this great metropolis. Note in that list how well the Episcopalian element was represented. So it is now. That historic Church of England lends again such assistance, that we of other Churches give thanks and take courage. We are glad to think that the Committee of this Conference do not misinterpret absences, which we deeply regret for our sake, if not for the Church's sake, and for the sake of mankind. We would like that, as of old, the right hands of fellowship were extended along the whole unbroken line to the many brothers from other lands who have, in a most gratifying manner and measure, responded to the invitation sent out,

Liverpool Conference, 1860.

by coming as deputies to give the benefit of their varied experience and wisdom.

We Britons are cheered by the presence of delegates from the twin countries, the United States and the Dominion of Canada ; and they, not less than the English, Scotch and Irish, gladly welcome the delegates from the Continent of Europe, which indeed is the original fatherland of almost every one here. The same blood runs warm in all our veins ; but still more and still better, we are one in Christ Jesus. To some extent we are fellow-workers. How much does India owe to the North American Continent and to the European? How harmoniously do American and British Missionaries co-operate in China?

Delegates welcomed to this Conference.

Medical Missions are of comparatively recent origin among us. The Early Church, no doubt, was distinguished for its hospital charities, a tradition of which stands out prominent before the stranger in New York, in' the distinctive names of their infirmaries, the Presbyterian, the Methodist, etc. There is the highest precedent for the principle. Of our Lord we read that He devoted His life to " teaching, preaching, and healing "—that He " spake of the kingdom of God, and healed them who had need of healing"—that He "went about doing good, and healing all who were oppressed of the devil." He performed these cures, it is written, because " He was moved with compassion." Observe, however, the quotation from prophecy that precedes. I do not remember any passage that suggests that it was any part of His design to use this power, to organise His benevolence, so as to be a means to an end. Rather otherwise : in one case he that was healed " wist not who it was that cured him." In another " He healed them all, and charged that they should not make Him known."

Christ's ministry of healing.

To proceed, when He commissioned the twelve, He " gave them power to heal," and said, " Preach, saying the kingdom of heaven is come : heal." To the seventy He said, putting the human body first, " Heal the sick, and say the kingdom is come." The Church of the Acts had the same power and like compassion communicated to it, and we read the consequence, "They were healed every one." Paul enumerates twice among the charismata, "gifts of healing." If we look to the language of the original, we recognise two things,—that healing, when one of the words so rendered is used, is applied indiscriminately to soul and body : sin is regarded as a malady. Our Lord was wont to regard the whole man. He is emphatically " the Saviour of the body." The other word, of extremely frequent occurrence, suggests to the mind what we still call " medical *attendance*," tender, loving, diligent ministration towards the sufferer, a characteristic of our Master and Example, which shines forth continually, and is seen in other miracles, such as the feeding of the multitude. Let every mention of *therapeutics* remind us of that kindness and thoughtful care, which *He* exhibited even on the Cross.

The disciples commissioned to heal.

It is in this spirit that the good Medical Missionary will work, and its voluntary character and its influence will be none the less apprehended and appreciated, because he is not endowed with Early Church gifts. It is the same spirit that still The Medical Missionary. works, though miracles have departed—the spirit which ought equally at home in *Christian* lands to be continually operating and equally manifest. The heathen should know that the same love abounds in us all, and dictates, much rather, let me say prompts, to corresponding deeds *at home.* Then will the Medical Missionary be strengthened indeed when Medical Missionary work is but local experience of universal charity. But to this we have not attained collectively. Let us use the divine remedy for this evil shortcoming. We are reminded in the inspired dictum, "No soldier engaged in a campaign entangles himself with the affairs of this life." This is "a hard saying"; but it is also a *problem* difficult for every individual to solve, difficult amid the complex ramifications of present-day life. But all can practise economy; most of us, more than we do, might practise self-restraint, curbing desire to possess, and ambition to be neighbourlike, which is a worldly aim and standard. The Churches must learn to give up attempts to combine the incompatible.

This is sure, that the spirit of Medical Missions is the spirit of Christianity; it is following in the steps of the Master: and it will *please* Him, whose career was love and work, as well as will exhibit "the benignity, humanity, and philanthropy of God our The spirit of it: pleasing to God. Saviour," "who healeth all our diseases." The University of Edinburgh, near the Medical Mission headquarters, is surmounting a dome, which the liberality of a citizen has enabled it to rear, with the image of a youth grasping firmly a torch and holding it up, to guide others and himself. So will the consistent Christian, though he stand alone, be a light in the world, especially to conduct personally to the Divine Healer, by his own example inflaming and stimulating his fellows, whom he may not judge, any more than does this Conference, which acts, in accordance with its designation, as a receptacle of information and opinions, leaving it to sanctified wise men to weigh and judge what is said, and trusting to love and zeal for determination to adopt and act. We do not presume to dictate or even to advise; only we urge to "work while it is day; the night cometh: then no man can work."

PAPER.

1. BY THE REV. JOHN LOWE, F.R.C.S.E. (Secretary, Edinburgh Medical Missionary Society, formerly of Neyoor, Travancore).

Medical Missions: their place and power.

The Medical Mission enterprise is, from first to last, we believe, Scriptural, Apostolic, yea, we might say, Divine. The example and precept of Christ Himself—the record of the work of His immediate

disciples, and the whole scope and spirit of the Gospel are a distinct
recognition of the Medical Mission principle; while experience,
especially during more recent years, emphatically testifies to the
value and importance of this agency.

Let us clearly define what we mean by a Medical Mission. It
is not merely a philanthropic agency,—not an enterprise for the
What a Medical provision in our Mission-fields abroad of the inestimable
Mission means. benefits of European medicine and surgery. If that
alone were the object contemplated, we should have no claim to be
heard here, and our Missionary Societies would hardly be justified
in using their funds for the establishment of Mission hospitals and
dispensaries abroad. What we mean by Medical Missions is, the
systematic combination of the healing art with the preaching of the
Gospel, and this in such a way as to make the ministry of healing
subservient to the winning of souls for Christ.

We cannot be too explicit on this point. Misapprehensions as
to the aim and object of Medical Missions are too prevalent. Many
Its true have the idea that this department of work is rather a
object. benevolent agency, than a directly Missionary enterprise;
and perhaps nothing has done more to hinder the progress of Medical
Missions than this misconception.

We hold that the true Medical Missionary is as much the
ambassador of Christ,—as much the messenger of the Churches,—
The Medical as much the preacher of the everlasting Gospel as is his
Missionary's ordained clerical colleague. As Medical Missionaries, we
position. claim for ourselves this position. We ask to be sent into
the Mission-field in order that we may do the work of an evangelist.
We ask that Medical Missions be recognised by our Missionary
Societies, and by the Churches, not merely as a benevolent agency,
not as an occasional auxiliary to Missionary work, but as an
embodiment of the Divine idea, enunciated by the Master Himself,
when He commanded the Gospel to be preached among all nations.
This Gospel views man as a denizen of earth, as well as an heir of
immortality—it has regard to the life that now is, as well as to that
which is to come,—it affects man in the whole extent of his being,
body, soul, and spirit. Christ's ministry was a ministry of word
and deed, that of His disciples was the same. We believe, therefore,
that the Divine meaning of "preaching the Gospel" (especially
when used with reference to the vocation of the Missionary to the
heathen) implies much more than the mere proclamation of the
Gospel message. We believe, that as He who is the sum and
substance of the Gospel "was made flesh and dwelt among us,"
that as His ministry was a ministry of sympathy with suffering
humanity, as He healed the sick, and went about continually doing
good, thus, ever manifesting while He taught it, the spirit of His
own religion, so His ambassadors must "preach the Gospel, not by
word only, but likewise, by a compassionate Christ-like ministry,
performed in Christ's name, and for His sake.

This then is the place we claim for Medical Missions. We believe that the consecration of the healing art to the service of the Gospel is not only in accordance with the Divine method, but that it actually forms a part of the Divine intention; therefore it follows, that Medical Missions are *a universally applicable agency*. Wherever we find man, there we find disease and suffering, greatly aggravated however in our Foreign Mission-fields by prevailing ignorance and superstitition. We often hear it said that in many of our Mission-fields, as for instance in India and Japan, medical aid is now so plentifully provided that, in such spheres, Medical Missions are not required. Apart altogether from the considerations already urged, scarcely a word is needed to show, from a merely professional point of view, how utterly erroneous is such a statement. In our own highly favoured land there is a doctor for about every fifteen hundred of the population, or twenty-three thousand for the whole population of the United Kingdom; let us suppose that there are ten thousand European or native qualified practitioners in India (an estimate far above the mark), there would be but one doctor to every twenty-four thousand of the population; or, in other words, to provide a medical man for every three thousand of India's population would require no fewer than seventy-five thousand practitioners. The recent official census of Japan reveals the fact that within the Empire there are thirty-four thousand native physicians, of whom probably less than five hundred are educated in Western medical science, thus giving one qualified physician to every sixty thousand of the population. The mere mention of such facts is an emphatic contradiction to the assertion that Medical Missions are not needed in such lands.

It will be admitted moreover that no country is better provided with parochial medical officers, with charitable dispensaries and free hospitals than our own, yet if anyone wishes to see for himself, the value of Medical Missions, and how effectively they subserve the promotion of evangelistic effort among our home heathen, he has only to visit our Medical Missions in this great City, in Edinburgh, Glasgow, Birmingham, Manchester, Bristol, and other large towns, and he will find that they are, as a rule, the most numerously attended of all public dispensaries, and, what is still more significant, that no agency is more manifestly blessed in bringing to the most degraded and sunken the glad tidings of the Gospel. *Their value at home and abroad.*

If in our own highly favoured land, Medical Missions are so successful in gaining access for the Gospel message, to the homes and hearts of the lost and ignorant, there can surely be no question as to their adaptation for the heathen, and as little doubt as to their need in all our Mission-fields abroad.

There are many considerations which strengthen our plea for the place we claim for Medical Missions, and which, at the same time, illustrate their power; we can do little more however than refer, in the briefest manner, to a few of these.

As bearing more directly upon Missionary success, there is a fact too much overlooked, which ought to secure for Medical Missions a very prominent place in every localised Mission; we refer to the remarkably suggestive fact that in India, China, Africa, Madagascar, among the islands of the sea, and, more or less, in every heathen land, the treatment of disease, barbarous and cruel as it is, and largely made up of idolatrous rites and ceremonies, is monopolised by the priests, or by others intimately associated with them, and entirely under their control. Let us suppose, for a moment, that an epidemic is raging in a mixed community of *Heathen remedies demoralise converts.*

heathens and Christians, and where no proper medical aid is available, what, in such circumstances, might we expect? Why, just what does happen in every Mission-field, causing sorrow and disappointment to many a Missionary's heart.

Every experienced Missionary could give such testimony as the following, which in a sentence or two will explain our meaning. A Missionary in Madagascar, after reporting the devastating effects of a severe epidemic among the people in his district, writes :—"This fearful disease threw back many of the converts upon their old superstitious rites and customs. It was a time of severe trial, and much of our work could not stand this crucial test. The people sought after 'wizards that peep and mutter, and ceased to seek unto their God.' For a season, there was a strong current of idolatry and witchcraft running throughout the district, and many went back from their faith. Everywhere, the churches were emptied of worshippers, and the schools of scholars ; while the charm-maker found his enchantments eagerly sought after, and liberally paid for. The most absurd things were done to effect cures by order of these diviners, and again and again, our eyes beheld things which showed unmistakably what a powerful reaction had set in."

An instance in Madagascar.

In view of the place Medical Missions should occupy in our Missionary organisations, and as still more strikingly illustrative of their power, let me ask what agency is there, humanly speaking, more fitted than a Medical Mission to disarm prejudice in a heathen community? to gain the confidence of the people? to win one's way to their homes and hearts? and to teach them, as by an object lesson, the saving truths of the Gospel? The blessed results of this agency in opening otherwise closed doors, in securing concessions which have greatly promoted the Missionary enterprise, in conciliating the goodwill of bigoted opponents, and in overcoming barriers to the spread of the Gospel are so well known that the place we claim for Medical Missions as a *pioneer* agency no one nowadays would venture to dispute. But they are *more* than a pioneer agency. We claim for this enterprise, that it is one of the most powerful, effective, and directly evangelistic agencies which the Church possesses. The array of facts and statistics in support of this claim are so remarkable and convincing that to us it is altogether unaccountable that Medical Missions have not, long ere now, secured a place in the very fore-front of our Missionary methods. We believe that, if the spiritual fruits of our Medical Mission in China could be tabulated, the fact would be revealed that in that great Empire no method of Missionary work has been more signally blessed in spreading the knowledge of the Gospel than our Mission hospitals and dispensaries. The seed sown in the hearts of patients has in many cases brought forth fruit in some thirty, in some sixty, and in some an hundred fold. In not a few instances native Churches have sprung up in towns and villages far distant from the headquarters of the Medical Mission, but where no other human agency had been employed, the patients having received the " double cure," had returned to their homes, and told out among their friends what the Lord had done for their souls. Medical Missions have not only broken down prejudices and opened " wide doors and effectual " among the exclusive Chinese, but they have been, in a very marked degree, the nurseries of the native Churches. The same may be said of Medical Missions in India. Were the triumphs of the Gospel won through this agency in India more widely known, we doubt not that in that land of caste prejudice Medical Mission hospitals and dispensaries would be multiplied an hundredfold.

Medical Missions evangelistic agencies.

Results in China.

In itinerant Mission work we can hardly over-estimate the value of this agency. Clerical Missionaries, when engaged in such work, everywhere feel the need of it, and, whether competent or not, are compelled in some measure to assume the character of the physician. The story of itinerant Medico-evangelistic work sent home from time to time by our Medical Missionaries reads like a continuation of the " Acts of the Apostles."

Valuable in itinerant Missions.

If it can be truthfully said of any Medical Mission that in spiritual results it is not so fruitful as we might expect it to be, we have no hesitation in saying that the fault is not in the *agency*, nor with rare exceptions in the agent, but in the exceedingly limited resources placed at his disposal wherewith to carry on the work. His work as a healer of disease is in many Missions so over- whelming, and the help he receives so inadequate, that it is utterly Spiritual results impossible for him, single-handed, to develop to the full the hindered. capabilities of his Mission as an evangelistic agency. Intimately acquainted as we are with Medical Missions and with Medical Missionaries in all parts of the world, to us, the wonder is, that with the comparatively little support they receive, and the amazing amount of professional work they have to overtake, they have, from a spiritual point of view, accomplished so much.

One word, in conclusion. In a paper which we read on " Medical Missions" at the Missionary Conference in 1878, we then said, "When I went out to India, in 1861, there were not more than twenty Medical Missionaries in the Foreign field; now there are between ninety and a hundred." It is with heartfelt thankfulness that we are to-day able to say that there are now over three hundred Medical Missionaries in all parts of the world engaged in this Christ- like work, and about thirty of these are fully qualified lady physicians.

PAPER.

2. BY MR. G. D. DOWKONTT, M.D. (Medical Director of the Inter- national Medical Missionary Society, New York).

Mr. Chairman, dear brethren, and sisters in Christ,—Being unexpectedly called upon, in the absence of the writer of a paper promised for this meeting, I shall confine my remarks particularly to the first division of the subject under consideration, viz. : " The Place and Power of Medical Missions," trusting to your kind sym- pathy and indulgence while I do so, my notice to prepare this paper having been extremely short. In the consideration of any subject it is desirable that the terms to be used should be clearly defined. While the majority of those present may be fully conversant with the meaning of the words Medical Mission, and Medical Missionary, yet for the sake of the few who are not, it may be well to explain them.

What is a Medical Missionary?—A fully qualified physician, who uses his or her medical knowledge for the relief of physical What Medical suffering, and to obtain an entrance for that Gospel which Missionaries he or she seeks to make known. In other words, one who are and do. takes the *fruits* of Christianity, and thus seeks to plant the *roots*.

What is a Medical Mission dispensary or hospital?—A place where the sick poor are gathered together to obtain physical relief, and while there have the Gospel preached to them.

It will probably save time if we shall consider interrogatively three more points concerning Medical Missions.

Why should Medical Missions exist?—Because of the *great need* for them, and their *immense value* in obtaining access, removing prejudice, and establishing confidence among the heathen abroad, and the almost worse than heathen at home.

What reasons can be adduced for their employment?—Chiefly four : *Christ commands it ; sympathy demands it ; wisdom dictates it ;* and *experience has proved their value.*

What are the special advantages of Medical Missions? Among others, *self-preservation, self-support,* as far as practicable, and *successful Gospel effort.*

The need for Medical Missionaries is a subject but little known, and still less *realised* by the vast majority of Christians ; but the following facts are adduced as affording some idea of it :—

Facts urged for their need.

1st. There are over *one thousand millions* of heathens and Mohammedans in the world.

2nd. They are perishing no less *physically* for lack of medical aid, than *spiritually* from ignorance of the Gospel.

3rd. There is *only one* Medical Missionary to nearly as many people as there are in the entire city of London.

4th. They are dying at the rate of about *forty millions* every year, the greater number of them without any knowledge of Christ Jesus.

5th. These poor sufferers *have bodies like ours ;* they have nerves, and *can feel* as we do. We know it? Yes, but are we not in danger of *forgetting* it, and almost unconsciously thinking of them as being made of the same material as the idols they worship ?

6th. We know what sickness is with all the aids of modern medical science . but what must it be without any of these ?

Many of the terrible things perpetrated under the guise of medical treatment among the heathen one cannot even mention in such an assembly as this, and yet they exist and should be made known. Think of such cases as the following :— The first student of the International Medical Missionary Society,—of which I have the honour to be the Medical Director—Dr. W. R. Summers, now in Central Africa, the pioneer of Bishop Taylor's work in that country, wrote me of two cases he met with, both little children, only a few months old. They had been sick, and their mothers' sought to cure them by scoring them from *head to foot* with a sharp instrument, and he counted *over four hundred wounds* on the body of one child. It is scarcely needful to add that both were dead.

Bishop Taylor narrates the case of a woman being sick in a native hut, and he saw the husband plunge a knife into the heart of his ten-year-old girl because he believed that she had bewitched her mother. Two cases were recently made known as occurring in China, in the one instance a daughter, and the other a son, had cut a large portion of flesh from their arms, which was *cooked* and *eaten* by a dying parent as a means of saving life.

The value of Medical Missions in removing prejudice, and evoking the deepest gratitude, has been manifested again and again the world over ; and the wonder to many of us is that we have been so slow to see the value of this agency.

Heathen gratitude for cures.

In Africa, Dr. Summers was loaded with the gifts of the grateful people he had treated at Melange ; and by means of these alone he was able to load thirty-six carriers, and succeeded in arriving at the further side of the Congo, a distance of more than a thousand miles, his Society not being able to give him at the time a single dollar.

In China, the late Dr. Mackenzie operated upon the eyes of two girls in one family, and gave them sight, and then the mother was operated on successfully. She had never seen her children, and her delight and gratitude knew no bounds. As a result all three were converted, likewise the father, and many others, and a successful church of a hundred or more is now in their village.

In Corea, Dr. Allen attended the prince when dying from a wound received in battle, thirteen of the native surgeons having tried in vain to stop the bleeding by pouring molten wax into the wound. The prince afterwards told the doctor that his people said, "The doctor did not come from America, but from Heaven!" and in a sense he certainly did so.

We might mention many examples demonstrating that wherever Medical Missions have been prosecuted in the true spirit of the Gospel, success, unattainable in any other way, has been experienced. *What is our responsibility?* *First*, to our hands alone has been committed the double gift of Medical Science to heal the body, and the Gospel for healing the soul; *second*, if we fail to take these things to them, they cannot obtain them in any other way, and as far as we are concerned they must perish body and soul. Let us suppose a vessel at sea; the crew are Our responsibility. dying of fever, when one day they sight a sail. The vessel comes closer and closer on her passage, and at last these perishing ones make known their need. "We've got the fever!" "Want some water!" "Send us a doctor!" But to their dismay and consternation, the steamer steers off and *leaves them to perish*. What is their crime?

A king learns that a famine is devastating a portion of his country, his people are dying by thousands. He calls together his ministers and leaders, and commissions a number of them to take the provisions, which *he provides them with* to their famishing brethren. A few go, but the majority do not, and instead of doing so, they consume all they can themselves, store up the rest, claiming the provisions the king has given them as their own, and thousands perish for lack of the aid which was provided for them. What crime are they guilty of?

And now, dear friends, in conclusion, permit me to present the following question for your prayerful consideration. *To know* that millions are perishing *body and soul; to possess* the means which *might save both; to withhold* the same and *let them perish,—is what?*

The Chairman: I am quite sure that this audience will have great pleasure in hearing a few words from another visitor from the United States,—Bishop Wilson.

Bishop A. W. Wilson, D.D. (Methodist Episcopal Church [South], U.S.A.) : I suppose I was requested to speak because I might have something to say on the question from a non-professional point of view, and not because I am an expert in medical work at all. I have observed Medical Mission work with interest, especially in the last ten years, and as far as the general questions are concerned, which have been so forcibly treated by Dr. Lowe and my brother from the United States, I can only give a most hearty endorsement of every sentiment and statement that has been uttered.

There are two things, it seems to me, that a Medical Missionary can do, with a distinctness and assurance of success, that a mere Clerical Missionary cannot do. The first is to teach the value of human life. Our Scriptures have done away very The Medical and Clerical Missionary compared. emphatically, I think, with the indifference to life that seems to be very prevalent among heathen peoples; and the lessons of our Scriptures was taught by our Lord in His care for all life from the life of the sparrow up to that of the man, and especially in His treatment of diseased life that He might restore it to its integrity, and make it capable of all its Divine uses. And I am very sure that while the Clerical Missionary may emphasise the truths of the Gospel in regard to this matter, the Medical Missionary by his direct contact with it, his care for it, his effort to preserve it, and build it up, and improve it in every possible way will instil more surely into the minds of heathen communities our sense of the value of life.

Another point, and it seems to me a most vital one, is that he in the same way by his direct dealing with it can teach the sanctity of The sanctity the human body as no other man can. " A body hast of the body. thou prepared me," he said. In some measure may we not all say it ? Does not God give the body to be just the expression of the individual life which He imparts to each one of us ? And is not it suited to our mental and spiritual quality and character ? I think that this view of it gives a special meaning to medical work, as we have a higher sense of medical work ever since the days that our Lord took our infirmities, and bare our sickness.

And then, too, we all know that in the advance that has been made in physiological science to-day, there is a closer and more intimate con-Intimate relation nection between the body and spirit than was formerly between body supposed. The body is not a mere tool; it is not a mere and spirit. instrument to be thrown away when it is done with. Our Gospel anticipated science, in that God taught us that the body has very intimate relations to the life that is to come : " And He that raised up Christ from the dead shall also quicken our mortal body because of His Spirit that dwelleth in us." I am one of those who place such value upon the Scriptures that even a hint *there* is worth a strong statement from any other quarter. There are intimations that if we want to do our work, even at home in more civilised communities with any sort of thoroughness, and any hope of permanent success, we must do it upon the line of the intimate and indissoluble association between the soul and the body. They must be cared for, not the one at the expense of the other, but each in its own sphere, and because each belongs to the other.

I will just add that after having gone through some of the hospital work in Pekin, in Shanghai, that large work of Dr. Kerr in Canton, some of the work in India and Beyrout, and along the Nile in Egypt, I begin to have larger and better hope for the success of the Gospel. I endorse Every Mission the statement that every localised Mission ought to have a should have a Medical agency in connection with it ; and I am sure we shall medical agency. find no more ready way of access to the people who need us most, and who are to be most largely benefited by our Gospel than this. So that from my point of view, evangelistic, if you please, I enter most cordially into any scheme that shall look to the enlargement and extension of this line of work, and especially endorse the intimation that we must look to our lady friends for a large extension of it on their side of the house. I have seen some of their work, and I have been extremely gratified, not simply that they have been successful, but that they hold their own with physicians of any grade from any country, and are doing work which will bear comparison with any that is done in civilised lands. I rejoice in this success, and pray that it may be greatly enlarged

DISCUSSION.

Dr. Robert Pringle (Bengal Army): Mr. Chairman, Christian friends, —Perhaps if no one else is going to take up the other three points in the Paper, I may cursorily run over them as the result of some thirty years' experience of medical service in India. The first is "The relation of the doctor to the Mission and Mission work." In my opinion it cannot possibly be too intimate. The two must go hand in hand; and perhaps the words of Sir Thomas Crawford, the head of the Army Medical Department in this country, may be of great value here. He said for himself he could not possibly understand how any Christian man, called in professionally to treat a case could not, when the opportunity offered, say a word for his Master, and he summed it up that necessity would be laid upon. him that he must preach the Gospel. I think, therefore, we may pass that over by the short answer that the relation of the doctor to the Mission and to Mission work is the most intimate that can possibly be held. *Relation of doctors to Missions.*

The next is "Ordained and unordained Medical Missionaries." On that subject, if we take first of all the unordained Medical Missionaries, there is a certain amount of University study necessary to qualify for a medical officer, and if the love of God is in his heart, and he feels constrained to go out to labour, no matter where, I utterly fail to see why the Churches should not put their hands on him and give him the commission of the Master. *The unordained Medical Missionary.*

Now, as to the next point, "The training of native medical students." As one who has seen something of what can be done by natives in India in the medical line, I must say this, I look to it with great hope for the future, but it must be very carefully done. I took a boy once out of the school, and I taught him, and I never shall forget the return that boy gave me for the medical knowledge I was enabled .o give him. Then, "Should it be confined to those who are designed for Mission work." I should say, undoubtedly. Select a man who gives his heart to the Master, and then you make sure the education that you give him will go out into the world sanctified and blessed. *Training of native medical students.*

It will be one thing for us working in that country to remember, that we have a very high character for professional knowledge to maintain, because the natives would not send for an English doctor unless in a very serious case. Now I must say with reference to this very important subject, we must not forget that Medical Missionaries have to try to heal the sick first of all; and if they go out with the blessed commission, "Heal the sick and preach the Gospel," we shall find they have a wonderful door open to them. It is astonishing what the natives will do when they hear the doctor has come. I have been perfectly astounded at the faith they had in me—infinitely more than I had in myself. They have come from all conceivable distances, and I know of nothing harder,—because they will come with "utter impossibilities" to you,—than to have to say, "Oh! there is nothing I can do." Oh! friends,—and with this I will close,—thank God, there is no *The natives and the doctor.*

incurable hospital in the Lord's blessed work. Be the disease of ever so long standing, be it ever so dreadful, the Lord can cure it, for He knows nothing about incurable. And may we never forget that in the East, medicine and religion are strongly associated together,—they cannot be separated.

Mr. Wellesley C. Bailey (Secretary, Mission to Lepers in India): Mr. Chairman, and Christian friends,—I would not have dared to intervene here to-day among professional men had it not been that I stand here as the representative of something like five hundred thousand of the most helpless and hopeless sufferers on the face of God's earth, of whom we may say, broadly speaking, that they have no more a portion in anything that is done under the sun, and who, if they were here to-day to plead in their own poor hoarse voices, would say to us something like this, "Have pity upon me, have pity upon me, O my friends, for the hand of the Lord hath touched me." I refer, dear friends, to the lepers of India: men, women, aye and children from all ranks of society, from among all castes, to be found in all parts of India, in the hot plains of Bengal as well as under the snow line of the Himalayas. These poor lepers, stretching out their mutilated hands to us, to-day plead through me, "Can you not do something for us?"

The lepers of India.

I am glad to see that it is on the Paper to-day as one of the headings to consider "The place and power of Medical Missions." I think I see here a very special place for Medical Missions, and I would like in a word to recommend it to Medical Missionaries present. In connection with our work amongst the lepers, amongst whom I may say I have worked myself twelve years, we have at least four Medical Missionaries, two working in Cashmere, one, Dr. Lowe's son-in-law, working in Neyoor, and another, one of the American Episcopal Methodist Church, working in Pithora, in the Himalayas, and all these men take the greatest delight in this particular part of their work. A short time ago Dr. Fry, at Neyoor, was followed for miles by eight poor lepers, begging of him to do something for them, and he wrote home to us as a Society and asked us could we do nothing to enable him to add a leper ward to his already useful hospital in Neyoor. I am thankful to be able to say that we were able to do something, and that our Committee at once voted a sum of money to Dr. Fry to enable him to commence this leper ward, and I had a letter from him only the other day telling me that the ward is already well-nigh finished, and asking how many lepers we are willing to take into it.

The claims of lepers.

One and all of these men, not only Medical men, but other Missionaries, both men and women, who have been engaged in this work amongst the lepers, bear this testimony, that of all the work they have taken up this is one of the most blessed and the most fruitful. It is extraordinary the number of lepers who receive the Gospel of the Lord Jesus Christ. As a class I do not know of any in India so accessible to the Gospel and who receive it so willingly. My own experience is this, that we have had amongst them some of the brightest converts we have ever made amongst any class of the community. I have met with lepers as bright Christians as ever I have met with in this or any other country. Let me just give you the testimony of one man. It went so deeply into my own heart that I never forget it and never shall to my dying day. I stood beside a poor mutilated form; I stood beside a man literally falling to pieces before my eyes, and that poor man in a hoarse broken whisper said to me when I commiserated him upon his terrible suffering, "No, sir; no, sir; God is very good to me. For the last nineteen years since I have trusted Christ, I have known neither pain of body nor pain of mind." So wonderfully had Christ lifted him above

An encouraging work.

Rich in faith.

all his suffering that he was able to say that. I was so struck by it, that I turned to my friend, a Missionary on my right, and I asked him whether I had heard the man aright ; I was so astounded I asked him again ; and again the old man said to me, " No, sir. since I trusted Christ, nineteen years ago, I have known neither pain of body nor pain of mind."

Now, dear friends, we have established a Mission especially for these poor lepers, and what I would like to say to-day is, that this Society of ours will co-operate with the Medical Missions or with any Missionary who is willing on his part to take the Gospel to the lepers of India. The **Object of our** first object in our work is to bring them the Gospel, to tell them of **work.** One who, as a special proof of His ministry, sent to John the Baptist in prison to say, "The lepers are cleansed." Oh ! dear friends, to look into these poor hopeless faces as I have done, and to see every now and then the light breaking across them as I told them of the love of Christ would rejoice any heart. I have looked at them over and over and I have seen them with a dull hopeless look, for a leper without Christ is one in whom the candle of hope is for ever extinguished. We cannot cure the leper,—the medical men will bear me out in that,— but we can relieve them. We can relieve them medically ; we can relieve them physically ; we can make life tolerably bearable to them, and above all things we can bring them the consolations of the Gospel of Christ.

Surgeon-General Gunn (Dublin): I came here feeling the importance of this work. I did not come to speak, but I felt my heart moved on seeing the numbers here, and I felt that I must speak. I have not the honour of being a Medical Missionary, although after my return from the Crimea I felt it my duty to leave the service and give myself up to Medical Mission work.

I volunteered for the west coast of Africa, and God gave me my handful of Mission work, but not in the way in which I expected to have it ; I was associated with the Basle Evangelical Society —there may be some of the members here to-day, and, if so, I shall be very glad to see any of them. I was enabled to work with them, and I may perhaps give you one case. In attending a boy whose friends objected to amputation, I had to change my treatment. I asked God to bless it as every medical man ought to do, and with this blessing the lad recovered. I attended him three months, but before he left the **Instance of its** Missionary with whom he was staying had preached Christ to him. **advantage.** He accepted Christ, as did also his father and uncle, and they went back with the love of Christ in their hearts. What was the consequence of this one case ? The consequence was, they they now have a school and church, with Sunday schools, as the result, showing you the advantage of Medical Missions.

One word about the natives. I think we must all feel that if India and Africa are to be overtaken by the Gospel and the Medical Mission, we must employ the natives—intelligent natives, and that is the only way in **Employment of** which we can overtake the vast field. With regard to the work **natives.** itself we have the greatest amount of encouragement. Everywhere that you go the Medical Missionary is appreciated ; and I must first say this although I am not a Missionary. I give my testimony, whatever that is worth to the devotedness of those godly men, who can leave everything for Christ and His cause in order to plead with these natives.

And now I leave this subject by just saying if there are young men or young women here to-day, my heart's desire is to enlist them in this noble work. God has given me four boys. Two of them are at college, and the other two will soon follow ; and if I know my own heart in the sight of God, I feel that for each of these boys my highest ambition would be that they should enter the Missionfield.

I do not think a year's training for a gentleman who has been at college studying his physiology and anatomy is sufficient. A little knowledge is a dangerous thing, and if you have Medical Missionaries, send them out by all means, the best qualified in the world. Christ wants our best talent, our gold medallists, and the best we have got. The silver and the gold are His, and the intellects are His, and the lives of the best and greatest men are His. Pray, therefore, that God will send out not half-class men, but men of the very best position, and then God will own and bless them. The other day when at a missionary meeting in Trinity College, Dublin, I felt as if I could hear the angels' song in glory. We'had asked those students, some of the best men, gold medallists and others, who would be willing to give themselves up for Christ's work in the Mission-field. I expected in my unbelief, out of one hundred and fifty or two hundred students, perhaps some seven or eight would come forward ; what do you think my feelings were when fifty young men came up to the platform so that it was not able to hold them ? I felt my heart full, I could hear the very angels joining in the song of praise. Are there not some men or women here who have not yet given themselves to this work ? Do not say you are too old. Qualified men, leave your practice. You may have a lucrative practice, but this is a practice that will tell throughout an endless eternity, showing that we have been enabled to do something for such a dear Lord as ours.

Thorough medical training.

Best men needed.

Mr. J. T. Fox, M.R.C.S., etc. (Friends' Mission, Madagascar) : I feel that some apology is due from me for drawing your attention to this island of Madagascar, when others have been speaking of the tremendous needs of India and China. I should, however, like to say a few words on the subjects that have been under consideration, drawn from my experience as a Medical Missionary in Madagascar, during the last seven years.

Madagascar.

With regard to the "place and power" of Medical Missions, it is rather different in Madagascar from what it is in many fields. There can be no doubt that the Medical Mission is one of the best forms of pioneer Mission work, with which to open up any new field, to open closed doors, and to remove prejudices. Such was the Medical Mission in Madagascar in time past, and such are some outlying branches of it still : but the work in which I have been principally occupied has been totally different from that. It has been mainly an adjunct to the general Mission work in the capital, in Antananarivo ; and it is only from that point of view that I am able personally to speak on the subject.

Different to other fields.

I should like to mention the last subject, that of the training of native medical students. This has been in the work in Antananarivo, the latest, and I think the most interesting, development. We have an hospital there, and when I went out there and re-opened the hospital, we found that it was absolutely essential to have some of the natives to help me, situated as I was and not even knowing the language. I therefore took a few lads from time to time, replenishing their numbers from the lads trained in the schools, and gave them the best education that I could. This work has gradually gone on and developed, until at the present time there is in Antananarivo a regular organised Medical Missionary Academy for the training of native medical students, and some ten lads have passed through and obtained their diploma. The reason why I wished to direct mention to this branch of the subject, as it has shown itself in Madagascar, is this, that it is principally for the object of medical education that the Medical Mission continues to exist in Antananarivo. I look upon it that as the great object of the Medical Mission is pioneer work, it is, so to speak, waste to have one in a place

Training work in Antananarivo.

like Antananarivo, where there are plenty of churches, plenty of schools, plenty of religiousness and Gospel hardening, and that sort of thing; but by this work of training native medical students, we hope the cycle of development will be completed, and that this Medical Mission will become the prolific parent of a great number of pioneer native Medical Missionaries in different parts of the island.

There is one other point about Medical Missions I would mention. One great objection to them, or difficulty with regard to them, is their frequently very great expense. I wish there were more time to go into that question, and inquire " How best can Medical Missions and other *The work a* forms of Missionary work be rendered more self-supporting?" I *great expense.* do think that in Medical Mission work we can set such an ideal before us, and endeavour so to work that within a measurable number of years the Gospel may be carried on by native Medical Evangelists to the distant heathen places where the Missionary has not time to go, and yet practically free of expense to the Missionary Societies: and that thus a much greater *Aim at self-* quantity of work may be done without any increase in expense. *support.* There is, however, one thing that must be said with regard to that. Judging by my own experience of Madagascar, we cannot, for a very long time yet, hope that such an extension of native Mission work, even though it might be self-supporting in regard to funds, will be able to proceed usefully without very efficient European oversight and direction by Missionaries sent out from here.

Mr. Andrew Jukes, M.R.C.S.L., L.R.C.P. Ed. (C.M.S., from Dera Ghazi Khan): It is, I think, a very important matter that this Conference, or rather those who give their opinion or give any advice in the conduct of the work, should express some opinion as to the necessity of Medical Missionaries, whether ladies or gentlemen, going out qualified or otherwise. I have had the advantage of very prolonged study, and of much hospital work—four years' hospital work after I was qualified, and five years' private practice before I went out as a Medical Missionary. I believe that the whole of my medical education was an education for the work in the Mission-field, and I do not think it was any too *Complete train-* long. I have met with ladies sent out as Medical Missionaries *ing necessary.* to the Mission-field, who have not had more than two years' study of medicine, and I know from what they have told me that they have experienced very great difficulty from not having had any practical work in medicine before they went out. This, I think, is a matter that ought to be looked into by those who have the instruction of our students, whether ladies or gentlemen. Those who are sent out are sometimes placed in positions of very great responsibility, and they feel, when they have not had a full education, that they are not qualified to take up the work which has been given them to do.

Our Saviour's command was *to heal* the sick. Some of our Missionary friends—I am speaking from experience, and not from hearsay—appear to have been or to be of opinion that Medical Missionary work is to treat the sick. I wish to protest against that position being taken up by *Medical treat-* the Medical Missionary. If the Medical Missionary goes out at all *ment should be* he should go out prepared to do his best, not only to treat, but to *thorough.* complete the treatment of those with whom he is brought in contact. For three years after I was sent out as a Medical Missionary I was itinerating, more or less. The Missionary I was with was a great itinerant and he had had opportunities of picking up some information about the treatment of disease. He had found that he was able to give here and there medicine to patients, which was a very great relief to them, in fact, which cured them; and he thought if he got a Medical Missionary to come out that he would be able to cure a great many people in the same way. Now a Medical Missionary when he is in the field, if it is known that he is a doctor, will have patients come to him who have been ill for weeks, or months, or years. If he tries to cure them by one or two doses of medicine, he will fall very far short of the accomplishment of our Saviour's command. When I went out I was expected to go from place to place, being here one day and going on to another place the second day, and so on, changing my location almost every day in the week, not stopping more than one or two days in each place. I saw hundreds of sick, and distributed much medicine ; but not to the advantage of the sick in a good many cases.

There is a matter raised in the Paper, whether Medical Missionaries should be ordained or unordained ? That is a matter which deserves very careful attention, because I think it is not a question that can be answered
Ordained Medical Missionaries. offhand. I mean to say the different position of our Medical Missionaries in different countries renders the answers to that question also very different. As I understand medical work in Africa, I think it may perhaps be an advantage to the medical man in that country to be ordained. It is only after the heathen have in a measure been brought under the influence of the Gospel that, in many parts, the Medical Missionary here has much medical work to do. In India and China the matter is very different. There, as Medical Missionaries, we have as much work as we can undertake without taking up any clerical work at all.

With regard to how the expenses are to be met, I should like to give my own experience of that matter because I think it is one that certainly affects every
Expenses, how defrayed. one of us. When I went out first I went with the expectation that the Society with which I am working would be enabled to do something towards defraying part of the medical expenses of the work, and it was only after I got out there, having provided myself with medicine and instruments, that I found that the Society could not do so. This was a very great disappointment to me, and in consequence I was driven to seek for help elsewhere, and the amount of aid accorded me was very little in proportion to the work which the raising of the fund entailed. I was therefore led to examine into my position, and it seemed to me reasonable that if this work was the Lord's work, I should expect the Lord to provide the means for that work. It did not
Have faith in God. seem to me reasonable that a master in this world should expect his servant to do the work and to find the expense of the work, and therefore I committed that matter to the Lord, much in the same way as the China Inland Mission commits the raising of its funds, or rather makes known the needs of the Mission, and asks the Lord of the harvest to provide the means for carrying on that Mission. So I was led in the Mission-fields to commit my way unto Him. And with what result ? From that time to this I have always had money in hand.

Mr. R. N. Cust, LL.D.: I read the reports of all Societies of all nations, and I find an insidious evil creeping in, which is called " faith healing." Should it not be opposed entirely by all reasonable men ? Is it not something, in heathen countries, very like the medicine man and
Faith healing to be opposed. witchcraft ? How are we to meet it ? It is creeping in, especially among our American Missions. I think it is one of the most dangerous and insidious errors that can be. It stultifies the medical man if a person can pray over the sick, and trust that by a miracle he can be healed. I should like a strong expression of opinion from this section on this subject.

Mr. Wm. Gauld, M.D. (Bethnal Green Medical Mission, formerly of Swatow, China): I have no doubt that China is pre-eminently the field for Medical Missionaries, for the telling of their work upon the heathen, and their assistance in the spread of the Gospel. I have been watching for many years the history of Missions in China, and I am very much surprised and pleased to find that the more I know of them and of their beginnings the more patent it becomes that their establishment and success in many parts of China has been largely owing to Medical Missionary influence. I was especially interested to hear from Dr. Lockhart the other day that Dr. Morrison, the very first Missionary to China, was enabled to extend his operations through the help of medical friends who were with him for a time.

China the great field.

Then another point I wish to emphasise is this, that in the Medical Mission agency you have an instrumentality which, more than any other that I know of, reaches *all* classes of the community in heathen lands from the very highest to the lowest. This has been very remarkably exemplified in the case of the late Dr. Mackenzie of Tien-tsin, whose early death we all exceedingly regret. He was the means in God's hand, through His help, of saving the life of Lady Li, and of getting the highest authorities there, even the *Viceroy, Li Hung-Chang* himself, interested in this Medical Mission work; and we have the remarkable illustration of a Mission hospital supported by the *heathen officials* of the place. Another way in which the Medical Mission is very helpful is in preserving the lives of valuable Missionaries.

Reaches all classes.

As to the value of native helpers, we are all unanimous about that, and at Swatow we have had some excellent native helpers. I remember on one occasion a patient came from a very long distance suffering from a tumour in the throat, and he told us if we could not do anything for him he would go and drown himself. The sea was very near, and he evidently meant what he said. I was afraid to meddle with it; it was in a position where, if there was much bleeding, his life might have been sacrificed; but he urged me, and so I ventured to take away a little bit, just enough to relieve his breathing, but I did not dare to do more. Next morning when I went to the hospital I found my native helper had done what I did not dare to do,—he showed me in a little phial the tumour, like a big cork,—and when I asked him how it was that he had done it, he said : " Well, when you went away the man would not give me any rest. He said I must take it away, and so I took the scissors and cut the whole thing off." Fortunately there was no bleeding, and the man went away delighted, thinking no doubt the assistant very much better than his master. I have at times left the hospital with between fifty and one hundred patients *entirely in charge of native assistants*, and I do not think we had much cause to regret our venturesomeness in so doing.

Value of native helpers.

Instance.

On the question of partial or complete training, I think I ought to say something, as I am guilty of doing something myself to help in the training of ladies going out to India as Missionaries. We are all at one, I believe, as to the value of *full* training for all Medical Missionaries,—men and women alike,—there is no doubt about that. The question is this. Are there at this present time either men or women in sufficient numbers to supply the need of the great heathen world? I may mention that when I first went to China we found our Missionaries there, whether they would or not, obliged to do more or less medical work. I found a bottle of eye water, a bottle of quinine, a bottle of liniment, a pot of ointment, in constant request, people coming almost every day for them. There is a brother here who was a dispenser of these good things many and many a time. It is the same in other fields, and with ladies too. They find that they must do more or less to help the sicknesses of those around them, and if they have a certain amount of training, all the better. A little knowledge is a dangerous thing, but I hold that no knowledge is a still more

Full training valuable.

A little knowledge useful.

dangerous thing. A little knowledge may be the means of saving many a life, and even the lives of Missionaries themselves. I believe if the Missionaries who go to Africa at present, knew more about how to preserve their own health you might not find so many dying almost immediately they reach their fields of labour.

At the same time I do not wish to be misunderstood. I think in two years an intelligent man or woman can obtain a great amount of practical knowledge,

Two years' training.

so as to enable them to deal with many diseases; and if they are wise enough not to profess to know more than they do, and not to call themselves doctors, they can do an immense deal of good. It is not a question of thinking, because at the present time we have the testimony of many that a vast amount of good work is being done. It is curious that the one lady who came home, and insisted upon the value of full training, was one who got her reputation when she was only partially trained herself.

Rev. I. H. Hacker (L.M.S., from Neyoor, Travancore): I wish it were adopted as an axiom of all Church life in respect to our enterprise, that a medical man must go with other Missionaries. I think the time has gone when it should be otherwise. I think your tone this morning in this discussion has been too apologetic; for the time has certainly gone by when there ought to be any question in the Christian Church and in the Missionary enterprise, about the value of the Medical Mission in foreign lands. Nobody who has had any experience of the work out yonder can fail to see that it is the very right hand of our service.

I believe that we want men, not doctors only, but men first of all, Christian men, struck through and through with a desire to live and die

Truest Christian service.

for the Lord Jesus Christ, and when they come out with their medical knowledge there will be good done, and not without. I can only say it is a great pleasure to me to render my testimony after ten years' experience of trouble and difficulty, that I believe the finest and truest form of the Christian service is along the Medical Missionary lines.

Mr. William Clark, M.B., C.M. (United Presbyterian Mission, Nusseerabad, Rajputana): With regard to the subject of the usefulness of Medical Mission work in India, I would desire to say a word. In Rajputana, nearly the central part of Northern India, we have had for twenty years a number of

Work in Rajputana.

Medical Missionaries at work; I have been for fifteen years there myself, and have had some experience of the usefulness of the work to the people around me. I wish to say simply this, that to the south of Rajputana there is a Mission more recently established, where the Canadian brethren have been seeking a footing in the native States of Central India. One brother, recently called to his rest while seeking an entrance into one of those Central Indian stations, was told by the people in authority there, and by the leading men in the community,

A Medical Missionary preferred.

that they did not want him as a Missionary. They said, "Come as a *Medical Missionary* and we will give a site at once for a house, and help you to a hospital!" That poor brother came in distress, seeking advice, to Rajputana. He was a man up in years, but still he thought it was his duty to go home to Canada to get a medical qualification, to return and take possession in the name of the Lord of one of the capitals of Central India; but the Lord called him home. His wife died—that was a sad blow to him—when he was considering this matter, and in a few weeks afterwards he was called home himself to glory.

One or two controverted points I have taken note of, and I would desire simply to bear my testimony upon them. I think that students who are to come to our aid as native Medical Missionaries should all be Christians. I have endeavoured during my fifteen years of Medical *Native helpers* Mission work to have only Christians, not only as qualified agents, *should be Christians.* but as subordinate servants,—even the sweeper, if I could have him, I would have a Christian within my hospital.

.With reference to the supply of medicine my conviction is simply this, that Medical Missions are not more expensive than Educational Missions, and if Societies are found incurring large expense for the purpose of carrying on Educational Missions, why should not the small amount *Providing of medicines.* necessary for medicine be found by the Societies, and the burden of that be taken from the hands of the men who are bearing the brunt of the battle in heathen lands and tropical climates. I think if this Conference is to be of any value, men who have had some experience of the thing ought to be permitted to give expression to their opinion upon such a controverted point.

Dr. Cust : I should like an answer to my question : Are we or are we not to protest against what is called faith healing ?

Mr. J. L. Maxwell, M.D. (Secretary, Medical Missionary Association, London) : I think what Dr. Jukes has stated with regard to the funds, and what Dr. Clark has taken up just now, is a point of great importance. It affects, not one Society, but quite a number of Societies in this country, and as Dr. Clark said, it is one of the very strangest things in connection with Medical Missions, that any Society should send out a labourer without tools. I cannot conceive anything more absurd in connection with Medical Missions, than that with the wonderful opportunities presented to a Medical Missionary as an evangelist, his hand should be hampered by having to write letters here and there, in order that he may secure the funds necessary to do his work. I confess, I cannot understand it at all, and if our Conference is to be of much practical value, *Should be fully equipped.* these things must be brought up, and this is one of the things that we should like to emphasise, so that our Societies should understand that it is not a right state of things, and that every Society which sends out Medical Missionaries should take care that year by year there is set apart a certain measure of funds, in order to meet their necessary expenses.

Dr. Cust has appealed to us on the subject of faith healing. That is a matter which I would approach very tenderly. My own conviction is that one of the causes why, in these days, faith healing has come to occupy such a prominent place as it does, is just this : that we *Faith healing.* who believe in using means—and I myself have no confidence at all in faith healing in the ordinary sense of that word—have not shown that we are, along with the use of means, at the same time trusting in the Lord. We have not shown that while we are doing our best, as God's servants, we are looking up to the Master for His blessing. If there had been more of that there would have been less about faith healing, and if we are really to fight faith healing, as we should do, it will be by showing that in all our use of means, at home and abroad, in private and in public, in dispensaries and in connection with private practice, those of us who are Christians are looking to the Lord for a blessing upon the means that we employ.

Bishop Wilson then offered prayer, and the proceedings were brought to a close.

MEETINGS OF MEMBERS
IN SECTION.

SIXTH SESSION.

MEDICAL MISSIONS.

(2) THE AGENCIES.

(a) The comparative value for Mission purposes of Hospital, Dispensary, and Itinerant Medical Mission work.

(b) Payment by patients for medicines.

(Tuesday morning, June 12th, in the Annexe.)

Sir Risdon Bennett, M.D., F.R.S., in the chair.
Acting Secretary, Mr. James E. Mathieson.

Rev. D. Sanderson offered prayer.

PAPER.

1. By Mr. J. L. Maxwell, M.D. (Secretary of the Medical Missionary Association, London, formerly of Formosa).

The relative value for Mission purposes of Hospital, Dispensary, and Itinerant Medical Mission work.

Happily the time is past when a Paper on Medical Missions requires to be introduced by a statement of the principles on which such Missions rest. Neither is it necessary to plead for their adoption, the Churches without exception having recognised their necessity. There is room, however, for a greatly multiplied extension of Medical Missions as one of the most powerful evangelistic forces in heathen and Mohammedan lands, and it may contribute to this desirable result if I place before the Conference my experiences of methods and results, an experience founded not only on some personal practical acquaintance with these methods, but also on a fairly wide knowledge of their working in the hands of others.

I premise by two observations, namely (1) that the scope of this 'aper is not the medical but the spiritual results of `Spiritual not` ledical Missionary effort, although the close relation `medical results.` etween the particular effects of the one, and the particular fruits of he other, will become apparent as we proceed ; and (2) that the xperience referred to is drawn in largest measure from the greatest nd most fruitful of Medical Mission-fields, that of China. Methods vhich are universally applicable throughout that vast Empire are for he most part applicable also in other heathen and Mohammedan ands, but the social and religious conditions under which they are pplied are so diverse in different countries that it would be unfair o judge of results obtained in one country by those obtained in nother. It might, however, be taken almost without hesitation as n axiom that the measure of difficulty in evangelising any people night be gauged with very fair accuracy by the results of Medical Missions in that country.

The three methods in common use among Medical Missionaries n heathen and Mohammedan countries are covered by the words HOSPITAL, DISPENSARY, ITINERATION. There is a fourth method which must not be forgotten, viz., HOME VISITATION. `Four methods.` It is already a power, and as time goes on will become a reater power in the hands of women engaging in Medical Missions. It is almost certain that in the hands of men also more may be looked for in the future than has yet been obtained from this method. My own acquaintance with it is so slight, and the published results of it in the hands of others are so meagre, that I do not venture in this Paper to do more than name it.

First, let me define as briefly and accurately as I can the conditions in relation to contact with Gospel truth which are to be understood by Hospital, Dispensary, and Itinerant Medical Mission work respectively.

The first condition of Hospital Mission work is, that at a given centre, in a suitable building, a number of the heathen `Definition of` sick, ranging from half a dozen to two or three hundred, `Hospital` should be brought together for a period of, at the lowest `Mission work.` average, fourteen to twenty-one days. The second condition is, that the atmosphere surrounding such patients be one strongly pervaded by a cheerful and yet earnest Christian tone and influence. The third condition is, that there be daily effort among these patients to teach them as much fundamental Christian truth as can be wisely and not offensively set forth in the time. And the last condition is, that the doctor and his assistants, his Missionary colleagues, and his native fellow-helpers, the men who, under God, are the instruments of conferring, or trying to confer, physical benefits on these patients, should also be the channels through which, as living epistles of Christ, the truth should be presented both in word and deed.

The first condition of Dispensary Mission work is also a fixed centre, with suitable hall in which patients may assemble and remain

until they pass into the doctor's consulting room.   To this hall
Of Dispensary a relatively large number of individual heathen patients
Mission work. gather together on fixed days of the week for *immediate*
treatment, their object being to return home the same day at as
early an hour as possible. The second and only other condition is,
that advantage be taken, as far as possible, by the doctor and his
helpers, both before beginning work and while work goes on, to use
the opportunity of inculcating some very simple view of the Gospel, so
that if the same patient should return once and again, as is not unfrequently the case (the average last year in Chin-chew being no less
than six times), there may be hope that in spite of the crowd, the
novelty, and the pre-occupation of the mind with the one purpose of
the visit, some ray of Gospel light shall reach the heart.

The first condition of Itinerant Medical Mission work, as I should
Of Itinerant describe it, is a variety of centres within a given area,
Medical Mission centres which are occupied at as nearly fixed intervals as
work. possible, for a brief period of days, or even weeks, and
during which period, patients and their friends come from the
immediate neighbourhood to receive medical attention and forthwith
return home. The second and only other condition is, that on the
occasion of such visits, advantage is taken to impress on all who
come around from day to day, the simple truths of the Gospel.
Practically, Itinerant Medical Mission work and Dispensary work
are very much the same in method, the peculiarity of the latter
being a fixed centre with abundant medical supplies, and that
of the former being a varying centre with limited supplies and
accommodation.

In attempting thus to define the conditions attaching to these
three forms of Medical Mission labour, I have endeavoured to avoid
too many details, the main intention of this Paper being to bring into
strong relief the relative advantages of these special methods in order
Relative that those who are interested in the extension of Christ's
advantages. kingdom may be able to judge for themselves, which is
most likely to repay the Church in its use, and how far each may be
used with advantage.

I.—HOSPITAL MISSION WORK.

Now, taking it for granted that the same fervour of Missionary spirit
prevails in the carrying out of the three forms of Medical Missionary labour
which I have described, it scarcely requires to be said that the first method,
that of the Hospital, offers *on the face of it* such manifest and great advantages that it would be very strange indeed if it did not prove more fruitful
in spiritual results than the others. And with this most natural anticipation agrees the almost universal testimony of Medical Missionaries. That
testimony is, that not only are far greater physical benefits secured to
patients by hospital treatment, and cases dealt with and operations undertaken that could not possibly be undertaken except in hospital, and so the
good name and influence of the Medical Mission spread abroad; but the
spiritual results obtained among hospital patients are so much greater than

those obtained by either of the other plans, that really there is no room for comparison.

Nor is this result hard to explain. For one thing, the kindly respect which your patients—not necessarily those who are themselves the immediate subjects of capital operations, but the whole body of patients in the hospital, who see and know all that is going on—entertain towards their benefactor, prepares them to listen with increased attention to the Word of God which he and his fellows preach.

For another thing, the opportunity afforded by the hospital of mutual acquaintance between the doctor and his patients permits of unreserved communication on both sides to an extent that is hard of attainment in any other way. Again and again, in my own hospital experience in China, I found myself face to face with men on whom the Word had taken hold, and who would secretly tell me that their difficulty—their one difficulty—lay in accepting what they realised to be the inevitable consequence of confessing Christ. Some of these men later on did accept the consequences; but I mention this just now only to illustrate how closely the doctor can get home to his hospital patients.

Further, and of great importance, hospital residence permits of an amount of detailed and explanatory Gospel teaching on the one hand, and of intelligent appreciation on the other, as enables the Word of God to be pressed home on individuals with a fair measure of force. It permits of frank discussion on these new topics among the patients themselves, and of easy intercourse with the native Christian helper who is attached to the hospital for the furtherance of spiritual work. Christian love in the heart of the doctor carries him, and sometimes with wonderful rapidity, within the whole range of *outer* defences wherewith the great adversary would seek to prevent the assault of the Gospel upon the heathen heart. And then, having got within the defences, there is the golden privilege given to him—golden both as to time and to opportunity— of plying the soul with the truth and the light of the Gospel of Christ.

Explanatory teaching possible.

Let me indicate as briefly as possible something of the precious outcome of Medical Mission hospitals, when the Missionary is a living and loving man of God. First, Conversions. I open some of the latest Missionary reports. What do they say on this head?

From Moukden, the capital of Manchuria, Dr. Christie tells in a single line what the grace of God has been doing in the hospital there last year. "Fifteen patients," he says, "were received during the year." That does not sound a large number; but really it means a body of candidates for baptism three or four times that number; and later on a fair number of those whom it was deemed prudent to delay would be received into the congregations most convenient to their own place of abode.

[After quoting much conclusive evidence, which we reluctantly leave out, from Dr. Mackenzie of Tien-tsin, and his colleague the Rev. Thomas Bryson, from Dr. Grant of Chin-chew, Dr. Cousland of Swatow, and Dr. Martyn Clark of the Punjab, Dr. Maxwell proceeds :—]

Another thing: the congregation in a hospital chapel is one of the most unique in its comprehensiveness. It is not merely one or two hundred souls, it is one or two hundred souls gathered probably out of fifty different towns and villages. And what does that mean? It means of necessity the diffusion of a fair measure of Gospel truth in all these different directions. As many as 1,200 to 1,400 towns and villages have been represented in a single year among the in-patients of a single hospital. Does

Another advantage.

not this speak of rare and glorious possibilities ? Is it possible to exaggerate the value of such opportunities as these ?

But not to linger too long, let me ask your attention to what is the most remarkable, as it certainly is the most visible, of the fruits of Hospital Mission work in China.   In the same last letter of Dr. Mackenzie's to which I have already referred, he says : " It is very wonderful to see **Spreading the tidings.** how, step by step, God has opened up this work (the Hospital work), and is now using it to spread *into all the districts round*, the precious word of Salvation." Shortly before his death he took a brief Christmas holiday. This is how he spent it—with one of his assistants he traversed one particular region of the country, from day to day hunting out former patients who had been baptised in hospital. In this way he visited no less than seventeen of them, to have the joy of finding that only one out of the seventeen was hiding his light under a bushel.

Dr. Christie of Moukden, writes : " Patients come to us from all parts of the province ; many not only learn the message of salvation for themselves, but carry it to the remote villages and hamlets." In one village, several days' journey from the headquarters at Moukden, he tells of a Church of twenty members gathered in by the labours of an almost totally blind man, who had heard of Christ in the hospital and went home with his heart on fire, to be called " mad " by his neighbours, but to have his reward at length in this blessed ingathering of souls.

II.—DISPENSARY MISSION WORK.

A sentence from a Missionary brother, Dr. Cousland of Swatow, on the spiritual results of Dispensary work at that centre, will express the conclusion of most Medical Missionaries in China—" *Here in Swatow our experience is that we very seldom influence out-patients.*" This testimony is the more striking as unquestionably there is no Mission centre in China where the spiritual fruits of Medical Mission work have been more rich and plentiful than at the Swatow Hospital. The explanation however is plain. The attendance of Dispensary patients is irregular and unfrequent. When they are present on any occasion they do not give themselves to listen and to understand the address. They have come simply for medicine, and wish to get it as soon as possible and be off. If they show any symptoms of interest their friends will probably crush it or persuade them to cease their attendance.

It cannot however be omitted. It diffuses rapidly through any district a very good report of the Medical Missionary's skill and helpfulness. It spreads also in many ways the knowledge of great fundamental truths, that there **Advantages greater than drawbacks.** is one God and one Saviour ; that the worship of the true God is dissociated from images and ritual, that is bound up with a kindly, upright, and pure life. Every patient can carry away a little, and this wide dissemination of even a few truths is of the highest importance in preparing the way of the Gospel. Again, we cannot do without the dispensary, for it is a great feeder to the hospital, and patients who might at first be unwilling to enter a hospital are much more willing if they have attended once or twice at the dispensary. Further, there have been not a few instances of souls whose first impressions of the truth were received in connection with Dispensary work.

III.—ITINERANT MEDICAL MISSION WORK.

Spiritually this is the least satisfactory of all. "It is useful," writes Dr. Anderson of Formosa, " for you thus benefit many who, if you did not go to see them, would never be able to come and see you." The effect of a passing Medical Missionary visit on a people not previously prepared must be looked for chiefly in predisposing to kindly feelings, rather than in definite spiritual fruits. Carefully repeated visits at *Preparatory work.* fixed intervals, associated with earnest evangelistic work, could not but lead to good results.

All three methods are needful to the complete manifestation of the Medical Missionary's efficiency as a servant of Christ. The intensive spiritual force cannot fail to be more fully shown in hospital work than in any other, the rapid diffusive philanthropic influence will reveal itself more readily through the dispensary, whilst the living presence of the Medical Missionary as he passes from village to village in itinerating tours will prepare the way most effectually for the labours of the evangelist.

In conclusion, let me say that a right comprehension of the spiritual range and power of Medical Mission work would at once clear the ground of not a few misconceptions which are still all too prevalent in this country, and in circles where they should not exist. It would remove at once the strange delusion that the Medical Missionary is one whose function ends with the healing of the sick. Nay, his function *Misconceptions removed.* is that which the Lord has given him, namely, to heal the sick, that he may joyfully say unto them, "The kingdom of God is come nigh unto you." It would remove at once also that other delusion, that the Medical Missionary's chief use is to look after his colleagues and their health. Of course he will look after his colleagues and their health; he will gladly do so, but to limit the great Missionary function of a Christian doctor in a heathen country to this is a terrible blindness of which Christian men who have the direction of Missionary work should be heartily ashamed. A right comprehension of the subject would also at once remove the strange ruling in some Societies that the Medical Missionary is himself to find the funds to *A grievous blunder.* meet the necessary expenditure associated with his work. To allow a man with such evangelistic opportunities as belong to the Medical Missionary to have his hands tied in this fashion is a grievous blunder, certainly a withholding of more than is meet and which tendeth to poverty. And once more it would remove the misconception that Medical Mission work is only good for pioneering purposes, and that its use ends there. A brief residence in any Mission-field in China would soon satisfy the most rigid upholder of this theory that his idea of pioneer work must be made to cover scores of years, during which time the Medical Mission is continually gathering fresh increase of power and efficiency. The fact is that the Mission hospital is not only a pioneer agency, but from year to year a great feeder of the Church.

I say it with an absolute conviction that I speak the truth that in heathen and Mohammedan lands there is no class of men to whom the Lord has entrusted more choice and blessed opportunities of sowing the seed of the Word in the hearts of men, than those which are enjoyed by Medical Missionaries, and I am satisfied that a right appreciation of the methods and opportunities and results of Medical *The Master's own work.* Missionary work ought to constrain the Church of Christ to enter with a far more confident and liberal heart upon a ministry which is so nearly after the Lord's own pattern.

PAPER.

2. By MR. JOHN HUTCHISON, L.R.C.P. and S.E. (Church of Scotland Mission, Chamba, N. India).

There can be no doubt that the example of our Lord and His command to His disciples to heal the sick was regarded as binding in the Primitive Church, for we know that an anxious care for the **Example of the** bodies of men, as well as for their spirits, was one of **Early Church.** the leading characteristics of the early Christians. In our day the Church, while fully acknowledging this obligation in her Home Mission work—as the innumerable forms of Christian philanthropic effort in our midst abundantly testify—yields a tardy and reluctant assent to the adoption of similar methods of work in the Foreign Mission-field. It is urged that the command to heal the sick is not obligatory on us, because we are unable to effect miraculous cures, and because obedience will therefore entail upon us costly and laborious service. This, however, can make no difference, in our obligation, for in this, as in every other form of Christian duty, we ought to be guided not by the letter only, but also by the spirit of the command, especially as interpreted for us by our Lord's own example. He "took our infirmities and bore our sicknesses" in a very real sense when on earth, and assuredly He does not care less for human suffering now in glory.

There are few forms of Missionary service so interesting and attractive as Itinerant Medical Mission work. It is the nearest **Itinerant** approach possible to us to the Divine model seen in our **Missions,** Lord's own ministry ; and in it, more than in any other, **Christ's method.** scenes and incidents are reproduced which carry the mind back to His life on earth, and bring before us, as nothing else could, a living picture of what His daily surroundings must have been. Wherever the Medical Missionary goes, the poor, the halt, the blind, the leper, the fever-stricken, in short, all forms of disease, and suffering daily present themselves before him. To many he can give complete relief ; to some only alleviation ; and in instances not a few, human skill will be of little avail. We cannot work miracles in these times, and of none can that be true which is recorded of the first and greatest of Medical Missionaries—"He healed them every one ;" but to all alike we can proclaim the old, old story of a Saviour's love.

In dealing with this important agency some of the disadvantages and objections which may be urged against it must first claim our attention. It must be admitted that grave forms of disease in **Disadvantages** heathen lands cannot be treated satisfactorily during itiner- **and objections.** ation. Such cases and others of long-standing chronic ailments, as well as those in which a major operation may be necessary, will often present themselves, and for them the Medical Missionary, during his short sojourn, cannot do much. And yet the little he can do is highly appreciated, and his kindly-spoken invitation to bring the patient to the central hospital, coming directly from himself, inspires confidence, and is often taken advantage of.

Then it is urged that but little can be done on a hurried tour for any patient whom one sees but once or twice; and that from difficulties of transport it is impossible always to have on hand the sort of remedy or medical appliance which is needful in every case. Now I admit that there is much truth in all these objections, but *Objections answered.* I still believe—as the result of long and varied experience— that with all its drawbacks and difficulties such medical work is in number-less instances a means of incalculable benefit.

As regards its Missionary aspects, I do not need to enlarge much upon them in order to convince you that opportunities are thereby afforded of the most signal value for presenting the Gospel message. Labouring as I have been for many years in a native State, where our Missionary operations are viewed with not a little jealousy by the authorities, I can bear emphatic testimony to the powerful influence which this agency has exerted in different parts of the territory—in disarming opposition and in gaining for us the goodwill and friendship of all sections of the community.

But valuable as itinerant Medical Missions undoubtedly are, they can hardly be said to have been brought as yet into anything like practical operation. Foreign Medical Missionaries are very few in *Need of extension and development.* number, and as a rule too much tied down by the charge of dispensaries and hospitals to devote much time to itinerating work; and however beneficial occasional tours may be, they are, as a rule, too desultory in their character to be productive of much permanent Missionary influence. In order to make this agency a real power for good, such as I am convinced it is capable of being made, it must be greatly extended and developed; and this can be done only by the employment of native agents. The field is very vast, and in India, even after making full allowance for the good medical work done in *Need of extension.* Government dispensaries and hospitals, there are still countless multitudes for whom practically no medical provision exists, and it is with these chiefly one comes into contact in itinerating work. Were it practic-able to raise up and maintain a sufficient staff of *fully-qualified* and fully-equipped native Medical Missionaries for this work—men of fervent piety and Missionary zeal—I believe it would be one of the most powerful evangelistic agencies which the Church could call into existence. But such an agency is beyond the hope of realisation except to a very limited extent.

It is in view of this that I venture to bring forward a proposal, which seems well deserving of earnest consideration. As one moves about in the midst of the sickness and misery so prevalent in heathen lands, the question *will* suggest itself, whether it is not possible to give *The employment of partially-trained natives.* a *partial* medical training to a considerable number of our ordinary Mission evangelists in every district to fit them for dealing with the simpler forms of disease, and to be of some use where the need is so great. This is a matter on which all will not be agreed. My own opinion is that while central and branch dispensaries should be in the hands of *fully*-trained men, a *partially*-trained native agency might be brought into existence in village and itinerating work to a far greater extent than has yet been done. I believe that nothing but good would follow the establishment of such an agency. Every Medical Missionary knows what a large proportion of cases presenting themselves in ordinary dispensary practice consists of diseases for which the treatment is fairly simple and uniform. I find from the statistics of my own dispensary that nearly one-fourth of the total number of cases is made up of the different forms of malarial fever, in almost all of which quinine is more or less beneficial. If to these be added all other cases of a fairly simple character, it will be seen that in a large proportion much may be done to alleviate or cure by one whose medical training may not have been very complete. I do not propose that such agents should in any way take the place of fully-qualified men, when these are obtainable. Nor do I mean to say that they would treat even simple forms of disease as efficiently as fully-qualified men ; but in the absence of an adequate number of these, and in face of the abounding sickness in heathen lands, agents such as I have spoken of would be an inestimable boon to many, and their efficiency as preachers of the Gospel would be vastly enhanced thereby.

Proportion of simple cases.

I have put this plan to the test of practical experience in my own field of labour. My Mission sphere comprises the whole of the Chamba State, situated in the bosom of the North Western Himalayas. A dispensary and hospital have been in existence in the capital for twenty years ; but it is only recently that anything has been done for the outlying parts of the State, which are very difficult of access owing to the mountainous character of the country. Beyond the outer ranges of snowy mountains and bordering on Western Thibet, there is a very interesting and beautiful valley called Pangi. I have long had a deep interest in the people of that valley, and some years ago I sent one of our native evangelists to labour among them. He had been in charge of the Leper Asylum of the Mission to Lepers in India under me for a considerable time, and had become pretty familiar with the uses of the simpler remedies ; and the treatment of ordinary forms of disease ; and I had therefore no hesitation in entrusting him with a small medicine chest. He found it of the greatest service in carrying on his evangelistic work ; the people were most grateful for the help he was able to render, and he was thus enabled to carry the Gospel to every village and house in the Pangi valley ; receiving everywhere a most cordial welcome. In the beginning of every summer, this noble servant of Christ, one of the most devoted native workers I have ever known. takes his departure from Chamba into the Inner Himalayan wilds ; and we often hear nothing of him for months. He has to cross and recross a lofty snowy range higher than Mont Blanc, to traverse mountain paths which are always difficult and dangerous, and to undergo much toil and hardship. His mode of work is to take up his abode in a village for a few days, or even for a week or two, and make himself quite at home with the people. All day long he is employed in visiting the sick ; preaching to and conversing with the villagers ; exhibiting and explaining the Bible pictures he always carries ; selling and distributing the Scriptures and tracts to all who can read ; and himself reading and expounding the Word of God to those who gather around him. I have myself on many occasions when itinerating with him had opportunities of witnessing the most gratifying evidences of the esteem in which he is held ; and as the result of his labours the evangelistic work in Pangi is now in a most hopeful condition.

The plan tested.

Method of native worker in Pangi.

The experiment which was so successful in this instance I have been trying to repeat in other parts of the Chamba State ; and my ideal, as yet only partly realised, has been to have a few branch dispensaries in suitable centres, under fully qualified men, and a band of partially trained medical evangelists itinerating among the villages in other parts of the territory.

Branch dispensaries.

Now it has often seemed to me that an agency such as this might be brought into much more extensive operation in village work on the plains of India. Something of the kind is urgently called for, especially in parts like the Central Punjab, where the Christian community is increasing very rapidly, and now numbers many thousands, scattered over a wide area. To these, our brethren in Christ, we are under special obligations, and in their times of sickness and pain they cry to us for that medical aid which they cannot provide for themselves. The day when every Mission centre shall have a fully-qualified Medical Missionary as a necessary part of its equipment seems as yet far distant ; but a partially-trained agency could be raised up without much trouble, and maintained at insignificant cost. It would be an incalculable boon to many, both Christian and heathen, and a most valuable auxiliary in the diffusion of the Gospel.

In order to the efficient working of such a scheme as this, it would be indispensable that the agents in each district should be under the supervision of a fully-qualified Medical Missionary, who would inspect their work, and help and advise them. They, on their part, would keep themselves in constant communication with him, sending, as far as possible, all difficult cases to the central hospital. It may be remarked here that such a method of work would not be new in any Mission station. It is one which every Missionary, however small his medical knowledge, is forced by the exigencies of his position more or less to adopt ; and all that is advocated here is its indefinitely wide extension among the native agents of our Missions, under careful and systematic conditions of training and management.

As regards the cost of maintaining such an agency, it would be just the ordinary expenditure for the evangelistic staff of the Mission, with that for the necessary medicines and medical appliances superadded, which would not, I think, be great. It seems very doubtful if, in India, any important help could be obtained by payments from patients. All Government dispensaries furnish gratuitous medical relief, and Mission dispensaries have hitherto done the same. The work of these agents also would be to a great extent among the low-castes and the poor, who, from their circumstances, have a special claim on our philanthropy, and are least able to pay for medical aid. It is among them, too, that the Gospel is making most rapid progress, and evangelistic work is most hopeful and successful.

As regards the character and extent of the training necessary for such agents, there will be difference of opinion—the more complete it can be made, the better ; but it is too wide a subject to enter upon now. All that is needful could be effectively carried out in connection with any Mission dispensary : and probably every Medical Missionary would prefer to formulate a course for his own pupils. It ought to be *practical* above all things ;

[margin note: Supervision necessary.]

[margin note: The cost very small.]

[margin note: The training of the best men.]

and I think it might be carried out without interfering to any extent
with the pupil's discharge of his ordinary duties as an evangelist.
The men selected for training ought to be the very best on the
Mission staff—notable not only for piety and zeal, but also for
evangelistic power—in fact, men who have already made their mark
as successful evangelists. With such a staff of workers, co-operating with central and branch dispensaries and other evangelistic
agencies, and growing in numbers and efficiency year by year ; and,
with that indispensable requisite,—the blessing of God on their
labours,—a blessing which assuredly would not be denied—there
would seem to be almost no limit to the possibilities of Missionary
success to which the Church might not hopefully look forward.

The Chairman: I will, with your permission, first call upon the
Rev. Mr. Lowe to address us. He has had large experience in the
training of Medical Missionaries, and will be able to inform us of
some of the difficulties attending the supply of men in sufficient
numbers, and of sufficiently satisfactory qualifications
for the purposes of Mission labour. I know that the
Training Institution in Edinburgh has had considerable influence
over the whole of this work, and I am sure Mr. Lowe will give us
some information that cannot fail to be valuable to us.

The Edinburgh Medical Mission.

DISCUSSION.

Rev. John Lowe, F.R.C.S.E. (Secretary, Edinburgh Medical Missionary
Society) : Sir Risdon Bennett, and Christian friends,—I represent a Society
which has trained a large number of Medical Missionaries, and has
provided men for all the various Missionary Societies,—I think we can say
that between sixty and seventy Medical Missionaries at present engaged in
foreign fields have been trained in connection with this Society.

I went out in 1861 to Travancore as a Medical Missionary. Dr.
Hutchison has just referred to the training of Medical evangelists for
Medical Missionary service. In 1862 I commenced a class for
native agents. We selected eight of the most intelligent and
best educated men from our Mission Seminary there. They
had received an English education and were devoted Christian men looking
forward to Missionary work. We commenced a class in connection with our hospital, and passed them through a course
of four years, and now these men, and others since trained in
connection with the Medical Mission, are carrying on their work most
successfully in branch dispensaries established in various parts of the
province.

Medical students in Travancore.

Experience of native agents.

The one great complaint made by Medical Missionaries labouring in all parts
of the world is that they do not receive the support necessary for carrying on
this important department of their work.

I should like more fully to refer to the importance of training native agents.
We have in connection with our Medical Missionary Society a very excellent
Training Institution in Agra. The students there attend the Agra
Medical College. They are devoted young men, chosen from all
the various Missions in Northern India by the Missionaries in
connection with all the various Societies, and sent to Agra to be under Dr.
Valentine's superintendence, and to pass through a course of four years' training

Agra Medical Institute.

both in medical and evangelistic work. Dr. Valentine has this session ten students in his Institution, and he has at the present moment applications from nine or ten Missionaries wishing him to take in students to be fully qualified for this great and blessed work. Dr. Valentine has had great encouragement in this department of service, and we look forward with much hopefulness to a large extension of Medical Missionary work through these native agents trained in Northern India, and I know in connection with Dr. Henry Martyn Clark's work in Amritsar and other Medical Missions large numbers of devoted young natives are being trained for Medical Missionary service. *Great encouragement.*

Mr. William Clark, M.B., M.C. (United Presbyterian Mission, Nusseerabad) :—I desire, Mr. Chairman and Christian friends, to say a few words briefly upon the comparative value for Mission purposes of Hospital, Dispensary, and Itinerant Medical Missionary work. Now it is not that either one or other of these forms of work should be adopted specially to the exclusion of the others ; they are each and all valuable in their own proper place. We might say the hospital work is the intensiform evangelistic department of Mission work. Your patients residing under your own roof and brought day by day under religious instruction receive an amount of knowledge which it is utterly impossible to impart to a mere dispensary patient who may only hear you once or twice in the dispensary ; and in comparison with the amount of instruction that is capable of being given in one Missionary address in a far off heathen village during the course of an itinerancy, you can see that the direct evangelistic influence brought to bear upon our hospital patients is very great indeed. *Value of different forms of work.*

This I look upon as the ideal form of modern Medical Mission work—hospital work, from which we may reasonably expect, I think, the greatest results considered in their intensity. In their expansive influence our Mission dispensaries are greater than our hospitals. We receive very much larger numbers, and are able to treat in our dispensaries greatly increased numbers in comparison with those we are able to take into our hospitals, and feed and treat through a long course. But the most expansive form is the itinerary, probably the pleasantest to the Missionary himself. I know of nothing pleasanter or healthier, in my own experience, than a five or ten miles' ride in the early morning, preaching to one hundred, or it may be to a thousand people, in a village that you had never visited before, and seeing from fifty to one hundred patients in the morning, during the course of the day, and in the evening ; preaching all day long in the tent to individual patients who come to visit you there, as well as to the great crowd in the bazaar of the village at which you happen to be encamped for the night. *Intensity and range of influence.*

I would like to say a word about payment by patients for medicines It is an exceedingly desirable thing that in every shape and form Mission money should be saved, and that contributions should be received from all and sundry, but as a Medical Missionary of fifteen years' experience in Northern India, I protest against the introduction of any commercial element between the Medical Missionary and his heathen patient. *Payment for medicines.*

With reference to the training of native assistants, I may say that I have sent five men to the Agra Medical Missionary Training Institution, who were trained under my friend Dr. Valentine. Those five have turned out splendid medical men, I am happy to say, and that two of them have turned out good Medical Missionaries is a pleasurable thing for me to announce to you.

Dr. Pringle (Bengal Army) : Sir Risdon Bennett, and Christian friends, —During thirty years' service in India, of which I may say the last twenty have been spent in itinerating, and nearly half of that time in tents, among a population of ten millions in the northern portion of Bengal, I have had considerable opportunities of seeing what the work under this head can do, and in saying this, I do so with deep thankfulness to God for the opportunity He has given me, and above all for this opportunity of telling you, that it is a work the value of which it is utterly impossible to estimate. The story just now told in those short but graphic words by my brother countryman is just the secret. You cannot tell the numberless opportunities that it opens out. One man is cured, and he goes home and tells the story. It is the old story of the love of Christ, how He had compassion on the multitudes, and that story will go far and wide and bear fruit.

Value of Medical work inestimable.

I know the Agra College well, as I was in that district for twenty years, and undoubtedly the action that Missionary Societies are now thinking of taking is the very best, being the one that the Government itself has been compelled to take. When great sickness prostrated the country, they sent out their educated native doctors through the villages with supplies of medicine, and I am satisfied that there are few modes in which relief can be afforded equal to that. When the body is so very carefully looked after, I feel we may leave it prayerfully and hopefully to the Church to see that the soul is not forgotten.

Government native doctors.

The Chairman: I am sure Dr. Pringle cannot render greater service to Medical Missions than by giving them the result of his experience, in the form of a small, condensed handbook, which might be given to every Medical Missionary, and not only to Medical Missionaries but to ordinary Missionaries, for they are called upon for medical help in a large number of cases. In conversation with my distinguished friend, Dr. Livingstone, again and again I have talked this question over with him, and he was very emphatic on the subject of the necessity of attacking the first initiatory cold stage of fever, in a very different way from that which had usually been resorted to, and he attributed his own comparative immunity to his adhering to his practice. There are a number of points of that sort connected with our own department, as well as the higher, which, if they were gathered up by those who have had experience in the Missionary field, and condensed into a portable volume, would be of inestimable value for every form of Missionary labour abroad. Of that I am quite satisfied.

Livingstone's opinion.

Mr. Henry Soltau (China Inland Mission, formerly of Burmah): I represent those who have only a partial training, and am not a qualified Medical man. I was forced to be a Medical man as a Missionary in Burmah by the people themselves. I had no intention, in going out, to give any medicine. I took a homœopathic medicine chest, just for my own personal use, but the people came and demanded that they should have medicines for their diseases. The medicines did not take much effect upon them, and I had to turn to Perry Davis's Painkiller, and Jayne's Expectorant, and the Almanack published to explain those medicines. I went on very well for a short time, until we had a Medical Missionary out there, Dr. Harvey, in connection with our Society, the China Inland Mission. I then got from him a year's training in dispensary work, which was very helpful. I was given a very valuable book, called "Moore's Family Medicine for India," and with that, and with

Compelled to practise.

the medicines recommended, which are not homœopathic, I began to get some good results among the people. When Dr. Harvey left, through ill health, he left the whole of the patients in his charge in my hands. I then went on with itinerant work, because the people demanded it. They sent messengers for us, and we had to go some distances into the country, on the border tracts between China and Burmah, places where no white person had ever been seen amongst people who are great robbers. We took nothing but medicines; no money, *Quinine and rupees.* excepting one bottle,—a quinine bottle, full of rupees, stuffed in with flour. It looked like quinine, and we carried that in our medicine chest.

In commencing work in two or three different villages I happened to have to treat people suffering from abscesses, and the use of the lancet gave great relief, and made a profound impression among the people. The result of our itinerant work has been that the American Baptist *Successful lancing.* Missionaries who followed us there, sent up some native evangelists, and they established Mission stations in several of the villages which we visited first, and have had the joy of baptising between twenty and thirty of those wild robber people, who have become consistent Christians; so that I think there is something in itinerant work and also in hospital work.

I used to charge a small sum for certain medicines that had to be given to people who had got diseases through their own fault. I found that rather a good thing, but otherwise we gave all the medicines free. I may add that I am now training fully in Edinburgh, and hope, God willing, *Who to take payment from.* to take my degree, and be sent out next year.

Mr. Andrew Jukes, M.R.C.S.L., L.R.C.P. Ed. (C.M.S., from Dera Ghazi Khan): I think, Sir Risdon Bennett, that it is important that those who have had practical experience of Mission work abroad, should give their opinion upon certain points, as you have so desired.

In the first place I fully agree with Dr. Maxwell in his opinion of the primary importance of hospital work as distinguished from dispensary and itinerant work with respect to its Missionary character. I do not think there can be any question that the longer a patient comes under the power of the Gospel the more likely is he to receive the truth of the Gospel, and to have opportunities of getting the various prejudices removed with which in the first place he generally comes to the hospital. We have had a very important paper from Dr. Hutchison, and I fully agree with him that the training of native agents is a most important part of the Missionary's work.

I do not think it is absolutely necessary to wait till the native agent is fully trained before you give him some opportunity of practically doing the work which he has seen carried on in your own Medical Mission. I think with Dr. Hutchison there are very many simple remedies which the *Learners can work.* native agent who is not qualified can with advantage take with him and give in his itinerations to many of those who are sick. The number of maladies which it is possible to treat by an unqualified assistant in certain districts is great. As we just now heard there is a very large proportion of malarial fever, and as almost every native has experience of this malarial fever himself, he can very quickly recognise it in the case of another, and I have found by giving instructions as to the use of remedies in these cases, that often very great good has been done.

The effect of itinerating work amongst people who have prejudice against Europeans and against Christianity is very great, although, I do not think it is so satisfactory, in bringing so many converts to the Christian Church as is the case of Mission work in hospitals; it prepares the soil for the seed.

Rev. J. McLeod (Philadelphia, U.S.A.): I am not a physician, but I am deeply interested in this work. My wife and myself are more deeply interested indeed in the establishment of a college in Ceylon, which is to have a medical department. I have more and more realised the importance of this in Missionary work, and my impressions have been deepened by every word that has been said this morning. I feel this, that *Actions eloquent.* a Medical Missionary can speak at once. Other Missionaries have to learn the language, but a Medical Missionary knows his language at once. As soon as he does something for the people they can appreciate his character, and value him. I have sometimes thought it was a good thing that Missionaries did not know the language, and that they had to spend some time in order to acquire it, that they might show what they had besides the language, what they had besides talk, what they had besides good advice—that they might show the people that they have something outside the mere teaching of high moral truths, which many of them have already, from their own heathen scriptures; but with regard to this Medical Mission work they have it not. For that reason I believe every Missionary, as soon as he is amongst the people, and can smile in a baby's face, and can *Preparing for higher things.* help a poor mother, or give some clothing or anything else to the people, is doing his work, and is preparing himself to obtain the confidence of the people, when he can speak their language.

The Acting Secretary said that Mr. Burroughs, of the firm Burróughs & Wellcome, had expressed a wish to present to Medical Missionaries, who might be at the Conference, two small cases of medicine, as an *Gift of medicine.* expression of his interest in their work. He thought they might propose a very cordial vote of thanks to Mr. Burroughs for this most generous and acceptable offer, which he had made to the meeting.

Rev. Dr. Schreiber (Rhenish Missionary Society): I am not, sir, even in the same case as some of the speakers. I only had half-a-year's study in Edinburgh before going out as a Missionary, but I was obliged to do as much as I could. I have learnt one thing, and that is that I could not do anything and everything, and so we are now on the way to look for real Medical Missionaries. It is a great fault with us in Germany that we have been so late in this respect. We have very few Medical Missionaries —only two from the Basle Missionary Society, and one from the Moravians; but now we in our own Society are just looking for two or three; one to go to China, to a new hospital near Canton, and one to go to Sumatra. I hope you will show us the way in which we are to get such men, because, I am sorry to say, I am afraid we shall not find them in Germany just yet.

Rev. F. Lion Cachet (Secretary, Dutch Reformed Missionary Society): I must say that I was in a more unfortunate position than the gentleman who has spoken a little while ago. He was called a doctor, and he was not "qualified." I was qualified, holding the Transvaal Government licence to practise medicine and surgery; but I did not feel myself quali- *No trust in self, but much in God.* fied to the work. I always had that dreadful cloud hanging over me, "Suppose anything should happen that I cannot treat, what must I do?" Well, I have had some medical training, and have studied hard, and had a successful practice for about ten or twelve years. I was forced to practise; I was the only minister at the time among the Dutch Boers—I hope no one will shudder—and my parish was three hundred, or four hundred, or five hundred miles in extent. I had to look after my people, and also after the coloured people. I was in connection with some friends in Natal, fully qualified men, and if I wanted them I could have their help; but how could I send for a medical man two hundred or three hundred miles, when they could only give a few minutes to a case, and they had no time to come. But still the Lord showed Himself to me many a time, and heard my prayers, when I was at my poor wits' ends. When a difficult case came before me, I would pray, "Lord, show me what I have to do; assist me in my diagnosis; strengthen my nerves and give me what I want!" If ever in my life I felt the strength of trusting in God it was at that time. I came back from Africa a second time, and became the Secretary of our Dutch Mission in Java, and the first thing I did was to say to our Committee, "We must send out a fully qualified Missionary to Java to do the work of the Medical Missionary, and to train others." God has given us the man, and he is at present under Dr. Maxwell's care in his institute. I plead with you, my friends, to send out fully qualified men. At the same time do not let any Missionary go out who does not know at least a little about minor operations. One gentleman has spoken about the use of the lancet, but the forceps goes just as far.

Mr. R. A. Macfie: It was suggested yesterday that if there were any difficulties felt or any doubts in the mind they might be put in writing, and I ventured as Chairman to say that if those questions were put together perhaps the Committee would allow us a separate session to consider them. With that view I have written out these questions. "Is it desirable"—I give no exposition of my reasons, they rather underlie than appear on the surface—"Is it desirable that Medical Missions be conducted by special Societies? Can and should one dispensary serve more than one Mission body, and should not the well-to-do brethren be encouraged to use it, of course paying? Might the contributions of the well-to-do be made voluntary, and, after paying for medicines, be applied to the Mission funds? Might there not be an office or offices, with correspondents qualified to advise with Medical men, who, from having private means or a desire to change climate combined with inward promptings of love and zeal, feel able to offer their services gratuitously for limited periods of engagement, and who desire information and guidance?" Then the last question is, "Might we not appoint a Committee to consider these questions and report?" My present object is merely to call attention to the last of these questions, "Might we not appoint a Committee to consider these questions and any others referred to it?" and also, I think, a special Meeting might be intimated to-night, at which any question sent in might be answered.

Mr. Macfie's questions.

The Acting Secretary: I fear it is quite impossible to expect another meeting. Every morning and evening is filled up to the extent of this building's capacity; but I will lay the matter before the Secretary.

The Chairman: At all events there can be no objection to collecting the main points that have been elicited at this meeting, so as to bring them before the public in a form that will be available abroad as well as at home. A number of points have been brought forward which it is very desirable should be put upon permanent record, and made available for those who are immediately connected with Medical Missions.

May I ask Dr. Pringle to let me know later on how far he thinks it possible that private soldiers connected with the stations where there are Medical Officers, would be available as Nurses or as Assistants to the Medical Missionaries in carrying on work? I mention this because I know in connection with the Army and Navy many of the privates make the most efficient aids to Medical men. A couple of the best nurses I ever came across in the course of my whole professional life were two men in the Navy. I was called upon to attend their captain, and I found that intelligence, efficiency, dexterity, and everything a nurse should have were evinced by these men to a degree that I have hardly ever seen approached by any other nurses, male or female.

Soldiers as nurses.

Miss De Broen (Paris): Mr. Chairman, and Christian friends,—I think I may say that mine is the worst of all cases, for I am neither qualified nor a little qualified. The reason, however, why I have been permitted to say a few words is this, that the Lord has used me as an instrument to establish a Medical Mission in Paris. We all know much of the value of Medical Missions in heathen lands; but, dear friends, in France it is almost more valuable than anywhere else. The heathen have a natural craving for God, so much so that they create themselves gods; but the French infidels say, "We have no God," as you know well enough. As one of the Town Councillors lately, when he gave away prizes to thousands of children, "Ah," said he, "my children, we are greatly abused, especially in English newspapers; they slander us because they say we send God out of our schools; but," he added, "it is not true, because there is no God; how can we send Him out of our schools."

Medical Mission in Paris.

Now, dear friends, this is the use of the Medical Mission in Paris that we are able to preach the Gospel to the patients. It is fifteen years ago since the Lord permitted me to open a Medical Mission, and I was very happy to see the first Medical Missionary sent out to me, Dr. Laidlaw, who was here yesterday; and now the Mission has so grown that we have had as many as thirty thousand attendances in one year, which has given us an opening to visit from six thousand to eight thousand new individuals yearly.

A great opening.

The Chairman: We shall be very glad to hear some information on the second point as to the payment by patients for medicines. If there is any Missionary present who has any experience on this subject, it will be desirable that we should have more information than we have at present had upon that point.

Pastor A. Haegert (Bethel Santhal Mission): I have been twenty years in India, and for sixteen years I have been doctoring the people. I have attended something like thirty thousand patients; every year the sufferers from one hundred and fifty villages have come seeking my medical aid. It has been my privilege to train, years ago, twelve native preachers for medical work. They occupy to-day twelve hundred square miles. They attended last year many

Native practitioners.

patients from one hundred and eleven villages. They have saved scores and scores of lives, and hundreds and hundreds have been visited by them, and I thank God for that. Now my medical men are not qualified according to Government diploma, but they know medicine, they know diseases; and the best medicines that money can procure, and the best medical works that money can buy, I have placed in their hands. Now, with reference to money matters, I was asked in years gone by, what I should charge. I began by saying, "Friends, you are to pay something for your medicines." Well, you know, they are Orientals. They are as keen as needles. They know that we have attended thousands Who should not and tens of thousands for nothing, and now, once in a blue and who should moon, we ask them for money. The result is they doubt our pay. honesty, and begin to dodge and argue like real Orientals, showing that they should not pay, while every one else gets it for nothing, so that instead of spending my valuable time in endeavouring to teach them the knowledge of God, and to draw them to the Saviour, I was spending my time, in order to get a copper out of these men. Well, I gave it up as a bad job, never to be done again. If a rich money-lender, who is the curse of thousands of people, comes to my house seeking my favour I say, " My friend, my charge is £5 to begin with, and after curing you it will be £5 more." "Sir, you take 10s." "No, I will take £10, if you please; if you do not like it, good morning, sir;" but then I know he has been making money fast by destroying hundreds of homes. "You pay for your medical advice; if you do not like it, good morning."

There was a correspondence last year in the papers, about Medical Missionaries complaining, that medical work made them *dry*, that it made them *secular*, that it robbed them of spiritual power. Sir, I have lived in India twenty years. Every day from morning to night, I have more or less been Is medical work removing pain and suffering. It has not made me dry. There is deadening? a house,—the good man of the house is dying; the wife says to me, "Come and see my husband, or he will die; and I shall be a widow, and my children will be orphans." I go to his house; there is sorrow, sadness, perplexity. My medicine makes the pain go away, death runs away from the house, peace, joy, and health come back. Is there anything in that to be sad about, or to get dry about, or to make you lose your spiritual power? Why, it makes me just glad to do it to thousands more!

The Acting Secretary said the next speaker was Mr. Alfred Sutton of Reading, who had sent three sons to be Medical Missionaries,—one to Burmah, one to Baghdad, and a third to Quettah.

Mr. Alfred Sutton (Reading): Mr. Chairman, and Christian friends,— As it has been my privilege to be called upon to speak, I will just say that there have been two thoughts in my mind upon points which have not been answered. The one is that medical men abroad should have a little more licence given to them perhaps than other More licence for Missionaries, but certainly they do require licence to act accord- medical men. ing to the circumstances in which they are placed; and then, the other point is that which has been mooted, but which no one seems to be able to answer; and it is very reasonable that they are unable to answer, because the circum- stances are so different in different localities. That question is, as to receiving payment from patients. I think, perhaps, I may Payment by illustrate that by the position of my three sons. One is in patients. Upper Burmah, surrounded by nothing but very poor people indeed. It would be wrong upon principle in every way to ask them to pay. And again in Baghdad, where my son Henry Martyn is, he is surrounded with such an immense number of persons requiring his services, that he is obliged to confine his attention entirely or almost entirely to the Mohammedans, wretchedly poor, and a few of the Jews, if possible still poorer; and therefore he cannot attend at all generally any of the upper classes. He has told us of one or two instances of the wives of merchants and others who have prayed him to come to them, and in that case he has gone, but he has refused to receive any payment from them, although they will insist on his receiving some curiosities from the ruins of Babylon or Nineveh, or something of that kind. But there is the other son in Quettah, altogether differently circumstanced. There are those here who know that Quettah is a totally different place to either of the other two; and in Quettah there are families who can well afford to pay. But I need hardly say my son will not receive payment of any kind in the ordinary sense, but it is of immense importance to him to have a hospital. He cannot possibly get on without a hospital, and therefore any persons who send for him in the upper ranks of life, put down in a book any gifts which they may feel inclined to make, to the hospital fund. I think it is both legitimate and desirable that medical men should under such circumstances receive fees.

Mr. William Gauld, M.D. (Bethnal Green Medical Mission, formerly of Swatow, China): There is a point which has been touched upon this morning, on which I should like to say a word. It was alluded to by a friend to whom I listened with much sympathy, namely the question of the Medical Missionary doing work before he has begun to learn the language, or before he has acquired it. Now I hold a very strong opinion on that point. I know that there are some Missionaries who have done noble work without knowing the language, but I hold that for a Missionary's own sake, for the influence he has amongst his patients, and for the preservation of his own spiritual life, it is most important that he should be able to speak to them, not only about their diseases but about the Gospel of the Lord Jesus Christ; and I think the very advantage spoken of, that the Medical Missionary has of being able to show the loving kindness of the Gospel in practical work before he knows anything of the language, is one of his greatest dangers. Missionary Societies would do well if they would strictly enjoin Medical Missionaries, especially, not to do more medical work than they can possibly help for the first year, and to give that year to the study of the language. Their future work will tell all the more powerfully for the Gospel of Jesus Christ.

Knowledge of language essential to work.

Then with regard to the relative value of the three forms of Mission work which have been spoken of, I am entirely at one with what has been said by most of the speakers, and especially with the Paper which has been read by my friend Dr. Maxwell; but I think the Medical Missionary would do well in his own person to combine all three. In our work at Swatow, where we had the privilege of building three hospitals at different times, in the winter months when it was possible and even pleasant to travel, it was a pleasure to me to take my medicine chest and go with a brother Missionary or native helper into the country, and spend as long a time there as I could. My assistants were always, after the first year or two, able to carry on the work in the hospital at Swatow in my

Relative value of three forms of work.

absence, so that the work there did not very materially suffer. The itinerant work will have this great advantage, it lets the people know you. Many of them know so little of your appearance that they Itinerant work. are afraid to come to the hospital. They do not know what a foreigner is; there are terrible stories told in China of what the foreigners are—demons, and all sorts of things. The Chinese in their various villages and towns see you, and they learn what you are, and in that way their confidence is gained, and they are more ready to come to the hospital. I think a great deal of good Missionary work can be done in these itinerancies, and good work for the body as well.

Then about the dispensary work. I had two dispensaries in connection with hospital work at Swatow, and in the town, where one dispensary was, the hostility to Europeans was of a very marked kind. On the first Dispensaries. two weekly visits there, we were stoned out of the town; and our boatmen would not go in again unless we got the Mandarin to protect us, which we did. On our way up the river to that dispensary once a week, almost every face we met was scowling at us, and the river boatmen were anything but friendly; still, having gone there week after week, and persevered with our work, the people came and heard the Gospel, and had their bodily ailments attended to. In the course of a year or two the change in that district was very marked; going up the river we were met with smiles, the whole feeling of the people had turned towards us, and in favour of our work.

With regard to the payment of fees by patients, I suppose the idea of requiring payment is to make the Mission as little expensive to the Home Boards as possible. Now in China we secured a great deal of work being done at very little expense, by making the patients who Payment by patients. came to the hospital pay for their own food. We did not feed any of them except in special cases, and in that way, at little more than the expense of the drugs, we were able to attend to thousands of patients in a year. Of course if any wealthy men came, they were welcome to help us, and occasionally we sent a subscription list round amongst the European and Chinese community, which was well responded to, so that the Chinese helped in that way to some extent. I think in China at least it is well not to charge the patients. Many of them are poor peasantry, and the very fact that they come from long distances and have to support themselves in hospital, is a guarantee that they really want to be healed, and secures us against being pestered by beggars or others who would simply come to live upon us.

Rev. Dr. Green closed the proceedings with prayer.

MEETINGS OF MEMBERS
IN SECTION.

WOMEN'S WORK IN THE MISSION-FIELD.

(1) *THE AGENTS.*

(*a*) The place of female agency in Mission work, and its relation to the departments of general Missionary Societies both in home arrangements and foreign work.

(*b*) The training of agents at home and on their arrival in the foreign field.

(*c*) Female Medical Missionaries.

(*Wednesday morning, June 13th, in the Large Hall.*)*

General Sir Robert Phayre, K.C.B., in the chair.
Acting Secretary, Rev. Gilbert Karney, M.A.

Prayer by the Rev. Gilbert Karney.

The Chairman: Dear-Christian friends,—As my time is limited, I do not propose to occupy much of it with anything that I have to say upon this important subject. I leave details to those who have practical experience and knowledge of the work. But I can say, that our subject of conference this morning, viz., the work of women in the Mission-field, cannot be surpassed for importance in the great work of Missions, in whatever part of the world it may be carried on; and I think that we have an evidence of this in the progress already made. It is, comparatively speaking, a very short time since this branch of Mission work was organised on a large scale, but in that time, and considering the slender means in operation, it has already begun to effect important changes in the heathen world. It has access where the Word of God never penetrated before, and as that Word carries power and light with it, I pray heartily that it may prevail more and

---

* This meeting, which was to have been held in the Annexe, was adjourned to the Large Hall, owing to the crowded attendance.

more, and have a fuller and freer entrance to those places which the Lord has opened up to us. It has been my privilege to be *Personal testimony.* associated with the Lord's work in India for about forty years and upwards, and all I can say is this, that I know no work that requires our support, our prayers, and our sympathies more than this " women's work," which we are about to consider this morning. It has supplied a want which for years the people of God have been longing to see met.

It was about thirteen or fourteen years ago that I had an exceptional opportunity of knowing the awful oppression to which women in the highest rank, as well as in the lowest, are subjected in the Zenanas and the harems of India, and I can assure you, when I heard of Zenana visiting, and Bible work, and schools for the young, and last, but not least, of lady physicians, with their trained nurses, taking up this work, it made my heart rejoice. In the instance to which I refer, I brought the matter to the notice of the proper authorities, and I am thankful to say obtained substantial relief. Just to show what progress is being made in that same *Signs of improvement.* quarter, I not long ago received from a native Christian gentleman of my acquaintance a letter in which he told me how, in that very country, where oppression of the worst kind had prevailed amongst women, the present ruler, a most enlightened and well-educated prince, sent to him and his wife, asking them to preach the Gospel to them and their Court. Now I merely mention this to show what results the Lord brings about when He opens the way according to His word. " All power is given to Me in heaven and in earth ; and lo ! I am with you alway." We learn from this, dear friends, that there is no amount of oppression, that there is no amount of hindrance that Satan may oppose to the progress of the Gospel, that cannot be removed by believing prayer and pleading the promises of the Lord Jesus Christ. Let us plead these promises on behalf of this glorious work which our dear sisters in the Lord have commenced under His leading and guidance ; let us pray that He may be with them, and that they may all of them receive a great accession of strength in this our Conference.

PAPER.

1. By Miss Rainy (Free Church of Scotland).

' *The place of Female Agency in Mission Work, and its relation to the department of general Missionary Societies, both in Home arrangements and Foreign work.*"

Woman's influence has been a potent factor in the world's history—too often, alas ! for evil, since that fatal day, when, having tasted the forbidden fruit, " she gave also to her husband, with her, and he did eat." Must we not carry with us *Woman and her Redeemer.* that old story of " Paradise Lost," while seeking to trace woman's place and function in the story of " Paradise Regained " ?

She owes a great debt to the race that she ruined. She owes everything to the Redeemer; for never was a creature more utterly undone than she, when first the Promise shed a ray of hope across her path, brightening, in the fulness of time, into that wonderful announcement: "Hail! thou that art highly favoured, the Lord is with thee;" and awakening Mary's glad response: "Behold the handmaid of the Lord!" (Luke i. 28, 38).

It was natural, that in the joy of a revelation like this, there should be a great burst of service. And so we find it in the Church of the New Testament, from Anna, the prophetess, who spake of Christ to all that looked for redemption in Jerusalem [1] to that elect lady who trained her children to walk in the truth.[2] Women ministered to Him of their substance.[3] The Samaritan woman gave Him her testimony;[4] the Syrophenician woman, her faith;[5] the woman that was forgiven much, her love and her tears.[6] It was well their part to bring Him what they could. It concerns us more to note how graciously He accepted their service, —how He delighted to draw it out and to vindicate it,[7] even when rendered by the poorest and the most unworthy. For more than knowledge or power, He prizes love,[8] and it is His glory to take the weak things of this world, to confound the things which are mighty, and base things of the world, and things which are despised, yea, and things which are not, to bring to naught things that are.[9]

Women in the New Testament.

Women were honoured to carry to the Church the tidings of His resurrection[10] they shared in the Pentecostal effusion,[11] and they were welcomed by the Apostles as fellow-labourers and fellow-sufferers in the Gospel.[12]

From allusions in the New Testament, and in the writings of the early Christian Fathers, it appears that while all Christians, men and women, were expected to take their share in the work of the Church[13] some women were specially set apart as deaconesses to care for the poor and sick, and to give private instruction to those of their own sex, who could not be taught by men.[14] Widows were often employed in this work. They were, in fact, the Zenana Missionaries of that age, when the state of society and of family life, especially among the Greeks, resembled, in many respects, what we now find in India. As time went on, and the primitive Church order was overlaid or superseded by human inventions, the deaconess was merged into the nun, and

Deaconesses in the Early Church.

[1] Luke ii. 38.   [2] 2 John.   [3] Luke viii. 3.
[4] John iv. 29.   [5] Matt. xv. 28.   [6] Luke vii. 38—47.
[7] John xii. 3; Matt. xxvi. 13; Mark xii. 43.
[8] John xxi. 16.   [9] 1 Cor. i. 27, 28.   [10] Luke xxiv. 10.
[11] Compare Acts i. 14; ii. 1—4, 17, 18; xxi. 9.
[12] Rom. xvi. throughout; Phil. iv. 3.
[13] 1 Cor. xii.; Eph. iv. 15, 16; Rom. xii. 4—8; 1 Pet. iv. 10.
[14] Rom. xvi. 1; 1 Tim. iii. 11; 1 Tim. v. 9, 10.*

* For further particulars, see Smith's "Dictionary of Christian Antiquities," vol. i., pp. 582—535; Heron's "Church of the Sub-Apostolic Age," pp. 295—298; Schaff's "Church History," vol. i., p. 185.

ultimately disappeared from Church history,* to revive again, in a new form, at Kaiserswerth.

In the wonderful work of the Moravian Church, women, both married and unmarried, have borne their part, very much as Priscilla, Phœbe, and Persis bore theirs in the first Christian Missions. When a Church is cleaving closely to the Master, there is a spontaneity in its gifts and services, and great results follow, without much fuss or elaborate organisa-tion. Persecution is often useful in preparing the agency and paving the way for such matter-of-course Mission work (Acts viii. 1—4). *[margin: Moravian women.]*

But the Church of the eighteenth century did not, as a general rule, consider it a matter of course that men—far less women—should go to Greenland, Sierra Leone, or Polynesia, to proclaim the unsearchable riches of Christ; and even after the Modern Missionary enterprise was fairly inaugurated, a considerable time elapsed before woman's place and power in connection with it were fully recognised.

In the earlier years of the century, indeed, such women as Ann H. Judson, Mary Moffat, and others, had shown that there is nothing unwomanly in braving the utmost trials and labours of Missionary life. But many of us can recall a time when these were regarded as rather exceptional instances, and when the sphere of women, and especially of unmarried women, in connection with the Missionary enterprise, was generally supposed to consist in collect-ing and contributing money, reading Missionary records, and remembering the work in prayer. Nor are these forms of service to be undervalued. Missions cannot be maintained without funds, and our Churches would need to be much more alive to their privilege and responsi-bility in the matter of giving, if ever we are to dispense with collectors. How thankful we might be, were we even at the point where collecting and contributing becomes a means of grace to both parties! Let us aim at this. And meanwhile let us prize the services of that great com-pany who have toiled as collectors for years together, and have borne and had patience, and for Christ's sake have laboured without fainting. Of these, the immense majority are women; whether the work for which they collect be for their own sex or not. May I not also say that some of the most liberal contri-butors, according to their means, are women—especially poor women; though in this we have all doubtless much to learn. If we cannot dispense with funds, neither can we do without that living personal sympathy which is more generally characteristic of women than of men, partly because the former have more leisure and more interest in details. Least of all can prayer be dispensed with. Who can tell how much of the success or failure of Missions depends on the rising or falling at home of that spiritual barometer of which prayer is the exponent? *[margin: Women's work in the cause at home.]*

Let us be thankful that ways are open by which every member of the Church, young or old, rich or poor, male or female, she who tarries at home, as well as they that publish the Gospel abroad, may be a fellow-worker with the Lord Jesus Christ in saving a lost world.

Yet it is also a matter of rejoicing, and it is becoming plainer every day, that the Lord has need of women, and especially of unmarried women in the foreign field itself. None of the Churches anticipated, on first entering the Mission-field, that the work among women would need to be a separate department. Their Missionaries were sent forth to preach the Gospel to every creature, and it was only experience that taught them that a large number of heathen women are absolutely out of reach of the ministrations of men, and that all of them stand specially in need of such womanly training as Christian women alone can give, to raise them from the degradation into which they have fallen, and to fit them for filling their rightful place *[margin: Women needed in the Mission-field.]*

* Concilien-geschichte von Dr. Hefele, vol. i., pp. 55, 278, 500, 664, 698, 736.

in the Christian family and the Christian Church. Missionaries' wives have done noble service in all our Mission-fields; but no one now believes that they can overtake all the work needed among heathen women.

But granted that this is so. "Why?" asks many a critical inquirer, "must Women's Societies be set up to carry on this work? Could not the existing Missionary Boards or Committees send out all the women that are wanted?"

In many instances in which this question has been put to me, I have found that it simply meant, "Why should we be asked for two subscriptions?" and all that was needed to silence the critic, was the very obvious remark that people would need to double their subscriptions to the General Committee if it undertook both sides of the work.

Why have Women's Societies? It is extraordinary how many people fancy that Missionary Boards might double their agency without any addition to their income.

But there are nobler critics whose misgivings spring from a higher source. "It is not Christianity," they say, "it is heathenism, that necessitates the division of the work abroad. At home, are we not all one in Christ Jesus, and would it not give more unity to the Missionary enterprise and be more in accordance with Apostolic precedent, if one Board or Committee managed both sides of the work?" Now as to the last argument, we read of no Boards, Committees, or Missionary Societies in the Acts of the Apostles; but we find Churches composed of men and women, filled with the Holy Ghost, under whose guidance the Missionaries were selected and sent forth. To these Churches of men and women the Missionaries made their reports, and there was a constant interchange of letters, messages, and prayers between them. One Church, whose first converts were women, sent contributions also.* We must go to Herrnhut or to Herrmannsburg to find modern Missions conducted in this primitive fashion.

As a Presbyterian, I believe in Churches carrying on Church work. But as the work becomes extensive and complicated, a division of labour may conduce to a higher unity. "All members have not the same office," and different departments may well be allocated to special Committees. Here we have a department in which women only can be employed, and their work lies among women and children; is it unreasonable to suppose that for selecting and corresponding with these agents, for creating interest in their work and raising funds for it, women may be better qualified than men? Is it reasonable to expect them to take all this trouble on behalf of work, in the management of which they have no voice? And in so far as Home management is available for the conduct of Foreign Missions, are they not, with their sisterly sympathy, with their aptitude for details, with the sense of an unparalleled indebtedness in their hearts to quicken love, courage and patience, and with their experience of woman's work at home, fully as likely as men are to manage this branch of the work well?

Fifty years ago, all that the few struggling Women's Societies could plead in their own defence was that a great and urgent work needed to be done, which **Our answer.** none of the existing Boards or Committees were accomplishing; and they must set about it somehow. But these fifty years have left their record, and in the light of their history, we venture to answer, when asked why Women's Societies should take up this work: "It is because the Lord would have it so." It is His voice that has called us; it is His hand that has led us; it is He who has cleared away difficulties at home and abroad, till the little one has literally become a thousand, and the women that publish the tidings are growing into a host.

It is now the exception for any Church that has Missions worth mentioning

---

* Philippians iv. 15. Does any one doubt that Lydia had a great hand in it?

to be without a Women's Society for the woman's part of the work. These Societies have an aggregate annual income of £250,000; and they are represented in the Foreign field by over a thousand European and American Missionary women, aided by several thousands of Missionary women from the races among whom they labour—themselves the first-fruits of a glorious harvest.

The work is manifold. Teaching in day schools, Sabbath schools, industrial schools; the care of orphanages and boarding schools; the Zenana Mission, or house to house visitation in India and China; evangelistic work among the poor in villages and country districts, at fairs and sacred places, in hospitals and prisons; Bible classes and mothers' meetings for converts; the training and superintending of native Christian agents; the preparation of vernacular literature; and, last not least, Medical Missionary work among women and children. The enterprise is yet in its infancy, but there are boundless possibilities before it. "This is the Lord's doing, and it is marvellous in our eyes." The work manifold.

II.

A few words now about the relation of our Woman's work to the general Missionary enterprise at home and abroad.

At first, the Ladies' Societies got little countenance from General Boards or Committees. It was in the Foreign field that the earliest relations sprang up between them. Young ladies sent to labour in heathen lands were placed under the protection of some married Missionary, with whose work theirs became associated; and whenever conversion led on to Church fellowship, women, as well as men, depended on the ordained Missionary for the administration of ordinances and for pastoral care.

At home, the field of Christian sympathy and liberality presented at first many spare corners where the ladies could reap or glean without interfering with their neighbours. But as Societies multiplied and Churches awakened to their duty, and Missionaries were sent out in greater numbers, the necessity for some mutual understanding and orderly distribution of forces became more apparent; and during the last twenty years, the Women's Societies, which formerly acted as irregular or unattached auxiliaries, have been endeavouring to fall into line, and to find a fitting place for themselves in the general *corps d'armée*. In proportion also as their work grew and bore fruit, the general Committees or Boards became anxious as to its bearing on their own. Hence many efforts to establish inter-relations, which are as yet of too various and tentative a kind to be minutely enumerated; though perhaps some general principles may be suggested by them, of which it is important not to lose sight. Women's Societies and the Churches.

First. The great majority of our Women's Societies now work in connection with particular Churches or denominations of Christians from whose adherents they derive their funds, and to whose Missions abroad their Missionaries are attached. There is an advantage in each Church knowing what amount of womanly aid it can count upon, and it ought to be able to count upon the loyal co-operation of all its own members at home and abroad. While doing so, it interferes neither with the resources nor with the work of other Churches, but can heartily bid them God speed.

Secondly. It is, of course, an object with each Church fully to engage the sympathies of all its members, and to enlist their help in this half of the Foreign Mission enterprise; and with this view to aim at more complete home organisation than sufficed when the work was on a smaller scale. Our friends in America showed an excellent example to all the Presbyterian Churches when they began the method, now adopted also in Canada and in this country, of forming a committee of ladies within the bounds of each Presbytery, to diffuse information and collect funds, and through its secretary to correspond, on the one hand, with a Central Ladies' Interest of Church members in the work.

Committee in which the execution is vested, and on the other, with the Congregational Associations in their respective districts.*

The Ladies' Societies of other Churches, which have not the same well-defined ecclesiastical divisions, generally have district committees or secretaries to act as intermediaries between them and their parochial or congregational constituents.

Thirdly. The exact relation of the Central Ladies' Committee to the General Board of its Church, varies according to circumstances. When a Ladies' Society, which had worked independently for years, entered into alliance with a General Board, it naturally preserved more of its autonomy than was conceded to Ladies' Societies formed at the instance of General Boards to aid them in work among women which the General Board itself had begun. In either case the Executive may be strengthened by the appointment of clergymen or laymen as assessors, office-bearers, or consultative committees. Some Women's Societies have conducted their business with remarkable energy, economy, and success,† with little or no aid of this kind; but even they may be sometimes glad of a manly voice to plead for them in the pulpit or on the platform; and emergencies may arise in which a manly breadth of view and knowledge of affairs may be of great service, provided these do not intervene in such a way as to impair the ladies' sense of responsibility and freedom of action. It is a simple way of establishing a good understanding between a Women's Society and a General Board that some trusted men should be associated with both, who can represent to each the views of the other. The same object might be served by having some women on the General Board. The ladies have shown a willingness and a power to work on any lines conceded to them, which ought, I think, to inspire confidence; and on the whole, there is a general disposition to let them work their own way, both in the details of their Home organisation and in the selection of Missionary agents.

Fourthly. These last are frequently placed under the same Local Mission Councils to which the ordained Missionaries of their Church are subordinated as to their work in the Foreign Mission-field. But some of the Missions allow them to have a voice in these Councils when their own work is under review. This, we think, is only fair. In other cases the Lady Missionaries have local Committees of their own, and their relation to the General Mission is simply that of friendly co-operation.

There are some Societies which still carry the so-called "Undenominational" flag. Of these, the London Society for Female Education in the East and the American Woman's Union Missionary Society took precedence of all Church Societies, each in its own continent. They have their own traditions, their own attached supporters, their own valuable and well-attested work. They were first in the field, and I don't think the most strenuous advocate of Church work would like to see them out of it. I may remark, however, that while the association of most of the Ladies' Societies with particular Churches at home tends, in my opinion, to prevent confusion, and to promote general good fellowship, efficiency, and economy of resources, yet in the Foreign field nearly all the Ladies' Societies are equally unsectarian. Nearly all of them have on their staff representatives of various Churches, and the native agents trained by each Society are available for all.

Relation of Ladies' Committee to General Board.

Relations of Missionaries in the field.

Undenominational Societies.

* The Great American Churches have Synodical Committees also.

† *E.g.*, the Society for Female Education in the East.

PAPER.

2. By Miss A. K. Marston, L.K.Q.C.P.L (Indian Female Normal School and Instruction Society, from Lucknow).

Medical work for Women in the Mission-field.

In speaking of Medical work for Women in the Mission-field, it may be well first to remind my hearers that all the arguments which have from time to time been advanced in favour of Medical work as an adjunct and aid to that which is purely religious are of equal force with regard to both male and female Medical Missionaries, the important difference being that the latter restrict their practice, as far as possible, to women and children. The special need of Medical women to work amongst women who are inaccessible to the ordinary male physician is well known, and now everywhere recognised. As in so many other branches of philanthropic work, Missionary Societies led the way in extending Medical aid to the suffering women debarred by their customs from obtaining it in the usual way. The movement thus set on foot has become widespread, and recently the Dufferin Association in India has undertaken the difficult task of providing some kind of female medical aid for all who desire it. *Female Medical work.*

Perhaps I may best occupy the short time at my disposal in bringing before you, as nearly as I can, a true picture—*first*, of the condition of women in India as regards Medical aid ; and *second*, of the work of a Medical Missionary among the women ; after which I may suggest some points which appear to me worthy of consideration with regard to our action in the future.

I. *As to the condition of Indian women.*—Although my experience is restricted to the North-west Provinces of India, the same description will probably apply more or less to women in all Mohammedan countries where the " Purdah" system is observed. *Condition of Indian women.* It is quite a mistake to suppose that Indian women are debarred from medical treatment altogether. From our point of view they are certainly debarred from sufficient or effectual Medical aid ; but from their own point of view they are, excepting in cases of special emergency, well provided for.

Take the case of a Mohammedan lady who becomes ill. The first person she will send for will be either a " dai " or a " hakim," according to circumstances. The " dai" is a native woman of the lower class, utterly uneducated, but possessing knowledge of a few remedies, so-called, which have been handed down from mother to daughter for generations. This " dai" will do her best, or her worst ; and if she does nothing to interfere with Nature, that great physician will in many cases effect a cure, and if so, the lady's confidence in her " dai " will be strengthened. Should a " hakim " or native male physician be sent for, he will be allowed to feel the lady's pulse, or, should he be a near relative, he will even be admitted to see the patient. This latter course, however, is by no means considered necessary for the accurate treatment of the case. The *pulse* is considered an index to the state of every organ of the body. *First resort in disease.*

Should all native remedies prove unavailing, and the case go from bad to worse, the lady's family will consider what is next to be done. It is at this juncture that the lady doctor is called in, but even here The next resort. there is another alternative, as "English medicine" may be obtained from various sources. First, there is the Bengali babu, employed in a Government hospital, or there is the native homœopathic practitioner. Either of these may feel the lady's pulse, and the gentlemen of the family will detail her symptoms, after which he will have no hesitation in prescribing; failing these, if the family be wealthy, the English civil surgeon may be resorted to, and will attend the patient on the same conditions. Should, however, the lady doctor have obtained a reputation in that quarter, she will probably be called in. She will carefully examine the patient, prescribe and give directions, which may or may not be carried out. The medicine prescribed will generally be taken, though in bigoted Mohammedan families, the "istikhâra," a kind of rosary, may be first consulted, to see whether it is likely to do good or not; should the result be unsatisfactory the medicine is not given. If the treatment is carried out, the effect of the first dose will be anxiously watched, and any untoward symptom that may occur during the ensuing twelve hours will be attributed to it. If relief speedily follows, and the malady yields easily to treatment, the lady doctor will be allowed to have entire charge of the case; if, on the contrary, it should be tedious, or any untoward symptom should arise, or worst of all, should surgical treatment be proposed, she will probably be dismissed altogether, and the unfortunate patient will again go the round of daies, hakims, babus, etc., etc.; perhaps when she is at death's door, and beyond the reach of human aid, the lady doctor may be again summoned as a forlorn hope. All this does not sound very encouraging, but we must remember that much patient effort is needed to overcome prejudice, and to educate the people to know their need and who are their true helpers.

The fact that the people of India are not fully alive to the need of adequate Medical aid for their women does not make that need the less. Words would fail me to tell of needless suffering undergone, lives sacrificed, and families desolated through the ignorance of native women supposed to undertake the care of the sick. From time to time I have been called just in time to see an unfortunate woman pass away who could, no doubt, have been saved by timely interference. Other lives I have been able to save which certainly would have been sacrificed had no adequate Medical aid been attainable. Doubtless the need is great, only it is needless to attempt to disguise the fact that female Medical work in India is uphill work, and needs patient waiting and persevering effort in order to reap the fruits of one's labours.

II. *As regards the work of a Medical Missionary among Indian women.* —The work of a Medical Missionary abroad differs less than might be supposed from similar work in our large cities. It is carried on largely and perhaps most satisfactorily among the poor, that is, among First applicants those who cannot afford to pay fees for Medical attention. To the poor. meet the needs of this class the Medical Missionary will open dispensaries in different parts of the city, so as to be within reach of all, and it is generally necessary, for the saving of time and strength, to make the rule that all who are not too ill to leave their houses, and are unable or unwilling to pay fees, should attend the dispensaries. Perhaps you will say, " How can ' Purdah ' women, who are not allowed to be seen abroad, visit a public dispensary ?" They do not come on foot, but are carried in doolies (a kind of framework, covered with a purdah), inside which they creep, and remain hidden from view until they are safely lodged within the dispensary precincts ; as an additional precaution a male relative generally accompanies the doolie as escort.

The work of seeing patients now commences, and they are admitted one by one into the consulting-room. When a certain number have been seen and prescribed for, and the late comers have had time to assemble, Medical work is suspended, and a short service is held, consisting of *The Zenana dispensary.* one or two bhajans, *i.e.*, Christian hymns to native tunes, and a short address. It is well if the doctor can give the latter herself. She has far more influence over the women than anyone else, and they will generally listen to her respectfully and attentively. Knowledge of the language is of course essential, but this every Medical Missionary ought to acquire thoroughly, if she is to reap any spiritual fruit from her labours.

On the whole, I consider the dispensary a most interesting sphere of Missionary work. Results are not to be estimated by the number of accessions to the visible Church, though these are not altogether wanting. From time to time the Medical Missionary's heart is gladdened by simple *Results of the work.* confessions of faith, and words of gratitude for spiritual benefits received. The good seed is being sown in the hearts of thousands, and in some it can be seen to spring up and bear fruit, even in spite of adverse circumstances, and opposing influence. Some are forsaking their idols, and are serving Christ in their homes, though home ties at present forbid their open avowal of Christianity. For the final estimation of results we must wait till the great Harvest Day.

After dispensaries, the next work of the female Medical Missionary is to establish a hospital for women and children.. This is not so easy as it sounds, for when a suitable building and all appliances are secured, and money for the support of the institution is *The Zenana hospital.* guaranteed, the next difficulty is to persuade the patients to avail themselves of the privileges offered to them. Many are the excuses offered by those whose only hope of cure, as the doctor too well knows, lies in the care and attention which they cannot receive in their own homes. " How can I come ? my house cannot be left. I have small children ; my brethren will not be pleased. What will become of my caste ? I cannot come alone, and there is no one willing to accompany me."

If all these objections are overruled, and the patient is at last lodged in the hospital, the next difficulty is to keep her there until remedies have had time to take effect ; probably she and her friends will allow about twenty-four hours for testing the success of hospital treatment, and if there is no decided improvement within that time you will be told "the friends have come to take her away." Years of patient labour, however, insure an increase of confidence on the part of the people, and as the doctor's reputation is established the hospital becomes a powerful agency for good.

There is still another department of work for the female Medical Missionary, the most difficult, and, in some respects, the most unsatisfactory, whilst at the same time it is very interesting and well worth cultivating. I refer to Medical attendance on ladies of the upper class in their own Zenanas. These are not so accessible to the Medical Missionary as is sometimes supposed. The question of religious bigotry among Mohammedans and of *Medical Zenana work.* caste prejudice among Hindus, both of which predominate in the upper classes of large cities, oppose the entry of the Missionary lady doctor, added to which there is still a steadfast adherence to native customs and a fear of offending the native hakims on the part of many wealthy natives of India ; in many cases they are slow to resort to European treatment, and when they do so it is under conditions and reservations, which are extremely trying to the doctor called in. She very soon finds that the case is by no means given into her hands. Her opinion is asked, but it is not necessarily accepted ; it is inquired of her what line of treatment she intends to pursue, but it does not follow that she will be allowed to carry it out, on the contrary, it is discussed by the (of course, non-medical) friends of the patient. The advice of some learned Moulvie or Pundit is then sought, and the family doctors or " hakims " are consulted, after which it is more than probable that the lady doctor will be told that her opinion and advice are quite wrong and she need not come again.

The difficulty of reaching the upper classes of India by the lady Medical Missionary is perhaps enhanced since the establishment of the " National Indian Association," for it has raised the question which now every native of India will have to ask himself, Will you have medical treatment for your wives, with religion or without ? The wealthy native, who prides himself on his adherence to the religion of his forefathers, will, in most cases, consider himself bound in honour to reply in favour of the latter, especially as any movement connected with or favoured by Government is in his eyes vastly superior to that which is the result of private or Missionary enterprise. At present, however, the number of lady doctors is so limited that the Medical Missionary will, from time to time, find herself summoned to the houses of the great. Occasionally she may find herself a guest in a Rajah's palace, with free access to the ladies of the family. Here, as opportunity offers, it will be her privilege to testify for Christ, perhaps not always by direct religious instruction but by trying to show them what Christ and Christianity really are ; sometimes Christian books will be accepted and read, friendships will be formed, and a bond of union established, which may be a means of influence in time to come.

Influence of the National Indian Association.

One word I would say as to the training required for Medical work in the Mission-field. The vocation is a high one. Let us aim high. Let us not lower our standard. All are not called to be Medical Missionaries. Let those who are grudge no time or labour to equip themselves for the great work they have undertaken ; they will be repaid in after-time. What hours of remorse and regret, and moments of terrible anxiety, as they see life ebbing away, and know that they could save it,—if they only knew how,—will be spared them ! Think what a female Medical Missionary's life is in India, and you will easily see what kind of equipment is needed for it. Her work is that of a general practitioner in England, with some differences. One is that she is the only female practitioner, probably within at least two hundred miles ; she stands alone. There can be no consultation over a difficult case, no one to call in for help in an emergency. Secondly, all kinds of cases are brought to her, which in England would only be trusted to a specialist ; either she must treat them, or send them away without hope of relief. Thirdly, she works in an enervating climate, where anxiety is ill borne, and health and spirits too readily break down under overstrain. It will not be difficult for you to answer the question for yourselves. Should the Medical Missionary's education be less or more thorough than that of the average Medical practitioner in England? I say from my own experience, emphatically,—more.

Thorough training required.

I would recommend in addition to the usual curriculum, qualifying for a diploma, a year given to the study of specialities, either in England or abroad, as opportunity offers ; but whether the extra year be taken or not, let no one undertake the difficult duties of a Medical Missionary who cannot bring to her work at least as much knowledge as is required from the ordinary English practitioner ; she will need much more. The difficulties which formerly lay in the way of women obtaining a full Medical education have

Study of special subjects.

now been removed. Shall we bring to the Lord and His work what costs us nothing? Women devote time and labour to entering the Medical profession for secular ends. Shall we say : " Anything will do for the Mission-field;" or shall we give ourselves with every power of mind and body we possess to the great work of giving Christ to the world? In no way can we better do this than by aiming to live His life among them, preaching the Gospel and healing everywhere. It is an encouraging fact, that of the sixty women, whose names are on the British Medical register, ten have given themselves to the work of Foreign Missions.

It is an important question—How can the Medical work of women be best utilised in the Mission-field? The number of qualified Medical women, willing to give themselves to Missionary work, is very limited. There are two courses open to them, *first*, to occupy large centres ; *second*, to act as pioneers in districts hitherto untouched. With regard to the former, the National Association is establishing female wards, and endeavouring to provide female Medical aid in most of the large cities. This movement makes it easier for Missionary Societies to concentrate their Medical works. They can *Utilising of female doctors.* choose a few stations and work them thoroughly, rather than aim to occupy a large number less efficiently. In the same way with regard to training. The Dufferin Association will, if it continues as it has begun, do much for the training of native nurses and midwives, and also of female hospital assistants. Why should not we have one Medical Missionary training college, with a hospital attached, and two or three lady doctors, the objects being to train native Christian young women of good character and education and Missionary spirit, as assistant Medical Missionaries ? I have only time to touch upon this subject, it is one for general discussion.

The second course open to Medical women in the Mission-field, applies especially to places not under British rule. In these there is often no satisfactory Medical provision of any kind, and it would be well if the female Medical department could be worked side by side with a *Zenana work in native states.* Medical Mission to the male population. All classes would thus be reached simultaneously, and the usefulness of both departments would be increased. As an instance of this, I might mention Cashmere, where a Medical woman has recently been sent to take charge of the female department, in connection with the long established Medical Mission there. Female Medical Missionaries are also much needed in China, and some have already taken up work there. The difficult work among Mohammedans, in Persia, might offer a promising field to Medical women wishing to act as pioneers, and doubtless there are many other openings of this description.

DISCUSSION.

Miss Cross (Free Church of Scotland Mission, Madras): Mr. Chairman, and friends,—I have only asked two minutes to lay before you two facts which I think no one else may be able to do. It has been my great privilege to visit India and reside there for five years in different parts. I know India from Cape Comorin to Delhi in many ways. On one occasion I was allowed to get into the female department of a prison, and I shall never forget during my life the sight I saw there of *Inside an Indian prison.* women condemned for life. I asked what was the chief crime for which those women were there, and the matron told me it was for the murder of their female children ; the fact being, as most of you know, they scarcely knew they were committing a crime.

In another large town I asked the permission of the English doctor to get into the Government hospital; and I shall never forget the gathering of poor Hindu women who were there considered as criminals, and yet you could hardly dare to say they were criminals, because they scarcely knew that it was a crime for which

they were shut up, and there was no sister to visit them, and yet there was a
crowd of poor women, many of them beautiful, intelligent-looking
women, some of whose hearts, no doubt, were very sad. Only once
had a native Christian been in that crowd. I just lay these two facts
before you, to show the terrible need there is for our Christian sisters going out
to India.

And a Government hospital.

Mrs. Ralph Emerson (Woman's Union Missionary Society of America):
I wish to say this, that the word "Union," in the title of our Society,
includes all denominations. The fact is, that in America every successful
Church has its own personal women's organisation for women's work,
and we rejoice in the children that have been born as it were to the
dear old mother Society. But I wanted more particularly to
give our testimony to the benefit of Medical training in our
Missionary work. We have found it invaluable in Calcutta,
in Cashmere, in Allahabad, and especially in Shanghai. We have physicians whose names perhaps are not unfamiliar to you. There is one
lady physician in Shanghai, who was educated in Philadelphia, and has
performed some of the most wonderful surgical operations known in
modern science. Her dispensary is opened at certain hours, and in the
interim between those hours the women are spoken to about their souls, and
they go forth with the seeds sown in their hearts. On Sundays the dispensary is closed, and then the physician takes charge of one of the Bible
classes in our Mission there.

Value of Medical training.

Mrs. L. R. Keister (Secretary, Woman's Missionary Association of the
United Brethren in Christ, U.S.A.): I need not make any apology for
speaking or for asking to have a word in this place. I have been
brought up in a Church where women and men are equally recognised
in the work of the Church. I just want to emphasise or ask a question with regard to Home work. Our hearts, ever since we have been
in Convention, have been stirred by the appeals of Missionaries from
foreign fields asking for more workers. We learn from the statistics
of the Churches, that two-thirds of the members of the Christian
Church are women. We learn from the papers of the different
organisations that but a handful of these women at home are
interested in this grand work of Foreign Missions. I want
to know how we are to get the women at home to interest
themselves in this work.

How to get the women interested.

These two facts—the want abroad, and the few women at home that are
interested—how shall we bring the two together? The money is in the Church ;
two cents a week and a prayer, or, as you would say, a penny a week and a prayer,
has accomplished all that has been done by the Missionary Societies. How are
we to get at the great number of women who are not yet interested ? In
the Christian home the woman has the first influence. Womanhood everywhere
is the source of life and influence, in heathen lands as well as at
home ; and nowhere more than at the family altar can a mother
impress upon the children that are committed to her care the importance of sending the Gospel to those who have it not. We can only reach
the women in the homes and in our Christian Churches, by bringing before them
these facts that Missionaries bring to us, and appealing to them to come out on
the Lord's side, because they have been redeemed and blood washed, and to
help to send this news to the millions of the earth. I came here to learn from
you how we are to do this, and I want when I go back to America to be able to

Woman's power for good.

tell the things that we have been told ought to be done in order to bring this subject before the women of our Churches.

Rev. B. T. Roberts (General Superintendent, Free Methodist Church of North America): I rejoice at the door that is opened for women's work in spreading the Gospel, and I want to say a word to try and open the door wider. My experience in America is like that of many from India. I find the women morally superior to the men; and, if so, I can *Moral* see no reason at all why they should not be permitted to preach *superiority of* as well as to labour in an inferior position. *women.*

My reasons for saying this are based on Scripture and on experience; and not to repeat what has already been said on the sixty-eighth Psalm, and Joel and Acts, we find in the sixteenth chapter of Romans, Paul sends his salutations to a great many women, and amongst others he sends them to "Andronica and Junia." Chrysostom, who understood the Greek language, was a Greek by birth and one of the brightest of scholars, says that Junia in that place is declared by the Apostle to be an Apostle. Our version is "of note among the Apostles," but he says Junia was an Apostle, and was a noted Apostle; and it seems to me that there is very strong ground for women to take an advanced place in spreading the Gospel in heathen lands as well as at home. And so, in experience, we find that some of the most useful labourers in America and in England have been women.

Mrs. Mary C. Nind (Woman's Foreign Missionary Society of the Methodist Episcopal Church, U.S.A.): I am here to represent the one hundred and thirty-five thousand women connected with the Methodist Episcopal Church of the United States of America; and as my first inspiration to Missionary labour was in Exeter Hall, being born within six miles of it,—in which I have heard a Moffat, a Medhurst, a Morrison, a Williams, and many others, I feel the spirit of those glorious men falling on me this morning. I am here simply to say, in the few minutes allotted to me, a word on behalf of the Medical Missions connected with the Methodist Episcopal Church of America. We have the honour of having *American* sent out the first woman Missionary to Asia, Doctor Clara *women first in* Swayne, who went from Benhampton, New York, and opened *field.* her wonderful Mission in India, where God gave her thousands of patients and very many precious souls. She was called from that work to be the private physician to an Indian Rajah. God has marvellously blessed her; and just before I took my steamer I grasped her hand and thanked God He had permitted her to come home for a little rest.

Then God permitted us to open the work in Tien-tsin. The Viceroy's wife being alarmingly ill God moved him to send for our Dr. Leonora Howard, stationed at Pekin. He sent down his royal yacht and brought her to the palace. God blessed her labours; the Viceroy's wife was restored, and she gave one thousand dollars to our Missionary work, and then opened a hospital for the high-class women of Tien-tsin; and then our brave *Women in* Missionary Society moved up; and these Medical Missions opened *Tien-tsin.* the work in Tien-tsin for both our Boards. At Fuh-chow we have a hospital, where we are training Missionary Medical students. God has sent one to our country, who is now being educated at Delaware, Ohio,—the daughter of one of our presiding elders—a consecrated young woman. She will go back when she has finished her Medical course to be a Medical Missionary. Now we are needing more Medical Missionaries; and now I am going to follow the example of my beloved sister from America, and say, Come over, *A plea for* and help us. I want a Medical Missionary to-day for Singapore; I *more helpers.* want another for Hyderabad; I want two for Fuh-chow, and if there is a good

Englishwoman we would just as soon have her as an American woman. Now I praise God for all that He has done for our Medical work. We are training our Medical Missionaries in Agra, in Cawnpore, and other stations, and we are seeking to reinforce from native agency the work which our women do not follow up as they ought to do from these home fields. I praise God for all this work; it is going to increase and multiply, and thousands and tens of thousands of souls in time and eternity will bless God for Medical Missions.

Rev. J. I. Pickford (C.M.S., from Colombo): Mr. Chairman,—I feel very nervous at speaking at a meeting of this kind; but I do want, if possible, to create a little interest in the Island of Ceylon. It is nearly ten years since I went out, and I was there just nine years. I returned a little while ago, and the reason why I mention it is this: We *Women needed in Ceylon.* have no lady Missionaries entirely devoted to the work there. We have Missionaries' wives, who give all the time they can; but, as Miss Rainy said they cannot give the time properly that a lady ought to do to Missionary work: they have their own households, and in some cases they have children, to attend to; it is altogether impossible for them to give regular and systematic attention to Mission work.

Now why is it so necessary, especially in Ceylon?—and I suppose it is the same all over the world? It is this. We receive girls into the boarding schools; *Work in schools.* they come and stay five or six years; in some cases they are daughters of Christian people, in some cases they are not; we have heathen as well as Christian children in our boarding schools, which is a great surprise to some of our friends in India. They come without our asking any questions about caste, or anything of that kind; they stay with us six or seven years, and then go out again, and then we lose sight of them. We cannot follow them up. And especially now do we want lady Missionaries, because we have day schools where Mohammedan girls are taught; they come to us when they are quite little dots, four or five years old; as soon as they can run about they are brought to the day schools; they are taught by a woman four or five years, and then we lose sight of them. We have tried to do something in the way of ladies' work, and I will tell you how very encouraging it is. We find in many places that there are copies of the Scriptures in Mohammedan houses, we *Work in homes.* find the children retaining the Scripture which they learnt in the schools, and we find very often that ladies are admitted and welcomed. Oh, dear friends, I would press upon the Missionary Societies here to do a great deal more for this work than they have done in the past.

Rev. H. Williams (C.M.S., from Bengal): It is my purpose to speak of one section of the work, and of one portion of the Indian Empire. The *Female evangelists.* part I wish to speak of is the evangelisation work that may be done by women in the Bengal villages. We are very sorry so little has been made of evangelisation work by the women in this morning's meeting—that so little reference has been made to it. I would just bring before you what our position is. I mean we men Missionaries, when we get into the Bengal villages. We go there: we have the men sitting before us, listening to us, arguing with us, being influenced by our preaching, but they go off into their villages, and the women are practically untouched by our teaching and uninfluenced.

In our work of preaching in the villages you may see a little gathering of women standing away off behind the men, or behind a hedge, or a wall, but practically we can hardly bring the Gospel to them to influence them in any degree, and then it goes on still further—a man is influenced, is baptised—and this has occurred once and again in my Missionary experience in Bengal—men ctually relapsing into Mohammedanism because their wives cannot be brought into the Christian Church with them.

I might say the two works ought always to go together; when men go to preach to the men, there ought to be a company of Christian women preaching to the women, because, unless you have that we are just in the position of fighting with one hand tied.

I am sure if you were to read the testimonies of your Zenana Missionaries, from Bengal, on the subject, you would find how the whole country is open for them; how they may go into the villages, and how they may gather these poor village women around them and preach to them. Of course Zenana work has many phases—teaching in the schools, and teaching in the houses of rich Hindus; but I think the work that needs the most to be developed, is the Village work. work of preaching to the poor Bengali village women, who are as much debarred from our influence as the rich wives of those who have Zenanas. As I say, these village women are kept altogether away from our preaching, and we want an army of English women to go out and do that work, which I say is easy to be done, because they are received kindly, and in the most friendly spirit wherever they go in these Bengali villages.

Rev. L. Dahle (Secretary, Norwegian Missionary Society): Dear Christian friends,—As I have come a long way, from Norway, with the special purpose of learning something about Women's Missionary work, I cannot abstain from expressing my great pleasure at the present meeting. I am sorry I am not one of those who can speak a word of guidance or of information with regard to the question before us. I am In want of information. one of those who want guidance and want information, and have come here just to get it, and I shall be thankful for any information I can get, or for any reference to sources of information. But would you just allow me in return for the pleasure and the information I have had, to state in a few words the position of this question in my native country at the present moment? When I, a few weeks ago, after nearly half a life spent in Madagascar, came back to Norway, I was met by my foreign secretary with a very startling remark. He said to me, "I tell you, you will have to face quite a new question in our Mission now." I Growing interest said, "What is that?" "Why," he said, "I believe that of Norwegian about half of the young Christian women in our country are women. ready to go into the Mission field;" and I tell you, friends, that I felt just like Peter and his colleagues in the boat when they had got all their fish in it, and they felt as though the boat was going to sink under their feet through the abundance of God's blessing; but then I remembered that the boat did not sink, because He was on board from whom the gift had come, and He would steer it to the safe shore; and so He will now. Now the position of women in the Missionary field up to this time in Norway has been that of collecting the money chiefly, as no doubt it has been in other countries very much the same. They have been very diligent in doing that work, and very patient—more so than the men. They have hundreds of Women's Associations, and they have done an immense amount of good. It has been a very great boon to the women themselves, and has helped to make them feel that they are A blessing to themselves. one great sisterhood; but now they have come to the front and long to do more. They have already a special paper for Missionary work amongst women, edited by a lady, and they have several female teachers out in the Mission-field. But presently our great assembly that meets every third year will have to deal with these questions, just in a fortnight from hence, and I shall go directly from this Conference to the meeting which is to deal with the question—" What we can do to promote Women's Missionary work among the heathen ? "   I am sure that we shall have to go through a battle with queries when we shall deal with this great work in our Assembly.   You Englishmen and Englishwomen have done infinitely

Norwegian queries, English energy. more than we in Missionary work, but there is one point in which I believe we can beat you, and that is in our ability in putting queries.   You go in for another method.   You rush into the work—sometimes very rashly it seems to me—but then you have a knack of proving your case.   You say to us, "Whilst you are discussing the possibility of converting the world we will go and do it, and then we will show you the accomplished fact to prove the possibility of doing it." That is good sound logic—a logic of facts.   I only wish, Christian friends, that God would give us an abundance of your practical sense, of your energy, of your sanctified common sense, and that He will give you a little share of our queries, and that He will help us to put in both the queries and actions at the right place, and give us His blessing.

Rev. W. Stevenson (Secretary, Free Church of Scotland Ladies' Society for Female Education): Mr. Chairman, and Christian friends,— There are just two things I want to say; the first is with reference to the relation of the Home Organisation for the two sides of the work.   Now, it seems to me that the ideal relation is just that of the marriage state. We do not want the men and the women to be confounded or identified,

Relation of men's and women's Missions. but we want them to do their own work in the very closest alliance that is possible; we want, not that they should stand quite apart from each other, but that while there is a woman's organisation and a man's organisation, where the work in the Mission-field has to be divided, we desire that they should have these separate agencies in as close alliance as is possible without the two being confounded or entirely identified with each other.   I think if anyone has anything to say further with reference to that question it ought be said. This is one of the meetings in which we are assembled for Conference on questions where there is a difference of opinion, and if anyone has difficulties with respect to the organisations, I think they ought to be spoken out now.

The second thing I want to say is this;—sometimes people are very much confused about India when they hear such different statements made with reference apparently to the same thing.   For example, you hear sometimes that it is impossible for men to get at the women at all, and then again you hear that male Missionaries can find very large audiences of women without any difficulty.   You have the Mohammedans and you have the Hindus, and generally people think that is all; that when you take away the Mohammedans, all the rest of the population,—barring

Explanation of contradictory statements. the few Eurasians, Parsis, and so on,—are Hindus; but the truth is that there is a great section of the population which is not Mohammedan, and not Hindu, although it runs very close to the latter,—I mean the large population of what are called the aboriginal races, such as Santhals, and other tribes like them.   Now, these are very often confounded with the Hindus, and they lie very close to them, and in some places it is very difficult indeed to draw a line of distinction between them; but you will never understand Mission work in India, and the necessity for a great variety of Mission work in India, unless you draw a clear distinction between Hindus proper,—who are bound up in the caste system, whose women are behind the purdah, who are inaccessible to the ordinary mode of Missionary operation,—and those aboriginal races, who, although in some cases they may claim a sort of caste, are really quite open to the ordinary public means of proclaiming the Gospel. If you keep that distinction in mind it will save a very great deal of confusion and avoid a great many of the objections which are often brought to various kinds of Mission work.

Where you have the women behind the purdah you can easily understand how utterly impossible it is to reach those women, except by calling in those departments of Women's Foreign Mission operations alongside of, and *pari passu* with the work carried on amongst the men, and this is the point which Christian women have really to look at. The work amongst the men,—I now speak of the Hindus proper,—has been going on for more than fifty years, and a very large class of the men have been reached by Christian influences, while their women have been untouched. The work amongst the women is at least a generation behind that amongst the men. If the work is to go forward, and if we are to reap the results,—even of the work amongst the men,—we must not only be content to do a little work amongst the women, but we must bring it alongside the other half of the work.

Mrs. Moses Smith (President, Woman's Board of Missions of the Interior, U.S.A.): Mr. Chairman, and Christian friends,—I take it that no nation ever rises higher than its mothers. As are the mothers of a nation, such is the nation. This fact must be taken together with the other simple fact, that at least two-thirds of the mothers of the world are practically among the secluded women of the world, and the other very essential point that only Christianity elevates a nation. It is only Christianity that has made England and America what they are; and we see to-day that the most essential feature of the evangelisation of the world is our Women's Missionary work, the Mission of women to women in the homes, to the mothers, and to the little children. I regard it as an essential factor in the work, both for the inspiration of those going abroad, and for the aid of those who have the equally difficult part to do to interest the Christian women of our Churches in giving their money to this cause that we should get them to comprehend the scope and the power of woman's work in evangelising the world. God has never before placed in the hand of any human agency the power which to-day is in the hands of Christian women.

It is truly womanly work, not taking us out of our sphere as mothers, and wives, and sisters, but binding us even more closely to the home consecration, that those in heathen lands may have the blessings that we have. One other point. One lady has spoken as to the means of awakening interest amongst the women of our Churches at home. That is a most essential matter. Let me throw out one suggestion. I believe we have not enough taken into our work the study of the Bible. Let us go to the people with—"Thus saith the Lord," for every point that we would make. We must make them familiar with Scripture—from Genesis to Revelation—this work is commanded; it is the essential work, "Go, disciple all nations, as the Father has sent Me." "As He has sent Me,"—remember, through poverty, through childhood, through misunderstanding, through Gethsemane and the Cross—"so send I you." I throw these thoughts out simply that we may perhaps gather from them an inspiration that we may give to others, and so brighten our work. I am glad to bring the greetings of the Board which I represent with a good hearty English hand shake.

Mrs. G. Stott (China Inland Mission): Eighteen years ago it was my privilege to take the Gospel to the heathen in the cities of China, and it was no small concern to know just how to put the truth of our glorious Gospel before them, that the dark heathen mind might readily comprehend what we wanted to teach. For a long time the course that seemed to be the most feasible was to give a sketch of what God had done, first of all in the creation of men, and of His dealings with men from the creation downwards, both without the law and under the law, and by easy stages to bring them to His having sent His only-begotten Son to live and die for us. But I was greatly disappointed in this method of reaching the heathen; being pioneers we had no Senior Missionary of whom to ask advice, and we were thrown upon God to find out just how to present the truth so that the hearts of the people might be touched. We did not want to touch their intellect, we did not want to manufacture Christians. We wanted to have souls born again for the glory and honour of our Master. We did not know just how to do it, until one day outside the city, at a village some little distance away, I was surrounded by a group of women, eagerly listening to what I should say. I was possessed with such a strong yearning for their souls that I forgot my former plan of addressing them, and I spoke something like this— "Dear friends, have you ever heard of heaven and hell?" They answered "Oh! yes, we know of heaven and hell"—that is, they knew the words. I said, "Well, I shall not speak of hell, it is not worth talking about; but let us talk a little while about heaven."

How not to preach to heathen.

I began picturing to them heaven and its freedom from sin, which they did not very much understand, because they had not yet felt the burden of sin, but I spoke of its freedom from care, and sorrowing and suffering of all kinds, and then their hearts were touched; every face was eagerly turned towards me, and then stopping short, I said: "Before you may enter that lovely place one thing is necessary." "What is that?" said one and another. "What is that?" Oh, that was the question I had so often longed to hear! "How can we get into that place?" and so their very hearts being touched by the power of God, I lifted up before them God's Middleman, which they can so easily understand. I pictured God's love for them and told them that in His desire for their salvation He sent His own blessed Son to be the middleman, whereby we could through Him enter into that glorious land. From that time till now, my dear friends, I have always begun just where I ended before, at the Cross of Christ. We have prayed, and proved very abundantly that that Cross is God's power unto salvation, and we have proved the truth of Christ's own words, "And I, if I be lifted up, will draw all men unto Me."

A chord touched.

There was an old woman who had come from her home twelve miles off to visit her daughter, and for the first time she saw a foreign woman and heard the strange things she had to tell. She went back to her own village and repeated to her neighbours what she had seen and heard. She said, "I saw the foreign woman there. What do you think she said?" and she told what I had said, though very imperfectly; and the question came from one and another, "And how did she say that we could enter there?" "Oh, I forgot; she said something about a middleman, but I forget just what;" and then one said,

Happy results.

"Will you take me to that place?—I want to hear more—I never heard anything like that;" and another followed and said, "I would like to go and hear more." The result was, not very long afterwards, that old woman and two or three others came twelve miles just to hear how they could be saved through God's Middleman. That old woman and others of her family are now Christians. Oh, dear friends, do let us hold up Christ who is God's power unto salvation to every one that believes!

Dr. Underhill closed the meeting with prayer.

MEETINGS OF MEMBERS IN SECTION.

WOMEN'S WORK IN THE MISSION-FIELD.

(2) THE WORK.

(a) Female Missionaries in school work.

(b) Female Missionaries as Zenana teachers and workers among women. Should secular instruction ever be given in homes by the Missionary Agent without Bible teaching?

(c) Training schools and homes for native female teachers and Bible women.

(d) The importance of working through established organisations in order to secure economy and avoid imposture.

(*Thursday morning, June 14th, in the Large Hall.*)*

Rev. Professor MacLaren, D.D. (Toronto, Canada), in the chair.
Acting Secretary, **Mr. C. E. Chapman.**

Rev. Dr. Parsons (of Toronto) offered prayer.

PAPER.

1. By the Rev. J. N. Murdock, D.D. (Secretary, American Baptist Missionary Union).

Woman's work in the Foreign Field.

Passing over the Bible account of the many women who were honoured to be fellow-workers with God, in carrying out His great purposes of mercy, in both Old and New Testament times, who have been repeatedly referred to in previous Papers, I now call attention to the records of Modern Missions which have been made illustrious by deeds of Christian women. No finer exemplification of Christian courage, endurance, patience, faith, and hope can be

---

* This meeting, like the preceding one, and for the same reason, was also adjourned from the Annexe to the Large Hall.

found in the annals of the Christian ages than is shown by the records of Christian women connected with modern Missionary Societies.

Woman's work in the Foreign Mission-field has been varied and most important. The records of the different Evangelical Missions will show what it has been ; a study of the New Testament will show what it ought to be. It is safe to say that in spirit and general form the work of women in the Missions abroad ought to be like that of devout and consecrated women at home, with only such variations as the changed conditions may render necessary. The work should be that of help to the men who have been sent out to make Christ known to the heathen. It should be labour for Christ, labour in the Gospel, and labour in co-operation with those who have been especially put in charge of the Gospel.

Woman's work abroad like that at home.

Assuming then that this work of women must be evangelical and co-operative, we may say that one important branch of it must be that of imparting instruction in Mission schools. In the legitimate school work of Evangelical Missions it may be justly claimed that women have taken a leading part. Women are the born teachers of the race. During all the earlier years of life children are under their forming hands. Their quick apprehension, their power of nice discrimination, their gentleness of spirit and winsomeness of manner, their plodding and reiterative patience combine to make them the wisest and most effective teachers of the young.

As teachers of youth.

It is no disparagement of woman's fitness for other departments of Christian work, to say that the Mission schools must always absorb the attention of a very large proportion of Female Missionaries. And certainly it is doubtful if any other sphere of labour bears the promise of results so large and enduring as the Christian school, which finds its beneficiaries most plastic and tractable, in whose natures the impression easiest made sinks deepest and lasts longest. It is the shaping of the soft clay with the gentlest pressure of the hand, compared with the hammering and chiselling of adamant into forms still imperfect and stony. If the school be, in fact, a school of Christ, it must produce its fruit in a culture which is of the highest form and the most enduring character.

In saying all this I would not be understood as justifying formal attempts to gather large schools of heathen children, housing, supporting and teaching them, with the moral certainty that, when their course of study is over, they will return to their heathen associations and customs. The schools of which I speak are those established in the new Christian communities for the education of the children of Christian households ; and where children of heathen homes and associations are received only on condition that they shall receive Christian instruction, and pay a proper fee for the benefit received.

Another form of service appropriate for woman in the foreign

field is a properly conditioned medical work. The restoring and
saving purpose of the Gospel embraces the whole man.
Medical work. Its relieving and comforting function regards the body
as well as the soul. Christ healed disease at the same time that
He forgave sin. And only he preaches a whole Gospel who presents
and illustrates its humane aspects toward physical infirmity and
suffering. And "woman's work for woman" is a phrase which
receives its peculiar and fullest significance when it is used to denote
the remedial treatment of woman by woman. It is a great and good
thing for women who go out to foreign lands as Missionaries to be
qualified to relieve their sisters from the horrors of medical superstition. A recital of the cruel torture inflicted on helpless women
under circumstances when they need the kindest consideration; a
torture often exceeding the pangs through which every member of
the race is ushered into life, were enough to curdle the blood of the
hearer. And so of the treatment of fever and delirium, and other
disorders in which a false system of religion converts what ought to
be the gentlest ministries into revolting cruelty. The woman who
can medicate the body as well as instruct the mind, who can heal the
sick as well as lead the wayward, will render a double service, and
win the suffering and heavy-laden to receive the balm of Gilead,
and the offices of the Great Physician.

But there are other departments of woman's work for woman
which come closer to the heart of Missions. One of these, in which her
agency is, and must be in the present condition of things, exclusive,
Zenana work. consists in visiting Hindu homes—if such a prison-like
seclusion deserves the name of home—for the purpose of
religious instruction. What has been known as Zenana work
has long been justly esteemed as a most valuable agency, and
the only one by which Christian Missionaries could gain access
to the caste women of India, the mothers and early teachers of
the multitude of Hindu youth. There can be no doubt that the
seed thus sown will spring up and bear fruit after many days.
How many thus reached and taught the way of life, receive the
truth into sincere hearts, may not be known to the present
generation. The traditional and utter subjection of the women
of India to their husbands, must, of necessity, prevent an open
confession of Christ by them; but when the final upheaval of the
foundations of Hinduism shall come, the potent work of the
Zenana Missionaries will appear in the preparation of those readiest
to be moved by the story of the Cross, and most open to receive the
pardon purchased by its exalted Victim.

But recently another form of work for a class of the caste
women of India, has been projected and actually begun, which
Schools for promises good results. Homes and schools of Christian
child-widows. instruction have actually been established for the enlightenment of caste women. There are, in the presidency of
Madras, several schools for this class, to which women, free to

do so, readily resort for instruction in Christian truth. The condition of the class of caste women, known as child-widows, has been regarded as the most helpless and abject in the whole range of woman's wrongs. These despised, maltreated, and helpless girls are only too ready to embrace the kindly influences of a Christian culture ; and the experiment, already made, gives promise of abundant blessings to them. We may well regard this as an opening for the advancement of the women of India, second only to the suppression of the cruel Suttee. The rescue of thousands of these child-widows from this inhuman custom, or the long lingering disgrace and oppression of those who survive the husband's departure, is, in itself, an attainment of the highest philanthropy. But if to this social deliverance we add the supplanting of a heathen despair by a Christian hope, we shall be able to estimate the richness of the blessing which awaits the women of India, through the agency just set on foot, when it shall be more generally adopted by Missionaries. This is a work worthy of woman's tender sympathies and glowing zeal.

Another form of woman's work in the Mission-field is the training and direction of a class of workers known as Bible women. This has already become a fruitful feature of womanly Training of enterprise. These women are selected for the qualities Bible women. they have displayed, and are taught to read the Bible and expound its vital truth to others; and as soon as they exhibit the necessary aptness to teach, they are sent forth into surrounding towns and villages, to impart the truths of the Gospel to the women and children, with a view of leading them to a saving knowledge of Christ. This phase of Evangelical labour has now become common in nearly all Evangelical Mission-fields. It has proved very successful, and it may not inaptly be regarded as an exemplification of that prophetic statement in the Psalms, which the Canterbury revisers have correctly rendered : "The Lord giveth the word, the women that publish the tidings are a great host."

Beyond this the plan of establishing itineraries of female workers for evangelistic purposes, is beginning to be more fully carried out. It is now no uncommon thing for single women, going in Female companies of two or more, to visit the regions around itinerants. some central station, telling the glad tidings to all who will hear their word ; and some of us can recall instances of the conversion of men through such labours. And doubtless this form of woman's work will become more general, and so more successful, as facilities for it shall open, and as experience may justify it. Why may not women now be sent on the same errand on which the angel at the sepulchre sent the astonished Mary of Magdala? It is well known that some of the most effective workers in the evangelistic movement of our time are women. And why may we not expect that well instructed, deeply experienced, and fully consecrated women, will yet reap large harvests of souls, renewed and sanctified by their proclamation of the glad tidings?

Moreover, the progress of Missions has been more than once illustrated by instances of the establishment of large and fruitful An exemplary Mission stations by women. One of the most successful female worker. stations in the Burman department of our own Missions in Burmah was opened by a woman, and has been led up to be one of the most prosperous and numerous Burman churches in the world, under the sole supervision of its founder.* Yet she pronounces no public discourses and performs no ecclesiastical functions. She teaches the women and the men in all that concerns Christian truth and Church organisation. She selects, indoctrinates, and encourages the native men for evangelistic service. She guides the church in the appointment of its pastor, instructs him in Bible truth, pastoral theology, including homiletical training, and supervises all the work of the station. She keeps an eye on the school at the station, and is sure to detect aptitude for teaching in any of the pupils, and sends them out to teach in the village schools. She has established zayat preaching, organised a circulating library, and keeps up a system of Bible and tract distribution throughout the district. She has encountered malcontents and awakened opposition in a few instances; but in every case her perfect mastery of herself, her good judgment, equable temperament, her firmness joined with kindness, her ready tact and her Christian spirit have brought her through in triumph. No jar has up to this time produced any violent change, nor has any impediment resulted in anything more than a temporary check to the prosperity of the Mission. Her greatest difficulty with her people has resulted from her persistent refusal to baptise her converts and to solemnise their marriages.

And yet so delicate is this woman's sense of the proprieties of her sex, that you could scarcely induce her to stand on a public platform and face a mixed audience, even though she might not be called upon to speak. A real overseer and leader of a numerous Christian flock, she does her work mostly in private, satisfied if she can only see her teachings reproduced in the public sermons and lectures of her native helpers, and bearing fruit in the lives of her people. And unless we misread the signs of the times examples of this kind will multiply, and greatly add to the increase of Missionary force and efficiency. At first the wish would sometimes arise that this woman were a man, but that wish long since was resolved into the prayer that God will give us more men and women too, of kindred spirit and equal faculty. "The tools to him who can use them," applies to women as well as to men. It seems that the Lord is a respecter neither of persons nor of sexes. He works by whom He will to the confounding of human customs and prejudices.

I have thus spoken of the work of women in the Mission-field; and here perhaps I might pause as having traversed the proper

* Mrs. Murilla B. Ingalls, of Thonzé, Burmah.

limits of the subject assigned me. But the treatment of the topic would be essentially defective without some more specific reference to the agents by whom this work is to be performed, and the relation sustained by them to the general organisations engaged in Missions among heathen races. Nearly all **Modern movements an extension of old plans.** branches of the work above outlined might be carried on to a limited extent by the wives of Missionaries. In fact, until within a comparatively recent period, all this work was really under the charge of Missionaries' wives, who were in some instances assisted by unmarried ladies sent out for the purpose by the Missionary Boards. The older American Societies began to send out such helpers within a very few years after their formation ; and the same thing is doubtless true of the English Boards. The present plan of sending unmarried women to the Mission-fields, therefore, is not new in substance. All the novelty consists in the increase of the number of this kind of agents, and the creation of organisations for their support. Single women have been employed in the Missions from the beginning, and the early annals of all the great Societies have been adorned by the names and enriched by the deeds of these devoted workers. All that is new in the present development of women's work in Missions consists in the more general awakening of women in the home field to the importance of the work, and in the measures taken to increase the number of labourers abroad. With the proper work of the women's organisations in the home field this Paper has nothing to do, **Unity in Male and Female Missions.** except as these Societies may tend to modify the relations of their agents to the general policy of the original Societies, composed as they were, and as they ought to be, of the men and women of the Churches in the home land. May I be permitted to remark in passing that it will be a dark day for Missions when our Missionary organisations shall become divided on the line of sex, and people shall begin to talk of "Men's Missionary Societies" and "Women's Missionary Societies" as separate factors in the one great work, whose essential condition is that it is neither male nor female, but one—indivisibly, indistinguishably one—in Christ Jesus for the renovation of our common humanity. The day that sees them separate will see them rivals, and where then will be the unity of purpose and spirit so necessary to insure efficiency and success. Let the noble Women's Societies be helpers at home of the Parent Societies, as those who are supported by their funds are helpers of the Missionaries in charge of Mission Stations abroad—always co-operative, but never co-ordinate.

And this brings us to the consideration of the true relations of the single women employed in the foreign field to the general work of the Missions. They ought to receive their appointment **Relation of female agents to Parent Society.** from the Board of the Parent Society, on the recommendation of the Woman's Board, and to go out amenable to the regulations and authority of the former in all the forms and details of their work. The single women, for instance, who labour in connection with the London Missionary Society, should receive their appointment from that Society, the funds for their support should reach them through its treasury, and all that they do in the Mission should be in the line of its general policy, and be acceptable to the Missionaries in charge of their respective stations. Not indeed that they should be in any sense underlings, or that they should move at the beck of their brethren; but that they should be subordinate to rules grounded in reason, tested by experience, and designed to secure harmony in counsel and effectiveness in action. This general conformity to rule need not and should not interfere with the exercise of freedom in methods, nor with the unhampered play of personal faculty in the attainment of the desired ends. While policies should be settled in tolerably well defined lines, there may be a wide range in the choice of expedients for their accomplishment. But whatever freedom may be accorded for the exercise of personal aptitudes, and whatever allowance may be made for personal idiosyncrasies, it ought to be accepted from the start that all female agents must abide by the rules and be governed by the policy prescribed for all other Missionaries. And to secure this end there must be a single source of appeal in cases of difference among Missionaries, and that must be to the General Society.

Moreover, while it must be accepted as the duty of single ladies to be helpful in all departments of the work, it ought to be expected Non-interference. of them that they will carefully abstain from any interference with matters not specially committed to their hands. It would be remarkable if no instance should ever occur in which the discipline adopted by the Missionary in charge of a station towards individuals or Churches, should seem to a looker-on to be strange or injurious. Natives who feel aggrieved by the decisions of the Missionary will often seek the interposition of his associates. Such interference, however sought or recommended, is more likely to widen breaches than to heal them. One must needs have a very perfect knowledge of the case to form an accurate judgment as to its merits, or, what is more, to justify anything like interference with it. Nothing is more to be deprecated in Mission-work among ignorant people than the well-meant but ill-timed mediation of otherwise efficient helpers with matters for whose wisdom or folly, justice or injustice, they are in no sense responsible. There is no sphere of Christian work in which it is so important for every Christian worker to be so utterly absorbed in his own duties as to forbid his mixing with the affairs of others. There may be cases, indeed, which will justify careful inquiry, and even call for loving and faithful remonstrance; but this is a different thing from those self-prompted intermediary efforts which are quite as likely to offend both parties as to reconcile them to each other. And when kind counsel and admonition fail to correct seeming errors, the next appeal should be to those whose advice will be likely to carry more weight, —that is, to the Home authorities—instead of writing to friends at home, who may make an incautious, but in no sense helpful use, of the information thus imparted. It often happens that Missionary Boards receive their first knowledge of misunderstandings in the Mission-field through the private correspondence of Missionaries who ought to have said nothing, or said it to those who might have applied the needed corrective.

Woman's work in the foreign field must be careful to recognise the headship of man in ordering the affairs of the kingdom of God. We must not allow the major vote of the better sex, nor *Man's headship* the ability and efficiency of so many of our female helpers, *in Missions.* nor even the exceptional faculty for leadership and organisation which some of them have displayed in their work, to discredit the natural and predestined headship of man in Missions, as well as in the Church of God : " Adam was first formed, then Eve," and " the head of the woman is the man." This order of creation has not been changed by Redemption, and we must conform all our plans and policies for the uplifting of the race through the power of the Gospel to this Divine ordinance. We may recognise with gratitude to God all that women have done in the past, and all they are now doing for the spread of the glad tidings ; but the work will not be done till men everywhere gird themselves for the task, and lead on to the final conflict with the powers of darkness, and to the crowning conquest of Him who is to subdue all enemies under His feet. Woman may not assume, nor may man shirk, the duty of leadership in the great enterprise of bringing the world to the feet of our Immanuel. The work of the new Societies is vastly inspiring and otherwise helpful ; but they will only yield their richest results when they follow in the train, and supplement the agencies, of those Societies which represent the whole company of the Redeemed, without regard to sex, race, or condition.

And it must also be accepted in all the Missions and by all the Missionaries that the providential help which the new organisations and their representatives bring to them, are to be assigned a place in the ranks of a mobilised Church, which is marching under the banner of the Cross to the conquest of the world. The *All under a* welcome of the new labourers to the field must be *mobilised* prompt and hearty, and the division of labour with *Church.* them should be open and ungrudging. Give widest scope to their powers and a broader field for their cultivation. Their work must overleap the bounds which, as I think, have been mistakenly fixed for it. Let it be no longer " Woman's work for Woman," but rather Woman's work for Mankind. Nay, let it be lifted to a still higher strain of endeavour, and become Woman's work for Christ. Let them labour to the supreme end, " that His way may be known in the earth, and His saving health among all nations." And so let the one work of the Redeemed Church go on by all agencies and instrumentalities till the "seventh angel shall sound, and great voices in heaven shall proclaim that the kingdom of this world has become the kingdom of our Lord and His Christ; and He shall reign for ever and ever."

PAPER.

2. By Miss Abbie B. Child (Secretary, Woman's Board of Missions, A.B.C.F.M.).

*Woman's Work in the Mission-field.**

Woman's work in the Mission-field may be considered in five aspects :—I. Its necessity ; II. Its aims ; III. Its methods; IV. Its results; V. The present demands, and the obligations they impose on Christian women.

I. Its Necessity.

The necessity of woman's work in the Mission-field is shown (1) by the condition and needs of women in heathen lands · (2) by their power in the family; (3) by the fact that their elevation must be brought about mainly through the efforts of Christian women.

To give a complete idea of the condition of women in lands without the pure Gospel would necessitate a long and pitiful story, Woman's position and attitude. and one too well known to need repetition here. . . . Most of these women accept their lot with a dulness and contented apathy that proves one of the greatest obstacles to Missionary work among them, but to many who have roused to a sense of their burdens they have become intolerable. This is specially true in India, where, we are told, some of the prisons are filled with husband murderers, and the graves with suicides. A prayer offered by a pupil in a Mission school in India expresses the soul-longings of many of these women.

She says, "O Lord, hear my prayer. For ages dark ignorance has brooded over our minds and spirits, like a cloud of dust it rises and wraps us round; and we are like prisoners in an old and mouldering house, choked and buried in the dust of custom, and we have no strength to get out. Bruised and beaten we are like the dry husks of the sugar-cane when the sweet juice has been extracted. Criminals confined in jails are happier than we, for they know something of Thy world. They were not born in prison, but we have not for one day, no, not even in our dreams, seen Thy world, and what we have not seen we cannot imagine. To us it is nothing but a name ; and not having seen Thy world we cannot know Thee, its Maker. We have been born in this jail ; we have died here, and are dying. O God of mercies, our prayer to Thee is this, that the curse may be removed from the women of India."

If work among the women be an important part of Missionary effort, what is the best way for it to be done—in the ordinary lines of labour, or

* We regret exceedingly the necessity for many omissions in this able paper ; but its length, like that of many others, exceeded our limits. Hence also the need for smaller type to save space, while giving as much as possible.—Editor.

ʜpecially by women ? The barrier that exists between the sexes in heathen lands is well known. A few women may gather about the Missionary preacher in the bazaars, a few may wander into a Christian chapel, but it is very seldom that one of the sterner *Many reached only by women.* sex can be a welcome visitor in their homes, or that there can ever be any freedom of intercourse between the teacher and the taught. A Missionary, who has spent many years in China, affirms that Missionaries might labouɪ thirty years in a place, and the women would never hear of Jesus. We must have female agency.

Another writes :—" Frequently when riding on the back of an elephant through the narrow streets of some city in India, I have had glimpses of the females of the shopkeepers' families, who occupied the upper rooms of the houses. where windows opened upon galleries overhanging the streets. My elephant lifted me to a level with this second story, and as the animal's tread was noiseless, the ladies could not be aware of my approach until my profane eyes were looking directly into their sitting or eating room. Instantly would be heard a loud scream, and the very first act would be to hide their face. Sometimes the doors and the windows would be closed with a slam and a curse ; sometimes the ready veil would be hastily drawn down, or the frightened creatures would throw themselves flat on the floor of the apartment and cover their heads with their chuddars until the infidel had passed.''

So strong is this prejudice, founded on the strongest principles of a woman's nature, fostered by the custom of centuries and the sacred tenets of her religion. many of them would rather die than permit the sanctity of the veil to be violated Is it not inevitable that it should prove a most formidable obstacle to the approach of any but those of her own sex ? In view of what has been said, remembering also that the women and children comprise two-thirds of the population of heathendom, is not woman's work in the Mission-field a necessity ?

II. Its Aims.

The aim of this woman's work we conceive to be *in heathen lands*—to be used as an instrument in the hands of our Lord, in bringing the women into His kingdom, in the creation of Christian mothers, and as a consequence Christian homes, and in the providing a Christian education for their daughters. To our fathers and brothers belong the task of opening the way for the Gospel, to make straight in the desert a highway for our God, to strike vigorous blows at the brains of heathendom, to superintend large educational and evangelistic enterprises, to plant the standard of the Cross and win many to its side. To woman belongs the quiet, patient labour in the homes of the people, striving to win the hearts of the wives and mothers, to gain the love of the children, first to herself *Woman's sphere in the Field.* and then for the Master whom she serves. While the men strike heavy blows at the citadel, women try to undermine the stronghold of heathendom, all working and waiting for the day when our God shall give the victory.

In Christian lands the aim of woman's work is to secure, equip, and send out single women to the various Mission-fields, to supply the needed funds, and forward, and in every way sustain their labours abroad To do this it is necessary to inform the women in the Churches of the needs of heathen women, to rouse and stimulate a prayerful interest in them, and to afford a channel for their efforts in their behalf.

III. Its Methods.

In the Foreign field the woman's work resolves itself into two chiǝf departments; (1) The Evangelistic ; (2) The Educational.

(1) The Evangelistic work consists mainly of personal effort with the women, either directly by the Missionary or through native workers trained for the purpose. The first problem that confronts the Missionary, is how to overcome the accumulations of prejudice and ignorance *As evangelists.* and win her way to the hearts of the women she longs to serve. To do this every womanly ingenuity has been taxed to its utmost.

Day by day these earnest Missionaries seek out the women in their homes, and, placing the lever of the Gospel under their feet, with the greatest patience and perseverance raise them from the ground upon which so many of them literally live. These untiring workers gather the women together for religious meetings. They teach them to read the Bible, and, when it is possible, gather them and their children into Sunday schools and chapel services; they meet them by the wayside, and win their attention by Gospel songs; they pitch their tents in the regions beyond, in the shadow of a tamerind or a banyan tree, or even of a great rock in a weary land, they gather little groups of women about them and proclaim the good news.

Perhaps the most important part of this evangelical work is the training and labour of native women. In the early days it was extremely difficult to find a woman of sufficient age, dignity and piety, *As trainers of* for so responsible an undertaking. In some cases they experi-*native sisters.* enced hardships and contumely of every kind, but as a class they have gradually won their way to positions of honour and respect.

Many of the Bible women whom they train are most valuable assistants of the Missionaries, as one of whom the Missionary writes: "She was my right hand, right eye, right ear, and tongue." Another writes: "These women are in many ways fitted to do a work which a foreigner cannot do." Their salaries are small, many of them working entirely without compensation, many of them are weak and ignorant, and there are sometimes utter failures among them; but under all disadvantages they are a power by which the mighty uplifting of their countrywomen is to be accomplished.

(2) *Educational work.*—The larger part of woman's work in the Mission-field is in the girls' schools of various kinds. The opposition to female education in all lands without a pure Gospel is well known. This is gradually disappearing, although the old objections are often heard.

This educational work, aside from what is done by the Bible women from house to house, may be considered as two divisions. (1) The day *As teachers.* and village schools; (2) the boarding schools.

Of the village school a Missionary writes, "At the foundation of all our educational, and, to a certain extent, of our Missionary work, lie our village schools. These are the feeders of our higher schools, and largely of our congregations, besides giving the first impulse to nearly all of those who afterwards become Mission agents. In many places the only foothold we have in the town is the school: but this in time leads to a congregation and a church. The school is welcomed everywhere. Not so the church. But if the school is first planted, the way is prepared for a church.

Most of the girls' schools in the villages and many of the mixed ones are taught by graduates from the girls' boarding schools. These graduates often find their best Christian service in their native village, where they gather the children together to teach them the first rudiments of learning and of Christianity.

It has been said that in no part of Missionary work can the immediate results be so plainly seen as in the boarding schools. To take a girl *Boarding school* away from the demoralising surroundings of her home, and place *work.* her under the constant influence of a Christian school, quickly brings about a thorough transformation.

In every school, so far as we know, the Bible is a regular and prominent study, and the religious atmosphere is so strong that it is a rare exception that a girl graduates without seeming a true hearted Christian. The special blessing on those schools in the way of spiritual quickenings has been very marked,—Over and over again the Missionary teacher has been able to write with full heart,—" We believe that, with two or three exceptions, every girl in the school has given her heart to Christ ; " and occasionally she can include every one in the number. A room full of girls weeping for their sins, and a house full of prayer and praise is no uncommon sight, neither is a scene like the following. " After the time of which I wrote, when many of the girls were under deep conviction of sin, there has been an uninterrupted season of prayer and praise. The scenes among the girls at night, after the lessons of the day were over, rival any- A school of Christians. thing I ever saw at home, and are beyond description. After the evening meal the whole school was one scene of rejoicing. In one corner a large group of girls were talking and praying with one or two girls who had not yet come into full possession of such joy and peace as the others knew they could have. In another place a number of girls were singing, and their songs would now and then be interrupted by some girl repeating in a clear, happy voice, some passages of Scripture ; then they would begin again with their accompaniment of clapping hands. Just outside the door was another group of girls kneeling in most perfect unconcern or disregard of those coming and going around them, praying in most earnest tones for a still greater blessing upon them all. In still another room a company of girls were crying, " More, more, more of thy Holy Spirit, O Lord ! " In short, the whole number of girls had given themselves completely up to this one thing. Like all orientals, these children are excitable ; but with all the excitement, I know there is depth and strength to their convictions."

Miscellaneous Work.—The miscellaneous work done by woman in the Mission-field deserves a special notice. A most important item is that of touring where the Missionaries visit the out-stations, where the school graduates are at work as teachers, Bible women, and wives of native pastors, advising, encouraging, and assisting them in their labours as necessity requires. In some places also the lady Missionaries have made a beginning in city Mission work. A few coffee houses have been established, many tracts distributed, and small libraries started.

The lady Missionaries have also entered the domain of literature to a certain extent, translating children's books and text-books and issuing juvenile papers. The largest undertaking of this line of which we are informed is a Christian Zenana paper cared for by the representatives of the Women's Foreign Missionary Society of the Methodist Episcopal Church in the United Literary work. States. It is issued fortnightly in four dialects,—Urdu, Hindi, Bengali, and Tamil ; and it is estimated that it is read by thousands of women in the Zenanas, the printed page reaching where no Missionary's voice can penetrate.

An important adjunct to all Missionary effort and one gradually assuming the proportions of a department by itself is woman's medical work. Access to the humbler classes, especially the women of the villages and interior cities, is often accompanied in the case of the ordinary Missionary, with rudeness and insults, but if the lady Missionary is known to be a physician she finds universally a prompt and cordial welcome, and has unparalleled opportunity to speak of the Christian doctrine.

IV.—ITS RESULTS.

In Heathen Lands.—Of the results of all this labour abroad who can tell ? The power set in motion by one redeemed soul only eternity can reveal. Among the visible results we find individuals and families rising to

a better life in every-day affairs.   We find cleanliness and order replacing
filth and confusion ; modest home with many civilised comforts,
Family life introduced. and decent dress instead of the miserable huts and half-clad condition of other days.   Husbands have learned to look upon their
wives with affection and respect, and the mutual burdens are more equally
shared.   Daughters and sisters are not scorned and blamed because they
dared to come at all, but are acknowledged as the possessors of minds and
souls, the equals of their brothers.   In short, the marriage rite and
relation begins to be regarded as sacred, and the family becomes a
Christian organisation.

Another blessed result is, that in many places the apathy of the women themselves is broken.   They are becoming restless under their thraldom, and long
for better things.   They are beginning to know what it is to have a hope
for the future.   They are gaining the desire and the power to bring their
dreary misery, so long dumb and hopeless, to the light of day.   They have
invited us to look into these homes, and our first impulse is to shrink
Hope inspired. back, sick at heart ; our next is to share our innumerable blessings
with them.

But best of all results, the aim of all the varied labour, are the redeemed souls
that are daily coming up out of every kindred and tongue and people and nation
to whom our Lord has permitted those young ladies to tell the power of His love.

In Christian Lands.—The result in general is a widespread movement to promote the interests of Foreign Mission work among the women
in the Churches.   The special effort and co-operation of women in Foreign
Missionary work is no new thing.   Our mothers and grandmothers laid the
foundation, upon which we find it comparatively easy to build.   There
came a time, however, when it was to assume a more definite, tangible
shape.   As the nineteenth century approached its meridian, there were
two contemporaneous movements.   The Missionaries in the Foreign field
began to see signs of awakening among the women around them,
Women at home aroused. and sent appeals for help to enable them to embrace the many
opportunities opening before them.   With our God the work
and the workers are never far apart.   In this instance they came together,
and there sprang up the various Women's Missionary Societies in Great
Britain and America.   The first in America was the Woman's Union
Missionary Society.   The first denominational Board was the Woman's
Board of Missions, working in connection with the American Board of
Commissioners for Foreign Missions.

The object and purpose of this corporation is to collect, receive, and hold
money given by voluntary contributions, donations, bequests, or otherwise, to
be exclusively expended in sending out and supporting such unmarried females
as the Prudential Committee of the American Board of Commissioners for
Foreign Missions shall, under the recommendation of the Board
Relation to the general work. of Directors of this corporation, designate and appoint as Assistant
Missionaries and Teachers for the Christianisation of women
in foreign lands; and for the support of such other Female Missionaries
or native female helpers in the Missionary work as may be selected by the
Board of Directors, with the approbation of the said Prudential Committee.

This is further explained by the Rev. N. G. Clark, D.D. (Senior Secretary of the A.B.C.F.M.), as follows:—"The work sustained by the Woman's
Boards* in the foreign field, in its general scope and in all its details, is under

* There are now three Woman's Boards, separated for geographical reasons, connected
with this Board,

the direction of the Prudential Committee of the American Board. Appropriations are made, Missionaries appointed, sent out and located, and their labours supervised by the Committee, precisely as in other departments. Efforts made for the social and moral elevation of women in the Mission-fields, are thus made to harmonise with the general work, and to constitute an integral and most necessary part of it. There is everywhere the heartiest mutual co-operation."

It is the confirmed opinion of the most experienced workers, both men and women, that for harmony both at home and abroad, for economy, for ease and efficiency of labour, the woman's work should be a part of the established organisation.

Among the indirect results of this work are the benefits to Christian women. "God thought of us as well as heathen women when He called us to this work," is a thought that finds a ready response in many hearts. The friendships formed, the dull lives quickened, the development of ^{Indirect results.} unknown powers of spiritual life are a part of the hundred-fold reward.

In this way, "with many hands and one heart," this woman's work is carried on. With no wrench from the sweet home ties and family life, so dear to every true woman, one here and another there has responded to what she believed to be the call of her Lord, and has taken her place in the work, fulfilling the prophecy, "The Lord gave the Word, and the women that publish it are an host."

V. PRESENT DEMANDS AND OBLIGATIONS.

The work for women in the foreign fields has increased fully fivefold during the last twenty years, and this increase could be doubled at the present moment, if there were the women to enter the places waiting for them and the means to send them. From Japan we hear that "the girls' schools are every one of them powerful influences in favour of Christianity, and that the feeling is so strong in favour of Christian education for girls that the prominent men are urging Missionaries to lay aside their direct Evangelical labours to take up this branch of work as offering a most successful method of propagating Christianity."

From China comes an appeal to the women of England and America for an increase of the number of lady Missionaries, "so as to meet the immediate and pressing wants of the work among native Christian women and girls, and among the heathen female population." In India there is an opportunity never known before to help millions of women in their heroic struggle to throw off the bondage that so cruelly oppresses them. In the Turkish Empire ^{Open doors.} the schools need our special support now that the Government, terrified at their success and influence, is endeavouring, uselessly we hope, to close them at least to all Moslems. Africa is open, and the evils of civilisation are entering this new field with terrible rapidity. Everywhere the cause demands the whole force of the Christian Church, the men, the women, and the children in it, to carry it on to a triumphant consummation.

This is a brief, meagre outline of woman's work in the Mission-field. Whatever of success has been achieved has been in one way. Consciousness of utter inability to cope with so great an undertaking has sent the workers to the foot of the Cross, there to wait for help and ^{The place of power.} guidance in every step of the way. Whenever there has been wandering from this place there have been mistakes and failures.

In one of the smaller college observatories in the United States, at nine o'clock on every clear night, there stands a solitary woman, with her eyes fixed on the stars, watching for the crossing of a certain star over the hair lines on a telescopic lens. Through the telegraphic instrument by her side, the mean time, as indicated by the stars, is given to all the time stations within a radius of many miles. The announcement of the correct time is passed on from one to another, till it reaches the city time

An Illustration. stations, the railways, the shops, the offices, the manufactories, the homes, the schools, the gatherings of people for whatever purpose, in hundreds of places. So it happens that the touch of one woman's hand controls the deeds of thousands of people; not of her own wit or wisdom, but because her eyes are fixed upon the stars. The moment her gaze falters her power is lost.

So it is in our Missionary work. So long as our eyes are fixed on the Root and Offspring of David,—the bright and morning Star,—we may go without fear to the uttermost parts of the earth. The instant our eyes wander to lower things we grope in the darkness. May we never lose this guidance, till the prophecy, written on the Royal Exchange of London, be fulfilled: " The earth is the Lord's and the fulness thereof."

The Chairman: Christian friends,—I have always entertained the opinion that the office of a chairman is to introduce the speakers, to keep order in the meeting, and to facilitate the good results at which the meeting aims; and I do not think that if I had taken up the time which has been occupied by these admirable Papers I should have done anything to advance the real interests for which the meeting is convened. If I am, as I believe, the first Canadian to open his mouth in this Conference, I am happy that it should be in connection with presiding over a meeting which is to consider the women's work. I think that all who were present yesterday, and who listened to the addresses which were given to us then by Christian women, and all who have been present this morning, must have felt how admirably women are prepared to take their part in making known the Gospel, and what a reserve power the Churches have in store

Canada absorbed in Home Missions. which to the present time, has scarcely been called into operation. I may say that in Canada we have not done very much in Foreign Mission work. Our Home Mission work is so vast, and so rapidly developing, that it has greatly taxed our energies; but I am glad to say that something has been done to advance the work of Foreign Missions. I have myself been connected with Foreign Mission work for more than twenty years, and if I thought that anything I had to say would really promote the best interests of this meeting I should be delighted to speak at any length in connection with the great work of evangelising the heathen.

I want to say, however, that in the branch of the Church to which I belong, we have about twenty-three ordained Missionaries in our various Foreign fields, including those now under commission to go out. In that section of the Church—I had the honour, I believe, of taking the initiative in the matter

Stimulus from Women's Missions. —we organised, twelve years ago or more, a Women's Foreign Missionary Society in the western section of Canada. Now I cannot say very much about the work in the Foreign fields, which is the special subject of to-day's Conference; but I can say this, that the reflex influence of the Women's Foreign Missionary Society, its monthly prayer-meetings, its diffusion of Missionary intelligence, its personal encouragement in Missionary effort—the effect of that throughout our Canadian Churches has been very manifest. I think we have received an immense blessing at home. I know that there is now a state of things very different from what there was twelve years ago. I was then the convener of our Foreign Missionary Committee, and often found it very difficult to secure labourers to go to the Foreign Missionary field, either male or female. At the present time we are not able, from lack of funds, to send one-third of the men or women who are prepared to offer themselves to go out and labour for Christ. In the Theological College of which I am a professor, the graduating class last year was a considerable one and more than half of the members of that class are prepared at any time to go to the heathen as soon as the Church is ready to send them. And I may say that we have offers upon offers of young men of ability and consecration who are prepared to go forth and labour in the Foreign Mission-field. Now, I do think that it is of the utmost importance for us in this Conference, as we are from every part of the world, to learn something about the way in which this great work, to which our women are directing their energies, may be best advanced in the heathen field, and that is the special matter we have met this morning to consider.

Theological students volunteering for Missions.

DISCUSSION.

Mrs. F. J. Coppin (Woman's African Methodist Episcopal Mite Missionary Society, U.S.A.) : Sometimes when a thought comes uppermost it is better to get it out of the way as it may be very troublesome afterwards. Now with reference to what we have heard this morning I wish to say this. I think there is nothing, in the law of God's universe, that was made without having ample space to move in, without trenching upon its neighbour's domain; and it may very well be said of women that while they are and were created second, they not only were created with a body but they were created also with a head, and they are responsible therefore to decide in certain matters and to use their own judgment.

A plea for woman.

It is also very true, as I will certainly say, that fools often rush in where angels fear to tread ; but then I question as to whether all the fools are confined to the feminine gender. Ladies and gentlemen, time is very brief indeed, and I am overwhelmed with the thoughts of looking upon English people and upon English faces—the historic land of liberty. No one here can understand how the women occupying the great seaboard yonder have looked upon this land—those who, like myself, bear the yoke with them. Now there are in the United States, distributed among eleven of the former Southern States, over eight millions of my people. Of these three millions are women, and those three millions whom the Lord God in His inscrutable providence has seen fit to pass through a hard school, distributed as I say along there, and very nearly in the majority,—they send greetings here to-day, and wish me to speak about what their feeling is towards the Christianisation of the coloured races of the earth. You will not, I am sure, deny us the very peculiar interest, as I say, in the Christianisation of all races. These poor women, less than a decade out of slavery, established a Foreign Missionary Society, and have their Foreign Missionaries in the Island of Hayti, in San Domingo, in Trinidad, in St. Thomas, and Sierra Leone, on the West Coast of Africa. They have not a whole loaf to share as we all know, they have not even a half-loaf to share with their sisters and brothers in foreign lands. They have but a crust ; but, poor as they are, they sent me here,—three millions of those women sent me three thousand miles,—to say to all who are here assembled that their hearts are in that work, and that they intend to devote not only what little they have of money and

Three millions of African women in America.

Missionary spirit.

of resources to sustain their Missionaries in those lands, but they are prepared
to give themselves. How I wanted yesterday to say, as Mr. Guinness spoke of
Africa, what wonderful transmutations under God's Providence

God's purpose
in their
enslavement

have been taking place amongst these people, and what a Missionary
spirit has been developed amongst them. The problem, how to
reach the coloured people on the Western Coast, has been for years
one which civilised nations have been unable to unravel, but He in His own time
will make it plain. Who hath known the mind of the Lord in these things ? and
yet we have been hampered on all sides by presupposed ideas of what was meant
by the enslavement of all these people. Now let me say something about them.
The spirit of Missionaries, the spirit of Mission work, is the spirit of sharing all
that we have. Those to whom God gives intelligence and wealth He gave it
simply that it might be shared. Did He give you more intelligence than
another ? then He gave some one else less, and it is your bounden duty to use it to
help that one who has not so much as you. Did He make you rich ? then He has

Responsible
for gifts.

made another poor, and the greatest of blessings and the truest
happiness is to share all that you have with those who need it
But if not from the grace and blessedness, I do think from the
very necessity of the fact that all history teaches that those who have had more
light from God, or more of the good things of this life, and who have not shared
it with those about them, they have had every bit taken away from them as you
very well know ; and the Light passed on and on and on through the Eastern
countries, westward, until it beamed equally on all men as the Lord God
intended that it should do.

Mrs. James Watson (Woman's Foreign Missionary Society of the
Presbyterian Church of Canada): Dear Christian friends,—I am not
accustomed to speak in audiences like this, but I am appointed by our
Woman's Board of Foreign Missions of the Presbyterian Church, in

Greetings
from Canada.

Western Canada, to represent them, and to bring from them
most hearty greetings to all workers for our dear Lord, who hath
so honoured us in this our day, by giving woman a large share
in the evangelisation of the world. We, from Canada, rejoice with our
sisters in England, America, and other countries, in the opportunity given
us to meet, to hear from each other's lips what the Lord is doing for us, and
for the heathen around us and abroad. When we each return to our homes,
may we carry back with us from this Conference such a baptism of the
Holy Ghost that nations may be born in a day, as the fulfilment of the
promise given to us by our Lord, "Ask, and ye shall receive." We ask
the Lord from these meetings to give us scores of Christian men and women
to go into every part of the world to evangelise it to His glory. We who
tarry at home divide the spoil. It is our joy as well as duty to uphold
our sisters who are working in heathen lands in constant prayer. Our
Woman's Board was formed in 1876, twelve years ago, by Professor

Growth of
Missionary life.

MacLaren and Mrs. MacLaren, who are here to-day. There
were present only forty women, but all filled with love for the
Master,—all praying for the Spirit's abiding presence and
guiding power, that this new work, which the Lord had laid before them,
should be undertaken only for His glory.

At this day, looking back on the past twelve years, we can say with all
reverence and humility that the Lord hath showered rich blessings on us, in
answer to the prayers of that meeting. We had at first only between three to
five hundred members. They gave at the end of the first year $1,000,
equal to £250 sterling, and this twelfth year we have sent £5,250 sterling to the
Mission-field. Five ladies are in the Mission-field, working in Central India,

two of whom are Medical Missionaries; one, Miss Oliver, having gone to Cashmere last summer for her health, through the grace of God was able to cure the Maharajah's wife, and we trust also to sow good seed for the Master there, as the Maharanee has requested that she should remain there as Court Physician. Our Woman's Board also supports Mission Schools in Formosa, Trinidad, and the New Hebrides, with many Missions among our own North-west Indians, who want much done for them, as they, too, live in deep soul-darkness and sin. Our French evangelisation forms also a part of our work. We thank this Committee most heartily for inviting us to attend this great Conference, the influence of which will redound to the glory of God.

Miss Anderson (United Presbyterian Mission, Nusseerabad, Rajputana): One of the points down here for discussion to-day is: "Should secular instruction ever be given in homes, by the Missionary agent, without Bible teaching?" ("Never.") That is just what I was going to say most emphatically,—never! If we leave our home and friends and go away to a foreign country, is it not that we may take the light of the Gospel to the people in that foreign land? I do not despise education. I would never say a word against education in Zenanas or schools, but I do say that it is a means, a worthy means, but still only a means to an end, and the end is that the women in the Zenanas and the girls in the schools may be brought to know the Lord Jesus Christ and what He has done for them. I do not see how any woman can go and be a Zenana Missionary without teaching the Bible. Secular instruction is good. I know some Zenana teachers say: "Only teach the Bible, and nothing but the Bible." I do not say that, but I do say: "Teach the Bible along with other things." *No instruction without the Bible.*

Miss Jessie Philip (L.M.S., from Pekin): Mr. Chairman, ladies, and gentlemen,—It is not on account of long or successful service that I venture before you now, but simply as having been in the foreign field, and having seen a good deal of various forms of work there, I feel impelled to speak upon one or two points.

One point touched upon is the interest and success of itinerary work. Of this I had a slight personal experience, and can testify to its value among the country stations. I had the privilege of going where no foreign lady had been before quite alone, and I received a warm welcome and generous hospitality. The women showed a willingness to listen. They said to me, "We can get near to our lady teacher. We cannot come so near the gentlemen when they come, but we can come close to you; we can hold your hands, and we can learn from you in a way we never dare learn from our gentlemen teachers." *Itinerary work among women.*

Next I would tell you before going out I availed myself of some opportunities of gaining some insight into Medical work, but I only wish I had learned a great deal more. Hundreds of people came to me for help, and what little help I could give I gladly gave. I found it always the road to their hearts and homes, such as perhaps nothing else would have been, and now my longing is to have fuller Medical training before I go back, and I can only urge it upon ladies who are thinking of going out that they should take, if possible, full Medical training, for I am sure it is most necessary. Before I went out it was a great longing of mine to be able to go independently. This was not within my power, but since I have worked out in China, I only wonder that ladies qualified by education and health and with means of their own do not devote themselves more often to this work. *Importance of Medical training.*

Miss Mann (English Presbyterian Mission, Women's Missionary Association): One of the subjects on the Paper this morning is, "Training Schools and Homes for Native Female Teachers and Bible **Women to train** Women." I am one of the many who believe that if heathen **women.** peoples are to be won for Christ, it must be done largely through a trained native agency. Ladies who go out to heathen lands will be doing work, perhaps the most far reaching in its results, by devoting a large portion of their time to training some of the natives, in order that they may go out and teach their Christian and heathen sisters both by word and example. The advantages of employing native agents was touched upon by Miss Child in her admirable Paper.

I would like to mention three advantages that natives have over foreigners. In the first place they have the self-evident advantage of speaking as a **Advantages of** native to natives. We can acquire a language after a great deal **native workers.** of study, but still we always speak to the people as foreigners. We never have that advantage. And then they are working in their own climate. In South China, which I know best, during the hottest months of the year, it is quite impossible for the lady Foreign Missionary to go into the country, but the natives are able to work as well in the summer time as in the cooler season. They have one advantage which we can never hope to possess, that is a perfect understanding of the people ; they know how they look at things ; they know what their own ignorance was, and they are able to suit their illustrations to the mind of the people, and to drive the nail home. There is another thing which might be referred to, and that is the zeal and earnestness of true converts from heathenism ; they all become Missionaries, because they cannot keep the good news to themselves, and we ought to take advantage of this and train these natives and send them out as Missionaries among their own people. The Medical work has been referred to again and again, and it is impossible to speak too highly of this department of work ; but it seems to me a very large proportion of the highest results of this work are lost, or will be lost as far as the visible Church is concerned, unless these patients are followed up into their own homes. It is one thing to profess to be a Christian in a hospital where there is everything to help you, and quite another thing to go away into a distant town or village, where perhaps no one else has ever heard of the one true and living God, and there bear witness to this strange religion about which **Converts need** your neighbours have never heard. You can readily understand **sympathy.** how much some of these poor people would be helped by a visit from one or two native Christian women who could live with them in their own homes, and sympathise with them in their difficulties, because they have passed through them themselves ; who could strengthen them in times of persecution, and could tell them, not of a foreign religion, but of a God whom they know, and of a Saviour who died for them. We heard yesterday of schools in which numbers of children have been trained for five or six years, who are afterwards lost sight of. That would not be if there were native agents who could follow up these children in their own homes and help them, for they need the help as much perhaps as hospital patients do. I think Mission stations are not completely equipped unless they have an ever-increasing number of trained native Bible women, who can follow the patients and the children into their own homes, and help them in their daily life.

Mrs. G. W. Clarke (China Inland Mission): Dear friends,—I am very glad, indeed, this morning, to have just a minute or two to speak, because I do want to plead for some more helpers in the great land of China. I have just come back from the borders of Mongolia, three days' distance **A solitary work.** beyond the Great Wall, where I was quite alone, the only woman for over a year We had opportunities of entering houses and of getting to the villages, but I wanted more help, and I come this morning to ask if we cannot get some. Above all I would like Medical ladies—fully qualified Medical ladies. Last year I had a very serious illness, and owe my life to the skill and kindness of an American lady there. Such is my experience of American lady doctors in China.

That lady spared no pains in her qualification, telling me that after she got her full diploma she went for six years' further study—making ten years' study—and the gift so offered to the Lord was no mean one. She is a most splendid worker, and has charge of an opium refuge ; I have seen her marshal twenty men into her service on a Sunday morning, and every one of them obey her like a child. In addition to that she has a dispensary and a large number of patients almost daily ; she also teaches women to read. She has taught about sixteen women in two years to read the New Testament, and nearly the whole of them are members of the Church, many going out without any money given to them to preach in the villages to their sisters. I want this morning to know if we cannot have some English ladies medically qualified to go out ; if not, those that do go I would strongly advise to get all the Medical *A call for Medical women.* knowledge they possibly can before they go. You are compelled, in a certain sense, if you get into isolated places, such as I was in, to use medicines ; if you are a quack, never mind : do the best you can. Nobody admires fully qualified ladies and gentlemen more than I do ; but supposing you are placed as I was—nine days and a half I had to travel to get medical help in one direction, thirty in another, and if I had gone south seventeen days. When you are situated like that you are glad to do something for the poor people around you, even if it is only to give a little ointment, or lotion, or a plaster. Something has been said about touring. Well, I had a little of that for three or four years, and I enjoyed it more than I can tell you. I had a donkey—for, of course, I could not go without it—and I had a little basket which contained a concertina in the middle (because the Chinese like to be taught a little singing) ; on one side I had my Bible and Christian tracts, and on the *Our mode of working.* other side just half a dozen simple medicines that one who is a quack could use. I went from village to village, and from town to town, with no assistant but a Chinaman, and he a heathen, and was well received in every place, never hearing an insulting word ; even at villages with fifty people in my room as tight as they could pack, and I teaching them until almost the sun was going down, and having a distance to go home before our city gates closed.

Miss Andrews (Society for Promoting Female Education in the East, from the Punjab) : Dear friends,—I will just state to begin with that the Chairman has made a slight mistake in announcing me as connected with the Presbyterian Missions. I am labouring in Lodiana, in the most friendly relation with the American Presbyterian Missionaries, but am myself an agent of the English Society for Promoting Female *In Lodiana.* Education in the East. That Society has now many ladies in Lodiana, and we are there by the invitation of the American Missionaries ; working in the most friendly relationship and experiencing all the benefit and help of the council and other aids which Dr. Murdock mentioned as so desirable in the case of women and men working together. Working hand in hand, as someone said yesterday, in the same spirit as the marriage relationship—that God created them male and female, and He meant them both to work, and that unitedly, on the lines of fellow help.

When I sent up my card to speak it was with a view of saying a few words on a subject not much touched upon in the Papers, viz., about the taking of the Bible into the Zenanas ; but what I had to say has just been said, and said so well that I feel there is nothing to add on that point except to emphasise it. If ever there were days when it was necessary to go first cautiously without the

Bible, those days are past, for the Punjab, at least, and I should say for the whole North of India. As far as my experience has gone, the days are past when there is any need for the Zenana lady to leave her Bible outside. We have in Lodiana more houses to visit than we can possibly attend to, and if there is any house where religious instruction is refused by the head of the house, we have no need to go, because we are invited to so many houses where they are willing and glad to receive Bible instruction.

Need of workers.

I will allude to one or two other points : one is the work of itineration, which has been mentioned. There are ladies in this hall from the Punjab like myself, who, I am sure, will endorse what I say when I affirm that the fields in the Punjab for women's work in carrying the Gospel to the women in the villages are indeed "white unto the harvest."

Since I came home for a short rest, whenever I have had the opportunity of speaking, my one desire has been to try and make English people realise what those fields are like. If only you could see a map of the Lodiana district, a map about three feet square, just simply representing one district (and there are many such in the Punjab), so thickly covered with names of small towns and villages, that you could not put your finger down without covering three or four, and then just try to realise that in ninety-nine out of every hundred of those villages we have free access to preach the Gospel to scores and scores of women!—going simply by ourselves, two and two, or with our native Bible women, we are never openly insulted, are very rarely slighted, usually received gladly, and have an opportunity of proclaiming the Gospel of God to crowds of willing listeners. All we want is more labourers that we may follow up the work. What distresses our hearts is that we cannot visit a village perhaps more than once in two years—there are so many villages to go to, such an immense amount of ground to cover, and there is the work in the city, in the Zenanas, and schools to be looked after, besides the Medical work—the result is that we rarely get time to re-visit a village under two years, and sometimes not then. Oh, if you could only see these fields "white unto the harvest," I think you would rise in a body and go forth !

Reception by natives.

Mrs. Mary C. Nind (Woman's Foreign Missionary Society of the Methodist Episcopal Church, U.S.A.): The Chairman has introduced me as Miss Nind, but I beg to say I am a mother and a grandmother, having six children in the Mission-field,—four in China and two in South America —so that I have a very deep interest in this work.

I cannot say too much in endorsing the training of our native agency. We have among our women, in India especially, on whom my thoughts now rest, some of the grandest women that God has ever given to us. We might speak of them by name, but you would not know them ; but standing out before me just now is that wonderful woman, Phœbe Rowe, who has just visited this country and looked in upon this city of London,—a converted Eurasian, who is like a flaming light all over India ; and our Bishop Foster says it is worth while going to India and back to look into her face and hear her sing the sweet songs of Zion, as she does in the Zenanas and among the women of India. I glory in these Women's Foreign Missionary Societies, differing a little from the brother whose Paper was read, because of their special work—women working for women. Beloved, there is so much to be done for women that our brethren cannot do,—that we cannot half do—and so we press on this wondrous line,—women educated by women ; ignorant women debased and enslaved, to be saved by women elevated and Christianised,—Medical women for the women of these foreign lands.

Native workers.

I think we shall have, in order to obey the Divine command, to keep this line distinct yet,—women's work for women. And you know the time is coming,—I am not a prophet, nor the daughter of a prophet, but the time is coming; I do not know that you dear English people will yet receive it; it may be a hard saying to you; and you will say, "Who can hear it?" but we can hear it in America, and we get our ears opened to it, and so should our brethren. The time is not far distant when we shall have to listen to the cry of the women in their Zenanas, that our Christian Missionaries and Bible readers will have to administer to these women baptism and communion. They Shall women administer the sacraments? may begin the education of women at the other end of the line: if that is God's will, let all the people say Amen. It is coming, let me tell you. Our dear Fanny Sparks, who has given nineteen years of her life to this Missionary work, found a woman in her Zenana converted to God, and really anxious to receive baptism; but how could she? She was a Zenana woman. Her husband was about to be baptised, and after a great deal of persuasion she was induced to go to the native chapel with a "chuddar" over her face, but only on this condition—"Now, Mrs. Sparks, I will never let a man put his hand upon my head except my husband, and how can I be baptised?" And so there the dear woman stood; the preacher in attendance, of course; but when the rite had to be administered, Fanny Sparks had to put the water on the head. She really did the baptism. That is a premonition of what is coming, and let us be ready for it. I propose to open every door that the Lord sets before me, as a member of the Women's Christian Temperance Union, or the Women's Foreign Missionary Society, or belonging to the White Cross Movement, or the King's Daughters, or anything else. Anywhere with Jesus, everywhere with Jesus; and put all my prejudices behind, and march on to victory.

Mrs. Middleton (Secretary, Ladies' Kaffrarian Society) said: I promise to be only five minutes in giving a report of a Society that has been at work fifty years—just one minute to every ten years. The Society is called the "Ladies' Kaffrarian Mission of the United Presbyterian Church of Scotland." This Mission was started more than fifty years ago. It took its rise in the deep anxiety felt by a number of eminent ministers and godly women, in the western capital of Scotland, to bring the knowledge of the Gospel of Christ to the despised and degraded tribes of South Africa. It was at first called the The Kaffrarian Mission. "Glasgow African Mission," and under this name was supported by all denominations of Christians. In the year 1847, the United Presbyterian Church undertook the sole responsibility of the Mission, and re-named it the "Kaffrarian Mission." From its outset, great prominence was given to the instruction of the native women and girls, it being felt that without their influence Christian homes would never be formed.

This was at first carried on by the wives of the Missionaries, but it was soon seen that the work was so great as to require the undivided attention of special agents. It was then that the women of the Church came forward and formed themselves into a Society, which should charge itself with the care of this side of the Mission work. This has ever since been known as the "Ladies' Kaffrarian Society."

It has held on its way amid much discouragement arising from the usual

causes—distance from the field of labour, and consequent difficulty in guiding
the agents and superintending the work. Besides all this there was
Perseverance the additional and grievous trial of frequent tribal wars, in which
rewarded. the stations were destroyed, the lives of the ministers endangered,
and their work apparently undone. But they always returned on the first sign
of peace, and their perseverance was at last rewarded by their seeing the Mission
take a firmer hold on the natives.

The Ladies' Society has concentrated its efforts on the station of Emgwali,
where it has a large boarding institution and school for Kaffir and Fingo girls.
These are received when young, trained in household work, taught English, and
have their minds steeped in Bible knowledge. They are thus separated for a
time from their heathen homes, and brought under influences which are calculated
to fill them with tastes for higher and better things than are to be found there.
It has at present a hundred and three boarders and scholars, with every prospect
of the numbers increasing. In a prominent place in the Glasgow International
Exhibition, now open, there is an exhibit of needlework from the Emgwali
school, which compares favourably with that done in our schools at home. If
Lessons from our small Society has any lesson for the friends of Missions now so
its work. largely assembled here in Council, it is that of the triumph of perseverance over obstacles and disappointments. What has been
beautifully said of Him by whose command we do all our Missionary work, we
venture to think is true also of the originators and older members of this Mission.
Unless their feet had been well shod with love they would soon have turned
back and said the way was impassable. We have desired to be represented at
this Council that we may secure a share in the interest and prayers of its members,
and that a report of the work done at this great Conference may be carried
home to Scotland, and may infuse fresh life and vigour into our quiet meetings.

The *boarding institution* and *school* for Fingo girls was built by the aid of
the students of the U.P. Church, and one of the present teachers is the daughter
of the well known Fingo Soga.

Mrs. Juliana Hayes (Woman's Board of Missions of Methodist Episcopal
Church [South], U.S.A.): I rejoice to be the representative of the Woman's
Missionary Society of the Methodist Episcopal Church (South), and I come
to you, my friends, bearing the greetings from what is really a very young
sister in this grand women's work. I was delighted with everything that
Development of the brother has said who spoke so admirably this morning, but
Missionary I do not want him to knock out that word, "Women's work for
spirit. women." It is for women that we are working. Our Society
is quite young—only ten years old. We in the South, as you know, have
had terrible trials; and out of the strifes, and out of the heart-aches and
heart-breaks of a nation grew a hitherto unworked power, which has
resulted in this "women's work for women."

We were wondrously delighted to find, beloved friends, that in the South
where we had not known much of women's work we should have an answer to
our petitions immediately, for although we did not know it we no sooner
organised than during the first year we had $4,000 in our treasury, and we have
gone on and on with no public speakers except your humble servant. We have
this last year paid to our treasury just before I left my home, at the annual
meeting, in which they insisted upon my bearing greetings to this body, $60,000
Reflex action for one year. We have gone on victoriously increasing. At the
on the same time I would not like to sit down without saying to you that
Home Church. the reflex action upon the Church at home, upon our beloved
women, has been far beyond what can be estimated by figures, for there is no
one who has entered into this work but has said that their spiritual life has been
quickened, and they have come nearer to God in this work than in any work

they had ever entertained. At first we knew very little of the work, and we sent out only one young lady without any home, to go out under preparation; and what she endured we can never understand. Then a young sister, a lovely blooming girl of seventeen years, followed her, and planted together in a small town. She opened a school, but at first she got no scholars because the natives said this foreign woman wanted to go there to take the eyes out of their children and send them over to America to make medicine of. We have one grave to mark our work.

The Doxology was then sung.

Rev. Mr. Blackstock pronounced the Benediction.

MEETINGS OF MEMBERS
IN SECTION.

NINTH SESSION.

THE PLACE OF EDUCATION IN MISSIONARY WORK.

(1) THE PRINCIPLE.

(*a*) The place of the education of the young as a regular part of Mission work.

(*b*) Should it be restricted in any way, either as to those who are to be benefited by it, or in its extent?

(*c*) The extent to which the employment of non-Christian teachers in Mission schools is legitimate or necessary.

(Wednesday morning, June 13th, in the Lower Hall.)

Sir J. P. Corry, Bart, M.P., in the chair.
Acting Secretary, Rev. W. Park, M.A.

Rev. Dr. Murray Mitchell offered prayer.

The Chairman: Ladies and gentlemen,—I see upon the programme that the Chairman is expected to say something at the opening of the meetings; but I think my better course on the present occasion will be to allow those who have prepared their Papers to read them, and then we can have a discussion upon them. I may say that it *Sympathy with* gives me great pleasure to be able to take part in this *the work.* great Conference. I have always taken a very deep interest in Missionary work, and the more I know of it and think of it the more I am satisfied that it is a work by which the present age will be greatly distinguished. The subject to be discussed this morning is one on which there may be many different opinions. There is no doubt whatever that the education of the young, either amongst our Foreign Missions or at home, is a very important work. Of course, in foreign countries it presents some difficulties that might not arise at home; but, so far as I am personally concerned,

I feel that the right thing to do is to get hold of the young. I am also in favour of combining secular education with religious training. That this work is carried on by our Missionaries in foreign countries is, I am sure, very well known to all present, and it is quite unnecessary for me to dwell upon it, because you will be very much more edified by hearing the gentlemen who are to read the Papers.

Importance of education.

PAPER.

1. By the Rev. N. G. Clark, D.D. (Senior Foreign Secretary, A.B.C.F.M.). Read by the Rev. W. S. Swanson.

Higher Christian Education as a Missionary Agency.

It is to the honour of Christianity, as compared with all other religions, that while its immediate object is the spiritual renovation of man, its work is not complete till his entire being attains to fullest development of its powers. The renewed soul then has scope for its varied energies, and can illustrate the fulness of the redemptive work, to the glory of God.

In the prosecution of the Missionary enterprise individual souls must first be won to Christ, then Christian institutions established for their nurture and growth in Christian character and power. It is not enough simply to introduce the leaven of the Gospel, and leave it to work out its legitimate results on the social and intellectual life of the people under the fostering care of Foreign Missionaries. Some degree of education must be added to enable believers to read the Word of God for themselves in their native tongue. So long as an uncivilised people can be kept free from unfavourable influences, such as the incursion of the errors and vices of an ungodly civilisation, this may suffice for a time, and the result is largely satisfactory, as notably among the Karens, the Malagasy, and in some portions of the South Seas. Native Christians are gathered into Churches under the care of the Missionaries, who are looked up to reverently as spiritual fathers, yet little progress can then be made toward independence; no native pastors are educated competent to take up and carry forward the work begun. Such was the experience of the American Board in the Hawaiian Islands. For more than forty years, during which tens of thousands had been enrolled in Mission Churches and the islands had been evangelised, no pastors had been prepared to take the places of the Missionary fathers. This was the natural result of the method pursued, and its weakness became apparent when disturbing influences from without seriously imperilled the work accomplished, and rendered necessary the most strenuous and persistent efforts to avert disaster.

Education a necessity in Missions.

In some Missions in India, where only the lower castes were reached, and where educational efforts were for a time limited to simplest elements, the native Churches continued in similar helpless dependence on their Missionary teachers, with little progress save in the number of Church members and of adherents.

It is only as the Native Christians gathered out of nature-peoples, or from the degraded masses in civilised countries, are encouraged to secure for them-

Influence of education. selves the advantages of a higher education,—only as their young men are brought under the personal influence of men like Bishop Patteson or Andrew Murray, and other equally devoted men, and so attain to some degree of disciplined intellectual character,—that they are prepared for the pastorate or for Missionary service in the regions beyond. Nor is it enough that a few be educated to become spiritual leaders while the masses remain in ignorance, differing but little from the heathen around them, as in the Roman Catholic Missions of Africa and India. Happily in nearly all Protestant Missions, education has followed the proclamation of the Gospel. Among a nature-people the school is at once established, to enable all, especially children and youth, to read the Bible in their own language. Their first reading lessons comprise passages of Scripture and Bible stories. The first book to be translated into their language is the Bible ; and it becomes, therefore, the beginning and the foundation of a Christian literature. Believers are thus nurtured in the truth, their faith confirmed and their religious character raised above the corrupting influences of old habits and associations.

Some measure of education is necessary to save our native Christians from yielding to specious forms of religious error, and to make them rise above their

Primary and training schools. old associations into a vigorous Christian life. The two lessons to be learned from the experience and observation of many Missionary enterprises thus far—particularly among nature-peoples and the lower classes in civilised lands—are (1) the importance of education in primary schools in order to the greater intelligence, the stability of character, and the more active Christian life of the native Churches ; and (2) of training schools to raise up a native agency, both teachers and preachers, adequate to make them the leaders in the new social and intellectual as well as religious life of their countrymen.

If a higher Christian education is necessary to the healthful growth and success of Mission work among nature-peoples when left to themselves, how

Greater needs in civilised races. much more, when all the elements · of our Western civilisation follow close upon the Missionary, if they do not precede him. No people can now long remain in isolation from the rest of the world, uninfluenced by its trade, commerce, and ungodly associations. Hence a more thorough education in the schools is demanded to ground men in the first principles of knowledge, to establish them in the truth, and to develop a force of character that will stand fast against the revival of old errors and the introduction of new. Yet more is such higher Christian education necessary in dealing with highly civilised peoples like the Chinese, the Japanese, or the high-caste population of India, with their sacred books, their priestly orders, their elaborate ceremonials and traditional usages, and where difficulties from these sources are increased by the imported vices,—the scepticism and the materialism of nominally Christian lands. The humblest native of India or the South Seas may tell his neighbour of the Saviour he has found, and awaken an interest where the foreign teacher has failed. But the teacher, foreign or native, who can command the attention of an audience of Brahmans in Bombay, or of one of the great theatre audiences in Japan, must be a man of culture and of disciplined character.

For the honour of Christianity and for its best moral influence, it is of great consequence that this higher education in Mission schools should be

Mission colleges. in substantial advance of what can be had elsewhere. This is easy among nature-peoples and in Mohammedan lands, and to some extent in India and China. If the Mission college or training school falls short of the variety and range of studies pursued n the Government institutions of India or Japan, it must more than make up the difference by the quality of intellectual and moral character secured.

The Mission college is not for professional studies, nor for the training of pupils in scientific pursuits; it is to educate the pupil in the use of his faculties, to ground him in the first principles of knowledge in the various departments of thought and effort, to enable him to take his bearings in every direction—in history, science, art, civilisation, government—from the great central truths and facts of the Gospel. This will give him strength and breadth of character and power among his fellow men. Through the use of the English tongue, the accumulated wisdom of the world is laid at his feet, and through the assiduous culture of his own native tongue he can make it tributary to the welfare of his fellow men. The power thus gained—the consciousness of a mastery of questions at issue, not to mention the respect and confidence gained for his opinions among those for whom he is to labour—may all be turned to account, or rather are necessary to success. Add to this the enrichment of the native languages by turning into them the current of English ideas, the fruit of centuries of thought and experience, to be carried henceforth through the thousand channels of influence, to regenerate the intellectual and moral life of the millions, and no words can adequately express the importance of using the English language as an agency to the grandest results of Missionary effort. Missions could be mentioned that have for years remained weak and dependent for want of a competent native agency; while others, like that of the Church Missionary Society in Sierra Leone, of the Free Church of Scotland in South Africa, of the United Presbyterians in Egypt, and those of the American Board in Turkey and in Japan, exhibit the splendid results of the thorough training of a native ministry.

When the time comes for the college, there will have been developed such interest in education as will make it, or should make it, unnecessary for the Missionary Society to be at any expense for the board and tuition of students—save possibly for grants in aid to promising Christian young men pledged to the ministry. It may be necessary to supply the needed buildings and school furniture as library and apparatus, but the fees for tuition should defray the expense of native teachers. Assistance must be given for a longer time to encourage and sustain educational institutions for young women, but already efforts to secure payment for the board and tuition of girls are meeting with success in Ceylon, in Japan, and in some portions of the Turkish Missions. *Time for and place of the college.*

In former years the mistake was made of establishing higher institutions of learning before they were called for by the natural growth of the Missionary work, and in the reception into them of heathen or non-Christian youths free of charge. It was not possible at so early a stage to exert a controlling religious influence in the schools, and while expenses were enormous the spiritual results were disappointing. Two guiding principles may therefore determine the use of higher Christian education as a Missionary agency,—first, that it is primarily for the discipline and culture of Christian youth for Christian work; and secondly, that the standard of instruction in training schools and theological seminaries is to be suited to the condition of each Mission-field, whether limited to Biblical theology and some little acquaintance with history and science, as in the South Seas for example, or extended through the English language to the best thought of the time, especially to studies in comparative religion and in religious philosophy, to meet the subtleties of modern scepticism and pantheism, as in India and Japan.

The development of self-supporting and self-propagating institutions of the Gospel is the one great object of Missionary effort. It is only to be reached as educational and religious institutions are made worthy of the support of the people. The teachers must show their competence by the result of their work; the preachers must be educated so as to command the respect and the regard of their own people, and to be leaders in their social as well as religious life. The Native Churches can then be led, with proper care and patient instruction, to assume the support of their own educational and religious institutions as at once their duty and their privilege. The most difficult of Mission problems will then have been solved, and success insured to the work in which we are engaged.

Development of Gospel institutions.

PAPER.

2. BY THE REV. JUDSON SMITH, D.D. (Foreign Secretary, A.B.C.F.M.).

The Place of Education in Missionary Work.

I. The immediate and controlling aim in all Missionary work is the awakening of faith in individual souls, and the raising up of a community of Christian believers. As soon as such communities, in any land, have been sufficiently developed and trained to become self-supporting and self-directing, and have been sufficiently multiplied to reach the communities around them that are still untouched, the proper work of the Missionary Society is done, and the further progress of the Gospel in that land can safely be left to these evangelised communities under native leadership.

Aim of Missionary work.

The conditions of Missionary work are not the same in every case, and the initial stages may well prove of diverse lengths; but in every case the Missionary stage is comparatively brief, and it delivers over the people it has blest to a long career within which they are to carry the work of the Gospel on to perfection, and to bring their special contribution to the increasing wealth of mankind. The Missionary work does not attempt everything which it is desirable should be done; it does not seek to carry everything through to perfection. Its aim is accomplished when the moral atmosphere of a people is changed, when the spiritual forces of a nation are revolutionised by the Gospel, and the Christian life has become so firmly seated, and so well in possession of its appropriate agencies, as to be capable of self-propagation and enlarging influence.

If we keep these things in view we shall much more easily observe the facts that bear upon our discussion, and we shall more accurately judge of the place which education holds in this initial stage of the Gospel's service to the peoples of the earth. There are many things we think of and speak of, when we consider the claims of Missionary work to our support, which belong to stages that follow long after the Missionary stage is properly ended. They will come, and when they come they will be the blessing we deem them; and the contemplation of them rightly fires our ardour and calls out our zeal for Missionary work. But they form no proper part of that work, and must be kept

Stages of Missionary work.

sharply separated from that work, if we would plan wisely and execute efficiently. The universities of England and the Continent are strictly an outgrowth of the Christian life of these nations, and a grand ornament and bulwark of that life.

II. It is obvious that in a sense the whole process of Missionary activity from first to last is in the nature of education. Mind must be appealed to, thought must be awakened and drawn out, in order to convey the simplest religious truths, or to awaken the most rudimentary religious *Educational* emotion. The first message of the Missionary, as he begins his *methods in* work amid a new people, is a lesson in the knowledge and fear of *Gospel teaching.* the living God. And the way is prepared for such truth to take effect, and for other truths to follow, and for all this to reach the mind, and stir the heart, and move the will, by educational methods. It is this natural relation of the Gospel to the human mind and to human society, as the cherishing atmosphere of man's noblest growth, as the mighty stimulus and guide of social graces and refinements, and as the heart and life of all high civilisation and human service, which makes the introduction of the Gospel everywhere and of necessity a grand process in education. And in this sense all Missionary work is education.

If we look more closely to the reason why education must have a place in any well-planned Missionary work, we shall find, if I mistake not, that it is a necessity which grows out of the very nature of the human mind and the character of the Christian faith. There is a harmony between the several powers of the human soul, which makes it necessary that the reason and judgment should approve, or tend to approve, what the will has chosen and *The mind must* what the affections have embraced. If this relation does not *be cultivated.* naturally exist, there is an increasing and unconquerable effort to establish the relation ; and so deep-seated and powerful is this instinct that it usually comes to pass that men love and justify what they choose and do, and the religious life and the intellectual life are continually acting and reacting on each other. Moreover, the Christian life is based upon certain truths, and is constantly shaped and reinforced from them ; and these truths are related to other truths and facts so as to constitute a systematic whole, each part of which is affected by all the rest. In its simplest elements the faith of the Gospel involves certain fundamental facts in regard to creation and Providence, and history, and human life and duty, without which it cannot hold its own, or even exist. Without attempting sharply to define and measure these facts, we see at once that Missionary work among an unevangelised people must involve a certain amount of Christian education, in order that the object of faith and worship may be truly discerned, and also in order that the elements and activities of the intellectual life may be in harmony with the elements and operations of the religious life, and may tend to reinforce and deepen that life.

As soon as the message begins to take effect, and a nucleus of believers has been gathered, the need of the training school immediately appears. Some of these converts give promise of power as teachers and preachers to *Training schools* their fellows ; and the efforts of the Missionary can be doubled, *for converts.* and often indefinitely multiplied, by associating with himself the more capable of these native helpers. The high school, more often called the training school, is designed to draw out and train such promising candidates for this special service. The importance of setting suitable men and women thus at work for their own people cannot easily be over-estimated. Other things being equal, the man who uses his vernacular, and speaks to his own people, must excel in efficiency the man who uses an acquired tongue, and speaks as a stranger and a foreigner.

For success in Missionary work, and especially for any considerable expansion of the area which is affected by its influence, it is needful that the labours of the Foreign Missionary should be seconded and supplemented by a native agency at the earliest practical day. Boarding schools for girls serve the same purpose in some degree, and other purposes also ; and they plainly constitute the

second most important class of Missionary schools. Christian girls, educated
in these schools, are prepared to teach, to engage in evangelistic
work, and especially to make attractive Christian homes for native
pastors and preachers, and thus to help in that profoundly important
task of planting the Gospel in the homes and at the centres of social and
domestic life throughout the nations.

Boarding schools for girls.

Education, thus, of some kinds and degrees, must evidently be an essential
feature of all wisely directed and successful Missionary work. We can scarcely
conceive a Missionary enterprise of much power or worth without this important
auxiliary of the Christian school.

III. But how much education and of what kinds may we appropriately
employ in our Mission-fields? This is the main point of inquiry. And in
the first place the nature of Missionary work, and the bearing
of all educational appliances on that work, at once fix certain
general limits. Education is not fostered and provided for
mere purposes of culture. We do not educate on the Mission-field merely
to educate. Some ulterior end is always in view. We train those men to
be teachers; we educate those men to be pastors; we furnish schools for
girls to fit them more efficiently to play their part in spreading Christian
truth and deepening its hold among their people. We foster day schools
for the children and youth because they open the way to the Gospel and
prepare a new generation of scholars for the higher schools and of
believers for the Church. Always and everywhere education, as an
auxiliary of Mission work, serves an end beyond itself, and finds its
justification in such further service.

Education, a means to an end.

1. We note the fact that Missionary work is carried on among peoples of great
diversity in point of development. There are simple peoples like those of the
South Sea Islands, and the undeveloped tribes of Africa, who must
be educated in some degree in order to understand the Gospel and
to make its hold upon their hearts and lives deep and permanent.
On the other hand, there are civilised and developed peoples, like those of India,
and China, and Japan, for whom this preliminary and elementary training is less
needful. The common school will here be useful chiefly as a natural point
of contact with the people, a centre of evangelistic activity, and a means of
selecting chosen persons for higher schools.

Diversity in development.

2. The second grade of schools, the training school for young men developing
on the one side into the high school, and on the other side into the theological
seminary, and the boarding school for girls have already been
named and described. Their importance as an auxiliary of Missionary
work, and as a preparation for the completion of that work, has
been sufficiently pointed out. Their pupils are picked youths of both sexes,
who are in special training for posts of service and responsibility in the work
of evangelisation; and their courses of study are shaped with reference to this
practical result, and afford liberal culture chiefly as a means to this practical end.

The second grade of schools.

3. The high school gradually tends both to enlarge its scope and to vary its
course, and to become on the disciplinary side the college and the university;
and thus the system of education moves toward theoretic
completion. These higher schools may be reached in some cases
before the Missionary stage is passed; in other cases they will follow the
completion of that work. The special features of that work in each field will
determine what is wise in each particular instance.

The High School.

There are two extremes, which should be sedulously avoided. First,
undue neglect of education, which fails to provide teachers who are
competent to lead the Churches and raise up a regular succession of trained
and able clergy. Second, undue enlargement of educational work, which

provides facilities beyond the real need of a people, or which turns the attention so exclusively to culture as to weaken the force of Evangelistic agencies. Some Missions, especially those earlier planted, have erred on the former side, and their work, remarkable as it was, has proved less capable of endurance and self-direction because there was a lack of educated men to lead the Evangelical communities, and hold up the work to the standard of the Missionary beginnings. Many causes have conspired to weaken and imperil the seemingly brilliant success of the Gospel in the Hawaiian Islands; but among them plainly stands an inadequate development of schools and an inadequate supply of mentally vigorous and competent native pastors and teachers. It may be a question whether the whole educational system now at work within the limits of the Turkish Empire belongs in propriety to the Missionary operations that are carried on upon that field; but it is obvious to remark that few fields are so fully furnished with a competent and trusted native pastorate, or are nearer the time when native talent may safely be left to replace foreign service in every principal department of Christian work.

But on the other hand the weak and almost inappreciable effects of Liberia College as an evangelising agency, and as a civilising force are quite in point here, as illustrating the necessarily secondary part which education, even in its higher degrees, must play in the development of a Christian civilisation. Culture is a valiant reserve, but a weak and inconsequent general. It never led a people or a single soul from heathenism or a false faith to the faith and fruits of a Christian civilisation. *Liberia College.*

4. There is a natural course of events in the progress of successful Missionary work which must be taken into the account in this discussion. An amount and a kind of education which answers every purpose well at the beginning will prove inadequate when the work has been carried further on, and the needs and demands of the people have enlarged.

Christian Missions cannot wisely be diverted from their one great aim of preaching the Gospel and planting the Christian Church amid the lost nations of the earth. This is the supreme service; there is nothing to equal it; nothing to be compared with it. And its successful accomplishment is the sure harbinger of every blessing that can visit man, and transform the home, and redeem the nations, and build the new heavens and the new earth wherein righteousness dwells. Let this work be thoroughly done, and the torch of Christian learning full soon will be kindled throughout the vast spaces of Africa, a Christian civilisation will spread abroad amid the teeming populations of China and India, and reach to every continent and island of the earth. Christianised China will not lack its schools of the highest order, and they will be the peers of the best that England has ever seen. Evangelised Africa will gradually fill with Christian states and schools of liberal culture and a nobler life, as Europe once emerged from its period of pagan barbarism, and assumed the Christian leadership of the world. And it is the glory of the Missionary work to start the nations upon this inspiring march, and to plant them thick and deep with the seeds of this prolific and glorious life. To the cry for help which rises from the countless millions of the lost nations, and comes with resistless appeal to the Christian heart, there is but one sufficient answer. Education cannot compass it; Civilisation cannot effect it; Science says, " It is not in me;" Philosophy says, *The object of Christian Missions.*

"It is not with me;" History says, "I have heard the fame thereof with my ears;" it is Christ alone who says, "Come unto Me, all ye that are weary and heavy laden, and I will give you rest." This is the good tidings of great joy which He bids us preach to every creature.

PAPER.

3. BY THE REV. PROFESSOR ROBERTSON (of Aberdeen, formerly of the Free Church College, Calcutta).

The Education of the Young as a regular part of Mission Work.

I take "Mission work," as here used, to denote the work of evangelising the heathen, whether as individuals or in communities. The subject to be discussed, thus, is the education of the young as a part of the ordinary means to be used in bringing under Gospel influences those that are outside.

I recognise most heartily that the great object of all Christian effort is, and ever must be, to bring about sincere personal submission to Christ; but history and experience alike show that even nominal submission is a result by no means to be despised. It is no small gain when men submit voluntarily to Christian instruction; the persistent use of the means of grace may, with the Divine blessing, secure the highest results. A complete view of the progress of the Gospel among men cannot ignore the wider aspect of the command to "disciple the nations." The Gospel demands immediate, personal obedience, but it does not ignore the future; efforts apparently fruitless to-day may be crowned with success in days to come. These two views of Mission work are not antagonistic, but complementary. The man who seeks immediate results is doing the best he can for the future. The man who has his eye on the complete success of the future knows that the results he aims at cannot come too soon, and therefore does not neglect the present. There is a coming of the kingdom of God which is "not with observation."

The great object to disciple nations.

The far-reaching character of the work to be done carries with it the necessity for equally far-reaching methods. All recognise the primary place assigned to the preaching of the Word of God, and the paramount importance of personal dealing with adults, by teaching and preaching. I know of no advocate of education as a Missionary agency who does not emphasise this position.

All agree that Scripture recognises a transcendent importance as attaching to the early training of the young. Divine truth, wisely treated, cannot too early be brought to bear on the rising generation. Even if we knew nothing of the place that Scripture gives to children; if we did not read, " Train up a child in the way he should go, and when he is old he will not depart from it " (Prov. xxii. 6); do we not know that God reveals Himself in providence as well as in grace? And has He not made it abundantly clear that the hope of the nations and of the Church is with the young? Christian parents are to do their utmost to bring up their children " in the nurture and admonition of the Lord ;" and no Christian, as he is true to His Master, dare neglect any opportunity of training, educating, influencing for God a non-Christian child. The education of the young as a regular part of

Importance of training the young.

Mission work simply means that Christian workers among the heathen should seize and use for God the most impressible years of every life. And whether the result be a real turning to God, or only a state of mind more or less prepared to receive "the Word of the Kingdom," in either case we have cause for thankfulness.

If it should seem to any one that in thus arguing I am substituting a process more or less human for the act and influence of Divine grace, a moment's reflection will show that such means or processes are to be found in all kinds of work in which human instrumentality is allowed to bear a part. The use of means in no way derogates from the glory of the Divine grace which alone gives the increase. Scripture and *The principle, that of the Sunday school.* common sense unite in telling us that we can be "fellow-workers with God" only in the use of means ; preaching itself is but a process. Up to this point, however, I do not anticipate any serious divergence of opinion. I have done no more than contend that in the evangelisation of the heathen the methods of the Sunday school are entitled to a place alongside the preaching of the Word. However strongly some may feel that education in the full sense of the term is a legitimate part of Missionary operations only when carried on among converts and their children, no Protestant can seriously dispute the duty and importance of using every opportunity of training young heathen in the knowledge and fear of God, and of instructing them in the great facts of sin and salvation through Christ.

But the education of the young as a part of Mission work means a great deal more than religious instruction and the methods of the Sunday school ; it includes moral and even secular instruction,—instruction in the three R's, in history, geography, grammar, mathematics, etc. Here lies the difficulty. Few doubt the utility of such education ; no one disputes its philanthropic character ; and yet, not a few shrink from allowing secular instruction a place in Mission work. If not prepared to regard it as absolutely antagonistic to the Gospel, some hold such secular work to be unfit employment for an ordained minister of the Word ; and we are often reminded of the *Secular and religious instruction combined.* Apostle's words, "I determined not to know anything among you save Jesus Christ and Him crucified" (1 Cor. ii. 2). A cursory reference to the Greek text is enough to show that the words actually used by Paul do not bear the exclusive sense usually attached to them. "I did not determine to know anything" is very far from being equivalent to "I determined to know nothing." Paul had made up his mind to know among the Corinthians "Jesus Christ and Him crucified ; " he had not made up his mind to include or exclude any other topic. These and other objections to the inclusion of secular instruction among Missionary operations may be met *seriatim*, and, if need be, I am prepared to meet them ; but in the meantime I content myself with indicating some of the considerations that might be urged on their behalf.

When a place is claimed for secular instruction among Missionary operations, it is always to be understood as accompanied by direct religious instruction. The education of the young, so understood, has been recognised as a regular part of Mission work by most modern Missionaries and Missionary Societies. To quote only one testimony, Carey, Marshman, and Ward, when reviewing their work in 1815, specify three distinct agencies required to plant the Gospel in a heathen country ; and one of them is " the instruction of youth in the truths of the Bible and in the literature suited to the wants of the country."

Such education is a necessary preliminary to the introduction of certain important parts of Missionary work. Without it the distribution of the Scriptures and religious tracts is useless among most heathen peoples. I well remember how, on my first visit to the Santhal country, I provided myself with a considerable supply of tracts *Education an important preliminary.* for distribution, but found them of no use, as very few, if any, of the people could read. No one who knows anything of the wonderful results of Bible and tract distribution among the heathen is likely to treat this consideration lightly.

Even when this education fails—as it does fail in multitudes of cases—to lead those who receive it to the Saviour, it is very helpful in destroying false religion, and in preparing the way for the reception of the truth. In India, for instance, it destroys the physical basis of Hinduism, and secures important advantages for the enforcement of Christian truth. The sacred books of the Hindus are "inextricably committed to a collision with the truths of astronomy, chemistry, medicine, geography, and all the facts of modern science."

Destroys idolatry and cultivates conscience. Instruction in the elements of physical science or geography not only upsets the old notions on these subjects, but so far forth uproots the Hindu religious system. Christian education, however, is not, like purely secular education, a merely destructive agency ; it is also constructive. It takes away the false, but it also endeavours to supply the true. I might urge that such education has a prophylactic and a corrective influence ; it reduces by anticipation and with ever-growing effect the strength of pantheism. It cultivates a sense of the reality of things, it develops a sense of individuality and responsibility, it educates the conscience, and so helps to bring the Hindu out of the mists and unrealities into which all things, even himself included, are resolved by his favourite doctrine of *maya* (illusion).

I may here quote a paragraph from the *Liberal*, the organ of the party of the late Keshub Chunder Sen :—" There is something in Hinduism which is not to be despised, and which must be recognised before any impression can be made upon it. What that something is, let the Missionaries find out. The religions of Greece, Rome, Egypt, Gaul, and Britain dissolved like ice before the summer sun at the advent of Christianity ; Hinduism threatens to maintain its conservative aspect in the face of all foes. Mohammedanism could not effect a single breach in the Hindu fortress." This is the view of men who have themselves given up Hinduism. Bishop Taylor, of Africa, when some *Chunder Sen and Bishop Taylor.* fifteen years ago he visited India, expected to see repeated among the Hindus the wholesale conversion of heathen which he had witnessed in South Africa. He preached the same Gospel in the same way ; he made repeated and varied efforts ; but he was compelled to admit that there were inherent difficulties in the case which made the result he desired at that stage impossible.

I do not affirm that education must precede preaching, any more than I affirm that civilisation must precede the evangelisation of the savage ; but I do *Education essential.* assert that without education a solid, self-respecting, self-governing, self-propagating Church is impossible, and that every Mission to such tribes should from the outset include the education of the young as a regular part of its operation. In short, whatever argument is available for Medical Missions is equally available for Educational Missions. The heathen mind is a mind diseased or deformed ; education is essential to mental health ; *mens sana* is at least as important as *corpus sanum.*

I might also point out how fruitful Mission schools have been among such tribes as the Santhals. A very large proportion, if not a majority of the converts connected with the Free Church Mission, have been the fruit of Missionary education. At this moment, I believe, the members of the highest class, about twelve in number, in the Mission school at Pachamba, are all Christians. *Fas est ab hoste doceri.* Hindus know what Missionary education has done, and make more or less persistent attempts to forestall or supplant it. One has only to read the evidence given before the Indian Education Commission, including in some cases a demand for a conscience clause in Missionary schools, in order to see how much this department of Missionary work is feared. To quote the organ already named, "Outside people have no idea of what education has done and is doing for the people of India."

All may not agree with me in holding such views, but I maintain that ordinary education, always including religious instruction, is not only a legitimate *Important, if not essential.* but an exceedingly important part of Mission work. And I hold that in circumstances like those of the Santhals and the tribes around Lake Nyassa, the education of the young is an essential part of Mission work, if we are to avoid the dangers of priestcraft, to have Christians able for themselves to read and understand the Word of God, and to see churches that are self-governing and self-extending. But in using education let it never be forgotten that schools are only schools; they are not prayer meetings or meetings for anxious inquirers.

I pass on to the second division of the topic before us: Should education as a part of Mission work be restricted in any way either as to those who are to be benefited by it, or in its extent? I need hardly say anything on this head, for my views on it have already been indicated. I have already said that among tribes without literary education, however readily they may yield to the preaching of the Word, education has a most important part to play in gathering converts and supplying the conditions of a stable Church. It is impossible to carry education too far down if we would have our Churches **What restrictions, if any?** formed of " the people of the Book." On the other hand there may be cases in which a sufficient education for ordinary purposes is given by the Government or otherwise; and it may be asked how far this affects the Missionary's duty. When the education thus supplied is anti-Christian or purely secular, Missionaries are bound to use every opportunity of getting the young under their care and instruction with a view to religious influence. If this can be done without undertaking the burden of secular work, by all means let us use what is provided. But if it cannot be done without undertaking secular as well as religious instruction, Missions and Missionaries must be prepared to carry on both, as far as means and opportunities allow. And this work of education should be planned and executed to the extent that promises the most telling and lasting results. I do not profess to lay down specific rules. Variations will occur from country to country, and even between different parts of the same country. A comparatively low limit may be laid down in some cases, while others may require the limit to be raised so as to include what is commonly called " higher education."

A further topic has been suggested for discussion : " The extent to which the employment of non-Christian teachers in Mission schools is legitimate or necessary." This topic has no necessary connection with the main subject of this morning's discussion, except on the assumption that without such teachers no Mission school would obtain pupils. Non-Christian teachers have sometimes been represented either as decoys or as guarantees that **On the employment of non-Christian teachers.** conversions were not desired; but for the most part by those who oppose either their employment or Missionary education. I know of no foundation for the assumption that such teachers must be employed in order to secure pupils. The real reason for their employment is two-fold : (1) Without them Missionary education would be seriously restricted in its extent; and (2) there is no bar in principle to their employment.

In the practice of the Missions with which I am acquainted, non-Christian teachers are employed only in secular instruction, and even then only in default of Christian teachers. I made it a rule never to appoint a non-Christian until I had tried and failed to find an efficient Christian. It should also be noted that the returns of non-Christian teachers in Mission employment sometimes include the Circle schools aided partly by local Missions, partly by the Christian Vernacular Education Society, on condition that the school books and the instruction are satisfactory, and that the teacher to whom the school belongs, usually a non-Christian, accepts the supervision of a Christian teacher and allows him on his visits to the school, once or twice a week, to impart religious instruction. These and similar cases swell the total of non-Christian employés of Missions in a somewhat misleading way. The fact, however, remains that by availing themselves of such agents, whether employed directly or indirectly, Missionaries are enabled greatly to increase the number of pupils under religious **Reasons for their employment.** instruction. According to the last Missionary census for India, more than twenty-seven hundred of the teachers employed were non-Christian; and on the lowest calculation, by relieving Christian teachers of secular work, they enabled the various Missionaries to give religious instruction to seventy thousand or eighty thousand pupils more than could otherwise have been reached. I believe the actual figure to be over one hundred thousand. Christian men will require something more than the exigencies of a theory to justify them in throwing away such an opportunity of extending the influence of the Gospel. If it is said that we ought to circumscribe Mission work so that it may be overtaken entirely by Christians, I reply that I find nothing in Scripture to prevent me from using for the advancement of Christ's kingdom even those who have not personally submitted to Him as Lord.

If I am told that in extending Christian work by the employment of non-Christian teachers we are going beyond the work assigned to us by our Lord, I reply that He has enjoined us to "disciple all nations," and "preach the Gospel to every creature," and that this command cannot be fulfilled too soon. Whatever exception may be taken to the influence exerted by non-Christian teachers, the additional pupils thus brought under the influence of the Gospel are in no worse case than they would have been had the schools they attended been entirely separate from Missionary influence; nay, the extent to which they are under Missionary influence is, as a rule, a distinct gain in disposition to attend to the Gospel. And to say that work among such persons is beyond the range of what has been given us to do, is to forget that, as a matter of fact, the work has been brought within our range. I do not deny that attempts may be made by non-Christian teachers, overtly or covertly, to defeat the work of the Missionary; but few actual cases have been adduced in support of this contention; and it should not be forgotten that not a few of these teachers are as near the kingdom of God as many nominal Christians. I quite admit that these non-Christian teachers are in many cases standing testimonies to the apparent failure of Educational Missions, and that by employing them we incur a limitation of the principle that at every point in his course of study the pupil should be directly influenced for God. I admit that all this means difficulty and even weakness, but I see in it no sacrifice of fundamental Christian principle, and so have no hesitation in availing myself of the greatly extended range of Christian influence. The employment of these teachers, however, should always be regarded as a temporary expedient to meet a temporary necessity; no Educational Mission work can be regarded as satisfactory until it has been provided with a full Christian staff.

DISCUSSION.

Rev. Young J. Allen, D.D. (Anglo-Chinese College, Shanghai): I wish to speak to you this morning on a revolution, and this revolution will determine, as I conceive, the place and the extent of education which we offer to China. In the first place we have forced upon China a revolution, and that revolution in its fundamental aspect involves the education of China. We have gone there as Christian nations to the number of about fifteen, and we have made treaties involving the extra-territoriality clause, which means that China shall cede to those foreign nations independent self-government. We have not only the ports open to us, but we have independent self-governing colonies. We have told China that she shall not have jurisdiction over us; that we shall have independent jurisdiction over our own people. We have therefore taken part of her territory, and established ourselves as a self-

External influence on China and Japan.

governing power. China and Japan are both involved in this extra-territoriality clause. Their wish and every-day thought is to retrieve their jurisdiction. We say to them, " No Christians will submit to be governed by heathen people; you must qualify up to our standard in your laws, in your moral principles, in your learning and in your general administration, and then we will yield back your territory and allow ourselves to come under your jurisdiction." We have thus placed upon China the necessity of learning, and I am glad to say that China has accepted the position. That is the origin of the revolution now going on in China and in Japan. It is not because they fancy or love our ways and esteem them better, but necessity is laid upon them, or they cannot enter into the comity of nations and be received as equals amongst Christians. We have forced upon them this necessity, not only of qualifying and educating a few people, but of qualifying and educating the nations; in other words we have been fulfilling what Christ commands as to teaching the nations. As I have said, China has accepted this, and she proposes to establish, and has established schools, and Missionaries have been called to take part in this great work of educating the nation.

(margin: Make educational changes necessary.)

This is not all. The Government has seen the necessity not only of teaching young men to have intercourse with these great nations with whom she has treaties, but they have found it necessary to have an educated empire, an educated cabinet, an educated council, and educated officials. And how is that to be done? By qualifying Missionaries to teach these young men, and to translate text books in history, geography, mathematics, and all these things, so as to place them within the reach of these high officials. That is the way that education is going on. The Government has found that it is necessary in order to retrieve its jurisdiction ; and in order to retrieve the integrity of its territory and to develop the resources of that magnificent empire, it has found it necessary to require the universities to accept questions on mathematics and the different sciences at their examinations.

Now, when you remember that in China there are one million five hundred thousand university pupils ; when you remember that they have their colleges in all the provinces, that they have their Provincial University, where they grant the M.A. degree, that they have the Imperial University at Pekin, where they grant the LL.D. degree, and that they have still higher degrees than that, and that all the officials of the Government are educated men,—when you remember that the Government has accepted the necessity of mathematics and foreign sciences in order to build their ships, to open their mines, to build railways, and to develop their resources, and place the country in harmony with the great enterprises of the West, and bring it into the comity of nations,—when you remember that, and also remember that the Missionary only stands there in China prepared to give the people this education, prepared to be teachers and to translate the books which they are to learn, you will then understand the place which education takes in the Missionary enterprise in China; then you will understand the limit which is to be placed upon it,—the limit should be the very best that we have got, the extent of it should be according to our ability to give it, and their capacity to receive it.

(margin: A growing necessity.)

Mr. Henry Morris (Hon. Sec., Christian Vernacular Education Society for India): The special subject I wish to speak about is education in India, which is the country I know best ; but, *mutatis mutandis*, what I say of India will apply to all other parts of the Mission-field. The first subject on the programme is "the place of education in Mission work." I consider that education ought to occupy the first place in the second stage of Mission work. I cannot enlarge upon

(margin: Place of education.)

this as well as on many other things, upon which I should like to speak, for want of time.

I would put in the forefront of this question the resolution of the Governor-General of India which was published on the 31st of December last, and which I think is one of the most important documents **Government and** ever issued from an official source since the Education Despatch **moral teaching.** of 1854. It deserves the most earnest and careful attention of all those who are interested in India. It is a most saddening document, as it is indeed, in many respects, a grave official announcement of failure in purely secular education. It is a remarkable fact that the Governor-General himself points to an increase in Christian colleges and high schools as the best solution of the problem, and almost asks that there shall be Christian instruction given in secular colleges after school hours.

I think that the Christian Church cannot let alone the question of higher education in India. Having come into contact with a number of educated Hindus, I feel the deepest sympathy with those who have given up one faith, and have not found another. I do not know anything sadder than the case of a man who, having given up his ancestral belief, is hovering about not knowing what he shall do. The last state of that man is worse than the first. We are, therefore, bound as Christians to give a Christian education to these men; and I would implore all those who take an interest in education in India not to leave the education of the higher classes to the Government alone, or to the Hindus alone.

I would also refer to another very important subject,—normal education, the teaching teachers how to teach. I believe that that is a subject into which the Christian Church ought to throw its heart, because if we do not teach these people something of the noble art and honourable profession of teaching, we shall really be leaving the education of the people in the hands of those who are not able to undertake it efficiently.

Let me say one word with regard to lower education, which also ought not to be neglected. It is the general policy of Missionary Societies to **Missionary** throw themselves almost entirely into the education of their **inspection.** own converts, and to give up the lower education of the people. I believe that all might, with the greatest advantage, use what might be called Christian inspection, by placing the indigenous native schools under the inspection of Christian Missionaries. I have known this system most successfully carried out in Bengal, and I could go on for half an hour telling you the admirable and splendid results of Christian inspection in native indigenous schools.

Rev. J. Murray Mitchell, LL.D. (Free Church of Scotland): In what I say I shall be as practical as possible. My friend, Mr. Morris, has spoken of India. I will also say a few words with regard to that country, as it is the field that I know best. Let it not be supposed that I advocate Educational Missions as opposed to other Missions. All my life I have heard the cry, "Teach, teach, teach," and then I have heard the cry, "Preach, preach;" and I have said, by all means preach and teach. Give as much preaching as you can possibly give, and as much teaching too. At present I will confine my remarks to teaching. Let it be remembered that the higher and middle-classes of India at the present day are determined to have education, and to have as high an education as possible. Who is it to give it? The Government has attempted to do so; but, as you have heard from my friend Mr. Morris, even by the confession of the Government itself, the purely secular education system Government difficulty about moral training. has been, morally, a failure. Then if the Government system has been a failure, what is to be done? If Government do not keep up schools and colleges, the natives will do it. Many of the natives are determined if possible to purify their Hinduism to a certain extent, and then to teach a kind of theism in their colleges. In Calcutta they are going on at a great rate in setting up colleges of their own.

Do you desire that the education of the mind of the heathen should be left to the heathen? I am sure no one desires it. And if we withdraw from the higher education—I refer to Protestant Missions—I will tell you who will be ready to take it up. The Roman Catholics will be so. They have sent out able men, Jesuits, men of high intellectual culture; and they have set up colleges in Calcutta, Bombay, and many other places. Well, are we to leave India in all its higher education to Hindus and Romanists?

But you will say, "Ah, but you have very few converts from those colleges of yours." I grant it. In the Mission with which I was connected in Bengal, for one Brahman brought out from the college there would be perhaps twenty converts in our rural Missions. But let this fact Character of college converts. be known, that when educated men are brought out, they are generally of a far higher type, intellectually, mora'ly, and spiritually, than the men of a lower grade. Let me give an illustration. We had the first Brahman conversion in Bombay in the case of a well-known man, my dear friend, Dr Narayan Sheshadri. Our institution was cut down to the ground. Every Brahman fled: almost every Hindu fled; and we had only some fifty pupils left. It was most disheartening, but we bore it because the conversion had come. Now that solitary man has been, under God, the instrument of bringing more than a thousand heathens into the Christian Church.

Take another case. There is my dear friend, the Rev. Baba Padmanji, who has devoted himself to a literary life. Now, there is certainly nothing more necessary for India than a pure literature. Missionaries were the first to write tracts. We have, many of us, done all that we could in that matter. I felt it my duty to do a good deal; but my friend and former pupil, the Rev. Baba Padmanji, has published literally more than sixty books and tracts; he has devoted himself to that work. He writes a beautiful Marathi style; and his productions are thoroughly Christian. His pen is busy at this hour, and as long as he lives he will labour in this infinitely important work. I call it so, for I am convinced that there is no more pressing duty than that of producing a pure Christian literature for India. But how can you have such preachers as Dr. Sheshadri, or such writers as Mr. Padmanji, if you neglect education, and even higher education?

Rev. Robert Tebb (Wesleyan Missionary Society, from Ceylon): I have had considerable experience in the educational work of a very successful Mission. We begin at the earliest stage of thought and feeling, and win the child's nature for the Lord Jesus Christ. Now to do that, we have, of course primary instruction. We begin our work in the jungle, and, there, of course, we want a centre for our work; we erect a place and appoint a Christian teacher. I must say that I have no confidence whatever in non-Christian teachers in any subject. I know it is a matter of opinion, but I have found these non-Christian Heathen teachers and fees. teachers doing more harm than they could possibly do good. Therefore I would pack them all out. We have to appoint Christian teachers. We have a place for evangelistic work, and the children are won in this way and gradually instructed in the elements of our holy religion. Then I would have these schools free from fees. I do not like the idea of any child being turned away from elementary, secular and religious instruction, because the father either cannot or will not pay the fees. If there is anything that a Missionary Society ought to support, it seems to me that it is vernacular education for every child that God has sent into the world.

Then the second thing is this : we try as soon as possible to teach English. English has a marketable value, and every child who comes into the Anglo-vernacular schools should pay a proportionate fee. I am reminded that our money is obtained from a number of our poor people, and we have no right, it seems to me, to give anything of market value to the people without making them pay for what they receive. Then, by way of scholarships we try to promote effective religious instruction. The secular education, of course, is examined by Government, and there is payment for it by results. With regard to religious instruction, we have a carefully prepared programme, and we have our Inspector of Schools who goes round and reports to our Church Courts as to the faithful attention to religious teaching in our schools.

I could give you many illustrations showing what a great blessing has been upon this systematic work, from the primary, through the Anglo-vernacular, up to English education in the higher class fitting them for this world and for the world to come.

Brigade Surgeon Cockell : I am going to speak about a very important subject. I heard Mr. Morris, or some one else, mention the want of Christian education in the Government schools in India. Now if we can get the Bible introduced as a text-book, by-and-by the whole nation Introduction of will become more or less Christian. I have a striking instance the Bible. in point. In the Government school at Dharwar, the Bible was introduced without asking leave from the Government, and, not only the pupils but the masters themselves attended, giving up the Saturday half-holiday for the purpose. The classroom or the examination room was filled with the highest class of English-speaking students with the masters. The Bible was read,—the first chapter of Genesis; and the first chapter of Matthew was also read from the New Testament. The students were asked questions upon it, and to the one who gave the best answers a prize was promised at Christmas—a prize of a silver watch. They were all anxious to win the prize, and they listened to the Bible and were able, three weeks before I left, to answer questions which perhaps some boys and girls in English schools could not have answered. Is not this then an important thing? The Missionary schools in India are a driblet as compared to the Government schools.

If God has given us India on purpose that we may make it Christian, do not let it be supposed that it is given for our benefit. The Mutiny is a sufficient lesson as to that. Look at the punishment that was inflicted upon us because we did not Christianise the people. I hope that the Jubilee of the Queen which was inaugurated last year will be completed by sending a deputation of one of our archbishops, together with bishops and clergymen of all denominations (I hope Mr. Spurgeon will be among them), together with laymen and noblemen (including, I hope, Lord Northbrook), to go before the Queen and ask that the Bible may be established as a text-book in the Government schools in India.

Rev. Professor T. Smith, D.D. (Free Church College, Edinburgh): The subject for this meeting, as I understand it, is: Education as a means of evangelistic work, as distinguished from evangelical, if I may make that distinction between education taking its place after men have become Christians, with a view to their education as Christians, and education with a view to bringing men to the acceptance of the Gospel. It is the latter subject, I think, that we are more especially interested in, particularly as regards the higher education. It so happens that for twenty years of my life I was occupied mainly in conducting this higher education in Calcutta, and this I will say frankly: it often fell to me to be the apologist of that kind of education, because we were much assailed in those days by men whom I greatly loved and respected, but whom I thought wrong on that subject,—it often fell to me to be the apologist, because I had the misfortune of being engaged in teaching little except mathematics, which was considered the most assailable subject. I generally took refuge in the principle of sour grapes.

Now, much as I have had to apologise for this education, and much as I am prepared to apologise for it now, I should be extremely sorry to see it become the only Missionary agency, or to see it have a larger part assigned to it proportionally than it has in the education of India. I do think that this is the danger that the educational method is subject to now. When I went to India in the year 1839, nearly fifty years ago, there were five of us belonging to the Free Church of Scotland, and we were *Education auxiliary, not exclusive.* the only educators in all Bengal, I may say in all India. Our success was such that we were imitated by almost everybody. In those days, while there were five of us engaged mainly, but not exclusively, in education ; there were at least twenty Missionaries in Calcutta alone who were entirely engaged in vernacular preaching. The state of things now, I think you may say, is pretty nearly reversed. The disruption of our Scotch Church doubled the educational work, and the London Missionary Society took it up, and Bishop Wilson founded his Episcopal College, which I believe is now considerably modified ; but the number of men employed in education is much greater than it was, and the number of men employed in vernacular preaching is considerably smaller. That is a thing I very much regret and lament. But the matter of education depends upon the circumstances of the people. When my beloved and revered friend,—I may say my father,—Dr. Duff, began the work, there were very few provincial stations. I look upon the matter thus. We are to preach the Gospel to every creature. Now there are creatures, the most important creatures you may say in regard *The only way of reaching a certain class.* to the future of India, and you can reach them in this way, but, generally speaking, you can reach them in no other way. It is not only that if you do not reach them in this way you cannot reach them by any other, but that they are determined to have education.

But the people will have education which is not only non-religious, but which is in its practical tendency anti-religious education, which by its necessary and natural result will reduce the nation that receives it to the condition of pure, simple, absolute atheism,—a system which will destroy all moral sense and all moral principle, and reduce that portion of the earth where it unhappily prevails to a condition very little different from that of pandemonium. This education they will have, or they will have the education that we can give them, an education not merely evangelical, as I have said, but evangelistic ; an education which ought at every step to deal with the consciences of men, and to persuade them by all means and instrumentalities to embrace the Gospel of the Lord Jesus Christ, which can alone bring salvation.

Rev. Arthur T. Pierson, D.D. (Philadelphia, U.S.A.): It impresses me more and more that all true wisdom on the subject of Missions is found in the New Testament. Our blessed Lord laid down distinctly the whole programme of Missionary enterprise, and we shall never improve upon it.

The first principle was the preaching of the Gospel by a man who under-
Preaching allows of many methods. stood it, not only theologically, but experimentally. "Preach."
"Ye are My witnesses." A man cannot witness anything that
he does not know. The preaching of the Gospel, with the
man behind the Gospel permeated with the spirit of the Gospel, is the first
thing. Secondly, teaching and healing the sick. First, "As ye go, preach;"
and the next injunction is, "Heal the sick." There are two words in
Matthew which are both translated "teaching" in the Old Version, but you
know very well that they should not be so translated. The first means to
make disciples, and the second means to teach. Now I want to give you two
pertinent illustrations of what can be done through education, especially in
reaching the more unimpressible, unapproachable peoples as a preparation
and as a handmaid to evangelisation. Years ago, among the Mormons of
Illustrations in Utah and Beyrout. Utah, there went a gentleman who undertook the superintendence of the Missions. Now we have had great difficulty
in reaching the Mormons, not only on account of their bigotry,
but on account of their stolidity and stupidity. He began by attempting
to reach them by means of a public lecture, and being unable to reach them
in any other way he gave a lecture on Humour, but they were so stupid
that he was obliged to repeat and explain his jokes. First, their muscles
would relax from their rigidity, and after the fourth or fifth explanation
they would burst into a guffaw of laughter. He was able, however, to get
sufficient hold upon them to persuade them that he could entertain them.
Then he gave lectures on scientific and historical subjects till he persuaded
them that he knew more than their ignorant priests. Then he set up
a school, and put a young lady at the head of it; and after she had got the
children together she opened a Sunday school, where they sang Sunday
school hymns. Then, having got hold of the children, they attached to the
school an evangelistic service, and got the parents to attend. My second
illustration is from Beyrout, where one of the most successful Presbyterian
Missions is established. They had schools there of a higher order, especially
for girls; and on one occasion,—when the girls were giving an exhibition of
their attainments,—the Pasha confessed to Dr. Jessup that they would
have to establish schools among the Mohammedan Arab tribes, in order to
prevent the children from being drawn under Christian instruction. That
was the origin of the Mohammedan schools in Syria. When they found
themselves unable to get any teachers from their own classes to teach
the children they absolutely went to our Christian schools for educated
Christian girls to teach those Mohammedan children.

Mr. Fountain J. Hartley (Secretary, Sunday School Union): I owe an
apology for standing up before such a noble gathering as I see before me
this morning, but I have taken some part in this question of high schools
in India, and I have come to the conclusion that upon the whole, though
they are undoubtedly useful institutions, they are diverting attention somewhat from the more evangelistic work. I will venture to say a few words
upon this subject, and I will chiefly put them in the form of questions.
First, Could we not be told what amount of money and Missionary power
Information desired. is expended on our high schools, and would not that information support the conclusion that too large a portion is spent in
educational as compared with evangelistic work? This is a
question very much of degree. We might go some distance in support of

these schools and colleges, but how far? My second question is: Could we be told how many high school pupils are Christian converts when they enter?—because, if a large proportion of the students were of this class, no expenditure of time or energy would be too great to fit them for future usefulness. That is a point that we should all agree upon. Then, thirdly, I should like to know whether any large proportion of the scholars trained in the high schools and colleges, do come to a knowledge of the truth while they are in those institutions, and do give themselves to the service of the Master at the close of their course of training? No doubt this information could be given to us, and on the nature and extent of that information would very much depend the conclusion to which many of us would come on this important subject.

The complaints made as to the want of teachers for our day schools and Sunday schools seem to me to show that a very small proportion of those scholars become teachers, or devote themselves in any way to the Missionary cause. Considering that we have had these institutions **Complaints made.** at work for two or three generations, I think they ought to have produced teachers sufficient to engage in Christian work throughout the continent of India. (I have been dealing chiefly with India, but what I have said will apply to other places.) Then I think we ought to know more fully the opinion of the Missionaries employed in the different districts in reference to this important subject. I know that some of them do feel that we are giving too much attention to education; not that they undervalue education, but they feel that our Missionary Societies are giving too much of their time and energy to this educational work, and that it does interfere to a great extent with our more evangelistic operations. One gentleman, the principal of one of our colleges in India, who had not heard the new translation given to us this morning of a certain text, did put on record, as will be found in the report of the Missionary Conference at Calcutta, the expression of his deep regret that he had so much to do in teaching classics, mathematics, and logic, that he was not able to carry out the resolution with which he went to India, " to know nothing among men save Jesus Christ and Him crucified."

Rev. F. A. Noble, D.D. (Chicago): I have ventured to send up my name this morning, because I have a profound conviction with regard to the question now under discussion. It has not been my good fortune to be in India, or Japan, or China, or any Missionary field, so as to be able to speak of it from the experience of a Missionary's life, but I have had occasion, in connection with my work in America, to study the question of the relation of education to evangelistic work—the relation of education to the Missions of our Christian organisations and enterprises in the great west of our country; and it is because I have had this opportunity that I have come to the conclusion, a very deep and profound conclusion, that we have too much omitted in our Missionary enterprise the educational element. Dr. Pierson has referred to an illustration in point drawn from experience in Utah. It has been my fortune during the last six or seven years to be closely identified with the Christian educational work in that and the adjacent territories.

It was at my suggestion that a Society called the New West Education Commission was organised in the city of Chicago. I have been at the head of that Society during these past years, and, of course, I have **Education as an** had to study the question, Why was that organisation suggested? **evangelistic** Why is it found necessary to spend sixty thousand dollars a **agency in America.** year in support of Christian teachers carrying on the work of education in that territory? Simply because it was utterly impossible for any

Minister of any denomination to make any sort of headway with the Mormon parents, except through that organisation. It could only be done by getting hold of the children by the process which Dr. Pierson has indicated in Salt Lake City and other cities and towns. It is only through the influence of education upon the children in the Sunday schools, and then through evangelistic work, that we could pave the way, so that ministers could establish themselves and win an audience. That is not only true of Utah and New Mexico, and that great sweep of territories where the population is being recruited from England, Wales, Norway, Sweden, and Germany, but it is true in the South. We have in the South from seven to nine millions of coloured population. They were emancipated only a quarter of a century ago, and the great masses of them are perfectly ignorant. They have Churches, and they have preachers who go forth who, as I have heard men in the South say, do more mischief by their preaching than they do good, simply because they are wild fanatics and know nothing of the Gospel of Jesus Christ by any instruction or sober experience. It has been found necessary to establish schools and colleges, to take these people and train them and educate them, and we are recruiting out of these coloured people in the South, men and women who can go forth and teach and preach. In that way we expect to save the coloured people of the South.

You have been reminded this morning that Rome gave England letters; you might have been reminded that John Knox saved Scotland by schools; you might have been reminded that the Pilgrim Fathers who went across the seas to lay the foundations of Christian institutions in America, carried schools with them wherever they went. It is the Christian school in England, in America, in China, and in India, that is at the foundation of Christian institutions.

Rev. Wilson Phraner (Presbyterian Board of Foreign Missions, U.S.A.): It seems a peculiar thing that I should follow brother Noble at this place and time, having myself been the acting Chairman of the work of Education of the Presbyterian Church at home, for years past, and I can confirm what has been said in connection with the evangelisation of our own land. We have found it necessary to go into educational work in territories where no provision has been made for the education of the people. We have been obliged in connection with our evangelistic work, to try and make our own land a truly Christian land,—we have been obliged within the last fifteen years to undertake school work, as it is called, among the children in different portions of our country. But in the opportunity that I have enjoyed during the past year of seeing Mission work in various fields, I admit that my views have somewhat changed as to the importance of educational work. I started from home with the thought that too much attention was perhaps given by our Missionaries to educational work, but as the result of a year's observation I have come to a different conclusion.

A travelled convert to education for evangelisation.

It is an essential part of all Christian evangelistic work. Christianity assumes intelligence on the part of the people. I have been surprised at the amount of excellent educational work that is being carried on, and the only criticism I would make is that in many points in foreign lands, as in the home lands, education is not sufficiently and distinctively Christian. I have been in a school in India with between three hundred and four hundred children and fourteen teachers, and there were only three Christians amongst them. I saw a Mohammedan hearing a lesson in the Bible; it is true it was only a recitation. I saw another school in India with three hundred children where there were only two Christian teachers. I said, "Why, is this, and how is this?" and the reply was, "We cannot get the men we want; the Government outbids us and pays higher salaries than we can afford to give, and so comes into competition with us and takes away the very men we want for our work." That is the process that is going on in India.

Let me say only another word as to the stimulus which has grown out of our Christian education, and I would take as an illustration the case of Dr. Harper in China. He wanted a Christian college there, and he went home and got one hundred and fifty thousand dollars. Five hundred Chinese then sent a petition to have the college located at Canton. The Viceroy heard of it and was disgusted that they should ask these foreigners for education. "If you want education," he said, "I will build you a college." I saw the building. It was an extensive institution, for they are going to have a large college there, where Western science is to be taught (for the mind of China has come to demand it), but no Christianity. He is now trying to prevent Dr. Harper from getting even a place to locate his college in Canton.

Rev. A. D. Gring (Reformed Church in the United States, from Japan): It is evident to all who are present here and who have heard these discussions that the work in the foreign field is more like the work at home than it is unlike. What the Christian schools and institutions have done at home for the Church, these institutions are doing, and will do abroad. This is seen and felt in Japan, where we are using schools as one of the greatest departments of our Christian work. We all feel as Missionaries that the fundamental principle of success in foreign work is that the great burden of the Missionary work must come upon the shoulders of the natives themselves. The next point is that we rear a native Church, with its ministers, its elders and its deacons, and its intelligent laymen. A Church without leaders is no Church at all; and a Church that has no intelligent laymen, as deacons, or elders, is no Church at all. For this reason, we are placing a great deal of stress upon educational work in Japan.

Then again, in Japan, our schools give us residence in the country. They enable us to go out of the treaty ports and to live wherever we please, so that while they serve our Mission interest in Japan *Missionary* they at the same time give us the privilege of living anywhere *education in* among the people. Then our Mission schools in Japan have *Japan.* elevated the Government schools in that country, so that to-day the Government officials in Japan have asked the Missionaries to supply Christian teachers for their schools. Of course, the schools must be carried on as much as possible by native money. We do not want foreign money to carry on our schools, and I am here to say that the Japanese are coming forward with their thousands of dollars and saying to our Missionaries, "You supply the teachers and we will supply the money." I know one instance, connected with the American Board, where they received ten thousand dollars from the natives, and have only supplied Christian teachers. Then in another school, forty-five miles west of that, the Governor, the Vice-Governor, and other heads of the establishments have come and said to us, "You provide us with teachers, and we will provide the money, and we will defray the running expenses;" and a large sum has been subscribed to establish in that town a Christian institution. The Governor has brought his son from Tokio and placed him in the hands of the teachers, saying, "Take this son of mine, and train him after the model of a Christian man." These are some of the influences of schools at work in Japan.

Rev. W. Park pronounced the Benediction.

MEETINGS OF MEMBERS
IN SECTION.

THE PLACE OF EDUCATION IN MISSIONARY WORK.

(2) *SPECIAL CASES.*

(a) The need of special provision for the children of converts.
(b) Are boarding schools necessary or expedient save when self-supporting ?
(c) The value of orphanages as Missionary agencies.
(d) The work of Sunday schools in Mission districts.
(e) Should education in Mission schools be paid for?
(f) The value of elementary schools.

(Wednesday afternoon, June 13th, in the Annexe.)

Theodore Howard, Esq., in the chair.
Acting Secretary, Rev. W. Park, M.A.

Mr. Henry Soltau offered prayer.

The Chairman: I am not going to take up your time this afternoon, because, like yourselves, I want to hear what our friends who have had experience in foreign fields have to say upon this most important matter. There are six different heads under which discussion may come this afternoon, which will fully take up our time, and therefore I will at once ask the Rev. Dr. Turner to read a paper which he has prepared for our edification.

PAPER.

1. BY THE REV. G. TURNER, LL.D. (L.M.S., from Samoa).

A self-supporting Boarding School and College combined.

1. Let me take you for a few minutes to a lovely spot, the finest islands of Samoa in Central Polynesia.

The place of labour. from the lagoon, you see six and tw nestling among the cocoa-p stone embankment protects the pat

Pacific Ocean. In the background there are three hundred acres of cultivation, bounded by a road three miles in circuit, and shaded all round by the cocoa-nut palm. This is MALUA, *the Samoan Mission Seminary* of the London Missionary Society. Here there are two resident tutors, an assistant native tutor, a hundred students with their wives and children, and a select class of twenty-five youths from fourteen to eighteen years of age, making up a population of two hundred and fifty; and here we have endeavoured to solve the problem of a self-supporting educational institution. But this was not the work of a day.

2. Five and forty years ago, heathenism was fast disappearing from Samoa; two hundred villages looked to us for instruction; a native teacher and preacher, selected by the Missionary, from his most intelligent Church members, was located in each village; but progress and permanence called for a higher education, by God's blessing on some steady and systematic course of training. The late Rev. Charles Hardie and I were appointed to leave our stations, and devote ourselves entirely to this work. We selected a central place on the island Upolu. It was an uninhabited bush, had a few bread-fruit and cocoa-nut trees, a spring of water, and was open to the sea and the trade wind. The chiefs said we might take, without stint or price, as much land as we required. We measured off about thirty acres, but begged *to pay* for it, which we did there and then, in calico, prints and cutlery, at the rate of fifteen shillings an acre, and had a title-deed drawn out and signed.

Commencement of the work.

3. Twenty-five youths, from ten to twenty years of age were selected for instruction. They put up temporary houses. The Christian natives brought presents of yams, taro, bananas, and cocoa-nuts, for planting as well as for food; the young lads laid under cultivation each a plot of ground for himself, bread-fruit trees sprang up as the bush was cleared, the lagoon gave a supply of fish, and on the 24th of September, 1844, we opened our first class.

Youths and adults.

4. In the following year, a **second class** was formed of twenty-one young men, some of whom had **already** been village teachers. As the years went on, the demand **increased** for better educated men. We added largely to the number of our students, and extended our land pur———— : ——e hundred acres, all of which was bought at an a———— y-five shillings an acre, and registered in the British ———— the property of the London Missionary ———— ys' class to twenty-five. We have no ———— have a room for a boy in each of the ———— the lad under the special care ————ber of adult students ————nd a demand for at ————ts of two hundred require that we he institution.

5. We commenced with two native cottages, and went on gradually adding house to house, principally by the industry of the students themselves, and now we have twenty-two stone cottages, 16 feet by 32, separated from each other by 32 feet, and arranged like a barrack square, as a naval officer one day called it. We have five and twenty other cottages. A classroom, 60 feet by 30, stands in the centre of the inland side, fitted up with desks, tables, and blackboards. We are also well supplied with maps, diagrams, steam engine, and other models. Two houses are for the entertainment of strangers and the friends of the students. The side of the square towards the sea is enclosed with a citron hedge, having an acre of ground in the centre, shaded with bread-fruit trees, and forming a fine place for out-door Missionary meetings, to which we occasionally invite the pastors and people of other districts. The two resident tutors have each a stone house, erected by the paid labour of the natives of adjacent villages.

Buildings.

6. Wednesday is our *industrial day*. From 6 a.m. to 2 p.m. all are then employed about the premises, building or repairing houses, road making, and other improvements. This one day a week, with an extra day on the first Monday in the month, on which the tutors, have a general inspection of houses and plantations, has overtaken almost all the building and other work we needed. While teaching the young men the mysteries of burning lime from the coral, stone and mortar work, sawing, roofing, weather boarding, door and venetian blind making, they learn much to aid them in the future, in superintending the erection of village chapels and cottages for themselves. During holiday or other spare hours, they often employ themselves in the workshop, making boxes, bedsteads, tables, desks, sofas, forms, or other useful things, which they take with them when they leave the institution. And thus, with the Christian and the mental, the material culture advances as well, raising alike themselves and their fellow countrymen, wherever they may be located. We strictly charge our native pastors, however, never to engage in any carpentry or other handicraft for the sake of gain, but to show to the people that their great object in living among them is the sacred and not the secular.

Example of an industrial day.

7. Had we to support our Malua pupils, a thousand pounds a year would not do it, but, by keeping up their fishing and agricultural habits, and without interfering with their studies, more than is necessary for the good of their health, they provide for the wants of their table, without drawing a penny on the Missionary Society. Our three hundred acres of land are all needed for the efficient working of this industrial and self-supporting system. Some may wonder what Missionaries do with so much land, but it is simply the "three acres" *minus* the "cow," and *plus* the fish and poultry, for we have *a hundred* students to provide for. The land has become stocked with well nigh ten thousand bread-fruit and cocoa-nut trees, and, in addition to these, there are thousands of bananas, and plots of yams, taro, maize, manioc, and sugar cane; amply sufficient for the wants of such an institution, for all time to come. We do not allow the young men to grow cotton, or indeed anything for sale. At one time we allowed them to sell spare produce, to help them to a little cash and clothing, but it brought in a flood of the secular, and had to be stopped. With a little help from their friends, and the occasional sale of spare poultry, they can

Support of the institution.

easily clothe themselves, and have something besides for the purchase of books, Missionary subscriptions, and other expenses.

For some time we gave presents of clothing once a year, from boxes which were kindly sent us; but that we have long discontinued. Good friends, however, and especially in Tasmania, help us still, by sending tools, paints, medicine, stationery, sewing materials, together with useful prizes, in the shape of workboxes, writing cases, inkstands, and portfolios. Our institution therefore is now, and may continue to be, free of all cost to the Society, beyond the salaries of the tutors; and that the directors may well afford to a people, who, for the last twenty years, and in addition to building village churches, paying for books, and supporting native pastors, have contributed an average of £1,200 per annum to the funds of the Society. And further let it be noted, that this Malua institution, with its houses and cultivated lands, has become an addition to the property of the London Missionary Society, of a beautifully situated South Sea island Missionary estate, worth at least £10,000— and all this, principally, the result of our industrial day, once a week, carried on during the last forty years.

8. We are much assisted in the management of secular affairs by three native monitors or superintendents. One has the oversight of the houses on one side of the square, another those on the *Monitors and rules.* other side, and the third looks after the plantations. In arranging work to be done on the industrial day, the tutors consult with the monitors, select certain men for each thing to be done, and the monitors share in and superintend the work. On the arrival of a fresh student the monitors show him his room, point out the ground on which his predecessor worked, the crops there which he can call his own, together with some forty bread-fruit and cocoa-nut trees, to the entire use of which he is entitled. It is also the duty of the monitors to see that each student keeps in order, and replants his plot of ground, up to the day he leaves the institution, so that when his successor arrives he may have a supply of food ready to his hand.

Our rules, which are read in class once a month, forbid quarrelling, intoxicants, tobacco, firearms, night fishing, lights after 9.30, leaving the premises without permission, and some other things adapted to the people and the place. Fines, from a shilling to a dollar, are carefully enforced, and all the more so as the students get the benefit of them. The monitors are the custodians of the fine money, lay it out in the purchase of oil, and divide it among the students for their evening lamps. Deliberate lying, stealing, immorality, or lifting the hand to a fellow-student, is followed by expulsion. In cases of discipline, the tutors and monitors form a court of inquiry, and, in some instances, take a vote of the whole house. These monitors have no special salary, the honour of their appointment is enough, and gives them a *status*, which villages in need of a new pastor bear in mind.

9. Many of our students are married, have their wives with them, and under instruction. The frequent adjunct to an application for a village pastor is: "We want a man whose *Married students.* wife can teach our wives and daughters something." To the general instruction given to the wives of the students at Malua, the ladies add sewing, shaping, making up garments, and so train them to be useful, in conducting a variety of classes, with the women and girls,

wherever they may be located. The children also come with their parents, and they, too, have a school, conducted by the students, six of them in turn, acting as teachers, for a month at a time, and thus prepare for future village school work.

10. And now let me describe the order and studies of the day. At dawn the bell is rung; after private devotions, and *Classes and services.* united family prayer, in each of the houses, some go to fish, others to the plantation, and others to the cooking house. At eight o'clock the bell is rung again, calling all to stop work, bathe, have breakfast, and be ready for the first class at nine o'clock. At this hour juniors and seniors meet together, as they do in several other classes. After a hymn and prayer, there is an exposition, in regular order, through some book of Scripture. At the close of this lecture, four pages of notes are left for each to copy. At the end of a book they stitch together their notes, and have a connected commentary from beginning to end.

From ten to eleven a class is held in another department. The two mid-day hours are spent in copying lectures, the children's school and a class for the women. From two to three medicine is dispensed, stationery given out, and the tutors' study is open for messages or inquiries on *any* subject, secular or sacred. From three to five the tutors have again a class each. From five to seven all are at liberty to go to the classroom, the workshop, the lagoon, or the plantation. They have their evening meal at seven o'clock; after that they have family prayer, and then they read, write, or converse. At half-past nine the bell rings the curfew, and all retire.

Monday, Tuesday, and Thursday are days of unbroken class-work. On the industrial Wednesday there is a mid-day class for the women and children, and an afternoon Scripture exposition class for all the house. Friday is devoted to the plantations, or messages to any near friend or village. Saturday morning is spent in fishing, and preparing food for the following day, and in the afternoon the week is closed with a prayer meeting.

On the Sabbath morning there is a prayer meeting at six o'clock; public worship at half-past eight; the children's school at eleven; an adult Bible class at two o'clock, and public worship again at half-past three. After each of these public services there is a prayer meeting in family groups, and conversation on the subject of the sermon. During the day some of the senior students preach in the neighbouring villages; and at 7 p.m. the family circles are again met for Bible reading and evening prayer.

We observe the "week of prayer" at the beginning of the year, and have also a Missionary prayer meeting on the first Monday of the month, at which we have a collection from the students, which amounts at the end of the year to about £30.

11. The course of instruction is in the vernacular, and embraces reading, writing, arithmetic, geometry, natural philosophy, *Course of instruction.* geography, geology, natural history, Scripture exposition, systematic and pastoral theology, and Church history. We have a class for the English language, in which *Young Samoa* is especially interested. To help in these classes we have nine printed text books, embracing arithmetic, the first book of Euclid, geography, natural

philosophy, natural history, a doctrinal catechism, Scripture history, Church history, pastoral theology, and popery. We have had a native assistant tutor for many years, who is most helpful in elementary branches, and in conducting classes in the absence of either of the Missionary tutors.

In addition to the text books just mentioned, we have an octavo marginal reference Bible, a small Bible without references, a large type Testament and psalter, and a book of four hundred hymns and chants. Other works on Christian and educational literature have been printed, and are also in the hands of the students. There is a condensed commentary on the Old and New Testaments, eight volumes of notes, practical and expository, embracing the book of Psalms, Matthew, Mark, John, the Acts of the Apostles, Romans, Galatians, the Epistles to Timothy, Titus, and Hebrews, together with the Epistles of James, Peter, John, and Jude. Two volumes of sketches of sermons, a translation of Bunyan and of the "Peep of Day," a Scripture concordance, a Bible dictionary, and some other works, making in all thirty-two volumes, and containing an aggregate of ten thousand pages in the Samoan dialect. We have also a grammar and dictionary of the language in English, a second edition of which was published by Messrs. Trübner, of London, ten years ago.

12. The term of study is four years; when that is completed the members of the youths' class return to their homes. After a time they often appear as candidates to fill up vacancies in the teachers' class, are received, and have *a second* course of ^{Term of study.} four years. Many of our best native pastors are those who have thus been eight years at Malua. For every vacancy there are a number of candidates, selected by Missionaries and native pastors in various parts of the group. Before admission all must pass a preliminary examination. There is also an annual examination, at which 75 per cent. of marks gains a prize, and if at the *exit* examination, a first-class certificate. Sixty-five per cent. entitles to a second-class certificate.

Before a student's time is up, he has, in most cases, a call to some village where there is a vacancy, but the completion of the four years' course is strictly adhered to. Some would gladly remain longer, feeling, like the late Dr. Chalmers, that, as we enlarge the circle of our knowledge, we, at the same time, enlarge the circle of our ignorance. One of these young men, not long ago, when dying, before he had completed his four years, said cheerily to a fellow-student: "My time is not yet up; but I am going to *heaven*, where my term of study will *never* end."

Of these students of former days many are dead, a number have retired from active service, some have become local governors, magistrates, secretaries, or are otherwise in official or commer- _{Results.} cial service, and upwards of two hundred are now ordained native pastors. We call them *Pastors* and not *Reverends*, and so distinguish them from the European Missionary. These Samoan pastors preach, and manage Church affairs; they have boarding and general schools, and are supported by the people in the villages where they labour. They have the oversight of six thousand Church members, and congregations embracing over twenty-five thousand, all in Samoa. In the sixteen out-station islands, from two hundred to two thousand miles to the north-west of Samoa, our native pastors have the care of two thousand five hundred Church members, and of a population exceeding ten thousand; and farther still, while the better qualified and ordained native agency has *increased*, our European staff of Missionaries has *decreased* from fourteen to seven; and the time may not be far distant when little more European help may be needed for the group and its out-stations, beyond a well sustained institution at Malua. And thus, we think, that the problem has, *there* at least, been fairly solved, of a self-supporting educational institution, and this, too, at a *minimum* of cost: the Samoan Mission Seminary has been, by God's blessing, a *maximum* of Missionary force for the conversion of the Polynesians, which no man can tabulate, a rich reward to those who have laboured there, and to the London Missionary Society who has sent them forth.

PAPER.

2. BY THE REV. JAMES COOLING, B.A. (Wesleyan Missionary Society, from Madras).

Schools for non-Christian Hindus in South India.

The value of education as a Missionary agency among a non-Christian people depends upon a variety of circumstances. Among one people it may be one of the most potent forces in their moral regeneration, whilst among another it may be of comparatively little value. Among one people, at one period of their history, or at one stage of their civilisation, its value may be small, whilst at a later period, or at a more advanced stage, its value may be greatly increased. My experience of Mission work has been confined to South India, and the applicability of my views to other places will depend upon the extent to which the conditions of work in those places correspond to those in India.

The Hindu community, in popular language, is divided into two great classes—(1) those who are regarded as within the pale of one or other of the recognised castes, and (2) those who are regarded as outside caste—the caste people and the non-castes. This is not a scientific division. But the Missionary, in his daily work, has not to do with a scientific ethnical classification of the community. He has to do with those divisions in their social life which actually exist, whether scientific or not. And every Mission worker in South India is confronted every day and everywhere with this broad distinction between the caste people and the non-castes. The so-called caste people comprise the upper and leading classes of the community, the members of the learned professions, the merchants, traders, artisans, the landowners, and most of the farmers. Though split up into numberless subdivisions among themselves, they all profess a religion which is one in name, and they are all bound together by that peculiar social and religious bond which it is so difficult for us Europeans to understand, and to which we have given the name of caste. The non-castes consist of the agricultural labourers, the menial servants of all grades, and the aboriginal hill tribes.

The caste people are the Hindus proper, *the* Hindu community. The non-castes are not considered Hindus. They are outside the community, but, from their close association with the Hindus, they have become *Hinduised* both in religion and in customs. In the Madras Presidency the Hindus or caste people are from 72 to 77 per cent. of the whole, and the non-castes from 23 to 28 per cent., according as the claims of certain classes to be within caste is admitted or not. It is from the latter class, who in South India number from ten to twelve millions, that the majority of our Christian converts have come. Their proportions.

The non-caste portion of the community are low down in the social scale. Very many of them for ages were slaves. Their long degradation has had a deteriorating influence upon them. They have scarcely any hope of bettering their condition, and consequently have little or no desire for education. Attempts to open schools in their midst are always regarded with suspicion by their high-caste masters or neighbours. Moreover, they are easily accessible by other methods. From these facts it will be seen that education holds only a subordinate place in Mission work among them. Education among non-castes.

On the other hand, when through any cause, these non-caste people have obtained an independent position, or when there appears to them the prospect of improving their social status they welcome the establishment of schools. Then since their caste ties are comparatively weak educational work has been most successful, not only as an indirect but as a direct means of conversion. In the city of Madras and in other large towns of South India, schools for the children of the non-castes employed as domestic servants have been markedly effective as evangelising agencies.

As a rule, in dealing with such non-Christian races as these, (1) efforts should not be spent in pressing education upon those who have no wish for it. If they are unwilling to receive the intellectual knowledge we have to impart there will be an equal unwillingness to listen to the moral and religious truth it is our duty to teach. (2) In every case there should be some tangible evidence given of their wish for education. In most cases this will take the form of the payment of a fee, either in money or in kind. (3) A Christian spirit must pervade every school whether for caste or non-caste children. In elementary schools that will best be secured by appointing none but a Christian as headmaster. But so long as the end is secured there need be no fixed rule as to the means. How to deal with them.

When we turn to the case of the caste Hindus almost all the conditions of the problem are changed. The majority of them are in an advanced stage of civilisation. They belong to the higher and middle ranks of society. They have had for a long period in the past a system of indigenous schools to which the highest castes have been accustomed to send their children. The schoolmaster and the religious teacher are both held in high esteem. In recent years a series of events have awakened a desire in all classes for an education superior to that given in the old indigenous school. The decision, fifty years ago, that the English language and literature should take the place of the ancient classical languages of Sanskrit and Persian as the instrument of education The caste Hindus.

for those natives who were to be employed in Government service was the beginning of the movement.   The creation of Government departments of education in 1855, and the establishment of universities after the model of the London University in 1857, mark stages of progress; whilst the introduction into the country during the last thirty years of all the appliances of modern civilisation has been a constant and increasing stimulus to this desire.   To-day a young man of respectable position in society would be ashamed if he had not some knowledge of English.   Last year nearly ten thousand candidates appeared for the Madras University examinations, all of which are conducted throughout in the English language.   When schools in which English is taught were begun the Brahmans were the first to take advantage of them; the other castes are following, and ere long we shall doubtless see all the well-to-do people of the caste population of South India giving their sons an education in which the English language and Western science will take a chief place.   The problem that the Missionaries of to-day have before them is not how to induce the Hindus to educate their children, is not how to mould that education after a European pattern—the problem before us is whether we shall take advantage of this movement and endeavour to utilise it for Missionary purposes, or whether we shall hold aloof from it as a something that does not concern us, and thus let the whole education of the highest classes of the community pass into non-Christian hands.

An English education sought.

In the earlier days of this wonderful movement, the Missionaries of South India saw their opportunity, and threw their energies into this work ; and to-day, though many other agencies are in the field, Missionary institutions still hold a foremost place.   But the question may be asked, As the object of these youths in coming to your schools is to obtain intellectual knowledge, are you not in compelling them to listen to your Christian teaching to some extent taking an advantage of them ?   Are they or their parents willing that you should teach them the Scriptures ?   And can you, under such circumstances, make your schools efficient Missionary agencies ?   The best answer to such inquiries is a statement of the facts.   The people know that we Missionaries have come to their country to propagate the Christian religion.   We establish schools, openly avowing that they will be conducted on a Christian basis, that every pupil will have to be present when prayer is offered through Christ to Almighty God, and that every pupil will have to spend a portion of his time in the study of the Christian Scriptures.   Those who object to these conditions need not send their children.   But it is a very rare thing indeed for the slightest objection to be raised.   The Hindus have no objection to reading the Bible.   They are ever ready for religious discussion.   And my experience is that Hindu youths can be interested in the facts and doctrines of Christianity quite as easily as youths of a similar age in Britain.   What Hindus do object to is any attempt to interfere with what they consider their caste.

No objection to the Scriptures.

There are then, it may be said, certain limitations attached to your work. Perfectly true.   But they are the limitations at present attached to all forms of work among high-caste Hindus.   To overstep these limits by a school teacher may lead to more disastrous consequences than to overstep them by a vernacular preacher.   In the one case a school may be broken up, which it will take months or years to gather again ; whilst in the other case a new congregation may be got in a few days or weeks.   But there are no limitations in school work as it ought to be, and as it can be carried on in South India, which in the slightest degree compromise the fidelity of any Missionary to his great Master's commission.

Limitations no bar to Missionaries.

It is not necessary for me to point out the importance of youth as a time for making a lasting impression.   The population of school-going age in India numbers many millions.   For influencing in favour of Christianity this large section of the community, there cannot be means more effective than well-conducted schools, where the truth can be adapted to the capacities of the children, and where it can be given "line upon line, and precept upon precept." But not only are Mission schools the *best* means of reaching the children ; in the majority of cases they are the *only* means. Hindu boys and girls, if they do not hear of Christ in a Mission school, are not likely to hear of Him elsewhere. In the case of high caste girls who, at the age of twelve or thirteen, are secluded in the Zenana (until our female Zenana teachers are greatly multiplied), their school days are the only opportunity they have of coming under the influence of Christian truth. *Schools chief means of evangelising children.*

What kind of results does educational work accomplish? In the first place it disarms the prejudices of the people against us, and enlists their sympathy with us. In the education of their children we and they find a ground of common interest, and this often proves the first step to a lasting friendship. The experience of every village evangelist is that nothing puts down opposition, disarms hostile criticism, and obtains for him the goodwill of the people so soon as the opening a school in their midst. *Results of education.*

But this gain, though not to be despised in a country where the Missionary's motive is almost always misconstrued, is small compared with the direct influence for good exerted upon the pupils, and through them upon the families from which they come. In schools for high caste girls, where the pupils leave at twelve or thirteen years of age, and are afterwards secluded in their homes, there can be little opportunity of witnessing any marked moral and spiritual results. Such work must be largely one of faith. We know, however, that these schools are working a change in Hindu female society. For many years in a certain part of Madras a number of these schools were carried on. A few years ago when Zenana work was begun in that neighbourhood, the Missionaries were astonished and delighted to find from the reports of the Zenana teachers how in many a Hindu home the seed sown in these schools was bringing forth abundant fruit. *In girls' schools.*

In the case of elementary vernacular schools, which the pupils leave at an early age, the chief result is that the teaching in the school is preparatory to the work of the vernacular preacher. Erroneous notions about Christianity are dispelled, a spirit of inquiry is awakened, the value of ceremonies which the pupil has been taught to observe from infancy is questioned, and he is made familiar with the main facts of Christ's life and work. With a congregation who have spent their boyhood in a Mission school, the evangelist will not have the old stock objections urged against him. On the contrary, he will not infrequently find a decided prepossession in favour of the message he delivers. *In elementary schools.*

In the case of young men who have studied for some years in a high school or college, the results are more marked. The majority of them lose faith in orthodox Hinduism. Their prejudices against Christian Missionaries change to respect and esteem, and in not a few cases to warm affection. Their ideas about God and their duty towards God, about sin, its nature, its consequences, its remedy will be poles asunder from those of their parents on these subjects. Their standard of morals is higher than that of those around them. Many of them honestly try to act up to this higher standard, and where they fail it is not without a struggle with conscience. A large number, at one period or other of their career, pass through a period of mental struggle, in which their conviction of the truth is so strong, that were it not for the terrible sacrifices they would have to make, they would openly confess their faith in Christ. The number of secret disciples from among such young men can never be known. Undoubtedly there are such, and from the frequency with which I used to be questioned on this subject, my impression is that they are not a few. *In colleges.*

But though the number of converts direct from our schools may be comparatively small, these are not all the gains to the Christian Church

from this branch of work. From careful inquiries, extending over some
years, I am convinced that a very large proportion of the
Indirect results. converts in and around the city of Madras (excluding village
communities, who usually come over *en masse*) have their first desire to
embrace Christianity implanted in some Mission school. In some cases the
desire has lain dormant for ten, twenty, and in one instance, I knew, for
thirty years, before there came the influence which caused it to spring up
afresh and led to open confession.

From these facts we may learn the place and the value of education as
a Missionary agency among such a non-Christian people as the Hindus.
Education complement to preaching. Its value is not so much as an agency complete in itself,—
though it is of great value as such—but as complementary
to all other agencies. Education and evangelistic preaching
should not be regarded as separate, still less as antagonistic modes of work,
but as two parts of one method, each essential the one to the other. The
full value of our educational work is lost, unless among our elder pupils it
is both accompanied and followed by some form of evangelistic work.

Evangelistic work, too, is carried on under disadvantages, when it is
not preceded or accompanied by education. The work of the Educational
Missionary prepares the way for the work of the evangelist, and the work
of the evangelist is the necessary sequence of the educationist.

It must be admitted that hitherto all agencies combined have made but
little impression in the way of conversions upon the caste Hindu community.
A change coming. Nor can these be expected in large numbers until such a change
has taken place in Hindu society, as will make that social
ostracism, which converts have now to undergo, a thing of the
past. As an instrument in effecting this change, education holds a foremost place. If all the young people of India could but pass through our
Mission schools, in a very few generations there would be such a change in
the attitude of the whole community towards Christianity, that the Indian
Missionary's great reaping time would quickly come.

DISCUSSION.

Mr. R. A. Macfie: The general theme on which I have written a
brief Paper is, "Co-working and concentration: where there are more
stations than one in the same city, why should not they do
Co-working and concentration. education in common?" The same might be done with
respect to Medical work. It would be economy of appliances
and money, would add efficiency, and would recommend, because illustrating, the Gospel spirit. The same comprehensiveness or communion should
be seen in the episynagoge, the assembling of ourselves together for the
Sunday services. The teaching, fairly paid for, might be open to children
unconnected with the Mission. An initial step should be taken—much
more than a step and much more than initial—in respect of school
grammars and school reading books.

Surely sanctified intelligence could hardly be directed and employed better
than to and in the preparing, in the English tongue, proper manuals that shall
not merely be devoid of heathen and anti-Christian teaching, but
Christian school books. be positively promotive of the Gospel, being books which would be
relished by the parents, and which would make the children in-
structors of the home circle, where reading aloud would be requested because
relished. The quality and influence of school books cannot be left out of

account in determining the great question of the place which education should have in Missionary operations. These manuals should be such as to bear and be worthy of translation, with due adaptations, into all languages, and of being adopted by the several Societies, European and American, who should undertake the joint production of them. This joint production, especially as there would be none of that cost-enhancing tax which we call copyright, would probably reduce prices one-half, with the happy prospect that the manuals would, in virtue of their merit, authority, and popularity, come to be regarded as standards, and come into general use in ordinary schools. To some extent this branch of Missionary activity, like teaching itself and healing, might possibly become the work of a separate Society ; but do not let us wait until such a Society is formed. Let the plan grow : it will grow when the home Churches and individual Christians become warmer, wiser, and by no means be it added wealthier, only more willing to part with their wealth. Let me beg those who can arrange it to have depôts of the school books which I have spoken of in the various parts of the world, where, if not Christian literature in general, these manuals could be purchased, or at least be ordered. *Depots for their sale.* And lastly (and be it reflected on deeply), let us put the question, Are the scholars, after their education is completed, kept in hand, or at least under eye ? Could they not be undenominationally registered as claimants of the Church's interest ? They might then be dealt with as youths whose faces look Zion-wards.

Rev. J. A. Taylor (Baptist Foreign Missionary Convention of U.S.A.): Mr. Chairman,—There is no question or subject that will come before this Conference during its deliberations in which I feel such a deep interest as the question of the place of education in Mission work. *Education among negroes.* Having had some practical experience of this work among my own people in America, I am prepared to say that education should have the very first place in the secondary course of Mission work.

Soon after the war, when we had been liberated from slavery, our good friends of the North,—following close on the heels of the Presidential message of emancipation to the Southern States,—built Christian Mission schools, and they gathered in from among our young men those who seemed to be readiest to receive educational training. The first to be trained from among our own people were for the ministry, and then young men and women *After the war.* for teachers. Twenty-three years ago when we started in the South we had not an organised Church of our own, not a particle of Church property, with but a very few exceptions in the more Northern States, but to-day the denomination that I represent have accumulated from their own earnings a Church property worth over $7,000,000 ; we have a membership of over one and a half millions ; and we contributed last year for Educational and Mission work over $300,000. I felt very keenly this morning when a gentleman stood on the platform in the Lower Hall, and asserted—only from theoretical knowledge—that he had been informed that the coloured ministry of the South was so ignorant that they did more harm than good. That man lives away *A protest.* in the far North, and no doubt he had never been South in his life where the bulk of the coloured people are. The earlier years of my life were spent the other side of slavery, and twenty-three years this side ; and when the war closed if you had painted my name in letters as large as that map yonder I could not have read it. For twenty-three years, starting out with a family of children to support, I have moved on to where you see I am now, living in the South. There are others who have not had the same burdens who have gone further still. We are moving on, brethren, and it is because of the work of education which was started among us twenty-three years ago. And this is not all. Not only have we done this work among ourselves, but *Negro Mission to Africa.* eight years ago we authorised the Baptist Foreign Missionary Convention, of which I am the humble representative here, to open, and we did open, a

Missionary station in West Central Africa; and we now have eight Missionaries labouring in the interior of Africa, supported and managed by the coloured Baptists of the United States.

Mr. Fountain J. Hartley (Secretary, Sunday School Union): Mr. Chairman, and friends,—The department of educational work to which I wish to refer is one which has a most intimate bearing on Missionary labour, and which deserves a very high place among the varied machinery employed by our great Missionary Societies—I mean the Sunday school. Considering the large extent to which our English and American Sunday schools have for many years contributed to the support of Missions, they have, I venture to think, some claim on the attention of the directors when we ask whether all is being done that can be done for the extension in heathen lands of the Institution which has done so much for the children at home. We have some notable examples of Missionary success achieved in this direction. The West Indies can boast of a large army of Sunday scholars, and the Wesleyan Missionaries in the Fiji Islands are able to report a proportion of Sunday scholars to the population almost equal to that of England, that is to say 20 per cent., or one in five. In these cases, however, the agency employed has borne something like an adequate proportion to the work to be accomplished; but when we come to look at the enormous populations of India and China, and compare them with the small band of labourers sent out for their evangelisation, it would be altogether out of place to expect a similar percentage under Sunday school instruction.

Sunday schools in Mission-fields.

Taking the last complete statistics which have been presented, England is much behind America in this respect. Grouping together the whole of the American Missionary Societies on the one hand, and the whole of the English Societies on the other, the Americans have double the proportion of Sunday scholars compared with the number of Missionaries employed, which the English stations can boast. How far this might be the result of the difference of districts in which the Societies are employed, or of the varying degree of attention paid to the higher education, or how far it may arise from other causes, is, I venture to think, well worthy of the attention of the Conference, and I hope our American friends will throw some light on the subject.

England behind in the work.

We are in the habit of saying that the most promising field of usefulness, and the brightest hope of the Church, lies among the young, and, looking anxiously at the mass of ignorance and irreligion in which our adult populations are engulfed, we are sometimes almost ready to despair. Acting on these convictions, the Committee of the Sunday School Union has established the Sunday School Continental Mission, and through its agency large numbers of children in the several countries on the Continent of Europe are being gradually brought under Sunday school instruction. If the same rules of action hold good in the East as in the West, we are bound in all our Missionary operations to look well to the young, and put forth our utmost energies to lay hold of the children and train them for Jesus. However difficult it might have been to accomplish this in time past, as far as India is concerned, it can be done now. The Rev. James Kennedy, formerly of Benares, confirms the testimony of the American Missionaries, that by visitation the children may be attracted to the Sunday School, and by means of international lesson papers, simple teaching, and plenty of singing, they may be retained and interested. But it is said, "We cannot find teachers."

Teachers the difficulty.

A respected Missionary (I think of Berhampore) wrote to the *Nonconformist* some time ago, in reply to a letter of mine, saying, "We cannot make bricks without straw; we have not got the teachers." But what then have our high schools and colleges been doing for so many years? Surely some of the pupils in these establishments become Christians, and might be enlisted as Sunday school teachers! Besides, we have our converts; let these be set to work. An hour or two spent once a week by the Missionary in training them, and preparing them for the lesson of the next Sunday, would be time well spent, and would soon be the means of making better teachers of them, while at the same time doing them good, helping them to grow in grace, and preventing them from lapsing into the condition from which they have been rescued. Whether too much is being made of the educational as distinct from the evangelising work of the Missionaries, and whether the high schools do not hinder rather than help in the development of Sunday schools, is a question which I hope will be fully dealt with in the Conference. *Teachers to be trained.*

Without any disparagement of educational culture, while fully admitting that the high schools and colleges have trained many faithful and efficient servants for the Missionary-field, and that even when failing to Christianise the pupils the influence exerted upon them is not without lasting and beneficent effects, my own opinion, notwithstanding, is that the measure of their success in producing Christians, as well as scholars, does not fully justify the amount of money and labour expended upon them. And this opinion I hold is shared by some of the Missionaries on the spot; one of whom has distinctly expressed his deep regret that his duties in connection with mathematics and the classics sadly interfered with the resolution with which he entered upon his work, "To know nothing among men but Jesus Christ and Him crucified." It is true that religious instruction is given in these schools, that some of the students listen to it without the impatience manifested by others, and that some of them also attend on the Sabbath-day for the study of the Bible; but this need not prevent the ingathering of the neglected children, for whom an hour or two of instruction on the Sunday is about all that can be done. *Need of Sunday schools.*

Rev. Principal Brown, D.D. (Free Church College, Aberdeen): I think it is not possible for any one who either goes out as a Missionary, or takes any interest in Christian Missions, to undervalue education in Mission work. What is it then that causes our American friends, and those who agree with them, to be jealous of education, and requires so many papers and addresses to-day to convince them of the indispensable necessity of education, particularly in India? I think it impossible to answer, among others, the Paper of Professor Robertson. I think that the arguments adduced, and the mode in which they were conveyed, were such that no one could resist them. Well, let us come to the essence of the whole question. It is not a question between education and evangelistic work, or between teaching and preaching. I think the primary question is—What does a Missionary go out for? It is to win the souls of the people; and, if that is the case, I hold that the first requisite for the Missionary is to have a passion for souls. *Cannot neglect education.*

The question is, Is a man having a passion for souls to object to being put into the teaching department? Very far from that. Let me tell you what I said to a student of my own who is now in Bombay. He was one of the most distinguished students of the hall in which I was then a professor. I said to him, "My dear man, what are you going out for? Are you going out to teach, say, Geography, Latin, English?" "God forbid," he said. "Well, then," I said, "Let me tell you what to do. Every morning before you go to the school, go on your knees and say to God, 'Lord, I have not come here to teach Latin, Geography, English, and other things, but to get the souls of these fellow-creatures.' But I must first gain their respect, and then I must gain their confidence, and then I must gain *Education a means of conversion.*

their affection; but every day let me drive at that object, and I will find opportunities in twenty ways to gain them." General Alexander, a noble character, who, though a Presbyterian in principle, was a director of the Church Missionary Society, which he loved and which I love, said to me one day in a **A frank opinion.** church where we met, "Oh! Dr. Brown, your Missionaries and Ministers are going to work in the wrong way." "Well, let me hear you, General." "Oh!" said he, "When John Anderson went out to gain the souls of the people, he said he could and would have them, and he insisted on having them; and he said, 'I am certain to have them,' and he got them. The noblest high-caste youths in the South of India were his converts. There was Rajah Gopal and Venkataramia, and not a few others. And now what are they doing? They are trying to beat the Government in educational matters, and now they have no baptisms." "Well," I said, "General, you are wrong. Education is a necessity, and they must go at it; but if there is any failure it is not in what they are teaching, but in what they are aiming at. If there is a want of that passion to get the souls of the people they will not get them; if they put the cart before the horse, or the means before the end, they won't get the fruit. Do not object to the thing they are doing, but object only to the way in which they are doing it. I do not know that they are doing it in the wrong way. But what I say is, let them aim at conversion; and remember that they are never to rest until they get it, and they are sure to get it."

Rev. G. W. Clarke (China Inland Mission): Mr. Chairman, and Christian friends,—There is one part of the world with which I have been connected for nearly thirteen years; and although it is not possible to speak at any length on these six questions, I may say that I have had to do with some of them practically. What strikes me to-day is this, that **Our ideas not clear.** we do not clearly distinguish what we are talking about. We do not quite make it clear. A Missionary is a Missionary; a schoolmaster is a schoolmaster.

If I understand the word Missionary aright, it is not a schoolmaster; it is simply to go out and to preach the Gospel of the Lord Jesus Christ, not to **What is a Missionary?** educate. To educate is one thing; you educate the intellect. I have met with a few educated Chinamen, and do not wish to meet with many. If you educate a Chinaman, and he is not converted, you have got the sharpest man to deal with on the face of this earth. Some of these men, who have been educated in various schools in America and in England, when they have come back, have been some of the sharpest knaves to deal with: one of them tried to raise a rebellion, and had to flee to save his head. Now, what have we heard to day? Have you heard once in any meeting such a phrase as this: "I believe in the Holy Ghost"? The cry has been, "Education, education, education!" just as if education is going to convert a man's soul, as if that is going to lift him from out of the power of the devil, and make him into a child of God. The Apostle Paul did not preach that doctrine. The Lord Jesus Christ did not give the command, "Go thou into all the world, and educate the people;" but He said, "Go ye into all the world, and preach the Gospel to every creature."

A Member of the Conference: He says also, "Go ye, therefore, and teach all nations."

Rev. G. W. Clarke: What does that teaching mean? I say it means, teach them the Word of God, and not teach them Hebrew, Greek, and Latin.

Mr. Henry Morris (Hon. Sec., Christian Vernacular Education Society for India): Mr. Chairman, and Christian friends,—After what has just been said, I begin by asserting that I firmly believe in the Holy Ghost. I believe this is one of the first principles in Christian educational work. I am a strong supporter of education, but it School work and preaching. must be *Christian* education. Mr. Clarke left the word "Christian" out; and I am sure that those Educational Missionaries who go on plodding day by day and hour by hour at the dry, dull, hard school work, are quite as much under the influence of the Holy Spirit as those who go out into the alleys and streets to preach the Gospel. And if they have the Holy Spirit with them, if they go to their work in the spirit which Principal Brown spoke of, I feel sure that they will have souls for their hire. I do not for one moment advocate education in Mission work, unless the teachers thoroughly throw themselves into *Christian* education.

I would like to say a word or two with regard to what Mr. Macfie said as to a series of Christian school books. I suppose Mr. Macfie does not know that there is an admirable series of school books already prepared for India by my friend, Dr. Murdoch, an indefatigable man, who, at an Christian school books. age when men are not usually working in India, has remained there in the spirit of self-sacrifice, and is still working for its educational wants. He has prepared a most admirable set of school books, thoroughly adapted to schools in India, and that is the principal point. It does not do for anyone, more especially Missionaries, to use in their schools books which are specially intended for England. The illustrations intended for English children cannot be understood by Indian children, and therefore I should like to impress upon all Missionary Societies the advisability of employing these educational books of my friend, Dr. Murdoch. I do not see how you can have school books prepared for the whole world, because what is adapted to India is not adapted to China, and what is adapted to China is not adapted to Japan.

With regard to the education of the children of converts, I believe it is absolutely necessary that all Christian Missionary Societies should take in hand the education of the children of their own converts. Whatever they may leave neglected as to education otherwise, they ought to Education of converts' children. take care of the education of the children of those whom they have raised up; and they ought to take care, too, that the converts themselves pay for the education of their children. With regard to boarding schools, I think they are most admirable institutions, and though not absolutely necessary, it is expedient to have them; but if we have them it is necessary that they should be self-supporting.

I do not like orphanages at all, because they bring up a sort of hot-house Christians; and if there is one thing that ought to be avoided it is making these "curry and rice" or hot-house Christians. And I think we ought in all our education, especially in boarding schools and under the The young to retain native customs. Missionaries' own eyes, to take care to bring these young people up like other natives. Do not allow them to eat with knives and forks, and adopt similar European habits; but keep them to their native customs and costumes, and see that they are thorough Oriental Christians.

Just a word or two about elementary schools. I wish that Christian men in England would realise the splendid opportunities which are placed before them now. You remember the Educational Commission in India, which did so much for the education of the masses in India of the lower orders; and I would like to ask those of this assembly who understand about education, what advantage has the Christian Church taken of that Education Commission? I believe that the time will pass by and do no good to Mission work at all, if we do not take care. We shall allow a golden opportunity to slip away, and ere long we shall repent it.

A Member of the Conference: What does the speaker suggest we should do about the Education Commission?

Mr. Morris: I wish that more were done in the way of Christian inspection. I think it is absolutely impossible to have a network of vernacular schools all over the country in order to get hold of the people we want to reach. We want to get hold of the peasantry in their homes: it is almost impossible to do that by ordinary schools; but if you have a system of Christian inspection and supervision, such as the Society with which I am connected has in Bengal, you will find how to reach the hearts and the homes of the native peasantry, and if the Christian Church would only throw its heart into that particular work, I believe you would do more to advance the cause of the coming of the Lord Jesus Christ than by anything else. There are marvellous instances that have come to my knowledge of the way in which the pupils are reached; their parents are reached, and the masters themselves are reached by this system of Christian supervision and inspection. I conclude, therefore, by pressing upon the Christian Church the extreme value of bringing the Gospel home to the very people you want to reach by Christian inspection and supervision.

Christian inspection.

Rev. George Wilson (Church of Scotland Foreign Missions Committee): Mr. Chairman, ladies, and gentlemen,—I am here in the interest and on the side of education. I have never been in India, and am not able to enter into the details of this subtle problem of the education of the Hindus, but I am interested in the Missionary education of the Church at home, and I would like in a word to state what view this discussion has presented to me this morning, as I long to go back to my parish and my church to add something to the Missionary impulse and the Missionary information of the people of Scotland. I long to hear this cry once and for ever silenced—the cry of teaching *versus* preaching.

In a Christian Church it never ought to have been raised. As I see it, there is essentially no difference. The teacher is a preacher and the preacher is a teacher, if he have any right to go to India at all. But I do think that there is at this moment a lack of perspective in the question. I was startled this morning at the statement that we have been marvellously increasing the number of our professional teachers, and we have been marvellously neglecting to increase the number of our evangelistic preachers, and therefore I do trust that the Churches will at once see that the picture is set in due perspective, because we must not by any means give up the old Divine institution of the direct proclamation of the Gospel even to educated Hindus. Our friend from China, perhaps, has not had to face the many and complex difficulties that are associated with what we all call the simple preaching of the Lord Jesus Christ. It needs a very fine culture, and it needs a very wise man; and the blessed Spirit of Almighty God always seeks the very best organ through which to pour His truth and grace into the hearts of people; and what I want to see is our best men going to India—men with deep insight into all the philosophic problems of India—men who know the currents of thought at home, and how these are affecting the Hindu mind—men who know that in the conversion of all Hindus there is a period of infidelity, almost atheism, in the transition stage between the false and the true—and who will go to these high-caste and highly-endowed Hindus, and preach to them the Gospel of the Lord Jesus Christ, in the light of all those subtle problems, resting upon this hope, that there is a hunger in the heart of these men for this very Gospel. I believe that we would have far more fruit, and that India would be a different Mission-field to-day if we had more direct work while we are carrying on the work of education. There is another thing I might say; I hope I shall not be misunderstood. I have been pained at one thing this morning. I do not know that we are to blame for it, but I think it is a thing to lay us in the dust before God. We have been preaching in India, we have been

The teacher is a preacher.

The right class of men.

Why so few native teachers

teaching in India, for many and many a year, and we yet cannot man our schools with Christian teachers. I think the remedy lies in this direction : it lies in the watching and the proper culture of your converts ; it lies in boarding schools ; it lies in paternal oversight ; it lies in the nourishing of that full and complete life of the younger Christians in India ; and until we make provision for that we will have to complain that we cannot man our schools with Christian converts and with Christian teachers. And above all, it lies in this—that our men who go to teach philosophy, who go to teach mathematics, who go to teach the ordinary elements of education, shall so teach them as to win souls, that they, through a lesson in **Use secular** geography or grammar, if they are men of a right Christian spirit, **teaching for** shall so teach these subjects that every one of these Hindus shall **spiritual ends.** feel that the purpose that has brought that man to make his home in India is not to gain a Government pass, not a Government grant, but is to win India for the Lord Jesus Christ ; and so your education and your direct preaching will both become organs through which the Holy Spirit will pour Himself into the souls of the natives of India.

Mr. Albert Spicer, J.P. (Treasurer, L.M.S.) : Mr. Chairman, ladies, and gentlemen,—I am sure I shall re-echo the feelings of many in this Conference if I say that I think Mr. Wilson has lifted the discussion this afternoon to a higher level altogether. It seems to me that we are in danger in this Conference, whatever the subject may be before us, of simply discussing that which relates to our own special garden and our own special opinion. Now, we have before us to-day, the place of education in Missionary work in certain special cases. I take it that the object of Christian Missions is to preach Jesus Christ and Him crucified, and as an **Object of** after consequence to lift the nations that we try to reach to a **Missions.** higher level. I have perhaps the advantage of looking at the question rather more in perspective, as Mr. Wilson has termed it, speaking not from the experience of any one individual Mission, but from having seen a very large field of Christian Missions all through India and in various parts of the South Seas : and I am perhaps therefore able to understand it in the whole even more clearly than one who knows only his special work or field of labour. It seems to me that if our work is to be sound, elementary education must form a part of it.

We have had our attention called this afternoon to the question of Sunday schools. I am glad Mr. Hartley has called the attention of this Conference to that question. I believe that, perhaps in the past, we, as English Societies, have not given it all the attention we should. I think I **Sunday schools.** may say that the American Societies have paid more attention to it because the American Sunday School Union perhaps has been more faithful with the Missionaries in these fields, and perhaps if the English Sunday School Union, of which Mr. Hartley is the secretary, had looked into this matter in bygone days, more might have been done in that way. But how are we to get teachers if we have neglected elementary education ? Some have preached and have gathered in the people as converts, but unless we are prepared to give them some elementary education the work of Sunday schools cannot go on. And let me point this out : if you commence training the Native Missionaries, and leave the mass of the people without elementary education, you are helping to train up a form of priesthood in its very worst sense. Questions have also been asked with regard to the matter of special provision for the children of converts, boarding schools, and orphanages. I think those of us who have seen much of this work will be prepared to admit that we would much prefer to do without **Boarding** any of these special organisations ; at the same time we believe that **schools, etc.** there are times when there may be required special provision for the children of converts, such as boarding schools and orphanages. In times of great famine, such as we have seen in recent years in India, I believe it would be a cruelty if we as Christian men and women were not prepared on such occasions to provide for special needs. At the same time let us remember that these are after all comparatively artificial means, which are only useful for a certain time, and must not be looked upon as part of our permanent organisation. I say, therefore, while we are all equally interested in preaching Jesus Christ, while we know that no Mission work is complete without that, which is the beginning and the end of all Christian Mission work; let us not cheat ourselves into the belief that we can do Mission work by ending there, to the neglect of all the different branches whereby a nation may be educated and grow up in strong Christian life.

Rev. W. F. T. Hamilton (British Syrian Schools and Bible Mission) : I stand here this afternoon as the delegate of a Society which is working in the Turkish Empire, as the representative of the British Syrian Schools and Bible Mission. I may say, at once, it is a Mission which I may call almost exclusively educational, but I should be grieved indeed if it were not to receive emphatically the name of a Missionary Society ; and I should like to say from personal knowledge of the workers that I do not think you would find any workers in the Mission-field who are more entirely consecrated to the service of Christ, and who are more filled with the love of souls, than those who are employed in teaching in these schools ; and I should like to say this further, that I believe, as regards Syria, the best way in which the Mohammedans and others can be reached is through the medium of schools.

British Syrian Schools Mission.

I came here this afternoon not so much to speak as to try and get information which would be useful to the Council of that Society, and perhaps those who speak after me may give me information on one point upon which I have been specially desired to obtain information, namely, this question of payments. I will briefly state our plan, and I should be very thankful if better methods could be suggested for our guidance. We have schools, and we have a training institution for teachers. Our system is to admit the most promising from the schools into the training institution for teachers, not by payment but under a contract. That contract provides that for a certain number of years they shall be detained, in fact until they pass a qualifying examination, and that after that period they are bound to serve the Society for a certain number of years as teachers. I may say at once with reference to the question of Christian education that we never permit any teacher to teach the Bible in our schools whom we have not reason to believe to be thoroughly converted to God. In regard to the smaller schools, we have through financial difficulty been obliged to impose a school fee. We adopt the plan of making it a higher fee for the first class, smaller for the second class, and less for the junior. We find that this system has certain advantages, inasmuch as it secures regularity and punctuality of attendance. But we are in competition with the Jesuits. The Jesuits seem to have unlimited funds, and they try every method to thwart our work. Not only do they tell the parents of our scholars that their children will go to hell if they come to our schools ; but, finding that fails, they tell them, as happened for instance in the Lebanon lately, that the Lord Jesus Christ has been sent to their school in a box, and that all who come to their school will be able to receive Jesus Christ and to enter into heaven. The nuns waylay our children on the way to our schools, and they bribe the children with money to attend their schools ; so that the system of school fees has this difficulty, that we are in competition with those who not only do not exact any fee but pay the children to attend their schools. Let me just say one or two words about the effect of this education upon the homes. We find in our work, which consists

Their plan as to payment.

Insures regularity and punctuality.

partly of educational work and partly of the work of Scripture readers and Bible women, that the key to the houses of the Mohammedans is found in the children; and it is when the children have learned to sing sweet hymns in our schools, and to repeat the beautiful stories of the Gospel, and carry them home, that then the doors of the houses of their parents are opened for the first time to our Bible women and Scripture readers. You will recollect that George Moore, the philanthropist, said that a child with knowledge was the best Missionary in a poor man's home ; and I would venture to say that a child with the knowledge of the Bible is the best of Missionaries in the Mohammedan's home. Let me repeat to you in conclusion the words of, I believe, one of the most sanctified workers who has ever gone out into the Mission-field, Elizabeth Seeley, sister of Professor Seeley, of Cambridge. As she lay dying in Syria she seemed to have forgotten this world and to be looking at the world beyond, and she said, " I see a great palace, and many are entering into it." And then, just before the spirit left the body, her thoughts once more turned to the blessed work in which she had been engaged in teaching the children of Syria, and her last words of exhortation, bequeathed as a legacy to the Church of Christ, were these, " Teach the children."

Influence of children at home.

Elizabeth Seeley's opinion.

Rev. Dr. Kalopothakes (Athens): Mr. President, and gentlemen,— It would take three hours to tell you my opinions, but I must confine myself to education. I heard brother Clarke say that education was nothing, but if he himself had not been an educated man he could not have done what he has been doing. Education ? Why, if you send an uneducated man into any field, you send a man to fail ; and it is the want of this Christian education amongst the natives that has compelled your Churches to send out new Missionaries from time to time. I say educate the natives and let them take the places of the Foreign Missionaries ; let *them* teach in your seminaries and in your colleges and in your schools, and also take the conduct of the press into their own hands. Why, in my country (Greece) or in Turkey there is not a native Protestant besides myself that is able to carry on the papers that are published there. Why so ? Fifty or sixty years should surely have been time enough to prepare Bulgarians, Armenians, and Greeks to carry on their papers themselves without the aid of foreigners. Why has not that been done ? I do not know. One American dies, and another succeeds him, and another, and another ; and why ? Because the natives are not educated. Are there no men amongst the natives clever enough to carry on that work ? Certainly there are among the Armenians as clever people as are to be found among the Americans; and also among the Bulgarians and among the Greeks. Now, educate them, and then you will not be obliged to send them money all the time, and have those poor Churches dependent upon you.

Education an absolute necessity.

I speak with all the more courage now because three years ago we in Greece, though very few and poor, undertook to carry on the work which a Society had been carrying on there for many years, and what they did formerly at an expense of $10,000 we are now doing for $3,000. If these things are not enough to convince you, then I do not know what else to bring before you. You say you want economy. Then educate the natives, and put them in the places of your Missionaries. You want the schools and colleges to be carried on by natives. Educate them. I recently had a conversation on the subject with one of the best friends I have in the Beyrout College. I said to him, " How many years has that college been established there ?" He said thirty. Then

Educated converts to replace the Missionary.

Results.

I asked, "If you now withdraw, have you any native Christian to take your place?" He said, "No." "Well, then," I said, "you are certainly in fault, for in the course of thirty years you ought to have educated not one or two, but scores of men who should be competent to be professors in the several branches of knowledge that you are teaching, and then the natives would come and say, 'We will support that school; we do not want to have the Americans and English sending us money.'" That is the way, dear brethren, in which you ought to act. It is by education that you must carry on the object of your Mission work. What is the object? You want to raise up native Churches to take up the work and carry it on for themselves. Now, if the China Missions are to do that, you must have Chinamen ready to take your places; and when you die you will have native men ready to take your places and do the work even better than you are doing it yourselves.

What colleges should do.

Mrs. Stott (China Inland Mission): I want to say a few words, dear friends, in favour of girls' boarding schools. I have had considerable experience of schools both for boys and girls, and I have found that there are difficulties attached to the carrying on of boarding schools for boys, which do not attach to boarding schools for girls. The difficulty of providing for the boys afterwards is great, but as every girl, in China at least, is brought up with a view to marriage, we have only to train them to make good wives, and their future is then provided for.

Girls' boarding schools.

We believed, however, that a girl could no more be a useful wife to a Christian man unless she were converted, than a woman in this country could be. A Christian man must have a Christian wife; and we most earnestly desired from God this great gift, the gift of the souls of our girls. We laboured on for some years without seeing fruit; but it came after long waiting and watching, when some of these girls, pricked by the Spirit of God, came to me one day with an expression of face I had never seen before; and the eldest girl, speaking for herself, said, "Teacher, will the Lord Jesus Christ save me now? You have so often asked me to come to Him; will He have me now? I have delayed too long I am afraid." There and then, with a glad, joyful heart, I told her of the Saviour who was not only able but willing to save her just as she stood; and in a great burst of sorrow she rushed from the room with tears flowing down her face. I ran into the study to tell the good news to my husband, saying, "The blessing has come at last! The girls are seeking the Saviour!" I ran back again after a word of thanksgiving, and went upstairs to the bedroom where she had gone, knelt down with her there, in the name of Christ the Saviour who had come to seek and to save the lost. Leaving her I went downstairs, and found more girls were in tears, and asking, "How are we to be saved?" They, too, wanted this salvation, and after praying with them they began one after another to confess their sins. I wish I could go into details, and tell you the history of that one day. They confessed that they were poor sinners; and brought out their sins, showing me little things they had pilfered; one confessed to sins three years before that I knew nothing about. In three weeks we had seven girls converted by the Spirit of God, in a most remarkable way. And what has been the result? These girls, by their earnest devotion in seeking the souls of the younger girls, have been the means of the conversion of others; and sometimes women who come in from the country stations to seek baptism, have gone into the school, and the girls have been the means of their conversion. The girls have pointed out what true life in Christ was, and how they must be born again of the Spirit of God. Oh! friends, if we bring our schools to the foot of the Cross, we shall find they won't be failures.

Conversion of pupils sought.

A rich reward.

The meeting concluded with prayer by the **Rev. James Cooling.**

MEETINGS OF MEMBERS
IN SECTION.

ELEVENTH SESSION.

THE PLACE OF EDUCATION IN MISSIONARY WORK.

(3) THE COLLEGIATE.

(a) The place of higher education as an instrument of Christian effort. India, China, Japan, among Mohammedans and unreformed Churches, among less civilised races.

(b) How far is the concert or co-partnership of different Societies in college education practicable?

(Thursday morning, June 14th, in the Lower Hall.)

The Rev. J. Oswald Dykes, D.D., in the chair.
Acting Secretary, Rev. W. Park, M.A.

Dr. Murray Mitchell offered prayer.

The Chairman: Ladies and gentlemen,—The subject of our Conference this morning, as you are aware, is the place in Missionary work of the higher or collegiate education by which I understand the place that may be legitimately filled, among the various agencies which are grouped under the general name of Missionary, by that education which is directed to the higher intelligence of the more cultured and civilised races of the heathen world. How far that place is a legitimate one, in what cases it is recognised as a necessary one, and to what extent and under what conditions it may fairly serve the general purposes of Missionary work in common with those other agencies which have been discussed at other meetings of the Conference, on this subject I am certainly unable to speak as one having any personal connection with the work. I am simply an outsider and observer; but I think I may venture to say that the experience of the past has justified the wisdom of those branches *Experience* of the Christian Church and those Missionary Societies *of the past.* which have undertaken this description of work. Of that I am not competent to speak from personal knowledge; but others will be able to do so. I think, however, that I may go further and say that the legitimacy, and even the necessity, of higher education in certain portions of the Missionary field justifies itself on general and abstract grounds to any one who understands what the Missionary enterprise really is, and to any one, also, who has an adequate acquaintance with the best history of Missions in early periods of the Christian Church. I think we ought, in looking at a subject like this, to carry with us the conception of a variety of methods with unity of aim, and the freedom which Christ has given to His people to adapt themselves to the varying necessities and conditions of human life and society in the promotion of the one object which He has set before them of bringing the light of the Gospel to men of all races and of all conditions of culture. If we firmly grasp the thought that no particular method has been prescribed by our Divine Saviour, that no limitation has been set by Him or by the principles which were acted upon by His inspired Apostles, to the freedom of the Church in making herself "all things to all men," and working through all channels which may seem to her the most suitable and the most effective for Christianising the mind and the heart of the world, then I think we shall feel that we need be under no misgiving whatever as if one particular department of Missionary effort trenched upon another department.

Variety of methods allowable.

I am well aware that there has been in some quarters a jealousy of the methods which we are to consider this morning, based upon the idea that the simple proclamation by preaching of salvation through the Cross of Jesus and the teaching of the most elementary Christian verities, is the prescribed method by which the world is to be evangelised and brought to Christ. Now I should like to say at the outset—and I think I shall carry the sentiment of those who are most interested in Missionary colleges with me when I say it—that there is no desire, on the part of those who are most anxious for the higher education as a Missionary implement, to supersede the preaching of the Gospel in its simplest form to all men, and under all circumstances and conditions. An agency like that of the Missionary college supplements the preaching of the Gospel in its simplest form; but it does not and cannot possibly supersede it. So at least it appears to me, and I am very much mistaken if that is not also the sentiment of those who have interested themselves most in this aspect of Missionary work. But along with the preaching of the Gospel there certainly must go in certain circumstances other agencies—agencies by which difficulties are taken out of the way of the Gospel, and the minds of men are prepared to give to it a more favourable and more intelligent hearing. I think if that principle be conceded—and I do not see how it can be disputed—then we have a foundation laid on which to argue for the use of higher education as a supplemental and accessory instrument in the propagation of the Gospel. For example, take the methods by which the progress of the Gospel is facilitated at the opposite end of the scale, so to speak. Missionary colleges are for the most cultured, the most intelligent, and the most civilised peoples.

Our methods challenged.

Preaching not always enough.

But take those least intelligent, least cultured, least civilised; take the barbarous races; is it not found there that we must approach them by civilising agencies, by agencies which contribute to their material development and prosperity as well as by the mere preaching of the Gospel? Is it not true that we find it necessary to take along with us the arts of life, —the elementary arts on which civilised existence depends,—to those who are utterly barbarous, as well as to carry to them the Gospel of Jesus Christ? And if it be justifiable in the case of the uncultured to open a way for the intelligent reception of the Gospel by civilising agencies, then I take it, by parity of reasoning, it must be **A simple argument.** equally legitimate and desirable to prepare the way for the reception of the Gospel by the cultured and civilised by other methods, such as those of higher education, which appeal to their peculiar condition. We have to disabuse ourselves, it seems to me, in this large subject of Christianising the world, of all narrow and sectional views of the work. We have to regard ourselves as custodians and propagandists of a religion which appeals to man's nature through all its avenues, and which aims at satisfying all its cravings and needs. Certainly, the needs of the intellect are not the least of these necessities; and to approach men of culture, men of thought, men of speculation on the side of their intellectual appetencies with a view of correcting their intellectual mistakes and of leading them into a position in which they can appreciate the intellectual side of Christianity, must be as legitimate as it is to approach less cultured men through lower channels of access. It appears to me that the whole history of the past demonstrates that the relation between Christian truth and the highest thoughts of the human spirit, as apprehended and developed by speculative thinkers in all ages of the world, is very close. If you will cast your minds back to the early centuries, and remember how the first teachers of Christianity in the Græco-Roman world found it necessary to approach the educated intellect of Greece and **Lesson from the Early Church.** Rome and of the countries which they had influenced, on intellectual lines, to explain, to defend, and to recommend the truth of the New Testament to those who were already saturated with the philosophical conceptions of the time, and so to gain a willing ear and a reception for the higher aspects of Christian truth from the educated men of their time' I think you will feel that without the efforts of these philosophical apologists and defenders of the faith in the first two centuries, and without the influence of the great catechetical schools founded at Alexandria and elsewhere by the first workers in this field, the progress of Christianity during that period of its early triumphs would have been very much less marked than it was. When we go to the East we find ourselves in the presence of races whose higher thought has been working at similar problems, and for many, many centuries has been working with an intensity, and with, as they believe, a success which claim at our hands the highest appreciation. We have to deal, therefore, with men who are to a large extent in parallel conditions to those in which the educated minds of Greece and Rome were in the first two centuries of our faith, and we have, it seems to me, to adapt ourselves to that condition.

There is another aspect of the matter. Not only does Christianity ally itself to philosophical speculations, and must necessarily take them into account when it has to deal with philosophically trained and speculative minds, but it connects itself with the whole view which man takes of the world as related to God, as a creation of God. It has to do with fundamental questions which underlie all our physical science, as well as speculative philosophy. And in relation to these questions of science is it not true that false conceptions and conceptions based on ignorance of scientific truth have so mingled themselves up with the theology, if you may so call it, and with the cosmogony of the Eastern systems of religion that there are no means by which you can destroy the hold of these systems on educated minds more rapidly and more certainly than by scientific instruction. The conception which man forms of this world, and of its relation to its Maker, and of his own relation to it, must be profoundly affected by the discoveries of modern and Western science. Now, that science which is so familiar to us and so unfamiliar to our brethren of the East, is a creation of the Christian spirit. It has been, in ways which of course it would be out of place here to endeavour to expound, but which those who have paid any attention to the subject will acknowledge, a child, a creation of the Christian spirit. The Baconian philosophy has been the production of Christianity at its deepest centre, and therefore it is only when you bring this ally and handmaid of Christianity face to face with the men to whom it is new, and introduce them to its discoveries and the marvellous revelations which it has made to us of the works of God, that you put them into the swim and current of Christian thinking as it is familiar to educated minds in Western Europe. These are of course general considerations, and I can only venture to speak of general considerations for want of special knowledge on the subject. I shall, therefore, content myself with having made these few remarks indicating the standpoint which personally I occupy in regard to this question, and I shall now ask your leave to stand aside that I may introduce to you those gentlemen who have undertaken to read Papers, which will no doubt put the matter before you with all the authority and fulness of information of those who have been themselves engaged in the field.

Science and philosophy.

Their influence on Missions.

PAPER.

1. By the Rev. WILLIAM MILLER, C.I.E., LL.D. (Principal of Madras Christian College).

The place of Higher Education as an Instrument of Christian Effort.

I am to speak of the exact place and function of higher Christian education as a part of Missionary agency, as an important auxiliary in Missionary work, not to engage in any defence of it. The time for that is past. In the place where it is best known in its practical effects, it is undoubted now that it has a special sphere, and that in this sphere it is most important. The unanimous resolution of the South Indian Conference nine years ago—a Conference containing one hundred and eighteen members, and representing twenty-five different Missionary bodies—settles this point. The vast majority of the members of that Conference were unconnected with education, yet cordially and unanimously they

A place for education unquestionable.

pronounced advanced Christian education to be an *indispensable part* of what needs to be done for the evangelisation of India. If there be any doubt elsewhere as to this agency being valuable in its own sphere, it is fair to expect that such doubt will pass away when it is placed on the same footing, and regulated by the same principles as in Southern India.

But, though formal defence is no longer needed, the time is not gone by when the Church still needs help in forming clear ideas as to the precise place and function of education among her varied methods. It seems to me that its place depends *Misconceptions remain.* mainly on the right application of two great principles. They are principles which no one will deny, but which men are in some danger of forgetting practically. The *first* of these principles is that the Church is meant, and commanded by God, to work not only for the immediate present. The second is that the form of the Church's work is intended by God to be determined *Two principles.* by the circumstances in which His providence places her. These principles must for our present purpose be applied to India. For this question is emphatically an Indian one. It does not seem to me that in any other portion of the Mission-field, particular prominence should be given to education in the meantime; or, at least, to that higher Christian education with which we are to-day particularly concerned. And even in India, it is in its bearing on a single section of the population that the function of Christian education can be best seen. This point needs some explanation.

It is too often supposed that there are but two elements in the Indian population—Mohammedans and Hindus. But, in point of fact, there are three; and, for any right understanding *Three elements* of the problem of evangelising India, the distinction *in population* between these three must be kept steadily in view. There *of India.* are some fifty millions of Mohammedans. There are perhaps a hundred and fifty millions of Hindus. The rest are neither Mohammedans nor Hindus. This third section are the descendants of those who never received the civilisation or the creed of the Aryan races, and were never embraced within the Hindu Society. It is as if Christianity in Europe had brought the larger part, but not the whole, of the population nominally within its pale, and had fused them into a Society completely marked off from such as remained outside it. It is as if the Society thus formed allowed those without to retain their creeds and customs, on condition of their becoming serfs to it.

Many of those thus outside the Hindu Society live amongst the Hindus, and speak their tongue; but morally, socially, and in point of racial character, even these are quite distinct from them. They are not marked, as yet, by any common name. They are known in different parts of the country by different names,—Mhars, Chamars, Santhals, Shanars, Dhonds, Pariahs, Madagas, and a hundred more. According to the rules of Hindu orthodoxy, it is sad to say that they are a species of brutes, whose very touch defiles. Across the deep chasm between Hindus and them there is no flow of thought or interchange of feeling. They number perhaps seventy or eighty millions, though it will not be possible to give their exact number till their essential difference from Hindus is adequately and officially recognised.

Now the Hindus and these outside races have each of them their own importance in a Missionary point of view. But it is in its bearing on Hindus that the scope of advanced Christian education can be fully seen. That great Society, the central and dominating mass of the Indian people, has remained on the whole untouched by any external influence. Revolutions have shaken it. Various creeds and cults have sprung up within it. One of its own heresies came near to subverting it. Its customs have changed, narrowing here and widening there. But every change has been from within. The Society, as a Society, has remained unbroken and unaffected. As regards the nature of this great Society, I can but remind you now that it is pantheistic to the core. To the Hindu, God is not only everywhere, He is everything. All that is, is not only caused by God, it is an emanation from Him—an expression of Him—a part of Him. To us, pantheism seems only the airy speculation of a few. The Hindu race are a standing proof that it can be a popular religion, and a religion with the strongest possible hold on those who rest in it. By means of ceremonies and forms and philosophic treatises and the all-pervading system of caste, this scheme of pantheistic thought has impressed certain features of character on every member of the Society. And if there be any truth in the principles from which we started, these features are intended *by God* to determine the Church's methods of action. I must touch on some specimens of these points of character. Take a state of mind very common among Hindus who are acquainted with Christianity. They accept all you say of Christ,—not feignedly in the least, but very heartily,—yet do not feel any call to confess Him,—cannot even conceive why any one should think that they are bound to do so. The thoughts awakened by what you say are mastered by the stronger thought that this is but one emanation from the Divine—good and beautiful and true, but only one among the countless ways in which the Spirit of the Universe has clothed itself.

Hindu pantheism.

The Church's methods, how determined.

Or take the absence of the sense of personal responsibility. Something like it may be sometimes seen in members of the Roman Church, who disapprove of many things in their Church, but to whom it seems monstrous to think that it would be right of *them* to oppose it. But the idea of personal accountability is not wholly lost in any form of Christianity. If you can imagine the state of mind of a devout Romanist intensified tenfold, you may have some faint conception of the feelings of a devout Hindu.

Once again, every Hindu idea of right is linked to the preservation of the one Society. The idea of right and wrong is often vitally and strongly present to the Hindu mind. To the Hindu, the main element of rightness is faithfulness to the social unity. To be what his people are, to think as they think, to move as they move,—this must be right. To separate from them is the greatest sin he can commit. We, too, acknowledge that there are lower and higher duties. To us the highest test of right is the will of the personal God. What obedience to God's will is to us, that adherence to the social unity is to the ordinary thoughtful Hindu. It is his highest test of duty.

These are the leading features in the character of that Society which from the day when it was formed till very lately has laughed to scorn all attempts to influence it from without.

There have been speculations lately as to the growth of Islam in India. A recent article, which is valuable in many details and just in many of its criticisms on Indian Missionaries, estimates the conversions from Hinduism to Mohammedanism at fifty thousand annually, and holds it to be "nearly certain that should no new spiritual agency intervene, the Indian peoples will at last become Mohammedans." *Influence of Islam.* Against this, I place the counter-statement that there is no visible token that Hindus will ever become Mohammedans, and that transferences from the one faith to the other are not taking place at the rate of a hundred per annum, or even ten. The accessions to Islam are wholly from the seventy or eighty millions which lie outside of the Hindu unity,—of what may allowably be termed the Hindu Church.

And something very similar is true as yet of Christianity. Between Protestants and Roman Catholics there are from one to two millions of Christians in India. It is however only the merest fringe of them that have been drawn from among the Hindus, and even of these the bulk have been influenced by Christian education.

When this question of education was coming to the front—say roughly some forty years ago—the attempt to influence the great Hindu Society had been going on in Southern India for one hundred and forty, and in Northern India for some fifty years. Speaking as men must speak about races and communities, the effect produced was *Origin of* practically nothing. It had become an important question *education* what policy the Church of Christ was to pursue. Side by *movement.* side with her failure to reach the Hindu and Mohammedan communities, she had had marked success with the non-Aryanised races. Among them— I do not forget the South Sea Islands—among them, particularly in Tinnevelly and South Travancore, the most remarkable successes of Protestant Missions had been gained. Might it not be wisest to push this great advantage, and to leave the Mohammedans and the great Hindu Society alone for the time? Much could be urged in favour of this course. This was the course adopted, if not avowedly at least practically, by those Missionary agencies that did not see their way to work education into their scheme of effort. And I have not the slightest inclination to argue that their course was wrong.

To some, however, it appeared that having put their hand to work upon the central Hindu mass they ought not to turn away from it. They did not doubt that the present Christ and the Word of God were mighty to the pulling down of all strongholds. The only question was as to the way in which the present Christ would have that Word to be applied. A force was beginning then to act upon the *Its rationale.* Hindu Society which was certain to produce change of some kind on that which had remained unchanged so long. With encouragement from Government, leading members of that Society were beginning to seek for acquaintance with English thought and the English tongue, and to desire that their sons should be trained after an English model. That desire has now developed into something approaching to a passion, and has resulted in the establishment of the present extensive apparatus of Indian education. It was decided that education supplied by Government should be non-religious and non-Christian. I shall not say whether this decision was right or wrong. The time for any profitable discussion of that question has long gone by. It would be mere waste of time to re-open it. But there can be no doubt as to what the effect of such a non-religious scheme of education would be if it should stand alone. In the minds of those who received it, there was no likelihood that Hinduism would stand the impact. With nothing to fill the place left vacant by its fall, all thought about the unseen would, for a time at least, be lost. Instead of a vast Society permeated with pantheistic thought and filled with religiousness, which, whatever else it was, was at least deeply earnest, the Church would be confronted, when the new influence should have had time to produce its full effect, by a vast population destitute of any moral standard beyond what the well-being of earthly life can yield, and destitute also of either belief or interest in anything Divine. Whether such a change would make the problem which the Church must solve, easier or harder on the whole, I leave to others to determine. But it seemed to some that Providence had opened a way by which the conditions of the problem were made at last more favourable. If the Western thought now flowing into Hindu Society could bear with it the influences of Christianity, the mighty mass might be awakened into new moral and spiritual life. And it was natural for this stream to bear such influences along with it. Our literature and language are saturated with Christianity. To teach the plan of God's love while teaching that which has flowed from it historically, was not to add a thing that was superfluous or intrusive. It was to do what good teaching called for, even if no advantage to the kingdom of Heaven followed. But certain benefits for that kingdom were likely to follow. And they were the exact benefits that the solution of the great problem called for. Let the historic truth be taught about the plan of love that was gradually unrolled till it was summed up in the life of lives,— and, by the Spirit's aid, it would bring hearts and consciences to the point of view from which the value of a Saviour is understood and felt. Let the proofs that God has revealed Himself be pondered in that great Society, and it would in time discern that however truly all that is, is in some sense a manifestation of divinity, there is one central manifestation that overrides and explains all others. Then, too, the sense of personal responsibility would awake from torpor. Then the will of the community would no longer be the test of duty. That and all other tests are nothing if on this common earth the eternal God has spoken. The consummation might be that as that Society had been bound into one by all its history as no other Society has ever been, so it might witness for truth on earth with all the untold force that unity confers.

Necessity for religious teaching.

Results hoped for.

It seemed to some that by such considerations Providence—God Himself in His living Providence—was making clear the path that His Church, or part of it, should walk in. Whether it might be years or centuries before the path led to perfect victory, this was a question for God and not for those whose highest desire should be, as their one true honour is, to be the instruments of His will. To refuse to follow that path because it was difficult and long, or because those who did not hear the heavenly voice might misunderstand and oppose them,—this would have been sin and shame on the part of those who saw the way in which God called *them* to serve Him. But if Christian education was thus to make plain the way of

A Divine call.

the Lord the education should be as influential as was possible. Hence it should be, at least in part, of an advanced description. The school influences its narrow circle. The influence of the college spreads wide and far. For both there was this great advantage that, in virtue of its wondrous unity, any thought spreads in the Hindu Society with a rapidity and force unknown elsewhere. But the speed and completeness of diffusion and the completeness of pervasion would be greater if the source of the new thought were prominent and commanding. That is the sole but sufficient reason why Christian education should be, in part, of the highest kind. The best thing of all would be if in any important centre the Christian college could take the foremost place. If it could thus be the leading factor in the guidance of thought and feeling, the leavening of the great Society might be antedated by generations. The place and influence of the Christian college.

Of course the mere teaching of English, or of English thought, would be valueless by itself. This higher education must be made the vehicle of a moral and spiritual power. It is only those who trust to spiritual forces and aim at spiritual ends that can make education—or any other agency—helpful in setting up Christ's kingdom.

Now, in India there are peculiar hindrances to an educational institution becoming a moral or spiritual power. And I am not here to deny that even the best of these institutions is far inferior to what we wish that it should be. As a specimen I shall mention one such hindrance. The present mania for examinations has appeared in India in its intensest form. To put passing examinations in place of thought, in place of training, in place of everything, is the prevailing danger there. The evils that arise from this are a terrible difficulty to those who try to mould opening minds according to the Christian pattern. Such difficulties are so great as naturally to awaken doubt whether a college which aims at moral and spiritual ends can attain the high position from which it will change the current of the thoughts that guide the Hindu unity. If it is impossible for a Christian college to gain any of this moral power, it plainly follows that the Hindu element in the Indian population must be abandoned for the time to the guidance of forces that are adverse to religion. But let me close with a few facts, well known in Southern India, which show that for this doubt, natural though it be, there are not sufficient grounds.

At Madras the establishment of such a college met with peculiar difficulties. Full advantage for Christian ends had been taken for a time of the desire for Western knowledge. But effort had been intermitted. For years the direction of the new current had been almost abandoned to influences that were not religious. Thus there had arisen an antagonism to Christian thought which has never ceased to be pronounced and powerful. It seemed that in Madras at least the channel had been stopped along which a tide of Christian thought might flow. Yet an attempt was made. From absurdly small beginnings, in the face of overwhelming difficulties, a college at last grew up that had some little power. It all along put training—Christian training—foremost. As to making the Word of God the centre Origin and character of Madras College. of its teaching, it never hesitated or faltered. By word and deed it avowed that its object was, not to make students *pass*, but to form their character and turn their thoughts on all that bears upon human duty and human destiny, and chiefly upon the Divine provision for man's guidance and redemption. Popularity might have been gained by putting the study of Scripture in a subordinate place, or by concentrating effort on success at the all-engrossing examinations. The temptation was resisted. The determination was to have a small influence such as might further the Divine purpose, rather than a large one of more doubtful character. For long years it was slow and up-hill work, little appreciated and little encouraged by most. But now for no inconsiderable time, that college has been admittedly the most influential in Southern India. It has been helped to become so by the fact that different Missionary bodies have co-operated in supporting it. This question of co-operation is one of those before us. But the only thing that need be said about it is, *solvitur ambulando*. For a dozen years, three Missionary bodies have taken part in the maintenance of this college, and taken part, through their local representatives, in its management. Others have given it moral though not yet pecuniary support. And no difficulty worth mentioning has been caused by the arrangement. It is impossible here to speak about details, but experience has fully shown that co-operation is quite practicable, and that it results, not only in economy of resources, but in great increase of moral power.

It should be further borne in mind that the college thus based on co-operation has won its place in spite of the telling fact that nearly all the fifty or sixty colleges of Southern India charge lower fees, and that the one which still charges a trifle more has external attractions to which the Christian college can make no pretence. And I believe every one who knows the facts will say that these outward things are but a token of the moral influence the college wields and the moral good it does. But these are points on which it is not fit that *I* should

Greater difficulties may come. dwell. Only remember that I build nothing on popularity. All that I have spoken of may pass away. Difficulty and danger are inseparable from a work like ours. Difficulties there are just now, though I believe these special ones will soon pass away.

But suppose that more than passing troubles lie before us. Suppose, if you wish to do so, that from this day forward the Madras Christian College should fall from its position and never be restored to it. Even then, the past is enough to show what is possible, to say the least of it. What has been done—done for many years—done where obstacles once were greatest and where antagonism has been always most pronounced—that, with the Spirit of the Lord to guide and aid, may be done elsewhere and done everywhere. And if higher Christian education can thus mould a people's thoughts, and find an entrance for saving truth to the great organic unity that was hermetically sealed against that truth so long, is it possible to doubt that the mighty work should be carried on by those divinely called to it, with patience and devotion, with hope and faith and courage!

PAPER.

2. BY THE REV. E. S. SUMMERS, B.A. (B.M.S., from Serampore).

Collegiate Education as a means of Evangelistic Agency.

This morning we are met to consider the place of higher education as an instrument of Christian effort in various lands. I speak as one who has had experience in and observation of this form of Missionary work in India, and more particularly in Bengal. I do not propose to justify Missionary effort in this direction on the

Educational work a felt need. ground that it is an exact imitation of Apostolic methods. To me, and I think to the majority of us, it seems sufficient if the peculiar circumstances of religious thought and social organisation in India render this form of aggressive effort useful and seemingly necessary. It may be a sufficient explanation of the fact that Apostles and other Missionaries of the first centuries did not employ it that their circumstances were so different that it is inconceivable that they should have done so. They in their generation had their special gifts for their special needs, and it is not unreasonable to suppose that Christ has prepared His people with special gifts and qualifications, and opened up to them special modes of operation for the special work of this century. I will not claim that India is the hardest field to which the efforts of the Christian Missionary have been addressed, though in my heart *I* believe it. But I think that I may claim that the simple influence of caste alone would make the field a unique one; and besides caste there India a unique are many other circumstances that make the attack of field. Christianity on heathen India, conducted as it is by Missionaries, so different in every respect from those among whom they labour, of an altogether unique character. The form of aggressive Missionary work, therefore, that we are considering, seeing that there is nothing in it contrary to Christian principle that renders it unlawful for us to use, must stand or fall by its practical results.

About these practical results there is much discussion. To a large extent we can only form an opinion upon the subject. Just as we decline to regard the question of the success of Mission work in all its branches as a mere question of statistics, so we Various must in this particular branch. We cannot allow its opinions. influence and success to be measured by the number of professed converts who have come from Missionary colleges. I think that Dr. Duff beyond all doubt looked for a numerical success that has not been achieved, but perhaps almost all earnest Missionaries have done that. It is easy to long for and to hope for results. We might like to grow a forest of oaks in ten years or even less, but God has chosen a century. In the longings of some after the evangelisation of the whole world in a generation, I recognise the throbbings of a Christian charity, by which I trust I am moved myself; Results are but I cannot help thinking that God has chosen a longer with God. time, and if so He has done it in wisdom and in love. It would seem, again, as though the number of converts from Missionary colleges is not so large now as in Duff's days, and for this fact various explanations are given. The rise and influence of the Brahmo-Somaj undoubtedly has had much to do with detaining many in a kind of half-way house who would probably otherwise have yielded themselves more to the influence of Chris- Hostile tianity. Others ascribe it to the influence of the Calcutta influences. University, which rules with too despotic a control over every educational institution in Bengal, and by its increasing claims seems to thrust the religious teaching more than formerly into the background. However the fact remains, that from the Missionary colleges and schools of Bengal have come a body of converts which may be small in numbers, but certainly has been influential, and so far as we can tell, other agencies would not have gathered such men in, and in fact have not done so.

But I believe that few supporters of Missionary colleges as evangelistic agencies would base their support on the number of conversions from among the students. In fact, a far more powerful influence is being exercised by them on Hindu society than can possibly be estimated, because it is an influence that works like an underground current, whose full effect can only be gauged after a time; but we know that the result must follow because the cause is present. These colleges are leavening Indian society with Christian thought and developing Christian feeling, and so preparing for a great harvest of conversions in the future. How common a thing it is to hear these Missionary institutions characterised as places for the manufacture of heathen B.A.s and M.A.s, as though such critics were unable to understand what was really going on and grudged the first apparent result because it seemed simply to be to the advantage of the heathen community. It seems to me that a considerable misapprehension exists on the part of many as to what really takes place inside a Missionary college. It seems to be assumed that the Missionary not only fails to be a teacher in any sense but sinks into a crammer for examinations. The students are crammed, whatever that may mean, and after a few years of such experience a comparatively raw, empty-minded, untaught young man, full of conceit and vanity, takes the degree of B.A. or M.A. with a great display of unidiomatic English. What is the real state of the case?

Results not shown by statistics.

For some of the most impressionable years of his life, the Hindu lad is engaged in the close study of English authors, some of whom, as Milton and Cowper, are deeply religious, others of whom if not so religious, are in sympathy with Christian truth in the main, or, if not in sympathy with it, are dominated by it, so that in the struggle with Hinduism such an author is compelled to bear witness to and exercise influence on the Christian side. Unconsciously, and yet most really as the young student studies this literature in which the Christian element is so important a factor, he imbibes new ideas and develops new feelings, which draw him from Hinduism towards Christianity. As surely as the heathenism of Greek and Latin literature has exercised a heathenising influence over the Christian nations of Europe, so will the Christianity of English literature exercise a Christian influence in India. Then the study of history, of philosophy, of science, work, of course, mightily against Hinduism, and though not so plainly, yet in the end, I believe, as decisively, in favour of Christianity. For truth of all kind has come from the same author, and those who accept it must be led by it so far as its immediate guidance is concerned, onward to Him. But you may say that I am speaking of nothing but what is going on in any Government college. That is true, and I believe that the Government colleges of India are doing a work for the evangelisation of that country, which their promoters do not contemplate, and their opponents do not suspect.* But the Missionary college differs from the Government in two respects. First, the teachers therein are not merely teachers, not merely Christians, but Missionaries, i.e., men who cannot help using every opportunity which their teaching supplies to fill the minds of their students with Christian truth. Is it nothing that Milton and Cowper should be explained by Christians, nothing

College influence on Indian youths.

Truth will prevail.

Missionary and Government colleges contrasted.

---

* We are told that 90 per cent. of the Hindu youth trained in Government colleges have ceased to believe in Hinduism, and are become sceptics. God be praised for so beneficent a result, if it be really achieved, and now may He who has delivered them from the shameful bondage of credulous belief in Hinduism, lead them on through scepticism to a reasonable faith in Christ.

that philosophy and science should be allowed to yield their proper lessons, and not be forced to become the handmaids of irreligion and unbelief? Is it nothing that that curriculum which in the struggle between Hinduism and Christianity must exercise an influence on the whole on the side of Christianity, should be directed with resolute aim and determination to that single end? And then, secondly, comes in, what so many assailants of the system seem to ignore, the direct religious teaching, the full and systematic statement of Christian principles, the study under Christian teachers of the Christian Scriptures. This element rightly absent from the teaching of the Government colleges (for who would tax Hindus and Mohammedans to propagate Christianity) forms an essential element in that of the Missionary college. How a Missionary, with the Christian Scriptures to teach, and subjects for instruction, which if not positively religious, have a religious side which can easily be brought out—how a Missionary so situated can ever sink into the mere schoolmaster, I cannot understand. I do not think that I did through the six years that I was engaged in this kind of work, even when teaching such subjects as Euclid and Algebra. I am sure that others, whom I know, *Teaching need not secularise.* did not, and I doubt whether any Missionary has ever so failed who would not equally have failed in any other branch of Missionary work. And then again, besides the mere instruction given in the college, there is to be reckoned the personal influence of Christian teachers exercised continuously, both in college and out of it; there is to be considered the amount of outside influence that can be exercised by means of the influence that has been acquired inside. We at Serampore know well what this means, because we feel that since we ceased to be engaged in this class of work we have entirely lost touch with the educated classes of the community. I trust that I have made it clear that the effect of the college teaching is to communicate Christian ideas. I know, from personal experience and observation, that a very large proportion of the students gain a fairly clear view of the facts and of some of the *Personal experience.* doctrines of the Christian religion; their minds are enlightened on the subject of sin and of their relation to God, and especially are they filled with intense admiration for Christ and for His moral teaching, even if they get no further. And if they do get no further—well sadly and sorrowfully we confess that as regards themselves individually there has been failure—they have not given themselves to Christ, they have not received the Holy Spirit. Like so many in more favoured England, they come to know, and in the same measure, to reject the truth. But that is not the end of it as regards our general Mission work. Though they reject Christ as their Saviour, they cannot eliminate from their minds what they have learned. They go forth to preach even for the very Christ whom they have rejected for themselves, and I have known cases where students of Missionary colleges have been the human instrument of conveying the knowledge of that salvation to others, which they have rejected for themselves. Wherever they go, they are more or less *Influence of students.* authorities on the subject of the Christian religion. They are glad to display their knowledge; they help in disseminating truer ideas about idolatry, about sin, about salvation, about the true idea of incarnation. They help to familiarise a community saturated intellectually and morally with the pantheistic conception of the universe with the theistic. They go where we cannot go; they speak where we should not be listened to; the truth, if uttered by our lips would be rejected without examination, is calmly considered and accepted; yea, we can rejoice with the Apostle Paul "that in every way, whether in pretence or in truth, Christ is proclaimed; and therein I rejoice, yea, and will rejoice." Thus in a hundred ways they help to prepare the way for the messengers of the Gospel of reconciliation. As a community the Hindus do not believe in the heinousness of sin, and do not feel the need of a Saviour, and hence so much of the labour of preaching a Saviour seems wasted. John the Baptist *Truer views of sin and righteousness.* went before Christ, and perhaps the systematic instruction upon the subject of sin and salvation given in the Mission colleges, and gradually percolating through the community giving new, higher, and truer ideas of sin, and producing a want for, a crying out after the living God, is the best preparation for the time when multitudes of evangelists shall traverse the land in all directions, and through a pouring out of the Spirit, perhaps in our own time, perhaps in a later generation, which in God's eyes shall be the fulness of the times, millions upon millions will speedily turn to the Lord. This class of work seems to me, therefore, a valuable auxiliary—I will make it no higher and no lower—a valuable auxiliary to the evangelisation of India.

This is the general theory of the subject as it presents itself to my mind, after actual experience of the work for six years, and observation of it through a longer period. I desire now as far as time *Objections to education.* allows, to answer some objections, which are not mere objections put up to knock down, inasmuch as I have heard them made by earnest opponents of this species of work.

The first objection that I shall note is this, that Missionaries allow themselves to sink into mere schoolmasters, and spiritual influence as a fact is not exercised. Now I readily concede that an institution may not be always worked as well as it might be, the influence exercised may not be as great as it should be, and this may even arise from defects, spiritual or otherwise, in the Missionaries chiefly concerned. But I do protest against the hasty and uncharitable *Character of agents.* criticism of those, who knowing little of a Missionary's work, and having little opportunity of seeing what influence he does exercise, pronounce their opinion that he has sunk into the mere schoolmaster. It avails little to put talk about the Holy Spirit into the foreground, if men attribute evil motives, and form unkind conclusions on slender evidence, about those who feel themselves as much called by the Holy Spirit, to witness for Jesus in the schoolroom, as some others feel themselves called to preach by the wayside.

We need common sense in locating and carrying on evangelistic work by means of colleges. If some men engaged in the work are not fitted to provide the result desired, remove them. If the place in which the college be situated *Colleges in great centres.* be unfavourable, remove the college. This form of Missionary effort is suitable only to large centres of population, and, on the whole, it is not desirable to introduce it where other educational institutions already fully cover the ground. Above all it is desirable to avoid competition with other institutions of the same kind, for where such competition exists, influences adverse to Christianity will be generated. How to avoid such competition I do not so clearly see. The idea of co-partnership of various Societies seems alluring, but I have my doubts as to the permanency of any such arrangement. Common sense and Christian love must be left to produce a solution of the difficulty wherever it may be felt. A specious objec- *Connection with universities.* tion is often put forward somewhat in these terms,—"Why do you work in connection with the Calcutta University; why not form a curriculum for your Christian students in which Christianity shall hold a more influential position, and allow heathen students to attend your classes if they please?" Like so many other objections this practically receives its answer on the spot. The influence of the Calcutta University at the present time on education in Bengal, is too powerful and too pervasive to be escaped. Your Christian youths, desirous of higher education, wish, and are required by their own people to pass the examinations of that university, and your refusal to teach them so that they might achieve that end, would result in loss of the best students and ultimately in the closing of the institution. I readily acknowledge the excellence of the suggestion, which to my mind is ideally perfect, but practically I do not think that it could be carried out. And further, though I acknowledge that there are objections to the examination system altogether, and to the curriculum of the university, yet practically you might go a long way, and search a good deal, without devising a better system, and without sensibly improving the curriculum. Another objection I have heard made is, that students of Missionary colleges are in after life often found as bitter opponents of the Christian preacher. I think that there is truth in the assertion that some are. We know that while a clearer knowledge of the truth attracts some and leaves many indifferent, it stirs others up to opposition. While we speak of the removal of prejudices and the dissemination of purer ideas of Christian truth, we acknowledge **Some students become opponents.** as the sign manual that we have indeed preached the truth in our colleges, the intelligent and bitter opposition of some. These are mainly of two classes ; first, those who are deeply attached to Hinduism, probably simply for race reason, possibly from deeper motives, who clearly recognise the incompatibility of our teaching with Hinduism and its overturning character ; and secondly, those who have nearly become Christians, but have drawn back at the critical moment, who seem sometimes stung by a bitter remorse, which can only find expression in bitter hatred of the truth they once loved and nearly accepted.

The last objection I shall refer to is aimed at the presence of the heathen teacher. His presence is essential to the carrying on of the work beyond all doubt, and if in principle it be wrong to admit him, practically this form of effort must be given up, at any rate for the present. But **Influence of heathen teachers.** I am not sure that those who somewhat ungenerously regard the Educational Missionary as a mere schoolmaster, do not treat the heathen teacher somewhat ungenerously too. They seem to imagine that every heathen teacher is striving might and main to subvert the Christian Missionary's teaching and influence. They do not see how it should be otherwise. They imagine that these Hindus are all as much aflame to resist Christianity as they are to propagate it. Experience compels me to say that in my opinion it is far otherwise. The suspicion that educated Hindus feel with regard to Hinduism, both intellectually and morally, is too deep to allow of such a position of hostility. Instances there may be where Hindu teachers have quietly and resolutely striven to hinder the religious work of the school ; such conduct would be more probable in Mohammedans, who, however, are not numerous in Mission schools. In my opinion, the present condition of Hinduism is such that as a body the heathen teachers are indifferent or favourable to the reception of Christian truth, as distinguished from the open profession of it. I can imagine many a Hindu teacher in a Mission school asked by a Hindu boy there whether Christ's teaching was good, saying Yes, and "Was idolatry wrong?" saying Yes ; and yet if the boy said to him, "Shall I become a Christian," saying No. But if that happened I should say that under the circumstances the teacher had done much to help the boy on his way to Christ, and that the negative answer could not be construed as disloyalty to the institution he served. The Missionaries must of course exercise common sense in the matter, and if they found a teacher who laid himself out to destroy their work, they would doubtless say, " Friend, your zeal from your point of view is commendable, but it will not suit our purposes." No Missionary that I ever knew or heard of ever failed to get as many and as good Christian teachers as he could get, and sometimes in our zeal we have known what it was to get a Christian who was so only in name, and whose conspicuous fall has wrought more harm than a dozen heathen teachers earnestly intent upon mischief could have effected.

Let me close with the ever-to-be reiterated observation that this mode of operation aims directly at the conversion to Christ of those with whom the Missionary is brought in contact, and where it fails of that end in any individual, temporarily or ultimately; it hopes to send him forth so changed, mentally and morally, that whether inten- *The one aim of the work.* tionally or not he cannot fail to influence those with whom he has to do in the direction of Christianity; it is not proposed as a substitute for other methods, equally legitimate and more directly practised by the Apostles—nay, rather where it has failed to gather in—it rejoices in being the auxiliary of those ·whom God permits to be the reapers. God grant that in another world, where we shall all see more clearly, the Saviour's purpose may be indeed fulfilled; and as we gaze upon the harvest that is gathered in, he that sowed and he that reaped WILL rejoice together.

PAPER.

3. BY THE REV. J. P. ASHTON, M.A. (L.M.S., from Calcutta).

English Education in Mission Colleges and High Schools, as an Instrument of Christian Effort.

The *primary object* of every Missionary college or high school, into which Hindus, Mohammedans and native Christians are admitted, should be the *conversion and salvation* of the *Original design of Mission education.* pupils. It was for this purpose such institutions were originally founded, and there is no reason to make any alteration. No concealment of motive was made nor is any required. The design is known to the pupils and guardians, and should be evident in the Bible lessons.

This is the Educational Missionary's *aim*. He may sometimes be troubled that, to attain it, so much time and energy has to be spent on secular teaching. The Medical Missionary feels the same amidst the absorbing labours of his Mission hospital. But as neither colleges nor hospitals can exist, still less flourish, without this secular work, it should be cheerfully undertaken, that through it the Great Master's kingdom may be advanced. At the same time both doctor and teacher should ever be on the watch, that they use all the *Opportunities for spiritual work.* varied opportunities of making known Christ, which are within their reach in so great abundance, and they, with other Missionaries, like the Apostle Paul, may beg that we strive together with them in our prayers to God that they may have utterance to speak the Gospel boldly, and to persevere in faith, whether results are visible or not.

There is yet another object which may be said to take precedence of intellectual culture and the attainment of certain standards of *Moral superiority of Missionary education.* knowledge; and it is the *moral and Christian training* of the young men. It has been publicly acknowledged by the highest authorities that the Government colleges, and those of indigenous growth are virtually godless and almost wholly destitute of moral influence. The very heathen perceive the moral superiority of Missionary education, and, except in moments of excitement, do not object to its continuance and extension.

But while emphasising the evangelistic and moral aspects of the work, it is desirable to look at it from some *special* points of view, which may serve to bring out more distinctly its Missionary value.

And, first, it is well to avoid the mistake sometimes made that the pupils in these English institutions belong to the higher and richer classes. All ranks and castes are admissible ; but, in fact, the overwhelming majority belong to the middle class, and to its lower rather than its higher half.   They are nearly all Brahmans, Kayasts, and Sudras, but, according to all analogy, these are the very strata of society which will form the bulk of the future Indian Churches.   Thus the Indian Educational Missionary reaches the very material which it is most desirable to evangelise.   Conversions still occur in our colleges, but in The classes reached. fewer numbers than before, for the recent Indian eclecticism in its varied forms and European scepticism now stand in the way of early decision.   In the old days these half-way houses were unknown.   But let Missionaries be earnest and faithful, and baptisms will continue and increase. The day of reaction and revival will yet come, and prayerful perseverance in Bible teaching will have its reward.   As it is, the results are such as may call for devout thankfulness.   The converts already obtained form a new and higher type of native Christian, with a wider Influence of native Christians. and deeper range of influence.   The twenty native Christians were but a small portion of the seven hundred delegates who met in Madras as a National Congress ; but their influence was felt on that memorable occasion.   Perhaps there were scarcely any whose eloquence surpassed that of Mr. Banerjee, from Calcutta.   This Brahman convert from Bengal was able afterwards, in another building, to hold spell-bound a large audience of Madrassee Hindus, as he discoursed to them in English from the subject: "If any man will do the will of God, he shall know of the doctrine whether it be of God."   The signs of true manliness and independence are showing themselves in the Bengali Christian Conference and the Madras Native Christian Association.   In such organisations there are life, and growth, and hope for the future, and the members will readily acknowledge the important part which the Mission colleges had in forming their characters.

It may be difficult for some to realise what *a wide field for evangelistic effort* the Educational Missionary and his Christian helpers Educational work gives openings for evangelisation. have, but no one who has visited a Calcutta Missionary college and has given a Bible lesson in English to one of its large classes, or has had the senior department gathered together for an English address, will have gone away without thanking God for the grand openings for the Gospel thus afforded.

The influence of college teaching is not confined within its walls.   The Bible knowledge and the Christian influence are carried to the heathen homes.   The Missionary who preaches in the bazaars, or who visits from house to house, or who itinerates in the villages, will testify that his most willing and intelligent hearers are Mission-school pupils.   He will also acknowledge that there is a much more widely diffused knowledge of the truth than before, and that more reasonable ideas of Christ and Christianity prevail. There may be various causes of this, but English education is the first and foremost. It was the same influence which opened the Zenanas to the Christian lady teacher. Government education may have had some share; but the chief credit is undoubtedly due to the more enlightened views prevailing in Missionary colleges, and the confidence which the Educational Missionary had inspired, so that the visits of the Missionary's wife and her native helpers were *desired* in the Hindu home. The female work has wonderfully developed, but the ladies still feel that some of their most hopeful pupils are the wives or sisters of Mission scholars, and the Zenana visitor will agree that the college teacher is carrying on a work parallel to her own. This is still more the case when the Missionary visits his pupils with some regularity, entering, perhaps, the Bytakhana of the men by the front door, as the lady enters the Zenana of the women by the back door.

Confidence inspired by Missionary education.

Another point of much importance is that higher English education gives opportunities of raising the status and influence of the native Christian community, and especially of the native ministry, which vernacular education, however thorough, cannot possibly afford. Of course, these English institutions might be maintained for the native Christians alone, but the great expense would soon bring such a scheme to an end. Whereas admit Hindu, Mohammedan, and Christian alike to the Christian colleges and the funds from fees and other sources, though not perhaps meeting the salaries of the foreign Missionaries, may yet pay for all the assistant teachers and other expenses and make the enterprise all but self-supporting.

Its effect on native ministry.

But this is not all. If the converts and sons of converts are trained entirely apart from the rest of the community they are made more than ever a caste by themselves, and the Missionary, too, is cut off from the sympathies of the people, and especially from that ever-increasing class, the English-speaking portion of the native community. Educate all the castes together, Christian and non-Christian alike, and it will be found that there is no place which has a more levelling influence than the college. Within its walls young men find that birth and rank and caste are of no avail, and that all depends on diligence, perseverance, and character.

Its levelling influence.

It must not be forgotten that the marvellous spread of the English language in India is a phenomenon of the times, and is entirely altering the conditions of Missionary work. In the providence of God it may be a powerful means for the extension and consolidation of Christ's kingdom in the land. For it offers a bond of union and common action of which every denomination may avail itself. India for many years cannot be one nation as Britain is. The races and languages are too numerous and diverse, but as English becomes more and more the *lingua franca* of the middle classes, the Bengali, Hindustani, Tamil, Mahratta, and other peoples will be welded into one great confederation.

English language a confederating power.

Another point to which reference should be made is the *important Sunday work* which these higher colleges afford. Some may suppose that a Sunday school can be gathered amongst Hindus in any part of the country. Experience is at present quite opposed to the idea. The very poorest classes, who can scarcely afford to send their children even to a primary vernacular school, may not be

Sunday work in colleges.

unwilling that their boys should pick up what they can in a Sunday class. Such schools, which are rather *ragged schools* than ordinary Sunday schools, have been opened in Calcutta and elsewhere, with undoubted advantage to the little children. But the *middle classes* are not likely to permit their children to attend what they can see is so exclusively Christian as the Sunday school. There is, however, a difference where there is a Mission high school, for the boys are attached to their teachers and to their school, and may either overcome their parents' scruples, or attend at the risk of their displeasure. A different plan is followed for the elder scholars, former pupils, and neighbours. *Printed notices of Sunday evening services in English*, with the subject of the discourse announced, are widely distributed. In this way a fair and regular attend- Sunday evening services. ance has been secured in the college hall. It is a full service, with singing to the accompaniment of the harmonium, reading of Scripture and prayer, as well as sermon or address. Occasionally when the speaker is of greater repute the audience is much larger. This is a hopeful form of work, which may yet more widely develop, and is another illustration of the many ways in which higher education may be made auxiliary to evangelistic effort.

To sum up : English education, both higher and secondary, is an important branch of Mission work. It is a means of direct conversion. It exercises a moral influence in a way which is impossible in other schools. It has been a potent factor in preparing the minds of multitudes for the reception of the Gospel. It has been the chief force which burst the bars of the Zenana and admitted the lady Missionary to the Indian home. It forms also the best introduction to the Bytakhanas of the men. It has raised the standing and widened the influence of the native Church, and especially Its results. of the native Ministry. And the college buildings themselves constitute an important centre for Sunday as well as weekday work. Looking at the subject in all its bearings, Providence seems to call aloud for the maintenance and extension of this educational work ; and if the Missionaries who carry it on be as wholly consecrated to the Master's service as those who were honoured to commence it, the results cannot but be such as will amply justify the labour and outlay bestowed.

DISCUSSION.

Rev. J. E. Padfield, B.D. (C.M.S., from Masulipatam) : When I left home this morning I had no intention whatever of speaking at this meeting, but it has been suggested that I should say something in support of what I so thoroughly believe myself. My only claim to be heard is that I have been some twenty years a Missionary of the Church Missionary Society, and that I represent that Mission where Practical experience. so much has been done in higher education,—I mean the Mission which is so well known in connection with the name of that prince of Missionaries, Robert Noble, of Masulipatam.

During my Missionary career and for several years I was engaged as the head of one of our Mission high schools. I can speak, therefore, of its difficulties, and I know something of its dangers and the needs of special grace, especially bearing in mind what Dr. Miller has said as to the great strain laid upon us with reference to examinations. I know its difficulties, I know its dangers, I know its needs of special grace to be faithful to our trust as Missionaries, and teachers and preachers of Christ. But surely that should not call for any animadversion on our work; it ought rather, brethren, to call more and more for your sympathy and for your prayers to uphold the hands of those engaged in it.

Difficulties no argument.

I want to speak of one matter of fact. In our Telugu Mission, the headquarters of which are at Masulipatam, we have had notable specimens of converts from the upper castes. The names of several leap to my lips, names well known in the Christian Churches in South India; but I must not mention names. We have had a goodly number of such men who have done much to advance the cause of Christ, *but we have scarcely had* a single convert in our whole Mission *from the upper castes who has not been a direct result of our Mission school.* Remember one thing, and I wish you to lay particular stress upon it, *that the low-castes, from whom the bulk of our Christians in South India are drawn, are not Hindus.* I have been engaged a great deal in evangelistic work, and I have been privileged by God to baptise a fair number of converts. I have also been engaged in training our Mission agents, therefore no one would be less likely to speak a word disparaging to our Christians. I know that in the eyes of God one soul is as valuable as another; but bear in mind this, that *when you have converted thousands upon thousands of the low-castes in India you may not have touched Hinduism one bit.* Granted that converts from our Mission schools are comparatively few; is it nothing, this percolating influence, this permeating of rising India with the Gospel of Christ? Is it nothing? Ask our military men whether the work of a sapper and miner is to count for nothing in actual warfare.

High-caste conversion by education only.

Low-caste conversions do not touch Hinduism.

I know we cannot write such interesting reports upon this work; it does not "tell" so well, perhaps, upon a platform; but I believe that in God's own good time—that good time that is coming, whether you or I live to see it or not—in that vast upheaving which is even now commencing in rising India, we shall see in a marvellous way the results of the work of those men who have spent their lives in faith, and labour, and patience,—the result of their work in our Christian colleges and schools. I will now conclude with one word of personal reference. I say it because it bears so directly upon the whole subject. I will speak of one individual simply because he is the embodiment, if I may say so, of higher Mission education in South India; therefore to speak of him is to speak of the opinion entertained amongst the Missionaries of such work itself. Of course, amongst the numerous Missionaries in South India, we do not all see eye to eye in everything. We are not mere machines; but I think I may unhesitatingly say that among the large body of our Missionaries in South India, of the different Societies and different Churches, there are very few who do not look with great respect upon the person to whom I refer for his work as such, and who do not look upon him with affection for his own personal qualities,—I mean my esteemed friend the Rev. Dr. Miller.

Dr. Miller and his work.

Rev. John Ireland Jones, M.A. (C.M.S., from Ceylon): Mr. Chairman, —For thirty years and more I have been a preaching Missionary. It has been my chosen work, but I went to Ceylon originally to start the institution which still flourishes there as Trinity College, Kandy, with its two hundred students. One may thank God heartily as one looks at an institution of that kind, and finds in it some answer to the question as to the place of higher education in our Missionary

Trinity College, Kandy.

work. One thanks God for it especially, because its principal can report that he has as his assistants, not merely men who bear the name of Christ, but men who, as far as he knows, in every instance have the love of Christ in their hearts.

I feel that in dealing with this great question of education, a higher education especially, one immense difficulty has been indicated in one of the Papers read this morning. As I stood here on Monday last and heard the qualifications of Missionaries discussed, my heart swelled with thankfulness and praise as I heard the unanimous opinion that we were to send forth none but God-made Missionaries, men in whose hearts the love of Christ was above all things, and who had no other object than that of making Christ known, and giving themselves for Christ. How can we, consistently with this, maintain that in our work of higher education we are at liberty to employ as our assistants men who do not even bear the name of Christ? *The character of a Missionary.*

The question was asked on this platform yesterday, "Am I to circumscribe my work because I cannot obtain a Christian teacher?" My answer was "Yes," and I answer "Yes" again. My own strong feeling, expressed without the slightest doubt, for my mind is fully made up upon it, is that where we employ non-Christian teachers we may be filling gaps and spaces, but we are going beyond that which God hath given us to do. The very same argument applies to the evangelisation of the world at present. I am told, as we were told yesterday, that such men are to be watched; that there is the greatest care to be exercised with regard to the work they do. I tell you that care cannot be exercised sufficiently, and that if you employ those men you are leaning upon a broken reed, upon which if a man leans it will go into his hand and pierce it. *Non-Christian teachers to be avoided.*

Mr. James E. Mathieson (Hon. Supt. of the Mildmay Missions): Dr. Dykes, and Christian friends,—I have never been in India, but I have read the Book, and I have some acquaintance with Christian history,— the history of the Christian religion and its victories. I am sorry to think that I may have an unsympathetic audience in the few remarks that I shall venture to offer to the meeting. There are a great many insidious forms of unbelief in the world, and I believe that there is a most insidious form of disbelief pervading many quarters of the Church regarding the wonderful power of the story of God's redeeming love presented to human hearts in whatever land —a disbelief in the mighty working of the Holy Ghost. There is a verse in the Scripture which illustrates exactly the position that I take upon this question. It is in Luke xi. 24, "When the unclean spirit is gone out, . . . the last state of that man is worse than the first." *Insidious unbelief.*

You may succeed in expelling the evil spirit of idolatry, but you replace it largely in these great educational institutes by the spirit of conceit of human knowledge followed by disbelief in God altogether, and you leave another evil spirit there—the spirit of how to get on well in this world, the spirit of covetousness which St. Paul tells us is the spirit of idolatry, a spirit which creeps into the hearts of these young men in the colleges. I do not say that there are not some who have been brought to Christ through these colleges, but it is notorious that the great majority of them remain in decided unbelief in regard to the Gospel of our Lord Jesus Christ. I do not think that this system honours God sufficiently, and a system which does not honour God, God will never honour; and He has put the stamp of His disapproval upon it in the meagre results which have followed. There is a great deal said in favour of this system because it goes to the high-caste Hindus. I say if you want large results, go to the common people, the pariahs and the outcasts; *Results of collegiate education.* *Go to low not high-castes.*

you will get them to accept the Gospel of our Lord Jesus Christ. I do not know if any of you were present on Tuesday evening, as I had the pleasure of being, at that great meeting on behalf of Medical Missions. If you were, you will endorse the sentiment with which I close, that if one-fourth of the sum which is expended upon Missions of this sort were expended upon Medical Missions you would have tenfold results.

Rev. R. Wardlaw Thompson (Secretary, L.M.S.): Mr. Chairman, and dear friends,—My good friend Mr. Mathieson's logic is admirable, and I always admire it. It now appears that we should give up all higher education, because what is bad for India must be bad for England. Let us be consistent. I speak as one who has had occasion to take a very special and practical interest in this subject, partly as Secretary of a Missionary Society, having large Missions in India and China, and partly because I have had the opportunity of visiting India and China and inquiring as to the result of this work, and I say without hesitation as the result of observation, and as the result of study of our annual reports, that I am becoming more and more convinced every year that the work which the Educational Missionary in India is doing for the future of India is far greater than its most sanguine supporters have ever imagined. I see in every part of our Indian Mission-field, as the reports come home, the indirect evidences of the results of educational work in the Mission schools. In the testimony from our Evangelistic Missionaries everywhere it appears that as they go about from place to place their best and most intelligent hearers, their most sympathetic listeners, those who help them most in reaching the people, are the young men who have been in our Mission schools and colleges.

Result of large experience.

I thank God for the three able Papers that have been read this morning, and I hope that our friends will study them. There is only one point, I think, about which the majority of the supporters of Missions in this country want to be satisfied. I think that the day is gone by with most of us for discussing whether higher education is a part of Christian work. I agree with you to the full that we ought to use every form of work that will bring Christ to the people. The only point that I want to be satisfied about is this—pardon me for saying it—that I think some of you have not kept us sufficiently well informed about this matter. We want to know that you are using education as a means of bringing Christian truth to the hearts and consciences of the young in their most sympathetic and impressionable years. If you are as Christian men and Christian teachers really trying to bring the truth of Christ home to the conscience as well as to the intellect, God be with you ; God speed your efforts ! But I am sorry that on this great question this morning all the remarks have been about India. Undoubtedly, the question presses most prominently and immediately in our Indian Mission-field, but I do want to hear something from Chinese Missionaries, about the question of education. We hear a great deal about China as an educated country. Well, after a six months' journey in India, and seeing the effect of education in the Mission schools there, I went to China and visited various Missions in the different parts of that Empire, and the first impression I received was a contrast for the worse, for the weakening of Mission work, in the absence of higher education. We hear about Chinese education, but I believe it is frightfully exaggerated. The idea is that China is an educated country all throughout. I am told by Missionaries in the North of China that 3 per cent. of the population can read. I call that a very small proportion. Chinese education, such as it is, is what ? It is the great bulwark, the great means of propping up and supporting the pride and prejudice of China in

Time for discussion past.

Education in China.

believing that it is the country of the world, and that all the rest of us are ignorant. The educated classes and the *literati* of China crammed with their old learning are our great opponents. Education in India has been the means of removing difficulty, removing old ideas and preparing the way for the Gospel. I believe that Chinese Missionaries will have to look at that part of the subject as well as the evangelisation of China—that we shall have to pay more attention to education there as well as in India, if we are to succeed rapidly in our work in that great country.

Its growing importance.

Rev. J. Shillidy (Irish Presbyterian Mission, Surat): This whole question of teaching is one of the most important that can come before the Conference. The aim of every true Missionary in all his work, whether of preaching or teaching, whether of tract distribution, Scripture translation, industrial work or any other, is to lead men to Christ; that should be the goal towards which all his labours tend, and I hold that the Missionary who does not use every means to the best advantage is not thoroughly equipped for his work, nor is he fulfilling the purpose of his life.

The Missionary's aim.

The real question at issue, as I understand it, is this, and it is a question that we are asked by people at home: "How can you Missionaries justify the expenditure of Mission money for the purposes of secular education for Hindus?" My answer to that question is twofold. First of all, Mission schools, especially of the higher grades, that is the high schools and colleges, should be virtually self-supporting. The receipts from fees and grants in aid should cover the entire cost of secular education. In the second place, the teaching of Scripture in all these schools and colleges should be as much a part of the regular work as any other subject. When Scripture teaching is thrust aside for good examination results, or when the work is done perfunctorily that some other object may be gained, I maintain that the management of the school is at fault, and the Home Society should deal with its managers. In a word, the whole of the secular education should be self-supporting, and I hold that the salary of a Christian teacher in these schools is a fair charge upon Mission funds; especially where the work is well done, and where the Missionary has daily under his charge many hundreds of the rising generation in India. You have few results to show, it is said, but the same thing might be said of other departments of Mission work in India, China, and elsewhere. Take bazaar preaching, which is one of the most general evangelistic agencies in operation. I maintain that there is very little in many parts of India to show in the way of results. I can say, from an experience of thirteen years, that there are very few high-caste men who are brought out by bazaar preaching. Again, there are very few results from Bible distribution, and the same thing might be said of other departments just as well as of school work. Let me say, in conclusion, that a distinction should be drawn between vernacular and high schools. The Society with which I am connected, has done a great work by its vernacular schools; and very many of our Christians in Gujerat have been led through these schools to embrace Christianity. Our high schools have not done so much.

Let secular education be self-supporting.

Results of bazaar preaching and Bible distribution.

Mr. Robert Paton (Christian Colportage Association): I would not have thrust myself into the debate at this time but I feel very deeply upon the subject, having had experience of it for nearly forty years, and having visited the seminary of our dear friend in Madras, and also that of Dr. Wilson and others in Bombay, during my Indian career.

I have formed a strong opinion on this subject, but it is not my opinion I wish to put before the Conference; it is something infinitely higher than my opinion, it is Apostolic practice.

From long observation, having come in contact with many young men who have come out of these institutions, having had from ten thousand to fifteen thousand natives under my own guidance at one time in connection with railway works in India, I hold that the outcome of these institutions, considering the vast sums of Missionary money spent upon them, is not adequate ; the Christian influence that comes from them is of a very meagre description and not at all proportionate to the amount of money spent. I rejoice in the education of the Hindu, but that is not the question. The point is: Do we collect money in this country and send men out to India to teach that the angles at the base of an isosceles triangle are equal to one another ? Never. I have seen English Missionaries in the Mission school in Madras, giving lessons day after day in arithmetic, in mathematics, and all the sciences. Now this, to my mind, deprives the Gospel of its urgency ;—it is an urgent thing, this Gospel of the Lord Jesus Christ. I come to the blessed Word of God, and I ask whether any Missionary in this gathering ever had a more interesting audience than the Apostle Paul when he went to Rome. And what was Paul's message to those men at Rome ? Let me read it : "I am a debtor both to the Greeks and to the barbarians, both to the wise and to the unwise. So as much as in me is I am ready to preach the Gospel to you that are at Rome also. For I am not ashamed of the Gospel of Christ, for it is the power of God unto salvation to every one that believeth, to the Jew first and also to the Greek. For therein is the righteousness of God revealed." It is the righteousness of God that we have to bring to bear upon the consciences of these Hindus, and not the wisdom of man.

Educational results not adequate to cost.

St. Paul's method.

I have come in contact with any number of Hindus who are exactly in this position ; they know the plan of salvation as well as Dr. Miller and myself, but they hold down the truth in unrighteousness. It has never come before them as an urgent call from God to repent and believe the Gospel. A previous speaker said : "We have no conversions outside the Mission schools, and the Christians that are brought out of these schools are very few." Of course they are, and they will be few until you go back to God's plan,—you will never get adequate results in any other way. You must preach the Gospel according to the Word of God, and then you will see the power of the Gospel.

Reason of small results.

Rev. G. E. Post, M.D. (Syrian Protestant College, Beyrout): I am very happy to tell you that one of the leading spirits in the Young Men's Christian Association of the Syrian Protestant College is a converted Druse, and his brother is also a converted Druse and a leading spirit in the Association ; and another converted Druse is one of the leading teachers in the College, and his brother was an efficient Medical Missionary of the Church Missionary Society in Jaffa for many years. Here are four Druses who have been converted by the Spirit of Almighty God through and in the Syrian Protestant College. What do you want better than that ?

Four converted Druses.

When the storm-tossed mariner is feeling his way along the dangerous harbourless coast of Palestine, and when he approaches the roadstead of Beyrout, he eagerly looks over the sandhills that he may see a tall tower rising there. That tower is laid down upon his chart as the landmark for the entrance to the harbour of Beyrout. It is the tower of the Syrian Protestant College. This college was established in 1865 by a vote of the Board of Missions occupying that country. It included in its board of managers twenty-four members, representatives of all the Missionary Societies in the East, the Church Missionary Society, the Presbyterian Society, the Congregational, the United Presbyterian, and it has included in its faculty and its corps of instructors Methodists and Baptists. We are therefore a Christian and a Missionary college, and we are established in the same spot and for the same pur-

The Syrian Protestant College.

pose as that of every other branch of the Missionary work. I will say further that we draw our students from every portion of the Mission-field, and those who select the students are the Missionaries themselves ; they are picked out as the best, the most hopeful elements of all those eastern communities, and with the express desire of training them, if already converted, to be evangelists throughout the East, and, if not already converted, to bring the concentrated influence of that Christian institution upon them to convert them to Christ. We have no other object ; that is the great purpose for which the insti- *Its one purpose, but varied operations.* tution was established, and to that purpose we dedicate our lives. I may also say that this institution is Evangelical to the very core. We teach the Bible,—it is a text book in the schools, and we teach every branch of Christian labour. We teach the students to become Sunday school teachers and evangelists in the neighbourhood : we teach them to be Medical Missionaries, and we aim to instruct their minds and to fire their hearts for the great work of spreading the Gospel throughout those eastern lands. The institution has trained, throughout its whole curriculum or a part of it, over eight hundred young men, and those young men are scattered everywhere throughout the Arabic, the Greek, and the Turkish-speaking world. We have some on the western coast of Africa, some in Senegambia, some in Morocco, some in Egypt along the valley of the Nile ; and at the time of the Relief Expedition to Gordon, twenty-three students of the Syrian Protestant College accompanied your forces in various capacities to aid in that work. We have them again all through Palestine in the service of the Church Missionary Society ; we have them all *Its students spread everywhere.* through Syria, in Constantinople, in Smyrna, in Cyprus, in Baghdad, and in the distant borders of Asia. I ask, Would you blot out this lighthouse, would you take down that landmark from the East ? Rather tear down the classic halls of Oxford and Cambridge and leave this standing to enlighten the Mohammedan world and bring it to the Cross.

One other remark and I have done. Four years ago a spiritual darkness and death had spread over the field of Syrian Missions and adjacent Missions, and we began to long and pray for the advent of the Holy Spirit. We had a prayer-meeting of the students of the college ; it was quite voluntary, and there were over eighty students present. It happened to be my good fortune to preside over that meeting. *A revival meeting.* I represented the state of things in the college and out of it, and then I asked the students to spend a moment in silent prayer. They bowed their heads, and you could have heard a pin drop anywhere in the room. After they had raised their heads I said, "Now, every one of you who is resolved to devote his life to the cause of Christ and His country rise." Sixty of those students rose by a common impulse; and the revival of religion that commenced in that prayer-meeting in the Syrian Protestant College spread all through the country, and there were gathered in that single year more converts to the Church of Christ than had been gathered in the six previous years' work of the Syrian Mission.

Rev. Silvester Whitehead (Wesleyan Missionary Society, from Canton): I am happy to have the privilege of saying one word upon this subject. Mr. Thompson, who, if I mistake not, represents the London Missionary Society, drew a contrast between what he observed *The Anglo-Chinese College.* in China and what he saw in India, and he said that higher education did not appear to be so prominent in China as it was in India. Now the fact is that Missionary work in China began with higher education. The Anglo-Chinese College was started and sustained by the ablest Missionaries of the London Missionary. Society. It is not in existence now, and Dr. Legge himself confesses that he considered it to a very large degree, a failure. Many of the men, who were therein trained, gained a knowledge of the English language and other subjects very valuable to them; they turned that knowledge to account, not by any service to the Mission at all, but in order to enrich themselves through commerce and the custom-house; and then they used their riches as a means of indulgence in all kinds of vice. That, of course, was not uniformly the case, but it was the case to a very large degree, and it was A question of one reason why the Anglo-Chinese College was given up. The proportion. question before us, I think, with regard to China is not, Are we to give up any arm of our Missionary enterprise? I think not. Higher education has its place no doubt, but the question for India and China to consider is this,—What is the due proportion between higher education in the colleges and Missionary work, preaching and teaching among the people? It must be limited to that.

Rev. William Gray (Secretary, C.M.S.): I should not rise at this advanced hour except just to speak on two points, which seem to me of very Government great consequence indeed, and on which I have not heard a opinion of its word said throughout the meeting. I think you ought not to own system. part without having a word about them. With reference to the subject of education, do you all remember that the Government of India has very recently stated its own opinion in very solemn words that its own system of mere secular education is breaking down discipline altogether, and that it is really deteriorating? Now we should all be exceedingly thankful if the Government of India, having made this announcement, would try and mend its ways in that respect, and give greater recognition to the Word of God in connection with its own schools. We shall even be thankful for a smaller mercy than that, if the Government would come forward and say, "We shall deal more liberally than we have ever done before in the matter of grants in aid to Mission schools, which will not break down discipline."

But there does not seem the least chance of Government doing anything of the kind, and I maintain in view of that, that it ought to be our duty to press forward this higher education more than we have ever done. That is certainly my own view of the case, and it is, I think, the view of the Society which I have the honour to represent.

Then there is another point that has not been touched upon, although it is a very important one, and is specially noted on the subject paper. I refer to the question of co-operation. I am thankful to state that the Church Mis-Co-operation in sionary Society is giving £300 a year to our dear friend Dr. Miller's higher college at Madras. Now why are we doing that? It is because we education. believe that the Gospel is faithfully preached in Dr. Miller's college. I assure you that if we found out that the Gospel was not being preached there not one farthing of our money would go to that college. Now, is there any prospect whatever of that principle of co-operation being more fully carried out? It would save us a great deal of money no doubt; it would do a far greater thing than that—it would show the people of India that Christians at home, who call themselves by different names, are able to work together for the cause of Christ. That would be a grand result to be attained, and I hope that we shall attain it more and more. How is it to be worked out? I believe if the thing is done as Dr. Miller has done it, we shall have a great deal more co-operation. As soon as you get an institution like his to be thoroughly successful, and as soon as you find a principal possessed of the same catholicity of spirit, and showing the same tact and power in managing the institution, so soon as you have his success attained, you may depend upon it you will find co-operation not so hard a matter. I believe most fully that we ought to put forward this matter of higher education more than we have ever done.

The Chairman pronounced the Benediction.

[*It was with extreme regret that we were unable to find a place for the following Paper in the programme. Its intrinsic value and the high authority of the author require that we give it in the appendix of the proceedings, of which it would have formed a part had time allowed.*—ED.]

APPENDIX.

PAPER.

BY THE REV. W. R. BLACKETT (late of C.M.S. Divinity School, Calcutta).

Conclusions arrived at from experience as a Member of the Viceregal Commission on Education in India.

I shall not attempt to treat this broad subject in a general way. It will be enough if I endeavour to state here the conclusions I arrived at from what I saw and heard as a member of the Viceregal Commission on Education in India in 1882.

In the first place it is evident that the education of the country can never be done by Missionary Societies. Were they all to devote at once all their funds and all their staffs to educational work alone they could not supply the education that is needed and demanded by the population. The work is far too vast to be accomplished by anything less than the resources of a nation, and of a rich one, which the Indian is not. To look *The Church* only at primary education,—in 1882 the children at school in *cannot educate the masses.* Bengal were reckoned at about a million. The number in schools where they were in any degree subject to Christian influences was about thirteen thousand. Now there are said to be two millions of children under instruction in the same province, and those in Christian schools are probably not more than they were six years ago. It is clear then that nothing which we can do can make Indian education generally Christian. I take it for granted that any national or governmental system of education in India must be founded on the principle of non-interference with religion. Were it possible it would, to my mind, be utterly undesirable that Christianity should be inculcated in any way by the authority of the Government. For one thing, not even the omnipotent " Sircar " could find Christian men to do all the teaching, and I have no faith in Christian truth taught by unchristian men.

Where then can Christian teaching come in, in relation to Indian education ? It might be useful to supplement it. Bible classes, or inquirers' classes, held near colleges and schools, have sometimes been tried with a view to draw towards Christianity such students as had any desire for something more elevating than mathematics and English literature. But the pressure of advanced education,—in other words the cramming for *Christian* examinations,—is so severe than even well-disposed youths have *alongside* little thought or time for what their spirits need. The earnest *secular teaching.* Missionary is always yearning to get these ingenuous youths more under his own control, that they may have more time for Bible study, and that Christian influences may surround them even amid their secular work. But when he has got them he finds his task not so easy as he hoped. He has to coach them up for examinations. If they find they have not a good chance of passing they will not stay with him. Their hearts are not with him in their Bible lessons—for these things will not tell in their examinations. His assistants are inefficient, at least in giving religious instruction. Sometimes they are Hindus, sometimes besides that atheists at heart,—and in their actual teaching, too, warning students after class against being so foolish to believe what they have been learning in the class. I have heard of such cases, and any experienced educationist will tell you that even native Christian teachers very seldom have sufficient Missionary zeal to make their Christian lessons at all efficient. Nay, the Missionary is liable to become in no small degree secularised himself. It is very hard to resist the despiritualising influence of educational drudgery and the rivalry and anxiety of getting up subjects for examination. The grace of God can overcome this or any other evil influence, but the average Christian shows and feels and laments the effect of it on his own spiritual state. To make the educational work really a Missionary agency conversion and religious instruction and impression must be made the first and foremost aim at all times. It is no easy task to keep it in any degree steadily in view. It can be done, and is done. But it cannot be strictly maintained that every Missionary educationist is first a Missionary and then an educationist.

If we look at the direct results of such work we might be inclined to regard it at first sight as disappointing. Not a great many students pass from our colleges into the ranks of the Christian Church. Some do, and those who do are valuable as testimonies to the result of the Missionary work that is done amid the distractions of modern education. More, perhaps, reveal in Direct and after life the seed that has been sown in their minds in school or indirect results. college, but has remained dormant it may be for many years. Often such cases are easily traceable to the impression or instruction received in the course of education at a Missionary institution.

The *soi-disant* educated natives are becoming blatant in their self-assertion. Doubtless they over-estimate at present both their powers and their importance, as witness the report of their Conference held last year at Madras. And sometimes they make themselves ridiculous. Yet they have that knowledge which in these days is power, and they have among their country-The educated, men the exclusive possession of it. Spite of all the resistance of the future rulers. caste and race prejudices and religious divisions, the possessors of English learning must sooner or later become, if not themselves the governing class, at all events, the class through whom their country must be governed.

A professor in Bengal asked his class what was the word in their language for *conscience*. After some hesitation an honest youth stood up and said, "Sir, when we have not got the thing how should we have a name for Missionary it?" And secular education has no tendency to awaken conscience teaching or inculcate principles of morality. The elder generation has cultivates discerned this. Loud and earnest were the appeals addressed by conscience. native gentlemen to the Education Commission for the introduction into all grades of schools of some sort of moral teaching.

Missionary institutions do in some degree supply the want. In some cases Hindu parents prefer these to the Government schools for this very reason. Yet we cannot in our schools do all that is required. But we can leaven the class that is being thus raised up. It is of the utmost importance that the educated class should comprise among its members an appreciable proportion of men, not only favourably disposed towards Christianity, but moreover actuated by its principles. To hand over the destinies of India, as they are being handed over in some degree, and must be handed over in an ever-increasing degree, to a class of men whose education leaves them thoroughly unprincipled, would be a poor and miserable result of our English Rāj. But if some among them are men of Christian principles then the people at large will find out sooner or later who can be trusted and who can not. The only hope for the educated class itself is that it should be permeated with an infusion of the high morality which is only likely to arise from a thorough and loyal acceptance of Christianity. We must keep up our Christian schools and colleges in order that there may be Christians among the rising class of our great dependency.

And again, the prestige of Christianity needs to be kept up. It has a prestige as a religion of culture and learning. The present popularity of English education springs largely, and consciously too, from the energy and enthusiasm of Dr. Duff. Missionary Societies, which find themselves *The prestige of Christianity.* now entirely unable to keep up the supply, were the original creators of the demand. And this is not unimportant in a country like India, where each of the prevailing religions has a culture and a learning of its own. We *have to* preach the Gospel to the poor, and endeavour to compel the outcast and downtrodden to come in to the feast. We may easily give the impression that our religion is fit only for such. The wealthy and the learned are ready enough in any case to despise the preaching of the Cross. It is by all means advisable to keep up, and to maintain at a high standard of efficiency, the colleges we possess, in order that Christianity may continue to be associated in the minds of the people with real culture and that learning which always commands respect.

Once more, our Christians want education. A very fair proportion of Christian students, sons of Christian parents, are to be found on the college books. God forbid that they should have to go to colleges where the influence is wholly secular, if not anti-Christian. They need special assistance, in order that the clever boys of our Churches may take their proper place, not only in the Church, but in the country, in the coming generation. It would be well worth while to keep up our Christian colleges, if it were only for the benefit of Christian people. At the same time, a good nucleus of Christian students is likely to have a beneficial effect upon the non-Christian students in the same institutions. It is impossible to keep our Christians wholly apart, although there are undeniable risks to faith and morals in the contact with heathens. But even for the work's sake such contact must be permitted, for faith and hope are propagated by contagion.

It must be noted, however, that all these aims, for which Missionary education should be kept up, bear not directly on the Missionary aim. They are pastoral, political, patriotic. Nor do they bear much upon primary education. Elementary schools appear to me to have passed out of the Missionary field, and entered into the pastoral. They must be kept up where there are Christians, as they are in an English parish, for the education of the Christians. The effect on the general education of the country of such schools as we can support is so infinitesimal, that it by no means justifies us in turning any of our limited Missionary funds into such a channel.

In female education, Missionary Societies still have the prerogative, and should strive to retain it, not by preventing, were that possible, other parties from doing anything in this line, but by extending their own operations, and making them as effective, as Christian, and as *Female education.* Missionary as possible. Native gentlemen often feel that great as is the danger of demoralising their sons by a purely secular education, with their daughters it would be greater still.

But whatever we do in Missionary education, let us do it well. Let it be efficient as educational work, and real as Missionary effort. To reach and maintain the equilibrium between these two is a constantly recurring difficulty. It is not to be evaded by regarding this work as *What you do, do well.* secondary, giving it inferior agents, and starving it as concerns domicile and apparatus. Our Missionary colleges and high schools ought to be at once good and cheap, and thoroughly spiritual in aim and character. Concentrate your efforts on a few such institutions, and do not be tempted to start new ones, which must both be weak themselves and weaken others, by any feeling of rivalry or competition.

But surely we have allowed ourselves too much time and care in the indirect work of Missions, in proportion to that bestowed upon the direct. "Preach the Gospel" is the foremost command. Do, teach, write, all that may tend to secure a favourable hearing for the Gospel, but do not wait for that to pour in the Gospel right and left, and straight in front, and everywhere. Let the heathen be exposed to a *feu d'enfer* of Gospel preaching,—or rather to a *feu de ciel*,—let us insinuate it if we can, but bring it to bear point blank as well at every opportunity. Let us believe that the Gospel, not education, is the power of God unto salvation, and let us keep in their proper places all those auxiliaries to the Gospel which are really in accordance with its principles and aim.

Evangelistic aims always foremost.

MEETINGS OF MEMBERS IN SECTION.

THE MISSIONARY IN RELATION TO LITERATURE.

(1) GENERAL.

(*a*) The place and importance of the Mission Press. Under what conditions should it be maintained ? Should it be confined to purely Missionary literature, or should it be used for and supported by general printing ?

(*b*) Should distribution of Christian literature be gratuitous or paid for ?

(*c*) The extent to which the Missionary may legitimately devote himself to the preparation of pure literature for the people generally—by newspapers, books of science, history, etc.

(*d*) How far may Missionaries of different Societies co-operate in the preparation of Christian literature ?

(*e*) The Missionary in relation to Science.

(*Friday morning, June 15th, in the Annexe.*)

Dean Vahl (of Denmark) in the chair.
Acting Secretary, **Rev. J. Sharp, M.A.**

Mr. Bevan Braithwaite offered prayer.

The Chairman: The theme upon which we shall dwell to-day is the Missionary in relation to literature, and the Missionary in relation to science. We find men who oftentimes disregard the higher work of the Missionaries, while they are quite ready to give them due credit for what they have done in the interests of literature and of science. Who is acknowledged to have been the greatest and the most noble of all the explorers of foreign countries in our days ? I believe it was he who died far away from his relations, whose corpse was borne to the coast by his native attendants, and was brought to his native country, and now is buried in Westminster Abbey among the most noble men of this country. He was a Missionary. The noble work of the Missionaries with regard to literature has also been acknowledged, and when we peruse the books of Dr. Robert Cust we can see how largely he has made use of all that the Missionaries have seen and written. The linguistic abilities of the Missionaries are very great.

In the spring of this year a Society was started in Scandinavia, having committees in all the three kingdoms of Scandinavia, with the special purpose of forwarding a native literature in the languages of the Meïh people in Assam, and of the Santhals, and this committee comprises the best Oriental linguists and scientific men, as well as the best men of our different Churches. What science owes to Missionaries we heard the day before yesterday, when Sir Monier-Williams, the distinguished Orientalist, said how much he owed to one of the late Missionaries for his knowledge about the old religions of India. In America a very thick volume has been published, stating what the Missionaries have done for science, literature, and commerce.

A Scandinavian Missionary Literature Society.

But that is not the only topic which we have to consider to-day. We have also to deal with the place and importance of the Mission Press. The Press is a very great power for good or for evil in our days, as all must confess. It has been called the eighth great power, and it is a very great power. It is necessary to make use of this power in the native countries where the Missions have been or are already established. There is a difference between countries which have had no literature at all and countries where literature has been found before our country had any literature of its own. There are many respects in which this question can be considered, but I shall not dwell upon them. We have able men who are to read Papers and speak, who have had much more experience than I have. I thank you for your forbearance in listening to me while speaking in what is to myself a foreign language.

Influence of the Mission Press.

PAPER.

1. By THE REV. H. U. WEITBRECHT, Ph.D. (C.M.S., Batala, Punjab, Editorial Secretary of the Punjab Bible and Religious Book Societies). Read by the Rev. Dr. Dyson.

The Missionary in relation to Literature.

It is, happily, needless to prove to persons conversant with Missionary work that the formation of a Christian literature is an essential part of Missionary work in any given nation. The question which practically concerns us now is the relative importance of literary as compared with other aspects of Missionary work, and the best means and methods for promoting it.

In treating this subject I can speak personally of India only. The Urdu language is, from a literary point of view, the most widely extended tongue in India; that is to say, it probably reaches the largest number of readers, and it is also the best furnished with general and Christian literature. Moreover India offers a wider field of observation and deduction than any

Experience of India.

other Mission-field, ranging from the most finished products of Western science and education in the Presidency cities and provincial capitals, to the merest savages in their hilly retreats. Hence the observations here recorded and the deductions attempted may, perhaps, have an application wider than the area from which they proceed.

What then are the special difficulties and special opportunities which the experience of the present juncture emphasises in respect of the literary work of Missions?

To mention the chief difficulty, first, I would say that excluding strictly spiritual opponents, it is the same which meets us throughout our modern Missions, the wide difference of race and civilisation between the evangelist and the evangelised. And this it is which renders it so difficult to adapt our literary work both in *Difficulties in adapting.* form and matter to those for whom it is intended, so that it may appeal to their faculties and influence them permanently. The area influenced by Western ideas is continually and rapidly enlarging, without a corresponding increase of power on the part of the Missionary body to cover it with Christian literature. To take only one instance. The early leaders of higher English education in India were Missionaries like Duff and Wilson; into the fruits of whose labours we have entered and are still entering. But since their day this higher education has fallen—not through *The need of literature.* a relaxation of effort on the part of Missionaries, but through the increased activity of the State—for the most part into the hands of Government institutions, while primary education has received an enormous impulse. Most of the youths who receive the higher education engage either in Government service or in the legal profession; and both during and after their training they are schooled in a system of religious neutrality often amounting to indifference. Thus, in addition to the old world of India, which offered its peculiar difficulties, Christian literature now has to reach a new generation. There are still the ignorant and illiterate masses; still a community educated on the old indigenous lines, with more or less of Hindu or Mohammedan classical knowledge. But there is also a community educated by Western methods, many through English, more through the vernacular tongues, some quite or nearly up to the standard of English scholars; others occupying every intermediate position between this and the purely vernacular reader, while even his language is receiving a strong dash of English words, uncouth as they look in their Indian dress. And yet, near as he may come to Western notions, the Indian is still an Indian in mind and disposition, and as such he must be approached. The many-sided sympathy in tone, the wide variety in form, needed to meet all these classes, must be found in Missionary literature, if it is not to fall behind in its great vocation.

With the difficulty of adequately performing a task of such increasing complexity, a corresponding opportunity is closely bound up. The *spread of knowledge* resulting from the rapid advance of education is opening an ever-widening door to Missionary literature. A supply of readers is being prepared much faster than a supply of good reading. Western knowledge and acquaintance with English is eagerly sought for, so that the Missionary—pressed as he is by his own proper work—finds himself seriously confronted by the question of pure literature for the people. At no previous period has the increase of the reading community in India been so rapid, and the ratio of progress promises to increase. Before the Education Commission in 1882, the number of scholars was estimated at 2,000,000 ; it is now computed at 3,500,000, the increase being chiefly in the primary department. Not all of these become regular readers, but the majority will require some mental food.

The third feature of the Mission-field which bears upon literary work just now is the *growth of the Christian community*. The rates of increase in the three decades preceding 1882, were as follows :—

1851-61	51 per cent.
1861-71	61 „ „
1871-81	86 „ „

At the end of 1881 there were 417,372 Protestant native Christians in India. For this community, as it increases in numbers and grows in intelligence, a Christian literature is more needed every year; and it is only in a well taught Christian Church that we have a reasonable hope of a permanence and self-propagation. To set forth the practical conclusions which flow from these facts it may be useful to borrow the terms of political economy, and consider Missionary literature in respect of its production, its distribution, and its consumption. And as its consumption is the practical end that we wish to attain, it may be taken first.

1. *The Consumption of Mission Literature.*[*]

Consumption depends upon demand. How enormously the demand for literature generally is being increased, by the educational work now going on, I have already pointed out. Between 1882 and 1885 the pupils in Government and aided schools in India increased by some eight hundred thousand.[†] Of the three-and-a-half millions now under instruction, some two hundred thousand are in Mission schools. For these readers literature of a sort is forthcoming. I have not the means of obtaining full statistics, but I may refer to the figures given by Dr.

---

[*] I use this term in preference to "Missionary Literature," as the latter might be understood to mean Missionary magazines, biographies, and the like.

[†] This increase may include a considerable number of schools already existing, which came under Governmental inspection and cognisance during the period named, but even this connotes an important increase in the effectiveness of the education given.

Murdoch in his Paper, showing that 8,963 publications were registered during 1886 in British India. Of these, the larger proportion, 1,485, were in Urdu; and, judging by the Punjab publications of a few years previous, we may roughly estimate that the percentage of subjects was as follows:—

Religion	25
Poetry, fiction, and drama	37
Education	25
Other subjects	13
	100

Of the first class a certain number, perhaps a sixth, are Christian works. The second class of books aud pamphlets are largely demoralising; while the third again include a sprinkling of Christian books, published by the Christian Vernacular Education Society. With the exception of these school books, most of the Christian works have a limited circulation, especially those of any size. The other languages of North India are relatively less well supplied with Christian books than Urdu.

From these facts we gather that the vernacular books which are read for purposes other than studious or professional are, to a great extent, morally pernicious. And this applies also, in great measure, to the English literature favoured by young India, so far as it is secular. Secularism and free love go hand-in-hand *Pernicious literature.* to furnish the mental food of many English-reading natives; nor is this a result to be wondered at, when we consider the secular character of education in Government schools. The Government of India, in its memorandum of the 31st December, 1887, on moral education, has shown its sense of this dangerous tendency, and its desire to check it, by the introduction into schools and colleges of moral text-books, and by other means. It is obvious that such efforts need to be accompanied by the provision of a pure literature, which will, in due course, be more largely demanded by a purer generation, and which tends to produce the frame of mind that perpetuates such a demand. To such efforts the Literary Missionary (when he has been evolved) will give all the help that he can spare from his direct Christian work.

The demand for literature, further, will depend not only upon the number of people who possess the ability to read, but also upon their will to use it, *i.e.*, on the reading habits they have formed. That reading habits are on the increase cannot be doubted; *Reading on the increase.* but, so far as my observation and the testimony I have been able to gather go, such habits are weak, considering the number of possible readers. The only literature excepted from this neglect is newspapers; these are overlooked by very few who pretend to education.

In this matter of reading the Missionary is able to influence substantially two classes of the community, the native Christians and pupils in Mission schools, and he should see to it that he

Christian literature in the Missions. does his best to promote reading habits and a taste for good literature among them. Every school and every congregation should have its lending library, to be kept replenished with the most attractive books to be had, and new books or tracts or new editions which come out, should be brought to the notice of the Christian community or the pupils of the school, by the colporteur and others. To do this systematically will prove no small stimulus to the consumption of our literature; and the student, once inoculated with a taste for it, will desire its further gratification. It is, however, most important for us to consider that, owing to the great extension of Government education, and the pressure on Mission schools of examinations and education codes squeezing down religious instruction to a minimum, the provision of Christian literature for the army of readers is rapidly over-shadowing the question of conveying a limited amount of Christian instruction to the comparatively few who attend Mission schools.

This leads us to two conclusions. First, *the importance of news-papers.* Each language area should have a good Christian vernacular

Importance of newspapers. newspaper, vigorously supported and well pushed; and each great centre, at least each Presidency town, an evan-gelistic organ, doing also the work of a literary paper—similar to *Progress,* so excellently conducted at Madras.

The second point is *the increasing importance of English as an element in Missionary literature.* Here the popular demand is really increasing. Mr. H. E. Perkins (C.M.S., Amritsar, late Commissioner of Rawal Pindi) writes: "Natives have in many places, *e.g.,* in Rawal Pindi, instituted English lending libraries among themselves." Many an English book of distinctly religious tendency will be acceptable for the sake of its literary merit or interest, where a vernacular book of similar tone would be passed by. The English sales of our religious book depositories, therefore, have a direct Missionary value, if rightly used.

2. *The Distribution of Mission Literature.*

Distribution must doubtless depend upon demand on the one side and production on the other, but the method by which it is carried on will do much to influence both. The question is raised in the

Distribution by sale or gift. Conference programme, as to whether distribution should be gratuitous or by purchase. If we are aiming to place our literary work on a solid and permanent basis, this can only be on the basis of a real popular demand for such literature as we supply. The demand which we can reasonably expect will be, first, on the part of the Christian community for its own edification and for evangel-ising purposes; and, second, on the part of outsiders who desire from motives of curiosity or spiritual unrest to know the Christian religion; or who are in part so favourably disposed towards Christianity that they welcome books with a certain amount of Christian teaching. Hence a rule has been adopted, since the Allahabad Missionary Conference of 1872, by the Indian Tract Societies, that all supplies of books must be paid for by the persons who order them, whether Missionaries or others. This throws the question of free distribution on the purchasers, and places a definite limit to it, inasmuch as Mission funds will seldom permit of free distribution of Christian books to any large extent. But it is obvious that the tendency of distribution should be from free gifts towards purchase ; and to say that a man, notably an Indian, will value and read what he purchases more than what he receives gratis, is to utter a truism.

What we need in the distribution of our Mission literature is that commercial principles should be more fully applied to it. I will take only two points. The first is attention to details. For *Commercial principles.* instance, in regard to the get-up of books. Such matters as the best arrangement of the title-page, proper tables of contents, the best style of binding, having regard to the nature and use of the book, advertising other publications on the fly leaves, the various minutiæ of typography, and a hundred other things demand attention. Again, in the sale room, showing up the stock without exposing it to damage from glare, weeding out old stock, advertising new arrivals, sending out specimens by colporteurs, looking out for new openings ; all this, and much more, has to be considered with care and vigilance. More especially, a *constant improvement* must be kept up, otherwise distribution infallibly suffers. In these respects, we must confess our Indian Publishing Societies have much leeway to make up. The second point simply follows on the first. I mean the need of *efficient supervision.* How can vigilance *Adequate supervision.* be without a *vigilans*, watchfulness without a watcher? And how can one watch the distribution of literature when he has his own proper work to look after ? Yet this is, with scarcely an exception, the position of every Missionary and layman in India, upon whom the guidance of literary work devolves. And, if we consider that the circulation of Mission literature has hitherto been carried on thus as a by-work, we can only be thankful to God for the extension which He has permitted it to attain. Moreover, if we regard the only instance that I am acquainted with, of a European Missionary entirely devoted to literary work,—I refer to my honoured friend, Dr. John Murdoch, of Madras,—we cannot but keenly feel how much more might be done were more men of the right kind assigned to subdivide the labour of this immense task. The Church of Christ must enlarge her ideas of Missionary work. We need lay- *Must enlarge our ideas.* men acquainted with the book trade, yet full of a desire to win souls, who will devote themselves, with no thought of worldly gain, on the same footing as other Missionaries, to the work of pushing the sale of Mission literature in Calcutta, Madras, Bombay, Allahabad, and Lahore, without neglecting the many opportunities for direct evangelisation that will come in their way. Will Christian England give us such?

Before passing on to the last part of my subject, I will touch on two more points connected with the distribution of literature. The

Two points. first is the desirableness of having in every town Mission something of the nature of an institute to supplement the ordinary bookshop or colportage; a place in which there is a lending library, books for sale, a paper or two to read, and a catechist, or other preacher in attendance; the same place serving also for preaching and lectures.

The other point is that, as already urged, pupils in schools and colleges should be encouraged to buy books and tracts not only vernacular, but English; and that these should be more widely used in prize distributions.

3. *The Production of Mission Literature.*

Production is of two kinds, material and mental. Under the first head comes the question of the *Mission Press*, mentioned in the programme; under the second that of *Authorship*.

The Mission Press.—The value of the Mission Press in a country such as India rests, of course, on grounds different from those which necessitate such an institution, say, in Madagascar. There is now an eager competition for printing work in the way of regular trade. Still the Mission Press has its value, if. efficiently supervised, inasmuch as it frees the Publishing Society from the disadvantages of competition, and affords a guarantee for correctness

The Mission of proof-reading and goodness of work. The Press
Press. should print Missionary work at a rate which will just cover expenses (not including the Superintendent's salary), and outside work should only be done as a resource when Mission work is not at hand, at ordinary market rates. Above all, the Superintendent of the Press should be a Missionary layman, acquainted with printing work, and assigned to that as his special duty.

Last, not least, comes the matter of *Authorship*. The Christian vernacular books that we have, do all credit to those who produced them; but the mass of them are only first attempts, and stand in great need of revision and improvement, to render them fitted for our present needs, and the rise in the standard of education. Useless will be the pushing of sales, vain all improvement in the get-up of books, only saddening the demand for Christian reading, unless we

Authorship. can improve in the matter of authorship, both by engaging the services of fresh talent and experience, and by developing the gifts of those who already work. Who, then, is to do this? Who is to watch the needs of his province, to inquire after literary workers, native and European; to suggest to them the part that each shall take, to unify and press forward the production of Christian books in each of the great languages of India? *We must have* LITERARY MISSIONARIES, one at least for each language area.

[Here follows an extract from what the Author had formerly written in the "Descriptive Catalogue and Review of Urdu Christian Literature." London : Religious Tract Society.—ED.]

I am not insensible of two qualifications to this plea for the appointment of Literary Missionaries. One is suggested by the Rev. R. Clark, of Amritsar, who has worked in this cause as few have, that well-known authors in England might do not a little to help us by writing short papers or articles with special reference to the religious doubts and difficulties of Indians. *Missionaries devoted to Literature.* Still it is only a small part of the needed work which can thus be done. The other consideration is of more weight. It is that we foreigners are but working to prepare the way for the natives of India itself, and that our chief care should be to train them for the work of providing a Christian literature for their own land. Most true this is. We Foreign Missionaries desire nothing more ardently than to be able to pass on the torch to Indians. But now there is the conflict, and in the midst of it the work to be set forward, as the walls of Jerusalem were built by Nehemiah and his companions, for at least a temporary shelter ; and in this the more highly-endowed brother who has come from without must, as yet, lead the denizens of the land. Moreover, it is just because the work of training or eliciting literary ability in the Indian Church, is so vastly important, that special men are needed to do it. When, in the name of Christ, will they be given?

The question is raised in our programme as to how far the Missionary may devote himself generally to the work of pure literature? I reply : Give the Missionary, whom God has so called, leisure, first of all, to devote himself to the work of Christian literature, and when he has surveyed and assayed this field in earnest, we will then begin to discuss what time he can spare for the remoter work.

The appointment of Literary Missionaries is part of a larger question : that of *Missionary reserves.* The Literary Missionary, as has already been shown, cannot be a neophyte. Experience in general Missionary work is a necessary pre-requisite for his calling. But how can Missionaries of experience be set free for this work under the present system of distributing our forces? No *Missionary reserves.* sooner, in the majority of cases, does a Mission appear strongly manned, than some of the staff are drafted off "to enter a fresh door." The first Mission is reduced to the strength barely necessary for the maintenance of the work ; a vacancy occurs through death or sickness ; and once more the mournful cry goes forth : "Under-manned." Is any earthly warfare carried on as we prosecute, for the most part, this campaign of Christ's kingdom? What general would dare systemically to fight without reserves? And what treatment would be accorded to one who did so when he met with well-merited defeat? Does any business succeed on such principles? If it is immoral to extend our pecuniary obligations, especially where others are involved, beyond the limit at which we can reasonably hope to meet them, what shall we say of the policy of extending our spiritual liabilities when we are already inadequately fulfilling those which we have contracted? Let us not in such cases speak of a "call": the best of works engaged in outside the line of God's moral guidance becomes a decoy. Nor let us cover the rashness with the name of "faith." By all means let us go forward in faith; but let us first apply that faith to the provision of proper resources for the prosecution of the work in hand, by accumulating some reserves to supply deficiencies which we know by experience will constantly occur, calls which must arise within the limits of the field already undertaken.

PAPER.

2. By the Rev. A. W. Williamson, LL.D. (China).

The Missionary in China in relation to Literature.

In another Paper* I have endeavoured to explain the exceeding importance of the Chinese race, showing that there is now an inner
The Chinese a and an outer China; that next to ourselves, they are the
colonising race. great colonising race of the world, and that they surpass us in being able to colonise tropical regions; that they have already virtually taken possession of all the chief centres in the Malayan Archipelago, and are fast occupying all the beautiful islands of the entire Pacific; and that, therefore, the evangelisation of the Chinese would be the enlightenment of the whole Orient.

I have also shown that they are the most difficult non-Christian nation in the world to deal with,—the ablest, most self-
Their conversion contained, and proudest; that they know more of truth
a gigantic task. than any other race, and have this truth set in the most attractive forms; for the moral aphorisms of the Chinese, polished in the finest minds of many generations, are perfect gems, of which they are justly proud, and which they are never weary of quoting; and that for these, as well as other reasons, the conversion of China is the most gigantic task the Christian Church has ever confronted.

At the same time, I have tried elsewhere to show, that there has been a providential preparation for the Gospel gradually progressing in China; and that, while her conversion stands forth as the most stupendous undertaking before the Church, yet Providence has so arranged that China is more within the compass of our efforts than many smaller nations. Among these Providential preparations I have placed the educational preparation, which is so marked in this land; and it seems to me that I

* The Paper referred to was not included in the subject assigned him by the Committee, and could not be classified, but we have given an extract from it in the Appendix to Missionary Comity—(1) Mutual Relations.—ED.

cannot do better in this Paper than summarise the leading features of this preparation, and add several others which have taken place during recent years.

First, then, the people have one written language, called *Wenli*, co-extensive with their race, not a dead language, as it has sometimes been called, but a wonderfully living, <small>The Chinese</small> expressive, and powerful language ; the language of <small>language.</small> their proclamations, advertisements, contracts, deeds, epistolary correspondence, and their newspapers, taught in all their schools, and used in all their transactions of life ; also a second written language—called the *Mandarin*, colloquial, not for one moment to be compared with the other for general use, but which has the advantage of being the vernacular of about two-thirds of the population. Literary men, as a rule, know both these languages ; merchants, in the north and west, also know both, to a lesser or greater extent. But the first alone is universal.

The proportion of *readers* varies in different parts and in different classes ; fewer in the south-eastern districts, and more numerous in the central and northern : and, of course, <small>Chinese readers.</small> fewer among the poor than the rich. Still, the number is very great, and ability to read is wonderfully widespread among all classes. Among the higher classes, and in wealthy families, all the *men* can read and write, and also a sprinkling of the women. In reference to the other classes, the proportion of readers decreases as you descend the social scale. Still there is even hardly a poor family in China in which there is not one, or more, who can read or write. *But in this case the whole family gets the benefit of the one who can read.* Again, every band of emigrants has, at least one, often several, who can read and write fluently. Thus we are justified in affirming, that a book written in simple idiomatic Wenli is intelligible, not only throughout all the provinces of China and her dependencies, but wherever Chinese live,—a very extraordinary fact, inasmuch as a book thus reaches three times the number of English speaking peoples.

2. These provinces, dependencies, and colonies of emigrants, scattered throughout the East, are all linked together to one another, and there is a marvellous system of inter-communication. <small>Their system of</small> They have river and canal ; highway and bridle-path ; <small>inter-communi-</small> lake and sea. For many centuries they have had native <small>cation.</small> post, courier and parcel companies, etc., connecting town to town, and province to province, in the most ramified and efficient manner. In addition, we have now steamers in all directions, a Chinese Government post office in embryo, and the telegraph already in almost every province, and fast extending. Thus we have the means of conveying truth into every district of China, and every part of the world wherever they dwell. And just as we find a book, and sometimes an article in our reviews, influences the whole of Christendom—Europe, America, and Australia, alike ; so, with God's

blessing, one book may be produced, which, in a short time, might arrest the attention, and influence the minds, of the entire Chinese race *in* China, and *outside* China alike. What an important fact this is! In India, as we all know, a book requires to be published in some twenty languages ere it can reach the population of that peninsula. In Africa, we have, I suppose, a hundred dialects, not yet reduced to writing. The Church has not men sufficient to carry the truth, *vivâ voce*, to the multitudes in these places. How can we convert them? China, therefore, as I said, in reality is more within the compass of efforts, than Africa, or many a minor state.

In the foregoing remarks I have had reference more to the male population, but this same literature can be made also to Ignorance of reach the women. We know that there are women— Chinese women. especially among the higher classes—who can read, but they are comparatively rare, and can only master simple works, as a rule, though the roll of distinguished women is no meagre one. Yet the great bulk are shut out from the scope of ordinary literature, but they constitute the half of the race! How, then, can they be influenced by books? There is a method, and a very efficient one, namely, *illustrated* books. Our Scriptures, treatises, and tracts may be bought and enter Chinese households, and be laid on the shelf without exciting the least attention on the part of the women. But let a picture book enter the family, the whole household at once gathers around it—especially one of our beautifully chromo-illustrated books. The children cry out about it; the women ask, "What is this?" and "What The influence of is that?" They compel their sons and husbands to picture books. read the explanatory story to them; and so these heathen lads become, for the time being, exponents of Divine truth. *The chromo-illustrated book becomes a family book.* Thus, by one instrumentality, we can, with God's blessing, reach both the men and women of China. We may, or may not, utilise it; *but the means are there*, prepared to our hand in a gracious Providence.

I know well what is being done for the women of this land: I am fully aware of the increased opening and facilities for *vivâ* Female agency *voce* teaching; and I rejoice that so many Christian inadequate. ladies are devoting their lives to this work; but, at the same time, I know that it is simply preposterous to imagine that we can ever supply female agency for the millions of women of China. Some time ago I made a calculation, which showed, that if all the women, rich and poor, between the years of eighteen and fifty, in Edinburgh, Falkirk, Stirling, Dundee, Perth, and Aberdeen, were to pack up, remove to China, and distribute themselves over the land, each one would have, I forget,—as I have not the data beside me,—how many thousands to teach. But the number was very large, showing, conclusively, the need of some other means for reaching the women and children of China and India. Beautiful chromo-illustrated books have been proposed; such books have been tried; and such books have been found eminently successful. If there be any other, or better, or more practical plan, let it be proposed; but if not let the women of Christendom see that this method be widely adopted. It is a plan eminently within our reach. Suppose a few years ago, our Lord had appeared in the clouds, with great glory, how very few of the women would have recognised His appearing! It would have been a prodigy to them, nothing more. We cannot change society; but let it be ours to distribute far and near, among these millions of secluded women, by sale or gift, such books as will tell of our Blessed Saviour, so that when He appears, multitudes of them shall be among those who shall bow their knees, and confess that He is Lord of all!

We have seen (1) that Providence has prepared an instrument by which we can reach, in a wonderfully true sense, the entire Chinese race; and (2) that Providence has also provided *Providential* a method—a perfect net-work of systems of inter- *provisions.* communication—by which this instrument can be used. The question now arises, Are they amenable to this instrumentality? Are they willing to receive our books?

3. This brings me to the last part of my subject, and I am happy to be able to show that there can be no doubt on this point.

From the very beginning of her long history, China has been distinguished, from all the other nations of the world, by her predilection for literature, and the high honour she has *Literary honours* always set upon it. The hero of the Chinese has not *in China.* been the warrior, nor even the statesman, but the scholar. And the arena of glory has not been the public games, nor the tournament, nor the battle-field, but the examination hall. They are the same still. Their schools are as numerous as ever; their students as earnest in their studies; their public examinations as largely attended; and the enthusiasm of literature as widespread and as powerful as ever it was. The consequence of this is, not only a larger proportion of readers, beyond all comparison, than any other non-Christian country, but a higher respect for scholarly men, and a higher esteem for books, than in any other quarter of the world.

And this respect is now being extended to foreign books. Thirty years ago they would hardly believe we had any books at all: admitting we were bold and fierce as tigers, with some *Their respect for* knowledge of mechanics, but as destitute of literary *foreign books.* tastes as the savages in their Eastern seas. By-and-by they found those fancifully-encased articles on our shelves were really books; that we could really read them; that we knew much they did not know; and, last of all, that we make books, which even they could read and profit by. This sentiment has grown wonderfully, and grows still.

The Government led the way, and to their infinite credit leads

still. When first addressed, their immediate act was a college at
Pekin, and the engagement of highly educated foreigners to conduct
it. Immediately afterwards they, at several of the ports, engaged
foreigners, some to translate books, and others to keep their eyes
upon the periodicals and whatever issued from the press, and translate every article bearing upon China, which translations
The Government were printed in a newspaper, issued every fifth day, but
and Western circulated among officials only. Since then they have
science. been advancing in this direction step by step. Two years ago they
instituted five colleges at Tien-tsin for teaching respectively—(1)
engineering ; (2) military tactics ; (3) naval science ; (4) elec-
tricity ; and (5) medicine ; and they are at present also building
a large and commodious seminary to provide for three hundred
students, who are to learn the elements of English and of science
preparatory to entering these colleges.

The Government of Canton is also erecting a similar institution
for the higher classes of China. But last year they took by far the
most marked departure from their old ways, and one which will
ultimately revolutionise the entire empire. I refer to the decree
The Canton issued last spring in the *Pekin Gazette*, the official
Government organ which is read everywhere, adding questions on
Colleges. *foreign science and knowledge* to the examination papers,
which are set before all the students who assemble triennially, at
their provincial and metropolitan examinations ; and not only so,
but encouraging the pursuit of sciences, by decreeing honours
and emoluments to the successful candidates, and crowning the
whole by the promise of an appointment to foreign countries, on a
mission of investigation, with a salary—very large for a Chinaman
—with a secretary to help, and travelling expenses all paid. They
have already redeemed their promises so far by selecting and
appointing some, who have already set out on their commission,
and they have shown their good sense as well as confidence in the
President of the Pekin College—the Rev. Dr. Martin, an old and
much-esteemed friend of my own—by appointing him as the final
examiner in the case of the competing candidates. The effect of
this decree will be most powerful and far-reaching. A friend
remarked at the time, " This will set some wheels agoing." Some
wheels agoing ! Yes ; it will touch the aspirations of every bright
youth, and every ambitious student, in every hamlet, in every province and dependency of China. The immediate consequence will
be a demand for scientific primers and text-books in Chinese, and
an ever-growing demand for foreign knowledge of all kinds.

We admire Japan, but China has now started on the same line,
and will advance with perhaps more cautious, but equally satisfactory steps. She cannot go back. She must move on as best she
China is can ; she feels this, and her best officials welcome light
awaking. from all directions. But this " awaking," as it has been
called by one of her most illustrious sons, is not confined to the

officials; it is extending among every class of the population. Emphatically, *China is awaking.* Every mail from the West increases the awaking; every steamer that enters the inland waters widens the awaking; every Missionary who traverses the provinces intensifies the awaking; every courier who speeds his way into the inland cities adds to the awaking; every foreign traveller heightens the awaking; every additional mile of telegraphic wire extends the awaking; every native newspaper morning by morning feeds the awaking; while every book and pamphlet distributed far and near strengthens the awaking. The whole country, less or more, is aroused. The schoolboys, especially in large centres, are alive with curiosity. Her best youth are all ear and eye when they get the chance of meeting us; her picked students are all pondering these matters. What next? they say; and the awaking will yet deepen and widen as months and years pass on.

There are those who say that this awaking is only for increased wealth, and carnal desires for foreign pleasures and luxuries. They would not be human unless these entered into their calculations. But it is a libel on China to say that that carnality Direction of new movement. explains everything. The Chinese have always set the intellectual above the material, and the moral above all. They deplore the advancement of foreign vice, and are at their wits' end to stop it. They distinguish between foreigners and foreigners. They appreciate the labours and works of the Missionaries; they receive our books, and the more we can help them on their way the higher will be our influence. They feel their need of new knowledge, new methods, and new guidance. The higher their mental capacity the more they see their need, and many of their leading men now feel distinctly that new knowledge is a matter of life and death to them as a nation.

But they make a great mistake as to the character of the knowledge requisite: they trust in science. Science alone is They believe in science. allowed in their schools and colleges; science alone is permitted in their translations, and they hope, through science, to renovate and strengthen their nation. In this, we all know, they make a grand mistake. Suppose a youth to study only science pure and simple, as geology, or botany, or any other, what better is he morally after having mastered the science? The truth is, in China he is a less promising man than he was before. For the teaching supplied in these colleges cuts at the root of their old faiths, and supplies nothing better. They go in with their old traditions and sanctions of duty; they come out without any fear of either God or demon, ancestor or sage. The truth is, that unless they take care, *science will be the solvent* of their ancient and great nation. If anything will do it, sham science divorced from its Author will be the ruin of their country. Science as taught in their schools destroys a personal God, a soul, a hereafter, leads to the denial of many moral and social duties which they prize, and undermines the very basis on which their government stands. Religion in conjunction with science—for true science is only one form of religion—can save them. The elevation and salvation of China in reality thus rests with the Church of God.

Above everything else, the Chinese need the conscience to be aroused, from the meanest to the highest, and sympathy awakened *The real need of* between man and man. These are the wants of China, *and hope for* and until they are supplied there can be no true strength *China.* or elevation. The nation will break up without them. Witness the spread of iniquity from their commercial centres.

I repeat, the salvation of China—even in a worldly sense—as a kingdom depends on their reception of Christianity. Here then is our opportunity, and here is our duty : a nation prepared to our hand ; one written language reaching everywhere ; means of conveying our books to all quarters ; a nation aroused and ready to look into whatever we present to them. What a preparation ! How shall we meet the present crisis ? By larger supplies of Missionaries ? By all means ; for there is nothing like the human voice and human sympathy. But as we have shown before, the resources of the whole Church would be inadequate thus to meet the wants of China.

The truth is that we *cannot touch China as a whole*, but by the press. But with books, and especially by well-conducted periodicals, *Far-reaching* we could, through God's blessing, influence the whole *influence of* population. China is almost, if not fully as prepared for *periodicals.* the apprehension and diffusion of knowledge as Europe was fifty years ago, wonderful though it seems. We may therefore reasonably hope that by judicious selection of subjects, careful preparation, striking and suitable illustrations, and wise measures for circulation, we may as thoroughly permeate the Empire, and as effectually change the opinions and action of China as has been done during the past half-century in Britain, Germany, and America. Periodicals now rule the world ; and it is a sad reflection on the Church of God that in such a literary country as China, so adapted for such work, we have no Christian periodical worthy of the name.

The Earl of Northbrook (President, Christian Vernacular Education Society for India) : I know how valuable your time is, and I shall take it up but for a very few minutes. The wide scope of the Paper we have just heard, shows the work to be done with respect to Christian literature, but my observations will refer only to that country of which I have some knowledge, namely, India ; and they shall be quite practical. The subjects for our meeting to-day are put down on this Paper. We have none of us, here present, any doubt for a moment that the Missionaries and *Increase of* Missionary Societies, are bound to do all they can for *readers in India.* the promotion of Christian literature. In India, I believe, about a million of natives of that country, able to read, are turned out of the different schools and colleges year by year. Before long the mass of the people of India will be able to use books, many of them books written in English, but most of them written in the different vernaculars of the different parts of India.

There is to be another meeting, in respect to literature, on Monday next, at which meeting a Paper is to be read by Dr. Murdoch, whose name is well known to many present as being, Dr. Murdoch's perhaps, the most indefatigable worker, in regard to literary services. Christian literature for India, that we have yet seen. Now that Paper is really addressed, and professes to be addressed, to the first three heads of the subjects before us to-day. As I myself shall not be able to be present at the meeting on Monday, I should like to say a few words as a supplement to Dr. Murdoch's Paper which you will hear on Monday next, because Dr. Murdoch has made a very great omission in the Paper which will be read on Monday— a very natural one to every one who knows what sort of a man Dr. Murdoch is ; but still it is an omission which ought to be supplied. I do not think that any one has a better right to supply that than I myself, because I happen to have filled, for a short time, in succession to Lord Shaftesbury, the position of President of the Society with which Dr. Murdoch is connected. What I refer to is the omission of Dr. Murdoch's own services, and of the work which he has done in this matter. I, therefore, have prepared, and shall put into the hands of the Secretary, a note, showing what the publications of the Christian Vernacular Education Society have been,—and when I say the publications of the Christian Vernacular Education Society, I do not wish to be misunderstood,—practically they are Dr. Murdoch's publications. The Society has been able to devote a very small portion of its funds to this work. The funds have been provided mainly by Dr. Murdoch himself, and the work has been done by him.

Let us look at the nature of the work. The nature of the work in the first place, has been the preparation of a most excellent series of books, written in the different languages of India. Now, I think, nothing can be more important than the provision for Nature of India, of good school books, to be taught in the different Mission the work. schools, not confined to one particular denomination of Protestant Christians, but applicable to all schools; and I have received, myself, testimony as to their value from Missionaries in different parts of India. The last that I had was one from Scinde, and another from Ceylon, two Missionaries I happened to see in the course of last winter. They said they did not know how they could have got on in their schools if it had not been for the publications of Dr. Murdoch, in respect to the school books.

Probably some of you have noticed, lately, a resolution, passed by the Government of India, I think on the last day of last The Government year, on the subject of the moral training of natives educated and moral in India, pointing out how, when youths leave school, they, training. at any rate in some instances, leave it without that moral and religiou training which is so desirable; and the provision of good books in schools must have a most important effect upon the moral training of those who go to those schools. I shall have occasion to refer to this afterwards, but that, I think, is sufficient to show what has been done in regard to school books.

There is another most important subject, and one which is growing in importance day by day, and that is, the provision for these young men, *Literature for those leaving school.* when they leave school in India, of some literature, part of it directed to explain the doctrine of Protestant Evangelical Christianity, but also good healthy Christian literature, to feed the desire which they must have for knowledge after they leave school. Now, as respects this part of the Paper, only a beginning has been made. It is, perhaps, the greatest deficiency at the present time, so far as I know, in respect to Mission work in India. Dr. Murdoch has taken this up with zeal. In the last year, 1887, he has written either himself, or with the assistance of others, a number of books of the very class to which I have alluded. There is a book upon "Popular Hinduism," of which three thousand copies have been printed; there is a book upon "Caste," and short papers upon "Caste," and "Popular Hinduism," also; there is a book on "The gods of the nations," showing the different systems of idolatry all over the world; there are "Stories from Early Christianity;" "Stories from Early British India;" a "Life of the Queen-Empress and Her Family, suitable for the Jubilee Year;" and besides that, those being all of them books with a direct Christian Missionary object, there are books upon travel by land, sea, and air; books respecting sanitary matters; there is Foster's "Essays upon Decision of Character, and Moral Courage," which has been re-published; and Dr. Murdoch is now, at this moment, engaged in republishing Sir William Hunter's interesting and important lecture, delivered at the Society of Arts the other day. Now this will show you what one man can do who takes up this most important branch of Missionary effort, and it should encourage us to proceed in the same direction.

I hope and believe that these meetings which we are having at this great Conference—in which I in common with, I believe, the great portion of the members of the Church of England—are delighted to see all Protestant Evangelical Christians meet together to co-operate in the same work, and I hope that some practical end will be attained by these meetings. For that purpose I will conclude what I say to-day by making one or two short suggestions. In the first place, I am sure that there is *The Indian press and pernicious literature.* some information connected with the Indian press which it is very desirable to put together in a really tangible and useful form. I have been informed, and I am afraid it is the case, that at this present moment at the different railway stations in India the contractor for the supply of books has at the same time certainly—whether it now continues I know not—("*Yes.*")—has supplied literature of a most degrading and disgusting nature, that is to say, translations made from the very worst of the most modern French novels. I should be very glad if those Missionaries and others who are assembled at these meetings of yours would be kind enough to supply me with any authentic information which may be in their possession upon this matter, because it is one, I think, of the greatest importance, and to which the attention of those who are interested in the welfare of India should at once be directed, and without absolute authentic information on matters of detail, it is impossible to take any action in the matter.

The practical suggestion that I have to make is that, if possible, some committee should be formed, after the meetings are over and the Conference is concluded, of those who are interested in this work, who may meet together and see how far the work can be promoted, what the wise way of promoting it is, and how far it is desirable or undesirable to divide *A practical suggestion.* it among the different Societies. Now we have here in England, certainly, three important Societies connected with the work; there is the Religious Tract Society, the Christian Vernacular Education Society, and the Society for the Promotion of Christian Knowledge. If those three Societies were represented together, and could meet together, they would be able, I think, to come to some practical conclusions, which would be followed, I am sure, by a very great extension of this work; because I am satisfied that it is only because the public in England are not aware of the importance of this work, and the best way in which it can be carried out· that the support—which we, for example, have received—is so very small, I think there are also ways in which the different Missionary Societies may assist in this work, and at the same time making a great move in the direction of increasing not only purely Missionary work, but the preparation of books for the diffusion of sound Christian knowledge in a popular form to meet the growing demands of the educated young men of the dominions of the Queen-Empress of India.

Mr. R. A. Macfie: Such a Society as the Indian Vernacular deserves the highest favour. Still there ought to be, somehow, inquiry how its funds can best be augmented; whether *The Indian* its books, etc., are in all respects the best selected, the *Vernacular* most likely to be useful; whether they could not be *Society.* increased in number and variety; whether it has a sufficient number of wisely and efficiently administered agencies and depôts; whether these could not, and should not, be available for other sound, English and other, non-vernacular literature; whether more of a business character might not be imparted to that Society.

It follows that earnest searching of heart should have been turned to the supply of vernacular literature to *all* the heathen nations— to other than Indian peoples—aye, to all nations.

In favour of gratuitous distribution I do not plead. But I do plead in favour of cheapness, and this is to be sought for in the following directions : contentment with moderate profits, *Cheapness* whether sales be made by "the trade," by colporteur, and *in distribution.* other itinerant vendors, or at depôts, and by diminishing the necessity of keeping large stocks, through receiving payment, in advance, for books *ordered* to be procured. Persons familiar with the trade will see the force of this "article" of hope. Commercial arrangements as to purchase, and return of surplus copies, minimising the baneful, and certainly not philanthropic ascendency of abused copyright law monopolies, which has hitherto received too little notice among Christian authors. Mention of copyright—that is, the artificial limitation of the natural right of the benevolent to reproduce and multiply and circulate, widely and cheaply, religious publications, for of such only do we take cognisance—leads to the fundamental question of the composition of suitable books. This topic, however, is too large to be dealt with now.

I conclude with a very practical suggestion. Should not there be a *Church Service Book* prepared for converts and the modern A practical *diaspora*, Christians of various nationalities, few in suggestion. number they may be, and unable to maintain a settled pastor to reside among them, but who, two or three gathered together towards and in the name of the Lord, would in a brotherly spirit meet to pray together and read the Scriptures together on the first day of the week, if they were encouraged to do so, and especially if they had assistance of the kind, for which I respectfully but urgently plead. The Church of England has prayers for use at sea. The Church of Scotland has a course of prayers for use by our country-men in India and by colonists. These are good examples. I may almost say, What more do brethren need? But as to the latter book it may well be asked, Is the work easily had—made readily accept-able in the proper places—and in their vernaculars,—by all the persons for whom it is intended, and others by whom it could be employed, and by whom—not least by the daily enlarging number of converts, whom Missionaries hail for their crown of reward, but cannot bring and keep under their personal ministrations? And, further, has the time not come for the joint preparation of one, or be it two, such manuals, directories, or *helps*, through mutual arrange-ment between the two sides of the Atlantic?

DISCUSSION.

Mr. Henry Morris (Hon. Sec., Christian Vernacular Education Society for India): I believe that it is the bounden duty of every Missionary Society to help in this matter, not only in India, but in every Mission-field throughout the world. My remarks here refer, however, to India only. The extension of education among the people, and the impetus which is thereby given to reading, imperatively demand the attention of every committee, or council, or board of directors concerned in Mission work. An opportunity for doing good has been given them, which they never anticipated. The preparation of Christian literature in the Duty of language of the people among whom they are labouring should Missionary be no mere by-work. It has been too long left to haphazard. Societies. It ought to be done systematically, thoroughly, and completely, as an integral part of the great work entrusted to their charge. Fully convinced of its vital importance, they ought to throw their whole heart and soul into it, and see that it is done, as their Lord and Master would have it done, thoroughly and well. To this end organisation is required. System and harmonious action are necessary. Intercommunication between the different Societies is wanted. In fact, in no branch of Mission work is careful system more needed. The following suggestions to this end are humbly offered, and I do hope that the great Missionary Societies will con-sider them; and, modifying them as they please, take action upon them for the benefit of the thousands in India, who urgently require good and wholesome books to read.

(a) In the first place there ought to be in every Missionary Society a separate department for the preparation of good vernacular literature. It should have a department to itself, just as much as the evangelistic or the educational departments. To prevent the matter becoming a dead letter, it should be seen that this department should not be merely nominal, or sink into dull routine. (b) To prevent this, sub-committees should be appointed, both at home and abroad. These should be in constant communication with literary men, whether European or native, corresponding with them, and keeping them up to the mark. (c) Special men should be set apart for this special work. It cannot be expected that good literary efforts should be produced by overworked and overpressed men. The sweetest drops have been exuded from the busiest workers. But a constant supply of good literature is required for the growing Christian Church, and this cannot be supplied except by specially selected men giving their whole time to it. One European Missionary in each linguistic area should thus be set apart, and he should be in communication with native helpers, who should work with and under him. (d) There should be intercommunication between the Societies as to this point. (e) These literary Missionaries and agents should all be in the pay of the Societies to which they belong, and as much under their control as any other agents. (f) The production of literary works should belong to the Missionary Societies, who should hand them over, when prepared, to the various Literary Societies for printing and publication. (g) To each of these Societies grants should be made in proportion to the work done. By the adoption of some such scheme as the above, overlapping and confusion would be avoided.

A series of suggestions.

Wherever the native Churches have attained anything like a separate organisation or self-government, the importance of this subject should be pressed upon them. They must be shown that what is really required is not so much translations, good and useful and necessary as these may be in their proper place, but original works, written in a bright, clear, simple, idiomatic style. The end which all desire is a Christian literature, thoroughly Oriental and thoroughly Indian—such as shall appeal to the heart and bosom of every Indian believer,— and appeals for Christ, which shall go home to the consciences of those who have not yet been converted to His blessed faith. May the great Missionary Societies take advantage of the present favourable crisis in Indian educational affairs, and do more to use the press in India thoroughly and effectively.

Mrs. Mary C. Nind (Woman's Foreign Missionary Society of the Methodist Episcopal Church, U.S.A.): I want to say a little about our literature in India, not that I am a Missionary, but as I am a representative of the Woman's Foreign Missionary Society of our Church, I want you to know that we are doing something for the women of India. And that you may know the means by which this work has been organised, you will permit me just to touch upon the literature of our own land. The organ of our Society is the *Heathen Women's Friend*, which has a circulation of 20,293; and it is one of the delightful things which will be encouraging to you women especially, that this paper, containing twenty-four pages, with a subscription of only fifty cents a year, edited by a woman, Mrs. W. H. Warren, of Boston, has been self-supporting from the very first month.

Organ of the Society.

It has been so admirably managed that apart from meeting its own expenses it has become a source of revenue for carrying on other Christian schemes, both at home and abroad. From this paper came the Zenana paper, and as the Methodist women of America have the great joy of being pioneers in Missionary work, we delight to praise the Lord that out of the surplus funds of our

Heathen Women's Friend, we have issued the first paper for Indian women that was ever published for them. This is also edited by a woman. Mrs. Blackman was our first editor, and now it is Mrs. B. H. Bradley, assisted by native women. It is published in Urdu, Hindu, Marathi, and Bengali. It has a circulation of several thousands. The way we raised the money for this paper, after we started it from the surplus fund of the Friend was this. We raised a fund of 20,000 dollars, one lady saying, in Boston, "If you will raise 20,000 dollars, I will give you the last 5,000." That money has now been raised, and the money has been invested at interest varying from 6 to 8 per cent. The capital is to stop there through time immemorial, until the millennium comes. Now this paper is a wonderful help to our Zenana women. It goes into the Zenanas, into the homes of high-caste women, and is a wonderful blessing. I am sorry I have not got copies in the four vernaculars here, but it would do you good to look at it. It is an illustrated paper, and though you could not read it, it might please your eyes. I hope you will pray for God's blessing on this Zenana paper.

A Zenana newspaper.

Rev. W. J. Wilkins : When did they begin that Zenana paper ?

Mrs. Nind: In 1886.

Mr. Wilkins : There was a Zenana paper in Calcutta, called *The Women of India*, in Bengali twenty years ago.

Mrs. Nind: Well, sir, I am very glad to hear it.

Rev. Young J. Allen, D.D. (Board of Missions of the Methodist Episcopal Church [South], U.S.A., from China): Mr. Chairman, ladies, and gentlemen,—I was exceedingly interested in the reading of Dr. Williamson's Paper. I have been associated with him for nearly thirty years, specially in the production of a literature for China. I have been, as I mentioned yesterday or the day before, in connection with educational work, engaged directly in the Government educational work as teacher and translator, and as editor of the higher class of text-books for the information and education of the Chinese nation. I have been working side by side with Dr. Williamson in the editorial or theological work, both for the Government and for the Missionaries. We are united together on three large committees—one for the production of religious books for circulation amongst the Christian Churches ; another committee appointed in 1877 by the General Conference of Missionaries for the production of school and text-books for use in Mission schools, and for use in China schools generally. We have done a great deal on that committee in the production of that class of books. We are also associated together in another large committee to produce books for the general public for the reading of the literary classes and of the officials. These books are to be composed from the Christian standpoint, and they are to be in the idiomatic Chinese. In all these departments and in all these committees we find a great demand for our books, and a recent letter from Dr. Williamson urged me to make arrangements whereby I could give more of my time to literary composition, for, said he, in all the range of our Missionary operations there are but very few men who are capable of producing books suitable for the reading of the Chinese literary men.

Engaged in translations for Chinese Government.

I referred the other day to the fact that there is a revolution going on in China. It has been forced upon them by us. It requires that they shall be educated up to our moral standards ; it requires that they shall accept our civilisation, in order that they may be admitted into the comity of nations, and have the amenities of Christian intercourse. Now, my dear friends, it is thrust upon us ; as a fact, the responsibility rests with us. We have got to teach them, and we have got to do that largely through a broader and competent literature. Now who is to prepare this literature ? who is to teach in these schools ? The Missionaries must to a large extent be detailed to do that work, and it is a glorious opportunity thrust upon the Christian Church to-day that it has Japan and China brought by diplomatic action to its feet as the pupils and wards of Christendom. And now we stand responsible for the situation, we must teach them, and we must produce the books necessary to enlighten them more largely than those they are able to come in contact with in the technical schools. When you consider the fact that the literature of China will circulate not only in China but in Japan, the Corea, in Manchuria and Mongolia, and covers an area of five hundred millions of people —when you think of that fact, and that one Missionary can, as it were, diffuse his Christian thoughts and ideas, not only through the eighteen provinces of the whole of the Chinese Empire, but beyond, to those countries that have got their literature from China, what a wonderful field is open to the Christian Missionary or to any other Christian worker !

Now is the opportunity in China.

I cannot do better than bring these few facts before you, and urge upon you that it is of the first importance that we devote ourselves to the production of the literature which shall embrace the country in its schools and in its general reading ; and this comprises the Bible, all kinds of Christian literature, and also science and other subjects written and issued from the Christian standpoint, by which we can guide the Chinese mind. I have translated for the Chinese Government about ninety volumes of history, geography, science, applied science, and so on, and in this I have been associated with Dr. Martin, Mr. Fryer, and others who have given themselves to this work ; and I know not of one solitary book issued by the Chinese Government that contains one character or one syllable that is opposed to the spirit of Christianity.

Earnest call.

Mr. Henry E. Clark (Friends' Foreign Mission, Madagascar): We have spent so long on India and China that I hardly know whether we can spare five minutes to think about the little work in the great African island of Madagascar. But let me say that the place and importance of the Mission Press in Madagascar cannot be exaggerated. I agree with every word that has been said with regard to India and China, and almost all refers equally well to Madagascar, except that there the Missionary Societies have the printing to themselves ; and they have been able by that means to keep out of Madagascar that pernicious literature of which we have heard as doing so much harm in India and China. Long may we be able to do so.

Mission Press in Madagascar.

I was rather struck by the expression in one of the Papers as to whether the Missionary should leave his own proper work to go into this literary work. I ask: Is it not a proper work for the Missionary to attend to this subject, and to make a pure literature for the native races in Madagascar ? I do not narrow the work of the Christian Missionary, but I widen it to its fullest extent to make it include this work. Neither do I agree with a gentleman who said he thought it would be well if a Missionary were separated rather specially for this Mission work, as I understand him, sitting in his study and preparing books, when all the time he is not mixing with the people. I differ from him, for I believe if you are to prepare books properly for the people among whom you are working, those books must be prepared by

The Missionary and literary work.

those who are working amongst the people and can understand their modes of thought and can enter into their feelings; and so those books get put into a language that the common people can understand; and they are written in a language which can enter into these, to some extent, dark minds. I can speak from some experience; for though I cannot say I have written ninety books, I have written some twelve or more in the Malagasy language; and I believe that work has been abundantly blessed to the Malagasy people, and will be in years to come.

Then again: Should our Mission Press be used for purely Missionary literature, or should it be used for, and supported by general printing? I believe it may be legitimately used for general printing, because by that means— **Missionary presses and general printing.** by making a moderate profit upon the general printing—we can reduce the cost of our own Mission works and so sell them for a less price. It may be interesting to know that only the last mail from Madagascar brings us word from our committee that we are printing for the Government a work of instructions to telegraph clerks. And then again, we have continually circulars, etc., to print for traders, and in this way our principles are sometimes put to the test, because we have to strike out always the items referring to intoxicating drinks; and also, as a representative of the Society of Friends, you will understand me when I say that we have to cross out all reference to warlike implements. Then, with regard to books of science and history, I am reminded of what John Bright once said. Referring to another member of the House, he said, "The right honourable gentleman makes up his history as he goes along." That is just what we have to do in Madagascar; we have to make up our school books as we go along; and will you tell me that that is not a proper part of a Missionary's work? I believe it is. School books, books of science, history, and agricultural books—I believe this is part and parcel of our Missionary work, for by that means we are moulding that Malagasy nation for God, lifting it up for God, and enabling it to take its proper part among the nations of the world. In Madagascar we are now almost independent of maps from this country. We have taught the natives to lithograph maps, and nearly all the schools are supplied with maps from our printing press.

I am very much surprised at the point which has been raised as to how far the Missionaries of different Societies may co-operate in the formation of Christian literature, as if it was rather a dangerous thing; that **Co-operation of Societies.** we might go a little way, but not very far. I think we may go as far as ever we can, and not only that we may do it, but that we ought to do it, and unless we do it we are doing wrong. In Madagascar, the London Missionary Society and our own Society's Press have an agreement one with the other that they will not enter into competition. And then again, with regard to the literature, Should it be paid for? I agree that, as far as possible, we ought to teach the people to pay for these books, for, as a rule, they will value them more if they buy them.

Rev. J. Murray Mitchell, LL.D. (Free Church of Scotland): To come back for a minute to the great land of India. I rejoice in the testimony that has been borne to what my friend Dr. Murdoch has done. It was **Natives employed to translate.** rather implied that he had written the books in all those languages. He writes, or compiles, in English; and then the natives have, I believe, in every case translated them into the different vernaculars. For example, in Bombay, one of our own pupils translated all the prose that Dr. Murdoch had provided; while others of us did our best to supply the poetry, for our translator was not much of a poet himself. We have all heard of the necessity for preaching; and we see to-day, I think, more clearly than we have seen before, that there is an equal necessity for printing. I am very much delighted to think that we shall

all go away with a stronger conviction than ever of the pressing duty of going forward in this work.

I remember when the printing press began to be used by the natives. Up to that time they had their sacred books all in manuscript. But then, seeing what the Missionaries and others were doing, they began to put their books, both in Sanscrit and Marathi, into print. Immense *Influence* numbers were thrown off, beautifully illustrated; and Hinduism *of the Press on Hinduism.* in a large degree reaped the benefit of the invention of the press. I remember regretting this exceedingly. But now I trust all are awaking to the necessity of using the press more and more. Some always did it. There were literary Missionaries from the very first; and I may venture to say, in Bombay most of the Missionaries, and myself among them, felt it a duty, as far as we could, to write tracts both in the vernacular and in English. The number of readers in India, as in China, is rapidly increasing; and the natives are circulating poisonous literature to such a fearful extent through the agency of the press that we shall be beaten if we do not put forth new efforts, and avail ourselves of the mighty agency of books to the same extent as we avail ourselves of preaching and of education.

Mr. John Archibald (National Bible Society of Scotland, from Hankow): My claim to address you on this subject lies in the fact that I have been privileged to establish a Bible Press in Hankow, and have had under my superintendence a large circulation of Christian literature—both Scriptures, tracts and other publications, amounting to some three-quarters of a million. I want to refer to several questions on the paper. The first is, "The place and importance of the Mission Press." I can only say what everybody says, whether he represents a continent or an island, whether he represents men's work or women's work, that *his own work* is the most important of all. Being on the Press, I think that the Press work is the most important of all. "Under what conditions should it be maintained?" In every station where printing facilities do not already exist. "Should it be confined to purely Missionary *Practical answers to* literature, or should it be used for and supported by general *questions in* printing?" It should be allowed to do general printing where *programme.* other Presses do not exist; but where other Presses do exist, and are conducted on commercial principles, the Mission Press ought not to compete, because it can undersell the trade, and cause the enemy to blaspheme over all the land. "Should the distribution of Christian literature be gratuitous or paid for?" Paid for; only there are exceptions, when distribution may be allowed. And we ought to make people pay for this reason: because what they pay for they appreciate, while they do not appreciate what they get for nothing. They not only waste it, but it demoralises the people and leads them to think they ought to get everything for nothing. Therefore, for their own sakes, I should make them pay. But in cases of triennial examinations, where thousands of students assemble at the provincial capital, we make a point of distributing the literature largely to these men, and we believe with good results. The Chinese themselves go in for the very same thing.

"The extent to which the Missionary may devote himself to the preparation of a pure literature for the people generally." That depends on the Missionary. It is not every man who can write books. But when we find a man who can, then he ought to devote himself to it as far as he can. I heartily agree with our friend from Madagascar that he ought not to give up his other work. The man who can do the best work is the man who knows the people best; and in China the best translator, the Rev. Griffith John, is also one of the hardest working Missionaries that we have in the country.

"By newspapers, books of science, history, etc. ?" *I* think all these things ought to be supplied; and they can be made self-supporting, as you have heard from our lady friend. The world appreciates newspapers and other publications, and the world will pay for them. The working man will subscribe for them. And with regard to scientific and other works, Government can help in the matter. Therefore we must not draw on the Missionary's pocket to carry on this kind of work. The rule is as plain as a turnpike, as the saying is. If funds are given directly for the spread of the Gospel and the evangelisation of the world, let them be so used; and if we want to carry on other work let it be by a commercial fund or let funds be separately raised for the purpose. If the Missionary has an opening to go in for this work, let him do so.

"How far may Missionaries of different Societies co-operate in the preparation of Christian literature?" As far as they can; the fact is that in China we have now nearly all the Christian literature produced largely *by committees.* We

Committees in China on literature.

have four committees all working together, composed of Missionaries of all the various Protestant denominations, and every book produced by your Missionaries passes under the examination of the committee, and is selected by them. This is important, because an author is by no means a capable judge of the value of his own work, and we have had such things as authors producing particular works, and getting funds from the Societies at home; printing the work on their own responsibility, only to be stowed away by the ton in the warehouse, and to be looked into only by the moth and the white ant. Therefore this work should be placed under a committee, and then you will be assured that the work will be carried on properly.

Rev. W. J. Wilkins (L.M.S., late of Calcutta): I should like to say a word or two in reference to the subject before us, as far as Calcutta is concerned. It was my privilege to be Secretary to the Bible Society and a member of the Committee of the Tract Society for many years, and I was

Zenana paper in Calcutta.

rather astonished to hear this morning that a paper for Zenana distribution had been produced for the first time two years ago. We had one in existence twenty years ago. It was very nearly self-supporting, and either that or its successor is in continuance to this day. It is an excellent illustrated paper, something of the style of *The Sunday at Home* or *The Leisure Hour.* It circulates in thousands. The publications issued by the Tract Society in Calcutta number yearly from eighty thousand to one hundred thousand copies. One very interesting feature is that the books that are provided and also these periodicals are very largely purchased by the Hindu gentlemen for their wives. Nowadays, as so many ladies are able to read, the gentlemen purchase Christian books produced by the Tract Society in preference to the native literature. I think, this being the case, it should be an immense stimulus to any man who has the talent and the time to engage in this work.

Let me say a word to inform our friends of the work of one man, who has since gone to his reward,—the Rev. J. E. Payne of Calcutta, a man who spent eight or ten years of his life in the preparation and circulation of Christian literature. He would, in some cases, find suitable English works; in other cases he would ask Missionaries or Missionaries' wives, or ladies engaged in Zenana work, to write suitable books, and then get them translated. And there

Bengali work by Europeans.

is one mark of progress that one should mention, and that is the possibility nowadays for Europeans to produce Bengali works such as the Bengalis themselves would approve of. Only about four years ago there was a most interesting case of this kind. A gentleman who had been spending a great deal of time in the preparation of Bengali literature, wrote a book in Bengali, and he was wishful to know what the judgment of the Bengali gentlemen would be upon his style. The book was submitted to a committee of the Tract Society, composed of four members, two Bengali and two Europeans. The two natives said the book must have been written by a native, as it was in excellent Bengali. The Europeans said it must have been written by a European, because it contained the marks of a European hand. We have solved the question that it is possible for Englishmen out there to write Bengali books such as the Bengalis themselves will appreciate. The fixing of a Bengali style has been one of the great difficulties in Calcutta. Possibly many of you are aware that until Missionary work commenced in the beginning of the century, Bengal had no prose literature. It had abundance of poetry, but no prose literature, and from that time till now the Bengali style has been in a state of transition. But as we have now a great number of Bengali newspapers, and the Bengalis themselves are writing books, that difficulty is passing away, and we shall very soon, I think, have a standard of Bengali style.

Rev. W. Stevenson (Secretary, Free Church of Scotland Ladies' Society for Female Education): I want to say a word in conclusion which may perhaps give a practical turn to our discussion, with a view to our continuation of it on Monday. The question comes up again on Monday and is put in this form: " How can religious literature and general literature on a religious basis be best provided for the *An organisation needed.* growing wants of the Mission-fields of the world? " We have three things very manifest to-day. First, the immense expansion of the field for Christian literature; secondly, the absolute necessity of supplying that field; and, then, thirdly, the fact that a very great deal is being done. But I think we must all feel here this morning that we want an organisation. There is no question that the efforts that are being put forth are being put forth without sufficient system and co-operation on the part of the different Societies. Now this is a work that cannot be done by one Society alone. It must be done by the co-operation of all the Societies together. This is one of the great fields in which we want a really undenominational Society. We should have a literature—a Christian Literature Society —for the Foreign Mission-field corresponding to the Bible Society, and the Religious Tract and Book Society at home. If this is to be arranged, this is the time to arrange it. We have representatives of all the Missions in the world here. We have an opportunity of conferring together; and I think that as many as possible who have a practical interest in this matter should come on Monday and take up Lord Northbrook's suggestion, namely, to appoint a number of those specially interested to confer together and perhaps to form a committee who shall consider this question, whether it is not possible to organise a great undenominational Society which will practically be a Book and Tract Society for the whole Foreign Mission-field.

Rev. Dr. White offered prayer, and the meeting concluded.

MEETINGS OF MEMBERS
IN SECTION.

THE MISSIONARY IN RELATION TO LITERATURE.

(2) *BIBLE SOCIETIES.*

(a) What prominence should be given to the printed Scriptures in communicating the Gospel to mankind?

(b) Translations.

(c) The management of Bible distribution.
  (1) By agents of Bible Societies.
  (2) By part payment of the agents of Missionary Societies.
  (3) By grants of Bibles, etc., etc.

(Monday afternoon, June 18th, in the Lower Hall.)

T. A. Denny, Esq., in the chair.
Acting Secretary, Rev. J. Sharp, M.A.

Rev. T. R. Wade, B.D., offered prayer.

The Chairman: Ladies and gentlemen,—I will not occupy your time this afternoon in dealing with the subject before us. It would *Desire a Bible* be unwise on my part to do so, as there are speakers to *for all.* follow, who are so much better qualified to deal with it than I am. There is one point upon which, I doubt not, we all have an opinion, and perhaps a right opinion, and that is as to the distribution of the Scriptures. I think every one in this room would wish that a portion of Scripture should be in the hands of every man, woman, and child on the face of the earth. The great difficulty is to accomplish any such grand and glorious result. We can speak for one Society that is represented on this platform, the Bible Society, which is now, I believe, in its eighty-fourth or eighty-fifth year, and which has been doing glorious work for Bible circulation, and for *How long* the race at large, by putting into their hands this precious *will it take?* book. I hope Mr. Sharp will forgive me if I say a word or two on that subject. I find from a little publication that I have been reading lately, that they have circulated one hundred and sixteen millions of Scriptures—Bibles, Testaments, and portions. That is an enormous number. But remember that the population of the globe is fourteen hundred millions, and that forty-five millions of the population are dying yearly; so that, let the Society do all it possibly can, and let all the other Societies do all they can, still it would be impossible, working as we are at present, to meet the tremendous necessities of the case. Then there is the question, as to whether to give or to sell. I think most *On selling or giving.* of us will be in favour of selling, if we can sell; but if I could not sell I would give. But the agency for giving is a difficult one ; and then we must remember that there are millions and hundreds of millions of people on the face of the earth who could not read even if we were to give them the Bible. This is a matter for consideration. When I first looked into the subject, I thought I could solve the question almost by the stroke of a pen, but the more I thought of it and looked into it, the more I saw the wisdom of the managers of the Bible Society in grappling with the difficulties of the subject. These, however, are matters that will be brought before you by others.

PAPER.

1. By the Rev. Edward W. Gilman, D.D. (Corresponding Sec., American Bible Society).

Power of the Printed Bible.

The Founder of Christianity having laid upon His followers the duty of extending His kingdom in the earth, the question is raised, What prominence is to be given to the *printed Scriptures* in communicating the Gospel to mankind ?

There are some who say that by the terms of the great commission the *oral* preaching of the Gospel is to be relied on as the chief instrumentality for proclaiming the good news of salvation. *Different views of Christ's commission.*

There are others who claim as a matter of observation and trial, that the printed page is distributed in vain, or worse than in vain, unless in connection with the living teacher.

And yet another class, assigning large importance to rites and ceremonies, avow that the Scriptures are not to be given, even to converts, except under such limitations and restrictions as the teaching Church may impose.

The object of this Paper is to maintain the thesis that *the circulation of the Holy Scriptures among the nations is of no less importance than the oral preaching of the Gospel.* We maintain that the conversion of souls and the extension of the Redeemer's kingdom are ever to be sought by bringing men into contact with the Bible as one book, complete, entire, and unique ; by putting them under the influence of the written Word, *The volume and the voice of equal importance.*

translated into their own familiar speech, reproduced by pen or type, circulated so freely that every man may see with his own eyes the words of the Law and the Gospel, and then if need be, expounded and applied ; until they believe to the saving of the soul. In other words, wherever the Missionary goes, and whether he is sent to Jews or Mohammedans, pagans or nominally Christian people, he is to hold out the Bible for their acceptance ; not substituting lessons, inferences, dogmas, rites, catechisms, hymnals, which he draws from the Bible, but giving the Book itself, as containing the truth, confirming his statements, authorising his embassy. And this involves the whole work of translating, printing, and circulating the Scriptures of the Old and New Testaments among all nations. We are to keep back nothing that is profitable to them, and all Scripture is profitable. Not until the words which the Holy Ghost teacheth have been made accessible to all people will the work of evangelising the world be done.

I. We are led to this conviction by considering the end which is sought. The heralds of the Gospel go to proclaim a coming king-
The same end dom ; to found an institution ; to organise a new order
sought by both. of things ; to set in operation a train of influences for generations and centuries. It is sought to build an enduring structure on the foundation of apostles and prophets, Jesus Christ Himself being the chief corner-stone ; to secure the evangelisation of pagans, the reformation of nations, the equipment of men with all that is profitable for mental development, for elevation of character, for renovation of heart and life, and to communicate the will of God respecting human salvation so far as that is made known in His Word.

The injunction to publish the Gospel in all lands and in all ages implies, of course, the use of such facilities as each generation in its turn supplies. The Master and His disciples journeyed on foot over the hills of Judea and Galilee ; but when He bade His disciples go into all the world, He did not limit their locomotion and that of their successors in all coming time to walking. He bade them preach ; and no doubt, the earliest proclamation was oral, but the commission does not limit them to spoken discourse, whether with individuals by the wayside, or among crowded assemblies in the market-place. The herald is to go on his mission, using whatever mode of travel shall bring him most satisfactorily on his way, whether it be by sail or steam, by diligence or rail, by ox-cart or camel's back. The chariots of God are twenty thousand, and all are to be employed as the exigencies of His work may require.

If to weaken the position I have taken, it be said that the Master Himself wrote no sacred Book, indited no catholic epistle, committed no sentence to parchment ; we answer that He was the exceptional Teacher. Jesus Himself baptised not, but His disciples. So He discoursed, and they treasured up His discourses ; made careful record of His deeds ; selected and set in order the things most worthy to be remembered ; and thus supplemented the ancient Scriptures by the new, and filled out the Book which we call the Bible.

It is true the Apostles did not organise Bible Societies, or solicit funds for the remuneration of scribes employed in multiplying copies of the law ; but they did show their appreciation of the Book ; they referred to it as of supreme authority ; they testified to its power to make men wise unto salvation ; they declared it to be given by the inbreathing of the Holy Ghost. They did not dispense with oral teaching, but the noblest of their hearers were those who like the Bereans not only received the Word with all readiness of mind but searched the Scriptures daily, whether those things were so.

II. We notice how it has ever been the instinct and practice of the Christian Church to publish its message of glad tidings by translations of the Holy Scriptures and the multiplication of copies.

The practice of the Church.

As we read Church history it is manifest that the instinct of the Church has been to translate and multiply copies of God's Word, and diffuse them as widely as its opportunities would allow. Syriac and Latin translations of the Bible and three Greek versions of the Old Testament had been made by the end of the second century. Within two hundred years the Scriptures could be read in Coptic, Sahidic, Armenian, Ethiopian, and Gothic.

That copies of the sacred Book were numerous may be inferred from the famous edict of Diocletian (A.D. 303), that all copies of the Bible should be delivered up and burned ; and from the statement that Pamphilus of Cæsarea, the martyr, was accustomed to make copies of the Scriptures, and keep them on hand for distribution among those who desired them. Eusebius says " that both Greeks and barbarians had the writings concerning Jesus in the characters and language of their own country."

At the very outset of his Missionary life, before leaving England, William Carey said to William Ward, a young printer to whom he was introduced in the streets of Hull, " We shall want you in a few years to print the Bible ; you must come after us ; " and when Phineas R. Hunt, a Missionary printer for thirty years, first in India and then in China, came to die, his heart poured out thanksgiving " that this grace had been given him that he should *print* among the Gentiles the unsearchable riches of Christ." The American Board was incorporated in 1812 to propagate " the Gospel in heathen lands by supporting Missionaries *and infusing a knowledge of the Scriptures ;* " and the Act of the Legislature provided that a certain portion of its revenues " should be used to defray the expenses of imparting the Holy Scriptures to unevangelised nations in their own languages." The Missionary Society of the Methodist Episcopal Church was organised in 1818 as a Missionary and Bible Society " (Reid, i. 30).

One of the firstfruits of Protestant effort for the salvation of the Indians of North America was John Eliot's Bible ; a great achievement ; a marvellous work ; commenced in 1659, less than thirty years after the settlement of Plymouth ; completed in eight years ; the version being made in a language which had no literature, and had never been reduced to writing ; comprehending the entire Bible ; not in paraphrase, nor with adaptation to liturgic use, nor with comment, but with strict adherence, from Genesis to Revelation, to the sacred text ; a *whole volume* of the Scriptures with just *one leaf* of catechism ; published in repeated editions at a time when bookmaking was costly and in its infancy ; absolutely the first case in history of the translation and printing of the entire Bible in a new language as a means of evangelisation ; and blessed of God to the enlightenment and salvation of souls. It is said that he lived to see six Indian churches with one thousand native members. This was English zeal transplanted to American soil (Reuss, " History of New Testament," par. 492).

Eliot and the Indians.

The work thus begun by the fathers has been continued by their sons ; and on both sides of the line, in British America and in the United States, the Christianisation of the Indian has been based upon the Scriptures in their own tongues as indispensable to success. Of the Dakota Scriptures alone more than thirteen hundred were called for last year.

The Jesuit Missionaries, on the other hand, have pursued a different plan in

their strenuous efforts for the conversion of the aborigines, at numerous stations
through the great valleys of the St. Lawrence and the Mississippi,
The Jesuits, a contrast. from Montreal to New Orleans; never, so far as I can ascertain,
printing the whole Bible, or even entire books of the Bible, but
aiming to circulate such portions of the Scriptures as they have found it desirable to print. Thus a volume of one hundred and fifty pages was printed at the
St. Ignatius Mission in Montana, in 1879, with the title, "Some Narratives from
the Holy Bible in Kalispel, compiled by the Missionaries of the Society of Jesus."
They were rather free translations of selected portions of the Old and New Testaments in the language of the Flathead Indians. I am informed that the
edition consisted of two hundred and twenty-five copies, of which some thirty
copies have been called for by librarians of Germany and other countries.
Seventy-five may perhaps be scattered over the country, while the rest are still
on hand.

III. We cite the results of repeated experiments made by the Roman Catholic
Church as a demonstration that if nations are to be grounded upon
No permanence without the Bible. the truth and built upon the foundations of apostles and prophets,
the Bible must be given them. The history of Congo is instructive;
that of Japan hardly less so.

In Congo, Portugal upheld the Romish Church from A.D. 1500 for two centuries. The Catholic faith flourished there. One hundred churches were built;
at one time all the adults had been baptised. One Missionary baptised thirteen
thousand, another fifty thousand in five years, another one hundred thousand in
twenty years; masses, penances, rosaries, crucifixes, medals, confessionals
abounded; but there were no schools, no translations of Scripture, no pains taken
to make the people acquainted with the Bible. And when the Portuguese power
was withdrawn from the land the priests also withdrew, and as the result of
their departure, it is said, every vestige and fragment of their religion died out.

Contrast this with the annals of the Martyr Church of Madagascar. In 1820
we see a pagan nation, untaught, with no literature, no books, no
Madagascar, a contrast. manuscript, no alphabet. In 1830, hundreds of pupils had been
under Christian instruction, a printing press had been erected four
years, a translation of the New Testament had been made, and five thousand
copies had been printed. But thus far there was not a single avowed believer.
On the 29th of May, 1834, twenty converts were baptised—the firstfruits of
eleven years of toil and prayer.

In 1835 and 1836 the Missionaries, forbidden longer to preach and teach, withdrew from the country, leaving behind them the printed Bible, complete, in the
hands of one thousand adherents, two hundred of whom were communicants.
Death was threatened to any native who should read the Bible, pray to God,
receive baptism, or join the communion of the Christians." * For a quarter of
a century persecution raged, and ten thousand persons were sentenced to penalties
of different kinds, including torture and death. Worship was held in secret; the
Scriptures were buried for safety, and read only by stealth; and when the
supply of printed Bibles failed, many busied themselves by copying out
portions with the pen. Says Ellis, † "I brought home no memorials of the
persecution in Madagascar more deeply affecting than some of these fragments
of Scripture, worn, rent, fragile, and soiled by the dust of earth or the smoke
in the thatch at times when they had been concealed, yet most carefully
mended by drawing the rent pages together with fibres of bark, or having
the margins of the leaves covered over with stronger paper."

Unlike Congo and Japan and Corea, the Church of Christ in Madagascar,
when bereft of its foreign teachers and guides, had the Bible complete in their
own tongue—a perfect rule of belief and duty in all things needful to salvation;
and fed on such spiritual food during those twenty-six years of persecution, the
Christians increased in number from one thousand to seven thousand, and the
actual communicants from two hundred to one thousand.

* Ellis, p. 269.   † *Ibid.*, p. 161.

IV. It may be admitted that there is some diversity of opinion among Missionary workers as to the value of the printed Book unaccompanied by explanations and comments. Such divergence of views is to be expected, and makes it reasonable and desirable to push our inquiries further. Is the printed page in this nineteenth century the power of God unto salvation? Is the Scripture profitable to all men? Have we not the testimony from China that instances are rare of persons converted by the unassisted reading of books? * Are we not told that the Bible is obscure in the extreme when circulated without note or comment among nations whose whole course of thought runs in other and different channels? Can one understand the Scriptures, except another guide him? Can a heathen get a clear conception of a gospel or an epistle which a zealous distributer has thrust into his hand without a word of explanation? † *Different views of Missionaries.*

Let us remember, however, that it is not a question between the Bible alone and preaching alone which we are called to decide as a practical matter. No one thinks of relying upon the Scriptures without explanation for the full enlightenment of the world. Missionaries, as well as books, evangelists as well as Bibles, must be sent to all lands where Christianity is unknown. But the Missionary without the Bible is like David going forth to meet the champion of the Philistines without any stones for his sling.

The testimony concerning the power of the printed Bible from those who have tested it in foreign lands is varied and conclusive. "The paramount importance of the services of Bible Societies on heathen ground has been forcibly set forth by an eminent Churchman when he declared that, "If the choice were to lie between the Bible without the teacher and the teacher without the Bible, he would unhesitatingly elect the former." ‡ *Result of comparison.*

Said Dr. William Goodell, "I never saw anything do such execution as the Bible does. It is becoming the great Book in the East;" § and again, apologising for devoting eight years of his life to translation work, "Our whole work among the Armenians is emphatically a Bible work. The Bible is our only standard, and the Bible is our final appeal. And it is even more necessary for us than it was for the reformers in England, because we are foreigners. Without it we could say one thing and the priests another; but where would be the umpire? It would be nowhere, and all our efforts would be like beating the air."‖

David Stoddard, speaking of the Syriac Bible, said, "This is a work which cannot die. We may all pass away, and much that we have done be forgotten, but this Bible will live and preach to young and old, on the plain and in the mountains, and bring forth the fruits of righteousness long after we slumber in the dust. Had the Churches of America conferred on the Nestorians no other blessing, this one thing would amply repay their efforts." ¶

From other and distant lands comes testimony of the same character. Rev. Mr. Day, of the Lutheran Mission at Muhlenburg in Africa, is quoted as saying that, "Moslems of the Mandingo and Vey tribes frequently come to his house and spend hours in reading the Christian Scriptures for the purpose of comparing them with the Koran." **

V. But the importance of the printed Book is further demonstrated by cases constantly occurring in every part of the world where, in advance of all oral instruction, the Bible is proving itself a power for enlightenment and salvation. The individual and special cases are so numerous and striking that no one hesitates which of them and how many to cite. *Frequent proofs.*

I might tell of those villages of Hindu-born peasants in Decca who were led

* "Middle Kingdom," ii. 343.
† *Bible Society Record*, November 1876, p. 164.
‡ "Proceedings of the Osaka Conference," p. 174.
§ "Ely Vol.," p. 228.
‖ "Forty Years," p. 282.
¶ "Ely Vol.," p. 243.
** *Missionary Review*, 1888, p. 380

by a copy of Carey's Bengali Testament to give up idol worship and lying, and were waiting for a true teacher to come to them from God.*

I might tell of an Armenian Evangelical Church at Perchenj, near Harpoot, of which the Missionaries knew nothing till a colporteur one day reported that he found seventy men assembled in a stable listening to one of their number reading to them from a Bible which he had bought in a neighbouring town. †

I might tell of a native of the Bassa country in West Africa, who was found preaching and baptising, and giving for his authority a printed book which contained the Gospel of John and the Acts, translated and printed by a Baptist Missionary forty-five years ago.

I might refer to the laying of the corner-stone of an *adobe* Church in an Indian village in Mexico, which I witnessed in 1879, built to shelter a little company whom an Indian had gathered around him, without any conference with the Missionaries, that he might read to them the wonderful things which he found in the Bible.‡

No less to the point is the story of the Chippewayans, who came twice a year, twenty days' journey in their canoes, to see the Rev. Robert Hunt ; and who were led to do this because they had heard an interpreter read from the Gospel of John in Cree syllabics. Said they, " Some of your talkers with God have been near our hunting grounds, and have talked to us from the Book the words of Jesus Christ, who loves us all and came to be our foregoer to His better world ; and we are come to the praying-master that he may show us Jesus Christ's track to those better lands."

VI. While we bring these proofs of the power of the Bible as an evangelising agency in lands that have been covered with a dark pall of ignorance and superstition, we must remember that that power is still greater in lands where for centuries it has been moulding the thoughts of the people, determining their beliefs, enkindling their hopes, regulating their morals, shaping their legislation, colouring their literature, dominating the language of the home, the school, and the Church. True, no occurrence in Christendom may afford an exact parallel to those which we have cited from heathen lands : from the nature of things we ought not to expect that. The power of the Book may be less conspicuous, but it is not less mighty, where it is best known.

More and more does it appear that the printed Bible, apart from all ritual, or hymnal, or catechism, or harmony, or comment—the *The Bible to be given to all.* Book, containing the Old Testament and the New, with every precept of the Master's, every incident of His life, every apostolic word of counsel, of promise, of warning, of revelation, every recorded fact of primeval history, every prediction of inspired men ; with all its wealth of parable and evangel and proverb and psalm and canticle ; historic, prophetic, didactic, poetic ; the things hard to be understood no less than the simple—this Book, faithfully, closely, fully translated, is to be given to the nations of the earth in their several tongues in which they were born, a stream of living water, whose perpetual flow shall gladden the wilderness and make the whole earth as the garden of the Lord.

* Smith's " Life of Carey "; see *Bible Society Record.*
† Wheeler's " Ten Years," p. 134.
‡ *Bible Society Record*, January 1880, p. 5.

PAPER.

2. BY THE REV. PREBENDARY EDMONDS, B.D.

Translations of the Bible.

I wish to make a few remarks upon translations of the Bible, as—

1. Witnesses to the authenticity of the original.
2. As, in some instances, expositors of its meaning.
3. As examples of primitive Missionary policy.
4. As pledges of permanence to a young Christian community.
5. As the crown of Missionary effort.
6. As a means of religious unity to a native Church.
7. As a searching discipline to the soul of the translator.

All these points are involved in my Paper, but it is not cut up into seven equal parts, and I ask to be excused from calling out when I pass from one to another.

Professor Salmon in his "Introduction to the New Testament," after examining the evidence which recent investigations have brought into notice, that the four Gospels, as we have them, were at the latter part of the second century of "immemorial antiquity" (p. 123), sums up one part of his argument with this striking observation : "Towards the end of the second century it is not only the fact that our Gospels are in sole possession all over the Christian world, but translations of them have gained an established rank. That is to say, at the time when it is doubted if our Gospels were born, we find their children full grown " (p. 45). *Children of the New Testament.*

This remark which Dr. Salmon makes for one purpose will serve admirably for another. It reveals to us by a flash of light the existence in the Church, from the beginning, of the principles and practices embodied in modern days in the work of the British and Foreign and other Bible Societies. The subject is of fascinating interest : that interest begins at once and follows on all the way. Three things almost immediately draw our attention :—

First : That the oldest documents of our sacred books, though highly prized, more highly now, perhaps, than ever before, are so prized as fountains of transferable authority, not as instruments of popular teaching, still less as part of the apparatus of worship. The Koran is read in Arabic, even where Arabic is not understood. So are snatches of the Vedas, in Sanscrit. So in Pali, are the sacred documents of Buddhism. The Bible, which is found everywhere, is everywhere a translation. To Christians it is of undisputed authority, yet it rests on history, and submits itself to criticism, bringing the truth not to men's ears only, but to their hearts and bosoms. We do hear it speak, every man of us, in our own tongue, wherein we were born. *Sacred books of the heathen not translated.*

Second : That there is no instance of an ancient Church, however remote in situation, however lowly in intellectual gifts, in which we *The Bible in the* do not find some early trace of a Vernacular Bible.   The *vernacular of* highest truth of which the world has ever been made *every Church.* conscious, has entered in at the lowliest doors; and the door, as far as we can ascertain, has been opened to receive it.   That is a noble sentence in the "Modern Painters," in which Mr. Ruskin remarks that to make communion possible between God and men "the Deity has stooped from His throne, and has not only in the person of the Son, taken upon Him the veil of our human *flesh*, but in the person of the Father taken upon Him the veil of our human thoughts."   And it may be added, just as an earthly father can speak his heart to his children who are immature, as truly, though not as explicitly, as to those of larger growth and fuller development; so the Father of all stoops to fill the words and idioms of His lowliest children with His manifold wisdom.   Thus He provides for them all, so that, as Origen says, they gather the Bread of Life according to their several capacities, they that gather much having nothing over, and they that gather little having no lack.   No language is wide enough to contain God, none is so narrow as utterly to exclude Him. The last, the least, the lowest in rank of translations, carries God's message to men, and may be as faithful a messenger as any uncial codex.

Third : That while the Bible is spread abroad in a translation, and while its distribution so translated is universal, it is also spon-*Translation* taneous.   There is no rule, or law, or canon of council, or *is spontaneous.* decree, enjoining it upon the messengers of the Churches. It is done now, it was done in days gone by, it will, we may feel sure, not cease to be done.   But it is done in obedience to a great spiritual instinct which has never ceased to operate, *Semper, ubique, ab omnibus.*

[*It is with the greatest reluctance we leave out a large portion of this paper on the Early Translations of the Bible by the Christian Churches of the East.   Abridgment was a necessity, and we naturally give that part which deals with translations of modern times, with which our Conference deals, though not the ablest part of the Paper. Room, however, must be found for the interesting quotation from Dr. Malan with which Mr. Edmonds illustrates the value of some of the early versions as comments upon the originals.   The learned author has a right to an apology, but our readers have the first claim on our fidelity to the task assigned us.*—ED.]

Let us listen to what Dr. Malan the erudite translator of the Gospel according to St. John, in "the eleven oldest versions except the Latin," says of the powers and capacities to convey the message of God to men, of the languages that were in use outside the circle of Greek speech.   I soften and shorten the first sentence, for it seems to me to go beyond the truth, but the rest is, I believe, unchallenged.

We must go to "the venerable idiom of the Peschito" for the "real spirit" of "our Saviour's teaching and conversation." *

"Likewise we must go to the Armenian for clearness and dignity of expression; to the Georgian for particles even brighter than the Greek ones, and for a double use of the pronouns which gives great force to many renderings; to the Coptic for a nicer use of the definite article than even in Greek, which has not, like the Coptic, an indefinite or partitive article, often indispensable to a right understanding of the text. In the Ethiopic we find a certain breadth as well as detail of expression which have great merit; and in the Gothic of Ulfila we have a faithful, a stern and noble Teutonic rendering of the Greek, which throws great light on the English version. . . . " Dr. Malan adds more words without adding much more weight, but this important and interesting sentence has passed into the literature of criticism, and it shows that the Bible message for five centuries after Christ lost nothing, but gained rather, by suffering the sacred violence of translation.

There is a third instance that must not be passed by. The Latin Bible, in its oldest form, is as old as the oldest Syriac, or the oldest Coptic Version. When the Church of Rome, at the Council of Trent, April 8, 1546, stood at the parting of the ways and only just stopped short of ana- thematising vernacular translations, she turned her back upon herself, and befouled her own nest. Her own Bible was a trans- lation and a noble Missionary gift. Let us for a moment trace it. The British and Foreign Bible Society was founded on the 7th of March, which day is linked in the Book of Common Prayer with the name of Perpetua. We may well be thankful for the historical instinct in the Reformers which rescued this precious fragment of Church history from passing away with a mass of legend that, compiled, as Hooker says, by "brainless men," had made England "ashamed of nothing more than saints." Now the faith that lifted Perpetua so high above all loves but one, was the faith that fired the whole North African Church. The Bible that fed that faith was a translated Bible, a Missionary version. It had not come to Africa from Italy, it went to Italy from Africa. It lent life to the Vulgate, and yet lived on in independence in Ireland, in Scotland, and even in England for centuries. The principle then established, viz., that Missionary work includes Bible translation, received, at least in the West, few illustrations for the next thousand years. We can hardly understand how slowly Latin died, how slowly crept on the tardy footsteps of the advancing nations who made the modern world. But they came at last and spoke with new tongues, and at once the old principlo was revindicated, the Bible learned their new tongues to speak to them.

I venture here to affirm two principles—(a) No Mission work is permanent or satisfactory that does not, as a main part of its responsibility, provide the converts with the Scriptures in the vernacular.

(b) No vernacular version can ever be permanent or satisfactory that is not in the loyal hands of a living Church.

I have dealt with ancient examples. I pass to such as are modern. I find nearly fifty versions of the Bible, I mean rather versions of the Bible

marginal note: Rome's Latin Bible a Missionary translation.

* His exact words are controversial and controvertible as to the Greek. "We can form no just idea of our Saviour's teaching and of His conversation, by reading them in the Greek of the Evangelists which He never spoke; but we must look for the real spirit of them in the venerable idiom of the Peschito " (Preface, p. vii.).

in nearly fifty languages, at the beginning of the present century. About forty are living books. Some of the dead ones were Missionary Bibles. For instance, John Eliot's translation for the Indians of Virginia, now extinct; the "first book," it is said, ever printed in America (1661-3). While John Eliot was then at work in the West, Dutch Chaplain-Missionaries were at work in the East, and a series of Malay translations began as early as 1629. Portugal, the last of the older nations in Europe to receive a Vernacular Bible, owed it when she got it to Missionary effort in the East Indies. The New Testament was printed at Amsterdam in 1681. The Old Testament at various times from 1719 to 1751 at Tranquebar. Thus Protestant Dutchmen and Protestant Danes gave the Bible to the Portuguese. They are slow in learning to read it. No praise can be too high, that is, for Christ's sake, given to the great band of South Indian Missionaries of the eighteenth century, the list of whom is headed by the name of Ziegenbalg. How is it that we know so little of him? He is our pioneer. His life is a model life, his plans and methods have never been greatly improved upon. Here is a man who dies at thirty-six, leaving behind him a version of the New Testament and half the Old, a dictionary of the language he has mastered, and a flock of between three and four hundred converts. I think it will be found that in breadth, depth, and permanence, that great achievement has never been exceeded since. Ziegenbalg's place is taken in 1739 by Fabricius, a fine Tamil scholar, whose work in the Tamil translation of the present time is as much alive as Tyndale's work is in the great Bible of England which we call the Authorised Version.

Modern translations.

Ziegenbalg, South India.

It is a startling thing to pass from Madras at the beginning of the eighteenth century to Bengal at the beginning of the nineteenth. Two East India Companies competed for the honour of carrying Ziegenbalg and his books and parchments. In the early time of the Serampore Missionaries, occasional passages were still given, but only to go away. The century called the century of progress, shows badly in comparison of the century of stagnation, but whereas the eighteenth century began well and then deteriorated, the nineteenth began badly and improved. Now the Serampore work begins, a work destined to be unequally divided into permanent and ephemeral—destined to illustrate both of the principles for which this Paper contends. The Mission that does not produce and provide the Bible is doomed. The Serampore Mission is safe there. The Bible that does not spring from the actual necessities of a living Church is doomed too; nearly all the Serampore versions are lost there. Now take the first principle, viz., that no Mission is satisfactory without its Vernacular Bible. Look at the Roman Catholic Missions of the sixteenth, seventeenth, and eighteenth centuries, in India, in China, in Japan. They cannot be dismissed in a sentence. They ought not to be so dismissed. In India we read in Dr. Hunter's pages of Father Beschi, scholar and poet, just the words that describe the Protestant Fabricius. Why is the work of the one so spiritually dead, and of the other so spiritually living? Because no Mission can live without its Bible, and the Roman Missionaries did not translate it. Think of Adam Schaal in China, master of the language, tutor of the Emperor, living under the palace roof. Think of his predecessor, Ricci—praised highly, of course, by the Jesuits, abused badly, equally of course, by the Dominicans, but clearly a man of high capacity and devotion. But no Bible did they give to their

R.C. Mission in China.

converts, although China is a land of books. Well, their work has not
entirely perished, but the carved work of their chief church is this very
year broken down by Chinese axes and hammers. And the great European
power that set itself, certainly not for any devotion to religion, to maintain
that building, has suffered a severe diplomatic defeat. The church is gone, in
spite of the French, to be rebuilt out of the Emperor's sight. Ricci died in
1610. It is a good while ago, but let us go back three hundred years more
to 1305. Listen to a voice that was silent in death before Wickliffe was
born. "I have myself grown old and grey, more with toil and trouble than
with years; for I am not more than fifty-eight. I have got a competent
knowledge of the language and character which is most generally used
by the Tartars. And I have already translated into that language and
character, the New Testament and the Psalter, and have caused them to
be written out in the fairest penmanship they have; and, so by writing,
reading, and preaching, I bear open and public testimony to the law of
Christ." And in a letter written a year later he says: "Since my coming
to Tartary I have baptised more than five thousand souls."

But the Tartar dynasty passed away, or surely on such foundations a
great Christian China had been built up. When Christianity came next
to China it was the Society of Jesus that brought it, and not the Church
of Christ. I pass by Japan for brevity's sake.

And now I wish to illustrate the SECOND PRINCIPLE, viz., *that no Bible
can be permanent that does not spring out of the actual necessities of a living
Church.* Bible Societies are bound by the very law of their
being to live by, and in return, to feed, the life of living <small>The Bible lives in a living Church.</small>
Churches. We cannot unroll a map linguistic, or ethnological,
and then finding a hiatus on our shelves, resolve to fill it up, whether the
living teacher is there or not. The Bible is, without doubt, the most
translatable of books, but it will only consent to transform itself when the
Spirit and *the Bride* say "Come."

No one has stated this principle with more force and insight than
Ward of Serampore. "I recommend to Brethren Carey and Marshman,"
he wrote, as early as 1805, "to enter upon the translations
which we can distribute with our own hands, and which may be <small>The Bible in India.</small>
fitted for stations which we ourselves can occupy. As to making
Bibles for other Missionaries, I recommend them to be cautious lest they
should be wasting time and life on that which every vicissitude may
frustrate. . . ." These were prophetic words, but the prophet *quâ*
prophet had no honour in his own country. It is pleasant to remember
that his frankness did not lose him a particle of Brethren Carey and
Marshman's regard.

Carey was a pioneer. He made better work possible. The subject of
Indian languages now mapped out with all the accuracy of an ordnance
survey, was then as unexplored as an Indian jungle. The languages and
dialects of the India he knew passed before Carey's eyes as the sons of Jesse
before the eyes of Samuel. Each, in turn, might seem to be the anointed
of the Lord. Carey saw no difference, and crowned them all. An Oriental
fate swiftly overtook the infant sovereigns.

All the Indian vernaculars have been re-translated since, and in only
two or three instances does anything of Carey's live in any language except
those with which he was in contact.

Thus Chamberlain lives in the Hindi, and Yates in the Bengali; like

Carey, too, with another life in the Sanscrit. And Martyn lives his inextinguishable life in Persian and in Hindustani; and Bowley, the diligent, the humble-minded, lives on in Martyn's Hindustani, taught to speak the old, old story more simply, that men might take it in. In all these cases, the men who made the versions had a pastoral link, official or voluntary, with the people for whom they made them.

I do not wish to exclude civilians or soldiers, who many of them, as I have known by happy personal experience, may be the most helpful of Missionary colleagues. The modern life of the Bible of Ceylon introduces us to two civilians, of equal devotion, but of lesser and higher gifts—Mr. Armour, a pious schoolmaster, and Mr. William Tolfrey, a scholarly civilian.

But look where we may, it is, as a rule, the Missionaries who are the translators. They start to our memories as we look at the map. It is hardly a hundred and twenty years ago that Captain Cook lifted *The Bible in the Pacific.* for most Englishmen the veil that hid the fiery jewels and calmer coral clusters that dot the Pacific. Some were "savage," some were "friendly," almost all are friendly now. Society Islands, indeed most of them are—a society more Royal than Cook thought of when he linked English science with the group that contains Tahiti. Some Missionary Society, English or American, some Bible Society, American or English, owns an obligation to guard and feed the life of these children of nature in her secret summer palaces. Here are seven and twenty versions of Scripture, nine of them whole Bibles—the oldest complete Bible is but fifty years of age this year. All these had Missionaries as their authors. They are a goodly band. Nott leads off in Tahiti. America follows at once with Hawaiian. Then to mention only a few names come John Williams, and Buzacott, and Bishop Williams, Yate, and Maunsell, and Hunt, and Calvert, and Pratt, and Turner, and Inglis, and Ella, McFarlane, and Creagh, and Lawes.

Look at Africa, and include Madagascar. Here are translations in forty-one languages.* Who made them? I must not forget that antiquity gave us the Coptic and the Ethiopic, and a studious Frenchman *Distinguished translators.* and a wandering Abyssinian provided us with the Amharic, at a time when £1,250 was thought not too high a price to pay for such a treasure as a version of the Bible in a new tongue. But putting these aside, who is there to dispute with Macbrair and Hannah Kilham, and Zimmermann, and Christaller, and Bishop Crowther, and Henry Townsend, and Schön, and Gollmer, and Goldie, and Robb, and Robert Moffat, and Shaw, and Shrewsbury, and Boyce, and Appleyard, and Casalis, and Mabille, and Freeman, and Jones, and Griffiths, and Rebmann, and Krapf, and Bishop Steere, and later translators still, for the palm of the successful translator? The Bible Societies do a good deal for Missionaries, but then it must be remembered that it is they who put it into her power to do them good.

I am speaking, it is more than likely, in the presence of Missionary translators. They work that they may finish their work. The native Church that can read with appreciation a Vernacular Bible can almost run alone, and if it can it ought. I do not plead for the production of Bibles prematurely. The early Church was a long while before hers was complete. In every case the Gospels, or one of them, should come first,

---

* The reference is to the list of B. and F. B. S.

then Genesis and Exodus, and then the Psalms; and I may just mention for those who have ears to hear it, and to take in all that follows from it, that a quarter of the Psalms are unintelligible, or only partially intelligible to those who are ignorant of Genesis and Exodus.

I have said that it is more than likely that I am speaking in the presence of Missionary translators. If it is right to envy any man his office, my heart would envy theirs. Let me make this plain. Every part of the Bible has an Apocalypse. *A word to translators.* There is a river which, in the Law, the Prophets, and the Psalms, makes glad the city of God. We see its predicted Catholicity in the fourfold streams of Eden ; we see its life and sparkle in the forty-sixth Psalm ; we see its deepening, widening, prevailing, refreshing, healing power, through the eyes of the Prophet Ezekiel ; and all these are gathered up in the perfect image which the angel of the last Apocalypse showed to St. John. You, my Missionary brethren, dig the channels through which the living water flows. No work is more honourable than yours. I am not entitled by age, by office, or by character, to speak a word of exhortation to those whom it is no effort to me to esteem better than myself. But, I believe, the man who, while digging a new channel, is drinking daily of the water which flows through the old, will not think more highly of his learning or his conscience than he ought to think, nor wish to stamp his own image upon his version of the Book of God. Nor will a translator who calls to mind that he is the last, and perhaps the least in a chain, whose links stretch through two millenniums, and engirdle the habitable globe, even be strongly tempted to do his work in an egotistical spirit, as if his name were to compete on the title-page with the Name above every name in the text.

Questions of judgment arise, and questions of conscience too. To borrow a convenient aphorism, "even the youngest" translator "is not infallible." There is generally some other judgment by which we can cross-examine our own ; there is a general conscience by which a private conscience can be proved. It is a serious thing for a race, a country, a Church to be without a Bible. The next calamity in seriousness is to have competing versions. Meantime we will answer for it that money shall not be wanting, nor sympathy, nor prayer, till by your work and ours

"The whole round world is every way
Bound with gold chains about the feet of God."

PAPER.

3. By MR. WILLIAM J. SLOWAN (Western Secretary, National Bible
Society of Scotland).

The management of Bible Distribution.

In a sentence, permit me to say that the National Bible Society of Scotland, with which it has been my privilege to be connected as one of its Secretaries for twenty-eight years, had in 1887 an income of

£33,432 7s. 1d., and an expenditure of £30,988 11s. 9d., of which £16,000 was spent on Foreign Mission work. It issued, or helped Bible Society to issue, last year 632,073 copies of the Scriptures, whole of Scotland. or in part, at home, in the colonies, and in seventeen foreign countries—two-thirds of the issues, in round numbers, being abroad. Its total circulation since 1861 amounts to 10,110,925 copies ; and its natural place among the Bible Societies of the world is just where it appears on this platform to-day, following immediately the British and Foreign and the American Bible Societies—though in respect of Missionary enthusiasm and circulation compared with resources, it claims to rank second to none. May I add one word to express the privilege I feel it to be to stand here side by side with the official representatives of the two great Bible Societies of England and America? Our Scottish Society is, compared with them, but a little one; but it has attained to the first three; and it is needed to complete this threefold cord of love by which, under the Divine blessing, souls are being drawn to Christ, and earth to heaven.

I proceed without further preface to the important practical subject committed to me, " THE MANAGEMENT OF BIBLE DISTRIBUTION."

1. *Distribution through Bible Societies.*

(*a*) It is important to bear in mind here that while Bible Not to be judged Societies claim their authority directly under the great by statistics. commission, " Go ye, therefore, and teach all nations," they have no other aim or object than that which is contemplated in that great commission, namely, " that men may believe that Jesus is the Christ, and that believing they may have life through His name." The number of Scriptures circulated is not the end, but only the means to the end, at which they aim. It is, therefore, not the extent or number of their issues, but the effectiveness of them, by which their usefulness has to be judged.

(*b*) *Bible Societies may well claim the sympathy and prayers of* *the Churches* in the peculiar difficulties with which they Peculiar difficulties call have to contend, such as ignorance of or indifference to for prayer. the Divine message ; the antipathy and active opposition of rationalism, which naturally recognises in the Bible its most formidable and dangerous opponent ; the superstition and bigotry of professed friends of the Bible, who affirm that our book is defective, because it lacks the apocryphal writings, or who, while they bless and offer it to the people with one hand, with the other commit it to the flames, or thrust it into an *index expurgatorius*, in the company of books declared by them to be unfit to be so much as named amongst us. Nor can we forget here the hardships and dangers which thus and from the nature of their occupation attend our colporteurs and other agents of distribution — hardships and dangers affecting liberty and even life. No one of the Bible Societies represented here but has its honour roll of sufferers and martyrs, men who have not counted their lives dear to them for

Christ's sake and the Gospel's, but have gladly worn them out or laid them down at the Master's call.

(c) *The chief agents of distribution employed by Bible Societies are depôts and colporteurs.* For ourselves we do not find *depôts* an effective means of circulating the Bible. They are sometimes a necessity, but a more aggressive agency is required. The sale of the book cannot be regulated by the ordinary rules of supply and demand. Here supply does not follow demand, but creates it. Hence the value of *colportage*—a value which cannot be computed by statistics or arithmetic. Nor is this agency necessarily Colportage. an expensive one. Many of the men employed by the National Bible Society of Scotland work on commission—obviously a cheaper method than giving the books away. Others work as colporteurs during only part of the year—the season most suitable for selling—while they carry on their ordinary avocations during the other months, thus reducing the cost of maintenance, keeping themselves in touch with their original occupation, and enabling the Society to drop at the end of any season, a man who shows himself inefficient without involving him in serious loss. But even though colportage appear in some instances a costly agency, judged by the number of sales, and though it may be true that the books might have been given away for less money than it costs to sell them, if our aim is not to thrust forth the largest possible number of books at the smallest possible cost, but that "souls may be born again by the Word of God," we are entitled and required to use what seems to us the most effective means to that end. Now I feel assured that no more effective means has yet been discovered than the sending forth of such colporteurs as are found in the ranks of the Bible Societies— men of the people, men of the book, men of God : "Missionaries to the ones " who abound in labour, but work as much on their knees as on their feet. When I study the records of their self-denying, God-honouring lives it seems to me as if a colporteur must have sat to John Bunyan for the portrait drawn in the house of the Interpreter, of one—"his eyes lifted up to Heaven, the best of books in his hands, the world behind his back, who stood as if he pleaded with men, and a crown of glory did hang over his head."

2. *Distribution through Missionary Societies.* The magnitude of this work calls for comity and co-operation all round. Co-operation Specially must the two great workers in the Missionary needful. enterprise go hand in hand in it—that which publishes the Gospel through the living voice, with that which publishes it through the written Word. These two are really one, for both are offshoots of the Church of Christ, which is the great Missionary Society of the world; and these two are really one because it is the one Spirit of God who alone makes either the reading or the preaching of the Word "an effectual means of convincing and converting sinners, and of building them up in holiness and comfort through faith unto salvation." The Bible Society has long been recognised as the fit

handmaid of Missions. The Missionary translates and the Bible Society prints and circulates the Word translated. But there ought to be still closer fellowship between these two whom God has made "not twain, but one flesh." It is not enough that they work side by side ; each must do not its own work only, but the other's also. The Bible-seller must be an evangelist, and the evangelist a Bible-seller, or each will be the less efficient.

The Society I represent has long acted on this principle. It supplies Missionaries with Scriptures under certain conditions, and *How they may work together.* gladly assists in the maintenance of colporteurs, or Bible-sellers, wholly under Missionary control. In China, for example, eleven Missionary Societies, of varied Churches and nationalities, have now forty or fifty colporteurs working under their directions, paid by us. But more is needed : Missionaries themselves must take this Bible-selling in hand, and Missionary Societies be asked to contribute towards the cost of colportage as a direct and fruitful branch of their own work. If the Bible Society provides the books, let the Missionary Society provide the seller or distributer, or share the cost. "I have always"—says Mr. Woodall, of the A.M.E. Church at Chung-kiang,— "I have always been interested in selling Scriptures after preaching. To give the people the written Word after they have heard it preached seems to me like clinching the driven nail." Yes, and a nail fastened by the Master of assemblies.

3. *Distribution through Tract Societies.*

In the statesmanlike paper read before the Missionary Conference at Mildmay, in 1878, by the ever-to-be-lamented Charles Reed, the *Value of tracts accompanying the Scriptures.* suggestion was thrown out that the time had almost come for Bible Societies to consider whether their agents might not be allowed to use other Christian literature as a help to the understanding of Scriptures circulated in heathen countries. The National Bible Society of Scotland has, from the beginning, granted its agents this liberty, and to the great advantage of its work. Our colporteurs carry and sell Gospel tracts and books, fitted to introduce, explain, and enforce, the teaching of Holy Scripture. This is not done at the cost of the Bible Society. The Religious Tract Society supplies the tracts or books, and allows a proportion of the proceeds of sale to be applied towards the maintenance of the agent of distribution—to the benefit of both Societies, and of the end contemplated by both.

Is it really honouring to the Bible to insist that it must be issued alone, literally "without note or comment"? Are the oral comments that accom-*"Note and comment," objections.* pany it,—unless only the dumb are to be employed as Bible-women and colporteurs,—are oral comments safe and helpful, and must written comments be dangerous and dishonouring? Is there not a possibility by our traditions of making the Word of God of less effect; and by a rigid interpretation of the "note and comment" rule, doing less honour to the Holy Scriptures than to the prejudices and jealousies of Christian men? As it is there has been, by common consent, a relaxation of the rule which, at one time, was thought to exclude marginal references ; and it is easy to see how readily a comment of a dangerous character might be constructed out of what is now, by a larger interpretation, allowed and welcomed by all. Had the Ethiopian eunuch received a good Gospel tract—I speak with reverence—along with his copy of the roll of the prophet Isaiah, he might not have been in doubt as to whether the prophet spake of himself or of some other man. But the Bible is not a charm, the mere touch of which will work a miracle; and Philip was used to explain Isaiah. As the written Word is not of use to him who cannot read it, neither can it be of use to him who cannot understand it. It is the *entrance* of God's Word that gives light, and shall we not use every fitting means that has been given us, to open the blind eyes that the healing ray may enter in and light up the soul! Rather publish one word with the understanding, than a thousand words which may be to the reader, though apparently in his own tongue, really in a tongue unknown.

The wisdom of this course has been shown by the experience of a quarter of a century, and by the universal testimony of those who have tried our method. The appeal of the Shanghai Conference of 1875 is evidence of the views held by Missionaries *Testimony from* on this question. It urges Bible Societies to supply such *the Mission-field.* explanations as are required to make the Bible, to some extent, at least, self-interpreting to the Chinaman into whose hands it falls for the first time; and, failing our consent, the Missionaries threaten to publish the Bible for themselves. The N.B.S.S. is, I believe, the only Society which has seen its way to respond to this appeal. Our concessions of leave to give an explanatory tract with the Bible, or to include in it marginal references and chapter headings, have not indeed fully satisfied the Missionaries. But, possibly, when their proposals are more clearly understood, they may prove less revolutionary and more feasible than they have seemed to be.

4. Distribution through Local Organisations.

We have always tried to work on the lines of local effort, as tending to a more economical and effective circulation, rather than to multiply agents of our own. Instead of maintaining a large staff of colporteurs in France, for example, we assist *Their* the Evangelical Society of Geneva in its French work. *advantages.* We believe that £1,000 per annum spent in aiding them to maintain fifty men, well organised and equipped, is spent to more advantage than in upholding, say, fifteen local colporteurs. The money does more work and better work. Our plan has the further advantage of drawing forth the sympathy of pastors and people in the various districts touched by agents partly supported by us.

5. Distribution through Voluntary Agencies.

An immense amount of unpaid voluntary labour is rendered in connection with Bible distribution, and may well be gratefully acknowledged here. At home our collectors, committees, and office-bearers, render services, the value of which cannot be *Their services.* estimated; while through other voluntary agencies a large home circulation is effected without cost, save the cost of the books, or a part of it. Many of our foreign correspondents and superintendents, too, discharge duties, important and onerous, without recompense, save the joy of service. Last year a young Scottish merchant was accepted by us as an unpaid agent in China; we sent him out, but he draws no salary from the Society, which would gladly extend its list of such helpers.

6. *Gratuitous Distribution of the Scriptures.*

This question, which has lately obtained considerable prominence, may be briefly looked at. I cannot think any principle makes it right to give away, and wrong to sell, the Bible. We cannot condemn sales because the Scripture commands those who have freely received to freely give. There is an equally authoritative and distinct command forbidding the indiscriminate distribution of precious things. The question is merely as to the wisest methods of attaining the end in view.

The gratuitous distribution of the Scriptures is certainly not preferred by those who have had the fullest opportunities of testing the comparative advantages of the two methods. We have constantly protests against it from those best entitled to speak on the question; and an earnest advocate for this method seems to concede the case when he says, in summing up his appeal: "Sell by all means wherever the people are able and willing to buy. . . . Throughout Protestant Christendom . . . Scriptures should, as a rule, be sold, and given away only to those who are too poor to purchase them." This is just what the Bible Societies do. But why should the advice apply only to Europe? There is not a Missionary in China, so far as I am aware, who does not stand side by side with Mr. Hudson Taylor in condemning the free distribution of the Scriptures, as having brought the Book into disrepute in that Empire, failed in the end in view, and made it difficult now to work on wiser lines.

Experience against gratuitous distribution.

We must not forget that the highest price charged for Scriptures in foreign lands, in rare instances, covers the cost of production, and that, in most countries, the Societies suffer a heavy loss on each copy they sell, so that even the buyer receives a gift.

It must also be borne in mind that, while the proceeds from individual sales are small, in the aggregate, they enormously increase the power of circulation. Last year, for example, the total cost of our circulation was only a fraction over $4\frac{1}{2}d.$ per copy, or $7\frac{3}{4}d.$ for each Bible and New Testament, taking twelve portions as equal to one Testament. If we gave all, we should only have half to give. It would not have furthered the cause of the Gospel if the Aneityumese, who honourably paid the British and Foreign Bible Society £1,200 for Scriptures supplied to them, had been debarred this privilege. Nor would the Bible be more honoured or more read, in any land, were it given to all and sundry, like the handbill thrust on your acceptance in the streets. It is said that we are mistaken in thinking that, because a man buys our book he will value it; that the reverse is true, and it is because he values our book that he buys it. But either way, the bought book is the valued book—which is all we contend for. That sale is so far a guarantee against waste few will be found to deny.

Sale adds to circulation.

I believe the best method comes between the two extremes,—and this is the method of the Bible Societies. We have no rule forbidding the free gift of Scriptures; and there is no Society which does not, on fitting occasion, distribute freely. But to make free gifts the rule is to pauperise the community, without cause, and without ultimate benefit; and to make it impossible to secure the advantages of even occasional sale. The discussion which has been raised by some of the best friends of Bible Societies, will probably serve its end by promoting greater freedom of distribution, in certain

The happy medium.

cases and on certain lines; few well acquainted with the facts would advise Bible Societies to make sale the exception rather than the rule.

I have spoken of the co-operation of Missionary and Tract Societies with Bible Societies, but I confess to a strong desire that the Bible Societies themselves should come closer together. There is probably **Joint action** at this moment, a better understanding among the leading **on the part of** Bible Societies, than at any former time—let us use it for the **Bible Societies.** largest possible practical results—for a more economical division of labour, and a closer agreement as to plans and prices.

It is important that our principles of action should agree in the various fields in which we work side by side. How, for example, are we to deal with countries wholly or mainly Protestant? These have not equal claims with Roman Catholic countries; and neither Protestant nor Catholic countries have claims comparable with those of the millions of heathenism.

Can we agree, for the development of self-help in Protestant countries, to offer there no Scriptures for general sale below cost price? It is the wholesome rule of the N.B.S.S. not to sell in Scotland below cost, while through other channels we make ample provision for the poor. We have no wish to monopolise the Bible trade of our country, or to do with benevolent funds what can be as well done through private enterprise. Could we in like manner agree to refuse to supply Protestant countries below cost, trusting their Churches to meet the wants of the poor, local Bible publishing, which now languishes, might revive, and local Christian efforts be stimulated, while our funds would be set free for use in such lands as India and China, which the next generation of Bible Societies will, I believe, deem to have a prior claim, not only from their appalling need, but from their rising importance among the nations which sway the destinies of the world.

Such action cannot be taken without concert. Other cognate questions, such as those formulated in Dr. Cust's letter of 31st May, which came to my hand after this Paper was in form, might well be discussed by a Pan-Biblical Council;—questions **A Pan-Biblical** relating to the production and sharing of versions, the **Council.** interchange of Scriptures, the possibility, by joint agents and common work, of reducing overlapping and friction to a minimum, while preserving to each Society the variety without which its interest would flag. In the discussion of questions like these, a beginning has been made by Bible Society Conferences within this Conference; but we need a great Missionary and Bible Society Clearing House, with autocratic powers, before we can hope to solve them all.

The romance that once attached to Bible Society work has largely passed away, and it is now but one of many Missionary agencies, pleading for the sympathy and help of the **Conclusion.** Church. But we believe there is no higher, truer, more practical, or more beneficent Missionary work, than that done by the Bible Societies : work in which there is less of man and more of God. May the prominent place given to it in this Conference increase its effectiveness, by deepening the interest of the Church, and evoking anew its prayers and enthusiasm on behalf of this grand means of making salvation known by the world-wide dissemination of the Word of the living God, in the mother-tongue of every tribe and people !

Dr. Maxwell gave the summary of a Paper by the **Rev. John Gibson**, of the English Presbyterian Mission in Swatow.

[*This Paper, which was not in the programme, is of such intrinsic value that we give the greater part of it in small type in the Appendix, to avoid spoiling the argument by too great abridgment.—Ed.*]

DISCUSSION.

Mr. E. H. Glenny (Hon. Sec., North African Mission): We have in North Africa a similar difficulty to that experienced in China. We have the North African Arabic spoken ; and a very large number of people, even those who can read the Arabic into which the Bible is translated, A translation needed for North Africa. cannot understand it ; they can read the words because the characters are the same, but do not understand their meaning ; and we feel sure that sooner or later we must have a translation into the Arabic of North Africa. I know there is a great deal of prejudice against it, but, although we have not yet had much experience, from the consultations we have had with Missionaries, and the colporteurs and agents of the Bible Society, we feel sure that we must come ultimately to a translation into the colloquial of North Africa. As to the distribution, I would ask that the Missionaries be allowed a sufficient grant of Scriptures that they may distribute them freely where they think it wise to do so,— not wholesale, but whenever a favourable opportunity is presented. Further, Character of colporteurs. I would suggest that those who are engaged as colporteurs should be chosen not so much on the ground of their selling powers as on account of their spirituality. I believe the difficulties lie more in this point than anywhere else. The man wants to sell as many books as he can ; and knows that his sales will be compared with those of other men, and in his anxiety may recommend his books in such a way that the buyer may purchase without knowing their true character, or think that they will act as a charm ; and when he finds that he has purchased a Gospel, insists upon it that he has been deceived, and so the agent has done actual damage by his selling. I know it is not the wish of the Societies that it should be so, but I have known such a case. I do not believe that the man had any intention of doing what was wrong ; but it shows the importance of seeing that the man who carries the book should himself be a living representative of the book he sells, otherwise the effect will be rather damaging than helpful. I do feel the great need of a much wider distribution of the Word of God.

Rev. Fr. Ziegler (Basle Missionary Society) : I want to say a few words with respect to the translation of the Bible. I have had great pleasure in listening to what has been said about the importance of Translations accurate but idiomatic. accurate translations, and I agree with every word that has been said on that point. But I wish to implore every one who has to do with the translation of the Bible and with Bible Societies to let the translations be intelligible and idiomatic.

Let me give you a few instances of what too close an adherence to the letter of the Bible may produce. Let me give you the English translation of the Canarese as it runs in the text, John iii. 16 : "In order that all who believe in Him not being lost should receive eternal life that God gave His only-begotten Son He so loved the world." Now I put it to you whether that is intelligible. I say it is not intelligible to the natives; and I know it, because I have had to do with school children who had to learn the text, and who could never understand it. There is a beautiful text in Isaiah, "Though your sins be as scarlet they shall be as white as wool." Now the majority of the sheep among the Canarese are black, and a literal translation of the passage therefore would be unintelligible. I once heard a catechist expound the text, "Let the word of Christ abide in you richly," as meaning "Let the word of Christ abide in you as your riches;" and he was quite right according to the Canarese translation. The word "richly" was taken too literally. It was forgotten that, although "richly" in English means abundantly, it has not the same meaning in Canarese. The translation should be as close as possible, but it should be intelligible. The closeness should never interfere with intelligibility. Never forget to read what you have translated to the natives,—not to those who have been instructed in your schools, and therefore know the drift of your thought, but to the heathen ; and take care to ask them what the meaning of it is.

Mr. John Archibald (National Bible Society of Scotland, from Hankow): Before I mention the subject on which I wish to speak, I should like to say, in reply to Dr. Maxwell, that I have been engaged in getting a large quantity of printing machinery from a house in London, and the manager said to me, "What do you want with such a lot of printing machinery for Hankow?" I said, "There are so many newspapers started, and there is so much printing going on; the Chinese are reading right and left; they have newspapers in Canton, in Shanghai, in Tien-tsin, and all over the country, pouring out from the press every morning, besides thousands of books that are circulated among the people."

Demand for printing machines in China.

It is one of the most difficult questions to deal with. I heard one speaker in this Conference say that not 5 per cent. of the Chinese could read, while another said that 90 per cent. could read. Again, one stated that Chinese is so difficult that it is impossible to read it in Chinese characters, and that the letters must be Romanised ; while another said it was so easy that a European who does not know Chinese can learn to read it in six or seven months. But that is not the question that I wish to address myself to—a question about which in China we have no dispute whatever. Eleven years ago at Shanghai there was a Conference and this question came up : recognising the great importance of the circulation of the Word of God, is it possible to do anything to render that circulation more effective? The Missionaries unanimously came to the conclusion that if we had liberty to circulate explanatory tracts along with the Scriptures, and also liberty to use annotated editions of the Scriptures, the circulation would be much more valuable. You have to consider that in China there are two classes of people amongst whom the Scriptures circulate, those who are under Christian instruction, and know something about the Bible, and then (which we have almost entirely in China) a great reading nation who have never heard of the Bible, and never met a Missionary, except perhaps the man who first introduced a copy of the Scriptures, and whom they may never meet again. There is nothing to show these people what the Bible is, what it claims to be, where it was issued, and what it is about ; and the man who has it cannot make it out. What we want is more means of telling the people what it is. Then there is another thing : Chinese is a very bad vehicle for conveying Christian truth at all. Those who have translation work to do, know that it is im-

An annotated Bible wanted.

The Bible misunderstood.

possible to put Christian ideas into heathen tongues without some explanation. The very term "God" they have no idea of, and whatever words you use for it give a wrong impression. So with regard to grace, mercy, and other things; if you simply translate those words you do not convey the truth, but you convey something which is not the truth. Therefore we require further explanations. An application was sent home to the Bible Board to this effect: a number of learned men sat round the table, and they considered the applications, and after a great deal of consultation, they came to the conclusion that there might be maps, and chapter headings, and tables of weights and measures, so that the Chinese might know the length of a cubit and the value of a shekel, but nothing further. Why is that? The Bible Societies are bound to circulate the Scriptures without note or comment, and they are not at liberty to do this thing for us. I know that the directors did not make the rule (it was not made for foreign countries), and that they cannot alter it without a tremendous storm. But we can enlighten the Christian public, and that is my main object in speaking to you to-day, to let it be seen that you may safely trust us to make comments, and to use explanatory literature, just as you trust the Religious Tract Society, with the best results. At present we are often putting the light into a horn lantern, which rather obscures it. What we want is liberty to thin out the horn till it gets translucent, and then more of the light will come through.

Rev. Thomas Richardson (Bible and Prayer Union): I was awakened, but I did not find Christ till I read my Bible personally. The chapter which is being read to-day by a quarter of a million of people says, "It is written;" and we find that Christ quotes from Moses, from the prophets, and from the Psalms, in each case referring as it were to the book. That

The Bible alone. is the only apology which I have to present for venturing to say a word to this Conference. I am personally deeply interested in almost every Missionary agency in the world, and interested in many places where Missionaries have not yet reached, and yet the Word of God is being read without a preacher; and taking the year round there is hardly a day when I do not hear from some part of the earth that there is some man or woman who has found help in the reading of the Word. We can do nothing in Bible reading without the written Word; we fall back upon that.

Rev. Principal Brown, D.D. (Free Church College, Aberdeen): Three minutes will enable me to tell two stories which will illustrate the remarks of the last speaker. One of them is ancient, the other modern.

In the last persecution of the pagans against the Christian Church there was in the Privy Council of the Emperor an apostate Christian. They were

First order to considering how best to crush Christianity out of the Roman
burn the Bible. Empire, and, said this apostate, "It is of no use to burn the Christians, for if you burn every Christian alive to-day, and leave a single copy of the Scriptures remaining the Christian Church will spring up again to-morrow." Accordingly the Emperor issued a decree ordering the destruction of the Scriptures. They did not succeed in their object. The sequel is an interesting one, but I have no time to tell it. Next I remember our dear old friend, Dr. Moffat, telling in my hearing a remarkable story. "I was wandering," he said, "with my party in an out-of-the-way part of Bechuanaland, when in the twilight, having fallen short of provisions, we came to a village and asked to be supplied, offering in exchange buttons and all manner of things which they liked; but they would not give us anything. After trying in vain we went away to a little hill where there were a few clumps of trees and were making a shake down for the night. When we were doing this a woman approached us with something on her head; and at

last she came into our presence and laid down a jar full of milk. We asked her what induced her to do this, but we received no answer; and she went away in silence. After some time the woman returned, A Bible in a and, to our astonishment, she had brought with her a pot with heathen village. the leg of some animal, and a bundle of sticks to kindle a fire with. Without saying a word she began to lay the sticks and kindle the fire, and then she put the pot on it. We then insisted on her telling us what could have induced her to do this. At last she broke silence, and said, ' Oh! when you do so much for that Master who has done everything for me, it is a very small matter for me to do this for you.' We now said, ' How is it that in this heathen village you come to be in this condition; and how can you keep the the flame alive without a Christian near you?' With tears she pulled out of her dress a Dutch Testament, and explained that when she was a little girl she was sent away some two hundred miles to the Cape to a Christian school, and that for her success in the class she was in she got this New Testament as a prize. 'And that,' she added, 'is what keeps the oil burning within me.' Oh, friends, the Church of Rome says that it gives us the Scriptures; but that apostate Christian thought the Scriptures give the Church. Nothing is to me a greater satisfaction than this afternoon meeting which tells us through so many voices, and from so many lands, that the Word of God is life to the soul.

Rev. J. Murray Mitchell, LL.D. (Free Church of Scotland): Some say that the Bible is to be read by the Church, and that it is not to be used as a means of making known the Gospel to the heathen. Our experience in India differs from that. I have known some Missionaries who said they decidedly preferred a Gospel to a tract; they found that it told more upon the heathen than even the best-written tract. Of course Select portions certain portions should be chosen. I have seen a man give for distribution. Ezekiel or Leviticus to a native who knew nothing of the Gospel. That was unwise. But the Gospels, the Acts of the Apostles, the Proverbs, Genesis, and part of Exodus,—the very books that have been mentioned this afternoon,—are welcomed even by the uninstructed heathen.

Often the educated heathen read the Bible in secret. They are not Christians; but their whole system of religious thought is steadily forming itself upon the blessed Word of God. I was struck the other day by a distinguished man among the Parsis saying, "We believe in the same God as is presented in the Old Testament, with all His sublime attributes." Only he had supplemented the Parsi doctrine, though perhaps unconsciously. Thus it is that the Heathen systems are, in consequence of the Bible as much as in consequence of anything else, gradually reforming themselves on Christianity. Among the Oriental Christians the circulation of the Scriptures is fitted to do a world of good. So among the Mohammedans.

The mere reading of the Bible does good; but when you have a Bible-woman to go into the Indian homes and lovingly read it, and explain it according to her own heart-felt experience, it tells immensely in all our Indian Zenanas.

One word more. Mohammed seems never to have known the Bible. Why was there not, by his time, a translation into Arabic? What was the Church of Christ about? Again, the Nestorian Missions in China were most noble Missions; there were none nobler in the history of the Evil of not Church. But they were all swept away. Why? I believe it was, giving the Bible. largely, in consequence of their not having the Bible translated into the language of the people. Let us by all means persevere in the blessed work of spreading the Word of God far and wide.

Rev. James Kennedy (L.M.S., late of Benares): We have heard much to-day about the connection between Missions and the Bible Society. To my mind Missionary Societies and Bible Societies are like the Siamese twins. If you kill the one you kill the other; the two have a common life. And the Tract Society is closely connected with them. They are a threefold cord that cannot be broken; they must be bound together in order that the work may be efficiently carried on.

I had the honour of taking a subordinate part in the translations into Urdu and Hindi, and in both cases we were closely associated with natives, from whom we derived great assistance; indeed, without that assistance the work cannot be done. The work of revision is now being carried on, and there is a great deal of discussion over it,—sometimes not very pleasant discussion. Alas! the " I " comes in too often with us Missionaries as well as with you at home. We all have the best motives, but now and then there is a great difference of opinion. You would be surprised if you knew the immense amount of discussion that sometimes takes place. It all comes from the desire to have the best possible translation of the Word of God, so that the whole earth may be filled with the glory of the Lord.

The Doxology was then sung.

APPENDIX.

BY THE REV. JOHN C. GIBSON, M.A. (English Presbyterian Mission, Swatow, China).

How best are the people of South China to get the Word of God in their own tongues?

The number of readers in China may be set down as certainly under ten per cent. of the men and one per cent. of the women, Number of giving a total not exceeding 12,375,000 readers in all. Dr. readers in China. Martin, of Pekin, states the case even more strongly than I venture to do :—

" We hear it asserted that 'education is universal in China ; even coolies are taught to read and write.' In one sense this is true, but not as we understand 'reading and writing.' In the alphabetical vernaculars of the West the ability to read and write implies the ability to express one's thoughts by the pen, and to grasp the thoughts of others when so expressed. In Chinese, and especially in the classical or book language, it implies nothing of the sort. A shopkeeper may be able to write the numbers and keep accounts without being able to write anything else ; and a lad who has attended school for several years will pronounce the characters of an ordinary book with faultless precision, yet not comprehend the meaning of a single sentence. Of those who can read understandingly (and nothing else ought to be called reading), the proportion is greater in towns than in rural districts. But striking an average, it does not, according to my observation, exceed one in twenty for the male sex, and one in ten thousand for the female."[*]

This estimate by Dr. Martin reduces the number of readers to 5,737,000, or under six millions, and I am not prepared to say that is too low.

The book language is not spoken in any part of China. The few who can read, therefore, read as it were in a foreign tongue, and translate as they go into their own vernacular. It is through this process of extempore

[*] "The Chinese : Their Education, Philosophy, and Letters." By W. A. P. Martin, D.D., LL.D., President of the Lung-wen College, Pekin.

translation from the book language into the local vernacular that the Scriptures reach our people in the Christian congregations. Each preacher gives his own rendering, and gives it anew and with variations at each service he holds. There is, therefore, no security for accuracy, and there is no fixity in the version of the Bible that reaches the people. **The book language unspoken.**

We cannot, therefore, reach the millions of China by one version of the Scriptures. They must be translated into all the vernaculars before we shall be able to say that the people have the Word of God in their own tongue.

There is a vernacular literature for Northern and Western China in the so-called "Mandarin Colloquial." This is quite distinct from the book language, and when read aloud as it stands printed it is understood without translation in those districts where Mandarin is the spoken vernacular. But it is not understood in the southern half of China, and there the only literary vehicle at present available is the book language with all its drawbacks.

In Southern China we must count at least the following six languages, namely, the vernaculars of Foochow, Amoy (used also in Formosa), Swatow, Canton, Hainan, and of the Hak-ka districts.

Further north there are other vernaculars differing more or less from the Mandarin, such as those of Ningpo and Shanghai; but I limit myself to the vernaculars of Southern China, of which I can speak with some personal knowledge.

These Southern dialects, with one exception, have not been reduced to writing by the Chinese. In Cantonese there is a native vernacular literature, but the other vernaculars of Southern China have not been written by the Chinese. Now my contention is that, inasmuch as these Southern vernaculars are the mother tongues of over thirty millions of people in the aggregate, we ought to have the Word of God and a Christian literature translated into each of them. This is vitally essential to the spirital life and nourishment of the Christian Church now growing up here. **Vernaculars of China.**

But these vernaculars, in which it is so needful to have a Christian literature, are almost wholly unwritten languages; and in some cases, as in that of Amoy, native scholars pronounce it impossible to write them in the Chinese written character.

What then is the solution of the difficulty? How can we lay hold of these unwritten vernaculars, write them down, and so form a literary vehicle on which we may convey to those who speak them the Word of God in their own tongues?

This is the question which I propose to answer now. The problem is how best to write a spoken langugage so that the whole body of the people may with least difficulty learn to read and write. **The question and answer.**

The answer I would offer is that the object in view is best accomplished by using our own Roman letters to write down phonetically the sounds of the Chinese vernaculars; *i.e.*, by the use of what is commonly called Romanised vernacular.

Not to speak of Europe, the problem has been solved in this way in Fiji, Samoa, Madagascar, and in the languages of Southern and Central Africa by the use of the Roman alphabet. The unwritten languages of barbarous tribes have been thus fixed, and a literature produced. Where two generations back there were only untaught savages, we have now instructed Christian peoples, who have bought up by the fruits of their own labour one edition after another of the Old and New Testaments, and who have a considerable Christian literature besides. The result is that among these once despised peoples the Christian Church is, in point of ability for self-edification by means of reading, in advance of the Church of this land of old literary renown. Those who were last have become first, and the Chinese, whose civilisation and apparent education seemed likely to give them the first place, are in danger of being found among the last.

When we come to China we find ourselves surrounded by a people who have already a written language. Its picturesque symbols meet the eye not only in books but on every signboard and doorway, where they relieve agreeably the grimy aspect of the streets and houses. To the new-comer this language seems to be everywhere present, and he fancies it must be everywhere understood. As we have seen, however, it is widely separated from the language of the people.

But our first inquiry is, Can the Chinese written language be adapted to express the spoken vernacular of the people?

Can Chinese character express vernaculars?   In the Mandarin speaking districts of the North and West it has been so adapted, and the native written character supplies symbols by which all the words in ordinary use can be written. In Southern China a similar adaptation of the Chinese character has been made for the Cantonese dialect. Elsewhere but little has been done in this way by native hands, and a large part of the vernacular speech consists of vocables for which no characters exist.

In Swatow and in the Hak-ka districts, as well as in Canton, efforts have been made by Missionaries to write the local vernaculars in Chinese characters. Books produced in this form are called " Character Colloquial."

The difficulty arising from lack of characters to represent many of the words is evaded in two ways. *First,* by avoiding the use of many of these words and choosing forms of expression approaching more nearly to the book language than the current vernacular. *Second,* by making new characters to represent words for which no characters exist in recognised usage.

The first of these expedients is manifestly unsatisfactory. It hampers *Attempts fail.* the writer, and instead of using the free mother-tongue of the people he is betrayed into a hybrid style which is neither good literature nor good vernacular.

The second is no better, leading to the multiplication of the characters whose excessive numbers are already an intolerable burden to the reader. These made characters, moreover, are not to be found in any native dictionary, and rest on the sole authority of the writer who invents them.

It will be remembered that a reader of the Chinese written language is confronted with two great difficulties. First, he must learn to read the sounds of the characters ; secondly, having done so, he must learn to translate the text into his own vernacular. Now this latter difficulty is removed by the use of " Character Colloquial." The words and forms of expression used are, with the exception noted above, those of the local vernacular, and if the reader learns the sounds of the characters, as intended by the writer, he can understand the meaning and does not need to go through the process of translation.

But the former difficulty is untouched. It is as difficult as ever to learn the sound of each character ; and the number of characters in each sentence is greatly increased. Many are used also in forced or unnatural ways, and not a few are not to be found in Chinese dictionaries.

I say nothing against this system, or any other which removes one obstacle from the way of people whom we desire to teach to read the Word of life. But it removes only one obstacle, and offers but a very imperfect solution of the problem with which we set out.

Is there then a better way of reducing to writing the vernaculars of South China? I believe there is. The Roman alphabet has been used for this *Use of the Roman alphabet.* purpose, and it has now been tried with great practical success. In the alphabet thus used, each letter has but one fixed sound, in which it is always read. In this way every sound that is heard in the speech of the people can be written down. Only nineteen letters and seven accents are required to represent all the sounds and tones of the Swatow dialect. The simplicity of the method may be seen from the following specimen :—

Goán ê Pē tì thin-nih, goán lí ê miâ tsòe sèng ; lí ê Kok lìm-kàu, etc., etc., etc.

I will note briefly some of the advantages of this system.

1. Every sound heard in the language can be spelled by a simple combination of letters, averaging three letters to the word, and in no case exceeding seven letters to one word.

2. The spelling is strictly phonetic, and each letter has only one sound. Any one who knows the nineteen letters and the seven accents has therefore complete command of the system, and can read anything he sees, or write down anything he hears or thinks. Four advantages of its use.

3. The writer of a book in this system has not to consider whether a word can be written or not. All words can be written with ease, and he is therefore free to use the purest vernacular as it would flow from the lips of any good speaker of the language.

4. Reading and spelling are much more easily learned than in English. It has been found that a very moderate degree of attention to the system for three months is sufficient to give any one, however untutored before, the power of reading any book printed in it.

A similar "Románised vernacular" system has been largely used in the Amoy Missions, and still more largely in Formosa, where the same language is spoken and the same books can be used. The experience gained there and elsewhere abundantly proves that in this method we have the means of making the whole body of Chinese Christians a reading people.

By the use of the Chinese book language this is absolutely impossible. For certainly over a thousand years a system of public examinations for admission to Government service has applied an extraordinarily keen and constant stimulus to the study of the Chinese written language in every part of the Empire. Yet with every advantage the result is the utter failure to produce a reading people, which we see to-day. In a country which imagines itself to be the one literary country upon earth, and which contains a population of three hundred millions, there are not thirteen millions of readers ; or, if we take the estimate of Dr. Martin, not six millions. Chinese characters only for the few.

This result is not surprising. The Chinese written language is undoubtedly extremely difficult. It can be acquired only by a literary caste, or those who can afford to begin in early youth, and to continue through life a sustained course of hard study.

A boy goes to school, and in three years or so learns to repeat "by heart "— i.e., without any heart at all—a series of books, containing in all some four thousand characters. He does not know all these characters. He has only learned to repeat the sounds of the books in which they occur ; but if he were shown the characters one by one separated from the context, there are probably hundreds of them which he could not recognise.

But he labours under a still more serious disadvantage—one almost inconceivable to any Western observer of his labours during these years. After all his efforts he yet knows nothing of the meaning of the books he has read. If you ask him to read, he will recite a portion ; and it makes little difference whether the book is open before him or not. In either case he is really repeating from memory. He gives, of course, the sounds of the book language, and if you then ask him to give the meaning in his own language, he will say, "I don't know ; I have not learned to translate."

At this stage, if not earlier, most boys in the ordinary ranks of life leave school. If the boy becomes a farmer, his slight acquaintance with books rapidly fades, until he reaches the condition described in the proverbial saying :—

"On white paper you write black letters ;
They may know me, but I don't know them !"

If he is seen looking at a book or a placard on the walls, he is liable to be chaffed with the saying, "Sweet potatoes ! six cash a pound !" which is meant to convey the suggestion that he cannot distinguish a character from a potato ; or, as we say, "Doesn't know a B from a bull's foot."

If he goes into business and becomes a shopkeeper, a small number of the characters whose partial acquaintance he has made become serviceable to him in keeping accounts. Numerals, and the names of the goods special to his trade, become familiar to him, so that he is able to note transactions and make out his bills. But any book or document Results of education.

outside of this limited range is to him an untrodden wilderness. His education enables him to conduct his business, and avoid the fate of the two heroes of a popular story. These two could not read nor write: one sold timber, the other sold sugar candy, and in an evil hour they entered into partnership. Each was in the habit of noting his sales by making a long stroke in his book for each stick sold. All seemed to go well till the end of the year, when it was found that the books had got mixed. It was plain, indeed, that so many sticks had been sold; but how many were of timber and how many of sugar-candy could never be ascertained; and the partnership was broken up in disastrous confusion!

Tradesmen who have some leisure often employ it in reading plays, novels, and such books, and it is from this class that the small percentage of readers in the ordinary walks of life is drawn. Those who really master the written character, so as to read and write it with readiness, are the men who make books a profession. Early and late they toil at their studies, reading aloud, and practising the writing of essays on which success in the public examinations depends. Year after year they go up for examination, and literally devote their lives to acquiring the art of reading and writing. The constant application required is set forth in the saying, "If for three days you neglect to read, your mouth will grow a whin-bush."

Now it is manifest that people who have to work for their bread, as happily most of our Christians do, can never learn to read on these terms. To many of them, too, the Gospel comes comparatively late in life, when even a very moderate acquisition of the book language is impossible to them.

Some do try, but with scant success, and though we urge all to do what they can, what can we say to people who go to their fields at sunrise, and return at sunset, stiff, and weary, and sleepy from a hard day's toil, to homes where the gloom is only slightly broken by a flickering, smoky, rushlight? They have their holidays, and their hours of leisure; above all the Christians have the blessed rest of one day in seven which the Gospel has brought them; but these times are too scant for the sustained effort that is needed to acquire the Chinese written character.

Disadvantage to Christians.

When we visit the country Mission stations we often in the evenings have a few of those who live near join us for evening worship. We often try to read in turn, "verse about," and it is a constant pain to wait for the slow, halting effort to make out the sounds of the characters. When this has been stumbled through, you say, "Now translate;" and the request generally comes, "Teacher, you please translate for me." Meantime, so much time and effort have been spent on the verse in hand that the previous one has been forgotten, and the connection lost. One is most painfully divided between the desire to encourage even these halting efforts to learn to read, and the desire to let these poor people taste for once the sweetness of God's Word by reading it continuously and intelligibly to them.

Among a people like this one should never lose patience, and yet it seems high time for some wholesome impatience in this matter of reading. I believe it is almost impossible for Christians at home to realise how little knowledge of God's Word there is among the native Christians here. I doubt whether there is any other part of the Christian Church where so few can read as in the Church of China. In the nation the Chinese character has had a fair trial for over two thousand years. In the Church it has been tried now through the lifetime of one generation. It is high time that we frankly recognised that, as a means of reaching the great bulk of our Church members, the Chinese book language has been a complete and conspicuous failure. I do not mean that the Church is worse in this respect than the rest of the people. I have no doubt that in point of education the Church as a whole stands rather higher than those in the same ranks of life outside. But to be only a little better is to fail. In the Church we must never be content to see one in ten of the men and one in a hundred of the women able to read. Even that would be an advance upon our present position; but we must have every

The Bible sealed to Chinese Christians.

man, woman, and child, who is not prevented by age or by infirmity, taught to read in their own tongue.

I believe there is one way, and one only, in which it can be done. It can be done by reducing their mother tongues to writing in the simple symbols of the Roman alphabet. "We must," writes a German Missionary, "find a means to make our Christians Bible Christians. The means for this, I find," he adds, "in the introduction of the Romanised Bible." *The remedy.*

I have already pointed out some of the advantages of using our alphabet for writing the sounds of spoken Chinese. Let us look at it again from another point of view.

All methods of writing fall into one or other of two classes :—
1. The Hieroglyphic or Ideographic.
2. The Alphabetic or Phonetic. *Two methods of writing.*

Were it not for misleading associations connected with the word, ' phonographic" would describe the latter class more exactly than " phonetic."

1. The former class—the Hieroglyphic—was probably the earliest, being based on the use of pictures to represent ideas. It includes the picture hieroglyphs of the Egyptian and other ancient monuments, the picture writing of the American Indians and the ancient Mexicans, and the characters of the Chinese book language. The last of these constitute by far the most ingenious, elaborate, and complete of all Hieroglyphic systems. Like the others, it began by taking pictures to represent objects, and such words as man, sun, moon, mountain, tree, fish, horse, etc., were written in the form of a small outline sketch of the object intended. Upon these were built up others to express abstract ideas, as the sun and moon put together represent brightness ; a tree with the sun seen through it represents the East, where the sun appears on the horizon shining through the branches. Finally, as in the Egyptian hieroglyphics, the idea was reached of using some of these pictures phonetically, *i.e.*, of using them to represent other words of like sound without regard to the original meaning of the picture, a mark being generally added to indicate this phonetic use. *Hieroglyphic language.*

These principles have given us the ample stores of the Chinese characters, of which some six thousand are in common use, and not less than forty thousand are to be found in the standard dictionary. Every word has a separate character, many single characters requiring from fifteen to thirty strokes of the pen in writing.

On this part of the subject it only remains to remark that a Hieroglyphic system, of which class the Chinese book language is the most perfect representative, has never produced a reading people. There has never been a period in any country where a people has learned to read and use a hieroglyphic system of writing. *Never made a reading people.*

The difficulty is not to be overcome by increased attention to education, nor by better educational methods. The conditions under which most men in all countries earn their bread put the acquisition of such elaborate systems beyond their reach. No people has ever learned such a system, and it is safe to prophesy that no people ever will.

2. Let us turn now to the other class of written systems—the Phonetic, or, as we may call it for practical purposes, the Alphabetic. This includes all the languages of the civilised world, and all the great literatures, with the single exception of the Chinese. The Alphabetic system seized on the profound and yet simple thought that, while ideas are innumerable, the sounds by which they are represented are very few, and are due to a small number of positions and movements of the organs of speech. The Alphabetic system fastened on these few elementary sounds, and with its twenty or thirty symbols enables us to write with precision, and to read easily all the infinite variety of thought and expression in all forms of human speech. *Advantages of the Alphabetic.*

What has now been said enables us to come back again to the question with which we set out, better prepared to estimate the conditions of a satisfactory answer to it.

If we are to reduce to writing the unwritten vernaculars of South China and to teach all classes of the Christian people to read them, all experience shows that we must make use of an Alphabetic system. The problem has never been solved in any other way, and it has been solved in this way over and over again for every fresh language with which Christianity has had to deal in its progress over the globe.

Of the three hundred and twenty-five languages into which the Bible has been translated, all, except the Chinese, are written alphabetically. The British and Foreign Bible Society has published specimens from two hundred and sixty-seven of the versions published by them, and of these no fewer than one hundred and twenty-eight are written in the Roman alphabet. If an alphabet is to be used there can be no doubt that the Roman is the simplest and the clearest. It is also that in which there is at command the largest and least costly supply of printing material.

Are there any objections to its use?

[We greatly regret that our space precludes us from giving more than the heads of these objections. They are ably met by argument and illustration.—ED.]

Five objections. 1. There is a strong prejudice among the Chinese—not against the Roman letters, but in favour of the Chinese characters. Prejudices are rapidly giving way.

2. The idea has been expressed that by translating the Scriptures into the Romanised vernacular we may "vulgarise the Bible." This objection I am not much concerned to answer. Chinese native scholars have told me that we vulgarise the Gospel by preaching it to the unlearned and in the vernacular. But this complaint is not likely to weigh much with us. We long to vulgarise the Bible in the true sense of the word, by making it familiar to all in the vulgar tongue.

3. It is sometimes said that the use of Romanised vernacular will hinder Missionaries from learning the Chinese character. If this were true one might still say, "Be it so! better let fifty Missionaries run this risk, if risk there be, than keep a people in ignorance because you fear that the means of their enlightenment may become a snare to dull and lazy Missionaries. Missionaries are made for the Church, not the Church for the Missionaries.

4. Another objection sometimes made against the use of Romanised vernacular is, that the use of a foreign method of writing gives a foreign aspect to our religious teaching. So does the employment of Foreign Missionaries,—but we have to strike a balance of advantage.

5. The last objection I will mention is the one which will perhaps be felt of greater weight than any other. It is said that a book in the Romanised vernacular of any district can only reach that limited region in which the dialect is spoken, whereas a book in the general book language reaches the whole of the eighteen provinces, and outlying countries besides. I have already pointed out that the book language, after its two thousand years of probation, reaches the eighteen provinces only in a fictitious sense. It reaches a small minority of the people,—less than thirteen millions, perhaps less than six millions, scattered throughout these wide regions,—but does not really reach the bulk of the people at all. On the other hand, each of these vernaculars is spoken by several millions of people; and the Church of Christ, which is already gathering in these millions as His disciples, aims at the same time at making them all readers of His Gospel.

The essence of the argument can be very briefly stated. It falls into a few simple propositions.

1. The bulk of the Chinese people cannot read their book language, and **The quintessence of the argument.** experience shows us that from the nature of the case they never will.

2. No people have ever learned to read except : vernacular.

3. The Christian Church must teach all its members to read (unless disabled by age or infirmity), and must therefore use the vernaculars.

4. No people has ever learned a Hieroglyphic system, and the native written character, being of this class, is too cumbrous to be made the medium for writing the vernaculars of South China.

5. The Roman alphabet gives an easy and complete solution of the difficulty, and experience has shown that even uneducated people easily learn to read and write their mother-tongue by means of it.

If these few propositions are true, as I have tried to show they are, our duty is plain.

MEETINGS OF MEMBERS
IN SECTION.

FOURTEENTH SESSION.

THE MISSIONARY IN RELATION TO LITERATURE.

(3) TRACT AND BOOK SOCIETIES.

(a) Tract and Book Societies as auxiliaries of the Missionary.
(b) How can religious literature, and general literature on a religious basis, be best provided for the growing wants of the Mission-fields of the world ?

(Monday morning, June 18th, in the Annexe.)

Col. and Hon. G. W. Williams, LL.D. (Washington, U.S.A.), in the chair.
Acting Secretary, Rev. G. S. Green, D.D.

Rev. E. Van Orden offered prayer.

The Chairman: It is only within comparatively recent times that the Christian Church in its efforts to evangelise the world has laid hold upon the Christian Press, and has organised and established Book and Tract Publication Societies in order to scatter the Word of God and auxiliary literature among the peoples of the earth, who thus far have not had the advantages which we enjoy in more highly civilised countries. Therefore we cannot over-estimate the importance of a discussion of this character, which leads us along the line of a desire to utilise every force and every power and every agency of Christian civilisation in order to scatter the light of the Gospel of the Son of God.

The Bible, of course, is the first thing to claim our consideration. It is not the sun nor the moon nor the stars, it is not Shakespeare, it is not Bacon, it is not the great poems of the literature of Pagan or Christian times, of mediæval or modern history, but it is the

The Bible supreme. Bible, revealing the Lord and Saviour Jesus Christ, that has done more to enlighten men, to give them an extended intellectual horizon than anything else in the world. More potent than armies, grasping the farthest bounds of civilisation, more effectual than navies, overshadowing the oceans of the earth, whenever the Gospel scheme has been proclaimed and scattered there light and there civilisation have begun. And I conceive that it is our duty as Christians to see to it that the Gospel of the Son of God shall be placed in the hands of the people to whom we go as Missionaries. I have listened with deep interest to many of the discussions which have taken place in this Conference. I have hung with rapt attention upon the earnest and inspired lips of Missionaries who are fresh from their respective fields of labour, and have been thrilled by the pathetic stories which they have told of the work Its power in of Christ in the hearts of the heathen. But I conceive evangelisation. that there is one thought which ought to have a place in our hearts above all other thoughts in this Conference, and that is the power of the Word of God, attended by earnest preaching and by prayer, as an agency for the evangelisation of the world.

Now, friends, while not trenching upon the time allowed to those who are to follow me, I have just a word to offer in reference to the character of Christian literature. Every man of letters will agree with me at once that the great products of literature, the great works of poetry, and the great creations of literary effort owe their influence, almost directly, to the Christian religion ; that they have borrowed its light, and that they shine in the borrowed light from the Word of God.

It seems to me that the one idea that we ought to keep before our minds in the distribution of religious literature is to preach Christ to the people through that literature, and to hold up the Bible as the sum total of all Christian effort as the rule of practice of our Christian conduct, and if we keep these ideas before us, it seems to me that we can use these Book and Publication Societies for the advancement and promotion of the Master's kingdom.

PAPER.

1. By Mr. John Murdoch, LL.D. (Christian Vernacular Education Society for India, Madras). Read by Mr. Henry Morris.

The Missionary in Relation to Literature.

The above subject may be viewed from different standpoints. The following remarks are chiefly intended to show the importance of literature, and how it may best be aided by Missionary Societies.

Evangelistic agencies may be classed under three main heads— preaching, education, and literature. The foremost place must be assigned to the living voice. In some Missionary fields, Evangelistic as in most parts of the dark continent, it is at first the agencies. only instrument that can be employed. Without readers, books are of no more use than spectacles to the blind. On the other hand, in countries like India and China, with a copious literature of their own, and where education has made some progress, the press becomes of great importance.

There is no antagonism between the three agencies : they are mutually helpful. Interest is best awakened by personal contact with the preacher; education gives the ability to read; while any impression produced may be preserved and deepened by the printed page.

No antagonism.

Though the influence of books is generally much less than that of the voice, they have the advantage of being able to be multiplied indefinitely, while preachers are comparatively few. Paul's address at Athens was heard only by a limited number : in its written form it has instructed countless millions, and will do so till the end of time.

While the relative value of some agencies may increase, under altered circumstances that of others may diminish.

Before the establishment of the Indian universities, Missionary colleges might teach any subject they pleased; now the all-absorbing desire of the students is to pass the prescribed examinations. It is not argued that Missions should withdraw from education; but there is the more reason why they should seek to influence those who have passed through their colleges and schools when the pressure of examinations has been removed.

Education.

Evangelistic agencies, it is evident, should be adjusted to the circumstances of each country. More or less prominence should be given to literature according to the number of readers and the demand for books.

Literature.

The following Paper refers specially to India. The arrangement mainly follows the heads given in the programme of the first meeting.*

I. *The growing importance of Christian literature in India.*

This will appear from two reasons :—

1. *The spread of education.*—Indigenous schools have existed in India from time immemorial. One of the earliest efforts of Ziegenbalg was to establish schools, an example subsequently followed by all Protestant Missions. The total numbers under instruction in Mission schools in India have increased as follows :—

Mission schools.

1851	...	Pupils	...	64,043
1861	...	„	...	75,995
1871	...	„	...	122,132
1881	...	„	...	187,632†

There are now about eighty European and American Missionaries and lay professors engaged in Mission colleges. The total Mission expenditure on education is not known; but it probably exceeds £60,000 a year.

As might be expected, much more has been done by Government for education. The statistics of Government and aided schools show the progress made :

Educational statistics.

---

* See p. 257.   † Statistical Tables of Protestant Missions in India, 1881, p. 63.

	1855-56	1870-71	1881-82	1884-85*
Institutions ...	50,998	83,052	114,109	141,304
Pupils ...	923,780	1,894,823	2,643,978	3,431,725

The grant of £10,000 has been increased to an expenditure from Government, at the old rate of exchange, of £798,930 in 1884-5, and from other sources to £1,574,224, making a total outlay of £2,373,154. Some progress has also been made among the fifty millions of people in native states. On a rough estimate, there cannot, at present, be fewer than twelve millions either under instruction or able to read and write. The number of readers must be increasing at the rate of nearly two millions a year. *Number of readers.*

2. *The increasing number of native publications.*—The Rev. J. Long says that the most ancient specimen of printing in Bengali that we have is Halhed's Grammar, printed in Calcutta in 1778. The *Friend of India* gave in 1820 a list of twenty-seven Bengali books issued from native presses, during the previous ten years. "Fifteen thousand volumes printed and sold among the natives within the last ten years, a phenomenon to which the country has been a stranger since the formation of the first, the incommunicable letters of the Vedas."

In 1835 Sir Charles Metcalfe removed the restrictions on printing, and soon afterwards native presses began to be established.

Government publishes an annual "Report on Publications Issued and Registered in British India." According to it, 8,963 publications were registered in 1886. Exclusive of periodicals, the numbers in some of the principal languages were as follows: Urdu, or Hindustani, 1,485; Bengali, 1,352; Hindi, 843; English, 679; Sanskrit, 445; Marathi, 436; Punjabi, 398; Gujerati, 373; Tamil, 258; Persian, 225; Arabic, 184; Telugu, 164; with smaller numbers in twenty other languages. Bi-lingual publications were also numerous. *Publications in the principal languages.*

Among the above are included Christian publications and some of an unobjectionable character; but the bulk are highly objectionable. Anti-Christian tracts are increasing in number. They are mostly translations from Bradlaugh, Ingersoll, and similar writers. Lately twenty thousand copies were printed for free distribution of a scurrilous and obscene attack on Christianity, and on English people through Christianity. *Anti-Christian tracts.*

Newspapers and magazines are not included in the language list. The first English newspaper appeared in Calcutta in 1780. The first vernacular periodical was commenced in 1818, by the Serampore Missionaries. In 1835 there were only six native papers published in India, and these in no way political. Luker's *Press Guide*, in 1885, enumerated 448 newspapers and magazines, published in India, in 17 languages. Of *Newspapers and magazines.*

* Statistical Abstract relating to British India, 20th No., p. 199.

these 175 were in English ; Hindustani came next with 102 papers.'

Native presses, some on a large scale, are multiplying. Several years ago, an establishment belonging to a Mohammedan at Lucknow, had upwards of 60 lithographic presses, and its catalogue occupied 116 octavo pages.

Both the spread of education and the increasing number of native publications are strong arguments for the provision of Call for Christian Christian literature on a much larger scale than here-literature. tofore. It is of little use to give the ability to read, if means are not provided for its beneficial exercise. The indigenous literature does much more harm than good.

II. *Classes of publications needed.*

These can only be briefly summarised. Books and tracts are wanted in the vernaculars for Hindus and Mohammedans, for Publications native pastors and Christians generally, for women and needed. children. They are needed in English for the large and influential class acquainted with that language, whose favourite authorities are John Stuart Mill and Herbert Spencer.

III. *What has already been done.*

Through the agency chiefly of the British and Foreign Bible Society, the Scriptures have been provided, in whole or in part, in the principal vernaculars, and colporteurs are employed to promote their circulation.

At first, several Missions took part in providing general Christian literature ; but for many years, with a few exceptions, Agencies. the work has been mainly left to the Indian Tract Societies, aided by the Religious Tract Society. The Christian Knowledge Society and the Christian Vernacular Education Society have co-operated on a smaller scale. The Missions which still assist are principally the Basle Mission, the American Methodist Episcopal Mission, and the Leipzig Evangelical Lutheran Mission.

The Madras Tract Society, established in 1818, is the oldest existing Tract Society in India. The Calcutta Tract Society was Societies formed in 1823, and the Bombay Tract Society in 1827. in India. There are at present eight Tract Societies working in India.* Last year, largely through grants of paper and money from the Religious Tract Society, they circulated about 3,800,000 tracts and books in the vernaculars and English.

Details are not available regarding the circulation of the Christian Knowledge Society's vernacular publications, but it was not large.

The Christian Vernacular Education Society, established in 1858, as a memorial of the Indian Mutiny, printed in 1886, 642,675 publications, chiefly school books.

* Exclusive of Burmah and Ceylon.

While thankful for what has been done with the scanty means available, the work of supplying India with Christian literature has only been commenced. The Hindi, the vernacular of about seventy millions, has not a single commentary _{Wants.} on any book of Scripture; only one language has a Bible Concordance. Wholesome interesting literature leavened with Christian truth, to take the place of vile native publications, is almost a total blank.

IV. *Printing.*

This is the next stage. The question is asked, Should Missions maintain Presses? These were at first a necessity, and they are still desirable at a few central stations. Cheap and accurate printing is needed, especially in the case of ^{Mission Presses.} the Scriptures. Private presses, under European management, generally charge high rates, and give themselves, as a rule, to English printing. In native presses the plant is often insufficient, and the work slovenly.

It is not desirable to multiply Mission Presses. They should not be established at out-stations, to turn out bad workmanship, and perhaps print what was not worth printing. With improved means of communication, such are now unnecessary.

Two examples may be given of Mission Presses which have been highly useful. The Baptist Mission Press in Calcutta, commenced on a very small scale in 1818, has since poured forth, in increasing volume, a continuous stream of Christian literature. The Christian Knowledge Society's Press in Madras has now thirteen hand-presses, and five machines, constantly at work. It has rendered great service to Missions by giving good workmanship at reasonable rates.

V. *Distribution gratuitous or paid for?*

Formerly tracts, and sometimes even octavo volumes, were given away freely. The opinion is now almost universally held in India, that, except in a few special cases, gratuitous distribution should be confined to leaflets and very small tracts.

Sale has three advantages:

1. *It tests the suitability of publications.*

2. *It tends to secure the use and preservation of* _{Advantages} *books.*—What a Hindu *buys* he intends to read. _{of sale.}

3. *It is the only way by which Christian literature can be provided on the requisite scale.*—Some progress has already been made in the direction indicated. The Madras Tract Society receives about twice as much from the sale of its publications as from money grants and subscriptions.

As already mentioned, there are a few exceptional cases in which a gift may be desirable, but sale should be the rule.

VI. *Agencies for circulation.*

As much effort must be expended in the circulation of books as their production, or they will lie as lumber on the shelves.

Two means may be employed :—

1. *Depositories and book shops.*—These will be of the following description :

(1) *Central depôts.*—Already each great division of India has a central depository, in which publications are kept in the languages current in the province.

(2) *Mission book shops, preaching halls, and reading rooms.*—The central depository should be under the control of the Presidency Tract Society. Branch depôts should be established and maintained by the Missions.

(3) *Native book shops.*—These are springing up in many places.

2. *Living agencies.*—These are of still greater importance as more aggressive. Three classes may be mentioned :

(1) *Missionaries and catechists.*—At present most of the circulation is effected through their means.

(2) *Colporteurs supported by the Missions.*—The Bible Society, with its comparatively large funds, is able to make grants for colportage.

(3) *Native book hawkers.*—In Ceylon about seventy men of this class purchase books from the tract depôt to sell again on their own account, receiving only discount, like that allowed to booksellers at home.

VII. *The Missionary and general literature.*

The third point in the programme is, " The extent to which the Missionary may legitimately devote himself to the preparation of pure literature for the people generally—by newspapers, books of science, history, etc."

There is no doubt that it would be best if the Missionary could leave this work entirely to others, and devote himself simply to the diffusion of Christian truth. Even where it seems advisable for him to take part in it, watchfulness is necessary lest it should engage too much of his time.

Still, everything that a Missionary writes should have, as far as possible, a Christian tone, and tend, indirectly, to the progress of his main work.

Need of present effort.—At no time in the history of India has there been a greater call for Christian literature. Various forces are at work powerfully affecting the condition *Effort called for.* of the country. Railways, schools, and colleges, Western literature and civilisation, are producing great changes. It is true that such influences yet reach only the upper strata of society ; but they are percolating downwards. A feeling of nationality has been awakened never felt before. The words of Milton have been applied to India : " Methinks I see in my mind a mighty and puissant nation, rousing herself, like a strong man after sleep, and shaking her locks."

But times of transition have their danger. Old restraints are removed, and no better principles have yet been established in their place. The recent remarkable Minute of the Government of India on moral discipline in schools and colleges shows that the gravity of the case is felt. Christianity is virtually acknowledged to be the only effectual remedy. *Transition periods dangerous.* While every evangelistic agency in India should be worked more vigorously than ever, Christian literature, in many cases, forms the only available means of reaching the scattered millions of readers. Will Missionary Committees regard it as coming within the sphere of their labours?

Summary of recommendations:—

1. Missionary Societies should set apart men for literature as they do for education.

2. Mission Presses should print Christian literature at cost price, charging market rates in other cases.

3. The Religious Tract Society should have at least one agent in India, and the number should gradually be increased.

4. Provision should be made in Mission estimates for preaching halls and book shops.

5. Every well-equipped Mission should have a staff of colporteurs.

DISCUSSION.

Rev. W. S. Swanson (English Presbyterian Mission, Amoy): I shall not occupy your attention more than two minutes. I think the subject with which we are dealing this morning is one of the very greatest importance, and it is especially important for me as a Missionary from China. I take it that we are dealing not merely with what may be called distinctive literature but literature of all kinds on a religious basis, and I think we should look at it in this light. *Consider literature of all kinds.* I am afraid from the current of what I have already heard that we are only looking at it in the light of a distinctive religious literature. Away out in China we have to face a new condition of things. The Chinese Government has done what some of us never thought we would live to see done. It was worth generations of us to get this done. The Chinese Government has now opened its literary examinations to competition on subjects of Western knowledge and science; and we who are Missionaries feel that we will have to face a new condition of things, and probably will have to draw up our work on some new lines. We must meet this demand on the part of the Chinese Government by literature of a general kind on a religious basis, and if we do not attempt this or do not set ourselves to it the future of China, in regard to the formation of its intellectual, moral, and religious character, may go out of our hands; and, if you will pardon me, I will say I think it will go into very much worse hands. I think one of the greatest dangers ahead of us is the multiplication of *On multiplying Societies.* Book and Tract Societies, because the more you multiply them the more you weaken your general position, and the more you weaken the platform from which you are going to proceed on this great work. Now it seems to me, whilst we have heard a great deal about India, we have not heard very much about China, and I wish the Christian Vernacular Education

Society would become a great deal widened in its basis; in fact, I think at this stage it should merge itself into something bigger and greater. And I may here say, as a matter of mere personal gratitude and in the name of my brother Missionaries in Amoy, that there is a Society ready at hand which will carry on this work. I refer to the Religious Tract Society. They have given us every facility. There is no kind of literature on a religious basis that we have asked them to help us in the publication of but

Religious Tract Society. they have richly done so. A great Society of that kind with the enormous force behind it, I think, should take the place of the Christian Vernacular Education Society, and should set itself to work to aid in the production of religious literature and of general literature on a religious basis in all the Missionary fields. I think they are admirably equipped for it. They have the funds; they have the public at their back, and the multiplication of Tract and Book Societies in China seems to me to have been a great evil. At the same time let me say if the Religious Tract Society would set themselves to this work they must add a new department to their already existing departments, and I hope from what I know of those in trust with the affairs of that Society and of the Committee that they will be ready to do so. I am not advertising; I have had no consultation whatever with any member of the Society, but

On merging smaller Societies. from my own sense of the great importance of this work and of what that Society has already done, and of the facilities it has given us, it seems to me that these Tract and Book Societies and Christian Vernacular Education Societies should all be merged in this Religious Tract Society. Let there be a new department, and then in addition to the other immense boons they have conferred upon the Missionaries,—for there is nobody to whom Missionaries are more indebted than to the Religious Tract Society,—they will take the place that they should take in giving us a religious literature and a general literature on a religious basis.

Mr. John Fryer (China): I am entirely unprepared to speak upon this point, but the subject is one in which I have taken great interest, and I may say by way of introduction that I have spent twenty years of my life in China. The Chinese are very anxious to have encyclopædias, and scientific and other books, and during my leisure time I have done all that I could in order to provide a suitable literature, both Christian and scientific, for the

Shanghai Conference and text-books. Chinese. In 1877 we had a large Missionary Conference at Shanghai, at which a series of text and school books were determined upon, of which I was asked to take the editorship. This has been in operation about eleven years, and I have already prepared some fifty or sixty standard text-books on various subjects of Western knowledge, not all of them entirely of a religious nature, but the majority have a religious bearing. I do not know whether in previous meetings notice has been taken of these school agencies and others, but I would make just two or three remarks on the subject of literature for China. We felt that the spiritual part of the nature of the Chinese was having too much attention at the hands of Missionaries, ad that the physical and intellectual portions were comparatively neglected. I regard a man as being composed of

Man, a tripartite being. three parts,—having physical, intellectual, and spiritual faculties. I regard the spiritual faculties, of course, as one of the highest importance, as the soul of one human being is of infinite value, but still we must not on that account neglect the intellectual and the physical; therefore my energy and that of my co-labourers in this work has been to some extent directed towards the intellectual improvement of the Chinese, and also towards developing their physical natures as much as possible. I may go on to say I was induced three years ago to try an experiment to see whether books of Western knowledge and of a religious character could not be sold to the Chinese, so as to leave a profit and make the work entirely self-supporting. I tried the experiment three years ago, and during those three years I established a depôt in Shanghai where about **A depôt tried in Shanghai.** \$16,000 worth of different books, some religious, some scientific, and some of a general character have been disposed of, and I have six different branches, one at Tien-tsin for Mission purposes, one at Uchang, another at Hankow, another at Swatow, and another at Foochow. These are branches, and the work seems to be going on. The Chinese are very anxious to have Western knowledge, especially as to some extent their examinations depend upon it. I heard the other day of an examination to which about three thousand students went and only thirty passed, and these thirty were told the reason they passed the examination was that they had attempted the mathematical papers. The others had not attempted them, and merely for the attempt these thirty men got their degree. From the small fund that has arisen from this three years' work I have been able to print about twenty thousand volumes, and those are now being spread over China. This is merely one little branch of the work that is being done there; but I feel that too much cannot be done in **The result.** the way of providing intellectual as well as spiritual knowledge for the heathen nations. The point I would impress more than any other is that such effort as far as possible should be made self-supporting. I found the Chinese look with great suspicion on any book which is offered to them, unless it is at a fair price. They suppose there is some sinister motive, and therefore put the book on one side and will not read it. The fact, therefore, that about \$16,000 worth of books have been purchased by the Chinese at a price that allows a fair profit, shows the need of such work.

Mr. Henry Morris (Hon. Sec., Christian Vernacular Education Society for India): I am going to ask the audience to take a jump to India from China; but to make the jump a little easier, I should like to say how deeply I sympathise with all that is being done for Japan. I do not know of any country that presents such an awfully interesting spectacle to us European and American nations. The Japanese are in search of a religion. They are one of the most intellectual **Japan, its present state.** nations on the face of the earth, and it remains for Christian England and Christian America to give them Christianity. The fact is that while we are hesitating, our agnostic friends are doing their best; and it would indeed grieve us all if Japan should become agnostic, for in the formula of St. Paul, which in order to give it point I must quote in Greek, " Οὐ γὰρ θέλω ὑμᾶς ἀγνοεῖν ἀδελφοί,"—" Brethren, I would not have you *agnostic.*" Now we will go to India, in which country I have the greatest interest. I believe there is an immense amount to do for the higher literature of India; and when I recollect what a number of young men are being sent out from the universities and other high educational institutions who really have no faith at all, my heart bleeds, and I pity them with all my heart and soul. They have given to them indeed the noble literature of England; but they do not read our literature simply from the love of it, but for the sake of passing examinations. And while they have our noble English literature, I am grieved to say that they have an ignoble English literature to read also; and I would desire, before going further, just to emphasise what Lord Northbrook said the other day, and I do hope the Christian public will take it up—there are at the railway stations some of the vilest books published in England, republished specially for India. Oh! let us deliver the youth of India from this terrible slough of Zolaism.

English literature in India.

Just one passing word with reference to my friend, Dr. Murdoch, who, in his seventieth year, is still doing a noble work for the people of India. Dr. Murdoch has been doing a great deal for what I would call the middle-class education of India, for the English reading population who do not enjoy the noble English literature of which I have been speaking, and I believe that he is doing a very great deal of good in that respect. What is really wanted is good, clear, bright, attractive little books published for the vernacular-speaking people of India, those who know only their own native languages. The only way to reach a man's heart is through his native tongue. I have been in huts in Ireland, and when I have heard friends with me speaking the Irish tongue the eye of the listener lighted up immediately; the people were able to appreciate what was said and to feel it. It is exactly the same with the Hindus. Just fancy what the literature of England would have been, if it consisted only of translations from the classics! We want books written by the natives themselves, which they will thoroughly and completely understand, and books written in simple and pleasing prose in their own common vernaculars.

The kind of literature required.

Good illustrations also are required, not the old cast-off cuts of the Religious Tract Society, to be used up in India. We want attractive illustrations in the Oriental style. I snatched from my table just before coming here a tract containing on its title-page an illustration of a very good, benevolent old gentleman separating two English boys from fighting—just such a picture as they would not be able to understand in India. Do recollect that the Bible itself is an Oriental book, and no one who has not been in an Oriental country can understand allusions in the Bible. Let me plead earnestly for India. My last words are,—"India is now thoroughly feeling national aspirations; do not leave it alone; do not leave it to Zolaism; do not leave it to agnostics; do not leave it to sceptics; do not leave it to the infidels of England. Do not let Herbert Spencer's and John Stuart Mill's be the handbooks of the rising generation. Give them Christian literature, and God will bless you and your rule in India.

Importance of illustrations.

Mr. R. A. Macfie: I want to warn you against a danger, and I do this from experience. More than fifty years ago, as perhaps my reverend friend Principal Brown may remember, when we had the benefit in Glasgow of his ministrations, some Christian friends collected money to give a prize for a work on behalf of Missions. We were encouraged by the late eminent Dr. Duff, Dr. Chalmers, and others. We were successful in God's good providence in getting perhaps the best book on Missions that ever was written. Unfortunately we reserved the copyright. We restrained others from reproducing this book. We sold

Prize essay on Missions.

the right to print the first six thousand copies to Ward & Co., London. They put a price on it of 10s. 6d., and for the style in which they did produce it, I am not saying it was too dear. But, mark this. So far as I know, the whole six thousand which we sold the right of were never printed, and those that were printed were never sold out. I am not aware that there was a second edition. The lesson is, pay people the proper price for proper work, but do not, by introducing a monopolist principle, prevent the diffusion of Christian literature which, in my humble opinion, ought to be as free as the Gospel itself. Now that I *Literature and copyright.* am speaking of principle that commends itself to the worldly mind, I will give the proof. American periodicals are being largely worked in our country. In the *Atlantic Monthly* of this month there is an extract from the works of Louis Blanc, a notable man, but I fear a socialist and an agnostic, and he speaks of it as a shame, as a dereliction of duty, as a wrong to society, for people who have God-given time and faculties to write books, to prevent others of mankind from getting the benefit of it. That, I think, is a wholesome Christian principle,—of course it must be applied with discretion and rectitude,—I commend this subject to the consideration of the Christian world. Then a second point. I think this matter of publication is so vast in its area, so wide in its aspects, that it is absolutely necessary that there should be a new organisation for the purpose, but it is not necessary that that new organisation should be separated from existing Societies. It might represent the Tract Society, the Vernacular Society, the Society for Promoting Christian Knowledge, and so forth ; but there are two things,—it must comprehend both sides of the Atlantic,—it must comprehend all languages.

Rev. Fr. Ziegler (Basle Missionary Society) : The remarks I am going to make have been partly called forth by some remark I overheard this morning, made by a gentleman who, I am afraid, is not here. He said, "The proceedings of this morning are unimportant,— *On Bible circulation.* give the people the Bible, and that is sufficient." Now I love the Bible, and I am sure that the Bible is the most important means of propagating the Word of God, but not as a charm, not as an amulet which will work by itself, but only when it is understood. Now I am afraid the translation of the Bible into foreign languages—I can only speak of the Canarese language in the southern part of India—is often such that the majority of the people cannot understand it. I know that of our translation of the Bible in the Canarese language, only the Gospels and the Psalms, and perhaps the historical part of the Old Testament are read or can be understood. The Epistles of St. Paul and others are understood scarcely by one out of ten. Now, till we get translations made by the Luthers of the natives, we are obliged to write tracts such as will explain the Bible, and therefore I advocate that tracts should be written explana- *Commentaries necessary.* tory of the Bible. The Rev. Mr. Bowen, of Bombay, who lately died, and who had a long Indian experience, proposed that the Gospel of St. Matthew, for example, should be written in a plain style, not exactly translated, but paraphrased as it were with some few remarks, explaining strange customs, and all those things that cannot be understood by the Hindus. Such things we are in want of. Now I want to say a few things about the pure literature that has been spoken of, *Pure fiction.* not exactly religious, but on a religious basis. I was once asked by a native inspector of schools to give him some little books that could be read by his wife, who had learnt to read. I felt the want of such books. We had some tracts, and had Bible histories, but he did not want those ; he wanted stories. Now if I had had such things to give him I should have been very glad. I know the females who learn to read in India can only read things that they had better not read. They learn by heart, and they read just the kind of literature that has been mentioned by Mr. Morris, impure literature ; and I know that agnostic literature, sceptical literature is very much read by the Hindus ; therefore we want a pure literature, resting on a Christian basis, although not exactly religious.

Rev. Emmanuel Van Orden (from Brazil) : Mr. Chairman,—When Luther threw the inkstand at the devil's head the devil did not get offended, but he said to himself, "Master Luther, you will find out what use I am going to make of that ink." Now the devil has made good use of the printing press, and it is high time that we should awake to the importance of the press. I have now given sixteen years of my life to Brazil, and I have been engaged in literary labours for many years and know its importance, and I feel it every day more and more. We have three thousand Church members in Brazil, all converts from Roman Catholicism ; our schools are filled with scholars,—they will need something, we must bring them good books. The Brazilian publishers are publishing all the translations of French novels. The devil is busy in Brazil ; why should not God's people be just as zealous to give good books to the people ? We have to make our text-books. I am going to Brazil in two weeks with a printing-press and with type, so as to produce more books than we have to-day. And, brethren, we must have books in the native tongue, but let it be the native tongue. There are a good many books in the native tongue which the natives do not understand. You may take my experience for what it is worth. The Missionary translates and lets the native revise, but when I can I let the native translate and I revise. We must have idiomatic translation. Now, if you take any German and let him translate a book from German to English, what would you say of it,—however well he may have known English ? It is the same in Brazil, the same in China, the same in India ; and we have translations of the Bible and other books which the people will not read. School books we must have ; histories therefore for our schools we have to make. We have a paper for our children and we have native ministers, and they write papers, they write the tracts, and we are on the right lines, I believe. And I must here acknowledge the great services which the Tract Society has rendered us in Brazil ; whenever I have made an appeal to that Society it has assisted me. The only Tract Society which has done great service for Brazil is the Religious Tract Society of London.

Importance of literature.

Translation by natives.

Dr. Robert Pringle (Bengal Army) : My only reason for saying a few words now is that I have had some practical experience, or rather my dear wife has had some practical experience, regarding one of the subjects laid down here,—" How can religious literature and general literature on a religious basis be best provided for the growing wants of the Mission-fields of the world ? " The way to answer that question is by every Christian man and woman with the love of God in his heart doing the best he or she can to circulate such literature,

Personal responsibility.

and I will tell you how it can be done. We started at Mussoorie a Bible and Book Society. We took it from a friend, General Anderson, on his going home, and my dear wife devoted considerable attention to it. We had a room in our house for it, and the books that were sold fetched just exactly what they absolutely cost. We had no wish whatever to interfere with the booksellers who were selling there, for we are believers in "Live and let live;" but we got a class of books that did not interfere with anything they sold, and by that means these books were circulated to an immense extent. And now we meet with one difficulty, and that is the question **Railways,** which has been referred to, of the railway bookstalls. Remember **Government** the railways in India are Government property, and everything **property.** done on a railway is done by the British nation; and let us see if we cannot have a voice in the matter as to the circulation of a pure literature along that line. And with reference to this pure literature I would here gladly say that it is with gratitude I acknowledge the help of that noble Society, the Religious Tract Society, in the books that it has enabled us to circulate throughout the North-West Provinces in India. I have before me a little pamphlet I got at the breakfast of the Religious Tract Society, with a little pioneer sketch and a story taken from the Word of God. If such were only sold in a cheap manner they would produce an incalculable benefit, because that is just the story that a native now wants to get.

Rev. J. Shillidy (Irish Presbyterian Mission, Surat): I have been engaged in connection with tract work for the last three years in Surat in India. We find this tract work one of the most valuable accessories we have in connection with our Mission. There are three principles which should be steadily kept in view by those who get up tracts; the first is, they should be got up neatly; the second, that they should **How to publish** be illustrated as fully as possible; and the third is, they should be **tracts.** sold as cheaply as possible. From my own experience I would say, following these lines, a great deal of work can be done, and I might illustrate this by what happened during the last three years. Formerly our tracts in Gujerati were not very fully illustrated, but we have been getting somewhat better illustrations in more recent times and hope still to get more, and the result is, by illustrating more fully, we have raised our circulation to more than double what it was, and our sales have more than doubled,—in some instances they are more than threefold what they formerly were. In writing tracts in the past, perhaps too much attention was paid to Hinduism, Mohammedanism, and Parsiism, and what was necessary for native Christians was too often left in the background. This should not be the case. The Mohammedans themselves at the present time are taking a great interest in tracts, and I have known Mohammedans publishing three or four tracts in reply to a series of articles in a Christian periodical criticising Mohammed's life and claims. There are Hindu Tract Societies being established both in North and South India at the present time to antagonise **Hindu Tract** Christianity. They have learnt a lesson from us, and are doing **Societies.** all they possibly can to oppose us, and we must do all the more to meet them. A Hindu does not care to give away money without getting something for it. A previous speaker has said something about approaching the Government of India in order to get our books sold at the railway stations. Practically we have been doing that for more than two years past without difficulty. Two years ago I wrote to the Manager of the Bombay, Baroda, and Central India Railway, asking him for permission to allow a colporteur to attend at the railway station at Surat to sell Christian books and tracts. This was permitted at all the stations along the line, and three-fourths of all the books sold by our colporteur were sold to passengers on the line of rail, so that we had no difficulty in this matter.

Rev. William Gray (Secretary, C.M.S.) : I take it that there is absolute unanimity amongst all the friends assembled here this morning about the immense importance of this work ; about the value of it ; that is to say, that we are called upon as fast as we possibly can to produce not only religious literature, but also general literature on a religious basis, for circulation in such countries as India and China. I take it for granted that if you have it produced, you will get it circulated easily enough. What I say is, you cannot leave the production to the Missionaries ; that is to say to the Missionaries, if they have other work to do at the same time. You cannot leave it to natives if they are not set apart entirely for it ; and, therefore, I simply ask the question as a practical matter, How are you to face this question ; how are you to do it ? How are you to produce this literature ? Now I venture to say, as my own distinct opinion upon this matter, that the Christian Vernacular Society has solved it ; and the way in which I think it has solved it is by bringing to light such a man as John Murdoch, because John Murdoch will not only see that the thing is done, but he will get the right men to do it, which is the great want. Well, how are we to get the John Murdochs? Mr. Swanson has said this morning,—I do not know whether he meant it,— that the Tract Society was to be like Moses' rod, swallowing up all the other rods. I hope that won't be done. I do not believe myself in absorption. I believe if you put two or three Societies together you won't get much more money for all united than you would for each one if it were separate. Therefore, I do not agree with that. I do most earnestly hope that we shall not part, without the Tract and the Christian Vernacular Society putting their heads together to get something practical done upon this matter.

Missionaries no time for translation.

No faith in absorption.

Rev. Principal Miller, C.I.E., LL.D. (Madras Christian College): My purpose in the Conference has been to listen and not to speak ; but I feel so strongly the importance of this subject that I would like to add a word or two about it. Much of what I should have liked to have said has been said already, especially by my friends, Mr. Swanson and Mr. Gray. I would add, however, this. We are all convinced of the immense importance of general literature upon a sound Christian basis in countries like India and China, but I am not sure that we all understand how thoroughly there is at present in India, or at all events in some parts of India, an opening for the intelligent and sympathetic reception of literature of that kind. There is a sort of general impression that students in India, and intelligent people generally,—those who are being educated,— read nothing, and care for little except what enables them directly to pass examinations. That is a very great mistake. Of course there is far too much of that sort of thing, but it is a very great mistake to think that there is no awakening intelligence. For example, amongst my own students, the last time I looked at the statistics of our library, some three or four years ago, I found to my surprise that a library containing no books directly

Openings for literature in India.

bearing on examinations, for those are provided in another department, had been made use of by the students to the extent of eleven thousand readings per annum; *i.e.*, books had been taken out eleven thousand times in the course of the year. I do not say every one of them had been read and diligently studied: that is a different thing. But at any rate, these books for ordinary reading purposes had been utilised to that very large extent. That was several years ago. I have no doubt the number is very much greater now. To some extent it is the same amongst all the educated and intelligent people of India. There is, therefore, a great and **Natives do read.** encouraging opening for the dissemination of such literature as is the subject of our thoughts this morning. But the one thing important is that something practical should be done in this matter. I thoroughly agree with every word that has now been said by Mr. Gray. There are many difficulties in the way, but we in the Mission-field cannot do very much to remove those difficulties. It is you at home that must lay your heads together. The one thing to be kept in mind is, that you have some central **Need organisa-** organisation or organisations to attend to this one thing. You **tion at home.** should get all possible help from others, but you must have a head to direct, and a central organisation to put things on the proper basis. What that is to be, you at home must decide, and I do hope that there will be earnest consultation before this Conference breaks up amongst those who have the best opportunities of knowing how this thing is to be done. There are many points to be kept in view if you are to utilise all Societies, as far as possible, in the best way. We cannot certainly let our **Points for** American friends depart without getting their advice, and getting **consideration.** them embarked in this great enterprise. It does appear to me, that it might be advisable that the work should be divided. Possibly it might be wise that this work should be done, say for Japan, entirely by our American friends. Or it might be wise that they take up certain of the many languages of India. But at any rate, let the thing be organised so that our American friends may know exactly what they are to do, and that you here on this side of the water may know what you are to do, and may set yourselves thoroughly to do it. Then there is the question about the various Societies. Of course I do not want to see any one Society swallowing up all the others, but there is also a danger on the other side, and it is for you here, at the centre of affairs, to harmonise these two sides of things. If there is the danger of destroying useful Societies, there is also the great danger of too much multiplying Societies. It does **Number** appear to me, for instance, that with regard to this noble Chris- **of Societies.** tian Vernacular Education Society for India, its proper field of operations has, to a large extent, in the varying providential circumstances, been changed. It started with this as one of its objects, the supplying of healthy, and Christian, and religious literature, and it has done much to meet the want. But there are other sides of work once undertaken by it which circumstances no longer call for so loudly as they once did. It is to my mind, at all events, a question of considerable importance whether that Society should not merge its separate existence with the Tract Society, or in some other way amalgamate itself. At all events, there are many things that we in the foreign field may suggest, but it is you here, who know how things work together, that must decide. The one thing I would press upon this meeting is, that the Conference should on no account be allowed to separate without some definite, precise, practical step being taken for bringing this matter to a point. The need of it is growing every day, and the opening for it is growing every day also.

Rev. Professor Blaikie, D.D., LL.D. (Free Church College, Edinburgh): I am afraid I may disturb the course this conversation has taken by introducing a matter which is in a different line from what has been so emphatically pressed upon us. It is evident that there are two departments of this subject: the one is the production of suitable Christian literature for our Missions, and the other is its distribution. My purpose is to say a word on the subject of distribution, and my apology for doing so is, that I happen to be Chairman of the Book and Tract Society of Scotland, which is the most extensive Colportage Society in this country. It employs some two hundred colporteurs, mostly in Scotland, partly in England. It is likewise affiliated with the Irish Colportage Society, and so we have studied colportage somewhat scientifically. I may say our Society is quite different from that noble Society which has been so often referred to, the Religious Tract Society of London. That Society is for production but not directly for distribution; our Society is solely for distribution and not for production. We have found it very essential in looking out for agents to appoint men not only of good character, but of evangelistic spirit. And here is a point also which we have found very essential, not to trust to haphazard efforts in the way of distribution, but to train the agents, so as to qualify them, to give them the best information as to the character of the publications which are available for distribution, and to encourage them, by every proper and suitable method, to find openings among the people among whom they go. Some are first-rate; others, though good men, are slow and not very capable. We have likewise found it of great benefit to bring them together so that those that have natural and special gifts for this work may influence others who are not so gifted naturally. It has been stated again and again to-day that colportage is one of the most useful methods of helping on the distribution of suitable literature in heathen countries. I think probably the experience we have had with regard to the necessity of an agency of this sort in a Christian country may emphasise the necessity of it in a heathen country, because I find that even in Scotland, the flood of publications (some of them pernicious, many of them very frivolous), pouring in upon our people, and finding distribution without any effort to put them into circulation, is sapping and mining the earnest spirit of many in our country; and the real way to dispossess that kind of literature is by systematic colportage. If that be the case in a Christian country, one can easily understand how much more evil is done by that class of publications in a heathen land, and my object in rising is simply to lay stress upon this, that in employing colporteurs, every endeavour should be made to get men of the most suitable character, train them for the work, superintend them in it, guide and direct them in the selection of the publications that they are trying to circulate, and then by God's blessing much may be done.

[margin notes: Experience in distribution of literature. Colporteurs. Colportage a corrective.]

Rev. Henry Rice (Church of Scotland Foreign Missions, from Madras): Having been engaged for many years in evangelistic work in South India, and having been associated the last two with Dr. Murdoch in the publication of two papers, one done in English for educated Hindus, called *Progress*, and another, a native vernacular sheet, started last November, called in the Tamil language the *Messenger of Truth*,—I wish to say I believe the time has come in India for a much larger, fuller, and freer use of the Press. There is no period in British history which I can at all compare with India at the present day, except the period, about three hundred years ago, which witnessed the reformation of the Christian Church, the revival of classical and Oriental learning, and the invention of the printing-press; and I believe the time has come when we should take a much larger advantage of the great openings in India. The latest infidel objections are just as current now in the streets of Madras, Bombay, and Calcutta, as in London, Oxford, or Cambridge; the consequence is that infidel books and publications which set forth objections to Christianity are freely purchased, while those which set forth the claims and authority of Christianity are disregarded. The difficulties in the way of belief are being pondered, but the far greater difficulties in the way of unbelief are being disregarded.

The Press in India, and the Reformation.

Scepticism rampant.

We know a great many educated Hindus think that Missionaries are preaching an antiquated form of Christianity which enlightened men in Europe are forsaking. Now, therefore, is our opportunity, and I wish to make one or two practical suggestions. One is this, that we should have men from each Mission, specially adapted and qualified, set apart to this work. The duty of these men should be, by elimination and adaptation of great English works, to publish them in the languages of the country. Another suggestion which has not been touched upon is this, that we should draw out by some means the latent native talent of the country; and the suggestion I make is, that the Tract Society or some Society should offer a money prize, say two or three hundred rupees a year to some native who would bring out an original book on some question of Christian evidence or Christian apologetics. I believe if you do that you will get a man who will write a good book. I know two or three men in Madras who, if you will only give them sufficient inducement, will come forward and write you a good book, which will be very useful at the present time. A third suggestion is that, whatever is done the books should be published cheaply. Large expensive books will never find a sale in India. The books should be cheap, and largely illustrated with Oriental illustrations. You should take a lesson from a native Bazaar-man in Madras. So long as tea was sold in boxes and by the pound, it was an unknown luxury in many of the Hindu houses. He hit upon the happy idea of selling it in small parcels of an ounce or less—what was the result? He sold large quantities.

Set Missionaries apart for literary work.

Cheapness a necessity in India.

Mr. John Archibald (National Bible Society of Scotland, from Hankow): The problem before us is one which the Bible Society has had to deal with, and which it has solved in this way. The Scriptures are circulated throughout the world. How is this done? The Bible Society at home raises the funds and superintends the work abroad. It has its agents in all its fields, and these agents work in harmony with the Missionaries. The Missionaries, more or less, assist the agents in every way, and the result is, throughout the whole world we have the Bible in every language. Now what we want is something similar with regard to Tract work. Speaking from my experience at Hankow, I do not believe it is difficult to find Societies capable of carrying on the work, but it is difficult to raise the funds. We are always engaged in raising funds, and I have had some little experience in corresponding with various Societies on that matter. The American Societies were engaged

The Scottish Bible Society's methods.

in supplying American Missionaries with large quantities of tracts at very much less than cost price, and the money was found by English Societies, and we did not think it fair. We wrote to them from Hankow. Our American friends sent a letter stating their great sympathy with us,— they would have been happy to send us a few dollars, but they had

not got them. We also remembered the Tract and Book

Difficulty in getting help. Society of Scotland, the largest of the kind in this country, and we thought, "Surely we shall get something from them ; " but we did not like to risk another refusal, so I was instructed to make inquiries indirectly to see if there was any chance of our getting anything. I did make the inquiries indirectly, and the answer was to this effect, "There is no chance of a single penny ; they need it all themselves for Scotland, and England, and Ireland." What were we to do ? We must find some means of raising a revenue for this work, and depend upon it it is a revenue that will require to exceed that of the great Bible Society. How are we going to do it ? I do not know except this that we more and more emphasise the work of the Religious Tract Society, and contrive in every way to get more funds, and in proportion as we receive the funds I believe we shall find the ways and means of carrying out the idea.

Rev. **William Stevenson** (Secretary, Free Church of Scotland Ladies' Society for Female Education): Following up the remarks made by Mr. Gray and others, I would say what we want now is simply organisation.

Better organisation needed. We have various Societies doing very good work, the Religious Tract Society especially; the Christian Vernacular Society and others are helping, but we want these to work on a more extensive and better organised plan. In India the work has been mainly done by the Christian Vernacular Society and the Religious Tract Society working together. The truth is that in India it has been done mainly by Dr. Murdoch. What he does he does at one time as the agent of the Christian Vernacular Education Society, and the next day as the agent of the Religious Tract Society; and it is all in his hands, and very good hands indeed. But Dr. Murdoch will not live for ever, and it is becoming too large even for Dr. Murdoch; and there is certainly a very urgent necessity that the matter should be taken in hand by these two Societies, and by other Societies also, which are taking a share in the matter. What has just been said shows the necessity of calling the Americans into the field ; they, too, have a share in it. I do not agree with Mr. Rice's suggestion

that each Mission should set apart a man for this particular work:

Need special men for translation. that is just where the matter will break down. Leave it to each Missionary Society, and they will do a little here and a little there. The Missionaries are engaged in other work, and are made responsible for other work,—they have not the time, and the Missionary Societies have not the means. It is absolutely necessary that we should have,—I do not say a new organisation, a new Society, but we must have an organisation, however con- stituted, which shall be accepted and recognised throughout both Europe and America as a great auxiliary to all the Missionary Societies, exactly in the same way as the Bible Society is recognised as a fellow-worker and auxiliary of all the Missionary Societies. If the Religious Tract Society, for example, takes up the work, then it ought to have a department for it quite separate from its work at home ; and it could go then to the public, and to the members of the denominations who have Missions in the field, and say, "See here, we are doing your work, and we have a right to claim your support in the doing of it." The Christian Vernacular Society is doing good work, but it cannot go to the public in that way. It does not appear on the face of it that it is a Literature Society. People naturally say, "This is an Education Society. What right has the Christian Vernacular to go abroad and claim funds for the same kind of work that every other Society is doing for itself?" But if the Society comes before the public, and says, "Here is a particular work which we are doing for all the Societies, which the Societies cannot do for themselves, and yet, which it is imperative should be done for them," then it has a right to claim the support of the whole Christian public in the doing of that work. This Literature Society should be in correspondence with all the Societies,— should be able to lay its hand upon the best men in the various Societies as they appear in the field ; it should be able to say to a Society, for example, as the Bible Society sometimes says, "Lend us one of your men for this particular work for a time, and we will employ him and pay him for it ; " and let it be put on as sound a financial principle as possible. What you want is agents in the field to manage the business department, and to lay hold of this man and the other man and say, "Here is work we want done by that particular man." If in some such way as that the matter were thoroughly organised, it would be one most important gain from this Conference for the whole Mission-field.

Christian Vernacular Society's position.

Special agents needed.

Mr. C. E. Chapman (late of the Indian Civil Service): I wish to say a word or two not only on the need of studying native lines of thought in the preparation of Christian literature, but also of studying the native modes of communicating those thoughts. Any of us who have been in Oriental countries, and have been kept awake during the midnight hours (which I am afraid too many of us have), have often listened to the low monotonous hum around us either of native servants or of the distant village,—singing generally to the tune of a native guitar, and we have wondered perhaps what this meant. If we could have got up to look what was going on we should have seen a circle of natives squatted on their haunches, and a story-teller seated in the midst, who was in all probability narrating stories of great heroes of the people told in their own vernacular. This is acceptable to the multitudes, it becomes a part of their modes of thought. Now can we not from a Christian point of view take a little lesson from this? If we want to saturate the masses, to permeate them, or get a little below the crust, we must not only adapt our thoughts or take in their thoughts, but we must also instruct our men to adopt their modes of narration.

Indian story-tellers an example.

Every native is a born story-teller and *raconteur*, and my own experience has been, after a good many years in India, if ever I have tried to take the Gospel to my servants I have gone straight to the Parables. I have taken the Parable of the Prodigal Son, and at once there was interest and attention, and you see the lowest amongst them with his whole mind in it. We want to take these Parables of our Lord, and clothe them in such a form as shall be acceptable to the native mind.

Let me also remind you how important a part hymnology must play— how important it is to take the native lute and to train up men who go into

the villages with their lutes to sing the Gospel. We want the Gospel sung
in such a way that every native high or low shall listen to it,—
A vernacular not to go in a stilted form just as a preacher will preach infinitely
hymnology. above the heads of his audience, but to go right down and take
their modes of thought and communicate to them. We want to get down to
the masses, to their everyday life, and if we can to saturate that with the
blessed principles of the Gospel of Christ.

Mr. Robert Paton (Christian Colportage Association): I do not think
there is any more important subject that can engage the attention of this
Conference than this. I feel quite burdened at the thought of what is going
on in India in connection with literature at this present time. Twenty years
ago I belonged to a Colportage Association there, and have watched the course
of literature in India from this country since I came home. I feel confident
that we have to wake up to the idea that the Gospel can be
Value of carried to men by the printed page as well as by the lips. I
colportage. have worked at the circulation of Christian literature in England
for the last thirteen years, and am deeply interested in a Colportage Association, so I have had opportunities for ascertaining what is being done by the
adversary with the press against the cause of Christ. It is utterly impossible
to describe what is going on at this present moment in London
Pernicious and throughout the kingdom. Now something like thirty or
literature. forty of the works of two of the most noted London atheists
are being scattered broadcast throughout India,—I have seen them advertised
in a Madras paper—so they are seeking to possess the minds of the natives
of India with their abominable and vile teaching, and no doubt they are
succeeding very largely. What is to be done? I feel certain that until the
Church wakes up and puts money into the hands of some Society,—I do
not care which Society,—that will enable it to produce Gospel
Aggressive literature on a large scale, we shall never have a large aggressive
colportage work. work in India. That it must be done by an undenominational
Society is perfectly evident, we do not want denominational literature
scattered in India.

I put into the hands of the Tract Society only the other day a letter I
received from Mr. H. E. Perkins, whose name is well known as a late
commissioner of the Punjab. That noble man has, I believe, determined to
devote the rest of his life to the spread of literature in India, and he asks
for a man to help in scattering the literature that is already provided. But
we also want men to do more aggressive work with literature, to go forth to
the Missionaries and tell them how important this work is, and to press it
upon them to devise new modes of circulation.

I know the consensus of opinion from India at this moment is that
this literature should be sold. Well, I believe most thoroughly in selling,
but I also believe in free distribution. I do not think there is
Free any man in this Conference who would speak to an intelligent
distribution. Hindu and tell him of his need of a revelation from God without
also putting in his hands a copy of the Scriptures. We find there are quite
as many conversions to God through tracts and Scriptures given away, as
through those that have been sold. I ask you to read the records of the
Tract and Bible Societies, and satisfy yourselves that God can use a printed
page whether given or sold. And when we get our minds fairly into the
thought that God has Himself condescended to put His revelation into type,

surely it is our duty to put that revelation of God into the hands of the people by some means or other.

Rev. L. Borrett White, D.D. (Secretary, Religious Tract Society): I need hardly say I have listened to this discussion with very great interest, and that it has been very gratifying to hear the testimonies which have been borne by those who have spoken, and who know so much about the subject —to what the Tract Society has been able to do in the way of aiding the production and spread of Christian literature abroad in the Mission-field. But I should just like to remind the Conference how it is that the Religious Tract Society have been enabled to give this help. In the first place, it has done so because it has conducted its operations at home on strictly business-like principles, and has made its own business self-supporting—and more than self-supporting, so that from the surplus funds which remain they have been enabled to make these grants. For though it is quite true we receive a certain amount of subscriptions and donations in aid of the work generally, I may say that almost the whole of that is consumed in our Missionary work at home. Indeed I have a strong suspicion that a great many of our subscriptions are given, not as a matter of interest in Missionary work abroad, but on account of certain advantages which subscribers to the Tract Society are supposed to obtain here at home ; therefore, if it were not that our work was self-supporting, and much more than that, we should not be able to give the help of which mention has been made. In fact, our experience shows that, for some reason or other, it is extremely difficult to arouse the enthusiasm or interest of the Christian public on behalf of publication work, and you may get subscriptions to a large amount for a Missionary Society where you would not get £10 for a Publication Society. I say this not only from our own experience at home, but if you look to the records of other Religious Tract Societies in India, if you compare the amount raised for the support of religious literature in India with the amount raised in India for the support of Christian Missions, you will see what a vast difference there is between the two. Therefore, you see, there is this initial difficulty to contend with, and unless we can overcome that feeling that Literary Societies do not want help in this way, I do not think that there is much prospect of our being able to extend our borders. We have always made it a rule to consider ourselves as a *producing* Society—a Society which supplies the wants of distributers, but does not undertake the work of distribution. Now I say this with the fullest appreciation of the importance of colportage work, both at home and abroad, and especially in the Mission-field ; at the same time experience shows that if a Society becomes a great colportage-supporting Society, it cannot at the same time be a Society which is able to make grants for distribution to those who want to colport. The representative of the Scotch Society has already explained that that Society gives itself entirely to the work of distribution. The American Tract Society, owing to the circumstances of its own country, has done very much the same, and finds it is impossible to make grants, except to a very small extent, for the aid of Christian literature in the great Mission-field. Mr. Gray has spoken about Dr. Murdoch; and it would ill become me to say anything on this subject without stating how profoundly the Religious Tract Society is indebted to Dr. Murdoch's incessant labours, and to his self-

[marginal notes:] A self-supporting Society. — Publication work not popular. — Production and distribution should be separate.

denying and encouraging liberality. We have Dr. Murdoch as the Society's agent in India, and I do not know exactly what we should do without him. It is a subject that fills the minds of the Committee with constant anxiety, in what way a successor can best be found for Dr. Murdoch when the time shall come for his retiring from the work. Dr. Murdoch receives no stipend from the Religious Tract Society for all the work that he does in their behalf; he only asks the Tract Society to bear the cost of his continual journeys from one part of India to the other. At his request we paid the cost of

Dr. Murdoch, his work in China. his journey through China when he visited that country, and when he endeavoured to bring the Christian workers in China into more complete union with one another, and to establish four Societies for the four different parts of China, so that energy might not be frittered away by a number of small associations. Dr. Murdoch in a great measure succeeded in that effort.

I will only add, that of course everything that has been said will receive our most serious and sympathetic attention, and we shall be very glad if any of those who are interested in the subject choose to come to us to talk over the matter further. At the same time, I wish you fully to understand the difficulties which would attend the establishment of any great Society having simply literary work for its object, and the importance of our work being strictly limited to production, and not going (except in certain exceptional cases) into the employment of agency, by which our funds would be consumed, and our efforts to help Missionary Societies in another way put an end to. While we do not employ colporteurs, it is our practice to encourage them as much as possible by the terms on which we supply our publications for their distribution.

A little time ago I took the trouble to single out a number of instances in the great Mission-field in which it was shown that books and tracts had

Conversion by books illustrated. been direct instruments used by God for the conversion and enlightenment of souls, and merely from these records, written without the object of bringing that particular subject forward, I was able to collect fourteen or fifteen successive instances in which these books and tracts, in one or two years, had done the work of evangelisation, and therefore I quite agree with that part of Dr. Murdoch's Paper in which he says that these colporteurs are a very important and necessary agency for every Missionary Society.

Dr. Underhill: Mr. Chairman,—In anticipating these meetings we were not without some grounds for hoping that the question might be stirred which has been stirred here this morning: and that some issue might come out of the gatherings that should call for further conference and

Value of these suggestions. arrangement, and probably for continued action. And I do not know that there is any part of the Conference more important than the suggestions which emanate from the various gentlemen who speak on these occasions. All these suggestions will of course be recorded and published, and will afford a constant source of inquiry in the various Societies which have these particular matters in charge. I do not think we should be able to gather together in any number so as to create some new Society or definite mode of action in regard to this special matter, but I may certainly say, on behalf of the Christian Vernacular Society, of whose Committee I am Chairman, that all that has been said to-day will be most heartily welcomed and conned over and studied in their Committee. I do not know that I am letting out a secret, but in point of fact this question of increasing the literature side of their work has been engaging attention for some considerable time past; and so far as I know the mind of the Committee, I think I may say that there is a purpose in the future to enlarge this particular feature of their work and to strengthen it to the utmost possible degree. We have often discussed the question of a Christian literature; we have made some attempts towards it. We have encouraged friends in India to write, and have assisted in the publication of books that were thought to be suitable; and more especially have we devoted much time and attention to the preparation of various grades of school books, those school books all of them having a Christian character and tendency. In point of fact, the great work that the Vernacular Education Society has done in the publication of literature and school books has come almost entirely from the profits gained upon these school publications, and they have formed a very important part of its annual income; the growth of schools, the multiplication of readers, the great extension of public interest in Christianity, and other things, are calling for a large extension of such publications, and we are attempting to meet that in various ways.

The C.V.E.S. a Literature Society.

I do not know that we should altogether like to be swallowed up in some great Society. I have perhaps a little feeling for a child that I helped to bring to the birth. I think its educational department is now losing some of its importance through the measures taken by Government. At the time it was instituted the Government were not favourable to education, for though the dispatch of 1854 was in existence it had done nothing whatever to carry it into operation; and so fearful were we of being blocked at the very starting, that we paid a visit to Lord Stanley (the late Earl of Derby) to ascertain whether he would oppose our endeavour to promote a purely vernacular education through the various districts of Bengal. He received us very warmly, and we found he would not, and that led to the formation of the Society. I think the Society has done good and excellent work in its time, and if in the progress of Divine Providence its powers can be strengthened and a work be accomplished of the first utility and most eminent necessity, I am sure we shall have the support of the Christian Church, the sympathy of all men who know India, and the help which we need to carry out a work so broad and so extensive.

Would preserve the C.V.E.S.

Rev. John Hesse (Calw, Würtemberg): I am Secretary to a small German Publishing Society, and I wish to say that we are perfectly self-supporting now. We used to give away our books and tracts largely. We do not do so now; we sell, and our circulation is immensely increased since we did so. We have the reputation in Germany that of all books ours are the cheapest, and of cheap books ours are the best. This morning I was asked whether I believed in free distribution or in selling. I believe in both, still I give preference to selling. There are English piece goods sent out to India for sale, which are marked with idolatrous emblems, made here in England,—little pictures of Krishna and other idolatrous things put on them; and there is now a gentleman in the Punjab who has taken up this matter, and proposes that Christian emblems should be put instead, even texts of Scripture, and has pressed that this should be offered to the selling houses that they might put

Books can be sold cheap to pay.

these emblems as trade marks on their goods. That is also a small department of Christian literature which needs attention. Then, as to adapting our methods to the native taste,—singing the Gospel.

The Gospel in song. I once came to the great city of Tanjore, and there I saw a fine building, half Oriental and half European in style. I was told it was the house of a native Christian singer and poet, a member of the Lutheran Leipzig Missionary Church in India. This Society is not represented here, and I wish to mention that because they do an excellent work in Southern India, and they ought to be here. This man and his whole family were given to singing the Gospel. They had evening meetings, chiefly during Passion Week, and the natives used to flock in and hear the whole story of the Passion of Christ by singing.

Rev. R. Glover offered prayer, and the proceedings terminated.

APPENDIX.

Christian Vernacular Education Society for India.

In accordance with the resolution come to at the meeting held on June 15th, we have much pleasure in inserting a reference to the work done by Dr. Murdoch in connection with the Christian Vernacular Education Society for India. The following is a brief abstract of the number and character of the works published by the Society, all of them under Dr. Murdoch's personal supervision, and of many he is the author.

I. *English Books for use in Indian Schools.*—Of these there are no fewer than thirty-one separate works in every department of a plain English education, including a series of graduated " Primers and Readers."

II. *Papers on Indian Reform.*—Under this head there are eight tractates dealing with social, political, and religious questions in a popular way.

III. *India.*—Five books chiefly on sanitary questions, and England's work in India.

IV. *Miscellaneous.*—Under which head there are nineteen books chiefly of a lighter character, such as are likely to induce a habit of reading among the young.

In addition to these we have much pleasure in calling attention to the very interesting series of little books and tracts adapted to Indian readers by the well-known authoress, A.L.O.E., which are also published by the Society, and of which further particulars may be obtained at their office, No. 7, Adam Street, Strand.

MEETINGS OF MEMBERS
IN SECTION.

FIFTEENTH SESSION.

ORGANISATION AND GOVERNMENT OF NATIVE CHURCHES.

(1) ORGANISATION.

(a) The extent to which the lines and forms of Western Church organisation should be perpetuated in the Mission-field ; in creeds and forms of worship, etc.

(b) How soon in the development of the Christian life should converts be left to manage their own ecclesiastical affairs ?

(Thursday afternoon, June 14th, in the Annexe.)

Right Rev. Bishop Stuart, D.D. (of Waiapu), in the chair.
Acting Secretary, Rev. W. J. R. Taylor, D.D. (U.S.A.).

Rev. Dr. Smith offered prayer.

The Chairman: My Christian friends,—I feel very deeply that the question which is to occupy our attention this afternoon is one of the most important, and, at the same time, one of the most difficult, and, in our peculiar circumstances, most delicate Important and questions, which can come before a General United delicate subject. Missionary Conference. There was a time when the supreme importance,—I think I may deliberately use the word—the supreme importance of organising of the Native Church, was not so generally recognised as, I am happy to believe, it now is. But that time—it was the initial stage of Missionary proceedings— has passed, and I may safely say, that every Missionary Society, and each branch of the one Church of Christ, which is engaged in Missionary work, now very fully recognises the importance of the Native Church.

But I have characterised the question as one of great difficulty, and also of peculiar delicacy ; I mean delicacy in handling it in a mixed Conference, in which, as a matter of fact, Missionaries, and the friends and supporters of Missionaries, belonging to various sections of the Church of Christ, are united. When we sang the hymn in which we have just joined, we could all accept the words without any qualification or any misgiving: we can all unitedly pray to the Heavenly Father:

> "Give tongues of fire and hearts of love,
> To preach the reconciling Word."

For up to a certain stage in Missionary operations, the work is very simple. We have to preach Christ and Him crucified; but when God has blessed these initial efforts with success, then comes the question of organising the company of believers into a Church, and on this particular form of organisation our opinions differ.

While I was in Calcutta we had practical co-operation, and one word in Dr. Smith's prayer just now, seemed to go to the very root of this question. I refer to the way in which he recognised the Church of Christ, that is the true invisible Church, the mystical Body of the Lord Jesus Christ; and I would say, at any rate as expressing my own conviction, that this question, and, indeed, all the questions relating to it, of the organisation of the Native Church, will never be firmly grasped or satisfactorily solved, if we lose sight

The Church visible and invisible. of the fundamental distinction, in the present state of things at any rate, between the Church visible and the Church invisible. I believe myself, that the confusion of these two, as it has been the source of manifold errors at home, so it has often been the source of much weakness in our Missionary work abroad. I would then say in discussing this question, let us keep firm hold of the truth of the mystical body of the Lord Jesus Christ as the Church spiritual and invisible. Then the question of the organisation of the outward Church of Christ, though it does not become a question of no importance, yet it will not assume in our eyes an exaggerated importance. And here, as I say, of course, we necessarily differ. Belonging as we do to various sections of that one Body of Christ, we shall all have our different opinions. Though we all, I trust, are united as to what is the real *esse* of the Church of Christ, we may differ in our views of the *bene esse*, of what may be best and most expedient.

I have had put into my hands a Paper which has been written by a Missionary of great experience in Ceylon, on the question of Native Church organisation. On my voyage home from New Zealand, I had the happiness of meeting this Missionary brother, and got his permission to make use of this

Ideal Church of India. Paper. It will to a certain extent supplement what I have already said. The writer thus concludes his remarks with reference to the idea of a great ideal Church of India. I must tell you the writer does not himself believe in a great ideal Church of India. He has pointed out in a previous part of his Paper how India really consists of many different nationalities, and that it is quite illusory to suppose they can be gathered up into one great national Church. He says:—

"If this great ideal Church of India is ever established, and English becomes, as it most certainly would become, the ecclesiastical language of its chief councils and principal members, the further step of making English the language of public worship would certainly follow in due course. The grand ideal of outward unity would be but imperfectly realised, so long as there were divers tongues used in Divine worship. To perfect that realisation there must be one authorised language of worship in the Anglo-Catholic Church, as in the Roman Catholic Church. Local Bishops might know the language of the people over whom they were set, but the higher dignitaries would need a fresh bestowal of the gift of tongues, to minister in the vernaculars, in every part of their provinces. How much better for them that worship should be all in one language! So one consideration combined with another, would ultimately lead to the repetition of the old error of having one authorised language for Divine worship. Doubtless the inconvenience of divers tongues, in a professedly one united Church, was one important reason, in old times, which led to the adoption of the language of the old Roman Empire, as the universal language of the Church. *One language necessary to formal unity.*

" But is not all this longing after a grand ideal contrary alike to God's dealings with the world at large, and to the New Testament idea of the Church of Christ? Difference in language is God's way of dividing nations, and it is useless to strive against it. Empires which include different races, speaking different tongues, can only be held together by one race, the stronger dominating over the weaker by the power of the sword and not by any power of affinity of sympathy. And it is equally useless and vain to try to unite different nations together in one Church. Here, as in secular matters, language must guide and rule. It is God's plan of dealing with men, and we can never improve upon God's plans. *Diversity in tongues, God's plan.*

" Each distinct people must have their own Church or Churches, and must model them to suit their own needs. We give them the essentials of Christianity, but its non-essentials,—things that are for edification, convenience, strength and progress, but not essential to salvation,—such things they must work out for themselves, and when the Christians in any country have become numerous enough and strong enough to do so, they may well be left to work out Church organisation for themselves, according to their own needs and circumstances. The Christian Churches of the future, if left to their own healthy growth and development, will differ much from us, and from each other, but holding the essentials of the faith, they will still, though many folds, be part of the one flock, and that surely is enough for every true Christian to desire. The wish to make one great Anglo-Catholic Church or one great united Church for India is unscriptural in conception, and it will prove hurtful to Christian development in working. The great bane of Christianity in the middle ages was the attempt to make an outward organisation the mark and symbol of the true Church of Christ, as the history of the outcome of that attempt, Satan's masterpiece, the Roman Catholic Church has only too clearly proved. May it not then be that the ' god of this world ' is at work again, dazzling the minds of good and earnest men now, as he dazzled the minds of good and earnest men in the past, that he may lead to the adoption of a line of action similar to that adopted in the days of old, and which will lead to similar results,—results which have done so much to enable him to retain his power over the hearts and minds of men. The events of past history show only too clearly how the power and influence of the ' god of this world ' have been exercised in the course of events, in the world, as well as in the Church; and perhaps that is the reason why history has so often repeated itself. A master mind has been at work, and what he has found to answer his ends in one age, he has tried again in another. *Diversity of Church organisation, useful.* *Roman Catholic unity.*

" It is well, therefore, carefully to consider how far the organisation of a grand Church system, such as the Romish Church (apart from its errors), is in accordance with the mind and will of the Lord as revealed in the New Testament. If it is *not*, then undoubtedly, even a distant and imperfect imitation of it, in Native Church organisation is fraught with danger to the spiritual interests of the infant Christian communities, and may result in spiritual disaster. The Lord Jesus Christ's kingdom is a spiritual kingdom. It is not of this world, though it is in this world, and is destined, when He comes, to rule this world, but not till He comes. Meanwhile, therefore, it is safer to trust but little to outward organisation, beyond what is *The ideal Church tested by Scripture.*

necessary for decency and order, and much to inward spiritual power, 'For the kingdom of God cometh not with observation.' "

With these introductory remarks (I have to apologise for the length to which they have extended), I have much pleasure in calling upon the Rev. Paulus Kammerer to read a Paper on the subject before us.

PAPER.

1. BY THE REV. PAULUS KAMMERER (Basle Missionary Society, from China).

Organisation and Results of the Basle Mission in China.

I. THE MISSION-FIELD.

The Basle Mission has its work among the Hakka tribe, in the province of Kwang-tung (Canton). The tropical clime
Condition of the Hakkas. renders the work there difficult and toilsome for foreigners. The Hakkas having come into the province after the Cantonese tribe had already occupied the fertile valleys, found for their settlements only the remoter and more sterile parts of the country. For this reason we meet with their villages, here and there, scattered among the settlements of the Cantonese. They have but few of the larger towns in the vast regions, whence they have driven out the former inhabitants. They are generally poorer than the other tribes, which, to some extent, look down on them as intruders. On account of the rapid increase of the Hakka people their settlements become too strait for them, hence many try their fortune in the towns of the Cantonese or in foreign countries. In Hongkong, the Straits Settlements, the Indian Archipelago, the United States of America and Australia, the thrifty, hard-working Hakkas form a large proportion of the working classes, and but a small number are found amongst the successful merchants. Like the Chinese in general they are an industrious, clever, frugal, and somewhat cunning race of a materialistic disposition, with but few religious wants.

In the year 1847 the Board introduced their work into China, and gave their first Missionaries instructions to carry the Gospel *to the inland population*,—a plan at that time not without its great
Basle Inland Mission in 1847. dangers—but after the opening of China through the "Treaties," was quickly followed by good results. These instructions faithfully carried out, gave us work amongst a rural population, removed from the old "treaty ports," the character of an "Inland Mission." Our experience tends to show that these country people are a more hopeful soil for the Gospel seed than the sly and crafty inhabitants of the large towns. Only lately one of the few Hakka towns, Chiayin-choo, was taken up as a central station, and here we had to meet much opposition in the endeavour to obtain a proper site and permission to build. And

after all, we find the chief success of the Mission work there among the surrounding country people much more than in the town itself.

This Inland Mission is to-day represented by twelve central, and twenty-five out-stations, spreading over all the country from the shore opposite Hongkong up to the borders of the provinces of Kiang-si and Fuh-kien, a distance of about three hundred miles, with 3,130 converts, of whom 1,900 are communicants.

II. THE LABOURERS OF THE MISSION.

1. *Missionaries.*

Since the commencement of the work (in 1847) twenty-six men have been sent to this field : of these four are dead, one returned invalided, two have left the Mission, four are at present in Europe on furlough, and fifteen are on the field ; nine of the fifteen are married. **Number of Missionaries.** Then we have four ordained native Missionaries, three of whom have received a good education at the Mission college in Basle, and the other in Barmen. Nineteen men, therefore, are in active service. The rule is, that two or more men work together at one centre, but at present want of men and money prevents the carrying out of this excellent principle. That the new comer shall first learn the language appears to us a matter of course ; for this purpose a year or two are given him before any definite charge is entrusted to his hands. Among the European Missionaries there is one layman who has charge of all money transactions, and also of other secular business.

Every three years all European and native Missionaries meet in a general conference. Decisions agreed upon by this body need the final vote of the Home Board. A local committee of three members is appointed by the Home authority for the superintendence of the whole work. The work is divided among them as follows : the Chairman of **Arrangements of work.** the general conference has the supervision of all ecclesiastical affairs, the second is general inspector of schools, and the layman has the charge of secular affairs. These three form the corresponding committee. On proposals and petitions to the Home Board, the members of this committee have to state their opinion, each on the subjects falling within his sphere ; proposals of a general nature require the signature of all.

The Mission-field is divided into two districts ; the Missionaries of each assemble once a year to discuss the affairs of their district. A Chairman of the district conference, a sub-inspector of schools, and a superintendent of secular affairs are elected for each district, who form a sub-committee. On stations, where there is more than one Missionary, the senior is the responsible authority. He carries on correspondence with the home and local committees ; he is also acting treasurer, though this branch can be transferred to another. All of them confer on station affairs as often as there is need. A division of work is agreed upon by the local conference, but must be sanctioned by the Home Committee. Except on private affairs all correspondence with the Home Board has to pass through the hands of the local officers, and the Home Board also transmit their letters to the stations through the local committees. Quarterly reports from every Missionary, and an annual review of every station, are expected at home. Petitions and topics requiring an answer have not to appear in the reports, but must be dealt with separately.

Every member of the Missionary body must be willing to take the charge of another branch of the work, or to remove to another sphere of work as a vacancy may occur. Removals are made easy, as the houses are furnished at the expense of the Mission.

2. Native Agents.

At present we employ in our Chinese Mission seventy-one native helpers who assist the Missionaries in all branches of work. They fall under the following classes—three pastors, nineteen catechists, eighteen sub-catechists, one evangelist, two Bible-women, twenty-two schoolmasters, and six schoolmistresses.

Six classes of native agents.

The pastors are ordained helpers selected out of the body of catechists; they generally superintend the largest out-stations. They have authority to baptise children and to administer the Holy Communion. The baptism of adults is reserved to the Missionary under whose charge the out-station is placed.

The catechists are preachers, who from early youth have been in the Mission schools. They are charged with the care and instruction of the congregations and with preaching the Gospel to the heathen.

The sub- or assistant-catechists are a class of agents who have not, like the catechists, received a theological education, but are recruited out of the ranks of adult converts, who have shown abilities for the work. They undergo a short training for the functions they have to perform, by private instruction, or by sending them for two or three years to the seminary. No one under twenty-six years of age is eligible. Being generally better acquainted with the habits, views, and capacities of the heathen, than the catechists, who grow up under the influence of Christian training, we make use of this class to stir up the heathen, and to act as preachers in newly-established congregations.

Evangelists are itinerant preachers mostly chosen from among the ablest catechists. Their task is, to travel through the whole field of our Mission, in order to preach the Gospel to Christians and to the heathen, and especially to awaken a feeling of union between the different congregations by relating in one the affairs of others, and by exhorting all to mutual intercourse and intercession. It is very difficult to find suitable persons for this kind of work; we have at present but one thus engaged

Of Bible-women we have only two; the fact, that suitable persons are rare, and also that the male agents in the work have much opportunity of reaching the Hakka women with the Gospel, makes this kind of agency less necessary.

Of the twenty-two teachers, eight have been educated in our seminary, and are employed in the parish schools. The remaining fourteen were formerly teachers in heathen schools. After their conversion we put them into vernacular schools, where some Biblical instruction is given by them. The schoolmistresses find work in the girls' schools.

All the agents receive a salary from the Board, and are thus not dependent on the congregations. The pastors receive a fixed salary. For the catechists a system of classified payment is in force according to their ability and to age. Single men have half as much as a married man, and for every child a further allowance is made. The payments of teachers are regulated by efficiency and age. All our agents must obey the call of the local committee to any place, wherever it may be,

Their salaries.

and submit to the orders of the superintendent Missionary. For the
assistance of widows and orphans, funds are established into which the
agents pay 2½ per cent. of their annual income; the sum thus collected
amounts now to about $4,000.

In speaking of the character and ability of our native helpers, I believe
I am not going too far in saying that no other Missionary Society has
more reliable and better qualified agents than the Basle Mission; yet, on
the other hand, it must be confessed that some do their work, as far as
men can judge, only for the salary's sake.

III. The Labours of the Mission.

We proceed now to take a view of the labour itself. I will first show
the mode of propagating the Gospel; next, the manner of organisation and
fostering the converts in the congregations; and finally, I will speak about
our school system.

1. *The mode of propagating the Gospel.*

Sermons for the heathen, such as are usually preached in the chapels of
large cities, are not usual in our inland chapels for want of a regular audience.
The chief work is done by itinerant preaching, distributing and selling tracts
and parts of the Bible. Unfortunately but few Missionaries are so free
from pastoral and educational duties, as to be able to spend all their time
and strength in travelling for this purpose; however, each tries to make
some preaching tours every year.

2. *Congregational work.*

The condition of a congregation on the Mission-field depends, to a great
degree, on the method employed in admitting inquirers to baptism. I
consider this to be one of the most important and difficult questions with which the Missionary has to deal. According to my   Dealing with
experience, it is best in admitting inquirers to be as careful as   inquirers.
possible, for, if mercenary elements once find entrance into the church, they
are not easily got rid of. In our Mission inquirers are mostly requested,
to attend the services regularly for some months at least, if not for a year
and longer, before they are put on the list of catechumens. During this
period they are attentively observed and watched by the agents. Having
given sufficient evidence of sincerity, special instruction to prepare them for
baptism is imparted by the Missionary. The minimum of Christian knowledge required for admittance to the rite, consists in a general conception of
Biblical history, and in knowledge of a short catechism.

The statistics of the Basle Mission in China are as follows: Christians,
3,130, namely 1,900 communicants, and 1,230 non-communicants and
children. There are also 160 catechumens and 280 heathen
boys who attend Christian instruction. But these numbers   Statistics of the
show but inadequately the real results of our work, as many of   Mission.
our converts have emigrated to foreign countries, where they form Christian
congregations, as is the case in Honolulu and Borneo. Emigrants to other
countries are scattered among their countrymen, where many of them
are lights among their heathen compatriots; but to our grief some turn
apostates.

All our converts are gathered into thirty-five congregations, each of
which has one of the native preachers as a leader. The more recent and
smaller gatherings assemble in the homes of Christians, others hire halls

for their meetings, or build chapels of their own, for which they get assistance from the Board.

We administer discipline in the following manner: first, private ex-hortation and admonition by the helper and Missionary; in case of disregard citation before the session, and the threat of exclusion; in failure of reformation, suspension for one year. And if then the delinquent shows no real repentance, his exclusion from the community is decided by the session, and publicly announced at the Sunday morning service. Re-admission is not allowed until the excluded person has, for the space of a year, given evidence of true repentance, and requires the unanimous vote of the session.

Mode of discipline.

I must now say a few words about the organisation of the native com-munity. Every community of fifty members elects a presbyter, and with every increase of fifty members, another is added up to the number of six. These together with the helpers form the local presbytery, under the presidency of the Missionaries of the respective stations. The duty of the presbyters is, to assist the Missionaries and helpers in their pastoral work, and they have also charge of the parish funds. Every congregation raises the following *funds :—*

Presbyters.

I. The church and school fund, which is raised by the Sunday collec-tions. This fund is not to be touched until the interest, together with the church tax, paid by each member, suffice to meet the expenses of the church and school. We have some congregations, whose church and school fund already amounts to over one thousand dollars, which money is laid out in estates.

II. The poor fund is raised on special occasions, such as marriages, baptisms, burials, communions, etc. It is usual, that at baptisms offer-ings are put into the poor box according to the ability of the family. Out of this poor fund aid is afforded to members, who are unable to earn their own livelihood.

III. An annual church tax of at least twenty cents is to be paid by every member over fourteen years of age; this money is collected by the Mission as long as the Board has to pay the native agents.

All these funds, together with the contributions, will by-and-by help us to make the native community self-supporting.

8. *The school work.*

The educational system of our Mission is admitted to be well developed, though perhaps somewhat too complicated.

1. *I first refer to the so-called heathen school.* For this work $1.50 per month is given by the Board in addition to the income of each teacher.

2. *Next to these come our parish schools.* All the children of our converts are urged to go to school. The schoolmasters of the parish schools are trained in our seminary, and have received an education similar to that of our preachers. Much time is spent in acquiring the Chinese book-language and in writing. The dialect is Romanised according to the system of Dr. Lepsius.

In this last experiment much time and money have been wasted by the Basle Mission, in the vain hope that Romanised might be a benefit to the native Christian community. But the effort was a mistaken one. In the eyes of the natives it was an attempt to extirpate the book-language from the Christian community, which meant as much as cutting off the converts from their political and social connections. Therefore, from the time of its introduction, the Romanised met with much opposition by the natives, and as soon as the Board refuses to pay the expenses connected

The Romanised dialect.

with this attempt, it will be thrown over. In the parish school an annual tax of at least twenty cents is collected from every pupil, which goes towards the teacher's salary.

3. *The boarding schools are established* on the principle of orphan-houses; but children of converts who have no opportunity of going to a parish school are received too; these pay a school-tax of forty cents and board-wages of about $2 each per annum. On stations with a boarding school no parish school is established, for the children of the congregation there attend lessons at the boarding school. We have at present four boarding schools for boys, with one hundred pupils in all, and two for girls, with sixty children. The plan of instruction of the boarding school is about the same as in the parish schools. The children generally attend the elementary school from the seventh to the fourteenth year, but there are many who come at a more advanced age, and spend only three or four years in study. Boarding schools.

4. *With two of the boarding schools secondary schools are combined.* Into these boys of all the elementary schools, who are fit and willing, and have their parents' permission, are taken, in order to be trained as helpers for the Mission work. In a course of two years the boys are taught—Bible knowledge, the elementary subjects, and the Chinese book-language and classics, to which a summary sketch of general history is added.

5. Next above the secondary schools *comes the middle school,* only one for the whole field, into which about twenty-five pupils are received, who are taken from the secondary schools. The course is four years, with instruction in the following subjects:—Bible reading, summary of Christian dogmas, Scripture history, singing, music, mathematics, geography, Chinese history, general history, essays on different subjects, Chinese classics and theory of style, and natural history. The lessons are given by a Missionary, and one of the abler catechists. For the special Chinese instructions a converted graduate is engaged. The pupils get board and lodging, but have to pay on an average $3 per annum. Only orphans are admitted free.

In all the above-mentioned schools, examinations are held once a year by the inspector of schools. These have perhaps more the purpose of stimulating the teachers than of measuring the literary attainments of the pupils.

6. Last, but not least, comes *our seminary.* After a training of thirteen years, viz., seven years in the elementary, two in the secondary, and four years in the middle school, the students enter the seminary at about twenty years of age. Another course of four years' study completes their preparation for Mission work. The plan of instruction includes an almost complete theological course. Two Missionaries, one native pastor, and a graduated Chinese teacher, share in teaching the following subjects: Chinese literature, critical analysis of Confucianism; the science and art of teaching, music, introduction to the Old and New Testament, Old and New Testament exegesis, symbolics, homiletics, Church history, dogmatics, Christian ethics, pastoral theology. To teach Greek and Hebrew, as we wished to do so very much, has hitherto been impossible, because the time is wanted for the study of the Chinese book-language. Board and lodging is given to all students free; to poor ones aid in clothing and other requisites is afforded. Training in the Seminary.

Our schools are a great advantage to the Mission work, as well as to the native Church, in more than one respect. A number of clever and trustworthy helpers have already come from them. They are the nurseries, in which not only new ideas are generated, but also new spiritual life is implanted in many young Chinese hearts. Influence of the schools on the work.
The young generation is growing up there free from Chinese superstition, and equipped with Christian and general knowledge. Though Christians cannot be made by training in schools, but only by regeneration through the Holy Ghost, nobody will doubt that Christian knowledge is the basis on which faith is founded. But I cannot help saying that our schools do also

some harm. The money expense is perhaps the least objection ; it is the elevation of our people far above their own position, and the attraction of mercenary elements into the Church by the foreign money spent in school work, by which we are entangled in many difficulties. In this respect, simplification of the educational system on the one hand, and making the natives to participate more in the necessary outlay on the other, would help us to attain still better results !

The Chairman : Bishop Caldwell has furnished a Paper on this important question. He is very well known to us from having laboured for many years in the Tinnevelly Mission in South India, and now for the last fourteen or fifteen years he has exercised the office of Bishop, being chiefly employed in the organisation of the Native Church in the Tinnevelly district. The Paper of Dr. Caldwell will be read by the Rev. W. Gray, formerly of the Madras Mission.

[*Mr. Gray wisely restricted his reading to those parts of Bishop Caldwell's Paper which bore directly on the special subject before the meeting; but we were directed to allow considerable latitude to the writers of Papers, owing to the want of time in making the arrangements. We print it in extenso. It is short; and as it gives the practical experience of organising a Native Church through the whole period of its growth, from a stage not far from its foundation, it is of much practical value, and being from the pen of one of the most esteemed and venerable of Indian Missionaries, will be prized by all.—*Ed.]

PAPER.

2. BY BISHOP CALDWELL, D.D. (S.P.G., of Tinnevelly). Read in part by the REV. W. GRAY (Secretary, C.M.S.).

Missionary Methods.

I have been asked to write a Paper on " Missionary Methods." In consenting to do so I must restrict myself to *giving some account of my own methods*, at the risk of appearing to be egotistical, as I can only speak of my own methods with the authority of personal knowledge.

On my arrival in Madras, on the 8th of January, 1838—now more than fifty years ago—my first work was, of course, to apply myself to the study of the vernacular of the district. After this, during the three years I resided in Madras, the only sphere of work I found open to me was amongst domestic servants ; and though this might be considered a very humble sphere of work, I devoted myself to it with all my might, and learned from it my first lessons regarding Missionary methods. My plan was, *to make the congregation the centre round which all work revolved.* I set myself, with the help of my native assistants, to invite individuals personally *to attach themselves to the congregation*, and as soon as any

Long personal experience.

person was in this way-brought under systematic Christian influences
I stirred him up to bring over his relatives and friends. In this way
it was hoped that each soul that was gained would become a centre
of light to other souls. The plan succeeded beyond expectation, and
before I left Madras the congregation became too large for the building. The essentials of the plan—viz., *the making the congregation the
centre of all work,* and endeavouring to make each convert a Missionary to his friends,—were such as I have ever since acted upon in
Tinnevelly, and are *such as might be safely acted upon in every part
of the world.*

I arrived in Tinnevelly about the end of the year 1841, and from
the moment of my arrival was resolved not to be content with pastoral work, such as ministering to Christian congregations, but set
myself to the work which I believed was especially incumbent upon
me as a Missionary of the Society for the Propagation of   **Evangelistic**
the Gospel—viz., the work of *endeavouring to propagate*   **work in**
the Gospel amongst those still living in heathen darkness.   **Tinnevelly.**
I found the majority of the inhabitants of Idaiyangudi itself still heathens, and multitudes of heathens all around, besides multitudes upon
multitudes within the distance of a few days' journey at most; and I
found all these people willing to listen, if not to learn, and especially
willing to come to me when invited, and hear patiently what I had to
say. The rudeness and violence occasionally met with by Missionaries in other parts of the country were here unknown. A wide door
was thus open to me for Christian teaching and the exercise of
Christian influences.

One object I had in view in *building schools,* as far as possible, in
every village, was that I might not only instruct the children of the
places, but that I *might have a convenient place in each village
which I could call my own, over which I had authority,* to which   **Double use of**
I could invite people of the neighbourhood to come and listen at   **schools.**
their leisure to my addresses, and receive such instruction as they were prepared for, with answers to their questions, and explanations of the difficulties
they felt. *This plan I always followed wherever I went, up to the last.* Though
I occasionally tried street preaching in the ordinary meaning of the term, I
always felt more or less dissatisfied with this plan as abounding in interrup-
tions and leading to frequent irreverence. Hence I was always glad to fall
back on the plan of assembling the heathen of the place in a schoolroom or
some convenient place where these evils could be avoided. Where I had a
congregation, however small, I erected for them, or (as was always possible
after a time) got them to erect for themselves, a place of worship, to be used
either as a church alone, or as a church and school combined; and there
after prayers with the Christians, and examination of the Scripture lessons
they had learnt, I generally took my seat outside, when numbers of the
heathens of the place would always come about, led doubtless partly by
curiosity, and then, as elsewhere in schoolrooms, I addressed the people
assembled, as circumstances seemed to require, followed by addresses from
our Christian teachers. On these occasions I was never content with lec-
turing to the people in an abstract, desultory way, without any definite aim,
but *always invited them to join the Christian congregation of the place,* **from**

which and from its ordinances they would receive the sympathy and help they needed to enable them to live to God. As I made it my duty to spend three days every week in the villages, this plan brought me into frequent contact with the people in their natural condition, and enabled me to acquire much useful knowledge as well as much local influence.

The results of my work amongst the heathen, though far from being equal to my wishes and aims, have been such as to give me much cause for thankfulness. The western portion of the district *Results of work.* developed to such a degree that it was formed into a separate district, that of Radapuram, and this is now included in the Idaiyangudi returns. The number of congregations in 1841 was fourteen. Now, in 1888, the number of congregations, or of villages in which congregations, large or small, have been formed, including Radapuram, is one hundred and twenty-nine. The number of Christians, that is, of persons under regular Christian instruction, in those villages, including Radapuram as before, and including catechumens, has risen during the same time from twelve hundred and one to eight thousand one hundred and sixty-seven. Radapuram has seventy-three congregations, and three thousand five hundred souls under Christian instruction. I was never contented with my own work alone amongst the heathen, nor even with working in conjunction with catechists ; but set myself to stir up the native Christians, including the new converts in each village, to work amongst their heathen neighbours, and to help them to form themselves into organised associations for evangelistic purposes. I made them promise to devote a specific time to this work—if possible, some portion of a day every week, and the associations were to send in their reports to me every month. This is done regularly in some districts ; still I endeavoured to induce *women* as well as men to engage in this work, as I could not but know that in India, even amongst the poorest classes, men cannot visit women in their houses to speak to them freely alone ; so that without the aid of Christian women the women of India must remain outside the pale of Christian influences. It is on this account that in large towns, amongst women of the higher classes, the work done by Zenana ladies is so necessary and valuable. I induced the Christian women engaged in voluntary evangelistic work to form themselves into associations, meeting regularly for prayer and consultation, and sending their reports to me from time to time.

I required every catechist, from the commencement of my work in the district, to devote a day a week to evangelistic work, and arranged that he should always invite a few of the members of his congregation to accompany him, that he might initiate them into the best way of carrying on this work and prepare them for carrying it on afterward alone or in connection with the associations which began to be formed.

A few years after my arrival I found the people and agents sufficiently advanced to enable me to form amongst them an

Evangelistic Association on a larger scale with wider aims. This was an association for evangelising the western portion of the district which was then almost wholly heathen. Funds were raised for this object among the people themselves and evangelists appointed, who were to work together on a definite plan, with a map of the district in their hands, and to come to Idaiyangudi once a month to relate at a public meeting what they had said and done in each place, and to join in a special service with special prayers for the wisdom and strength, the patience, love, and zeal they so much required. This association was very popular, and received much better support than the Church Councils, which were afterwards established with the object of inducing the people to support their own agents themselves. The latter object appeared the more necessary if we were ever to have a self-supporting Native Church, but the former, *the work of the Evangelistic Association*, appealed more directly to the Christian sympathies of the people. I considered that this association was favoured with remarkable success, inasmuch as the district in which it worked became in time an important independent district under the name of the district of Radapuram.

I found in the district a few isolated congregations which had been formed by the Missionaries of the London Missionary Society in those parts of the district which were contiguous to Travancore, but those congregations were, after a time, generously made over to me by that Society, so that the whole of the western division of the district came under one head and one administration. This new district was first placed under the care of the Rev. D. Samuel, a native of Idaiyangudi, trained by myself, now a B.D. It is now under the care of four native pastors.

Evangelistic work amongst the heathen still goes on, and wherever I go *I do what I can to stir up the native pastors, agents, and people to be more and more earnest and zealous in this important work.* Last year at Idaiyangudi during the three months' preparation of twenty-five candidates for ordination, I sent them out two by two one day every week to gain experience in evangelisation, in the hope that the benefit of this part of their training would appear afterwards in the districts to which they might be appointed.

In 1876 I commenced and carried on for about a year a series of Evangelistic Missions in places inhabited by the so-called higher castes, who had not yet been induced to join the Christian Church by any of the agencies and influences hitherto at work. I wrote and printed five journals of my work in this department, giving the fullest particulars with regard to each place. I was anxious to try for myself the effect of endeavouring to make converts among that class, not by means of schools, but by means of direct preaching. I enlisted a band of competent, zealous assistants. The result, however, was that I found I was obliged to look, as before, *almost entirely to teaching in Mission*

An Evangelistic Association formed.

Catholicity of L.M.S.

Experience among the higher castes.

schools for direct fruit. I have had some experience in the work
of conversion myself, and have tried in succession every variety of
method, but the remarkable fact remains *that during the whole of my
long Indian life I believe that not one educated high-caste Hindu
has been converted to Christianity in this part of the country except
directly or indirectly through the influence of Mission schools.* Such
converts may not be very numerous, I regret that they are not, but
they are more numerous than has been supposed, and *they are all
that are.* No other system can claim any conversions at all amongst
persons of that class. In 1881 when I made some inquiries on this
point, I found that in the Noble School, in Masulipatam, they had
had twenty-five high-caste converts, of whom sixteen were Brahmans, and that the number of converts of this class in Palamcotta
was thirty-six, of whom three had relapsed. In this way we have
had conversions in connection with all the Society for Propagating
the Gospel schools in Tinnevelly and Ramnad. The conversions in
connection with the Society for Propagating the Gospel colleges and
schools in Tinnevelly number between forty and fifty.

The only place where my evangelistic work among the higher
classes and castes bore direct fruit was a place called Alvar Tiru-
Nayari, a Brahmanical town with a famous temple, where
we had a flourishing Anglo-vernacular school, which at
that time was under the care of a headmaster, who used
every opportunity for filling the minds of his pupils and the young
men of the place with Christian truth, and who had acquired much
influence for good. The Brahmans of the place were so friendly
that they allowed me to make use of the great entrance hall of the
temple as a lecture-room. On one occasion when the Rev. Luke
Revington gave an address in that place, there were more than two
thousand Brahmans and high-caste people present, besides about two
hundred native Christians. After this address I devoted several
days to more private addresses to inquirers, when fifteen or twenty
pupils professed a desire to become Christians. They told me one
evening that they had just then been holding a meeting for prayer
by the river side, when they had resolved to follow the example of
Lydia, whose heart had been opened to receive the truth preached to
her by St. Paul, in a similar place. Six of the young men referred
to have been baptised, two of whom were baptised by Mr. Revington,
in a stream, during a subsequent visit. All these have remained
steadfast, though one of them, the leader of the party, was removed
by death some time after.

Famine Relief and the Gospel.—All through the period of the great
famine in 1877 and 1878, but especially during the period when famine
relief was being distributed, the accessions from heathenism
were very numerous. The number of souls in this way brought
under Christian influence reached in all the large figure of nineteen thousand. Of course the motives of persons who joined the Christian
community during a period of famine would necessarily be open to some

[marginal note:] Conversion of Brahman students.

[marginal note:] Accessions during the famine.

suspicion, but the fact remains that whatever their motives were at first, they were carefully instructed in Christian truth and duty, and that the great majority have remained steadfast to the present day. *It was a very important consideration that we had the children of all those people under our care from the beginning to train up for God.* Two classes of influences had been brought to bear upon them from the first,—one was the teaching they received from the evangelistic associations which had everywhere been formed, and the other was the impression produced in their minds by the wonderful kindness of the Christian people of England in sending such large sums of money for their relief in a time of extreme distress, when their Brahman priests had left them to die.

If our first work in any place was the endeavour to bring non-Christians into the Christian fold, our second, and not less important work, was that of instructing and training those new *Training* people in Christian doctrines and practices, so as to make *Christian* them, if possible, Christians worthy of the name. Here *converts.* the congregation was, as before explained, the basis and centre of our work. Generally each congregation was under the care of a catechist, but sometimes, if funds were deficient and the congregations were small and contiguous, one catechist would have the care of several congregations. There was an abbreviated service daily in every village in addition to a more fully developed service on Sundays. A speciality of the services was the reading of the Psalms for the day in alternate verses by all who were able to read, and the number of whom was continually increasing. After the Sunday service a Bible class or adult Sunday school was held, divided into two portions, one consisting of those who could read, and the other a very necessary class at first, consisting of those who were unable to read and who had to be instructed orally. A portion of Scripture was always appointed to be committed to memory and repeated at those Bible classes, and appropriate lessons were appointed to be learnt by the others. I used to employ an inspecting catechist to visit each village in turn for the double purpose of examining the schools and examining the lessons the people of the congregation had learnt. Now that we are well supplied with native pastors this work is undertaken by the pastors themselves, who exhibit to me, from time to time, the returns of their work.

The most important part of the work of the district was the weekly meeting of the catechist and schoolmaster, attended afterwards by the native pastors also. At this meeting all *Weekly meeting* who lived within six miles were expected to be present, *of catechists.* coming in the morning, and returning to their villages in the evening, except once a month, when there were special services and when they stayed over the night. This meeting comprised two classes ; a superior class, instructed by myself, and an inferior one, under the care of a catechist, or native minister. On these occasions, one portion of the work done was the exhibition of returns of work, with *vivâ voce* reports of any special event, including accessions, if there had been any. Another portion of the work was an exposition of some portion of Scripture, when notes were taken of the principal points in the lecture. Another point was the composition of a sermon. The plan I adopted was to give out a text, and request five or six persons to go out for half an hour, and prepare themselves to preach extemporaneously on the text for five or eight minutes in the presence of the assembled body. After they had done this, I called upon those who had filled the position of hearers to make any remarks on the sermons they thought fit, and I then went over the sermon myself, and made such amendments as seemed to be required. This final revision was written down at length by every person present, and thus a sermon appropriate to the people and the place was provided weekly for every congregation. We then concluded with a prayer, offered by some of the catechists in turn. One of the most important parts of our plan was the general annual examination of all our catechists, schoolmasters and mistresses, in the books of Scripture, and other subjects set them to study at these weekly meetings, with prizes for proficiency. At one time they were all assembled for this examination in one place, from all parts of the country, but this was found rather inconvenient, so that, afterwards, we adopted the plan of examination by written questions and answers.

In addition to the ordinary instruction of the people in the congregations, we have always had special classes for special purposes. Special classes. One class is for preparation for baptism, another for preparation for confirmation, and another for preparation for Holy Communion. The last class always precedes the celebration of Holy Communion, being held the evening before. To help forward the work of these classes, I have prepared in Tamil a series of elementary books. One is an elementary catechism, in very simple language, on the most essential Christian facts and doctrines for the use of candidates for baptism; another is a catechism on confirmation; another is a companion to the Holy Communion, containing instructions, meditations, and prayers, for use especially at the preparatory meetings.

I conclude with a brief reference to the means adopted for the promotion of self-support and self-government. This is by means Self-support and self-government. of a Church Council established in every district, composed of members elected by each congregation, subordinate to a general council representing the division. This council has the control of the funds of the district, and much administrative power, which it is learning to use wisely.

I trust that these *miscellaneous notes on Missionary methods*, though so exclusively local, will be found interesting by those who are engaged in similar work in other parts of India, or in other parts of the great field of the world.

DISCUSSION.

Rev. W. McGregor (English Presbyterian Mission, Amoy): My Lord, and Christian friends,—I wish to say a few words with regard to our experience in Church organisation in Amoy, in South China. We have felt that Church organisation is of the very utmost importance for carrying on the work of the Gospel in China. When a man becomes a Christian he is very apt to sink down gradually in his Christian character and conduct; and our experience has been that which is indicated in Bishop Caldwell's paper, that the congregation is the centre from which one has to work. Our work has to be done through the congregation. *Experience in Amoy.*

Being connected with a Presbyterian Mission, our method has been to organise congregations. Where a few members have been received into the Church, they are organised into a congregation, under the care of a preacher, and by-and-by, as the congregation grows, some of their number are selected as elders. We visit these congregations, preaching every Lord's day, evangelising the neighbourhood, and looking after the character and Christian life of the converts. We visit these congregations as often as we can overtake them, administer ordinances, examine candidates for baptism, and preach the Gospel. By-and-by, when a congregation becomes strong enough to maintain a pastor of its own, we encourage the people to call one of our preachers as their own pastor. We take means to make the various congregations acquainted with the character of the preachers, by causing them to circulate among the Churches, and we ordain no man to the Christian ministry until a congregation is prepared to support him. These congregations then have their native ministers and their elders, according to our Presbyterian order. Alongside of us, in Amoy, we have another Presbyterian Mission, the Reformed Church of North America. Their method is the same as ours, and the congregations that are gathered by them, and the congregations gathered by us, are formed into one native Chinese Church, with a common Presbytery. In that Presbytery at present, there are the Missionaries belonging to our Mission, and those belonging to the Reformed Church of North America: there are eleven ordained native ministers, supported by their own congregations, and there are seventeen representative elders, from their respective congregations. *Plan in the Presbyterian Mission.*

The Chairman: Native?

Rev. W. McGregor: All natives. We have found this Presbytery of the very greatest importance in carrying on our Mission work. Supposing, for instance, some question arises with regard to the social life of the Chinese: it may be a question whether some particular custom is idolatrous or not, whether it should be distinctly forbidden and Church discipline exercised upon those who practise it, or whether we should simply try to restrain it. Such questions as these come up continually. We have them discussed in our Presbytery. We have there the best representatives of our Native Church; we can get them to express their opinion freely; we express our opinion freely; and the decision carries with it much greater weight than it would if it were merely the decision of Foreign Missionaries. The Chinese are a people who, like many oriental peoples, have a great deal of pride of their own, and the more we can make them realise that this Church is a Chinese Church, the better in every way, and our effort is to bring our native members to the front and ourselves retreat into the background. We may exert a good deal of *Natives in the Presbytery.*

influence in the background, but the more prominent the natives are the better. Our hope is, and our aim is, in this way to produce a self-supporting and self-propagating Native Church; for even if a Foreign Missionary were stationed in every village in China, that would not make China a Christian land. The Christianity must become indigenous to the soil, and our hope, our aim is that the Church itself shall thus grow and spread until it fill the land.

I wish to say one thing also with regard to creeds. I am a Presbyterian, and you know our creeds are pretty definite; and we in China had our own creed, the Westminster Confession, and the shorter Catechism; and alongside of us we had the Reformed Church of North America, with the Heidelberg Catechism and the Belgic Confession; and if we were to lay all this as a burden upon our native Presbytery, it would be pretty heavy, and rather more than they would be able to understand. Instead of this we proceeded—not we, the Foreign Missionaries alone, but with the assistance of our native Presbytery—we proceeded according to Presbyterial order, and appointed a committee to prepare a confession. This confession was sent to the various congregations, to be examined by all the office-bearers, and reported upon to the committee. It was passed through the Presbytery on two separate occasions, first for approval, and then for final revision, and it has been approved and printed and published, and is now *the accepted confession of this native Chinese Church.*

The native Church's confession of faith.

It is a brief confession of eight articles, which all the children in our native schools can commit to memory, and do commit to memory, and upon which they can be examined. I think this is really the way in which these things will be settled in the East. I have found that the same thing has occurred in Japan. In that country there are various Presbyterian bodies, and they each wished to bring their own confession to the front. The Japanese have declined, and insisted upon having a confession of their own. "Formerly," they said, "there came to us one confession from America, and there came another from Great Britain. Why should not we have some symbolic work of our own?" And they have, I believe, at the present time, virtually decided to accept the articles of the Evangelical Alliance as their confession, for they are negotiating just now for a union not only among all Presbyterian Churches in Japan, but with the Congregational Churches, so that all the Congregational Churches and the Presbyterian Churches may be united in that one bond of union.

Pastor A. Haegert (Bethel Santhal Mission): My Lord, and gentlemen,—I was sorry at one time to perceive that in our Church there were some members who did nothing for Christ. One Sunday morning I begged that the men would remain as I wished to talk to them. The service having been completed the congregation retired and all the men remained. After prayer I said, "Well, friends, what do you say; to-day is Sunday. 'Remember the Sabbath and keep it holy.' Will it be sanctified by us all going home and having our dinner and going to sleep? The heathen might do that, but that would not sanctify the Sabbath. Would you not rather go out into the villages and preach?" They said they would. Then I asked them to choose their partners so that they might go two and two. Each chose a partner, and they formed about ten parties to go into the different villages to preach Jesus. Well, then we had prayer and separated.

Organising evangelistic work.

Afterwards the Christian women of the place had a meeting, and they formed the plan of going two by two into the different villages on the Sunday to speak for Jesus; and they said, "Father does not think much of us, he did not ask us to the meeting. Now," they said, "we will do the same as the men. Why should we not? There are lots of women in the villages, heathen women, and why should not we go to them?" They chose partners, two and two, and went to the different villages on a Sunday afternoon to speak for Jesus: and this was continued for months; but then the opposition, the insults, the sneers, and the abuse the women received were so painful that they thought they would do better by dividing into two companies to go in different directions to preach for Christ. I wish to say that in Mission work the first thing in my humble opinion is to form a Church among the heathen ; secondly, to organise them by urging them to choose their leaders ; and thirdly, to set all the congregations to work for our Saviour. May I say that in this Mission we have now seventeen chapels, a big church, and Christians in forty villages.

Rev. C. F. Warren (C.M.S., from Japan) : My Lord Bishop,—Really when I entered this room I did not think that one of such short experience in the Mission-field as myself would be in a position to address a meeting like this ; yet I have seen some little of the working of the Church of Christ in Japan, and I am very anxious to give utterance to two or three thoughts, and to state two or three facts regarding it.

I am very sorry that we have not got to the real point of the discussion. The question before us is, " The extent to which the lines and forms of Western Church organisation should be perpetuated in the Mission-field." I think the first essential thing to be remembered is this, that Christianity is not a form, it is a life, and it is a life that is to show itself in its own characteristic developments wherever it may be *Christianity is a life.* found ; the Christianity of Great Britain may be very different, and will no doubt be very different, from the Christianity of Japan, that is in the way and the forms of its manifestation, and I take it that it will be the same also in the forms of worship which the Churches will adopt in due time.

As a matter of course we gather our converts into our Churches, and try to model our institutions on, I will not say, the same lines, but something like the same lines, as those which were adopted by the old Missionaries. Well, now, that is all very well so far as it goes, but I feel that is only the initial stage of Church organisation. Then you have heard from the dear brother who spoke just now, how that the Presbyterian bodies in Japan have *The union of Churches in Japan.* united into what they call the one Church of Christ in Japan, or the Union Church of Christ in Japan ; and the Congregational Churches, although each congregation is in itself a separate unit according to the Congregational idea, has nevertheless formed something like a Congregational Union, and they are going, or trying at any rate, to bring about this union between Congregationalists and Presbyterians, leaving the poor Episcopalians, like myself, out in the cold. But, my dear friends, much as one may sympathise with all this drawing together, and I do sympathise with it myself thoroughly, I think there is danger lest we should after all emphasise Presbyterianism on the one side or Episcopalianism on the other, or some other division, and so bring about a permanent division of the Church of Christ in Japan. What I would prefer is that we should all work on our own lines, keeping steadily in view the United Church in the future, and not so lay down our rules for ourselves and our brethren doing the same for themselves, as much as to say, These are the lines upon which the Church of the future must run. Rather, let us do all in our power to foster union and communion between the different bodies of the Christians, while carrying on our work on our own lines, and keeping steadily before us the idea of a United Church in the future if we can well bring it about. And that is what the Japanese desire, and that is what I desired when I first went into Japan, and that is what I still desire when I go back this year to that country.

Now there is another important question, and that is, when the converts are to be left to manage their own ecclesiastical affairs. That is, I think, a very vital question ; but it is a question which will not receive the same answer in all

Mission-fields. It is a thing you cannot measure by years; it is a question of development, and a question for the Churches themselves. The Self-government Church in Japan will be much more ready to govern itself in a few of native Churches. years than some Churches which have been established much longer. It is a question of the development of the spiritual life and the spirit of self-support, and of the power of the Churches to govern themselves; and surely God will guide us in regard to that matter. Let us ever keep before our minds this fact, that we are to plant in these distant countries Churches not dependent on the Mother Church, and not dependent on the Church of England or on the Presbyterian Church or any other body of Christians, but that we are to establish independent Churches, national Churches, if you like, certainly independent Churches, growing out of the spiritual life of the peoples among whom they are planted; and when these native Christians have got to that point of development, when they are prepared to support their own institutions, I should like that no power outside their own country, ecclesiastical or civil, shall in any way interfere with the development of God's work in their midst. I think that is what we are working to, and although I am a loyal Churchman, a member of the Church of England, loyal to my Prayer Book and loyal to my Articles, loyal to the constitution of the Church to which I have the privilege to be a minister, I shall go back to Japan with that thought in my mind, and it will be my one prayer to do all in my power to bring about a United Church of Japan.

Rev. Robert Tebb (Wesleyan Missionary Society, from Ceylon): My Lord,—I have the pleasure of standing here to say a few words, because I think the subject which is before us this afternoon has reference to Churches that have been for some time in operation. I think a great deal has been said about the initial work, and of course in all Churches there is that initial work, but the Church with which I have Personal experience. been connected for several years has passed out of the initial stage, and we have now several self-supporting, self-governing, and self-propagating Churches. My own view of Western creeds and forms of worship is what has been wrought into my own soul:—

"Let names and sects and parties fall,
And only CHRIST be all in all."

And I would therefore say let the arrangement of these matters be made entirely subordinate to the development of the spiritual life that was so earnestly inculcated by the last speaker.

We have in connection with the Church to which I belong a large central gathering, where we have a proportion of, at any rate, six or A council of seven native ministers to one European Missionary, and all these native ministers. native ministers have an equal vote with the European Missionaries in the management of the affairs of all the Churches connected with that large district.

A Member of the Conference: Where is it?

Rev. Robert Tebb: In Ceylon. We have had sometimes three Missionaries with twenty native Ministers, and so you can see that my view is that the Church should be distinctly a Native Church. As I have travelled about from station to station I would never preside in one of the native Churches where the native minister was present. I would say, "Here is the person who is appointed to regulate these matters, and I am here as his 'guide, philosopher, and friend,' and as the friend of all of you; but I want you to look to him as your pastor, and treat him accordingly." Therefore you can see from our mode of working we are Connexional. Then, of course, we have all affairs brought before this central authority, which we call the District Meeting—schools, itineration, and every matter pertaining to the Church. Well, now, just to come to the Native Church itself. Of course the pastor comes from the Native Church to the District Meeting, and we want as soon as we can, to get the native minister attended by, at all events, two delegates from each Native Church. We have not got quite as far as that, yet; but that is the idea that we have, that each Church should be fully represented on the central authority. Then if you go to the station, or as we call it, the Plan adopted by Wesleyan Church. circuit, we make the station the centre of a number of villages, from perhaps three or four up to ten. Then we get the native minister supported by a native council, who as laymen—call them by what name you like—gather round him, and they form the court for the regulation of the educational, evangelistic, and every other agency in the locality. The Missionary occasionally goes to see that things are going on well; but really the authority is vested in this meeting of the Church over which the native pastor presides.

I will just give you one illustration of the blessing which has attended it. We arranged one of our circuits in this way, gave its officials the authority I have mentioned, and they had a decreasing grant to support their Illustration of its effect. institutions. Then in a few years they took complete charge of the schools; they built a large chapel which cost in English money £700; they built their native minister a house which certainly was equal, I should think, to anything a native would wish to live in, and, indeed, equal to what any European would be quite willing to live in, and also a splendid school hall; they raised an amount of money to send the Gospel to another station which they formed themselves; and, therefore, my full conviction is that if we as Christians are to do anything really effective in evangelising the world, we must insist on a Native Church: bring every native forward that it is possible to bring forward, put them into positions of authority, because that is the way to develop them; trust them, love them as brethren, go with them, be with them, and you will find if you treat them in this way that they will speedily come up to their responsibilities; but if you treat them as children, we shall have a burden upon us which we cannot bear, and the Church of Christ will not prosper. Mind you, I do not care whether it is Presbyterianism, or Episcopalianism, or any other ism, if it is only advancing the kingdom of the Lord Jesus Christ; and I think this may be done very extensively if we cultivate this spirit of self-sacrifice, and allow the Lord to work through His people to the extension of His own kingdom.

Mr. Henry E. Clark (Friends' Foreign Mission, Madagascar): Mr. Chairman,—We seem to have all sorts and conditions of men on this platform this afternoon. I am a member of the Society of Friends, a Quaker. I confess to being a little disappointed with the character of the two Papers which were read to us. After more than fifteen years' work in Madagascar among the Churches there, I came here to learn something of what other friends are doing in different parts as to this Church organisation; I came to learn and I have hardly found that instruction which I wished for. We have heard a good deal about the formation of Organisation in Madagascar. Churches, but in Madagascar we have had what I might almost call a spontaneous formation of them. Many of you know that the London Missionary Society and the Society of Friends have worked now in harmony in Madagascar for many years in the central province, doing what we can shoulder to shoulder in carrying out the work of Christ in the centre of the island. Many of you will know the history of the Church in Madagascar. When the Queen adopted Christianity in 1868 all the people thought they must adopt it too, and there was a mighty rush of people into the Churches, and almost every little village formed its own Church; they did not wait for us to form it, they formed it for themselves. What we have had to do is to unite these Churches, and to teach them and to help them to govern themselves.

We have at Antananarivo a six months' meeting very much after the character of the Congregational Union of England and Wales, but containing also some elements of the yearly meeting of the Society of Friends; but we allow the Malagasy to carry out that form of worship they feel most adapted to, and which best meets the genius of the people. In this meeting of representatives of hundreds of Churches,—for we deal with hundreds there, not with one, two, or three,—for one year a Missionary takes the chair, and another year a Malagasy takes the chair. There is also a large meeting connected with it, a prayer meeting, and one six months the Missionary gives the address, and another six months a Malagasy gives the address. We do whatever we can in Madagascar to let the Malagasy Church carry out that form of worship and that form of service which they feel and which we feel is most adapted to the wants of the people. It is a Malagasy Church; it is not an English Church; it is not an Independent,—it is not a Quaker Church; it is not Episcopalian; but in some way it resembles them all. The Missionary is like a little Bishop. I had forty churches under my care, who looked to me for help, upon whom I might almost say the responsibility of the Church devolved; and people were continually coming to me for advice and for help.

Organisation of the Malagasy Church.

This Malagasy Church has, during the past fourteen years, raised nearly £2,000 for the extension of the Gospel in the outlying provinces. You will say that £2,000 is not very much; but when you can buy a sheep for a shilling and beef for three farthings a pound, you will see that a little money goes a long way. And it is interesting to find that these Malagasy, with the gift of talk so largely developed, when they receive this Gospel, these glad tidings of great joy which they find bring such comfort to their own hearts, must go and tell somebody else the glad tidings that they have heard. Are we to tell them they must not go? Not in any way. We are to help them as far as we are able to do so in carrying on by themselves with our help this Church organisation in Madagascar; and I fully agree with those who have gone before that we must not try to transplant our English opinions out there in Madagascar, and say, "Unless you follow our customs we won't have anything to do with you." We are to be with them, to help them, to lead them; but do not drive them. The Malagasy will not be driven; but they may be led, and they may be helped, and they may be coaxed into right ways; and that is just what we have been endeavouring to do there.

Its Missionary zeal.

Rev. Professor T. Smith, D.D. (Free Church College, Edinburgh, formerly of Calcutta): My Lord,—Allow me first of all to reciprocate the kindly sentiments which you expressed at the beginning of the meeting, and to express the satisfaction which I have in renewing in London the intimate acquaintance that we had long ago in Calcutta. I gave my name to speak;—well, let me just say that I very cordially agree and rejoice in the sentiments expressed by the gentleman who said he was from Japan—Mr. Warren. I dare say you may remember, my Lord, that I was a pretty stern Presbyterian, and had a great desire that all people should be such as I am.

I have always maintained, I did in India, and I have since I came home from India, that the Government of India and the Churches of India should conduct their operations with a view to their own effacement, that is to say, that the Government should govern India in such a way as to prepare the natives at as early a period as possible for governing themselves; and so I say that our Missions ought to be conducted in such a way that as early as possible our native Churches should

Missions should lead to self-government.

be self-dependent, self-supporting, self-governing, independent of us altogether. Now, that is precisely the second point in the consideration of our subject for this afternoon. "How soon in the development of the Christian life should converts be left to manage their own ecclesiastical affairs?" As I have united the two, the Government of India and the Churches of India, I may say I have long felt that the Government of India have been going a great deal too fast in their pushing forward of the natives, when they are not prepared for it. I think it would have been better if they had been kept longer outside of the positions that they have been forced into before they are ready for them. Very well, it is apt to be so in regard to our Church organisation. We must have these organisations rising up, naturally, not with our European systems and our European methods patched on, but they must grow out of a developed Christianity, and they will run into their own peculiarities or into our peculiarities soon enough. I do trust that we shall be wisely guided in regard to this matter. It is one of extreme difficulty, and as you stated at the outset one of very great delicacy. It is one in which a great deal depends upon the wisdom of those who shall have a part in the regulation of it.

Rev. John F. Gulick (A.B.C.F.M., from Japan): Christian friends,—I shall confine myself to a very few remarks on the second point. "How soon in the development of the Christian life should converts be left to manage their own ecclesiastical affairs?" And I shall not promise to answer in categorical terms the number of years, or the exact definitions by which we can tell exactly the day and the year, but I think there are certain general principles by which we may safely test Christians in the Christian world, and in the heathen world as Churches are gathered. One or two of these principles have been incidentally referred to. I think it was Mr. Warren from Japan who has already said that he advocated this view of the subject, partly because it led to self-sustaining and self-supporting and self-propagating Churches that should be permanently planted in the country. Now I think it may be said that no Mission has been planted, and that Christianity has never been planted in a country until it gains root, first for its livelihood, second for its management and organisation, and thirdly for its propagation in that country. When that has been attained then Christianity has been planted there. It will go on to triumph, and the country will become Christian.

Now, how soon can we venture to throw this responsibility on the Churches. First, it is evident that the number of years, the period of Christian tutelage and of continuous teaching and direct organisation of the Church will differ in different countries somewhat, according to the intellectual capacity and development of the people among whom they exist. The work at the Sandwich Islands very rapidly developed, a large number of the population were gathered into the Churches early in the history of the Mission; and though it may very reasonably be asked whether the management of those Churches was not delayed too long, still I think it is very manifest that the whole responsibility could not have been thrown upon the Hawaiian Churches, the Churches of the Sandwich Islands, as early as it could safely be borne by the Churches in Japan, where the development, the natural resources of the people, their culture, and the culture found amongst many of the leading members and the Church pastors, is of a much higher grade.

Still, further, I think we may lay down as one principle that as you can develop in them a spirit of working, and a readiness to give assistance to the work, so you may begin to throw upon them the responsibility of managing the work. The two things go together. If you never throw upon them any responsibility, you cannot expect them to come up to the full measure of giving and of consecrating their lives and their time, and their thought and enthusiasm; for this consecration of life comes with the feeling of manhood that is associated with being the ser

Capability and responsibility of converts.

vant of Christ rather than the servant of any Foreign Missionary; and the two things act and re-act on each other. If you are very slow about throwing responsibilities upon them, the development of their independent energies and enthusiasm for Christian work will be dwarfed, and on the other hand if you throw on to them large responsibilities in the way of managing an organisation which is largely supported from abroad, why, I think the results will be disastrous, clearly disastrous, in almost any country ; I make no exception. Perhaps the more intellectual, and the more ambitious the people are, the greater would be the danger ; but if the two ideas are kept together, I believe that we may trust and commit the Lord's work to the hearts that have shown an interest in it. If the Lord has moved the hearts of the people so that they are willing to undergo self-sacrifice for the kingdom of God, then they are beginning to show the leadings of the Spirit, which will guide them and enable them to do the work properly. Now, our methods of Church organisation are very different. The traditions with which we start, and the exact lines along which it is thought the best results may be attained, will differ with each organisation, and somewhat with individual minds. But, at the same time, this last principle that I have just thrown out is one that might guide us all ; and I believe that the great results in regard to union, which are to be hoped for in certain countries, are not to be gained by our organising a Union

Union Missions in Japan.

Church for them. I do not believe we are able to do it ; and I want to tell you a secret. The larger union Missions in Japan have not been originated or carried forward specially by the Missionaries or the Missionary Board. We were so placed that we felt paralysed. The old traditions held us. The old connections held us to our Churches that are contributing to the work ; but when a Church has through the discipline of God, Providence leading them forward in the direction of Christian work for their fellow-creatures, gained some liberty, some knowledge, some vigour and growth, it begins to feel around to find other communions, other societies, filled with a similar spirit, and to want to be united with them, and I believe the time will come when these hopes of union will be realised, not specially by our doing, though we should be very careful not to interfere.

Rev. F. Lion Cachet (Secretary, Dutch Reformed Missionary Society) : Mr. President,—I did not come to this Conference to speak, but to hear and to learn. Though I have had some little experience in Mission work, still in many respects I feel that we know very little about it ; and I am thankful for whatever we have been able to achieve. As we say in Holland, " We are thankful, but not satisfied." I have heard some brethren, who have a right to speak with authority, say that a Church must not be constituted an independent Church unless it can support itself, and must not

A limit to independence.

have its own pastor until such time as it can support him. I have asked myself, Is that true ? I take up my Bible and I read therein in Hebrew, in Dutch, in English, in Greek, in Latin. I do not find that the Church is any the less a Church because it requires assistance. There are, for instance, Churches in Venice, and in Hungary, and in other places. Are they less the Churches of Christ because they are liberally supported by English or Scotch Christians ? Does a Church actually cease to be an independent Church because it wants some support ? I do not think any one of us will say Yes ; and so with the native Churches. We have heard a great deal about China, and not only about China, but a great deal about Japan and other places, though not half enough. I could stay here a whole month if we only had meetings like this, and heard things discussed as they are. But you have heard very little about the

Dutch settlements in all this, and I thought you might like to know a little about them, and about the work there.

We have in our Dutch India about thirteen millions of souls; in Java, eighteen millions, of whom two hundred thousand are Chinese, and among these I do not think there is one single Missionary. We have our Mission in Central Java, and we have there between forty and fifty Churches. Our belief is, that we are bound not so much to found stations as to plant Churches. I do not say that is the only plan, but we, Dutch, have that plan; **Presbyterianism in Java.** we think we are bound to plant Churches. Being Presbyterians, and Dutch Presbyterians, it is no wonder that we wish the Churches that we do plant to be Presbyterian Churches holding by the same principles as the mother Church. Our Missionaries there do not enforce them, I believe, but they give them the Heidelberg catechism,—I am sure that all Presbyterians will say that is a very good catechism,—translated into Javanese. We do not give it away, but they buy it. There was an edition, I think, of one thousand or fifteen hundred copies; they buy it all over Middle Java. They want to have it. So gradually these Churches are formed according to our Presbyterian lines When there are a number of Christians in a Society, say twenty or thirty, with their children, they appoint elders and deacons, and there is the nucleus for a Church of Christ. One of our Missionaries wrote to me lately : "The sooner my work is done the greater glory to God. I am working that I may have no more work to do here." I think that is the right principle. One of the fundamental rules of our Missionary Society is that, we give up the work as soon as possible. As soon as the Churches in Holland will take up the work, we cease to carry it on as a Society.

Next month we have our Synod, and this is one of the things that will be brought before the Synod and discussed there. Now, Mr. Chairman, and dear brethren, are we wrong? Must we not give these people their own pastors, and must we not recognise them as Churches, because they are far too poor to support themselves ; and why are they poor? It is because **The Church must support evangelists.** of that cursed opium in our Java colonies ; it is because the people have been held for years and years by it. I have not done it myself, nor you, but Christian nations have made them poor. Now we say we cannot recognise you as Churches until you have the means of support. Brethren, it is for you to guide us, to give us a little more light in this matter. If you will do that, I for one shall be very thankful.

Rev. Robert Craig, M.A., Edin. (L.M.S.): My Lord, and Christian friends, —I must express a certain delight at the sentiments which have been uttered by the Missionaries from many countries, indicating a great willingness on their part to give liberty to their converts to determine their own form of religious life in the future. It seems to me that that is on the right line. But I have also to express a little disappointment that some reference was not made to the second part of the subject, which seems to me of very great importance : in truth, I was going to request you, my Lord, to ask whether we had here any Missionary of experience from the West Indies, or from South Africa. As a director of the London Missionary Society, I know the difficulties connected with this question; for whilst under the superintendence of this great Society, you will find groups of Churches that might be regarded as partly Episcopalian, and partly Presbyterian, yet it rests chiefly on the Churches of the Congregational order. And then we admit freely that the strength of that system of Church government depends upon the moral character of the members; unless a pure Christian life is preserved in a Church it seems to me that of all forms of ecclesiastical polity the Congregational is the weakest.

The next question is this with reference to the subject of time—when

should converts be left to their own care? I want Missionaries of experience to
tell us how soon they think it right for European superintendence
to be withdrawn. That really is a most important point. When
Churches have been formed; when they have professed their
loyalty to Jesus Christ, and, so far, have done well for many years, it has
been found in different parts of the world that when the European influence
is withdrawn there is a tendency for the moral character to become degraded
again, and for the converts to go down to their old level. Now if any
Missionary here can give us information upon this point, I shall be delighted
to listen to him.

Withdrawal of European supervision.

Rev.. G. H. Hanna (Superintendent, Moravian Missions in Jamaica): I
should be glad to be allowed to say a word or two on this
subject. I am a Moravian Missionary, and have been so for
thirty-two years, spent chiefly in the Island of Jamaica; but
after more than one hundred and fifty-six years' work as Moravians in the
West Indies, we do not find that we can as yet entrust the supervision of
our Churches altogether to the natives. We must not be in a great hurry
about it. No denomination has given its Churches right over to the natives
as yet. But all are making very great efforts in that direction, and all
hope for it in time.

Experience in Jamaica.

Rev. William Gray (Secretary, C.M.S.): Confessedly, my Lord, this is
one of the most difficult and important subjects, I suppose, that we could
possibly have taken up at this Conference, and one does wish,
very much, that we had had a more thorough discussion upon
it. I dare say we shall have it at future meetings of this great
Conference. The Church Missionary Society, of which I am one of the
representatives here to-day, has, as your Lordship knows from very real
experience, been prominent rather in the planting of Churches. We love
to plant Churches, and we like to talk of them, and we venture to make use
of the expression sometimes in connection with them, which St. Paul made
use of when he spoke of "that which cometh upon me daily, the care of
all the Churches." We have been planting Churches, up and down, through
India and other parts. Perhaps we have gone farther in India than we
have in other parts of the world in this matter. Well, now, we feel the
difficulty about these native Churches, as we call them, very greatly indeed.
May I say, first of all, what we are doing about them? One point is, we
are trying to make these Churches self-supporting. We are trying to make
our Bengal Church self-supporting, our Tinnevelly Church self-supporting,
and so on all through India, and in other parts also.

C.M.S. and planting of Churches.

In some parts the advance is more evident than in others. We have a set
principle in this matter; we have laid it down clearly and distinctly, and we are
trying to carry it out as far as we can. We give grants to these
native Churches to help them to go on; but we have introduced
the system of every year reducing the grant. In some cases we
have said we will reduce the annual grant by one-twentieth. If
that were done for twenty years it would, of course, amount to a giving up of the
grant altogether, and in twenty years, in some cases, the Churches would become
self-supporting.

Gradual withdrawal of grants.

There is another thing in regard to these Churches which we have in view.
We encourage all our native Churches to look at the Protestant
Christians of other denominations face to face. We try to avoid
everything that would bring out into prominent relief any non-essential

Encouraging Catholicity.

points of difference between our Christians and the Christians of other denominations. We try to avoid anything that would stereotype differences, which would tend to division ; and, therefore, we encourage them to look at Christians of other denominations face to face. Where we find them meeting together we are pleased. Meanwhile, of course, being Episcopalians, we are bringing them up—we are obliged to bring them up—in the doctrine and discipline of the Church of England. One great point of our system is, that we are having the pastors, catechists, and others taught the great fundamental verities of the Christian truth ; that is our great point, and that system is going on. The work of self-support is progressing, will progress more and more. What will follow ? I do not know. We must leave it to the Providence of God. All that we can do is to draw up our system, lay down our principles, and to go on waiting. We drew up a kind of constitution some time ago ; we came just to about the point I have been describing, and we ended our Paper by saying, *Domine dirige nos.*

I quite agree with Dr. Smith in what he said, You cannot have a native Church for all India. I think that is impossible. We can have provincial Churches. Let the boundaries of language settle that matter ; in all probability they will settle it. I should like for myself Provincial native Churches. to see a Bengal native Church, composed of the native Christians of all Protestant denominations, which the Providence of God might guide them to. And yet it would be a very serious thing to say to a number of native Christians of all denominations, "Gather together, and form a constitution of your own!" I think on the whole, dear friends, we had better be content with laying down sound principles : do not let us do anything prematurely ; let us work upon those principles, and let us ask that the guidance of God may be given to us with regard to the future. I think that is the conclusion to which we should come.

The Chairman pronounced the Benediction.

MEETINGS OF MEMBERS
IN SECTION.

ORGANISATION AND GOVERNMENT OF NATIVE CHURCHES.*

(2) TRAINING OF WORKERS.

(*a*) The best method of training native workers—by individual Missionaries; in central institutions; in the vernacular only, or by means of the English language.

(*b*) Shall an American or European education for natives of Mission-fields be encouraged?

(*c*) In cases where preachers and physicians have been thus trained, should they be put upon a higher footing than other native helpers?

(*d*) Would the difficulties relating to such cases be relieved by sending persons thus educated to a different Mission-field?

(*e*) In Missions where high order of qualification on the part of native teachers has been attained or is possible, shall such attainment be encouraged by enlarged privileges and powers?

(*Friday morning, June 15th, in the Lower Hall.*)

Hon. Eustace C. Fitz (U.S.A) in the chair.
Acting Secretary, Rev. F. F. Ellinwood, D.D. (U.S.A.).

Professor Welch offered prayer.

The Chairman: I shall beg your indulgence for a moment before proceeding with the business of the day, only just long enough, however, to express how heartily I am in sympathy as an American with the objects of this Conference, and how earnestly I hope for its largest success and its broadest influence in extending the knowledge of God throughout the earth. I have the honour to represent, in part, one of the oldest Missionary institutions in America, the Baptist Missionary Union, having its headquarters in Boston, an institution which is nearly seventy-five years old, and which has

---

* *Owing to the value of the evidence on the important subject of discussion in this meeting, we have not struck out repetitions; but have used a smaller type to reduce the undue length of the report.*—ED.

its Missionaries in Europe, Asia, and Africa. The question before us is a practical question, a question which can be spoken to best by gentlemen who have been upon the field, who have come in contact with the natives, who know how to organise a native Church, who know the best methods which can be adopted and ought to be adopted in order to build up those Churches. I have been connected some fifteen years with the administration, mostly financial, of our own organisation; therefore I am sure I am not qualified to speak on the question before us this morning, but I have taken the liberty of asking the Rev. Dr. Murdock of Boston, the Secretary of the American Baptist Missionary Union, to address you on the subject after the regular Papers have been read. There is another reason why I do not feel it my duty to speak to you this morning from the chair. I have an idea, and it is one that we rather cling to in America, that the duty of a chairman is rather to guide others in speaking than to speak himself, and I know that I shall relieve myself and relieve you if I keep my seat and adhere closely to that rule.

Subject of meeting.

PAPER.

1 By the Rev. Robert Stephenson, B.A. (Wesleyan Missionary Society, from Madras).

It is an axiom of Missionary policy which has been stated more than once during the Conference, that the evangelisation of a great heathen land, like India, must be accomplished mainly through the agency of her own sons; men to whom the language of the country is their mother tongue, who from childhood have been familiar with the feelings, the modes of thought, and the habits of the people, and to whom the climate is native and genial; among such men, when converted to Christ and filled with His Spirit, we look for those who shall leaven native society with Gospel truth, shall uproot heathenism, and extend far and wide the kingdom of Christ.

In *Ceylon*, where the W. M. S. began its work in the East, it may claim to have done not a little in the raising up of a native ministry. By the side of *sixteen* English Missionaries, it has now *forty-nine* native ministers, and forty-six catechists or evangelists. Of the native ministers several are venerable and grey-headed men. On the continent of *India* the work of the W. M. S. is not so advanced; but it is with the Southern continental Districts of that Mission I am best acquainted, and from them chiefly I gather illustrations of the remarks I have to offer.

The W.M.S. in Ceylon.

The first inquiry proposed in the programme is as to " the best method of training native workers; by individual Missionaries, or in central institutions?" In reply, I would point out that there is no antagonism between these methods. To secure efficiency they must be combined. There is much that can be done with greatest advantage in a theological institution; on the other hand the full benefit of such an institution can be realised only where much work to the same end, both preparatory and supplementary, is done by the individual Missionary.

Subject of Paper.

First, to secure good native workers, there is needed *the training of the native Church*. It is ever possible that God may raise up an evangelist of special zeal and power in the midst of a feeble and worldly-minded Church; nay, He may call such workers directly from heathenism. Of these stones He is able to raise up children unto Abraham. But a succession of men spiritually and morally fitted to become ministers, we are

Human instrumentality.

authorised to look for only in a Church which, though it may be small and socially uninfluential, is vigorous and active. Dr. James Hamilton described Methodism as "a Church which finds a work for every talent, and a talent in every member." This is the ideal of all well-organised Churches, and to this ideal the Missionary seeks to lead the native Christians. He begins at the lowest point, and labours to train even the feeblest to do work of simple kind for Christ, not only in
Growth of zeal. the Church, but in the heathen world. In this, progress is being made. In the report of his visit to the East three years ago, the Rev. E. E. Jenkins writes : "There is more heart religion in the native Churches than I ever remember to have witnessed during my own Missionary course. For instance, you will seldom see a native preacher or catechist standing in a bazaar of a town, or the open square of a village, a solitary witness for Christ. He is now escorted by a voluntary band of helpers; and these are generally armed with musical weapons, and fight down all opposition by lyric melodies." "The members of the Church are in the midst of the people ; the leaven is in the meal ; the witness, the example, and the life of the native Church penetrate the mass."

2. Increased attention is called to *the training of the children of Christian people.* This subject is more and more pressing itself upon the attention of the
Instruction of children. Wesleyan Mission. There is a strong feeling that heretofore too great effort, proportionally, has been given to the higher education of the Hindus, and too little to the education of our own people. This evil there is now an effort to remedy. In each village where a congregation is formed a school is opened, primarily for the instruction of the children of the converts. In Hyderabad and in the Mysore, it is a wise practice to select the brightest boys in these schools and send them for more thorough teaching to the boarding schools, which have been established at central stations. "In these schools the children of our own people are trained in home and school life, under the eye of the Missionary; they become familiar with Christian doctrine and polity, and they are held to the Church by higher considerations than those of salary and social advantages. The fruit of this work ripens slowly, and we cannot force it, but when it is gathered it will confer almost equal gain upon every class of Mission work." The Rev. W. Burgess declares the "guiding principle of action" in his own district to be :—"Let us look after the children of our own people, and educate them at all cost. Those Missions are the most successful which devote their energies to the uplifting of the children of their congregations."

3. It is a foremost duty of each Missionary to give personal attention to *the training of his native helpers,* especially those likely to be admitted to the theo-
Training native helpers. logical seminary, and of those who, after a course of training, are on probation as catechists. The Missionary must maintain a constant and loving oversight of their conduct, must direct their studies, and accompany them on their preaching excursions. He must assemble them weekly for consultation about their work, and to give such instruction and exhortation as may seem requisite. These arrangements on the different stations are amongst us supplemented by similar arrangements for the district. A yearly or half-yearly convention is held of all the native ministers and catechists in the district. At these conventions, which extend over two or three days, all on probation are subjected to examination on a prescribed course of study, and are expected to preach before their senior brethren. Special services are held, and it is sought to make the occasion one of spiritual enjoyment and profit.

But, however valuable training of this kind may be, it does not furnish a substitute for the more complete course of study and training, possible only in
Collegiate study a necessity. an institution where a number of students for the ministry are placed under the tutorship of a Missionary, or Missionaries, separated for the purpose.

In the four districts of the W.M.S. in South India, three principal languages are spoken, and hence it is found needful to have three theological seminaries. In each, accommodation is provided for about twelve or fourteen students.

In *Hyderabad* the institution is located at *Kurreem-Nugger*, and the language in use is the *Telugu*. One suggestive peculiarity in the arrangements is thus described : " When a number of persons in a village place themselves under instruction, we take the most likely man in the village Village readers. itself, and train him for a year or so, and then send him back to do the work of teacher and conductor of village worship," an experienced catechist, or a native minister visiting the congregation as often as possible. " The men in training for this work of village reader form a class by themselves, and in teaching them, the only books used are the Bible and the first and second Catechisms." In the other classes students are prepared as teachers, and for the various grades of catechists, and for the native ministry.

In the *Mysore* the work is more developed. A normal school for teachers is conducted at Shemoga, and a theological institution at *Bangalore*. The latter for nine or ten years has been under the efficient care of the Rev. Josiah Hudson, B.A. Here the language is Canarese. The students are instructed in the Bible ; in doctrinal theology, from a manual prepared by the Rev. J. Hutcheon, M.A., and translated into Canarese ; with the evidences of Christianity and Church history. They study also the history of England and of India, geography, arithmetic, and the Canarese language and literature. Special attention is given to both English and native singing, and A theological almost every student learns to play some musical instrument. college. Proficiency in music is found of great service, both in brightening Christian worship, and in attracting a congregation of Hindus in town or country. The students are taught in class four hours daily. Every other morning they go to the surrounding villages two and two ; and almost every evening they attend schoolroom services, etc., taking their turn in giving addresses and helping in the music.

After completing their course in the institution, the students are employed as catechists or evangelists, and undergo further probation before being advanced to the position of native Missionaries on trial.

The institution at *Trichinopoly* was opened in 1885, and has been conducted with promising success by the Rev. R. S. Boulter, assisted by the Rev. Elias Gloria, a native brother of great ability and experience. Several of the students have some acquaintance with English, but the instruction is given entirely in *Tamil*. As at Bangalore, those only are admitted as students who it is hoped may become evangelists or native pastors. Several youths are being trained as vernacular schoolmasters at the excellent normal college of the C.V.E.S., at Dindigul.

It seems, however, that in a Mission like that of the W.M.S., addressed to peoples speaking various vernaculars, but amongst all of whom the higher classes are eager to learn English, there is room for a central institution where training should be given through English. In such an A need for institution the subjects of instruction would take a wider range than higher in those I have described, and especially an attempt would be made education. to teach the Greek Testament.

I will add a few general remarks :—

1. It is a principle in the Wesleyan Mission, and I believe also in most of the Missions represented in this Conference, *that only those men be accepted as candidates for spiritual office, or admitted as students in our Theological Institutions, who give evidence of spiritual conversion, of high character, and of zeal for evangelistic work.* Before acceptance, they must evince by voluntary effort a desire and a fitness for the work of soul saving. Only those who do so can we hope will become efficient evangelists.

2. In a *theological institution in India it is necessary to make Bible teaching specially prominent ;* and it is well, I think, that in all, or nearly all cases, teaching in this subject should be in the vernacular. Even students who are proficient in English should be encouraged in their private devotions to use the Bible, each in his mother tongue, and to cultivate the power of frequent and accurate quotation.

The Rev. G. M. Cobban urges the importance of instructing students for the ministry in the principles of Hinduism and Islamism, and in the arguments by

On teaching the principles of Hinduism.
which the upholders of these systems may best be refuted. The Rev. Henry Little writes: "We want men able to meet the statements of Bradlangh and his party translated into Tamil." The brethren would, however, agree with me while insisting that a preacher in town or village should be able to realise the standpoint from which his hearers receive his message, and to adapt himself to it; that it is of supreme importance that he be himself absorbed in that message, and filled with Christlike sympathy and love for souls; and also that theological students should be exhorted to avoid rather than to encourage controversy, and to give their utmost effort to the clear, full, and sympathetic proclamation of the Gospel, seeking to bring it home to the apprehension and to the hearts of their hearers. The instruction given should have this object constantly in view.

3. *Students preparing for the office of pastors and evangelists should be taught daily to practise their Divine calling.* They should learn to delight in preaching and to look earnestly for results. In their evangelizing excursions they should be accompanied, as often as possible, by their Missionary tutors, who should not only offer faithful and affectionate criticism, but set before them an example of effective preaching.

4. In the institution I have described, many of the *students are married men.* They usually live in cottages erected on the Mission compound. Where this

Training for wives.
arrangement prevails, it is an excellent rule that training should be given to the wives as well as to their husbands. They should be regularly taught in Holy Scripture, and trained to such ministrations as may devolve upon them in the future.

5. An experienced Missionary, writing with much satisfaction of the character and diligence of the workers under his care, nevertheless adds: "*They give us most trouble by getting into debt.* Indeed, in the native Church generally, debt causes us more worry and annoyance than all other evils put together." If the evil thus indicated can be kindly but effectively dealt with among our students, the result will be of great practical value.

6. *For the charge of these theological institutions, it is essential that the best men be appointed:* men not simply skilled in theological or other lore, but having large loving hearts, and strong faith in God; who will inspire their students with confidence, attract their love, and bring out the very best that is in them.

The power and influence of teachers.
Such men were Anderson, Johnson, and Braidwood,—men whom I cannot name without reverence,—the pioneers of the Free Church of Scotland Mission in Madras. They took their converts not merely to their homes, but to their hearts, and were reproduced in them. These students never lost the impression of their intense enthusiasm, and of their mighty power in prayer, and in wielding the sword of the Spirit. Such a man was my dear friend and comrade, William O. Simpson. His students were his companions and sons. His lessons were given not more in the classroom than in evangelistic tours, during which the lads ate and slept in his company. His ambition was to place an example before them in all things, but especially in vernacular preaching.

7. Lastly, *there is no work that will bring a greater reward to the Missionary than the training of native agents.* It is a work demanding diligence and patience

The reward.
and invincible hopefulness. It has its sorrows and bitter disappointments. It can be successful only when conducted in the spirit of intense prayerfulness and in the power of God.

"The harvest truly is plenteous, but the labourers are few; pray ye therefore the Lord of the harvest, that He would send forth more labourers into His harvest" (Matt. ix. 37, 38).

PAPER.

2. BY THE REV. JOHN HEWLETT (L.M.S., from Benares).

Training of Workers.

The subject given to me, not chosen by me, to deal with for this Conference, is the training of workers as a branch of the still wider theme of the organisation and government of native Churches. No question can, it seems to me, be of more vital importance to the success of our great Missionary enterprise. The history of Missions strikingly proves to us how inadequate for the Christian conquest of the yet vast heathen countries of the world, is the number of Foreign Missionaries which the Church can hope to bring into the field; with what success the Holy Ghost has *Need for* already crowned our prayerful endeavours to enlist native con- *trained* verts into the great Missionary army; and what powerful *native workers.* appeals are presented to us by ever-multiplying opportunities, as by so many summonses from our Saviour King, to enlarge the forces of our native Christian workers, who have so faithfully and successfully begun to take part in this holy warfare already grown, and always more and more growing, beyond the power of Foreign Missionaries.

Now Missionaries abroad, like ministers at home, find the Churches richly blessed by God with spiritual life to be homes from which spring in considerable numbers devoted men and women who prove, under such training as His providence supplies, successful workers in advancing His kingdom in the world. But as Churches strong in spiritual character have been of rare and slow growth in that obstinate part of the battle-field of Missions, the North-Western Provinces of India, *Personal* where my past Missionary life has been spent, and where the *the N.W.* nature of the work is still warfare rather than victory, pulling *provinces.* down rather than building up, enlightening rather than converting, the difficulties we encounter in training native workers, caused by the still comparatively weak character of most of the Churches, considerably exceed the difficulties experienced in many other parts of the Mission-field, where more prosperous Churches lend their co-operating influence. So important, however, do I feel it that friends of Missions should as much as possible encourage by their prayers, and by all the aid in their power, the development of this work to meet the growing wants of Missions, that I have gladly undertaken, in compliance with the request of the Secretary of this Conference, to answer from my own experience the very important and apparently exhaustive list of questions on this subject in the programme. But before I proceed to speak of the various plans adopted by Indian Missionaries to secure bands of faithful native workers, let me bear testimony to the fact that, whatever be the success or failure met with by Missionaries in these endeavours, it has been unquestionably their first object to raise up around themselves as fellow-workers, men and women full of the Holy Ghost, enthusiastic in their devotion to the Saviour, and burning with zeal for the salvation of souls. For the strong conviction, universally indispensable for the supremely important tasks of selecting and training Christian agents, is kept up in Missionaries by the ever-pressing necessities of their work, that none but those who have experienced the change from death to life through the Saviour's indwelling presence, and who have been especially qualified by His grace for His service, can be instrumental in making their fellow-men partakers of His salvation.

As to the first question in the programme—the best method of training native workers—Missionaries in the earlier stages of Mission work necessarily felt themselves shut up to adopting the best methods available in God's providence rather than left free to choose the ideally best. Accordingly it has often happened, that when a convert appeared to give evidence of strong love to Christ and of the Divine call to Christian work, so eager was the Missionary to secure his services that, without delay, he Individual arranged to devote what time he could upon the convert's training training ing by such personal methods as conversation, prayer, by Missionaries. expounding God's Word, taking the convert to open-air preaching, and putting him through some suitable course of study. This was the kind of preparation received by the native pastors and evangelists of the London Missionary Society, who have rendered good service to its Missions in the North-Western Provinces of India. This is the history of the training of the Rev. Peter Elias, a native Missionary of that Society, who has laboured with great zeal and success in both gathering out and building up a church of converts from amongst the aboriginal inhabitants of Dudhi, a rural station in the Vindhya range of mountains, about one hundred miles from Mirzapur. He is, I rejoice to say, only one of many such earnest and successful native ministers trained by individual Missionaries of different Societies in India. Similar also is the preparation for Christian work received in that country by large devoted bands of evangelists, school teachers, colporteurs, Bible women, and Zenana visitors, many of whom are known to myself as having greatly helped to lead numerous precious souls out of heathen darkness into God's marvellous light. So that when God's providence seems to suggest this method of training as the only practicable one for making the most of a convert's services for Missionary purposes, experience has amply justified its adoption.

But the gradual increase of Christian Churches and of candidates for Christian work has in God's good providence led to the establishment of Establishment central institutions to raise up an educated class of agents well of central equipped to teach the Churches, to educate the youth, and skil-institutions. fully to meet heathen opponents. Admirably organised theological institutes are now successfully worked, one by the Church Missionary Society at Allahabad and another at Lahore, one by the American Presbyterian Society at Saharanpur, and one by the American Methodist Society at Bareilly. Numerous servants of Christ trained in these divinity schools are now making full proof of their ministry as successful pastors of Churches of their countrymen in various parts of those provinces. Many more are labouring as faithful evangelists in different Mission stations to win the heathen around them to the Saviour. As to the training of male school teachers, no special provision seems needed, since the numerous flourishing institutions employed as evangelistic agencies to impart higher education are admirably adapted to this purpose.

Then again a valuable normal school in connection with the Church Missionary Society has been for many years successfully employed at Benares, to fit female converts and the daughters of native Christians to become teachers of girls' schools and Zenana visitors. The growing need of effort of this kind is seen in the recent establishment of a similar institution by the American Presbyterian Society at Allahabad. There is no more important work carried on for the advancement of the Saviour's kingdom in those parts of India than the training of Christian workers of both sexes in these central institutions by Missionaries, who seek not only to impart to the students good instruction, but also to infuse into them a holy ardour for the Redeemer's service.

The question of training in the vernacular only, or by means of the English language, hardly admits of one short reply. As the spread of English education in India leads to imparting English instruction in the higher schools, in which boys acquire such learning as fits them to become teachers, **Training in** and in the normal schools, in which girls receive the same advan- **the vernacular** tage, the question is happily settled in favour of English for both **or English!** of these classes of workers. As to training for the ministry, and for evange- listic work, since some of the candidates are from amongst those who have acquired a knowledge of English, it would seem highly desirable, especially in the case of those full of promise to labour for the conversion of natives educated in English, that their theological training should be carried on at least partly in that language. Then again, if native ministers are taught to draw from the English treasury of knowledge, which is so rich with all the wisdom of the Christian Church, to say nothing of the best thought of all countries, they are necessarily far better qualified than they would be if they had only access to the yet comparatively scanty though growing Christian literature in their vernacular, to prove valuable instructors of their Churches even through the medium of their vernacular, provided they received grace also to avoid the danger of rising above sympathy with their people. Moreover, it is exceedingly desirable that we should provide for the securing of increasing numbers of ministers as highly educated as possible, gradually to take the places of the European and American Missionaries, as the native Churches become, what we earnestly pray to see them, self-supporting, self-governing, and self-propagating. But for the present, in the case of the great majority of candidates who do not know English, it hardly seems advisable to require them to learn that language, partly because of the time and expense involved, and partly because it would tend to lift them too much above the level of the mass of the people, Christian and heathen, who are ignorant of English, and who form suitable spheres of labour for a greater number of agents than can well be educated in English.

The remaining four questions of the programme on the subject of the train- ing of native workers, each of which, if there were time, might profitably receive a separate discussion, are yet sufficiently connected by a common principle to receive a joint consideration. They are all concerned with the perplexing problem of imparting a high order of qualification to a select class of native agents. In such a country as India, where Mission work is so varied as to give scope to workers of almost every kind and degree **Educating** of qualification, and to call for some workers of a very high order **agents in** of training, there can, in my opinion, be no doubt whatever as to **Europe and** the wisdom of encouraging an American or a European education **America.** for a fair number of natives of Mission-fields whose Christian character seems sufficiently strong to resist the temptation to be spoiled by such an advantage, and who would be likely to return to their own country, to become wise and able leaders of the native Christian Church. It will probably sometimes happen that men of high qualifications, whether gained in America or England on the one hand, or in India on the other, will, from a spirit of Christian self-denial, prefer that no difference in status should be made between themselves and their less favoured brethren. But as the universal operation of this principle can by no means be calculated upon, it would seem safest to provide, while carefully guarding against making rules in the spirit of Hindu caste, for those who have enjoyed exceptional advantages to receive in consequence higher duties and higher salaries. But as to seeking to relieve the difficulty by **Sending such to** sending such men to a different Mission-field, it would certainly **another field.** appear that, while cases are conceivable of natives of the Indian Mission-field receiving such a call from God to go to labour for Christ in foreign countries as it would be wrong to resist, yet to give to them unsought encouragement to go to receive a training for this purpose in Europe or America is hardly justifiable, at least, in the present stage of the progress of Indian Missions. But I would say, in passing, that it must be one of the glorious ends for which we are seeking the best methods of training native workers, to see India speedily become so Christianised as to imitate the South Sea Islands in sending forth, not out of the desire to relieve herself of difficulty, but out of a spirit of love to Christ, and of zeal for the salvation of souls, some of her best sons and daughters for the evangelisation of other heathen lands, if indeed there be any heathen lands then remaining.

The success gained in India by the methods which I have now sketched are such as to fill friends of Missions with gratitude and hope. It is, however, sometimes objected to us that we Westernise too much the natives of India by planting amongst them our own Christian institutions. The advice is given that we should rather encourage the converts to develop a Christian life in forms adapted to the spirit of their own country. We at once respond that we ardently desire and pray to see the natives of India, who have been so long devoted to false religions of their own invention, blessed with such a fulness of Christian life as will manifest itself in types of character and *Western* forms of institutions adapted to the highest good of their country, *methods* however different they may be from our Western developments of *objected to.* Christianity. We believe that when the Gospel, through the outpouring of God's Spirit, lays strong hold upon that great country, which has been so long remarkable for her zeal in founding religious sects, she will produce enthusiastic Christian leaders of her people, who will, by the course they take, astonish even Missionaries and friends of Missions. We think it not unlikely that, just as the Christian Church—in the course of her history—received her ascetic institutions from Egypt, her creeds from the Greeks, her Papal form of Government from Rome, and her Protestant love of freedom from the Teutons; so too, India, when the Spirit of Christ works mightily within her, will develop Christian life and character, not uninfluenced by the strong national characteristics of her several peoples. We long to see her manifesting a Christianity in forms peculiarly her own, provided they are the genuine outward expressions of her zeal for the glory of God, of her trust in the Saviour's atonement, and of her baptism by the Holy Ghost.

But our task in India will be completed when God begins to make Christianity in that country blossom into such spiritual wonders. Meanwhile, in working for this blessed end, what better plan could we adopt than to begin, in reliance upon the guidance of God's gracious Spirit, to Christianise India by the *The methods* methods which have proved such mighty Christianising agencies in *justified by* Western countries? Thank God for our native Christian Churches *results.* in India and other heathen lands, although they have been built up after the models of our several Western Churches. Thank God for our native Christian workers in those countries, although they have been trained after our Western models. We rejoice in the assurance which we believe He has given us that both our native Churches and our native agents are the workmanship of His Spirit, wrought through the only means supplied by His providence. We rejoice in the assurance which we believe He has given us that He is graciously employing these agencies to bring the nations of the earth to a saving faith in the Lord Jesus. May He mercifully both pardon all the errors, which He cannot but see in our methods of work, and show us how to remedy them; so that they may no longer hinder the spread of His blessed kingdom over the heathen world. May He increase within His Missionary servants those Divine qualifications, which will fit them efficiently to train, according to His will, the native workers of His own choosing in heathen lands, for the enlightenment and conversion of the many millions of human souls still without a knowledge of Christ. May the Christian Church be stirred up fervently to pray that the native workers so trained may receive a Pentecostal baptism of the Holy Ghost, in order to reproduce within them the apostolic character, to make them successful in bringing many of their countrymen from the power of Satan to the kingdom of God's dear Son,

DISCUSSION

Rev. John N. Murdock, D.D. (Secretary, American Baptist Missionary Union): Mr. Chairman,—It is not without a touch of sensibility, under the peculiar circumstances of the occasion, that I address you by this very familiar title. I may explain to this audience that the occasion of that sensibility is that my valued friend has felt constrained by the pressure of other duties to resign his place on our Executive Committee, of which he has so long been Chairman. I trust, however, that he may so far renew his Missionary interest, and so far complete his Missionary education in these great convocations that he will be willing to return to the office which he has so long occupied and to the duties which he has so well performed. The first line in the scheme of this morning presents both the *modus vivendi* and the *modus operandi* of Christian Missions: the organisation of the native Churches (the spring of action and of success must lie in this), and then the training of native workers. My friend Mr. Stephenson well said that the hope for the conversion of the world lies in men raised upon the field, educated for their work and made effective in it. We shall never bring the world to the knowledge of Christ through the instrumentality of Missionaries imported into the various countries of the earth. We have not the men, and great as may be the resources of Christian Churches and of Christian lands, and fully as they may be consecrated to the great work of evangelising the race, they never will be equal to the adequate supply of the vast, populous and fearfully destitute regions of heathenism. If the world is to be brought to a knowledge of Christ, it must be through the instrumentality of a native agency, and if there be one human cause for the success which has attended the work of the great Society which I have the honour to represent it is that our chief reliance has been upon native work.

A mode of living and working.

We have never hoped to send forth Missionaries in sufficient number, or with adequate means, to convey the message of grace to all the peoples to whom they are sent. Our success from the beginning has resulted from the work of natives. Take, for example, that wonderful work among the Karens in Burmah under the early ministrations of Ko-Thah-Byu, the Karen Pioneer, a man not learned in human learning but rich with a knowledge of a Divine inspiration and with the teaching of the Holy Scriptures. That man went forth an instrument of power: light followed in his train, and multitudes were brought to Christ through his instrumentality. The Karen Churches owe their origin to the work of this lowly, yet most consecrated and most successful Christian preacher.

Success from native labour.

Then, of all men who have wrought in Burmah, none has occupied so conspicuous a position in this work of evangelisation as the man whom the venerable Dr. Anderson of the American Board has named the Karen Apostle (Sau Quala). He was the means under God of originating that great work in Toungu, where there are now six thousand Karen disciples, organised into a large number of effective Christian Churches, maintaining an order that would be a credit to the Churches in any Christian land, and accomplishing a work that will redound to the glory of Christ and the salvation of men. This work of training the native agents must be done in the field; it is not helpful to these men to bring them to England or America. It is only a hotbed growth that they experience, losing

Another example.

all the fervour of their original spirit, and losing their hold upon the people. Let them be educated upon the field with such facilities as you can give them. In the early days of the Missions the Missionary was the teacher of his helpers, and those early native helpers were well taught; but we have now theological seminaries and Biblical and training schools. We have the seminary in Rangoon, which is sending out scores of men every year into destitute fields; the theological seminary for the education of multitudes of Telugu preachers, coming forth to preach the Gospel; we have the training school of Swatow, and the training school of Ningpo; we have relegated the work to these institutions, and we have felt it our first duty to the Mission to provide these schools for native evangelists and Christian pastors, in order that the work of the Lord may prosper to the remotest parts of the Mission-field.

Training seminaries.

Rev. Professor Aiken (Princeton, U.S.A.): The announcement of my name and connections will show that I approach this subject from a somewhat different point of view from that of the preceding speakers,—the point of view of the theological seminaries under which, more or less, the young men come, with or without the consent of the Missionaries, and the Boards that have had charge of their earlier life. Lest the inexorable five minutes' bell should cut off my conclusion, I will, in defiance of rhetoric and logic, state the conclusion first, and then use what time I have in supporting it. With regard to the question in the programme, "Shall American or European education for natives of Mission-fields be encouraged?" I say emphatically, No, if you mean indiscriminate education; but I say emphatically, Yes, if you mean the encouragement of selected men, who have commended themselves to the pastors and to those in charge of the Missionary work at home, and whom you wish to prepare for commanding positions afterwards, e.g., in the training schools of their own country.

Western education.

It seems to me that unless we wish to give some colour to the charge which is brought against us, that we mean to keep these native peoples and Churches in leading strings, unless we mean to give some colour to the charge, that we mean to keep the moulding of these people and the pastorates in our own hands, we must as rapidly as possible be developing among them men able to take these positions themselves; and it does seem to me, as was said by Mr. Hewlett, that an education, broader, richer, and more stimulating than has yet been provided in the Mission-field, should be given to selected men sent to the West for training, in order that they may as soon as possible take the positions occupied for the time being by Missionaries from Europe and the United States. This question involves some embarrassment to us in the seminaries to which these young men come. Whether encouraged or not, they do come and they will come. They have aspirations for a higher education, as they regard it, than they can get at home, and they will make their way, surmounting probably great difficulties, to the doors of our institutions. Shall we refuse to receive them? We cannot do it, unless we lay down conditions in their case that we impose on no others. If they come properly accredited, if they come with a character indicating a worthy purpose, if they fulfil the conditions we lay down for candidates for theological instruction, we cannot say No to them. We receive, for example, in the Presbyterian seminary at Princeton, men from the Southern Methodist Church. We have had some of the most prominent men from the Baptist Church, some from the Congregationalists, and some from the Episcopalians. Four or five American Episcopalian Bishops, have been educated, in whole or in part, at Princeton. We have had coloured men, and we have had men from Ireland, from Scotland, from Wales, from Germany, from Spain. Shall we then say to the Armenian, to the

Natives to take the place of Missionaries.

Bulgarian, to the Greek, to the native of India or Japan, "We cannot receive you, because you are from these lands occupied at present as Mission-fields"? We are not prepared to make that discrimination against them. Therefore, when they come, we receive them and do the best we can with them. Although it has been sometimes said that the methods of our theological seminaries kill out piety and spiritual life, even in our own land, we do not quite admit the justice of that: we do not admit it as an inevitable certain tendency of our institutions. We do not mean that these young men when they come to us shall lose their piety, their zeal, their love for the Master, that they shall lose their competence to serve God well when they go back. We have had several cases of men within the last four or five years, to whom I should like to refer if I had time; I will only refer to one of them. *Do seminaries kill piety.*

Ten years ago a native of Athens, a graduate of Robert College, came with the strong feeling that young men from his country have often manifested to us,—a feeling that was stronger eight years ago than it is now, a feeling of distrust in regard to the attitude of Missionaries toward native pastors and native work. He at once took a position in a large class as one of the two ablest men in it. He went through our course with great credit, and he became a pastor, first of a country church in Pennsylvania, then he became a Professor in the Forest University near Chicago. Two months ago, he was selected as Professor of the New Testament Department in Hartford Theological Seminary, and next September he enters upon a position where he will become one of the trainers of American pastors and American Missionaries to his own and other lands. Now if that man, instead of coming under the frown and disapproval of the Missionaries and teachers by whom he had been trained in Turkey, had come with a measure of support and countenance and sympathy from them he might have been sent back to work there,—to do such work as he is now doing and is likely to do for us. He is a man of rare power. There are other cases I might refer to as involving embarrassment to us, on some account or another, but I have not time.

Rev. W. S. Swanson (English Presbyterian Mission, Amoy): I shall begin like the last speaker by taking my second point first, because he has so strongly insisted upon having our native workers trained in Western lands. I think that would be damaging, I think it would be disastrous for us, and it would be very difficult for our friends in Princeton or any other college to carry it out. I listened to hear whether in the range of countries from which students have gone from Princeton, China was included, and I was happy to find that that name was not mentioned. I wonder whether they would have a staff of professors to speak Chinese! Those who have watched this subject feel that if this plan was carried out it might rob foreign fields of the best possible agents. We have cases of men who have come from the foreign field to study in our colleges in Scotland, and have remained there; they have not gone back to the foreign fields. We do not wish our Chinese agents to take on an American or an English polish. We wish to have a native Church; we do not wish to have an exotic. We wish it to be native in its organisation, and I hope I may not be mistaken—for I am orthodox—in saying that we wish it to be native also in its theology and in its view of looking at things. We wish our agents to be trained in the face of the conditions in which they are to carry on the work, and we do not wish to separate them from the social condition of their own country and their own people. We go, not to Americanise, nor to Anglicise, but to Christianise. *Against education in the west.*

Then I pass on to say a single word upon the organisation of native Churches, a point which I think has been overlooked. This point rises in importance just as we examine, as it is always well to do in matters of this kind, what it is that we go to foreign lands to do. I think there is a great amount of misconception upon this point. Are we working out there until the several countries in which we work have as many ministers from foreign lands as there are ministers in our own country? I hope not. I do not think anyone conceives that that is the goal towards which we are working. Are we there simply to proclaim the sound of the Gospel over as wide a region as we possibly can? Well, I accept this; but I say what the Churches and Societies are doing in sending Missionaries to foreign fields is this, they are sending them, as God's grace and strength may enable them, to build up a native Church, self-supporting, self-governing, and self-propagating. We have been hammering away at this point; we have been trying to keep it before Christian people. It is a point that lies very near, not only the polity of Missions, but very near its economics. We began as soon as possible in my own field to organise our native Churches, and to train our native pastors, and to make our Church a self-propagating Church. We have now our organised congregations, we have our native pastors entirely paid by our own people, and we have our own Missionary institutions supported by the native Church. We have passed the initial stages; but I do not think that we should ever have got beyond them if we had sent our native workers to Oxford or Cambridge, or any of our home universities to be prepared.

What are we working for?

Rev. G. Owen (L.M.S., from Pekin): Mr. Chairman, and Christian friends, —If we are to give our native preachers an English education, it should be thorough. Now that requires a long time,—several years of study. Unless we give a thoroughly good grounding in English it is a waste of time. They have to spend much time in this way, which might be devoted to better purpose. But if they are to spend a number of years in learning English they must begin comparatively young, and I doubt whether it is wise to take mere boys from our schools and train them with a view of making pastors and evangelists of them; I doubt whether we should be doing God's work, or carrying out God's ideas in pursuing a course like that.

Reasons against an English education.

In teaching English to our prospective pastors and teachers in China we should be leading them into very great temptations. Along the coast of China the English-speaking Chinese can command very large salaries in connection with our large commercial houses, and their services would also be in demand by the Government. Thus the ablest and best of those whom we were training would be open to the temptations of being drawn into mercantile or Government life. The only way probably in which you could save them would be to raise their salary. Are we prepared to do this? To raise their salary would be to create caste among our native evangelists. On the one hand there would be the English educated evangelists, and on the other there would be the native educated evangelists, and on the ground that a man could speak English he would get three times the pay of a man who only knew Chinese; yet the English-speaking Chinaman might not be a whit better in mental power or in effective service than the Chinese evangelist who was only getting one-third his pay. Nay, in everything except his knowledge of English, he might be an inferior man. Now that will raise dissatisfaction; it will create a spirit of covetousness, and all our natives will be looking for large pay. I deprecate the creation of that spirit. It will also be preventing the possibility of our native Churches maintaining their pastors. Let us not make a fetish of English; let us not think it is impossible for a man to be an able, an effective, and a noble worker unless he knows English. Again I say give Chinese education. A thorough training in the Bible, a spiritual education, an evangelical education is the only education we need for the wants of China.

High education and high pay.

Rev. C. F. Warren (C.M.S., from Japan): There are just one or two points I should like first of all to emphasise. The first is that in the matter of training native workers, nothing should be done practically to weaken the conviction that all the converts are workers for Christ. I think that is a point that sometimes Missionaries, especially in the initial stages of Mission work, have forgotten. Then there is another point that I should like to put before you, that not every earnest worker should be specially trained for special work. Many of us have had experience of this particular point. We have seen a man perhaps thoroughly in earnest, doing very good work as an ordinary Christian; we have taken him in hand, we have trained him and put him in office, but he has proved sooner or **Selection of men to be trained.** later a failure, and I think it requires very great discrimination on the part of Missionaries in the selection of men to be trained. Then I think there is another thing we should bear in mind, that is, that the number of persons trained should not be large when compared with the great body of believers. If we train a larger number of men than we can really find work for, except by the use—I had almost said the indiscriminate use—of foreign money, we are doing greater harm to the cause of God, in the land where we are carrying on our Missions, than if we did not employ them at all.

Now I come to the question more immediately before us. Our friend who has just sat down has been referring to China. He has been speaking from a Chinese point of view, and he says you must not give this people any English education, because they do not want it. In Japan the circumstances are entirely different. We are there in the midst of a people who are now teaching the English language in their primary schools, and consequently it is almost impossible not to have men who are acquainted with the English language. I thoroughly endorse the sentiment that has been expressed, that the training **English or vernacular?** should be native, and I think in the main that the training should be in the native language; but, nevertheless, the students in our colleges, more particularly, should be encouraged to carry on the study of theology in English. You might even use English text-books, but the recitations should be in the vernacular. The person in charge of the seminaries should be thoroughly conversant with the native languages, so that he might be able to carry on the education of the students in the vernacular, whilst they are getting a great deal of help from books which they have not in their own language. As to whether men should come to Europe or America for education, this I conceive to be a matter upon which there will be of necessity a difference of opinion. We have had the standpoint of the Professor in the college at home, and the standpoint of the China Missionary. I think the true course is somewhere between these two extremes. Take for instance, Japan. I know one of the most earnest workers in one of our Missions there—the American Board of Missions—and I cannot, as an English Missionary, speak too highly of that American Board. One of the most earnest men there, was a man who came to America for another purpose, and he went back a thoroughly consecrated man, **An example of Western education.** and he has been one of the most able, devoted, and successful workers and pastors ever connected with the Church in Japan. So that European or American education, theological or otherwise, did not unfit that man for his work. The real question is this: We want men who are thoroughly consecrated, and if God has given us such men, if in His providence He leads them to Princeton, or Oxford, or Cambridge, or anywhere else—not necessarily sent by the Societies—but if in God's providence they find themselves there, in due time they will get good and carry it back to their own country. I think it would be disastrous to introduce a large body of young men to these places indiscriminately, to carry back to their own countries a state of living which would be altogether incompatible with the simplicity which is necessary to those who are to carry on Christ's work in the native Churches.

Rev. Professor T. Smith, D.D. (Free Church College, Edinburgh, formerly of Calcutta): Having the fear of the bell before me, I will follow the example that has been set, and begin at the end and go back to the beginning. I thoroughly agree with the friend who has just spoken, that if men must come to England or America, we cannot help it. But I have used any influence that I have had very strenuously and strongly in the way of discouraging their coming at all. I have had a great deal to do with men who have come to study law, medicine, and so on, and I am grieved to say that in every case the results have not been good, while in some cases they have been very bad. I think we ought all to set our faces against it when it can be helped. Of course I speak as a theological professor now, but I speak as a Missionary of former days, and I think it is an evil. If it be a necessary evil we must meet it in the best way we can. Going back to India, I am sure there is a work to be done there by the native Church that cannot be done but by English educated natives; therefore, I strongly advocate the continuance of those institutions which have the power of educating natives, through English, in the highest way possible. At the same time, I think that there might be a considerable amount of economy there.

On education in Europe.

I have taken part in training a great number of native Missionaries, for not only have our own Churches been supplied from the Calcutta Institution, but we have sent dozens to our American brethren and to others all through the country. Almost every six months I get letters from some of the men who tell me they are employed at Lahore, Peshawur, Amritsar, and all kinds of places in the North-West, in the American service. Then, I think, the example ought to be followed that has been set in Madras, of uniting the forces in order to train these ministers. I do not think it fair in our American brethren to come upon us little Scotch people, and expect us to train for them, at a considerable expense of men and money, the people who are to be their agents. They are of course ours, because they are theirs. Then as to this matter, I very strongly feel that we have had an injury done us, through what I must pronounce to be the most injudicious conduct on the part of the British Government in their treatment of the natives, in raising their salaries to an amount that is almost impossible for Missionaries to pay, and thus placing a temptation in the way of our educated natives, which it would require an enormous amount of Christian principle to resist.

Temptation to English-speaking natives.

We have had our resources drained again and again by the offer made to our best men of high salaries, with which I presume they are discontented now, whereas they formerly would have been contented with salaries a fourth or a fifth, or even a tenth part of the amount. That is a difficulty that I think is to be surmounted.

Rev. William Gray (Secretary, C.M.S.): Whether we realise it or not (I am not entirely sure that we do realise it, from the tone of the speeches delivered and the Papers read), the question before us this morning is about the most difficult and the most critical of all the questions which Missionary Societies and Missionaries in India have to deal with at the present crisis of Missions. The reason why I say so is that nowadays we have a different sort of thing to do in dealing with native agents from what we had to do in former days. In old days, as far as I know, we could do pretty well what we liked with the native agents. They were all a different style of men, often poor men, entirely dependent on the Missionary, and the Missionary could train them as he liked; and after he had trained them he could employ them as he liked, and give them

Cannot do as we did formerly.

any salaries he chose. That day has gone by. We are now looking forward to a different kind of men coming to us, and we cannot deal with them in the way in which we dealt with the men of old days. I therefore think we ought to look this matter very carefully in the face, and try to get a solution of it. The great difficulty does not lie in the training. We may be all pretty well agreed upon that.

I think Dr. Smith has hit the mark in reference to the really important part of the question—What are we to do after we have trained them, and how are we to employ them, and what salaries we are to give them? That is a very difficult question, and it is a burning question in India. I speak specially of our experience in the Church Missionary Society at the present time. The very best men I myself ever knew as native agents were a few men educated in Mission schools, and afterwards brought forward and put into the hands, for thorough careful training, of a very superior and devoted Missionary. I do not say that against training institutions. It happened in the cases I speak of that the men were thoroughly well educated in our Mission ^{C.M.S. methods.} schools; they were matriculates of the Madras University, and they were thoroughly taken up and trained in the field. They were admirable men. But they were not sent to England, and I may say on my own part, and on the part of the Society I represent, I do feel it is not a good thing to send them to England if we can help it; and we do not send them. We think it far better for them to get the training in the field itself in our theological schools, and to get a further training under superior Missionaries. If you send them to England they will learn to wear English clothes, and very likely will learn to despise their own language, and if they do that they will certainly not be the men to preach the Gospel in their own language to the people. The great point to which we should direct our thoughts is this. What are we to do with these men when we have trained them? How are we to deal with them, and what salaries are we to give them? Nowadays, as Dr. Smith has said, the Government is bringing us into difficulties by their high salaries. The natives are coming forward and saying, "You must give us as large salaries as the European Missionaries get; at all events you must give us two-thirds of what the European Missionaries get, in accordance with the Statutory Service plan of the Government of India at the present time." The great solution that our Society has is this; we are endeavouring to encourage every educated Christian into whose heart the Lord has put the desire to serve in the Gospel, to think it ^{A way of solving the difficulty.} the highest possible honour to be connected, not with a Foreign Missionary Society, but with his own native Church. Men like coming to the Foreign Missionary Society, and they think they will give the best pay. Let us not encourage that. Let us strike that system down; let us encourage them to go to their own native Churches, and then say that all questions with regard to privileges and salaries do not belong to us at all. We say, "The Foreign Society have nothing to do with that; let the native Churches settle it for themselves."

Rev. G. E. Post, M.D. (Syrian Protestant College, Beyrout): Mr. Chairman, and dear friends,—Trust your Missionaries or else recall them. You have various opinions among the Missionaries about Church policy, about doctrine and other matters; but you have solid unanimity on this question all over the world. On this matter of the education of the natives, I have never yet met with a Missionary, or heard of a Missionary, who did not believe that they ought to be trained in the field. Now if your Missionaries are all mistaken, call them all home and seek good men for your Missions; but if they are right support them. I ^{Cost of education East and West.} speak of a thing which is a very serious evil. I made a calculation during my recent visit to America that there was money enough spent on candidates from the Turkish Empire, of Greek, Armenian, Syrian and other nationalities, to support seven colleges in Turkey; and every one of those students is supported by benevolent people who believe that in that way they are furthering the cause of Missions; but we who are in the field know that there is no outcome whatever to the cause of Missions from all that vast outlay. Dear friends, we should decide the case for ever; it should not be debatable hereafter.

Let me tell you what perhaps may be a surprise to many, that in the Turkish Empire there is not the slightest necessity for any student to come to any American or English college or theological seminary. We have seven colleges in Turkey; two of them are of the highest rank,—Robert College at Constantinople, and the Syrian Protestant College at Beyrout. The latter is a university fully equipped, and I may further say that the basis of instruction in that university is the English language, so that there is not the shadow of a shade of excuse for any student to pass by its doors and come to Princeton, or Oxford, or Cambridge.

They teach in that institution all the sciences which are taught at Princeton, but no Greek or Latin. In place of them they teach the imperial Arabic, which is a full equivalent in every respect. At the head of the theological seminary is a graduate of Princeton Theological Seminary, the Rev. Dr. Dennis, and there is a professor from Princeton Theological Seminary, the Rev. Dr. Ady, and one professor from Union Theological Seminary, Dr. Jessup, besides other teachers. The theology is as orthodox and thorough in every

A comparison. respect as the theology taught in Princeton. We can support a young man in that seminary for a hundred dollars a year. I suppose the most economical in Princeton does not spend less than five or six hundred dollars a year, and those five or six hundred dollars come out of the pockets of benevolent people who believe that in that way they are furthering the Mission cause in Syria. I wish to say that practically those who are trained in European countries do not go back in any evangelistic capacity. We know of what we speak; we know our men, and we know they do not come. Brethren, if repeating will make it forcible, let me say again, they do not come. Yet you have them all over England. In America I believe there is money enough spent to support six or seven colleges in Syria; I believe that in England twice as much is spent, because it is easier and cheaper to get to England. The day has come when the Christian public should be enlightened on this subject. We are not narrow-minded in the field; we are carrying with us the light and education of this country; we love that country and we love those people, and the motive of our conduct and principles is to elevate them as fast as we can, and to elevate them altogether. I will say one word to the brother who spoke of the debt of Americans to the college in India. We have paid it tenfold in Syria in this college, for Irish, for Episcopalians, for all branches of the Christian Church, and we are glad to do it for them. He can turn over the Bill of Exchange on India to the Syrian Protestant College.

Rev. A. D. Gring (Reformed Church in the United States, from Japan): —I represent the Union Church of Christ in Japan. In that Church we lay down the principle of a self-supporting, self-propagating, self-sustaining Church. That is why we have our schools. We have a great many girls' schools and boys' schools, but, as it was urged upon us yesterday, these schools are emphatically Christian. They are for the prepara-

Education in Japan. tion of our young girls and boys, and our young men for Christian work, and if there are any heathen who wish to come in and take advantage of them, we welcome them, but they are emphatically Christian schools.

We have seven thousand young men and young women in them to-day. Then we have fourteen theological schools with two hundred and sixteen students. We begin with the Church, and we try that every member of the Church should be a worker for Christ. We ask that every member of the Church should be at least willing to pray in public, women or men ; indeed there is not a member in my Church that I am not privileged at any time to call upon to lead in prayer or read the Scriptures. That is the beginning. And then, those who develop any special gift we select to be evangelists. They are unordained, but they have to be taught especially in the Scripture and in the Catechism, and then we place them as evangelists or leaders of little churches in groups.

We take in women too. There is a good theological seminary or training school for women in Japan to train these women for evangelistic work. Next to the evangelistic work we have the seminary. After the evangelists have passed two or three years in successful work amongst the Churches, we select the best of them and put them in seminaries, and there, through the English language and through Japanese as well, we teach them the higher studies in theology and thus prepare them for ordination. Our Presbyterian Government suits excellently for this kind of work. We have what in Japanese is called the Session or small body in the Church. Here come our elders and our deacons, and we sit down with them and talk over the interests of the Church. Next we have the Presbytery, and here again we sit down with our elders *Presbyterianism* twice a year—the elders, ministers, and evangelists—and talk over *in Japan.* the general interests of the large section of the Church. Then every year we have the General Assembly or Synod, where we meet in a large hall with our elders and deacons and the great mass of the people, and discuss questions at large. We all sit down on equal terms in that great Home Missionary Society, which is one of the grandest developments of the native Church in Japan. We teach these ministers, and evangelists, and elders, and deacons, to carry on Home Missionary work, and we place them on an exactly equal footing with ourselves. They have a vote as we have, and they are placed exactly alongside of us. We come in not so much to lead them as to help them. The Japanese are sharp enough to know the difference between our coming there to propagate our own denominationalism, and our coming there to propagate the Gospel of Christ ; they distinguish clearly between these two things. Let me say, in conclusion, that the prospect for the future of the Church in Japan is splendid.

Rev. F. Ziegler (Basle Missionary Society) : Dear brothers and sisters,— My excuse as a foreigner for coming forward to speak here must be, first, that I am one of the representatives of the Basle Missions ; and, secondly, that I have been about thirty years in the service of that Mission, twenty-two of which were spent in India. As to the best method of training native workers, the experience of our Mission has been the same as that of others. At first each of the Missionaries trained his native assistants himself, and some of the men who were thus educated were, and are still, very good and effective native workers. I wish there *The course* were more such. But now we have come to the second stage *pursued.* of training our men by central institutions. If the head of those institutions is himself a superior man, filled by the Spirit of God, and having the gift of bringing his pupils and his teachers to the knowledge of sin and to conversion to Christ, the education is a very useful one.

But we must take the boys when they are not yet developed, and we must bring them up in our schools. If they do not come to be converted in our institutions, they will do more harm than good ; that has been my experience and the experience of others. Our practice is to give the necessary instruction in the vernacular only, but we teach the English language as a means of enabling the students to read English books and have access to English literature. The second question on the programme, " Shall an American or European education for natives of Mission-fields be encouraged ?" has been answered practically by our Missions. We have had a considerable number of men from Armenia, from India, Africa, and China, who came to the college at Basle, and were educated there. My experience is that this practice ought not to be encouraged, but my experience only goes as far as India. They say that in China the outcome has been better than in India. When a man is to be sent home to Europe, I think the native Church ought to pay for it, but of course in such cases the natives should be induced and encouraged to take no higher salaries than their other native brethren receive. But when they are sent by Europeans they must be paid higher salaries.

Professor R. B. Welch, LL.D. (Auburn, New York): The question before us is interesting, not only in regard to Foreign Missions, but in regard to the Home Missions. We need instruction, deliberation, conclusion on this subject, clear and strong for the home field as well as for the foreign. We have been taking the standpoint abroad, and we may as well take the standpoint at home. What shall we do at home? The young men are coming to America and to England, what shall we do with them? Now it

Have a fixed policy regarding Western education. seems to me that abroad and at home there must be light thrown on this question, so that young men abroad, if they propose to come to America or England for education shall know precisely the issue,—shall know precisely how they will be handled if they come to England or America. If they come it must be at the peril of their not being sent back, or their being sent back precisely on a level with those who stay. In such a case, would it not be wise to encourage them? You cannot stop their coming. If God puts it into the mind and heart of a young man abroad to come to America, he will come; you cannot stop him if he is urged by an impelling force. You may discourage him and hold him back, but if he comes and is willing to undergo all hazard, and to put himself with all his new training on the same footing as that of the native helpers, I say let him come. But let him not come with the understanding that he shall gain a breadth of education, and a denationalised character, and a strength and excellence that shall carry him back and lift him up above his fellow natives.

Now if he comes independently, with the influence of Christ in his heart, with the desire to get all the information he can in a short time, and then with rededication and reconsecration, goes back to the native field and puts himself forward for God's service in the broadest way, then I say let him come. God means something in such a case. I know one or two such persons who have come to our seminary and have gone back again. I could mention one name that

Example of a seminary student. many of you would recognise, the name of one who has gone back to the intensest work, not chilled in spirit, but with glowing fervour from the first day to the last, and we look to him now as a man whom God is blessing with continuous revival. That man went back a strong man, filled with knowledge, and above all things filled with the Holy Ghost and with faith. I say further, if seminaries at home or abroad are so miserable that they chill faith and destroy ardour, and weaken a man as a Christian, they ought to be disbanded, the Church ought to frown upon such institutions; God's frown must be upon them. If it is said in truth we ought to pray for such seminaries; we ought to see that they come up on the plane of Christian working motive.

Mr. Andrew Jukes, M.R.C.S.L., L.R.C.P. Ed. (C.M.S., from Dera Ghazi Khan): Mr. Chairman,—I think it is important that every Missionary, as far as time will allow, should express his opinion upon this subject, particularly upon the subject of bringing natives to England or America for education. Coming from the Punjab, I think that our experience there has been decidedly against this practice. Some of our native brothers have come to this country; more, perhaps, may have gone to America; but I cannot point to any single instance where this practice has been followed by any good result to the Mission in the Punjab. In the first place, the natives who come back have not only taken upon them- **Natives** selves a certain amount of Western polish, but they have lost **who return are** touch with their brethren at home. They have a difficulty in **out of touch.** taking up the same place upon their return that they occupied before they left. Again I repeat what Dr. Welch has just said, that our native brethren who are urged to come to this country or to America for educational advantages should come at their own expense, and their education should be at their own expense, and that if, having acquired such education, they are willing to consecrate their services and talents to their Master, we should by all means receive and encourage them.

Rev. John Ross (United Presbyterian Mission, Manchuria): Mr. Chairman, and Christian friends,—I do not know that it is necessary for me to say much upon the subject, inasmuch as all the remarks which I had intended to make have been in a scattered sort of way already laid before you. It seems to me that difference of opinion is more apparent than real. The last speaker, I think, cleared up the difficulty in **Western culture** stating that we Missionaries are quite willing that the natives, **at the natives'** whether Christian or not, should receive the highest possible **expense.** advantages in educational establishments abroad or in this country, but that, if they go beyond the Mission circle, and seek for higher education than is absolutely indispensable for effective Mission work, that higher education should be carried on at their own expense.

As far as our own experience goes we have found that it is not necessary to instruct natives in any foreign language in order to make them competent, useful, and successful agents. In the beginning of our work in **Effects of** Manchuria there were two or three who became Christians. I **training natives.** gave them such Biblical instruction as I could, and then sent them to their work. But every Christian man is also told to preach the Gospel where, when, and how he can, so that, of all the members, nine-tenths are preachers of the Gospel. I mentioned in the Great Hall the other evening that there are about a thousand members connected with our small cause. I wish to emphasise the fact, that the foreigner has been the means directly of the conversion of not more than one dozen out of this number,—that all the others have been directly the results of the private and public instruction of their fellow countrymen. The manner in which we carry on our Christian instruction is this. We first of all enjoin upon every believer, **Methods** men and women, aye, and upon children too, that they are to **in Manchuria.** impart Christian knowledge when and as much as they can. We soon discover who of these Christians are the most apt in imparting Christian instruction. These we teach in class, not paying them in any way, but giving them instruction at their own expense. They carry on their own business, whatever it is, and they come to us for more complete Christian instruction three times a week. Then, if we discover, after a course of study, that there are some who are peculiarly fitted for the work of preaching the Gospel, we set them apart. But the native Church itself is now raising funds to send out men of their own choice under their own instructions, amenable to their discipline. They have already sent out two such men, and I hope that within another year they may send a third. We are endeavouring in this way to raise up a native ministry for the native Churches. If they can learn anything outside

Christian instruction we shall be delighted, but we do not wish to impart that further instruction at the expense of any funds which are raised for the direct work of preaching the Gospel to the heathen.

Rev. L. Dahle (Secretary, Norwegian Missionary Society): Mr. Chairman, ladies, and gentlemen,—The Society which I have the honour to represent is a very small body compared with your big English Societies. Nevertheless, we have a good deal of school work, especially in Madagascar. There are 15,000 converts there, but we have 30,000 pupils in our 220 schools, and about 500 native schoolmasters. We have therefore a good deal of experience with regard to the training of schoolmasters. I have myself been a teacher in our college for about fifteen years. Our native teachers have Mode of training. had a very different education. Some have been trained in a college where they had about the same education as you give people in your colleges in England and America, with the exception of the ancient languages. Some few have been taught a little Greek, to read the New Testament.

In the normal colleges for the training of schoolmasters, the training is not very inferior to that which we used to give in such colleges in Europe. But then a great number of our teachers have got their training at the station where I work, because we could not train them all in these seminaries. Some of them are very good teachers indeed. The Missionary tries to gather round him out of his schools, picked men, the best scholars, and to give them special training for school work. They receive very little pay. Some work for twopence a day; the most they get would be about five dollars a month—those trained in the college—with the exception of sixteen ordained men, who would get from five to eight dollars a month. With regard to the question of educating men on the field, or sending them home, I agree with a former speaker who said that there is only one opinion amongst Missionaries about that: give them their training on the field. We have sent home only three men. Let me only say further, whatever training you give them, do not give them such training as would dissociate them from their people. Do not try to lift them as high as to make them hover over the heads of the people in the air. In the next place, whatever training you give them, train them thoroughly in the subjects you select. Do not attempt too many things : *non multas sed multum* is a good old proverb that you should stick to. Do not try to cram them too much, but rather try to develop their brains and their hearts if you can, and especially to inspire them with a burning love to Christ and their fellow-countrymen, and a wish to do them good. That is what I desire above all things. I have known some men come out from the college almost like an electric battery, so brim full of knowledge that you could hardly touch them at any point, without drawing forth an electric spark. I tell you, gentlemen, I have the profoundest disrespect for that kind of knowledge.

Rev. William Lee (L.M.S., from Nagercoil): Mr. Chairman, ladies, and gentlemen,—I should not venture to intrude upon your time if I had not been connected with a Mission in which we have an institution that has been most successful, under the blessing of God, in training men for Christian work. I believe we are not legislating for special cases this morning, but dealing with broad general principles, and I say from my own observation as a Missionary that you can train men for Christian work in their own country and amongst their own countrymen far better in the field than you can possibly train them by sending them home either to America Method in or Europe. We have in connection with the London Missionary Travancore. Society, in South Travancore, a large and important Mission which God has greatly blessed. Side by side we have the European Missionary working, and we have lay native catechists, and native pastors, and native evangelists. Our natives have been trained, those of them who knew Tamil, in the Tamil language, those who knew English in the English language. We have never lacked men, competent to dispute with their fellows, in the Hindu bazaars or in the public streets of the capital, and we have never lacked men competent to instruct their young brethren in Christian faith and love.

If you get men to come to England at their own expense, who will go back and work side by side with their own brethren upon the same platform, and at the same salaries, who would refuse to receive them and help them ? But if you are to send men at a great cost home to England to be educated, and then send them back again to the Mission-field as an experiment, I for one, as a Missionary of upwards of twenty years' experience in India, entirely dissent from that view of the case. We have men coming to England from India to study law and medicine. Now if our Christian men will come and study on the same terms, we shall be delighted to welcome them in every way possible. We have our Mission plans in Travancore, which have been the result of a great many years' experience and thought, and we believe that we have to some extent solved this question of training native agency. We have in our seminaries and schools, boys who are receiving an ordinary education, and also boys who are receiving a superior education. Such of them as wish to be employed in Mission work are employed as schoolmasters, and also as catechists, and amongst those who have developed very superior ability, we have selected some who have come back again into the college from which they had gone forth and have received a little more special training to fit them for higher and more responsible duties as Pastors and Missionaries.

Rev. R. Wardlaw Thompson (Secretary, L.M.S.): I am sorry to intrude with another part of the question at this late hour. The question of training native evangelists in India and China is an exceedingly tempting one, but I shall entirely avoid it, only saying that in the management of a Missionary Society, at any rate, it is a grievous thing to think of having to send away from their own country to receive European training, men who shall be denationalised thereby. I want to ask a question and obtain information for our own practical help in other fields of labour—for after all there are other fields. Important as those two great fields are, we want to know what is to be done in regard to training in some of the simpler and more elementary fields of labour, which are now undergoing a great transformation from their youthful condition. What training are the native pastors to receive, and what medium of instruction is to be used in such fields of labour as South Africa and the South Seas, where you have had in the past peoples separated from all others, so that you have been only able to use the native languages; but now they are coming in contact with Europeans. Is it advisable or not to adopt English in such cases, as a medium of instruction and training for evangelists and pastors of the native Churches? I know that the difficulties are very great. I know the danger of lifting up pastors in those places, out of sympathy with their own people, and making them so much superior by their knowledge of English that they take a false position. But I know, on the other hand, from reports that are continually reaching me, the danger to which they are exposed in knowing only the native language, now that Europeans are coming into these isolated parts. I know also the labour of giving small and detached communities which have languages of their own instruction requisite to provide them for their advancing position, by the laborious process of writing out lectures or printing books. This is a matter of serious importance as a practical question of Missionary arrangement. This may seem a small question by the side of the great Indian and Chinese fields, but it is a difficult question in the management of some of our Missions. I had hoped that some hint would have been dropped by our American friends who have had experience in Asia Minor and the South Seas, in regard to this matter, and if any one can give me an answer privately I shall be thankful to receive it.

Dr. Cairns pronounced the Benediction.

APPENDIX.

[It is a fact too much overlooked that the African race in America is the largest result of Missionary effort of modern times, consisting, as it does, if we include the West Indies, of some ten millions of nominal Christians, descended from a heathen ancestry, all brought within the pale of the Church during the last two hundred years. In this light the Paper by Dr. Strieby has much significance and importance.—ED.]

1. By THE REV. M. E. STRIEBY, D.D. (Corresponding Secretary of the American Missionary Association). (*See* page 58.)

The Training of American Freedmen as Factors in African Evangelisation.

The presence of the freedmen in America is an anomaly in the world's history. European nations have gradually abolished serfdom, and the master and the serf being of the same race, the line of separation has soon broken down. America is a nation of immigrants, mostly from Europe and Africa. The Europeans soon assimilate, and only the tradition of the individual family tells of the particular nation from which it came. But the African immigrants are still, after three hundred years' residence in America, separated

African residents in America. from the white race by visible and ineffaceable marks of colour and features; and are thus at the same time identified with the land of their fathers. They are here in great numbers, are strong in body, bright in intellect, and of a peculiarly religious temperament. Are not these facts suggestive? Does not the persistent race-identity of these people, linking them still with Africa, suggest a duty they may owe to it; and do not their vigorous intellects and warm religious characteristics indicate that duty to be a high and sacred one.

On the other hand, Africa, the land of their fathers, is another anomaly in the world's history. For a thousand years it was unknown to the civilised world; its people are the most degraded on earth, and it is a shame and reproach to the Church that it has done so little to enlighten them,—yea, a double shame when, as is now well known, Mohammedanism is spreading most rapidly over the whole continent.

These added facts emphasise with marked significance the question already asked: Are not these freed negroes peculiarly fitted and providentially called to carry the Gospel to their fatherland? Is there not here a Divine purpose that

The freed negroes and their fatherland. the Church should be quick to see and prompt to carry out? As the Hebrews were taken to Egypt, disciplined by bondage, and made familiar with the arts of the most enlightened nation then on earth, and were thus prepared for their high destiny in developing the plan of salvation, so, are not these children of Africa, chastened by their severe bondage, brought into contact with the civilisation of America, and fitted by their ardent religious impulses, destined to bear a large share in the work of Africa's evangelisation ? It is to the development of this thought that I invite attention.

Let me first revert to the slow progress of Christianity in Africa. One of earth's earliest and brightest civilisations skirted its northern border ; Egypt ruled the ancient world in letters and arts as well as arms. One of Christianity's early triumphs covered the same lands. St. Mark is said to have planted the Gospel in Northern Africa, and Origen, Augustine and Cyprian, great lights in the early Church, were teachers and Bishops in Egypt, Carthage and Hippo. When the dark ages settled down on the Roman Empire, their gloomy wings covered Egypt also ; but when the day dawned once more on Europe, it did not spread to Africa. It is true that the Saracenic civilisation of the middle ages brought a gleam of light to Northern Africa which Europe was glad to borrow, but it did more good to Europe than it did to Africa, for it helped to bring to Europe the glory of modern civilisation, but in its own home in Africa, it sunk again into deep night. But while these lights shone on the northern shore, none has come to the rest of the great Continent. So far as is now known, darkness has hovered over it— ignorance, superstition, degradation, cannibalism, slavery and war have made and perpetuated that darkness. *Early Christianity in Africa.*

It is now in order to ask if the freedmen of America can be fitted to take a special part in the evangelisation of Africa. I think it can be shown that they have race advantages similar to the Mohammedans, and that they can readily obtain the acquired advantages of the white Missionary. In the first place they are numerous—eight millions now, and increasing at the rate of five hundred per day. They are not soon to disappear, but are destined to hold a place among their fellow-men. In physical proportions they are stalwart and vigorous, inured to toil and capable of great exertion. Their mental powers are quick and susceptible of wide culture. They are eager to learn. Perhaps there never have been so many millions in one group, that showed such an earnest desire for knowledge, as these negroes did when they were emancipated. Their capacity to acquire learning, even in its higher branches, has been abundantly tested in the schools they have attended. This testimony has been confirmed by every added year's experience in the schools which these people have been permitted to attend. *Qualifications possessed by the freedmen.*

The religious characteristics of the race are very marked ; faith, hope, and love, are leading traits. They endured a bondage that would have crushed other races ; their faith and hope never deserted them. Their bitter experience in those long and weary years drove them to God as their only source of help, and the " Slave Songs," with the sad history out of which they grew, are among the most pathetic utterances of patience, trust, and triumphant hope that human literature presents. The furnace was hot, the gold was refined. The love element was manifested in their attachment to their masters through all the years of their bondage ; and during the war, waged by their masters to rivet their bonds, as they well knew, their fidelity and attachment in their care of the families, were abundantly shown ; not a single instance has been found where the homes, wives and daughters of the masters, were not sacredly guarded. The war was long, but they never lost their faith in their ultimate deliverance. The Jew in his journey from bondage to Canaan, often became despondent and murmured ; the negro never did either.

Their worship is fervent and their zeal is often without knowledge or virtue, but these are the results of their warm blood, and of the inevitable influences of slavery. But it has been found that as they rise in knowledge, their worship becomes decorous and their piety intelligent and pure.

Such a people are surely destined to develop a rich and beautiful Christian life. If they should be specially fitted, and their warm hearts inspired for the work of Missionaries to Africa, who can doubt the success of their efforts ? They would stand on a better vantage ground there than the Mohammedan, for he is a foreigner transplanted on the soil ; they would come back to the homes of their fathers, and would meet the native *Their fitness to be evangelists.*

as brothers—long separated, yet as brothers; their colour and personal characteristics would attest the kinship, their Christian love would kindle their zeal towards the degraded of their race, and their holy ambition would be fired by the grand work to which they were called—the uplifting of the millions of long-neglected Africa.

It would be reasonable to expect that they would endure the African climate better than the white men. They are a tropical race, and in America they love and cling to the sunny South, seldom migrating to the North; they do not suffer from the malaria that is so fatal to the whites in the South. Doubtless, the change to the intenser heat, and more intensely malarial influences in Africa would try them at first, but in all probability the change would be to them an easier process than to the white man.

The experience of the past in Mission work in Africa, brief and limited as it is, ought to throw some light on the questions we have been considering. With a view of learning the results of that experience, I addressed letters to the Secretaries of all the larger Societies in Europe and America doing Missionary work on that Continent, and in due time received courteous replies from nearly all of them, giving opinions and facts with more or less fulness of detail. My inquiries mainly centred around two points: First, the ability of the coloured Missionary, as compared with the white, to endure the climate; *Compared with the whites.* and secondly, his relative success as a Missionary. The opinions given in these letters, as might be expected, are various, and the facts themselves, gathered from widely different sources, and relating to very different climates and local circumstances, point to somewhat different conclusions. But the whole testimony may thus be summed up:—

1. The coloured Missionary *does* endure the climate better than the white man. Leaving out of account the northern and southern extremities of Africa, *Endurance of climate.* which have the climate of the temperate zone, and are therefore healthy alike to both races, and confining our attention to the hot and malarial regions which, alas! are the larger share of the continent, the testimony decidedly preponderates in favour of the greater healthiness of the coloured Missionaries. The true point of comparison, for the purpose I have in view, is where coloured Missionaries, born in America or in the West Indies, have been employed in the same localities with those of the white race; and here again the evidence is in favour of the greater endurance of the coloured man. The more specific statement stands thus: No Society reports that the coloured man is *less* healthy than the white; one or two Societies discern no special difference; but the larger number say he endures the climate much better than the white man. 2. On the second point—the *Success as workers.* comparative success of coloured Missionaries—the testimony bears very decidedly, as a rule, as yet against them, while a few and very favourable exceptions indicate that the fault is with the individuals, and not with the race, and hold out the hope that time and better training will remove the difficulties.

The more full account may thus be given: Some of the Societies charge a want of carefulness, perhaps a want of integrity, against the coloured Missionaries *Weak points in coloured Missionaries.* —that coloured treasurers will not render accounts, teachers will not make reports, Missionaries desire to control, and very seldom are sufficiently respected, especially when of younger age. Now these are manifestly the vices and infirmities of an immature and imperfectly cultured race. We must recollect that centuries of civilisation and Christian influences are behind Europeans and Americans, while the native African, converted and trained in his own land, has behind him only the few years of his own life separating him from the densest degradation of heathenism; the African born and converted in the West Indies has been a freedman only since 1840; and the American negro was perhaps himself a slave, and his race had the shackles struck from their bodies only in 1863, while the fetters of ignorance and vice still manacle the minds and hearts of the mass. We ought not, therefore, to wonder so much at the failure of many as to rejoice and take courage at the success of the few, especially as there is another side to the dark picture.

The Christian world has known and honoured some of the successful coloured Missionaries in Africa, and the letters I have received joyfully refer to these, and mention others not yet widely known, but whose work attests their wisdom, piety, and usefulness. Thus one Society refers to a Missionary, born a slave in America, and educated here, as "the most scholarly man in the whole Mission." Another says :—" Some excellent and useful Missionaries are found in their ranks." Another Society testifies, and our personal knowledge of the men referred to confirms the testimony, to the remarkable success of one of its coloured Missionaries as a business manager, a preacher and a teacher, showing himself fully equal to any emergency, and remarkable in his influence with the heads of the tribes and his success in winning souls. The testimony in regard to two others of its Missionaries is almost equally emphatic. Other Societies give similar testimony, and the Secretary of the Missionary Society of the Protestant Episcopal Church of America writes :—" All the ordained men on our Missionary staff in Africa, from the Bishop down, are coloured men. I think we have concluded that, all things considered, except for the work of higher education, coloured Missionaries are more available in that field than white." He refers with gratification to the career of Bishop Ferguson, the only coloured man who has a seat in the American House of Bishops, who was born in America, educated in the Mission schools, and has risen through the positions of teacher, deacon, priest, and rector until he was consecrated the Bishop of Cape Palmas in 1885, and has worthily filled all these positions." The Church Missionary Society of London refers to the remarkable career of Bishop Crowther, too well known to need repetition.

From all these facts the inferences are plain : 1. That negroes have succeeded in this work, and that those in America can be prepared for it. They can endure the climate, find ready access to the hearts of the people, and be eminently successful in preaching the Gospel. They should have the best training for the purpose, and great care should be exercised in selecting and sending forth only those of good education, mature character, sound judgment, and unquestioned piety. 2. America owes it as a debt to them and to Africa that they be furnished with the means for this training. The guilt of man-stealing and of slavery can have no better atonement than in sending back to Africa the sons of those stolen from those benighted shores, who shall take with them the light and blessings of civilisation and Christianity. 3. The coloured people of America should be aroused to this Providential call to this high Mission on behalf of their fatherland. We do not question nor minimise their great duty and destiny in America. Their warm affections, their easily-kindled zeal, their gift of song and eloquence, will yet add an enriching pathos to our piety and a wider range to our patriotism. But this call to Africa, while not interfering with duty here, will broaden their vision and deepen their piety. There will be a grand uplift to them in grasping and endeavouring to realise this great work. It will lift them above petty ambitions, it will give a practical turn to their religious enthusiasm, and bring them into closer sympathy with Jesus Christ. They have been in fellowship with Him in suffering ; they may now be co-workers with Him in redemption.

[For the same reason that we insert the Paper by Dr. Strieby, we give the following by Mr. East (see p. 51), as an illustration of the results of the conversion and organisation of a heathen race. That slavery has been the means of bringing these idolaters under the influence of a Gospel agency of any kind, is one of those mysteries of Providence which we cannot understand. We can only recognise the fact, and try to learn the lesson which it is meant to teach. *The fact is* that under the rough discipline of slavery, an hundred times more Africans have been brought into the Church than by all the

Missionary agencies of all the Societies labouring in Africa. *One lesson* which seems to be taught is, that in some way *native agents* may be found in America and the Indies, for carrying the Gospel to their ancestral home. We can only find room for *the summary* of the long and able Paper.—ED.]

2. BY THE REV. D. J. EAST (President of Calabar College, Kingston, Jamaica)

The Results of Emancipation on the African Race in the West Indies.

This review of the results of emancipation on the African race might be largely extended. But enough has been said to confute their traducers, and to satisfy the friends of religion and of freedom, that good progress has been made in every relation in which the emancipated African and his descendants are concerned.

The social condition of the West Indies prior to emancipation has been briefly noted: It has been shown how the Act of Emancipation legalised the manhood of the black man; how some of the evils fostered by slavery still cling to him; how, notwithstanding he has risen to a full, though at times it may be an inconvenient, consciousness and self-assertion of his independence; how amazingly his voluntary industry has been developed; how from the date of emancipation, as a taxpayer, he has borne far more than an equal share of the burdens of the State, and is the main supporter of the social improvements which modern science and art have introduced; how the black man is housed in favourable comparison with some parts, even of the United Kingdom, and how he is making progress in this direction; how he is qualifying himself as a citizen for the duties and offices of citizenship; how the cause of education is advancing through the agency of Government-aided elementary schools and training colleges; how widely general and religious literature is being circulated amongst the masses; and, above all, it has been shown how the Protestant Churches of every denomination are increasing in numbers; how these Churches have become self-supporting by the voluntary contributions of their members and adherents; how large the amount of contributions annually raised; how, notwithstanding every drawback, the power of vital godliness is exemplified by *attendance on the means of grace*, and the zeal and devotedness of a great multitude of Christian workers, as lay-preachers, native pastors, leaders, and other Church officers, Sunday school teachers, and specially appointed delegates and visitors.

METHODS.

After this review, but little need be said with reference to the methods by which these results have been reached. Beyond all question they are largely consequent on the influence of religion through the agency of our Protestant Missionary Societies. It was the Christian Missionary who prepared the slave to receive the boon of freedom, as it was to the Gospel that the emancipated slave ascribed it. It was through the Missionary's teaching that the freedman acknowledged and accepted his liberty as being as truly an act of Divine mercy, as was the liberation of the Israelite from Egyptian bondage. It was under the influence of the Gospel, as taught by the Christian Missionary, in numerous cases, brought home to the heart by the Holy Spirit, that former injuries were forgotten, and resentment was suppressed on the part of the emancipated. It was through Missionary teaching and influence that the Act of Emancipation came into force without popular excitement and commotion, the liberated slave population instead thronging the houses of prayer, to lift up to God the voice of thanksgiving and praise. It was thus that in Jamaica three hundred thousand slaves, looked upon as chattels before, having their fetters snapped asunder, rose to the conscious dignity of free men and women. And to the same gracious influences working directly and indirectly, I believe it is mainly owing that the African race in the West Indies may be pronounced to be the most quiet, orderly, and peaceable peasantry in the world.

Influence of Protestant Missionary.

The methods of the Christian Missionary have been very simple. Their work has mainly consisted in the preaching of the grand distinctive truths of the Gospel. This has been done in the true Evangelical spirit, *Preaching the Gospel, principal method.* without any admixture of science or philosophy, falsely so called, and without reference to the controversies which have agitated other parts of the Christian world.

Next to the preaching of the Gospel, the most potent influence has been the exercise of New Testament discipline in the Churches. As soon as it becomes known that a member is walking "disorderly," the case *Church discipline.* is brought before a meeting of the officers for investigation. If the charge be proved, the name of the offender is brought before the whole Church, and dealt with according to its merits. Gross and scandalous sin is uniformly visited with exclusion. The effect of such discipline is not only to preserve the purity of the Church, it exercises a salutary influence on others; and outside the Churches the moral standard thus set up tends to raise the moral tone of the community. I believe the discipline of the Churches has a far-reaching beneficial effect on society at large.

The meetings of Church officers constitute a kind of ecclesiastical courts, in which not only cases of discipline are considered, but in which the general business of the Church is transacted. The annual *Officers' meetings educating.* gatherings in Conference, Synod, or Union are of a similar character, only on a larger scale. In the annual meetings of the Jamaica Baptist Union, not infrequently between forty and fifty delegates, and as many ministers, assemble. These meetings serve as a school of practical education to those who attend them. The black man, equally with the minister, shares in the duties. And hereby they become instructed in the art of conducting deliberative assemblies, and in the modes of carrying on the business of such assemblies in a becoming and orderly manner. They serve not only to qualify them for the business affairs of the Churches, but for the business of social life. They are, to all intents and purposes, eminently educational institutions. They are training the more influential members of society not only in the interests of the Churches, but in the interests of the State; and there cannot be a doubt that they are exercising an eminently useful influence in promoting self-government and good order.

The general organisation of the Churches of almost all communions may also be cited as tending to good and useful results. The Wesleyan and Baptist Churches are, as has been shown, organised on what is called the *Class system.* Class system. Each congregation is divided into classes, with officers appointed over them. As many of the Churches are large, numbering from five hundred to one thousand members, this system has become absolutely necessary to a proper supervision, especially as in the country the members reside in villages some miles apart from each other. Thus again, our leading black men become practically exercised in the art of government, and the people in the duty of subordination to constituted authority.

Another efficient means of training is in the periodical meetings of teachers, both day and Sunday school. The schoolmasters of Jamaica have, during the last few years, formed themselves into voluntary asso- *Meetings of day and Sunday school teachers.* ciations, with a view to mutual improvement, and to deliberate on schemes of school work, together with such kindred objects as occasion may bring to the front. There are also numerous associations of Sunday school teachers, in connection with which periodical meetings are held. I have noticed with satisfaction the practice, on the part both of male and female teachers, of writing and reading essays on the practical methods of Sunday school work. I have read some of these essays with astonishment and delight. Twenty years ago not only were no such associations in existence, but no such papers as are now commonly read could have been produced.

The Christian Missionary uses every means in his power to develop native talent. And year by year this endeavour is yielding more and more fruit, while it is tending to the desired social elevation of the African race in these

Western Isles. The fathers of our West India Missions were the founders of our
elementary schools, and have been the pioneers in all social improvements. Underlying their endeavours has been the solemn conviction that God hath made of one blood all nations. The manhood
of the African from the first has had a full and unquestioning recognition;
the Missionary has thus become the defender of his rights as a man. This, even
after his emancipation, made Missionary advocacy necessary to his
protection against the oppression of those who were unwilling to
admit the doctrine of human equality. This sometimes exposed
the Missionary to the charge of being a political agitator. But the
sympathy thus shown towards the black man inspired his confidence, and gave
the Missionary pastor an influence over him which he still continues to exercise
for both his spiritual and temporal good.

Such in brief are the methods which Protestant Missionaries have
employed, by which the good results of the emancipation of the slave have
been achieved.

CONCLUSION.

The results of emancipation in the West Indies are inspiring of bright hopes
for the future of the African race. They clearly demonstrate the capacity of the
African, equally with other races of men, to receive intellectual,
moral, and religious culture. They show that he can be raised
from the lowest barbarism to a high degree of civilisation. They
make it plain that he is competent to fulfil all the duties, and willing to bear all
the burdens and responsibilities of citizenship. They show that under the
influence of the Gospel of the grace of God he may be delivered from the
bondage of the most degrading superstitions, and be transformed into the
image of God in righteousness and true holiness.

There is one remarkable feature in the African race which, in looking to its
future destiny, should never be lost sight of. While some races have become
almost extinct, the African is as numerous and prolific now, as at
any period of the world. This is true alike in the West Indies, in
the Southern States of America, and in Africa itself, notwithstanding the devastations of the slave trade. And who shall say, as the race continues
to multiply, how grand the future which is before it? Receiving Christianity at
our hands, the African may reflect it, associated with the gentleness, the meek-
ness, and the long-suffering patience which were so conspicuous in him in the
days of slavery,—qualities which still distinguish him,—and thus practically
become the teacher of the more refined and cultivated nations of the earth;
while from both the West Indies and from America, his sons and daughters
become the heralds of salvation to their fatherland.

Development of native talent. (margin)
Advocacy of black man's rights. (margin)
Results of emancipation. (margin)
Future of the African race. (margin)

[The following Paper has been forwarded from Canton. Though not
in our programme we give such portions of it as deal with points not taken
up by others.—ED.]

3. BY THE REV. R. H. GRAVES, M.D. (American Southern Baptist Mission, Canton).

Training Converts.

*After having shown the importance of training converts, from their great
need of it, and from the commands of Christ, and the example of the Apostles, he
deals with the question how this is to be done.*

How is this to be done? Of course no Missionary entirely neglects the
training of the converts. Attendance at public worship every Lord's day, or
attendance at the Lord's Supper every two or three months, is expected of all
who join the Church. But, in heathen lands, even these ordinary
opportunities of obtaining Christian instruction are not always
enjoyed. Converts come from villages here and there, miles away
from any place of public worship; it is often very difficult for women to attend

Unattainable conditions. (margin)

church at all, and, to add to the difficulty, they are generally unable to read and thus to obtain any Christian instruction for themselves through books. The weekly Sabbath instruction and training in Divine truth is all that many converts receive. It is the Divine plan for the training of Christians; and must, therefore, always hold the first place in any attempt towards Christian culture. Week-night Bible classes are generally out of the question for the bulk of the membership, and an impossibility for the females. Even when our members do attend regularly on Sunday, the time spent in worship is occupied by prayer and praise, as well as by the sermon; and the sermon is often hortatory and consolatory, rather than didactic. So, even with regard to those members who regularly attend our Sabbath services, the question occurs: How can we best carry out our commission, and *teach* our converts?

(1) The plan I have been accustomed to follow, and that I would suggest to others, is this: *First*, have before or after the ordinary Sabbath service a Bible class or a Sunday school, in which the Scriptures may be studied in the vernacular. Let pains be taken to get *all* the members, old and Bible classes. young, male and female, to attend this Bible school. *Secondly*, expound the Scriptures in order, as an essential part of the Sunday service. This may be done, either by reading *selections* as the lessons for the day, according to the Episcopal Prayer Book or the International Sunday School plan; or by reading the Bible narrative just as it is, which is what I prefer. What we want is to give our Christians a *connected* idea of the Gospel history and the historical portions of the Old Testament, as well as some knowledge of the Psalms and other devotional portions of the Word of God. In expounding the Old Testament I have found an opportunity of teaching many *practical* truths needed for the every-day Christian life. Andrew Fuller's lectures on Genesis seem to me an excellent model for such expository talks. My experience is that the mere *reading* the Bible without any comment, or drawing practical lessons, is not so efficient.

(2) But all Missionaries who feel the importance of training their converts desire to give more time to this teaching than the hour or so we have them under our instruction on Sunday. All realise, too, how important it is to have at least *some* of the converts well taught in Bible truth. How is this instruction best accomplished? The usual plan has been to establish schools where boys are taught a knowledge of the Bible, in connection with some branches of secular learning. It is freely admitted that some good preachers and useful intelligent Church members have been raised up in this way; but it must, on the other hand, be candidly acknowledged that as a means of securing an adequate supply of earnest, useful ministers and active Church On schools for membership this plan is a failure. It always will be so, for it does the heathen. not proceed on Scriptural lines. To train unconverted heathen boys, hoping that they will be converted while at school, is not the Divine plan for securing a Christian ministry or a well-trained Church.

My plan has been to give the converts some systematic teaching, and in this I have been seconded by my colleagues in the Mission. We spend a month in each quarter in studying the Bible. Instruction in the evidences of Christianity, Scripture, geography, homiletics, and Church history is given in connection with this, but exegesis is the great thing. Our assistants A residential and colporteurs, and as many Church members as can come, are course for urged to attend. Especially do we try to get every new convert in converts. the country Churches to attend this class in Canton for at least one month. It introduces them to the brethren of the City Church, it gives them an insight into the practical working of Christianity, it encourages them by the sight of the large body of fellow-believers, and promotes a feeling of unity among our Churches. But the main object is, to teach them how to study and how to understand the Bible. The course extends over three years, that is twelve months of study, which is nearly equal to two sessions spent in a theological seminary at home. The assistants are expected to take the full course. During this time, the historical books of the Old Testament are gone over, in the form of lectures, and questions are put both oral and in writing; the New Testament is read in class, verse by verse, and expounded in detail: and the Psalms, Proverbs, Job, or some of the prophetical writings are explained. All who attend are required to memorise an analysis of the book we are to take up for the quarter, and all who can are expected to write a sermon or an essay on a text or a subject previously assigned.

In order to accommodate those in the country, who cannot attend this class, the Missionary in charge of a station is accustomed to hold a Bible class at the station for a week or a fortnight, when some book of the New Testament is studied. We have not yet applied this system, except in a limited degree, to the women; but my opinion is that the lady Missionaries should have similar classes, visiting the country churches for this purpose, for it is difficult for the women to come to the city.

The expenses of this mode of instruction are much less than those of schools. The travelling expenses are paid, and $1.00 is allowed for food. Those who are able are expected to pay their own expenses, and paid assistants have only their travelling expenses paid. All who can are expected to spend part of the day in preaching at the chapels, or in selling tracts in the streets. The amount of aid given might, of course, vary in different Missions, but the principle is not to offer any pecuniary inducement to a man to leave his labour, and spend his time in study, but merely to help to defray any extra expense which he may have. By having these men under our training we ought to get to know them—their mental capacities, their spiritual attainments, their earnestness of purpose, and their ability to express themselves. If any of them feel called on to devote themselves to Christian work we know what advice to give them, and what department of the work to put them in. We look to these men for our supply of colporteurs and native helpers.

One result of system.

There is a pressing demand for labourers to take the places of those, who, having "served their generation, by the will of God, have fallen asleep." May God give us wisdom to leave behind us a native Church, "mighty in the Scriptures." Then we may lay down our burdens in peace, and commit our flocks in confidence to "God, and the Word of His grace, which is able to build them up, and to give them an inheritance among all them that are sanctified."

[This short Paper was prepared by the writer at the request of his brother Missionaries.—ED.]

4. BY THE REV. P. A. EUBANK (Southern Baptist Convention of U.S.A. Mission, Yoruba Country, Africa).

The Character of Native Converts.

Perhaps the most serious and important question that faces the Missionary in the Yoruba country, and calls for his solution, is the character of those who profess conversion to Christianity. On this depends the value of his work. If the profession is a mere empty one, leaving the individual still a heathen, but wearing the name of Jesus, his time is worse than wasted. If, on the contrary, those who profess faith prove faithful; if they show the Christian graces and develop strong Christian character, then he is abundantly repaid, though the numbers be few. With what interest then does the Missionary watch the growth of character in his converts?

True conversion the first condition.

Why it is thus, and what is the remedy for the tendency to a low standard of profession and practice in native converts are questions hard to answer. Doubtless their previous training and present surroundings are to be credited with this state of things in a great measure. The babe, the child, the youth, the man have been made so familiar with sin in all its phases that it has never been to them the "monster of so frightful mien." Deeds that would cause us to shudder and turn away in abhorrence make no impression on the native because of their very familiarity with them. Can the new convert from heathenism be expected to pass at a bound to a clear discrimination between good and evil, between holiness and sin?

The native Christian has not the help of public opinion, that strong incentive to right action and restraint from wrong in Christian lands. The only public sentiment here is that formed and controlled by the heathen. Here "Vox populi" is "Vox Diaboli." It is hard for the individual to rise far above the public mind. And let us remember the growth of public sentiment in Christian countries; for instance, in regard to religious toleration within the last three centuries. *Public opinion no help.*

Such reflections palliate the evil we are considering, though they do not excuse it.

We turn to an equally important question, and one not yet answered to the satisfaction of the Missionary, How can the evil be remedied? I can but briefly mention some things that will help toward this end.

We must begin with the beginning. Preach against sin to the heathen. Expound the Bible teaching concerning sin and God's abomination of it. Show the sinner as deserving death and hell. Try to ensure true conviction and repentance in the professing convert. Every Missionary is impressed with the absence of deep penitence in inquirers. *Remedies for the evil.*

Let every native convert, if possible, learn to read the Bible in his own language, that he may get the direct influence of its teachings on his life.

The Missionary must be a living example of the truth he preaches, mingling freely with the people, that he may have the greatest influence over them, and may impress on them his own godly life. *Good example and prayer.*

Give instruction publicly and privately, "line upon line." Create a distinctive *Christian* public opinion.

Following these lines with persistent fervent prayer to the Giver of all good, we may hope for improvement in time to come. But let us "learn to labour and to wait."

MEETINGS OF MEMBERS
IN SECTION.

ORGANISATION AND GOVERNMENT OF NATIVE CHURCHES. *
(3) SUPPORT OF WORKERS.

(a) The support of native workers. How far should this be undertaken by the Missionary Societies? Other means of support—by personal labour, or by the alms of the people, or by the native Churches.

(b) Industrial self-supporting Missions.

(c) How far shall Church architecture and other non-essentials be adapted to the native styles and tastes of the country?

(d) The importance of projecting Missions and Missionary expenditures upon such a scale, that the native Churches may at the earliest possible day be able to reach entire self-support.

(Friday afternoon, June 15th, in the Annexe.)

Rev. F. E. Wigram in the chair.
Acting Secretary, Rev. G. D. Boardman, D.D. (U.S.A.).

Rev. Canon Hoare offered prayer.

The Chairman : My Christian friends,—The subject for discussion this afternoon is one of very great importance indeed. I think that it brings very prominently before us the very solemn responsibility which rests upon the promoters of Missionary work with regard to the way in which the native Christian communities that may be raised up through the agency of the foreigner, may become really independent and really indigenous. First of all we have to support native workers. How far should this be undertaken by Missionary Societies? I suppose we should all agree at once, as little as possible. But yet we should find it impracticable to abstain altogether. To a very large extent it becomes necessary in the initial stage of the Mission to do something towards the support of the native workers, or else to do without the valuable, or rather invaluable help of the native workers ; for there may be indivi-

Reasons for
an indigenous
Church.

* This chapter is put in smaller type like the last, and for the same reasons.—ED.

duals brought out who may be duly qualified to be evangelists to their countrymen before there is a body of Christians in the country sufficiently numerous and sufficiently wealthy to support these workers. There are other means of support—by personal labour, or by the alms of the people, or by native Churches. I will not dwell upon these, because we shall hear a good deal about them presently from the readers of the Papers.

Then we come to industrial self-supporting Missions. I should like to say that one gentleman very high in office in India, pressed this subject upon me most earnestly, and spoke with great thankfulness of the Industrial Missions that were being organised by Missions in the country. I believe that as far as our own experience has gone we have not had very much to encourage us with respect to the industrial self-supporting Missions. But the idea of this gentleman, who from his position ought to have known, was this,—that if instead of giving the secular education which the Government are prepared to find for the growing youth of India, and which the Missionary agencies avail themselves of as a grand evangelistic agency, we were to open industrial schools and get out first-rate mechanics from England to teach, then we should be doing an incalculable benefit to the country, and we should be securing what we want, namely, access to numbers of young people whom we might so influence. *Testimony to Industrial Missions.*

Then I do feel very tenderly with regard to the next point, How far shall Church architecture and other non-essentials be adapted to the native styles and tastes of the country? I must confess that as I wandered about in the different Mission-fields that I passed through, my heart did yearn to see something which looked as if it really did belong to the native people in the way of a church, not Gothic structures such as would commend themselves to any of our own people in England, but not adapted, as I thought, to the ideas of the people. It appeared to me that it was just putting into exhibition a most false idea of Christianity as the religion of the foreigner. We want to see something that really comes from the minds of the people, and will represent their ideas of what the House of God should be. One day on the hills of Santhalia, amongst the Paharis, I did at last come across a place of worship which evidently had not been touched in any way by a European, and I felt I could thank God for it. I am not going to describe it to you. It was as unlike a place of worship such as we should think of, as could possibly be, and yet the whole of it was so neat, so carefully reserved : a little trellis of bamboo enclosed the raised platform within its open space, and everything was so clean and nice, that it was evident they had given it their best efforts ; and when from it I went into the hut which was the house of the head man of the village I realised the contrast, and I realised that they had been taught that their place of worship should be very much better than anything they were accustomed to in their own way of living. *Church architecture.* *A model native church.*

Then we have to consider the importance of projecting Missions and Missionary expenditures upon such a scale that the native Churches may at the earliest possible day be able to reach entire self-support. This is one of the most difficult problems possible. We must not starve our Missions, and yet we must keep this great object in view. And then, again, we foreigners are at a great disadvantage from our inability to accommodate ourselves to the climatic difficulties of many of these places, where we are obliged to shelter ourselves in a way that is not at all necessary to the natives of the country. And we have to build larger houses and lead a different mode of life in many respects. We know that there is a noble effort being made not to dissociate the Missionary from the people more than can be helped, but I am afraid we shall always find it is absolutely necessary for the foreigner in a tropical climate to protect himself in a way that the native need not do if he is *The foreigner's disadvantages.*

to keep himself—as he is bound to keep himself—in vigorous physical and mental health, that he may do his work powerfully. I would just end with what I began by saying, that I do look upon the question as one of very serious moment indeed. Are we going to be used of God to raise up native Christian communities, that shall be really vigorous, manly, and independent, belonging to the country, and able to reach the people of the country as from within and not from without? or are we going to keep the communities that God permits us to gather together in tutelage, in swaddling clothes, not allowing them to develop and mature and

Danger of encouraging dependence. be independent? I think that a great many people who talk about Missionary work, and who love to give a few shillings or a few pounds for this, that, or the other object, or for the support of this or that native Christian community, little realise the gravity of the question or the mischief that they may be doing by encouraging that dependence upon the foreigner which we desire to check. We want the natives as soon as possible to supply their own workers and support them, in order that they may be really going forward as the Lord's workmen to the great work of evangelising their countrymen. I have now the pleasure of calling upon the Rev. Professor Lindsay, of the Free Church of Scotland Foreign Missions Committee, to read Dr. Stewart's Paper.

Rev. Professor Lindsay, D.D.: The Paper I have in my hand is by Dr. Stewart, who is at the head of the large educational institution at Lovedale. He has recently published a record in black and white of the results obtained at that institution. The numbers of men sent out must be reckoned by the thousand, and the failures and those who have gone back by something like ¼ per cent.

PAPER.

1. By the Rev. JAMES STEWART, M.D. (Free Church of Scotland Mission, Lovedale, South Africa). Read by the REV. PROFESSOR LINDSAY, D.D., of Glasgow.

Industrial Education: Its Place in Missionary Work.

In the Paper I have the honour to submit to this Conference, I do not profess to do more than state some points in connection with the subject of industrial education, as an agent of Missionary operations. The limits of the Paper preclude anything further. But this may serve to introduce the discussion, should there be representatives in the Conference from those regions where such operations are carried on.

The subject is not one which will probably occupy the Conference long,—amongst the many more important matters which will claim attention. In case of misapprehension it may be as well to state that the spirit of this Paper is

Spirit of the Paper apologetic. apologetic and explanatory—though why it should be necessary to apologise for so useful a kind of work as the teaching of honest industry, is not very clear, even to the mind of the writer himself. Most Missionaries who have had to do with this form or adjunct of Missionary work have been obliged to adopt this attitude. The reasons for this will appear immediately.

I propose in this Paper to briefly touch the two following points :—

I. The extent of this agency in Missionary Work, and the means by which it is carried on.

II. The necessity for such training and its moral value as a Missionary means.

I. The extent to which industrial training is carried on, as a portion of

the greatest and most important work which occupies the world to-day, is
not after all, very great. The reasons for this are easily found. It is not
necessary to introduce the arts of civilised life among a people who are
already civilised. In India and China it is not as necessary as it is in
Africa. And even in South Africa, there are only a few centres Centres of
of such operations. Two of the oldest are, Lovedale in con- industrial
nection with the Mission of the Free Church of Scotland; and training.
St. Matthew's in connection with the Church of England. At the former
of these places the work has been carried on for more than thirty years, and
and is more varied than at any other similar place in South Africa. It comprises printing, bookbinding, carpentering, waggon work and blacksmithing.
Telegraphy is also taught to a few; and for all there is some practical instruction in field or farm work. The number in the trades department varies
from thirty to fifty males, and in the girls' school from twenty to thirty; in
all about seventy-five. At a few other places, as the French Mission in
Basutoland, Blythswood in the Transkei, the Kaffir Institution in Grahams-
town, there are one or two trades taught at each. But the extent of their
operations is as yet not great.

We come now to what is after all, the real cause of the limitation of this
mode of work. It is this. There is a doubt in the minds of many of the
constituents of Missions at home, whether this is a legitimate
expenditure of Missionary time and energy. And this doubt Cause of
hardens into very practical shape in the minds of Home Com- the limitation.
mittees whicha dminister the funds, and appears in this form generally—
that these Committees undertake no financial responsibility in connection
with such industrial work. This is, I believe, the rule, whatever exceptions
there may be. This is not stated in the way of complaint. Probably all
Committees feel painfully, and chronically enough, that the funds at their
disposal annually are all urgently needed for more direct forms of Evangelistic
educational work; and until this special kind of training is more fully
recognised, and authorised on the part of the different Churches or the constituents of Missions, Foreign Mission Committees cannot do otherwise than
act on their present rule.

The next question to be answered is, How are such industrial agencies
called into existence and maintained? Generally at first by the generous
aid of individual Christian men, for buildings or material; by How
aid in the shape of grants from the Education Department of the originated and
Government, if a Government exists in the country, or if such supported.
grants are available; and by the proceeds of the industry itself.

For this form of work then the individual Missionary, or body of Missionaries on the spot, must make themselves financially responsible. All this
points to limitation. Industrial enterprises also, on a large scale, involve
both the possession and expenditure of capital. But Missionaries are not
men possessed of capital, hence also a limitation on another side. There is
a further conclusion. The little that has been already accomplished does
not owe its origin to large expenditure, either in the way of commencement
or maintenance, but to rigid economy, and to persevering work. Where the
work does not contribute largely to its own self-support, it soon dies out.

The fear, then, if it exists, that any large portion of Missionary funds is
devoted to this kind of work, is without foundation. Missionary Committees, so far as the writer's experience goes, are disposed to act generously,
that is as far as their rules allow. In years where the deficit balance is

not very heavy, they may give occasional aid in such ways as paying the passages of trade teachers, or in other forms.

This fear may be further shown to be groundless, by the fact that nowhere—in Africa, at least—so far as the writer's knowledge goes, are *Subordinate to evangelistic work.* such industrial operations carried on otherwise than alongside, and subordinate to, other more important work,—the evangelistic and strictly educational. In this way, it is a useful addition to those higher forms of work, besides affording a wholesome variety; for human nature is a varied thing in individual tastes, capacities, and inclinations. There are other uses which will be referred to further on.

II. The necessity for such training and its moral value.

Though I have not visited India, I believe that even there industrial work is carried on in connection with some Missions. There were, and probably there are still, such institutions in Mangalore in connection with the Basle or German Mission, as well as elsewhere. The Americans also have in several of their Missions not neglected this form of work.

The object in India is to aid the native convert in securing a livelihood, and to afford him assistance and protection if needed. In Africa we have to go further back. It is the moral training of the individual man primarily; *Object of such training.* the aiding him to a better livelihood than that of a day labourer is secondary, and yet inseparable. Industrial training to a people in the condition of native Africans may be a secular means, but the object aimed at is not secular but moral. This ought to alter the whole aspect of the question in the eyes of the home Missionary public, and ought to be weighed by those who maintain that Missionaries have nothing to do with affairs so secular as teaching of handicrafts. It is very difficult to say where, in the complex life of man in this world, the distinction between purely secular and sacred is really to be drawn. The spirit and the aim of the worker alone gives the work its character, and converts even secular work into a service of the Church, or it may be a religious service into a secular work.

There are very few Missionaries, I mean ordained Missionaries, who have to do with industrial work who would not very gladly be free from its care, *Three reasons for their existence.* worry, and responsibility. It may be asked then why they trouble themselves with it, and lade themselves with the thick clay of such occupations and distracting responsibilities? The answer is threefold. They have done so, from a contemplation first, of the life of the people among whom they labour, if they are a barbarous or uncivilised people. Second, they see that the tide of advancing civilisation is rolling so rapidly over certain portions of the globe, that barbarous peoples must accommodate themselves in some measure to its conditions and requirements, or be swept away. Third, among barbarous peoples one of the most formidable barriers to the acceptance of the Gospel is the indolence, or in plainer words the absolute laziness, which marks the social and individual life of such peoples. This indolence is the result of generations of hereditary influence, of social habits and customs, and is also partly due to the influences of climate. These are formidable powers to be vanquished by the Missionary's Sunday sermons—if he contents himself in such circumstances with preaching only. Preaching is the main power no doubt, but individual human wills are moved by many powers, seldom by a single influence only. Most Missionaries also find that it is very ineffective teaching which is limited to precept only; that it is little use saying; Do this; be industrious and cleanly; adorn the Gospel by your life—when each and all of these, both as to the means of accomplishment and the thing itself, are unknown and unintelligible. Example, and showing the way how, is the most effective method. Admonitions and recommendations are powerless in comparison. But it is impossible to teach everything useful. And some handicrafts, suitable to the country, and to the capacities and necessities of the people, are selected and commenced as systematic training in one particular branch of the arts of civilised life. Thus the industrial school, as an integral part of the varied work of a Missionary Institution, emerges. And for a time, amidst many difficulties, it is maintained; and later on, its results begin to tell in the improved condition of the native workman, in his higher wages and increased intelligence. He is thus rendered a more useful member of the community; and on the frontiers of a British Colony, if he is a steady and attentive workman, he is always sure of employment, and much higher remuneration.than if he had remained untaught. If he is a member of the Christian Church, his better social position enables him to contribute more easily and largely to its funds, and thus to aid the consummation so devoutly wished for, and so dear to finance committees of the Home Societies—the self-supporting condition of native congregations. *Its benefits to the natives.*

The process involved in this method, as one amongst many others, may be slow and not according to our views of what Missionary work is and should be as its ideal form; but the results as obtained at Lovedale, and elsewhere, are such as show the practical soundness and beneficial effects of the method.

It is true that some still say such work is not according to Apostolic forms and example. This is true. It is also true that the world is a very different world to-day from what it was in the days of the Apostles; and there are many additional methods of work subsidiary but important now in operation. None of them will supersede successfully the one great method that has lasted from Apostolic days; nor, taken all together, can they equal it in effect and power. And we may assure all our friends that we try to *Objection to such work.*

> "Raise men's bodies still by raising souls,
> As God did first."

The objection, however, is difficult to overcome. It really resolves itself into this, whether Missionaries should concern themselves with the temporal or secular affairs of the people among whom they labour. The warning, "No man that warreth entangleth himself with the affairs of this life," has surely more reference to entanglement for one's own personal benefit, than bearing burdens to assist and instruct the ignorant. To meet this objection, which is the only one with any force, there are three sources from which we may gather information and guidance. These are the example of Christ; the method of the Apostles; and the modes of working of the Christian Church to-day. We have also to remember that we have to deal with men who have bodies as well as souls; and that the needs of the body if very clamant will extinguish all anxiety about higher needs. *The Scripture argument.*

If we were to count the miracles of Christ, and see how many were directed to relieving the wants of the body, we should find that in His mode of working there was no forgetfulness of the fact that men have both souls and bodies to be cared for; and in what we have recorded of His doings there is none of that exclusiveness which would limit His work, then or now, solely and only to spiritual forms.

The Apostles again, if their doings are carefully studied, seem not to have been above interesting themselves in the bodily welfare of all with whom they came into contact,—but always with one object, to commend, and practically exhibit the true nature of the Gospel of Jesus Christ, as something fitted to man's earthly condition now, as it is also to his spiritual state hereafter.

But the strongest argument in favour of the soundness of industrial operations, as an auxiliary Missionary agency, among uncivilised peoples at least, is to be found in the varied forms of practical benevolence adopted by the Christian Church of to-day in most civilised countries. Proof of this is at the doors of the Missionary Conference. Let it be supposed for a moment that all those multitudinous forms of Christian activity which are to be found at work, even within the City of London itself, were to be suddenly compelled to assume only one form,—namely, that of preaching,—what would then become of the sick, the hungry, the helpless of all sorts and conditions, who are now being assisted by the very variety of work, which Christian experience assumes, in addition to that special form which stimulates and perfects them all? There is a stupor of misery among the helpless and despairing at home,—among those who have sunk beneath a certain level,—which prevents the message of the Gospel reaching the heart at first, by direct moral or spiritual address. There is also a stupor, though of a different kind, among the heathen, which has to be gradually dissipated by indirect means, and to this class of methods belong all forms of industrial training among barbarous peoples. It is purely a supplementary agency, and in no way takes the place of the higher methods.

The principle acted on at home.

It is the combination that benefits for both worlds at once. And the Missionary plea for industrial training for moral ends is nothing else. It may be asked whereto all this tends, as to the meaning and intention. Simply to this, that the recognition of a variety of method in Missionary work abroad as well as in Christian work at home, is probably both wise and necessary.

There is one part of the Apostolic method that every true Missionary keeps well before him. It is this. The preaching of these truths,—the forgiveness of sin, the love of God, the death of His Son as the Substitute for men,—briefly summed up in the words, "God so loved the world that He sent His Son, that whosoever believeth in Him might not perish but have everlasting life." With this in its due and prominent place there is no fear of industrial work in Missionary operations doing any harm, but rather good; and if this be so, it is worthy of the recognition of the Home Church on a more extended scale.

Evangelistic work kept prominent.

PAPER.

2. By the Rev. JOSEPH C. HOARE (C.M.S., Ningpo, China). Read by the Rev. J. GURNEY HOARE of Canterbury.

The Training of Native Candidates for the Ministry, and of other Native Workers.

That training is necessary few indeed will dispute; differences of opinion on the subject arise rather with reference to the nature and method of training required, than with reference to the necessity of it. I assume, therefore, that the invitation which I have received from your Committee to write on this topic, means that I am to endeavour to put before you the result of my experience in this special work, as regards methods. This I will attempt to do, premising only two points:—first, that I write only as a learner, thankful indeed for spiritual blessing vouchsafed to students during the past twelve years, but very conscious of the utter weakness of the human side of the work that has been done; secondly, that what I write has reference only to my experience in China, and that I do not pretend to any knowledge or opinion as to the nature and methods of training best suited for natives in other lands.

In dealing with this question it seems important at the outset to lay down one general principle, viz.: *that the means should be adapted to the end.* This principle seems so simple and obvious as to render it unnecessary to mention it. But effective work is usually carried out on simple principles, and the neglect of such principles usually leads to failure. I believe that it will be found that in many cases much valuable time has been wasted, much labour mis-spent in the training of native agents, either from a misconception of the object to be attained, or a miscalculation of the means required to effect that object. That this should be the case is not surprising. A young man fresh from the university is often set down in the midst of new surroundings, and informed that he is to undertake the training of native agents. He does not know, he cannot know (I speak from personal experience here), the mental and spiritual attitude of either the native Christians or the heathen. *A principle laid down.*

Now we shall all agree that *the end of all training should be to send forth men who will work for the glory of God in the conversion of individual souls, and the building up of the Church of Christ.* To effect this it must be borne in mind that the masses, amongst whom the work of native agents will for the most part lie, are—whether they be Christian or heathen—very ignorant, unversed in philosophy, unskilled in science. To do the work of an evangelist or a pastor amongst such people, a man does not require a knowledge of Western arts and sciences, but a knowledge of the Word of God, and a personal experience of its saving power in his own soul. This, I believe, holds good with regard to the vast majority of Christian workers in European countries; much more is it the case in the East, or at any rate in China. We want, in short, not Europeanised, but Christianised native workers. *The object of all training.*

What then is the method of training best calculated, with God's blessing, to effect this end? I shall first speak of *the course of study,* next of *the training for active work.* With regard then to *the course of study,* I enumerate, in what appears to me to be the order of importance, the subjects which should be taught.

(1) *Saturate the students with Scripture.* The expression is, I believe, Mr. Venn's, and it was passed on to me by the late honoured Bishop Russell. For our own spiritual life, for work amongst others, it is of the chiefest importance that we should all be imbued with the spirit of Scripture. It is, therefore, our first duty in training our native brethren, that we should lead them to study it with care, to commit to memory, to keep it in their hearts, to have it always on their tongues. Without it their own souls must starve, their work must be powerless.

(2) *Theology* should be systematically taught. It is by "sound doctrine" that the faith of believers must be built up, and the gainsayers convinced. There is a tendency in the present day to depreciate dogmatic teaching; but I believe that it is impossible to over-estimate its importance. Often have I detected in my students the germs of heresies which have grievously troubled the Church in times gone by. If we do not want to have the battle of the creeds fought over again in every newly-founded Church, we must hand down "all the counsel of God" as we have received it from our fathers, not indeed with *Dogmatic teaching.*

the undue assumption of authority, but helping our students to prove all things, and to hold fast that which is good.

(3) *Native philosophy, religion, literature, and history* should be carefully studied. This is absolutely necessary, in order to enable an agent rightly to gauge the mental attitude of even the illiterate. Personally, I am strongly opposed to the method of endeavouring to attract the mind of the heathen by showing them that their own religion and philosophy approximate to Christianity. I believe with Sir Monier Williams that between the best of the sacred books of the East and our Holy Bible there is " a veritable gulf which cannot be bridged over by any science of religious thought," and I believe that we should endeavour to win the heathen, not by showing any fancied similarity between the two, but rather by pointing out the immeasurable superiority of the Word of God over the doctrines of men. But, at the same time, it is essential that a preacher should know the minds of his hearers, and it is undoubtedly the case that a quotation or illustration from native sources may often help to clench an argument, provided that it be always borne in mind that the sword of the Spirit with which we must fight is the Word of God.

The agents and heathen religions.

(4) Knowledge of *Western science*, etc., should be imparted so far as time and opportunity allow. Not that a knowledge of Western science is likely to be of much use to a preacher in working amongst the masses of his fellow-countrymen; indeed it may often be a hindrance, through their making statements incomprehensible or incredible by their hearers. But scientific training has its use as an instrument of education, and may be well introduced for this purpose. At the same time it must be remembered that Scripture itself, if one may with reverence say so, is as fine an instrument of education as the world possesses. History, poetry, philosophy, religion, are all treated of in the Word of God as no mere man has ever written of them. The Missionary, therefore, who finds that he has no time to lecture on science, etc., may well content himself with imparting such knowledge of these matters as his students will not fail to draw from him in constant daily intercourse.

Training in Scriptures.

(5) The question remains, as to whether *English or any other language*, such as Greek, Latin, or Hebrew, should be taught; and whether it is desirable to make English a vehicle of education. To the latter part of the question my own answer is a direct negative. *Native agents* have to work amongst natives; they must teach them from the native translation of the Bible; they must present the truth to them in a native dress; they ought, therefore, to study and habituate their minds to think of these subjects in their own language. If it be difficult to express religious ideas accurately in the native language, this is only an additional reason for carrying on all teaching in that language; for it is of no use to fill a preacher with ideas which he cannot convey to his hearers in an intelligible form. It should be the object of the Missionary to enable his students to expound the native Bible; and, if necessary, to develop a native Christian phraseology and literature, which shall be clear and intelligible to their fellow-countrymen. To effect this, the teaching must be carried on in their own language.

On English training.

As regards the teaching of English or of any other language, as a subject, there can be no doubt that a man may be much benefited by it. At the same time, it must be remembered that the cost in time and labour is very great; and unless the course of study be made to extend over many years, the time and labour may be spent with but very scanty results. I have, therefore, advisedly placed this last on my list of subjects; for, having tried the experiment of teaching Greek, with a fair measure of success, I have come to the conclusion that, on the principle of adapting means to the end, the four classes of subjects mentioned above claim priority and require all the time that my students can give.

To pass on now to the *training for active work.* A Mission agent must be an active worker; his training therefore should be carried on, not only in the lecture-room, but also in the *open air*. It should be a standing principle in every training class, that active work is as necessary a part of training as study. At special times, therefore, the Missionary should, if possible, lead his students out into unevangelised districts, to train them in the warfare of evangelistic work, to teach them to endure hardness as good soldiers Training in Mission work. of Jesus Christ. Such active work may hinder study, but it deepens the spiritual life, and familiarises the minds of the students with the difficulties to be encountered, whilst there is yet time to obtain counsel and guidance, or even, if it seems best, to withdraw from a work for which a man may lack qualifications. Two months of such work have in my own experience proved more beneficial to several of my students than two years of steady collegiate training. It would be most undesirable to let active work take the place of study, but it is essential for the thorough preparation of an efficient native agent.

Above all, the students should be trained both by precept and example, to be *men of prayer*. They should be constantly reminded that all our doings without God are nothing worth. In the chapel, in the lecture room, before preaching, whilst preaching, after preaching, at all times, in all places, all things should be begun, continued, and ended in the spirit of prayer.

From what has been written already it is obvious that in my opinion *training must be carried on in central institutions*, and not by individual Missionaries. Good teaching requires time, study, and practice ; but it does not require much more time to teach a dozen men than to teach three. If each Missionary attempts to train his own native agents the inevitable result will be that in many cases the training will be very badly done, and in most cases the Missionaries will be much hindered from the performance of their other duties.

There are two questions which have an important bearing on the question of the training of agents, which ought to be at least mentioned in a Paper on the subject. The first regards *the source whence the students should be drawn*, the second refers to *the manner of employment* of the men when trained. I propose, therefore, briefly to discuss these points.

With reference to *the source from which students should be drawn*, my own experience leads me to insist strongly on the advantage of, if possible, taking men who have had a Christian education in their youth. Recent converts from heathenism are not like well-educated Jews in the times of the Apostles, "mighty in the Scriptures," and it is very difficult to familiarise them Agents drawn from Christian youths. with the Scriptures in the same way as those who have in their youth been carefully taught. No doubt many will object that a boy trained in a Mission school is like a hothouse plant, and that there is a danger of his knowing the letter, but not the power of the Gospel. No doubt there is some truth in this ; but it is at least equally true that God has promised His blessing on early training, and that He gives the blessing which He has promised. My own experience leads me strongly to advocate the training of agents from their youth up. It has, however, been found to be a great advantage in our Mid-China Mission, to interpose a period of probation in some subordinate position, between the time of a youth's leaving school, and his acceptance as a theological student, and a candidate for definite spiritual work.

The other question relating to *the employment of men when trained, and the sources from which they should be supported* is a difficult and complicated one ; and I should not have ventured to touch on it, if it had not been definitely put before me by your Committee. As regards employment, indeed there is no lack of that ; the native Christians require pastors and teachers, the heathen require evangelists. But how are these pastors, teachers, Support of native agents. and evangelists to be supported ? Can they support themselves ? Is it desirable that they should do so ? If not, is it a right and sound principle that they should be supported by Missionary Societies, or should none be employed unless they are supported by native contributions ? In the conflict of human opinions on the subject, it is well to turn to the Word of God and see what principles we can gather from that.

(1) In the first place then, "*the Lord Himself hath ordained that they which*

preach the Gospel should live of the Gospel." This inspired statement puts it beyond all question, not only that pastors and preachers may be supported, but also that it is best that they should be supported by the contribution of others. Independent unpaid workers should be encouraged to the utmost extent; but the Divine ordinance should never be ignored; and those who are specially set apart to preach the Gospel should be freed from the anxieties and temptations of business carried on for their own support.

(2) Scripture clearly teaches us that *pastors should be paid by their flocks.* "Let him that is taught in the Word communicate unto him that teacheth in all good things." "Who feedeth a flock and eateth not of the milk of the flock?" The duty of supporting their own pastors should therefore be impressed upon native Christians from the outset. But with regard to this principle, we meet

Duty of members to their pastors. with a difficulty. Whilst the foundations of a Church are being laid, when Christians are few in number and poor in this world's goods, it is often impossible for them to support the pastor or pastors required for their spiritual necessities. They may be willing and able to contribute a portion of the sum required for his sustenance but cannot pay the whole. In such a case what should be done? Some Missionaries have solved the problem to their own satisfaction by deferring the appointment or ordination of any pastoral agent, until the native Christians are able entirely to support him without help from foreign funds. But in so doing they seem to ignore the fact that so long as they continue to act as pastors themselves, as in this case they must do if the native Christians are to have either teaching or sacraments, they practically teach these Christians that they may look to the Foreign Society to supply them with pastors, and that too at a far greater cost than would be the case if help was given towards the support of a native pastor. At the same time the Missionaries themselves are much hindered from doing their proper work as evangelists to the heathen.

(3) It seems clear from Scripture that *it is right that evangelists should be supported by contributions from foreign funds.* St. Paul when in Thessalonica "once and again" received help from Philippi. When in Corinth he

Evangelists supported from foreign funds. "robbed other Churches, taking wages of them." St. John writes of those who "for the Name's sake went forth, taking nothing of the Gentiles." And to descend from Scripture to the question of expediency it seems obvious that if it be the object of Missionary Societies to send forth men to preach the Gospel, it is a wise and prudent policy to extend the native agency. Our European Missionary requires an outlay equal to that required for some twenty natives, whilst one native who is filled with the Spirit of God, may often be able to do more effective work than several Europeans.

I have written at length—too great length, I fear—about methods and plans. I know that what I have written will not commend itself to the judgment of some of my Missionary brethren; for opinions differ, as, indeed, it is well that they should differ. We ought indeed all to consider humbly, carefully and prayerfully, what are the best methods, and how we can best work for the glory of our Lord and Master; and deeply thankful shall I feel if what I have written may in any way conduce to that end, even if it only be by drawing out superior arguments against the plans which I have suggested. But I write in the full conviction that our human plans are but of slight importance. One man works in one way, another in another way, and God blesses both to the salvation of souls. We have this treasure in earthen vessels, and the excellency of the power is not of us, nor of our plans, but of God.

PAPER.

3. By HERR G. PFLEIDERER (Basle Missionary Society).

Industrial Training.

Having been called upon by the Executive Committee of this
Conference to prepare a Paper on Industrial Education, I intend to
describe in a few words,—

1st. The way ; how the Basle Mission came to take up the task
of Industrial establishments.

2nd. The manner ; how these establishments are founded and
carried on, and

3rd. The results of the same.

[*We omit a short introductory sketch of the Mission begun in
the year 1833, and give fully the practical part of the Paper.*—ED.]

Within the space of ten years from the commencement of the
Mission, they had a small congregation at Mangalore, and a number
of boys had been collected in a boarding school, and placed **Mangalore**
under the immediate direction of the Missionaries, who **Mission.**
took a deep interest in the bodily and spiritual welfare of those
entrusted to their care. The number of Missionaries had also been
considerably augmented, and as early as 1842, the reports sent home
to the Committee had to state this fact : " That the real sorrows did
only commence with the baptism of the converts, because whole
families had to be looked after, and because body and soul had to be
cared for." The brethren began to think of plantations, colonies,
and other agricultural undertakings, for the benefit of the converts.

In the same year, the Missionaries in charge of the boarding
school requested the Home Committee to send out some truly
converted artisans in order to teach the young Hindu **Origin of its**
Christians how to earn their own bread. Two years later **Industrial**
we hear again of consultations concerning the purchase of **establishment.**
land, as it had become evident that the Mission was in duty bound
to assist the converts in gaining an honest livelihood, and to prevent
their being obliged to go about idle or living by alms. Meanwhile
the Missionaries endeavoured to get the boys instructed in useful
trades ; and in the year 1846 it was reported that six boys of the
boarding school were apprentices,—that two were going to become
bookbinders, two weavers, and two locksmiths. By this time the
Home Committee resolved to take up the question, but on a closer
inspection, so many details presented themselves for consideration,
that it was necessary to form a special Sub-committee for this
purpose; a number of suitable gentlemen were selected, and thus
our

Industrial Commission

was established, which thenceforth directed the Industrial branch of the

Mission. At first no decisive steps were taken, and it was rather a series of
experiments, which had to be gone through, before a certain
stability was acquired; as above mentioned, some boys were
apprenticed with native tradespeople; some were sent to
Bombay; others to military stations (viz., to Bellary and Cannanore), in
order to learn some trade; thus bookbinding, tanning, shoemaking, weaving,
tailoring, baking, and so on were learnt by them with more or less success,
but not sufficiently well to be of any use. Therefore, two artisans were sent
out from Europe, a locksmith, and a clockmaker. They at once opened
their workshops and took in a number of boys for instruction; but both
experiments, though made in good earnest, had not the desired success.
Next a weaver was enlisted, and sent out to Mangalore; here he found some
Christian weavers at work, and by leaning upon what he found at hand, by
improving the original looms and implements, and by gradually bringing up
men and materials to a more European standard, a firm footing was first
established in the trade of weaving: a good deal of this success was owing
to the fact, that amongst his workmen he had a number of converts, who
had been weavers by trade before, and that he had not to deal with mere
apprentices only.

Failure of experiments.

Whereas these trials were made in behalf of the newly-converted Christians and of the boys growing up in the orphanages, two lithographic presses
were procured, to assist the Missionaries in their task of publishing tracts
and portions of Scriptures in the vernacular languages.

In the years 1850-51 the then Inspector, Rev. Mr. Josenhans, paid a visit to
our Indian Mission; he took great pains in ascertaining the wants of the
Mission in all its bearings, and returned with the conviction, that in our part
of India Industrial training of the young congregations was part of the
Missionary work, which should not be neglected, though of course it was
only a small part of the whole, that is of the task of establishing the Lord's
kingdom also in India.

On his return to Europe the Industrial Commission was reorganised, a
distinguished Industrial of the town was asked to step in, and this friend
soon became the leading member. In a circular of the 1st
February, 1854, he laid down the principles of the Commission,
as follows:—" The object of the Industrial Commission is a
twofold one; *first*, to lessen, and as far as possible, to remove the social
difficulties which the institution of the caste in India opposes to the Missions
in their endeavours to establish new congregations. Our second aim has
more of a lasting character. The former is merely intended to be a support
to the Mission; the *second* may perhaps be called a Mission itself, a Mission
not by preaching, nor by direct promulgation of the Gospel, but if possible by
the power of example, by Christianity in its practical everyday life, a Mission
by the introduction of Christian diligence, of Christian honesty and respect-
ability, a Mission by showing conspicuously as far as possible, that godliness
is profitable unto all things, having promise not only for the life to come, but
also for that which now is.

Industrial Commission reorganised.

This was our new starting point. The shops of the locksmith and
watchmaker were closed, and more attention was paid to the weaving. New
funds were raised independent of the Mission, and the whole
affair was placed on a certain mercantile basis; for meantime
the Mission had also expanded. Stations had been founded in
Malabar and the Deccan, and the Industrial Commission was ready to give a

Weaving industry.

helping hand whenever it was required. In Malabar the situation was similar to that in Canara; the converts were there in need of support, and weaving on European handlooms was commenced in Cannanore, Tellicherry, and Calicut. At this latter port, which has a well supplied timber market, a carpenter workshop was set up, which turned out furniture and articles required for building operations.

In the Deccan, however, things were different. The weaving trade in native fashion was there at home long ago, and amongst the converts there were some who had been manufacturers before. But as soon as they became Christians they found their credit gone, and they were on the verge of ruin, because also their customers kept aloof. Some friends at Bombay and the Industrial Commission stepped in, supplied them with twist and with silk, and the result was, that they could go on though under altered conditions. So the difficulties were soon overcome; moreover, our Mangalore superintendent paid them a visit and remained several months with them, introducing improvements, by which they were considerably benefited.

About twenty years ago tile making was taken up; the heavy rains of the monsoon on the western coast of India are very trying to the roofs. The native style of thatching is not suited to larger buildings, and the native tiles are so bad, that most of the tiled roofs are constantly leaking. A better kind of roofing material was therefore an urgent necessity. Clay is plentiful along the coast and of an excellent quality, so the thought of making a better roofing material was quite natural. One of the lay brethren, when at home on furlough on account of failing health, acquired the art of tile making, and commenced operations on his return to India in 1865. There were at first many difficulties, but by his painstaking perseverance, and by the help of the Lord, they were overcome, and we soon were enabled to manufacture really good grooved tiles, which are now extensively used in the whole of Southern India as well as on the west coast, from Kurrachee and Bombay in the north, down to Ceylon in the south; for they are the very thing for covering in houses, and factories, and magazines, and completely meet the requirements of the land and its climate; but these tiling establishments, in quite a special way, meet also the wants of the Mission, because they can give work to a great number of men, women, and boys, without any previous training; every inquirer and new comer who asks for work can be employed there, and is thus at once brought under Christianising influence, every day's work being commenced by the reading of the Word of God and by prayer. *Tile-making industry.* *Benefits to the Mission.*

As machinery had to be used in these establishments, especially when it was found necessary to employ steam power, another industrial branch had to be added, viz., a mechanical establishment, which has to keep the machinery in good working order and repair, and which made itself useful in many ways to Government and to the general public; because in due time it even succeeded in constructing and setting up iron bridges, besides doing all sorts of job work, for which there is a considerable demand. *Further development.*

Now all these undertakings require a certain organisation; the establishments, multiplied and enlarged as they now are, require a good deal of money, and had to be placed under proper directions from home. The Industrial branch of the Mission was therefore amalgamated with the Mercantile branch, which had already an office of its own at Basle, and it is from thence that now the financial, technical, and practical wants of all the Industrial Mission establishments are attended to. The funds, as mentioned above, are quite separate from those of the Mission, having been raised by a Joint Stock Company. The shareholders, however, get only 5 per cent. interest on their invested capital, whereas the remaining surplus is yearly handed over to the Mission as a free contribution towards its expenses. The chief thing, however, in the task is to have the right man at the right place; the superintendents of the establishments have to be real Missionaries in every respect, and, besides, they have to know their respective trades, technically and practically as well, that they are able to stand their ground and to meet such difficulties as are sure to arise in a country where they have no assistance from auxiliary establish-

Qualification of superintendent. ments, as is the case in the industrial centres of Europe. The weaver, for instance, has to be not only a thoroughbred weaver, but he has to be at home in the art of dyeing, in the art of preparing, or at least of repairing his implements, and so on. Such brethren, therefore, as are willing to serve the Lord in the Mission by their own handicraft, are generally first sent to training institutions at home, to go through a full course, before they can be placed at the head of an establishment; and when once there we find that they cannot thoroughly fulfil their calling unless they be placed on an equal footing with the other Missionaries. Our committee therefore considers the lay brethren, though not in holy orders, as full Missionaries, who have the same rights and the same duties as their ordained colleagues, each, of course, in their sphere of labour. They are full members of the Presbyteries and of the Station Conferences, when they have once attained the proper knowledge of the vernacular, and in matters of government and Church discipline their intimate knowlege of the bodily and spiritual condition of those employed under them is found to be of the utmost importance.

Another part of the organisation is that it was found necessary to connect the industrial establishments intimately with our Mercantile

Conducted on mercantile principles. branches, so that the accounts are kept in proper order, and that the whole management is carried on on sound mercantile principles. This is most necessary for the success of the whole, as well as for the interest of the workmen themselves; an establish-ment that is not self-supporting in the long run should not be kept up, because it has a demoralising influence, inasmuch as it affords temptation to neglect commercial reckoning.

When our Mission entered upon industrial undertakings it was not intended to found large establishments, but rather to teach the Christians different handicrafts, which they might carry on as a kind of house industry. We succeeded in inducing several weavers to do so, but not to that extent as had been desired. We were gradually convinced that we had to reckon with facts, and that, as in other countries so in India, the days of the small tradesmen were numbered. The single individual cannot go ahead against the general competition, and it was only the system of improved machinery and combined labour by which success could be attained. Notwithstanding this we do not lose sight of the desirability of introducing house industry wherever possible, and we are ready to make another trial as soon as we see our way in doing so.

We conclude by stating :—

That about the tenth part of the native members of our Indian congregations find work and earn their livelihood in these Mission Industrial establishments.

That much care and work for the outward concerns of the converts is thereby taken off the hands of the ordained Missionaries.

That the Mission staff is considerably increased without adding to the expenses of the Mission.

That many of the young men and boys are trained up under a careful supervision.

That people not accustomed to work are trained to industrious habits.

That inquirers can easily be tested as to their motives.

That the congregations are kept together, and the Christians to a large extent are kept from being dispersed and roaming through the country and through the world.

That Christians without means of subsistence find a livelihood.

That many of these workmen who entered absolutely poor and penniless now possess small houses and gardens of their own, in which a decent family leads a Christian life.

And that, though progress is slow and trying, and even drawbacks make their appearance, we rejoice at the results gained, knowing that it is worth a deal of trouble and care to cause men to grow up as honest workers and Christian fathers of families.

A close and critical observer, who some years ago paid a visit to our Mangalore Industrial establishments, said : " What is the impression which the visitor takes away with him ? First of all, it is clear, that our lay brethren have a very tedious work to perform, that they <small>Impression of a critical observer.</small> must possess a great amount of patience in order to fulfil their daily task ; but none the less that this education to a well-regulated labour and to a practical Christianity is a source of rich blessing, though it cannot be indicated by ciphers. Finally " (he said), " I take leave of these workshops with the words of the Apostle in 2 Thess. iii. 12, 13 : ' We command and exhort you by our Lord Jesus Christ, that with quietness they work, and eat their own bread ; but ye, brethren, be not weary in well doing.' "

PAPER.

4. BY MRS. BISHOP (Author of " Unbeaten Tracks in Japan," etc., etc.).

How far shall Church Architecture and other non-essentials be adapted to the Native Styles and Tastes of the Country ?

This question in some of its branches comes up for settlement in the earliest stage of successful Missionary effort, and forces itself strangely on an outsider as bearing upon the permanent existence of the Christian communities which we are striving to plant.

My opportunities of personal observation of un-Christianised, and Christianised coloured races, have been chiefly among the North American Indians, the Sandwich Islanders, the Ainos of Yezo, <small>Range of observation.</small> the Japanese, the Malays, the Chinese of the Malay Peninsula, the Tamils and Singalese, the Nomads of the Sinaitic Peninsula, and the mixed race to which we give the name of Egyptians. The necessarily cursory, even if painstaking observation of a traveller during a period of three and a half years, who, for the most part, gained a knowledge of the

opinions and feelings of the people through a more or less efficient interpreter precludes dogmatism or confident assertion, and if I appear to be
guilty of either it is because the necessity for brevity forbids the use of the
courtesies and apologies which would qualify my remarks.

The Europeanising tendency of Christianity is inevitable, and perhaps
desirable, under some circumstances, certainly regrettable under others.
European customs excite opposition. Wherever the white preacher goes he carries with him the
religion of the stronger, the religion of the race whose footsteps
throughout the world are marked by conquest, or absorption,
or gradual displacement, or swift destruction. So dreaded is this ascendency of the West as a fate near or far off, that it is easy for the astute
among the leaders of false faiths to rouse a popular opposition to Christianity
on purely patriotic grounds, by representing it as the veiled herald of the
gleam of the British bayonet and the roll of the British drum, the first
political move of a series which will bring about the destruction of the old
manners and customs, and eventually of the nationality itself. The fear of
us, and the dread of us, or at least the suspicion of our good faith, is more
or less on all the dark-eyed, and dark and yellow-skinned races, from the
Red to the Yellow Sea.

To meet this difficulty, it is a matter of extreme importance for
Christianity to show a deliberate intention to conserve nationalities by
conserving all in their architecture, costume, social customs, including
etiquette and modes of living which is not contrary to its precepts and
Native customs should be considered. spirit. Such careful guardianship of those peculiarities which
should be, and often are, sacred, which climate and economical
reasons render suitable, and which have the sanctity of the past,
may tend not only to remove some of the native dread of the new faith, but
to rejuvenate and strengthen the nations themselves. We must respect
customs differing from our own where they are not sinful. Possibly we give
a little colour to the notion that Christianity is a *Western* religion, as
opposed to the religions of the *East* by our usually pertinacious adherence
to our own style, and our thinly-veiled contempt for customs which are not
our own, though the Bible was given as an Oriental book, full of the state-
liness and courtesies of Oriental life as the surroundings of the history of
the two Oriental revealed religions.

With regard to *architecture*, whatever the native style of building may
be, I have almost invariably noticed that the Christian Church
Architecture. edifice is fashioned more or less upon that model of bald and
unredeemed ugliness which we associate with the name conventicle, hideous,
often inappropriate to the climate, and unsuited to national habits : a building of stone and lime, with a roof with shallow eaves, and big windows
admitting the blazing sun of the tropics, is an example. Is this complete
departure from the style of domestic or even temple architecture, necessary
or desirable ?   Is it not the introduction of that foreign and Western
element which excites prejudice, and makes towards the subversion of
national habits ?   Are pews desirable, or even benches, where the custom
is to sit upon a matted floor ?   Is not the solid foreign building also an
element of expense ?   I should think it possible and desirable to adopt such
styles of building as are found in Hawaii, Japan, the Malay Peninsula, and
Ceylon to every purpose of Christian worship, and to the requirements of a
Missionary household, and in so doing to ally that worship with the archi-
tectural traditions of these countries. In looking forward to a day when

Japan will receive the Gospel and cast aside for ever the old faiths, I cannot imagine any buildings more fitted for Christian worship, from their convenience and simplicity than the temples of the Monto sect, which could be utilised for such worship to-morrow by the removal of the shrine of Buddha and its accessories. Others know better than I whether there is anything repulsive to the Christian Japanese in the consecration of such temples to the worship of God, but no objection could be urged to the adoption of the native style to churches, rather than the imported conventicle style.

With regard to *dress*, decent covering cannot be regarded as among "non-essentials," but the fashion of such covering may be. In countries in which it has not been the custom to be clothed at all, the clothes' question must assert itself as soon as a Christian impression is produced, and with no inventive genius at hand to aid, it is most natural that the Missionary and his wife should supply the converts with the only patterns they possess, those of European garments. We do coloured people an injustice by inflicting our European style upon them, for we simply make them grotesque and ridiculous, and the tendency is for people so clothed to become feeble imitations of white men, and to go from coats and trousers to whisky and so on. To provide them with European dress, as is done in some parts of Africa, or to aid and abet the popular movement in favour of wearing it in Japan, is to introduce a very heavy expense, which tends to increase the general expense of living, and to place life under the same burdensome conditions as those which at home are daily becoming more perplexing. Possibly such a dress as the Malay jacket and short *sarong*, or the short, girdled robe of the Bedaween might be found exactly suitable for the African man ; while the Sandwich Island *holoku*, the single full loose garment, which, I believe, is owed to the genius of a Missionary's wife, might be safely taken as the inexpensive and perfect model for female dress, wherever Christianity touches a previously unclothed people. With such, clothing is another name for expenditure, and expenditure is mainly a new thing, and a difficult thing, and it seems well, when dealing with dress, to bear this difficulty in mind. It does not seem that there is anything calling for interference in the costume worn in many Eastern countries ; and in China our Missionaries, specially those of the China Inland Mission, show their wisdom by paying the tribute to its propriety and fitness of wearing it at all times inland. Possibly, more concessions to native modes in dress, architecture, diet, etc., would tend to remove prejudice and conserve nationality.

As to *social customs, manners, and etiquette*, all are agreed that these should not be interfered with unless they are at variance with the spirit of Christianity, while no one would contend for the retention of the scalping lock, or of the custom of tattooing, or of crippling the feet of girls, or of cutting slices from living fish ; in practice, however, difficulties appear. Our Missionaries go to countries which have an elaborate civilisation and complicated etiquette with which, if they do not conflict with Christianity, they are not at war. But each Western man and woman represents that resistless West which it seems essential to defy or imitate. Our Missionaries frequently live strictly European lives in dress, diet, houses, manners and habits generally. They get their food and clothes as far as is possible from home. They stamp in heavy boots, where the native is lightly shod or sandalled. They nod, where he bows profoundly. They are curtly unceremonious, while ceremony is the atmosphere of the East. Many American Missionaries have told me that it is "impossible to have patience" with the tedious courtesies which national etiquette enjoins ; and the abrupt disregard of native customs and feelings shown by many Christian people in my presence has been simply shocking, when its possible, or rather probable, effect is considered ; and I cannot but think that many Christian men and women do much to alienate and prejudice, and much by the mere force of insularity and disregard to sap national life and produce a mongrel civilisation destitute of the dignity of the East or the rational freedom of the West.

I have often seen a Japanese go up to a Missionary with two or three profound and graceful bows, which have been responded to by an abrupt and most ungraceful nod, suggestive of disrespect.

On this subject I have heard very much from natives, and in some cases from English-speaking native Christians, who were unable to understand our abandonment of the courtesies of which they and we read in the Bible. Is there not a more excellent way,—truly a way of self-denial, but of self-denial for the Master's sake—by which our devoted friends may adapt themselves wisely to The Missionaries the etiquette of highly civilised heathen or Musalman countries? and native The courtesies are indescribably tedious and wearisome ; but when etiquette. people have left all to preach Christ, could not the tedium be borne if it helped forward the Gospel ? Our Western manners are indescribably repulsive to an Oriental, while any adaptations in non-essentials which we can make for Christ's sake, are warmly accepted and appreciated by men of native races. Are they not a means, not only of helping the Gospel message, but of Christianising and conserving coloured nationalities, without being faithless to our own ? Dr. Berry, now of Kioto, whose singular success as a Missionary is well known, and whose influence has penetrated into the upper class in Japan, doubtless owes much of this influence, which has been so valuable to the cause of Christ, to the fact that he has been a careful student of the niceties of Japanese etiquette, that he does not shrink from the tedium of its elaborate courtesies, and has learned to bow in the most invertebrate oriental fashion. May we not make it our aim to conserve very much that is found in the customs of Japan, China, India, and Arabia, permeating if possible the elaborate courtesies with Christian truthfulness and sincerity, carefully guarding the respect for parents and for old age, and the unquestioning obedience of children ; transforming the superstitious reverence for the dead into the tenacious tenderness which decks the last resting place with flowers, and even there, sorrows not even as others who have no hope, while giving place to customs which are blended with idolatry and superstition, no, not for an hour.

In secular teaching in Mission schools it would be well for the text-books to make the country of the pupil the centre, making its geography, ancient and modern history, its botany and zoology bulk very largely. As at home, the leading feature in the teaching of history is English history, so in China it would be Adapt all Chinese, and in Japan Japanese history. In brief it is wise to non-essentials. make no compromise as to essentials, but to go very far in adapting all non-essentials to the native style and taste in every civilised country, and in regions where the Missionary has to create a civilisation, to create it as much on native lines as possible. All are agreed at this Conference that the work of the Church is not to Europeanise, but to Christianise the nations, to build up Christian nationalities which shall develop after their own fashion their Christian ideals, as provinces of the Empire of Him unto whom one day every knee shall bow, having received of the Father the heathen for His inheritance, and the uttermost parts of the earth for His possession.

DISCUSSION.

Rev. George Piercy (Wesleyan Missionary Society, from Canton): Mr. Chairman,—I wish to speak to one point only, which I think is a most important point in our discussion this afternoon, viz., the support of workers. Support of Many here were present this morning, and heard a long, interesting, workers. and most comprehensive discussion as to how to train men and put them to work. Then, I take it, the most important thing of all, after men have got to work, is the means of supporting them in it and keeping them in it. I am not going to speak about how English, American, and other Missionaries are to be supported in the work abroad ; it is the support of a native agency that I wish to speak about for a minute or two. Now we are told that native agency is to do the largest part of the work, and I suppose there is more general consent on this point than perhaps on any other in our Missionary work or enterprise ;

that idea seems to have won very general and almost universal consent. When native agency is put into the work, it has to be for a time maintained by funds from this or other Christian countries before being taken over entirely by the native Churches, and the important question as to the support of native agency is as regards the scale of pay. Now there will be a great many different opinions about that, and I think we should agree upon one simple law for dealing with this matter. I will give you my own idea. I have been for thirty years in China, connected with a Mission there from its very beginning. We now have a prosperous Mission, with a number of well-trained native agents and some fully ordained native ministers. You will remember that according to the generosity of the native Churches will depend in the future the number of native agents, and the reproduction of native agents and the extension of this work, which is to come ultimately into the hands of native people.

Now as to payment I lay down this principle: that the scale must be a native scale. It must not be English, American, or even German,—but a native scale. Then we simply add one word to these two, and say a reasonable native scale; and I think this ought to command the consent of all **Payment of native agents.** Europeans, and the approbation of all natives. I think we should call in the native Churches, and consult with them, and ascertain their views, and that, before this matter is settled, we should have the guidance and help and the thought of the native people. Just one word more, sir, and then I will sit down. I think every one can see that by keeping the scale of remuneration down to a reasonable point we can have a multiplication of native agency to an almost indefinite extent, and that without any very great lapse of time there can be a marvellous host of native agents put into the Mission-field, working right and left and everywhere towards the conversion of the world.

Rev. George Smith (English Presbyterian Mission, Swatow, China): Mr. Chairman, and Christian friends,—I quite endorse what Mr. Piercy has just said, and I would add a few remarks in the same line. I may say, to commence with, that we Missionaries who are connected with **Aim of the Presbyterian Missions.** the Missions of the Presbyterian Church of England consider ourselves to be in China only temporarily, for a short time. The object which we have in view is to raise up a self-supporting, self-ruling, self-propagating, and self-teaching Church, and so our Missions are doing what, in our opinion, most accords with the end we have in view.

With regard to the support of the natives, we think that as little should be given to the natives from foreign funds as possible, and that every native who becomes a Christian should give more or less, according to his **Duty of converts to contribute.** ability, for the support of native agency. As soon as any one becomes a Christian, it is his duty to contribute of his means for the support of the native agency. That is a very important principle. The labourer is worthy of his hire, and we must remember this also, that it is doing no good to the natives not to ask them to contribute. The Apostle Paul considered he had done a wrong to the Church of Corinth in not taking of their funds; and he says, "What is it wherein ye were inferior to other Churches, except it be that I myself was not burdensome to you? Forgive me this wrong." There is more meaning in that than we usually attach to it. Christians are wronged when not asked to take their due part in contributing to the support of the Christian ministry. All Christians are to contribute to the support of the Church, and in so doing they are fulfilling the law of Christ. "Be not deceived: God is not mocked; for whatsoever a man soweth, that shall he also reap." That statement is made in connection with the support of the Christian ministry. Those who contribute to the spiritual needs of their hearers have a right to temporal benefits from them, and if the latter fail to fulfil their part they are doing themselves a wrong. That is an important principle, and we must remember that every Christian, when he is created anew in Christ Jesus, has a heart responding to every precept of Christ, and we must seek to develop that, and he will feel it a privilege to contribute to the support of his church.

I remember on one occasion a heathen Chinaman came up to one of our Church members, and said to him, "How many dollars a month do you get for giving up your work and going to church to hear these fellows!"
"A share in the concern." "I get dollars!" was the reply. "Why, I contribute towards the funds. I have a share in the concern myself." So that it appears from that he gloried in what he was doing, and that is as it should be. As soon as a native pastor is called by a native Church to be its pastor, we do not contribute a farthing to his support; it is entirely left to the native Church. One word more, sir, and I will be done; it is this: In our plan of adjusting the native salaries, we look to what the Chinese give a man under similar circumstances, and do not raise them beyond what they are able to pay, and that is our only hope of getting a self-supporting native Church.

Miss M. A. Cockin (L.M.S., from Madagascar): I just wish to say after living eight years in Madagascar, and having visited the industrial schools at Lovedale, that I feel the need of some such institution in Madagascar. Those
Industrial school needed at Madagascar. of us who have lived there know that the people have very few industries of their own, and I am sorry to say that the conduct of Europeans has taught them to distil a great deal of rum; and a great deal of their revenues (I do not mean the public revenues, but the riches of a great many of the Malagasy) is derived from the distillation and sale of rum. Now I think we ought to give them something better than this. They are in a very backward state as regards civilisation, as they want almost everything that we are accustomed to,—I mean to say they want to be taught to build proper houses, and to make the furniture that is necessary for such houses. They are very capable of being taught, but if we do not teach them thoroughly and well, they will only learn to do things in an inferior manner, and I think we ought to take this subject into consideration. This is all I wish to say beyond bearing my testimony to the high value of the work that is being done in the institution at Lovedale.

Rev. James Sleigh (L.M.S., from Loyalty Islands, South Pacific): Mr. Chairman, and Christian friends,—For twenty-five years I have been in one place, in a large district of Lifu, the largest island in the Loyalty group. When the French sent away the Samoan and Raratongan teachers, we at once set up throughout the island twenty-four native teachers, without asking permission from them, and the priests were dismayed.

Now with regard to their support. The Missionary Society at first gave out a few little articles of clothing, and a few tools and things of that kind, and still
Practice of L.M.S. in Loyalty Islands. defray some expenses of the institution where they were trained at Lifu. Then we have taught the members of the Church to contribute to the support of their teachers, and during the last fourteen years my people have contributed fully five thousand francs a year, partly to their pastors, and partly to the London Missionary Society. Their teachers cultivate a piece of land. We do not now give anything from the Society; the teachers are supported themselves by personal labour, and by gifts from the people, and they are in a position superior to the people quite as much as the clergy are here.

As for the architecture, they build these churches in the "beehive" style or oblong. One only is of lath and plaster, and eleven are substantially built of
Native Church edifices. coral rock. Mr. Jones has built a very pretty church at Maré, but too much like the English, though, of course, a good deal altered. Our churches are simple in construction and airy. We always let the people choose their own teachers. We may suggest a man, but if they do not like him and want another man they have him, and I say to them, "It is like a marriage; you choose your pastor and your pastor chooses you: keep the obligation sacred, for you are like husband and wife.'

Rev. C. F. Warren (C.M.S., from Japan): My friends,—As the time is so limited, one can hardly touch upon the different subjects, but I should like to say just a word or two about the payment of natives. It is a subject to which I have given a great deal of thought and attention, and one about which I have very strong opinions. "The importance of projecting Missions and Missionary expenditures upon such a scale, that the native *Payment of native agents.* Churches may at the earliest possible day be able to reach entire self-support," embodies a principle which we all wish to be guided by ; but it is so easy for Missionaries to dole out the money sent out by the Societies ; and it is so much easier to spend money lavishly than it is to bring the expenditure down to such a point that this object shall really be gained. I am speaking among Missionaries here. I think we ought to keep that well in mind. Now we want to create in the mind of the pastors, or the future pastors of our Japanese and other Churches, an idea of the duty and privilege of self-sacrifice. There really is not time for argument upon the matter, but I want just to give one or two instances illustrating this. We had in our Church Mission at Tokio some time ago, a man who was receiving from the Society a salary of $12 per month, which was a very moderate salary indeed, compared with what was being *Self-sacrifice of a native agent.* eceived by members of other Missions, some of whom were giving $15, some $20 per month. When the Church came to the resolution that they would try and support him themselves, he actually asked to have his salary cut down to $10 per month. That shows what can be done when the natives really put their minds together, with a view to independent self-support. We want men of that sort. There are a great many such men connected with other bodies, the American Foreign Missions for instance. I remember the case of a young man coming from America, who had had a good education, and was originally intended for quite a different sphere of life, but came and threw in his lot with the Mission work. He undertook to receive $5 per month. He won't receive a penny from the Society. His is now one of the most vigorous and liberal Churches in the city of Edrawàk ; and when I left it three years ago they had established a girls' school, which is one of the grandest institutions of the kind in the country. That is the spirit we want in our natives. That is the spirit which should be fostered, and everything should be done with that intention.

[*The following we have transferred from the meeting on "The Turkish Empire and Central Asia," to this chapter, to which it properly belongs.*—ED.]

Rev. Dr. Kalopothakes (Athens): Mr. Chairman,—I have just come to the City of London, and I do not feel well prepared to speak. I should not have ventured to appear before you, were it not for the fact that I wish to say a few words about a subject which I think will interest you. The question about which I am going to speak to you is a very important one. It is about how the Churches that are formed by the Missionaries of native converts are to be self-supporting. This is a question important in several aspects. I am sorry that there has not been given to the natives an opportunity to *Self-supporting Churches.* express their own views before the Christian Church. In Athens this important subject of self-supporting Churches has been presented in a new light, and under some very peculiar circumstances, and they felt themselves obliged to take it up, although at the time we were not ready.

I was a Missionary with full powers and privileges, but I felt when it was presented to me that it was my duty to cast in my lot with my native brethren. It was three years ago. We were in the Presbyterian Church. We had no money, and we did not know how the work, which needed at least £500, was to be carried on. Yet we said, "Brethren, we are *Experience in self-support.* better off than the Apostles. We are in better circumstances than the first Christians. Why should we not undertake to carry on the work ? Wo know the language. We have the work in our own hands. We have our papers. We work with the Bible Society. Why not let us go and trust ?" And so we did, and this is the third year ; and although, of course, we did it with the sacrifice of a good many things that we were accustomed to, still the work is carried on this third year. Well, we not only paid our own expenses, but we paid a debt which the Mission had left us, of twelve hundred francs, the first year; and the last year we had a surplus of about £4. The way in which we decided to do the work was this. We were three ordained ministers. We said to the native brethren, " Now, if you promise to contribute one-tenth of your income, then we will give you our work gratis;" and we were also to contribute all that we could make out of our own personal work outside the pastoral work, and so we did. And those native brethren who never paid a dollar before, because they said, "Why, we have a Society that can pay all the expenses—why should we pay?"—those very brethren gave one-tenth—10 per cent. or 8 per cent. of their income.

Now, I say, that this is a very important question for you, and it is a very important question for the Church at large. If I understand the Gospel properly it was the way in which the Apostles did in the first Missionary work, they went about. They preached the Gospel. They gathered two or three or four disciples, and they left them to put their heads together and carry on the work, which they received from the Apostles. When the natives come to understand that, and to feel that it is their work, then they are willing to make sacrifices. But the Missionaries and the Missionary Societies must prepare the natives to do the work. And it is to this that I should like to turn the attention of my brethren. Prepare the natives for the work so that you can leave it to them. It will be then done better, and it will be more economical, and the effects will be better. We have had several accessions since we declared ourselves independent. My fellow-countrymen cannot say to me now, "You are a Missionary, because you receive a large salary." I hope that you will help the natives in this —not only among the Greeks, but among the Armenians, among the Chinese, among the Turks. Wherever Missionaries can, let them raise up the natives. Wherever there is a chance, put the natives forward. That is the way to have self-supporting Churches.

Rev. A. Merensky (Superintendent, Berlin Missionary Society): Mr. Chairman, and friends,—It is on behalf of Africa that I want to say a few words. We have heard a great deal about Lovedale. I want to say it is not simply a Missionary institution. It relies to a great extent on Colonial grants. We have in the Transvaal many stations at which the people are much

Industry of Transvaal natives.

admired by the colonists and the travellers for their works and for their industrial habits, and we accomplish that simply by developing the resources of the country and encouraging the natives to improve their own African industries. The natives cultivate maize and Kaffir corn, which they sell, and by that means they are able to buy cattle and clothes, and they give the tithe to their Church, so that in that way the station is nearly supported, the children working for their teaching very often a few hours. The men are able to do some kinds of common work, but with regard to skilled work, such as the making of window-frames, doors, benches, and better houses, although some of them were instructed by our tradesmen to become carpenters and masons, the people in Africa do not very much take to European trades. Where there is soil enough, I believe they must first support themselves by agriculture, and they must remain agricultural in Africa; but the agriculture of the natives may be improved a little by European experience. If we do that then African natives will go ahead, and I believe that Missionaries by their teaching will draw down the blessings of God on that poor country, so that Africa in these respects, industrial efforts and so forth, will go ahead by its own resources.

Mr. R. A. Macfie: Mr. Chairman, and friends,—I am desired to say that it is only for secular work that money is received from the Government at Lovedale. I quite agree with what has been said here, and what has been well said upstairs a few minutes ago, that churches ought to be very simple buildings.

They ought to be as cheap as possible, so that they can be multiplied, and they ought to be characterised by a good Christian style, rather than by an ornate ecclesiastical style. There ought to be no pews, and there ought to be no consecration, so that buildings can be moved about and sold and put up in better places if required. There should be no idea that a Christian church is a temple, for then you cannot make it too fine, because it will be the dwelling place of God; whereas our Presbyterian ideas, which were established three hundred years ago, and which have worked comfortably up till now, is that a church is a place made for the use of man where he may meet his fellows. The effect of the introduction of costly buildings amongst the heathen would be to produce amongst them evils which all of us feel to be very severe in our own country; it would introduce class ideas, separate brother from brother, and probably cause diversity or divergence within and between Churches. Although no doubt I might enlarge upon these topics, I think I have said quite enough to express what is felt to be an underlying topic of great importance.

Native churches should be simple.

Rev. **Arthur Jewson** (B.M.S., from Comillah, E. Bengal) : Mr. Chairman, and friends,—In India wherever a few Christians were gathered together we have found it necessary, or thought it necessary, to place a pastor over them. The Missionary Society paid his salary, and hoped that in time the natives would contribute a little, and eventually pay the whole of it. I believe we have appointed many of these pastors, because we thought a long prayer and sermon were necessary. I believe we should have done better if our worship had consisted in the shortest of prayers, a verse or two of the Bible, and some of the simple stories expounded, and instruction in a Catechism and the art of reading. For such a service as that no pastor would be necessary. Each Christian in such a community would become a teacher, teaching what he himself knows. Christianity would spread, and by the time the community had got so far as to need a pastor, with his sermons and long prayers, they would be able to support him themselves.

Support of native pastors

Rev. **D. Rood** (American Missionary, from Natal) : Mr. Chairman, and friends,—I shall not occupy a moment in giving any argument, but will simply state something of the manner in which we have succeeded in carrying forward the work amongst the Zulus in Natal. We have been there a little more than forty years, and we commenced with these people in a very low, ignorant, and savage state. We commenced first by worshipping in God's temples under the shadow of trees. After that the natives began to encircle these, something after the shape of their own houses, and when they wished for something better—some of them becoming Christians— they went to work to try and imitate English people in their houses of worship, and with their own hands they manufactured the bricks, and brought the wood, and erected the building without any help from any white person, save with the doors and window-frames, which they purchased. Later on, they have erected a better class of buildings, by subscribing amongst themselves, and even among the heathen people in the kraals. They have built several churches by that means, and have employed educated labour in their erection, so that they are now getting a better class of buildings. In regard to the support of native preachers, there are many native preachers who go out to preach on the Sunday, and also hold service during the week, without any support whatever. At fixed stations, where we have preachers, a few ardent native Missionaries are supported, chiefly by the natives, but assisted somewhat at first by a subscription from the Society. That is the principle we go on,— endeavouring to get the natives to take the work upon themselves, and to carry it out amongst their own people.

Zulu church building.

Rev. **S. Macfarlane**, LL.D. (L.M.S., from New Guinea) : Mr. Chairman,— It was thought by friends that as I had had a good deal to do with the organisation of Christian Churches, and with the training of native agents, I might perhaps say a word or two upon one or two of the topics here. I may say that I have had the pleasure of establishing about twenty churches; and, therefore, *Organisation in New Guinea.* know something about their organisation; and of baptising about five thousand natives; and establishing two training institutions, one on the first Mission that I went to in New Guinea; and of sending out nearly one hundred natives all trained, as we think, and fit for the work. I will just tell in a few words what we do. There has been a good deal said as to adaptation. That is precisely what we aim at. I listened with intense interest to a good deal that was said this morning, and it seems to amount to this: that you want different men for different positions. Well, we try to see what we want a man for, and then we educate a man for that. We want these natives, for instance, amongst whom I have been labouring, to make better houses, and to make roads, and to build better canoes; and we establish for that purpose industrial schools. In the organisation of Churches, too, we try to make them self-supporting, as soon as possible—that is our object.

We do not go out there to Anglicise the people. I believe that many of us, in our first years, have done a great deal of harm in trying to do that. We do not go out there shouting, "Down with everything that is up," but "Up with *Industrial training.* a good deal that is down," and we try to adapt our work to the wants of the people. The first institute I founded was at Lifu, which we tried to make self-supporting. The next was at New Guinea where the men have three hours per day manual labour. We have a turning lathe, a circular saw, a blacksmith's forge, and all the paraphernalia of a good workshop; and what may be done in New Guinea may no doubt be done elsewhere. We teach them to make boxes and useful things for the people, and the people supply them with native food, which keeps them while they are at work in the institution. As soon as we can get the natives to stand on their own legs in the way of Church government, we shall do that too. We tell the natives: "You must select the man you want, but you must provide for him." It is rather a difficult lesson sometimes to teach the people. One native pastor was obliged to tell the people that he did not go to heaven on Monday morning and come back again on Saturday night, but he was there all the week, and required something to eat. But, although it may be difficult at first, the people soon drop into it. In the Lifu Mission, the churches have been self-supporting for years. From the New Guinea seminaries we have sent out some thirty teachers already, and the churches are beginning to support these men. Therefore, I would say let us try industrial schools, where they are necessary. I do not know whether they are necessary in India or in China, but they are necessary in places like New Guinea, Madagascar, and Africa. And so I *Adapting to native wants.* would say, with reference to ecclesiastical architecture, you must try and adapt it to the people amongst whom you are, and the same observation applies to clothing and other things. Let us also try and adapt our Church organisation and our instruction and everything else to the wants of the people, and we shall soon find the people rising up, and moving in the direction in which we wish to lead them.

The Chairman: I should like to say a word as to what was said just now about the pastor who had to remind his people that he did not go up to heaven on Monday morning and come back again on Saturday night. *Converts and pastoral work.* That reminds me of the very serious importance of our leading our converts to realise what pastoral work is, and that it does not consist merely of Sunday work, but that they must be doing their pastoral work from Monday morning to Saturday night. I think that is one very important point we have to keep in mind. Then with regard to the great desire we have for the native work, to go forward without expense to Foreign Societies, do we keep in view the immense importance of voluntary work amongst the natives themselves ? As was very well said, 40,000 communicants among the native converts ought to mean 40,000 Missionaries ; but it does not, I am afraid, abroad, any more than it does at home. I think that is one point we ought to keep very prominently before them, that any one who has received the grace of God in his own heart, and knows his Saviour, is bound to be telling others. With regard to Japan in particular, I was very much struck with the way in which they seemed to be doing that.

I remember at one place I called at, there was a band of some four-and-twenty Christians gathered together, and I was told that they were all the fruit of the labours of the village innkeeper, who had himself only been baptised a couple of years before. That is the kind **Native voluntary work.** of thing we want. I recollect that in another place, in the Nizam of Hyderabad's dominions, the work was carried on by a native Missionary of the Church Missionary Society. He was supported by native Church Funds, partially aided by the Church Missionary Society. He is doing the work entirely without European help, and he has a band of catechists and has converts scattered over an area of forty miles round. He has converts in eighty different centres ; and he said to me, How can I possibly attend these scattered sheep with such a small body of catechists as these (twenty-four), and I can get no more money from the Society for it ? So what has he done ? He has got a dozen more to become catechists on these terms. He has given them enough to clothe them (and that is little enough), and they are to look for their food from those amongst whom they labour. That is the kind of voluntary work we want. I could continue for some time longer on this topic, but I am afraid we must close punctually.

Rev. J. Hesse offered prayer.

APPENDIX.

[This Paper, though not read, we print here, both on account of its own merits, and being asked for by Bishop Fitzgerald (of the Methodist Episcopal Board, U.S.A.), who was unable to be present at the Conference in person.—ED.]

On the Training and Support of Native Workers.

BY THE REV. S. L. BALDWIN, D.D. (Boston U.S.A. ; for over twenty years Missionary of the Methodist Episcopal Church, U.S.A., at Foo-chow, China).

Understanding that the Papers to be presented at the General Missionary Conference are intended to pave the way for a general discussion of the topics treated under consideration, I propose to treat in as concise a form as possible the questions submitted by the Committee.

The best method of training native workers—by individual Missionaries ; in central institutions ; in the vernacular only, or by means of the English language.

It is very doubtful whether any one method can be picked out, and confidently affirmed to be in all cases "the best" method. Experience abundantly shows that all our methods must be adapted to varying local conditions, to national and tribal characteristics, and to individual peculiarities. That in all large and well-established Missions, a central training institution is very desirable, will hardly be disputed by any one. Such schools have so fully demonstrated their usefulness in all our great Mission-fields, as to make it unnecessary to cite examples, and to leave no opportunity for debate. This does not, however, rule out the training of native workers by individual Missionaries. In many Mission-fields, the circumstances of the case do not allow the organisation of a great central school; but it is perfectly feasible for the Missionary to gather around him several native helpers, and by spending a few hours with them,—two or three days in the week,—to give them instruction in Biblical knowledge, in exegesis, in systematic theology, and in the practical work of the ministry. Some of the very best results have been reached under this system of training native workers. It is always very highly to be commended, where circumstances prevent the institution of a training school; and it is often found useful, after the very best training of such a school, in the graduate's practical introduction to the work of the ministry. Happy the native preacher who, having made the most of his school days, and having fully equipped himself mentally and spiritually for his great work, falls into the hands of an intelligent, devout, and experienced Missionary, and has a supergraduate course of training *in the work,* under such a man.

Best method of training.

As to the use of the English language, or of the vernacular only, in such training, there is no question that will come before the Conference, the decision of which must be so absolutely controlled by the providential circumstances of each case, as this. In some portions, at least, of India, where great attention is given to the acquisition of the English language, where large numbers of the more intelligent natives are becoming conversant with it, the native worker will be at a great disadvantage, if he knows only the vernacular. So, too, in Japan, where the Government is giving instruction in English in its schools; and there is quite a general movement among the awakened minds of that Island Empire toward the study of English. The native preacher ought to be fully abreast of the best thoughts of his time, and ought to possess the highest intellectual advantages that can be secured in his field of labour. Where the English language is necessary for this purpose, it is eminently proper that provision should be made for its acquisition by our native helpers. But where the English language is little used, where the best results of Western thought have been, or can readily be translated into the native languages, the time which would be spent in the study of English, can be more profitably employed in the study of the Scriptures, and of other Christian books, as well as of scientific and literary works in the vernacular. Within the last ten years, it has been stoutly asserted by some able Missionaries, that the time has now come for introducing the study of English, and opening all the stores of Western knowledge, not only to theological students, but to all others who choose to avail themselves of the privileges of the schools. Anglo-Chinese colleges have been instituted at several of the larger stations; and, while the Missionaries in charge of them are enthusiastic in their belief that they are on the right track, there are still many who vehemently oppose them. The best course, probably, is to quietly await the result of the experiment, taking a little counsel of Gamaliel, and believing with him that, "if this counsel or this work be of men, it will come to nought; but if it be of God, ye cannot overthrow it." And as none of us wish "haply to be found even to fight against God," we can afford to wait, without undue excitement, or violent controversy, the result which time will surely show.

Training in English or vernacular.

In regard to the specific question, "Shall an American or European education for natives of Mission-fields be encouraged?" while there may be exceptions, my answer would be decidedly in the negative. I do not remember a single instance, of all that came under my observation, of a native helper sent to America or Europe for education, where the outcome was satisfactory. The general tendency in such cases is to adopt

Western education for native helpers.

Western habits, to grow away from their own people, to demand higher salaries than native congregations can afford to pay, and to become unduly exalted. I knew one native preacher who went to America at his own charges, obtained a very limited education in English, and returned to labour contentedly with his brethren ; but there was no evidence that his usefulness was materially enhanced by such English knowledge as he had acquired. I am sure that the experience and observation of the Missionaries in China generally is decidedly against sending helpers abroad for education.

Another question raised by the Committee is, " In cases where preachers and physicians have been thus trained, should they be put on a higher footing than other native helpers ? " Still another question is very closely allied to this— namely, " In Missions where a high order of qualification on the part of native teachers has been attained or is possible, shall such attainment be encouraged by enlarged privileges and powers ? " The answer to these questions will depend largely on the view which is taken of the work and of the obligation of the workers. Where the work is viewed as one *A place for English culture.* of deep, spiritual consecration, in which the workers are to receive only a reasonable support, and not to be paid for natural or acquired talent, it will naturally be determined that the highly educated helper shall be put on no higher footing as to pay than his less educated brother. It will be taken for granted that, in his consecration to the work, he will be glad to bring all his acquisitions to the Master's service, without expecting to be paid more money because he has enjoyed and improved greater privileges than his neighbour. If he enjoys any " enlarged privileges and powers " they will be only those which naturally accrue to superior talent and ability,—not any which are artificially created as a sort of reward for acquired merit. For instance, he may be made chairman of a council, moderator of a Presbytery, or delegate to a convention, by reason of his brethren's recognition of his ability ; but he will not be paid a salary largely in excess of that paid his fellow-workers.

Still another question is raised : " Would the difficulties relating to such cases be relieved by sending persons thus educated to a different Mission-field ? " My answer is, Seldom, if ever. Suppose a native of Oude, thus educated, to be sent to Bengal. What advantage would there be in the transition ? Or what difficulty would be overcome by sending a Cantonese thus educated to Pekin ? It would only relieve Canton of a burden to pile it upon Pekin. I do not imagine that any elysium can be found for English educated native workers, where their new tastes and habits can be gratified without creating friction and greater or less disturbance in the workings of the Mission to which they return. I come now to the last part of the subject assigned—the support of native workers.

I take it for granted that there will be no disagreement among the members of the Conference as to these propositions—(1) That the native Churches ought to become self-supporting at the earliest practicable moment. (2) That all possible effort should be made to secure this result. But, *Self-support of native Churches.* with these propositions granted, there is still a wide field for differences of opinion ; and we find that all shades of opinion are held—from the extreme of never employing a native helper until he can be supported by his own people, to the opposite extreme of paying increasingly large salaries to native preachers out of the Mission treasury. Truth does not generally inhabit the extremes.

In the beginning of Missionary work in any field, when there are a few converts, and some among them have the " gifts, grace, and usefulness," which indicate their call to preach the Gospel, it is evident that one of two things must be done. Either their preaching must be confined to what they *Support of native preachers.* can do on Sunday or in the evenings, while daily labouring to support themselves ; or they must be assisted from the Missionary treasury to give themselves up wholly to the work. If the former course is followed, we have the advantage of being able to say that no native helper receives foreign pay ; while, on the other hand, we lose the continuous labour of a good man, who might be winning many souls for Christ. The Rev. Dr. Blodget, of Pekin, said very forcibly at the Shanghai Conference : " The principle of love in the hearts of Christians hastens to supply every want of a Christian brother, and every need of the whole Church. Those who have, help those who have not. By this principle, young men in Christian lands are aided while preparing for the ministry of the Gospel; and Missionaries are supported among the heathen by the same principle. This law of Christian love does not admit of distinctions of nation or race. The Church in Shan-tung may educate young men from Shan-si, and may support them while preaching in that province. The Churches in China may educate at their own expense young men from Mongolia or Corea, and support them afterwards, while preaching the glad tidings to their own countrymen. Why may not the Churches in the United States, or in England, in like manner, educate and support Chinese preachers? The Chinese Christians are poor. There are among them those who are desirous of preaching the Gospel. Is there anything in the Word of God, **How to decide the question.** or in the example of Christ, to hinder our affording to them such aid as they may require?" And the Rev. Dr. Mateer, of Tung-chow, expressed very tersely the same principle, when he said: "All the Churches at home raise funds, and send out evangelists to preach in destitute places, and there is no sufficient reason why the same principle should not embrace China. The Church is one and the work is one; and there is no reason in the nature of things why the gifts of Foreign Churches should be limited in their use to Foreign Missionaries." The strong words which were uttered by the Rev. Dr. Crawford, of Tung-chow, at the same Conference, against the "employment system," were based very largely on the assumption that the preachers employed were preachers *because* they were employed. No one would defend an attempt to *make* preachers of the Gospel by paying men to preach. But when the members of a Mission are satisfied by proper evidence that certain native brethren are called and qualified to preach the Gospel, why should they be restrained from giving their full time to the work, because there is not yet a native Church to support them? There are Christians ready to support them, and Christians upon whose heart the Master has laid the commission, "Go ye into all the world, and preach the Gospel to every creature;"—men who are making money for God, and who are anxious to use it in His cause. Why should they be prevented from supporting a Chinese, a Japanese, or Hindu preacher, while there is not yet a congregation to support him on the field?

MEETINGS OF MEMBERS
IN SECTION.

EIGHTEENTH SESSION.

MISSIONARY COMITY.

(1) *MUTUAL RELATIONS.*

(*a*) The desirableness of having a common understanding between Missionary Committees and workers on their relation in the field as to boundaries of districts, employment and interchange of workers, and transfer of converts and congregations.

(*b*) Is there a stage in the progress of Christian work in any district when such an understanding cannot be applied ?

(*c*) The adjustment on each field, as far as may be, of a common scale of salaries for native helpers, with a view to removing all temptation to a mercenary spirit through the anticipation of larger compensation.

(*Tuesday morning, June 19th, in the Lower Hall.*)

H. M. Matheson, Esq., in the chair.
Acting Secretary, Rev. R. Wardlaw Thompson.

Rev. Dr. Judson Smith offered prayer.

The Chairman: Dear friends,—We have now arrived at the last day of this great Conference, and the subject before this Section is one that concerns us all, and one upon which I feel sure there will be no difference of opinion amongst us who are assembled in this room. What is meant by "Comity"? The word means Meaning of "Comity." mildness, suavity of manners, courtesy, civility, and good breeding. It may seem strange to those who have been witnessing and so greatly enjoying the spirit of unity and brotherly love which has so remarkably prevailed among us, that it should be needful to discuss a matter of this kind, affecting so closely as it does the principle of brotherly love, mutual respect and consideration which fills all our hearts. But we are not always in circumstances such as we have been in during the last ten days, seeing one another face to face, strengthening one another "as iron sharpeneth iron," and comforting and encouraging one another, in the great work in which, through God's goodness, we have been permitted to engage in. our *Its consideration* different callings. Human nature is weak; the old *important.* Adam has not yet died out, and the consuming zeal with which Missionary agents are filled and animated, is not always tempered by that discretion which it is so needful for us all to cultivate. It is therefore desirable that this subject should be considered among us, in order that some wise Christian considerations may be brought before us to govern the action both of Committees and of Missionaries in the field. It is important for us all that there should be an earnest desire and even determination to respect each other's boundaries, to repress every feeling of rivalry, and to cultivate instead that holy emulation in faith and good works which will have the Master's smile and benediction. I will not, of course, enter into any detail upon this subject ; it will be treated by our venerable and beloved Dr. Thompson, who will address us upon this important matter, and I am sure we shall listen not only with respectful attention, but with a desire to carry into practice the suggestions of Christian love and wisdom that will be brought before us not only by him but by other speakers who are prepared to address us this morning.

I remember an instance in the Mission-field with which I am best acquainted, one large district of which is occupied by three Missions. The Missionaries on the field have an honourable understanding as to the division of the land among them ; one goes in *An example of* this direction, and another in that. These boundaries *true Comity.* have been recognised, and this has been helpful to all. The Missionaries have not been treading upon one another's ground. But once a zealous Missionary of one of these bodies sought to open a station within the ground of one of the others. It happened to fall to my lot to call upon the Committee in the Home field to talk over the matter with them ; and I was at once met by this statement : "We have already considered that action of our dear brother, and I will read you the despatch which has been sent out to the Missionaries requiring the withdrawal from the field occupied by your Society ;" and that was immediately done. I know of no instance except that, that has ever occurred in the forty years of the Mission with the management of which I have had the great honour of being connected during the whole of that time. No doubt there are zealous men who sometimes forget the things to which our attention is to be called this morning, and who do not always respect the fields occupied by others, and the feelings of those who are engaged in the work. Let us cultivate the spirit of brotherly love. We have been singing that sweet Psalm of David :—

> " Behold how good a thing it is,
> And how becoming well,
> Together such as brethren are
> In unity to dwell."

It is more blessed than can be told; and if the spirit of love and harmony prevails more and more, it will not detract in the smallest degree from the true liberty of the labourers or from their success, but will contribute to it in an eminent degree.

The Acting Secretary: Mr. Chairman,—The gentleman who was to have read Dr. Warneck's Paper has been summoned on a jury, and is unable to attend, and Dr. Warneck has had to appear before a Court of Justice in his own country in connection with some of his writings on Missionary subjects. It was accordingly proposed to take the Paper as read. *Dr. Warneck's Paper. An explanation.*

PAPER.

1. By the Rev. G. Warneck, D.D. (of Rothenschirmbach, Germany).

The Mutual Relations of Evangelical Missionary Societies to one another.

When we make the brotherly relationship of Evangelical Missionary Societies to one another the object of our counsels,—for such indeed is the meaning of Missionary Comity,—we may be sure in an especial degree of the blessing and intercession of our great High Priest, who is enthroned at the right hand of His Father. For not only did He repeatedly designate as the mark of His disciples that they should "love one another"; but in His sublime sacerdotal prayer He explicitly made supplication "that they all may be one; as Thou, Father, art in Me, and I in Thee, that they also may be one in Us: that the world may believe that Thou hast sent Me." *The blessing on unity.*

We know that the Son of God intended to convey by this *Oneness* something far deeper, more spiritual, and more free than the Romish Church understands by the hierarchic unity which is to-day especially her proudest boast. But, on the other hand, we should degrade this Oneness to a mere pious expression if we were to consider it as merely something spiritual *and not intended also to be outwardly recognisable in our practical relations with one another.* *Unity to be visible.*

The mechanical unity of Rome, which is the necessary consequence of her plan of a Church culminating in papal infallibility, is an impossible thing upon Evangelical ground. The fundamental Evangelical article of justification by faith is the root at once of Evangelical *freedom* and of the *diversity* of movement and life for which there is neither an understanding nor a place in the unyielding unity of Rome. But it would nevertheless be fatal shortsightedness, were we to see *only strength* in the freedom and diversity of Protestantism. Truly, they form our strength, but they are just as truly allied to our weakness, perhaps *Union with freedom and diversity.*

even *in* this strength itself. The words of Paul, "When I am weak, then am I strong," still embody a truth when read the other way, when I am strong, then am I weak. The Romish Church has lost its freedom to gain its unity, and the Evangelical its unity to gain its freedom.

Unfortunately the domain of Protestant *Missions* is not free from the general weakness of Protestantism. Still the division there, is not so great as the derision of Romish opponents represents it to be. *The concord among the Missionaries of the different Protestant Societies is greater than the discord, the esteem shown on all sides stronger than the distrust, and respect for one another's boundaries is more general than infractions of them.* Were it not so, it would have been impossible to hold this General Mission Conference in which we are now assembled, and to which delegates have been sent, with few exceptions, by all Protestant nations and Church communities. And at all events such a unity, founded upon freedom, has a far higher value than that of the Papal Church, purchased as it is by the sacrifice of liberty.

The Conference an evidence of concord.

Evangelical Missions suffer heavily from their divided condition. For this division breaks up and squanders our powers, it is a temptation to unbrotherly rivalry, and occasions not a little perplexity, and even scandal, among the heathen.

Is it not possible sensibly to diminish this evil?—I will not say to completely do away with it, for that would be but an illusory hope. Nothing can be done in the way of ecclesiastical regulation, just because we have no supreme authority among the Churches. Something however might be accomplished by means of *unconstrained brotherly union*, and, if appearances are not deceptive, it will be one of the most glorious tasks of this *General Mission Conference*, meeting from decade to decade, to bring about gradually, by such fraternal alliances, a certain amount of unity in Protestant Missionary labours, which are to-day still so split up into manifold rivalries. There is no doubt that an *impulse towards unity* is already passing through the different denominations; and this is shown not only by the Mission Conferences in India, China, Japan, and South Africa, but also by the coalescing of many Mission congregations belonging to different Missionary Societies into *one Missionary* Church; for example, those of the Presbyterian Societies in Japan.

Decennial Conferences.

The question as to *what is to be done on the part of the individual Society to institute and maintain this Missionary Comity,* must now become the subject of our deliberations. I content myself with a threefold reply:—

I. We must become mutually *acquainted* with each other;

II. We must mutually bind ourselves to avoid all *overstepping of borders;* and

III. We must more constantly *hold out helping hands* to each other.

I.

Evangelical Mission work to-day covers a wide extent of territory, and has many ramifications, and there are in Europe as in America but few of those interested in Missions, who possess a thorough grasp of it. One reason for this is that not much interest has been shown in the acquiring of such a *general* comprehension of it. Want of knowledge.
No doubt, in Germany this general knowledge of Missions is most fostered. Here—in addition to about six popular Mission papers—it is made the subject of two Missionary reviews of some literary value, and with a circle of readers to be numbered by thousands, quite distinct from the special reports of the separate Societies, and having as their particular task the treatment of Mission work *as a whole*.

There is no doubt that the consideration that Evangelical Missions—in spite of differences among the Societies promoting them—are something *united*, are a *whole*, forms, together with brotherly love, the first condition for the practice of Missionary Comity. A restricted circle of information generally results in narrowed sympathies, while, on the other hand, a wide gleaning of facts opens the heart itself. So far as my experience goes, all those who have acquired a thorough *general acquaintance with Missions* and extended views of the whole work, have been free from narrowness of heart.

With insignificant exceptions, our friends in England and America are strikingly *unacquainted with German Missions*, and not only with our Missions, but generally with our religious condition at home.

Incorrect reports concerning Germany frequently amuse us, still oftener they pain us. The further result of these perverted judgments on Germany and German activity is naturally a *lack of Comity*, that is to say, an injurious contempt for our performances, a condescending treatment of them, as though we were not Mission workers of An illustration of absence of Comity.
equal standing, and even in our literary Mission labours were yet in leading strings, not to speak of the various ways in which unfriendliness is experienced in the various districts of Missionary labour. This lack of Comity, which we often experience painfully, has, it is my firm conviction, its origin in the *great ignorance* about the situation in Germany.

It is far from being my intention to idealise this situation. It is a German characteristic to criticise ourselves very severely, and pharisaical self-glorification is not a German national failing. But we may say without any vain glory, and you will acknowledge it as a fact, *that we in Germany are better acquainted with Foreign Missions, especially those of England and America, than you in England and America are with German Missions*, and *that we are more just towards you than you are towards us*.

But whether it be indifference to the Mission work of others, or a contempt for it, in either case it shows a narrow-heartedness which hinders the formation of what may be called a *Missionary esprit de corps* within the circles of Evangelical Christianity, which would look Narrowness mars unity.
upon Missions as the *common* concern of all Evangelical Churches. Of course, it is the business of the official organ of the individual Missionary Society to furnish precise information as to its own work; but, even if this special branch of news must form its principal contents, denominational politics need not on that account be urged therein. God's kingdom is being built up among the heathen on the outer side of one's

own boundary fence, and the band of workers of a single Mission can but form a company, a battalion, or a regiment of the whole Evangelical Mission army.

Just lately things have somewhat improved. The *Boston Missionary Herald*, for example, has for a long time regularly contained " Notes from the Wide World," and so a number of other Mission papers have now for some few years past given notices of " Other Missions." I am convinced that no inconsiderable service would be rendered to the cause of Missionary Comity, if the organs of all Evangelical Missionary Societies would keep at least a couple of pages free for regular news concerning the doings of their co-workers, especially those whose districts of work lie nearest their own.

II.

We must mutually bind ourselves to avoid all overstepping of borders.

For where one Missionary Society forces itself into the field of labour already occupied by another, the assured result is a lack of Christian brotherly kindness. Again it is of the highest importance for Missionary Comity that the different Societies should entertain due consideration and regard for the *boundaries of their respective spheres of action.*

Let us consider for a moment the fact that in Evangelical Christendom, there exist already many Missionary Societies. The smaller a Missionary Society is the more expensive it is, and the greater will be the difficulty in working, especially in tropical lands. But the evil increases as the number of Missionaries are multiplied, who, unconnected with any Missionary Society, go out as individuals to undertake independent Mission work. By this system the already much divided and split up Protestant Missions will be altogether anatomised. Our watchword to-day must be, " *Working in connection with the already existing Missionary Societies, and decreasing their number by association.*"

Danger of multiplying agencies.

Stringent limits and regulations are impossible here, and we can only appeal to brotherly Comity.

Two rules, however, should be held binding.

1. It is the duty of an Evangelical Christian to keep faith with that Missionary Society which he has once freely chosen, so long as such Society remains true to its principles.

Rules for agents.

2. It is incumbent on every worker holding office in any particular Missionary Society, never to entice away the friends and supporters of other Missionary Societies ; but should an increase of income be desired, to try and obtain it in the first place, from their own friends, and secondly from those who have not yet subscribed to any Missionary Society.

Before I refer to the Missionary work abroad, among the heathen, permit me to add a few words in a free and brotherly manner as to *Proselytism among Protestant Church communities*, particularly in Germany, for I am at a loss to comprehend how it is possible to exercise Missionary Comity in heathen lands, if this Comity is not first exercised at home. In my opinion systematic proselytising amongst different Evangelical Churches *should not take place* at all ; and it is particularly wanting in tact if this system of proselytising is pursued in making converts among the *heathen.*

Lack of Comity at home.

I will make no mention of names ; but up to the present time Missionary reports have passed through my hands, in which Africa, Central America, South America, China, Germany, India, Turkey, and Japan are being mentioned in one sentence as Missionary fields. Suppose a Hindu or a negro were to read such reports, he would necessarily be led to believe that Germany was a heathen country, standing on the same footing with India or the Congo. And what are we to say when a Methodist preacher writes from Berlin: "Here is a field for work with over one million souls, with *only one worker*"?—viz., this Methodist.

Our Missions to Germany.

Dear brethren in England and America, I believe that I speak in the name of all my German fellow-believers, if I urge upon you to cease.from looking upon Germany, the land of Luther and Melanchthon, Arndt and Spener, Francke and Zinzendorf, Tholuck, Fliedner and Wichern, as a half heathen and rationalistic country.

Even to-day great religious battles are being fought in Germany, the issue of which will be of the utmost importance to England and America.

Do not, I beseech you, take this request amiss, but show us brotherly Comity by so working with us, as to remove this proselytising spirit from our midst.

I take the liberty of laying before the Conference the following suggestions:—

1. If an Evangelical Missionary Society desire to enter on a new field of labour, let her choose one not already occupied by another Evangelical Society, or in the event of the sphere of labour, like East Africa for example, comprising a very large space, let boundaries be arranged, in a brotherly spirit, with any Evangelical Mission already at work, and each consider the regulations as binding.

Suggestions to Societies.

2. Where a Missionary sphere, as for instance, South Africa or India, is already occupied by several Missionary Societies, avoid as far as possible intruding into the districts belonging to other Societies, or proselytising amongst the members of such Societies, thereby fostering a deplorable spirit of desertion.

Furthermore, we should agree on certain principles respecting the reception of members from other Missions; and I suggest the following as a basis for such an agreement:

Receiving members from other Missions.

(*a*) No member of another Mission should be received or admitted to Communion without informing the Missionary of the district to which he formerly belonged of such proposed admission; and his answer being duly considered.

(*b*) No member of another Mission to be received who has been expelled or is about to be expelled from his former Communion, or against whom Church discipline is threatened.

(*c*) As there is danger that native helpers may exchange one community for another, purely from selfish motives, they shall receive no appointment, or at any rate no higher salary than they had in their previous position; in fact, it is recommended that Missionary Societies working in proximity to each other should agree on terms for the stipend of their native helpers.

3. *Regular Conferences* are of special importance for the cultivation of friendly union between Missionaries, at which all Evangelical Missionaries in surrounding districts may have the opportunity to cultivate each other's acquaintance, and in brotherly love, endeavour to be of one mind, touching all important Missionary questions. Such Missionary Conferences as those held at Allahabad, Calcutta, Madras, Shanghai, Osaka, and King William's

Town, have done more for the mutual edification and benefit of the different Protestant Missionaries, than all admonitions; and I would suggest that more such Conferences in smaller districts are greatly needed. An altogether new danger to Missionary enterprise has arisen from the modern colonial **Dangers of** policy; which introduces into the international field of Missions **colonisation.** those national jealousies and passions which it rouses; this is not only the case in Germany and France, but also in England. Within the bounds of this Paper I can only touch lightly upon this all-important question, which alone might have formed a subject for a Conference.

The Evangelical Missionary Societies cannot be accused of having aroused these colonial political jealousies, still less are they able to remove them. So far as my knowledge extends, they have, with a few exceptions, given evidence of the danger of nationalising Missions. We, in Germany, have done as well as our brethren in France, who stand perhaps in the greatest degree under the pressure of such national passion. (I take this opportunity of calling attention to the Conference of the German Missionary Societies, held in Bremen in 1885, of which it seems little is known in England, and I refer to the " Allgemeine Missions Zeitschrift " of 1885, p. 545, etc. ; and 1886, p. 39, etc. ; also 1887, p. 269, etc.)

It is to be hoped that this era of extravagant national sensibilities will pass away as soon as colonial political relations have been consolidated, and the new colonial era has passed through its infantine maladies. **Modified** The desire of European colonising powers to have in their **by time.** colonies, or the territories over which they exercise authority, Missionaries of their own nationality, is up to a certain limit very justifiable, for colonial possessions make Missions a national duty. But the duty of *Missionary Societies* will be a double one. *First*, to take care that this national duty does not produce injustice to, and intolerance of, the Missionaries of other nationalities. *Secondly*, that Missionaries of other nationalities shall not give cause by their irritating behaviour for well-founded complaints from the presiding colonial power. We must earnestly guard both sides that neither *colonial policy be mixed up with Missionary enterprise*, nor the *Mission be mixed up with the colonial policy.*

The indispensable *assumption* for the cultivation of true Comity amongst Evangelical Missions belonging to different denominations in the Church is the double acknowledgment: *Firstly*, that we all possess in common such measure of doctrinal truth as is sufficient to show a sinner the way of salvation. *Secondly*, that salvation is *not* by any *Church*, but alone by the *Lord* Jesus Christ. If this basis is lacking, then complaint of unfraternal intrusion is futile, and every request for brotherly consideration frivolous.

In China, India, Japan, and Africa dwelling-houses are built in a different style to those in America and Europe; and if we learn to consider our European and American ecclesiastical systems, as far as Missions are concerned as only the scaffolding, which is indispensable, but not the building itself, then I believe that Comity in the Protestant Evangelical Missionary Societies would take a mighty step in the right direction.

III.

We must more consistently hold out helping hands to each other.

With regard to the third point, viz., that of reciprocal aid, I venture to lay before you only two propositions.

I. We must look upon defence against attacks on Evangelical Missions as a battle which we have *unitedly* to fight, even should the attack not concern us personally or the Mission with which we are associated. Such attacks are made principally from two sides, viz., by the Church of Rome and by the adversaries of Missions in our own Church. *Union for mutual defence.* The enmity of Rome against Evangelical Missions shows itself today more vindictive than ever, and goes so far as to manifest this animosity by systematic aggression into the spheres of Evangelical Missions, as well as by systematic libels. It is high time that our sanguine fellow-believers should have their eyes opened to the enormous danger which threatens us from Rome.

An equally pernicious principle is it to say: "What has it to do with me, so long as the attack is not aimed against me, against my Missionary Society, or against my countrymen?" I have had some painful experiences in this matter. English Missions, for instance, have more than once been attacked in Germany, and I considered *Want of sympathy in this.* it my bounden duty to defend them publicly. For this purpose I needed authentic information, which I endeavoured to obtain from the Committees of the Missionary Societies in question. From some I received no reply at all, and from others a reply to the effect: "We do not care what is written about us in Germany!" I did not ask for a personal service from the English Missionary Societies, but was anxious to render them a service to the utmost of my power and ability. Can this be considered Missionary Comity?

II. A Standing Central Committee, with headquarters in London, and composed of delegates from all Protestant Missionary Societies, should be formed, not only to act as leaders in matters where the united action of all Missionary Societies is desirable, but also to act as arbitrators where differences threaten to disturb the harmonious *A Standing International Committee.* working of the different Missionary Societies. In order to give the Central Committee a sound basis, Missionary Conferences should be formed in every Protestant nation, to include all existing Evangelical Missionary Societies of that nation, and elect deputies to represent them on the Central Committee. Such national Missionary Conferences already exist in Germany, Scandinavia, and Holland; it would therefore only be necessary to organise them for Great Britain, North America, and France (with Vaud and Italy). The duty of this Committee would be: (a) to organise a general Missionary Conference once in every ten years; (b) to undertake the regular publication of a general Missionary statement as above; (c) to initiate united action in cases which recommend themselves to the general policy of all Missionary Societies, as for instance, the restriction of the drink traffic; (d) to settle differences with regard to boundaries of spheres of labour. And now, in conclusion, my *ceterum censeo*: if Missionary Comity is really to become a virtue for all Missionary Societies, we must learn to look upon Missions as a *common cause*, in spite of all our differences, to kindle a Missionary *corps d'esprit*, and cultivate *Missions a common cause.* it, to accustom ourselves to a *solidarity of Missionary interests*, and to place in the foreground the *vital* truths of the Gospel common to us all. If we are really in earnest concerning the foregoing, we shall be able sincerely to pray, with the assurance of being heard, for the manifestation of Christian brotherly love, which is the surest guarantee of Missionary Comity.

PAPER.

2. BY THE REV. A. C. THOMPSON, D.D. (Chairman of Prudential Committee, A.B.C.F.M.).

Missionary Comity.

What is Missionary Comity? The observance of equity and Christian courtesy in foreign evangelisation. No human authority can have jurisdiction over the numerous Missionary organisations. There is therefore need for the exercise of inter-mission comity, a subject which should have place in treatises on Christian ethics. Foreign Missions, being eminently a department of Church work, ought surely to be conducted by all branches of the Church with marked conformity to the requirements of our holy religion. In no sphere of duty should Christian principles have more complete control. To the golden rule there can be no geographical or denominational exceptions. One of the most marked defects of social ethics hitherto is limitation of range. The actual breadth of obligation as binding upon the entire human family, irrespective of zone, race, culture or political status, has had small space in scientific treatises, and sometimes too small space practically in the thoughts even of professed pupils of the Great Teacher. The pithy remark of Lord Coke that "corporations are without souls," would seem to be quoted sometimes as if a Gospel maxim sanctioning the absence of corporate conscience.

Comity universally binding.

PRIMARY PRINCIPLES.

There are certain truths concerning Foreign Missionary proceedings on the part of Evangelical Churches, Societies, Boards and individuals, which may be deemed axiomatic.

I. *All have rights which are entitled to respect by all.* A share in the work of discipling the nations being incumbent on every believer and every body of believers, that duty should command the common regard of others. It cannot be legitimately interfered with. No one Church is charged with the evangelisation of the whole world. It is as truly the obligation of each to respect the interests and duties of fellow-Christians while obeying Christ's last command, as it is the duty of each to take part in the work, for the authority under which each one rightfully acts is alike divine and supreme.

II. *Equality of rights* is another prime principle. The smallest Missionary organisation may lay as unimpeachable a claim to its function as the largest. The rights of any one are the rights of all. To assail or affront one is to assail and affront all. Right is one thing, rank another. In the evangelistic realm no balance of power requires to be maintained owing to jealousy of growing resources and enterprise on the part of any member of the great brotherhood of Societies. On the score of jural parity it is here as among sovereign *states.* The more powerful have no privilege of eminent domain over others, even the most circumscribed. "Russia and Geneva have equal rights," said John Marshall, Chief Justice of the United States. To offend one of Christ's little ones is a grievous offence.

But there are considerations more evidently concrete.

III. *Evangelistic economy* is required. Whatever may become true in the future, at present there is sufficient territory unoccupied or but partially cultivated, to admit of Missionary operations by all with no danger of interference. The same considerations which lead to any foreign movement, should inscribe on every banner, "The greatest good to the greatest number." Nothing can be plainer than that it is a dereliction of duty for two or more evangelistic agencies to enter the same field, while there are unevangelised regions beyond. Wise division of labour is as imperative as the labour itself. It cannot be questioned that the history of Missions and the present distribution of forces reveal more or less of unauthorised expenditure of means and overlapping of agencies. Intermingled fire brigades need to disentangle their engines, and betake themselves to different sections of the conflagration. " Yea, so have I strived," says the Apostle Paul, "to preach the Gospel, not where Christ was named, lest I should build upon another man's foundation ; but, as it is written, To whom He was not spoken of they shall see ; and they that have not heard shall understand" (Rom. xv. 20, 21).

IV. *Priority of occupation* establishes a right that deserves to be recognised.

This is analagous to the claims of discovery, exploration, and military or colonial occupation, which are admitted in international law. * Any evangelistic agency has the undisputed right to enter any part of unevangelised heathendom. Arrangements in progress, such as give rational promise of speedy occupancy, or an earlier published intention soon to enter a given field, confer presumptively the same right.

Certain limitations to this right are to be observed.

1. One is that great seaports like Constantinople, Bombay, Madras, Calcutta, Singapore, Canton, Shanghai, Tokio, Osaka, may well admit of co-existing labours by different Societies.

This arises from the populousness of such places, and also from their convenience as ports of entry and, in some instances, as bases of communication and supply for inland operations. Certain interior cities also, like Benares and Pekin, belong to the same category, on account of their size alone.

2. Another limitation may exist, sometimes at least, where different nationalities with different languages occupy the same towns or territories.

3. Yet another exception may also proceed from prolonged and wholly inadequate cultivation of some part of a field. This would be particularly obvious where the region is extensive and densely peopled. It is true that opinions will vary concerning what constitutes an occupancy sufficient to bar a new comer. No question, however, can reasonably be raised touching

* Phillimore's " International Law," I., pp. 273, 274.

localities where there is a resident Missionary, or where there is a school or congregation in charge of some native agent, and which is occasionally visited by a Missionary. Any evangelistic operation that reaches or has fair prospect of reaching a considerable part of the population—accessibility being considered in estimating population—without unreasonable delay, should prevent the incoming of another agency. Yet every Mission ought to beware of excessive claims, and of an unwise multiplication of outlying posts, with no rational probability of anything but a languishing existence.

There are, however, maxims not limited to mere territorial rights, and which relate to—

V. *Equity in administration.* Where Mission-fields are conterminous or not far apart, there is liability of embarrassment, owing to difference in policy and methods, especially respecting the natives. One perplexing matter suggests that—

1. Agreement between contiguous Missions as to the scale of wages is a great desideratum. The closer the proximity the greater this need. Any noticeable difference in the stipend paid to native agents of about the same grade is sure to be known and to occasion uneasiness. In neighbouring Missions there are often divergent views relating to the value of labour and the proper limits also of charitable assistance. It is then plainly a duty that some common understanding and adjustment be reached; otherwise the evils of injurious competition, instead of the benefits of co-operation, will be felt. It is alleged that here and there offers of large salaries have been made to teachers and other native assistants, which act as a virtual bribe. Mercenary motives are called into exercise. Heart-burnings and jealousies ensue upon such violations of evangelistic Comity.

2. No Mission should employ a native agent who has been in the employ of another Mission without an amicable understanding between the two. The chief underlying reason is that such persons are either unworthy of employment, or that, in seeking a change, they are influenced by unworthy motives.*

3. Inter-mission Comity should be exercised in relation to Church discipline. Discarded agents and Church members under deserved discipline are sometimes welcomed from one Mission to another. There may be instances in which this proceeding brings a measure of relief to one of the fields, and no extradition treaty would be desired. But the tendency is to convert a Mission into a cave of Adullam. Christian fellowship is in this way set at naught, and benefit accrues to no one, while the general standard of religious character is lowered. Common honour and the plain requirements of good neighbourhood should be enough to prevent such occurrences. This was among the points specified in a resolution adopted by the Missionary Conference at Allahabad 1872—73, which body had a membership of 136, representing twelve different nationalities and nineteen different Societies. The united sentiment was embodied thus:—

* Dr. Carstairs Douglas of Amoy, gave utterance to an opinion common throughout the wide field of Protestant Missions : " We should be very suspicious of any person coming to us professing to have conscientious objections to the principles of his first Christian instructors. It is in the highest degree probable that any such profession is either a cloak for improper motives on the part of the man himself, or the result of underhand dealing on the part of some one who hopes to reap some advantage by the change" ("General Conference of the Protestant Missionaries in China," Shanghai, 1877, p. 444).

"It is their solemn conviction that the progress of the Gospel in a heathen land can only be retarded by the Missionaries of one Communion receiving the converts of another Church, who are as yet imperfectly acquainted with Divine truth, and unable to enter intelligently into questions which separate the various sections of Christendom, especially those who are under discipline." *

Decision at Allahabad.

4. Unauthorised appropriation of the fruits of one Mission by another is a violation of Comity that should be sedulously avoided. If anything ought to be superfluous in evangelistic operations, it should be the need of quoting the eighth commandment. Let there be only an ear open to request for sectarian interference, and requests will be sure to come. What would the great Apostle do in such a case? Regarding "other men's labours," his avowed principle was "to preach the Gospel in the regions beyond you, and not to boast in another man's line of things made ready to our hand." If the Decalogue were antiquated, the New Testament injunction, "Let him that stole, steal no more," is not antiquated.

Missionary annals supply noble examples of Christian honour touching this matter. I will cite but one, the refusal of the Church Missionary Society, a quarter of a century since, to listen to urgent solicitations that it would enter among Armenians either in the provinces of Turkey or at the Capitol. Strong appeals were made for aid to a company of converts in Constantinople, who, under the lead of an able pastor, had unreasonably withdrawn from connection with the American Mission, and pleaded conscientious convictions in favour of an Episcopal "Reformed Armenian" movement; but the Committee of the Church Missionary Society, after mature deliberation, unanimously declared "that the Church Missionary Society could not give "the desired" countenance or support, as it would be an unjustifiable interference with the great and good work for so many years carried on by the American Board of Missions in Turkey, with the manifest blessing of the God of Missions." The return, soon afterwards, of the disaffected party to cordial relations with the Mission of the American Board, as well as other subsequent developments, attested the wisdom no less than the Christian courtesy of that decision.†

C.M.S. and A.B.C.F.M.

5. Inter-marriage between Missionaries of different Societies furnishes occasion for Comity. The number of labourers and the proximity of fields having increased in recent years, instances of the kind now referred to have also increased.

When a lady's term of service has been short, and has been spent chiefly in acquiring a new language or in other mere preparations for usefulness, and she then enters into a domestic arrangement that involves connection with another Society, no equivalent has been rendered for the outlay attending her appointment. The Society that sent her out will have borne the expense required to place her in the field and sustain her there for a season, and must now have further inconvenience and loss of time in securing a substitute, along with, probably, a serious embarrassment at the station from which the lady retires. The least which equity demands is that the expenses of outfit, journey to the original place of destination, as well as support there for a longer or shorter period, be refunded. Marriage is indeed honourable in all, but it may be attended by circumstances not so honourable.‡

* "Report of the Allahabad Missionary Conference," London, 1873, p. 485.

† "Annual Report of A.B.C.F.M.," 1866, p. 18.

‡ The Manual for Women of the American Board has the following: "In case of a Missionary retiring from the field within a limited period, as five years, for other cause than failure of health, it is expected that an equitable return will be made to the Board,—due regard being had to expenses incurred and services rendered" (p. 12).

COMITY OBSERVED.

The annals of Protestant foreign evangelisation record a prevailing and most gratifying observance of Christian proprieties on the wide field. Allusion has already been made to this. There are Societies not a few which make little or no mention of infringement. Numerous instances have occurred in which unintentional friction, actually existing or imminent, has been promptly obviated.

In 1829 the United States ship *Vincennes* touched at the Marquesas Islands, and its chaplain conversed with natives in regard to the establishment of a Mission among them. No Missionary from any quarter of the world was there at the time, nor was the American Board aware that other labourers had an eye upon that region. Learning afterwards, however, that such was the case, the Board relinquished its contemplated movement, and placed on record this avowal : "It is contrary to their principles to interfere with other Missionary Societies." * Since then that sentiment has been repeatedly expressed and similarly acted upon. An experience not dissimilar took place also at Singapore. So, too, when the Mission of the American Board was about to be established at Madras, a most friendly correspondence ensued with the representative of the London Society, then residing there, and happy results followed. Noteworthy was the honourable course pursued some years since by the American Methodist
Illustrated in Bulgaria. Episcopal Society, in relation to dividing Bulgaria for evangelistic purposes with the Board just named. More than once has that Board had occasion to recognise the high-minded and courteous attitude taken by the Church Missionary Society when a question of Comity arose. Public mention is also due, in view of the honourable course of the American Baptist Union, regarding a recent mischievous invasion of territory in Western Asia, occupied by the American Board.

But the present hour is not the time for an exhaustive mention of similar illustrations in the history of other kindred organisations. Many an instance has there been of friendly co-operation and material aid, as well as many an instance in which one Mission or individual has gratefully acknowledged hospitality and kindness in various forms from members of other ecclesiastical
Brotherhood general among Missionaries. connections. It is a delightful fact that, in general, Christian brotherhood is nowhere felt so warmly as among labourers from different sections of the Church, toiling in the same great harvest fields of heathendom. Honourable sentiment and conduct are the general experience. Dr. Alexander Duff, in his forcible utterance, only voiced a prevailing conviction among non-sacramentarian Missionary bodies : "I would as soon," said he, "leap into the Ganges, as venture to go near Tinnevelly, except as a brother to see the good work that is going on." †

COMITY INFRINGED.

While in this regard the avowed position and actual practice of many Societies are all that could be desired, exceptions exist. Missionary journals and annual reports show this. Now and then a narrative pamphlet is published, and Missionary memoirs not infrequently contain notices of the same. Cases are known, of which for the sake of peace, or for other reasons, aggrieved parties make no public mention. Sometimes these infelicities are the result of—

I. Inadvertence or insufficient information. During the earlier period of Modern Foreign Missionary movements, the habit and the means of giving publicity to intentions and operations were by no means what they now are.

* Annual Report, 1833, p. 88.
† Speech in Freemasons' Hall, London, 1858.

On the other hand the number of organisations—between one and two hundred—is now so large that territorial relations are becoming more intimate. A little or a good deal of indiscretion is no strange thing. Missionaries abroad, rather than Home Boards, are sometimes chiefly at fault, and yet oftener perhaps, native agents, rather than Missions, are responsible for disturbed relations. All such cases can easily be condoned. With kindliness in negotiations an early removal of the offence may be confidently anticipated.

But unhappily that anticipation cannot be so confidently entertained where intrusion takes place—

II. Under less pardonable circumstances. Reference is not now made to Roman Catholic methods. No regard for Comity is expected from that quarter. The propaganda avows the design of establishing a counter-movement beside every Protestant station in the heathen world. This proceeds from the monstrous assumption by the Roman Curia, of jurisdiction over all nations of the earth. Having large resources and a measure of governmental aid, that Church is enabled to confront nearly all Protestant evangelism with a perpetual menace or actual hostilities. We neither expect to make the journey to Canossa, nor to make terms on any other basis than a universal triumph of the pure Gospel of peace.

There are, however, occurrences within the limits of Protestant foreign operations, for which no valid pretext can be pleaded. The prospect of schism would seem in some cases to awaken no dread, and its *Evangelistic* bitter fruits no compunction. It is notorious that here and *piracy.* there a lofty indifference has been shown to the local rights and the successful labours of faithful Missionaries. Evangelistic piracy has been practised. The only apology at times offered for it is an alleged defect in ordinances. Church members and catechumens are plied with objections to the teachings of those men who, at an outlay of no small time and self-denial, have brought to them the Gospel of our Lord. The ministrations of such are pronounced invalid. Industrious endeavour is made—and with a measure of success—to entice them into a different fold. Is that Gospel propagation or sectarian spoliation? Home authorities have, by sufferance, if not by formal permission, sometimes sanctioned such vexatious proceedings.

But Churchly arrogance is not the only form of mischievous interference. There are free lances, whose errantry is, at times, pursued with heedless disregard of Missionary rights. This differs from the organised plunder just spoken of, as freebooting differs from regular warfare.*

III. Consequent evils. Of course sad results follow. Not only is there a needless waste of forces, but a sort of evangelistic anarchy ensues. The welfare of newly-established Churches is imperilled. Rivalries, perplexities, discords are inevitable. If a thorn in the flesh is needed, the perseverance of saints may thus be helped on. The Apostle Paul, referring to those who preached Christ of contention, thinking to add affliction to his bonds, rejoices thus: " I know that this shall turn to my salvation." But while Divine

* It is not yet six months since the organ of a religious body which patronises a proselytising irruption into a Mission-field amply occupied by another denomination, gloried thus in the schism : " A man stronger than you has entered your house, and bound you, and is spoiling your goods." The long and successful occupancy of that field is coarsely ridiculed as " Squatter Sovereignty " (" The Apostolic Guide," Cincinnati, Ohio, Feb. 3rd, 1888).

Providence knows how to strike straight strokes with crooked sticks, it is not for such to set themselves up as a means of grace.

EMBARRASSMENTS FORESTALLED.

Can these mischiefs be mitigated, if not prevented ? Certainly they can and ought to ibe. There are principles of propriety, indeed self-evident maxims of morality, which cannot fail, sooner or later, to be accepted by all as applicable to Foreign Missions. Certain precautions may suitably be formulated at this time ; and if they, as well as the principles already enunciated, are approved by so large and representative a body, they will tend to unify general sentiment and practice.

I. Missionary candidates and Missionaries should be duly instructed. Home influences, emanating from just views on this subject in the Churches and in administering Boards, are indispensable. It is needless to enlarge upon a point so obvious.

II. The intention to establish a new Mission should be published seasonably and widely. Simultaneous independent movements in the same direction may thus be obviated. When the thought is entertained of entering a field already occupied in part, early correspondence should be had with those who have pre-occupied the ground.*

Territorial allotment should be carefully sought and regarded. This may seem to be only a reiteration, but it is demanded both by good neighbourhood and by evangelistic economy. The co-existence of different nationalities and languages may constitute a reasonable exception in some cases, as has already been stated. A general consensus has also determined that exceptions may be made in favour of certain populous seaports and interior centres. But if no adequate reasons, local, linguistic, or racial, exist for joint occupation, then should a geographical distribution be made between different agencies, circulation of the Sacred Scriptures included, and that distribution should be strictly observed. The history of Missions shows but too plainly that there is occasion for introducing this topic. At the Second Union Missionary Conference in London, the autumn of 1854, a paper was read which included the subject of territorial relations.†

* It is now half a century since the American Board took action as follows :—
"Resolved, that this Board respectfully suggest and recommend, whenAn old resolution ever a Society has a Mission already in a district of country where another
of the
A.B.C.F.M. Society contemplates operations, that it be deemed suitable that the
Societies, whose Missionaries are already in the field, be apprised of the fact, and consulted before such operations are commenced" (Annual Report, 1838, p. 34).
The observance of this obvious rule has often already resulted happily. The Prudential Committee of that Board having, for instance, conditionally instructed the Sandwich Island Mission to send some of their number to the Marquesas Islands, three brethren sailed from Honolulu to the Society Islands (July 18, 1832), and discussed the whole subject of Missions in the Pacific, with the English brethren. The latter proposed that the contemplated Mission should be postponed till word could be had from London, but if that were deemed inexpedient, they consented to give up the Northern Marquesas group (Washington Islands) to American occupation. The three men visited those Islands, and reported a fair prospect of success. But the Prudential Committee, upon learning that the Islands were regarded as a part of the field occupied by the London Society, sent instructions to take no further steps in the line which had been thought of.

† By the Rev. J. B. Marsden. "Evangelical Christendom," vol. viii., p. 432.

The same has received attention at sundry similar convocations, both general and local, that have since been convened. The latest assembly of the kind, held in the City of Mexico, the present year (January 31st to February 3rd), composed of the representatives of eleven denominations, divided into eighteen distinct Missions, adopted pertinent resolutions, without a dissenting voice.*

An equitable division of fields and labours is in accord with Scripture teaching and example. From the college of Apostles one devoted himself to the circumcision and another to the uncircumcision. Nothing more is needed than that the Oriental courtesy of Abram become prevalent : " Let there be no strife, I pray thee, between thee and me, and between my herdmen and thy herdmen, for we be brethren. If thou wilt take the left hand, then I will go to the right ; or if thou depart to the right hand, then I will go to the left." Pleasing illustrations have occurred within the present century. Among many, one occurred fifty years since. When labourers, under the Church Missionary Society, were dismissed on account of irregular proceedings, but refused to yield the ground to other Missionaries of that Society, the London Society declined their offer of service unless they would remove to a different district.

REMOVAL OF DIFFICULTIES.

It is supposable—and unhappily facts confirm the supposition—that serious embarrassments may arise. The forenamed and other cautionary measures being imperfectly observed, there comes an antagonism of interests. Trespass is charged, and complications seem to forbid the hope of adjustment by any of the methods hitherto suggested. What shall be done ? No positive human enactment can be made or enforced. Yet some irenic device is required. Mediation naturally suggests itself. Of course, nothing like the High Court of Appeal in England can be contemplated. We would not employ even the term *arbitration*, implying thereby an authoritative umpire to decide difficulties. But—

1. *A Committee of Reference can be appointed.* It may consist of one or more members. An impartial referee, or Board of Referees being constituted, will receive statements, oral or written, and then give, not a decree, unless so requested, but an opinion on the merits of the case submitted. Something analagous to this is found in Denmark, called Courts of Conciliation. They have no official standing, and neither party is legally bound by the judgment rendered. The object *Danish Courts of Conciliation and Arbitration.*

* " 1. Resolved : That in towns not occupied by any Christian denomination, where the population is fifteen thousand or over, more than one denomination may enter. And that it is recommended that in places of less than fifteen thousand, where there are already established more than one denomination, the *Resolutions of Conference in Mexico.* place shall be ceded to the one which first occupied it, save in the case of private agreement between the interested parties. In case of difficulties about the arrangement of the particulars of disoccupation, the matter shall be resolved by the Committee of Arbitration, hereinafter provided for.

" 2. That a place formerly occupied by a denomination, and afterward abandoned for one year or more, may be occupied by another on invitation by any one in the place, or even without such invitation.

" 3. That by the occupation of a place is to be understood the organisation of a congregation in said place, and, furthermore, the holding of stated religious services in the same."

of these Courts is to prevent needless and irritating litigation, the judge aiming to give an opinion which will reasonably prevent the carrying of a controversy into the regular law courts. The expedient is said to work well, especially by economising in time, expense, and hard feelings. Something analagous may also be seen in the resort to arbitration for the settlement of international differences. In the more civilised political world there is now an auspicious drift favourable to the establishment of a Court of Reference, to which matters in dispute between Governments may be sent for adjudication. A permanent peace policy is gaining in the esteem of all the wise and philanthropic. It would be superfluous to remind this assembly of a recent deputation from England, embracing Members of Parliament and other gentlemen, who were bearers of an address to the President and Congress of the United States. That address, signed by over two hundred and thirty members of Parliament, contemplates a provision for the adjustment of complications that may arise between Great Britain and the United States. It is already a third of a century (1856), since forty-six nations bound themselves, in the Treaty of Paris, to abide by a declaration of certain maritime regulations. Since 1815 there have been between fifty and sixty instances of arbitration for the adjustment of international differences. Does it become the Christian Church, in her aggressive, yet peaceful movements, to be behind civil governments in efforts for peace ?

2. *Appointment of the Committee.* No costly and elaborate machinery is required. This Conference might designate one permanent Committee of Reference for the entire sisterhood of Societies ; or one in each of the three or more countries of leading Missionary enterprise ; or might recommend a method of appointment as occasion shall offer. An experiment, somewhat in this line, has already been proposed on one Missionary field for its own better guidance.*

3. *Advantages Resulting.* Instead of heated public discussion and chronic alienations, Missions and Missionary Societies may thus have the prompt arbitrament of Christian candour. Delicate questions relating to precedence, to geographical boundaries, to pecuniary claims, to conflicting methods, and whatever assumes a grave aspect, might—by mutual consent—be thus referred. Provide properly for adjustment, and grievances will be less likely to arise. When the

---

* The recent Conference of Protestant Missions in Mexico, besides resolutions already cited, adopted the following :—

" 4. That a Committee of Arbitration be named by this assembly, to be composed of one member of each denomination herein represented, to examine and Resolutions resolve the questions that may arise in connection with the subject of Conference treated of in the resolutions. The decisions of the Committee shall be in Mexico. without appeal, and therefore final, when two-thirds of its members vote either affirmatively or negatively on any subject presented for their decision.

" 5. That this agreement shall be valid until the next meeting of the General Assembly.

" 6. That if any other Evangelical denomination shall begin Missionary work in the country, its attention shall be called to this agreement, and it shall be invited to enter into the same, by naming the representative to serve on the Committee of Arbitration.

" 7. When a Mission represented by a Chairman of the Committee of Arbitration, shall be an interested party in any question presented, the Committee shall name another to preside in such a case."

need of justification before the Christian world shall be felt, a restraint will be put upon doubtful movements. Christianity is, by way of eminence, the religion of love and peace. May this great Missionary Conference lead to a cosmopolitan concordat.

The **Chairman** said that Dr. Warneck had asked for the sympathy of the Conference in reference to the subject to which he had drawn attention, and to his own position at that time. He would, therefore ask Dr. Murray Mitchell to lead them in prayer on behalf of their friend.

Dr. **Murray Mitchell** offered prayer.

DISCUSSION.

Rev. J. N. Murdock, D.D. (Secretary, American Baptist Missionary Union) : Mr. Chairman,—I have asked the privilege of saying a few words for a special purpose; but lest I should not be able to refer to the matter again I wish to express my hearty approval of the admirable Paper which has been read by my very distinguished friend Dr. Thompson.

In a " Manual of Evangelical Protestant Missions," prepared by Dr. H. Gundert, the Society which I have the honour to represent has been noticed in a peculiar way. We have been charged with over-reaching and over-grasping in the case of the Lutheran Mission in the Telugu country, and also in reference to the Bostonian Mission (I sup- *American Baptist and* pose the American Board of Commissioners for Foreign Missions) *Lutheran* in Asia Minor. My friend has disposed of the last charge and *Societies.* statement. We have not interfered with the work of the American Board of Commissioners in Asia Minor, and, God helping us, we shall never interfere in the way indicated in the charge. But with reference to our Telugu Mission you may not be aware that we entered the country twenty-two years before our Lutheran friends in the United States, for whom we entertain the very highest regard. Whatever trespass we may have committed upon other Societies, we have not consciously committed any trespass upon these dear brethren. We occupied the town which became their central station many years before they did, and we withdrew from it simply because we had not the men to occupy it. We recommenced there, as you know, in the great movement running from 1868 to 1878, during which more than twenty-five thousand converts were gathered into the churches of our Telugu Mission.

Our native preachers traversed the whole region. The Church at Ongole had become so great that it was impossible to work the field from that centre, and we found it necessary to establish a line of stations to the north of us. We had already gone north to Secunderabad and to Hanamaconda, twenty-five miles north of Secunderabad, and we found it necessary to establish stations that we might guard and nourish the disciples who had so suddenly and unexpectedly come to our charge. We established a station at Bapatla on the coast, and at Vinukonda. Our Lutheran brethren complained that we had trespassed on their territory. They appointed a Commission to visit us, and we on our part appointed two brethren, myself being one of them, and after a care- *A mutual* ful survey of the whole question we came to this decision : In the *agreement.* first place, that under the peculiar circumstances of the case it was impossible to separate our work by any geographical lines ; they had so interlaced without our intention, without any purpose of ours, that it was impossible to separate them. In the second place, we agreed that the Missionaries be instructed to press it upon the native preachers that they refrain from any denominational appeal, or from an appeal to any caste prejudices, with a view to win disciples from one Society to the other.

In the third place we agreed that wherever either Society had so much as a school established, the agents of the other Society should refrain from going there. And in the fourth place we agreed to instruct the Missionaries to be very careful in receiving members from either party until they had ascertained that they came free of all taint, or in any way subject to any form of discipline. We thought that the observance of these rules might obviate all difficulties. In making this statement I do not wish to cast any reflection upon our Lutheran brethren, but I simply wish to clear ourselves of a thing that we never contemplated, and that we never would have done. Unhappily fresh difficulties arose, on which I must not say more, in the absence of the other party, than that we feel quite guiltless of any violation of these rules.

Rev. H. Williams (C.M.S., from Bengal): My object in saying a few words is to emphasise the desirability of a common understanding about the interchange of workers. The Mission to which I belong in Bengal has enabled me in a special way to become acquainted with this part of the subject. It is a large Mission about seventy miles north of Calcutta, and a great many of the workers in Bengal are drawn from that Mission. I see, therefore, the necessity of such an understanding as is here *Violations of Comity.* referred to. I regret to say that again and again in the experience of the last ten years I have seen men and women going from our Mission, and being employed in other Missions without any reference to us—native men and women whom they never would have appointed if they had first made inquiry of us. With regard to the women I may give you one very clear instance. A woman had misconducted herself; she was an agent of ours, and she was excommunicated in our churches. She went down to Calcutta, and the next we heard of her was that she was being employed as a Bible woman there. It was only by our making a strong protest that she was taken out of that position as long as her excommunication lasted, but then she was taken on again. I do think that we need to have something said about this matter here.

With regard to the subject of boundaries and districts, in Bengal, as far as my experience allows me to judge, we do not feel the difficulty so much in the country parts; on the contrary there is a very good understanding, I think, between the Missionary Societies. Honourable mention has been made of the Society to which I rejoice to belong, the Church Missionary Society, and as one of its Missionaries I should like to pay a tribute of respect to the *Comity between C.M.S. and Baptists.* noble Society of the Baptists, and to the way in which they have worked with us in Bengal. Some dissatisfied persons in our Mission have before now sent to some of our Baptist brethren begging them to come and establish a Church in our district, and the practice of our brethren in Calcutta has been to put such a letter into an envelope and send it to our Missionaries. How is this kind of common understanding to be brought about? I think, first of all, it should come about here at home among the Secretaries and Boards in England and America; and then on the field there should be the Committees of Reference which have been proposed in the Paper which has been read to us.

Rev. Professor Aiken, D.D. (Princeton, U.S.A.): The single point upon which I wish to say a word is a point lying directly behind the one brought before us in Dr. Thompson's Paper, and touched upon again and again already, namely, the refusal to employ in one Society the agents of another. I want to go to the back of that, and suggest the greatest caution in taking up the candidates of one Society for employment in another. Let me illustrate what I want to say by a single case in connection with our own training of theological students at Princeton within the last year or two. Eight years ago two young Bulgarians came to Princeton, and both entered upon the academic course in the college of New Jersey. After completing their academic course they entered upon a theological course. One went to a Presbyterian seminary in Allegheny, and the other came to us. When they reached the end of their course the question was how they should find employment among their own people.

Employing the agents of other Societies.

One of these two young men accepted an overture made to him by the American Methodist Board, and he goes back as one of their employés. The other, who was our student, came to me for advice. I said, "Do not seem to change your faith for the sake of a commission; do not take employment there unless your own conviction leads you to do it, and enables you to do it heartily." He is now pursuing a course of medical study, that he may have two modes of working for the benefit of his people. This suggests the point on which I wish to lay stress, that there should be the greatest tenderness and carefulness in dealing with candidates for employment in the Mission-field.

Mr. John Archibald (National Bible Society of Scotland, from Hankow): I do not enter into this matter on my own account, but rather on behalf of some who would gladly have been here this morning, only they are at the other side of the globe. "Behold, how good a thing it is for brethren to dwell together in unity." If you wanted to see that you would only have to go to the other side of China on the banks of the Yang-tse, and there you would see it for yourselves. I do not believe in geographical divisions, because we find that by working together we can help one another a great deal more than we hinder one another.

Much real Comity in China.

In China some years ago there was a Mission manned by a brother who was a kindly, God-fearing man, and was a great help to us all; but a change occurred. A new Bishop came out who had new clergy and new views, and he made a new departure. There was new teaching with regard to the subject which we are considering this morning, and it is that which I wish to bring before you. There is no harm in my naming the Church, because nobody will find it out. The Chinese name of it is, "The Holy Catholic Church." The Bishop, teaching his converts in a catechism issued about two years ago, says this: "In regard to the sin of sectarianism, how are we to pray? The Common Prayer Book says: 'From all sedition, privy conspiracy, and rebellion, from all false doctrine, heresy, and schism, deliver us.' Has Jesus said anything in regard to it? He has spoken words of warning to us. 'And many false prophets shall arise and shall deceive many' (Matt. xxix. 11). What does St. Paul say? 'The time will come when they will not endure sound doctrine' (2 Tim. iv. 3, 4). Are there any other arousing words with reference to this? There are in the second Epistle of Peter, second and third chapters, and the whole of the Epistle of Jude. What about those who have been brought up from their childhood among the sects? Their sin is comparatively lighter because of their ignorance. In regard to sectarians, may we lead them with words? No one has ever seen a blind man on the point of stepping into danger without informing him (of the danger); we must act like-

A striking exception.

wise. Is there anything else we ought to do? We ought to pray the Lord of Heaven, the great Shepherd, to lead these lost sheep into the fold."

The Bishop was immediately followed by one of his own clergy, who also wrote another book which was issued at our centre. It is much to the same effect, but it is too long for me to give quotations from it. The writer says: "Now why do I desire that all the Christians in China should join the Holy Catholic Churches of England and America? This is my reason: The converts connected with the Gospel Halls (Nonconformist Churches) cannot join the Roman Catholic Hall without giving up essential doctrines, but they can join the Holy Catholic Churches of England and America without giving up any essential doctrines. The converts connected with the Roman Catholic Hall cannot join the Gospel Halls without giving up essential doctrines, but they can join the Holy Catholic Church without giving up any essential doctrine. Thus the important thing for all believers in the Lord Jesus is to become united in the Holy Catholic Church." These are the principles; now what is the practice? Although, numerically, but a weak Mission, they began at Shanghai, multiplying stations, and they have planted their stations all up and down the Yang-tse, alongside other and older stations and nowhere else. Wherever they have gone they have carried on this work of enlightening the blind and the ignorant, and leading them to the truth. And what has been the result? The result is this— that confusion has been introduced. I hold in my hand a protest issued by one Mission against this work. There are twelve cases of men who have been, in a measure, bought over; in one instance a whole Church,—a little one—the whole congregation—was taken away. Hence this protest has been issued.

Now what is to be done I do not know. It seems to me that, as we have been denouncing agnostic literature, we should have some indignation for this kind of literature that I have referred to. We have been denouncing the opium traffic and the traffic in rum and gin; I think we ought also to denounce this trade in babes in Christ. It is working a great mischief. I can read letters written by converts to an old Missionary showing how this thing works. This is one of them:—"We, the undersigned disciples, had in our former state been long lost in the devil's world. We are indebted to the venerable teacher for our rescue from the sea of misery; surely no good fortune could have been greater than that. Now we have been searching the Scriptures, inquiring into the root and branches, and we find that the Holy Catholic Church is the root; we therefore ought to revert to the Catholic Church. On this account we write a few words to thank the venerable teacher for his kindness of former days, and to make known to him our present good fortune. Moreover, it is our hope that the venerable teacher himself will return to the Catholic Church."

Such letters as these have been written; and as an old Missionary says, "Is it not a pitiable thing that after labouring thirty years in this land I should find that men, whom I baptised in their infancy twenty years ago, are to-day discussing the question whether I am a minister of Christ or not?" I think that something ought to be done. There seems to be a conspiracy of silence on the subject. We have to meet the same difficulty that Paul met in the case of Judaising teachers, and we ought to meet it in the same way.

Their method of proselytising.

The disturbing influence.

The system should be denounced.

Rev. A. H. Arden (C.M.S., from South India): Upon this subject, it is most important that there should be some definite outcome from this Conference. I am afraid that many persons in speaking of it will say, "It was all very nice and interesting, but what was the outcome of it?" It is twenty-five years since I went to India, and I must say that we have suffered severely in our Mission work from the lack of brethren recognising those great principles which we have been laying down. Now what I would ask is this, that we should at this Conference pass some strong resolutions condemning the practice of one Society making inroads into the territory of another. I may give you one illustration. I had in an interesting Mission district a cluster of four or five villages. One of them was particularly unsatisfactory. The people had asked for baptism, but they were utterly unfit for it. An agent of *An illustration of non-recognition.* another Society passes through that village : he does not stay a week there, but he baptises a considerable number of the natives just in the very middle of the circle of my villages, and he then leaves them, and, as far as I know, he has never to this day been near them again. That is the sort of thing we sometimes meet with. I have no doubt the man did it in earnestness, and that he thought he was doing a great work. At the same time it is the upsetting of all rule and order in the Mission-field.

I was exceedingly sorry to hear a speaker say that we cannot respect or regard geographical boundaries. Now I think that is just the thing that we ought to do. If geographical boundaries are not *Geographical boundaries* observed, what *is* to be observed ? Why should an agent from *to be observed.* another Society come into another Missionary's district, and stir up ill-feeling ?

In regard to Tinnevelly, I believe that one of the greatest reasons for the great success in that Mission has been concentrated effort, and its being left to one body of Christians ; and I believe that Missions will make great progress, if certain districts are left in the hands of certain definite Societies. I know that we make a great deal of differences at home. Thank God, we make uncommonly little of them abroad, and I most firmly believe that the natives think very little of our differences. You may get half-a-dozen Brahmans in a room who will not eat, and who will not intermarry with one another, because they hold different doctrines with regard to the soul. But I have known men trained in very high Church ideas, who, nevertheless, because the Wesleyan Chapel was two hundred yards nearer their own house, constantly attended it ; and they did not see much difference after all. They had given up their Vishnu : and they had grasped the great and glorious Christ ; and that is the main point.

I would emphasise most strongly the undesirability of taking agents from other Societies without a mutual understanding. When I was in Madras a very intelligent Brahman Christian offered himself to me. I said, "Whom do you belong to ?" He replied : "I have been work- *Taking agents from other* ing with the Wesleyans." "Then," I said, "I will go to the *Societies.* Wesleyans, and see the secretary, and we will discuss the subject." There was no difficulty ; and the matter was arranged most pleasantly. A short time ago I was speaking to the Missionary who was the means of bringing that man to Christ ; and he rejoiced (as we can all rejoice) that the man made a change in an honourable and proper way, and went on well under new circumstances. I do most strongly emphasise the point that we should not break up this Conference, without at any rate passing some very strong resolutions that we can point to and say, "The united Conference completely condemned an inroad into another Missionary's territory, or an exchange of agents without reference to those by whom they had been employed. If a strong protest were made upon this point, I think there would be some practical outcome of this intensely interesting Conference.

Rev. E. Van Orden (Brazil) : If we cannot pass resolutions I hope the outcome of this Conference will be a Board of Reference ; for difficulties in Missions multiply not only in India but in Brazil, and I would *Suggests* call attention to the fact that the Bible Societies should divide *a Board of* their fields better than they do at present. I have been in *Reference.* Brazil for the last ten years, and I have employed a colporteur partly paid by a Society in Glasgow, and a Society in America sent a colporteur into the same field, followed by a colporteur from some Society in London. Now that is a waste of time and a waste of money,—a waste of time because there are millions of people who have not the Bible in Brazil, and a waste of money because we have not money enough to supply the men that are wanted. Why should not these Societies divide Brazil among them? The same thing goes on still. Why should not one Society take the north of Brazil, and the other Society take the south, each being responsible for its own field, instead of leaving many places in Brazil where not a single Bible can be had?

Then I wish to call attention to the fact that the Presbyterian Board of Foreign Missions has had Missions in Brazil for twenty-eight years, along the coast, and that another Society of the Southern States has entered into our field, and created some unpleasant feelings by setting forth their peculiar doctrines and making some mischief among the members of our Churches.

Now, brethren, when the field is so large, when we have entire provinces in Brazil that have no Missionaries, I ask you in the name of common sense and in the name of the Gospel, is it right that Missionaries of other *Evil of inroads.* denominations, which differ in some points from ours, should not rather go to these provinces where there is no Missionary than go to provinces where Missionaries are already established? More depends upon the men sometimes than upon the Societies, therefore I advocate the creation of a Board of Reference, such Board to be chosen by the different Societies, to which they pledge themselves to submit all questions of this kind. We agree in many points on the Mission-field, and I am sure that these little difficulties in due time, with the help of God, and with prayer and supplication, will all be removed, and God shall be glorified.

The Acting Secretary: I would suggest that our brethren should avoid naming Societies in their speeches. Our friend, Mr. Van Orden, has named at least four Societies. Probably the representatives of all those four Societies may be in the meeting, and may want to answer him, and they will certainly not get the chance because of the number of names already sent in.

Rev. J. E. Padfield, B.D. (C.M.S., from Masulipatam): As an old Missionary of some twenty years' standing, let me say that, from bitter experience in our Mission, we do feel the importance of this subject. I fully agree with all that was said in the admirable address to which we have listened. Would that its sentiments were always carried into action in the Mission-field! It is pleasant to hear of the action taken by one Society. Would that all Societies acted in the same way! But unfortunately they do not. I do not know that I should have spoken this morning had it not been for a report from our own Mission, which only came to me three days ago. It is so thoroughly *apropos* of this subject that I felt I must speak. The report to which I refer is from one of our Missionaries who went to the field where he is now labouring, some thirty years ago. There were then little more than a hundred converts in the whole of that part of the country, whilst at present there are more than eight thousand, and the Mission is well manned both by European and native agents. Yet this brother Missionary speaks in the most bitter terms of interlopers coming to his own doors and interfering with his work. Ought these things to be so?

I do think that, in spite of what has been said, it would be a good outcome of this influential gathering if we could send out to our brethren in the Mission-field some rules for corporate action, and lay down some definite lines on this subject. Let it not all end in mere sentiment and **Desirability of rules for guidance.** words. People at home cannot fully understand the evil that is done by this sort of action that we are deprecating. It interferes so much with our work, both as regards the heathen before us, and also with our infant Churches. Remember how weak they are. Surely you have room enough in England and America for your bitter controversies about mint, anise, and cummin! Ought we not as Missionary Societies to attend to these "weightier matters," brotherly love, Christian charity, the unity of the spirit in the bond of peace? With regard to the second point, as to the agents, I have myself had agents whom I have been obliged to dismiss for great un-satisfactoriness, and they have simply gone to another Mission and been employed without the slightest reference to me. This is not an uncommon thing, and I am sorry to say men are taken on without any reference, and they also sometimes get higher pay. Is not this a premium upon bad conduct on the part of native agents? I would strongly emphasise the desirability of taking some corporate action in this matter.

Rev. Paulus Kammerer (Basle Missionary Society, from China): I only want to give additional testimony to the fact that we have great diffi-culties on our Chinese Mission-field in regard to this question. Three German Missionary Societies have hindered each other in the province of Canton by such rivalry. I assure you that all the troubles I have met with in the course of eleven years' Missionary life have not caused me so much pain and discouragement as the trouble arising from **Suffering from disregard of boundaries.** rivalry in regard to boundaries. Not only has this rivalry no blessing attending it, but it is just the reverse. The evil can only be removed by the Boards at home; and it would be a very good thing if the Boards at home would agree to recall their Missionaries from fields where such rivalry takes place, leaving such fields to those who first occupied them. I could give you specimens of my own experience in other Mission-fields. I have been asked by the Chinese how it comes about that near an old Missionary station a Missionary from another Society started another Mission and received people who have been dismissed by the Missionaries of the other station. "How is this?" I have been asked. " They are now showing hostility one against another. What does it all mean?" I could not give an answer, and I felt ashamed of myself. We should all take care to avoid such deplorable occurrences. The matter should be dealt with, as I have said, by the Boards at home, and I trust that this Conference will induce them to take it up.

Rev. A. Merensky (Superintendent, Berlin Missionary Society): I only rise to state that our Berlin Missionary Society has been working in perfect harmony with the other English, Scotch, and German Missionary Societies in South Africa. In British Kaffraria our Missionaries are working side by side with the Presbyterians of Scotland, who have their beautiful station of Lovedale. In Natal they are working side by side with the **Examples of Comity.** American Board in perfect friendship. The Missionaries of the American Board have taken the coast, and the German Societies have taken the upper parts of the colony. In the Transvaal we are labour-ing with the Hermansburg Society, and are taking the whole country of the Transvaal between us. We take the east, and they take the west. When a chief came to us, and pleaded to have a Missionary, he was sent to the Missionaries who had charge of that part. In the northern part of the Transvaal the Swiss brethren came after us, but there was no difficulty with them; they took the whole country of Makwamba lower down, leaving to us the tribes amongst whom we had been working hitherto.

But I am sorry to state that we have of late years had great trouble on account of another Society having come in behind us. In the country of Sekukuni, where we had been fifteen years, and where Christians of our Church had shed their blood for the faith, they sent their Missionaries, although there was no need to do so, as we told them that we were fully prepared to occupy the whole country. There we had three Missionaries among a tribe of thirty thousand souls, but still they sent another Missionary. I do not think it wise to over-stock one country, and leave others without the Gospel. We have had painful incidents of this kind. It is really not a pleasure to mention such things. A farm where we had erected a chapel was bought by this Society, notwithstanding our remonstrances. Native helpers have been almost bought over by them, and so on. Such things must create great confusion in native minds. If there is not one method with regard to baptism, with regard to instruction, with regard to heathen customs, and with regard to discipline, great confusion must be created, and not only is great damage done to the promotion of the work, but I believe that souls will be lost by such a practice. I wish to press the responsibility upon those who are the cause of such proceedings. Could not this Conference do something by which these lamentable occurrences might be avoided in future ?

The contrary.

Rev. G. E. Post, M.D. (Beyrout): Sixty-five years ago the Mission of the American Board was commenced at Jerusalem. After a certain period there was an intimation that the Church Missionary Society wished to enter into the work in those sacred lands. The American Board and their Mission in Syria in a spirit of Christian Comity set apart Palestine for the work of the Church Missionary Society, and retired from it. This was done in the interests of peace and brotherhood. The Mission in Syria has continued on that basis ever since, and I am happy to say that the Mission of the Church Missionary Society has also continued to preserve its territorial boundaries. But there are influences at work in Jerusalem to overstep these boundaries. There was an Episcopal visitation made into Mount Lebanon last year, and two members of the Presbyterian Church were confirmed and admitted into the membership of an Episcopal Church which does not exist. Christian brethren, is this right, and will you endorse it ? I might go on to speak of other infusions of the same character. Let me emphasise this, that the Church Missionary Society has no earthly responsibility for what has occurred, and I believe they are as much grieved over it as we are. In Syria, which is so small in its territorial extent, in addition to the original Mission of the American Board which has been transferred to the Presbyterian Board, there are no fewer than *seven different Societies belonging to as many different Churches, besides the schools of the Plymouth Brethren*, who belong to no denomination, and a *multitude of free lances corvetting* from end to end of that land, and now we have another Church Society hovering about our northern border. Brethren, this is contrary to the spirit of Christianity, and I call upon you, if not by resolution, by your single voice to spread it throughout the world that these things shall not be. We love peace, but we do not want to go to pieces in our efforts to Christianise the world.

Dr. Post's practice and experience.

Rev. T. W. Chambers, D.D. (Reformed Church in America): It seems to me that this is the most important thing that has come before the Conference. In other things we are propagating Christianity, here we wish to carry it out in action. We all know a good deal of this matter privately. These things are not put in the papers, because people do not like to publish them; but what a revelation we have had this morning. I thought I knew something about it; after what these brethren have said, I find I do not know anything.

It seems to me that every member of this Conference is bound henceforth at home with his own Missionary organisation to stand up for the principle of Christian charity and Christian comity. The Apostle says, "Giving diligence to keep the unity of the Spirit God gives, let us in the bond of peace." Now you did not make that unity, the keep, unity. Holy Ghost made it, but you can mar it. Hence the Apostle says, "Giving diligence *to keep* the unity of the Spirit in the bond of peace." Each Missionary is bound to do that, and each member of each Missionary Society is bound to use his influence at home constantly in this direction. Bear and forbear, act your Christianity as well as preach it.

If another man intrudes on your territory, go away; try to get him to go, but if you do not succeed go yourself. That is the spirit of the Sermon on the Mount; that is the spirit of Christianity as I understand it. Mutual It is the hardest thing for Christians to learn and act upon. The forbearance. great object of Christians should be not to assert their rights but to perform their duties. They too often want to assert their rights, cherishing revenge and retaliation. What we need is to create a strong influence at home so as to help our Mission Boards to proclaim these principles and act upon them so that we may show the spirit of Christianity while we are proclaiming its precepts far and wide throughout the heathen world.

Rev. J. Hudson Taylor (China Inland Mission): I most cordially echo the sentiment to which we have just listened. I believe that the great way to win a battle very frequently is not to resist. But there are circumstances such as those which our friend Mr. Archibald has brought before us this morning that are causing very great embarrassment in China, and I think that some of those who are most tried about them are not tried, because The injury to the proselytes. they find eight, or ten, or twelve of their worst and poorest members who are open to being bribed, so much as for the sake of the souls of these poor people. It often happens that persons under discipline are put prominently forward as teachers and catechists. One feels that it is almost hopeless to try and do them good under such circumstances, and that very great sorrow and evil is the result. Now I think we must discriminate between occasional difficult cases in which possibly there may be differences of opinion between good men and a general principle. Is it right that such publications as those from which Mr. Archibald has read to us should be circulated among our native Christians? Is it right that there should be circulated authorised publications stating that all Presbyterians, Congregationalists, Methodists, Baptists, and all of every other section of the Church than the one which issues these things are without the true root and have not the doctrines of salvation, but are left to the uncovenanted mercies of God.

Dear friends, could not something be done in the way of remedying these things? I can scarcely think that the Boards at home would not be open to a wise and courteous Christian representation of the evils of these things. Time,

I am afraid, will not admit of going into this matter further in detail. One sees the difficulty that there would be if we were to attempt to pass resolutions here, but I think that many of the leading Societies are here represented ; and could not some Committee of Secretaries or others deal with this question in such a way as to bring the united influence of a large part of the Christian Church to bear upon those bodies that neglect this important matter? One word before I sit down. After an experience of thirty-four years in intercourse with Missionaries of nearly every denomination, let me say that *I hope this audience will not go away with the idea that these discourtesies are the rule. Brotherly love is the rule.* I have experienced it to an extent that it would take a very long time to relate. But, unfortunately, these sore feelings do arise at times, and then we cannot help sympathising with our brethren who are so afflicted.

Lack of Comity the exception.

Dr. Underhill : I wish to refer very briefly to two points. One relates to a remark that was made to-day as to whether some Board of Reference could not be appointed in this country to take up such questions as these. Our brethren do not seem to be aware, that the present happy relations that exist among all the leading Missionary Societies of Great Britain, have been greatly brought about by a monthly meeting of the Secretaries of these Societies in London. At that Board I sat for many years, and I know that many of these questions came before us, and were settled in a way in which you would desire that they should be settled. Similar Boards exist in heathen countries amongst the Missionaries. There is an admirable one that has been constituted for many years sitting in Calcutta, and that Board has been influential in creating permanent peace among the Missionaries working in various parts of Bengal. Now why should not Missionaries in all countries associate themselves together in that way? A large proportion of these cases cannot be settled at home, because we could not get all the essential facts before us. But let the Missionaries in any district or country have their monthly or quarterly meeting, and you would soon find that their assembling together would create a sense of unity, of affection, and of esteem, which would prevent a great many of these unhappy occurrences.

United prayer meetings promote Comity.

The other point is one which I will only briefly allude to, as it would take too long to discuss it. It is referred to in the programme under the letter (a) "Transfer of converts and congregations," and under (b) "Is there a stage in the progress of Christian work in any district where such an understanding cannot be applied ?" Now, brethren, there is such a stage, and it is a very difficult thing to deal with when it comes. I mean the formation and existence of independent Churches. You know perfectly well that you have no control or power over the Christian conscience, and when a Church of Christ is constituted, that Church has the inherent right to follow the Master's laws whithersoever they lead. An independent Church is not to be controlled by any organisation or Missionary Society whatever, and as fast as you create congregations and Christian Churches, those congregations and Churches will assert their rights. There is the difficulty. The question is how to prevent collision and strife amongst them. I do not know how it is to be done, but I beg my brethren to take the matter into their most serious consideration. The Missionary Societies feel that it is one of the great difficulties that spring out of our work, out of its great triumphs and glorious successes—the formation of independent ecclesiastical organisations following, as they believe, the laws of the New Testament. I hope you will look at that point and seek for some solution of the problem.

Mere rules ineffectual.

Rev. John Ross (United Presbyterian Mission, Manchuria): Though I am well acquainted with the state of matters existing in Mission-fields among foreign nations, of which we have had some glimpses to-day, I question whether the majority of the influential members of this Conference are so familiar with these facts. It seems to me that one effect of the statements made to-day will be to cause perplexity in the minds of those interested in and anxious for the propagation of the Gospel in foreign parts. For the last week or two we have been pleading for funds, and for men to send into the unoccupied parts of the earth, and during this whole forenoon we have been told that we have been treading on each other's heels, and interfering with each other in all parts of the world. I should like as a Christian and a Missionary to urge upon those who have influence to take steps to utilise more effectually, and scatter in directions in which they could be more useful, the forces already in the field.

I do not join in the cry for an enormous increase of Missionaries in China, but I do urge upon those interested in China to utilise with greater efficiency the forces already existing there, and to break them up. We do not want a great host of men sent into Manchuria. What we do want is to see the stations occupied by two or three men working all round that neighbourhood, one at one station and another *Utilising of forces in the field.* at another. I believe that China will be better evangelised, that it will have far brighter notions of Christianity, and a better acquaintance with the spirit of Christianity in that way than by agglomerating several Societies and a large number of Missionaries in little centres. At one time this distribution was impossible because the ports were the only places where Missionaries could live ; now it is possible because the Missionaries can live in any part of China. It seems to me that the root of this whole difficulty is what I would call sectarianism.

In nearing a port in China the coasting steamers hoist two flags : the house flag occupies the most prominent position, while the national flag occupies a position much lower down. Now that is what some sectarians do— the flag of the sect is hoisted on the topmost point to be seen of all *Which flag is uppermost!* eyes and at all distances, but the flag which has on it the name of Christ is on a lower level, to be seen only when you come very near. Now I wish that to be reversed. Hoist the flag with the name of Christ on it to the highest point. I do not oppose sectarianism or even friendly rivalry, but let there be no bitter hostility : let the name of the sect appear, but on the lower level, with the name of Christ high above all. Then we shall hear the last of these bitternesses and feuds on the Mission-field.

Rev. D. T. Maylott (Primitive Methodist Missionary Society): I claim the indulgence of this Conference for a minute or two, first, because I represent a Society that has had no voice in this Conference until the present time, and secondly, because having been a Missionary in Western Africa, and having visited the island of Fernando Po twice, I am glad to bear my testimony this morning to the fact that so far as that part of the Mission-field is concerned there is unity in the truest and best sense. I quite endorse what Dr. Underhill has said about *Comity in West Africa.* Missionaries meeting and conferring together upon these things. The Missionaries at Old Calabar, the Cameroons, and the Gaboon River, in connection with the Fernando Po Primitive Methodist Mission meet at stated times to confer together and help each other in their work, and we find it a matter of very great benefit for our individual stations as well as for the work of God in that part of the world. I wish to bear my testimony, too, to the brotherliness, to the kindness beyond expression, of the agents of the different sections of the Mission work in Western Africa.

The island of Fernando Po was vacated by our Baptist friends about forty years ago through the persecution of the Spanish priests. Some twenty years ago the island was visited by Bishop Crowther, and the Rev. Robert Smith, the Baptist Missionary from the Cameroons. In the meantime, however, the people had sent to this country and asked our Committee to send out Missionaries. While that message was on the way Bishop Crowther went over to the island, and visited the Europeans who subscribed £200 towards a church. While he was there Mr. Smith, the representative of the Baptist Missionary Society, also went, and claimed the Island, as the Baptists had been there previously. They heard, however, during their stay that the people had written to our Society, and to the honour of both these dear brethren be it said, Bishop Crowther said to the Europeans, " Here, gentlemen, is your money, and I will retire," and Mr. Smith said on behalf of the Baptist Missionary Society, " As you desire the Methodist brethren, though the island really belonged to us, we will retire and wish them God speed." We have had the co-operation of the Presbyterians, the Baptists, and the Church of England Societies in such a way as to make us feel that it is one Lord we all serve, and that we are one brotherhood seeking to evangelise that part of the world.

Bishop Suter, D.D. (of Nelson, N.Z.): I think it is high time that a Bishop put in an appearance upon the scene. I come from the lower part of the Pacific, and it *is* the Pacific, judging from what we have recently heard. I wish to say a word on behalf of the Melanesian Mission, which has been conducted from the very first upon the principles of Comity. Bishop Selwyn, rather a high type of Churchman, when he went out, seeing the work of the Wesleyans and Presbyterians, avoided a difficulty by communicating with them, and stating that he would take one particular part and would not interfere with the work they were doing. It is a pleasing circumstance that his son, the present Bishop of Melanesia, is carrying out exactly the same principles.

I was asked by our General Synod to go and visit the islands of Fiji, Samoa, and Tonga the other day, and in Fiji I saw one who certainly ought to be its Bishop, the Rev. Mr. Langham. In fact, brethren, you are having the thing without the name, and I believe if you had the name as well you would have much greater unity. They are Bishops, doctrinally descended from the Apostles, as I am, historically as well, but they have not the name of Bishops. If you Presbyterians would only have your Superintendents, according to the definition of John Knox, we might easily arrange matters. We would give the older ones, Dr. Post, for example, an episcopal designation *honoris causâ;* younger ones we would ask to come into the episcopal position in the way in which we ourselves do.

I believe that a good deal of this difficulty might be overcome by double ordinations. Well, what is laughed at at one Conference may become the rule ten years afterwards. I believe that to be the solution of the difficulty. If some of our young clergy were ordained both by Presbyterians and Episcopalians they might minister to both congregations. But now the work is done at the cost of two agents, practically doing the same thing. I myself would not mind going before a Presbyterian Board in order that I might be accepted by them on their principles. I have confirmed a great many Presbyterians, and I have ordained Presbyterians too, but when I have ordained them I have said, " My ordination casts no slur upon your previous ordination, it merely says that you were not ordained according to the rites and ceremonies of the Church of England, and that is what my ordination is." I think these are pregnant questions which come up for solution.

I know that there is too much of "*our* converts," "*our* Mission," "*our* Society." The whole difficulty arises, as Dr. Underhill has said, from this. There are two stages of Missionary work. You convert men from darkness to light, from the power of Satan to God. That is one stage. Then they form themselves into Churches, and then comes the difficulty: and the difficulty will increase in the next five or ten years; but it will be a shame upon us if we cannot solve it; it will be a shame upon us if we have not the Spirit of the Master and the wisdom of the Master who said, "Forbid him not, for he that is not with Me is against Me." "We saw one casting out devils in Thy name, and we forbade him because he followeth not us." "Forbid him not," said Christ, "no man can do a miracle in My name, and can lightly speak evil of Me." That is the principle which will solve this rising difficulty. *[Second stage of work: the difficulty.]*

One word more. You are anxious about your converts. Never mind; perhaps men may give to A. the honour that belongs to B., but it is all right in God's book; when He puts it down there He does not put it in the wrong column.

Rev. L. Dahle (Secretary, Norwegian Missionary Society): Mr. Chairman, ladies, and gentlemen,—I rise chiefly to state my agreement with, and my great delight in the Paper read to us by Dr. Thompson, which gave me the impression of not being the outcome of speculations in the study, but of its being built upon a very broad experience in the Mission-field, which is the very thing we want in such a Paper. As to the question before us, there are only two alternatives, either a geographical distribution or a harmonious working together side by side in the same field. There can be no doubt, according to my experience, that the first is, as a rule, the best where you can have it, I mean a geographical distribution. I wish a Conference like this could sit down and map out the world, as it were, and divide it between the Societies, so that each Society should have its share, and each nation have its share. That would really bring system or order into the work, but I suppose it is impracticable. *[Geographical limits or harmony.]*

The next best thing is to work harmoniously, and I know that can be done in most cases. I have tried. We have in Madagascar five Societies. One is a Roman Catholic Society, and the other four are Protestant. As to the Roman Catholic Society, the Jesuits, you have only two courses to choose between, to leave them alone or to fight them. With regard to the Protestants I am exceedingly happy to say that it has been my privilege to get on exceedingly well with them all, and I am of opinion that you will get on if you make up your minds to get on.

Do not keep aloof from them, do not try to leave others out in the cold; draw nigh to them, heart to heart, and hand to hand, speak to them out of your own heart, and you will find their heart. Break a lance with them if need be, but do it as a Christian warrior. Let them feel that what inspires you is not the fire of party, but the true fire from the altar burning for the salvation of immortal souls. But let nobody begin by assuming that he has the right to say "We are the Church." No, brethren, we are all the Church if we are Christians, the totality of those who believe in Christ and love His Gospel makes the Church. *[Mutual intercourse a remedy.]*

Next let us remember the golden words of Augustine, "Let there be unity in what is necessary, liberty in what is doubtful, love and charity in all." The matter is too earnest now, friends, for a petty quarrel between brothers and sisters. When the powers that break down Christianity are at work everywhere we should say, "Down with all talk of mine and thine in the work of the kingdom of God." Let us claim respect for the royal truth that the kingdom is Christ's, and that His is the glory; let us march on hand in hand under the standard of our common Master, and, under the guidance of His Spirit, let us all join to take the strongholds of the powers of darkness.

Rev. W. J. R. Taylor, D.D. (Reformed Church in America) : I desire to emphasise two points, referred to by Dr. Thompson, in regard to the question of intrusion.   I would refer to a fact in connection with our Arcot Mission.   A few years ago a Missionary from one of the English Missionary Societies came into a district which had been occupied by our Missionaries exclusively for many years.   There were signs of trouble.   Our Missionaries complained, or rather made representations to our Board in New York.

A good example. A correspondence was initiated with the Board in London, and the result was, that the Missionary was withdrawn, and I am happy to say, he was withdrawn by the Society for the Propagation of the Gospel in Foreign Parts.   It was done most cheerfully.   I do not know whether it came from the better kind of Ecclesiastical or Missionary diplomacy or not.   At all events, it was done in a spirit of Christian Comity and love.   With regard to the marital relations of the Missionaries.

Dr. Thompson alluded to the fact that very frequently expenses incurred by one Board had been paid by another.   In Japan one of our most valuable female Missionaries recently married a Missionary of the Church Missionary Society, but from the first it was understood, and it was practically complied with, that every dollar of the expenses incurred in sending that lady to Japan should be repaid ; apparently, it was paid by the Missionary herself, but really, as I learned, from the funds of the Church Missionary Society.

Rev. Principal Miller, C.I.E., LL.D. (Madras Christian College) : I think that one of the most important things to secure harmony in the Mission-field

Binding influence of a common work. is that the various Missionary Societies, when they are acting in the same place, should have some common work.   Those who are engaged in the same place and are interested in the same object, are drawn together powerfully, so that there is very much less danger of their clashing, or of any disharmony arising between them.   Those who have some one thing, however simple it is, in which they all have a common interest, are most likely to feel that they are servants of a common Lord, and to harmonise in all that they do.   Such opportunities are given by the Educational and Medical Mission work, and similar things ; and I think it is one of the most important things we could press upon our Missionary Societies for its indirect, as well as its direct benefits, that those who are labouring in the same field should have something, be it a school, or a college, or a dispensary, or anything else, in which it may be possible for them to have a common interest, in order that they may thus in all the rest of their work harmonise and recognise that they are fellow-servants.   Theory shows that, and practice shows it too, and I think there are those present, like my friend, Mr. Arden, who has already spoken, who can testify that the fact of Missionary Societies having some one thing in which they are interested, helps them to get on well in all the rest of their relations with each other.

Rev. Principal Brown pronounced the Benediction.

APPENDIX.

EXTRACT FROM A PAPER BY THE REV. A. W. WILLIAMSON, LL.D. (China).
(See page 266).

After describing the vastness, importance, and difficulties of the field, Dr. Williamson goes on to say :—Such is our common aim, and it is surely our duty to lay our plans so as to facilitate this grand achievement, and not retard it.

What then is the state of matters ? I almost fear to state it in all its reality, lest I should excite myself. But the truth must be faced. To begin with, we have all the leading Societies of England and America, with their separate organisations and customs, and all their articles, creeds, confessions, and formulas, reproduced on the soil of China. But this is not the worst aspect of it. One denomination has eight subdivisions, and several others are split in two and three parts. *The Foreign Churches introduced into China.*
What a spectacle is here to a thoughtful Chinaman, and there are many such ! Nor is even this the worst view of the situation. Look at the matter locally ! Take a few of the places with which the worker is most familiarly acquainted. Begin with Shanghai, with the representatives of no fewer than seven different denominations in England and America.

I know of the movement among the various Presbyterians and Missionaries towards union ; and I hail it, and I wish I saw a similar movement among the Episcopalians, Methodists, and others, for it would always be a step in the right direction. But my contention is that this is not sufficient ; I would gladly rest content with such union did I see it *Unions effected or aimed at.*
to be satisfactory. But the truth is, it only reduces the evil in a very small degree. In Shanghai, for instance, there are at present seven separate Mission agencies, as we have just pointed out ; in the supposed case there would still be six. In Tien-tsin there are four, and there would still be four. In Pekin there are five, and there would still be five. So also with other places. Would this be satisfactory ? I know the advantages of healthy rivalry. I respect conscientious scruples ; and I do not condemn sects. They have generally been the offspring of Christian principle, a rebound from error, or from some flagrant violation of Christian privilege or duty. They were a necessity of their times ; but as the times pass and the circumstances alter, the need for them also passes away. Why should we perpetuate them ? Above all why should we seek to introduce them into China ? I beg to emphasise my question by several other considerations.

(1) We can never, humanly speaking, Christianise China on the present system. We have neither funds nor forces sufficient. The resources of the whole Church would be inadequate. It would take thirty-six thousand Missionaries to work China alone, giving each ten thousand people, and we would require *four hundred and fifty new Missionaries every year*, on the same scale to meet the wants of the increasing population. We must either give up the hope of Christianising China at all, or adopt some other method. Unless there be some change, increasing *A Chinese Church for China.*
heathenism and growing immorality will lessen our proportion, and diminish our position every year, and swamp us. The tide of evil, as I said, is rising fast and ominously. Our present method is self-destructive. The Chinese won't have it. We are aiming at the impossible. Those who advocate denominationalism commit a serious mistake in contemplating their work in China. China is no small island of the sea ; the Chinese are no tribe of uncivilised heathen who may be easily won over, and on whom we may impose almost any system of religion we please. Nor is this empire like some nations, comparatively limited in area, and destitute of powerful national proclivities. As we have shown, there is no nation like it in the world for national sentiment, pride, and jealousy. The Romans despised the early teachers of Christianity ; the Chinese take a sounder view of the circumstances, and they dread us. They suspect our movements ;

and are prepared to resent anything which looks like the undermining of their
hoary institutions or national prestige. Nothing they fear so much
Chinese aversion to anything foreign. as a society, guild, or organisation outside or independent of themselves and their control. Can we suppose that such a nation will
allow us to impose any Church system upon them ?—much less six
or eight? The thing is out of the question : we must modify our aims if we
would secure influence in China. A foreign yoke may be imposed on a nation
by the sword. Commerce may be initiated and promoted by force ; but, I need
hardly say, religion can be advanced by no such means. In seeking to promote
religion in such a country as China, we must first of all win the respect and
confidence of the people, command the assent of the intellect, and
We must gain their confidence. secure the affection of the heart. Or rather, we must instil our
faith into the life-blood of the nation, and allow it to work its own
way in developing its benign character, and renewing the body corporate. They
will certainly resent the attempt, as they did in relation to Romanism in the
time of Kang-hi ; as they do at the present moment ; and as the Japanese also
now do.

Worst of all, we do the Chinese great injustice in keeping them isolated from
each other. We narrow their sympathies. We create controversies and bicker-
ings. We deaden their Christian instincts. We positively retard vital religion
among the native converts. There is strength in numbers ; there is warmth in
numbers ; there is life in numbers ; there is expansion in numbers. They feel
that themselves ; they say plainly, " It is you foreigners that keep
The Chinese desire union. us apart." Only lately one of the leading native pastors said to a
friend of mine, " We have thought the matter over, we are prepared
for union. It is you Foreign Missionaries who keep us separate. You are to
blame." My friend asked, " What about baptism ?" " We have considered
that, too," he replied ; " we would immerse those who desired it, and baptise by
effusion those who preferred that form." So it is, they, for the most part, can
see no force in our differences. They feel its evil effects, and had they the
power they would unite. And they certainly will follow those who unite, and
leave the others out in the cold, as the Japanese are doing.

Am I asked, What do you propose? Details can be arranged by-and-by ;
but I would respectfully submit that, in the interest of Christianity and all that
this implies, we should lay aside our particular denominationalism ; that the
Missionaries in one province should form a definite ecclesiastical organisation,
and place themselves loyally under this organisation, and take such work as that
organisation appoints ; that those who can unite should unite ;
A plan for a Chinese Church. that those residing in the same locality should throw their churches
and congregations together, and carry on their work by division of
labour and co-operation ; that they should, as far as possible, meet in the same
place on the Lord's day ; that one of the Missionaries should be appointed as
pastor, either permanently or for a time ; that the public preaching in the Church
should be conducted either by rotation, or as may be agreed upon ; that another
Missionary be set apart to superintend the schools ; others to Evangelical work,
and so on ; that all should work for the common Church, give in their reports
to it, and in reporting to the Home Board should not merely relate their
individual labours but the progress of the common Church. Also that there
should be a common Church in each province, related to each other ; that there
be a constant correspondence and frequent exchanges ; that these Churches
should institute common seminaries for the training of the native ministry ; and
that there should be stated local, provincial, and general assemblies as may be
determined on. Thus we should seek to create and foster a native common
Union Church in China—the Chinese Church of God.

MEETINGS OF MEMBERS
IN SECTION.

MISSIONARY COMITY.

(2) *CO-OPERATION.*

(*a*) How far has union among native Christians in heathen lands been found practicable or desirable ?

(*b*) At what stage of Missionary work should Independent National Churches be encouraged ?

(*c*) How far may fraternal counsel and co-operation be maintained between Missions on the same fields, though not organically connected ?

(*d*) Is it desirable to concentrate Missionary effort on fields of special readiness and promise ; and if so, what measure should be recommended by this Conference, in order that such fields may be immediately and thoroughly evangelised ?

(*e*) Is it possible or desirable to map out the whole heathen world among different Missionary Societies, or Churches, so as to ensure its more rapid evangelisation ?

(*Tuesday afternoon, June 19th, in the Annexe.*)

Robert Paton, Esq., in the chair.
Acting Secretary, Rev. R. Wardlaw Thompson.

Rev. Dr. Welch offered prayer.

The Chairman: I regret extremely that an important engagement prevents Lord Harrowby, whose name appears as Chairman for this meeting, from being with us at this hour. We hope that at a later hour he may be relieved from his important duties on the Education Commission in time to come into our midst and take charge of the meeting. I have been suddenly called upon to occupy this very prominent position, so that it would be presumption on my part to occupy any of the time of the meeting. I had the privilege of being present in the morning when the same subject was under discussion and felt most deeply interested in what I heard. I feel sure that it is of extreme importance that this subject should be thoroughly thrashed out,—not that I personally feel that resolutions can be arrived at, but the information which will be given, and the suggestions made may help towards some conclusions on the subject. I have the impression very strongly in my mind that just as the Church is at home, so the Church will be in the Mission-field: as different Churches draw closer together in the home field so the different Churches will draw closer together in the Mission-field, and I think a great many of the difficulties in the Mission-field will be solved when men on this side of the water get to know more of each other, and to love each other more.

Difficulty of this question.

I have had put into my hand quite recently a pamphlet by a friend, and was exceedingly struck with one paragraph, entitled "The heroic Missionary and the heroic Missionary Society," in it referring to the martyrdom of Bishop Patteson in the South Seas. Along with Bishop Patteson there was murdered one of those youths that accompanied him from Norfolk Island; and when he saw his leader's dead body he left most remarkable testimony which I should like to read, as it opens up to us a view of God's thoughts concerning Missions, and our interest in them, which it is very profitable for us to consider. This young Norfolk Islander probably had never seen a thousand people in his life, for his life had been spent on Norfolk Island, which was populated by the descendants of the mutineers of the *Bounty* who settled on Pitcairn Island in 1790; therefore he had no opportunity of coming in contact with the Christian Church. Hear what the youth said before he passed away: "Seeing people taken away when we think that they are most necessary to do God's work on earth makes me think that we often talk too much about Christian work. What God requires is Christian men. He does not need the work. He only gives it to form a perfect character in the men whom He sends to do it." It was very remarkable testimony from this youth evidently taught by the Holy Ghost; and I am quite sure recognition in the Mission-field and at home, more and more, of the presence of the Lord Himself in our midst, is the solution of all the difficulties that come in our way and the only solution. Without further preface I will call upon Dr. Taylor.

Testimony from the Field.

Workers not the work.

PAPER.

1. By the Rev. WILLIAM J. R. TAYLOR, D.D. (Reformed Church in America).

Union and Co-operation in Foreign Missions.

This is *the* problem of Foreign Missions in these last years of the nineteenth century. Its principles are immanent in the teachings of Christ, in the terms of the Great Commission, in the first Pentecostal blessings, in the Acts and letters of the Apostles, in the planting and training of the Apostolic Church, and in the first three centuries of Christian life and Church history. The primitive Churches were one, and continued to

Unity in early Church.

manifest the unity of the Spirit in " the common faith," and in the
propagation of the Gospel among the nations until heresies and
schisms rent " the Body of Christ " asunder. Islamism, Buddhism,
Brahmanism, are severally one and undivided, and they are mighty
by their oneness. The Church of Rome is a unit in her aggressive
work throughout the world, and we Protestants have much to learn
from her Missionary annals. The divisions of Protestantism are
its diseases whose infection and contagion have been carried into
the unevangelised nations ; and which can be healed only by Him
who restored the withered arm and made the lepers clean. Had
it not been for the Catholicity of the Missionary spirit and the
essential oneness of Christian Missions in foreign lands, and the
goodly fellowship of Missionaries themselves there would have
been the same barriers to union abroad that divide the Churches
at home.

But, by the grace of God, we have reached a turning point
that compels a halt from old ways and a new departure, or rather,
a quick and decisive return to New Testament methods, Tendency
and a facile adaptation to existing facts. We are learning to it now.
over again the lessons that should never have been forgotten, that
the Church of Christ is organised on the basis of the Great
Commission; and, therefore, to use the language of the late Dr.
W. Fleming Stevenson, " The Mission is not an organ of the
Church, but the Church is an organ of the Mission—Divinely
appointed, Divinely endorsed, Divinely dwelt in. The Church has
been consecrated to this work by its Master, and when the consecration is accepted, penetrating not only into assemblies and
councils, but into every little group of Christian people, penetrating
like a fire that burns into men's souls, and then leaps out in
flame of impulse and passionate surrender, we shall see the Mission
as Christ would have it be." (Address before the Belfast Council
of the Alliance of Reformed Churches, 1884, p. 178 of Volume
of Proceedings.)

Assuming that this subject is in full accordance with the
principles announced on the call for this Conference, and in order
to " turn to account the experience of the past in actual Mission
work abroad, and in its conduct by the Home Churches, The Conference
and to seek the more entire consecration of the Church is call to unity.
of God," I propose to treat, as briefly as possible, the several points
suggested in the programme in their order.

I. How far has Union among Native Christians in Foreign Lands
been found Practicable or Desirable ?

The answer is, that wherever Missionaries of the Cross of Christ have
been animated by supreme love to their Saviour and their work they have
usually and readily found their ways to some kind of closer Unity practic-
fellowship and co-operation in the service of their one Lord. able without
Co-operation ought to be and is practicable and desirable uniformity.
even where actual union, and particularly organic union, may be

impracticable. Actual union has been happily maintained at Amoy, China, for more than a quarter of a century between the Missionaries of the Reformed (Dutch) Church in America and those of the Presbyterian Church of England. Having laboured together in the faith of the Gospel, gathering converts into the fold of Christ, and founding native Churches, these brethren could not and would not spoil the unity of those infant Churches by making two denominations out of one company of believers; nor would they sow in that virgin soil the seeds of sectarian divisions which have long sundered the Protestant Churches in Europe and America. The result was the organisation of the *Tai-Hoe*, or Great Council of Elders, which is neither an English Presbytery nor a Reformed Church Classis,

Tai-Hoe.   but is like them both. It is not an appendage of either of these foreign Churches, but is a genuine independent Chinese Christian Church holding the standards and governed by the polity of the twin-sister Churches that sent them the Gospel by their own messengers. The Missionaries retain their relations with their own home Churches and act under commissions of their own Church Board of Missions. They are not settled pastors, but are more like the Apostolic Evangelists of New Testament times—preachers, teachers, founders of Churches, educators of the native ministry, superintendents of the general work of evangelisation.

This *Tai-Hoe* is a child of God, which was " born, not of blood, nor of the will of the flesh, nor of the will of man, but of God." It is believed to be the first ecclesiastical organisation for actual union and co-operation in Mission lands by the representatives of Churches holding the Reformed faith and Presbyterial polity. Its history has already been long enough to give the greatest value to its experience.

More recent, and in some respects more important, are the results of co-operation and unity in *The United Church of Christ in Japan*, which has assumed national proportions, and is constantly developing The United new phases and forces. Originally composed of the Missions Church of Japan. of Presbyterian and Reformed Churches in Scotland and the United States, together with native Churches and pastors under their care, it has now its own general assembly with its subordinate courts, and its doors are opening for a still wider union, embracing the Congregational Missions and Churches. Should this union be consummated the United Church will become so strong and so planted in the most important places of the Empire, that it may work out its destiny by the grace of God in every direction.

For confirmation of these statements, and in proof that organic union is both " practicable and desirable " in that wonder-land, I venture to quote a few lines from a recent personal letter of one of the wisest and most experienced Mission leaders there. " If there be any who fail to sympathise with the proposed union with the Congregational Churches here they fail only because they do not understand the degree to which our Japanese spirit Missionary work has been developed, and the spirit of the Japanese of self-support. Churches. Mission Churches, when once they become self-supporting, cannot be kept in mere leading strings. In the United Church of Christ in Japan there are to-day more than twenty-five self-supporting congregations, and there is an equal number in the Congregational Church; and when fifty or more self-supporting congregations are animated by a strong desire to come together, all the Churches in America and Scotland cannot stop the movement. And I am happy to believe that they will not want to stop it or hinder it in the least."

On a smaller scale, but on the same essential principles, the various Presbyterian bodies in the Island of Trinidad, in the New Hebrides, in South Africa, in India and China, in Brazil, and elsewhere, have been gradually drawing together; some in organised ecclesiastical assemblies, and others in voluntary alliances for mutual counsel, and concerted movements for the propagation of the Gospel and for the establishment of the Missions and Churches within their bounds.

In all these efforts towards greater co-operation and union *the labourers in the field have taken the initiative*. They could not stay apart and work successfully in the presence of united heathenism. Their very necessities have made them one in spirit and services. And as the work advances it will put increased pressure upon them, from within and without, from the Cross and the world, *for Jesus' sake*.

Union begins in the Mission-field.

From these examples of what has been already accomplished, and is being done towards actual co-operation and organic unity, it is comparatively easy to conclude how far union among native Christians is practicable and desirable elsewhere. The answer is that it is to be desired and secured wherever it is possible, so far as circumstances in each field will permit, and just under the guidance of Providence and of the Holy Spirit. But no one field can furnish rules for another in this great concern. It is enough to add that the tendency of the best Missionary work in the world is strongly towards co-operation and closer union; and that every specific case must be governed by its own conditions: and especially by the spirit of the Missions and of the native Churches. Any true and abiding union must grow from the good, imperishable seed of the kingdom. It cannot be made, much less forced by human devices. But it can, and should be cultivated as a tender plant, a precious vine, in the Lord's vineyard.

No one rule for all.

II. At what Stage of Missionary Work should Independent National Churches be encouraged?

That depends upon the intelligence and ability of the native pastors, officers, and members of the Churches. We stand alone. The first and most conspicuous example in this line of Missionary development occurred when the American Board of Commissioners for Foreign Missions decided to confide their great and glorious trust in the Sandwich Islands to the care of the Churches that had been planted and trained by their veteran Missionaries. The latest experience of its kind which has already been referred to in this Paper, in the Empire of Japan, speaks the last and loudest word for the cause. In both instances dependence upon the foreign Churches that gave them the Gospel was needful only until they had grown to such size, and strength, and vigour, that they could be trusted to manage their own affairs. But in each field there has been, and long will be room and requirement for the counsel and assistance of Mission workers from abroad. It is simply a question of ripeness and maturity; and that will vary with every separate people; from the most intelligent and educated and self-sustaining Christian communities, down to those that need

In dependence a natural growth.

the personal oversight of successive generations of Missionaries, and the help of the home Churches. Among barbarous tribes and amid hostile hierarchies and persecuting powers, and especially among the poorer and more humble classes, it might be cruel to Churches still leave the natives alone under the Cross. But whenever need oversight. and wherever they have been sufficiently educated and trained to take care of themselves, it will be wise and proper to encourage self-support, self-propagation, and self-government by the native Churches. And especially is it desirable to promote their unity and co-operation upon their own national lines—so that there shall be but one great Independent National Church of each great family of Churches, holding the same faith and order in India ; another in China ; another in Mexico ; another in the Orient ; another in Brazil; and so on, until even these shall flow together as the rivers into the seas.

III. How far may Fraternal Counsel and Co-operation be maintained between Missions on the same Fields, though not organically connected ?

The best answer to this question will be found in the proceedings of Missionary Councils, Conferences, and Alliances, which have been held of Present late years in India, China, and other countries, and notably in Conferences to the annual gatherings of returned Missionaries in America, in be extended. the summer time, representing nearly all of the Evangelical Churches in Canada and the United States. This very Œcumenical Conference is itself the type and promise of what may be expected hereafter in Mission lands. Every Mission band ought to have a "solemn league and covenant" with every other Mission band in each contiguous field of operations, binding them together for the discussion of important problems that are frequently arising, and for mutual help and co-operation with each other, for Christ and His Church, and against "the powers of darkness." And the home Churches should encourage and foster all such "fellowship in the Gospel." We can never forget that the tongues of fire at Pentecost made a united Church out of the converts of all nations, and that it was not a Church shivered into pieces like a broken mirror, but that one Holy Catholic Church of the primitive Christian ages that drove the whole rabble of pagan gods from the Pantheon, and struck the oracles dumb for ever.

IV. Is it desirable to concentrate Missionary Effort on Fields of Special Readiness and Promise ; and, if so, what Measure should be recommended by this Conference, in order that such Fields may be immediately and thoroughly evangelised ?

To the first part of this question there can be but one wise and emphatic reply. By all means concentrate. But concentrate as the Apostles did in their day, always in order to diffusion. The Saviour's own Concentrate command, just before His ascension, contains the ruling principle, to diffuse. which will yet become the ruling passion of the Mission service in all lands, "Ye shall be witnesses unto Me, both in Jerusalem, and in all Judea, and in Samaria, and unto the uttermost parts of the earth" (Acts i. 8). The grand strategic points must be seized and held. Plans of campaigns that cover whole continents, like those of the late American Civil War for the Union, must include innumerable details, as well as vast systems of defences on land and sea, great marches and battles, as well as the bring.

ing of rivers and picket lines, and the last struggles for final victory. In many a field the man is more than the place. The personal equation is an element in every problem. One single man may embody in himself the whole Gospel and the kingdom of God, as the first pilgrim who leapt from the deck of the *Mayflower* on to Plymouth Rock, seemed to incarnate in his own person the unborn republic of the new world.

The second part of the question now before us will be best answered by those wise men from the East, who have followed the star of Bethlehem from their own land to the places where it has reappeared, and where they have taught the wondering pagans to worship their king. I therefore leave the treatment of this part of the subject to those for whose guidance this Conference so earnestly waits ; for " they are the messengers of the Churches and the glory of Christ."

V. Is IT POSSIBLE OR DESIRABLE TO MAP OUT THE WHOLE HEATHEN WORLD AMONG DIFFERENT MISSIONARY SOCIETIES OR CHURCHES, SO AS TO ENSURE ITS MORE RAPID EVANGELISATION ?

Answer : If the whole heathen world were still a *terra incognita*; if its greatest Mission-fields were not already pre-occupied, it might be possible thus to map it out as heathen Canaan was divided among the twelve tribes of Israel. But, as it is, the very attempt at such *Past experience.* a project would probably lead to a historical repetition of the tribal feud of ancient times, when " Judah vexed Ephraim and Ephraim envied Judah." Let the unoccupied fields be given up to those who first enter them ; let great care be taken everywhere to prevent intrusion, and confusion, and conflict in the field of one Mission by the labourers in another field ; and as soon as possible let a Federal Union be formed, composed of Missionaries and Churches of all Christian communions that can affiliate, to " carry the Gospel into the regions beyond, and to take advantage of those critical opportunities which are opening unevangelised nations, such as Corea, Thibet, and large regions of Central Asia and the dark continent for the coming of the King and His kingdom.

The views and conclusions thus presented are fortified by recent deliverances of several of the most important Ecclesiastical Courts in the United States of America, and especially by those in Europe and America belonging to that large family of *A proposal.* Churches represented in the Alliance of Reformed Churches throughout the world holding the Presbyterian system. During the last ten years this subject has engaged its General Councils and their Special Committees with profoundest interest, urgency, and success, of which ample evidence will be given in the Report which is to be presented to the Fourth General Council at its meeting in this place, a fortnight hence. Without anticipating its action, but inviting careful attention to its proceedings and its successful prosecution of this great work, I close this Paper with a single suggestion,—Why may not this Centennial Missionary Conference " prepare the way of the Lord " and of the Lord's people for a still greater Œcumenical Council to be held, towards the close of the nineteenth and the opening of the twentieth century, in some capital city of the old world or the new world, not to frame new creeds, not to fight over old battles, but to organise more completely, and to start more powerfully, the most extensive and practical system of Gospel propagation that the world has ever seen since that day of Pentecost which was the type and promise of the conversion of all nations under the Great Commission, and by the power of the Holy Ghost?

PAPER.

2. By the Rev. C. C. Fenn (Secretary, C.M.S.).

Of the questions connected with *Missionary Comity*, those which it has been agreed I should speak to in this Paper are the following, (*a*), (*b*), (*c*) of the programme for this meeting.

I will venture to consider these questions in their chronological order, which as it seems to me is the inverse order to that which is followed, and not improperly followed, in the
<small>Order of treatment.</small> extract I have just read from the programme. Before there can be native Christians in heathen lands, there must, as a rule, have been Missions to those lands; and before the various bodies of Christians thus gathered out from heathenism can consider, with much practical utility, how far and in what respects they can unite with each other, they must have some power in their own hands, they must have attained some degree of independence.

I therefore propose to consider :—

(1) What kind and what degree of union can be attained and should be desired between Missions carried on by different Christian communions, and what steps should be taken to bring about such union?

(2) How soon should the native Christians in heathen lands become so far independent of the religious bodies through whose Missionary efforts they have been brought out from heathenism, as to be able and to be called upon, to consider and decide respecting their own religious organisation and respecting the relations that should subsist between the various sections of native Christians which may be found at the time in those lands?

(3) So far as we can judge from our present standpoint, what kind of union and what degree of union should be ultimately aimed at, or are likely to be ultimately aimed at, by these different bodies of Christians, and what steps should be taken to bring it about?

Speaking roughly, my first question is, What kind of present working union should there be between different Missionary Societies labouring in the same country? My *third* question is, What union should be ultimately looked forward to among the different bodies of Christians gathered together by these Societies? And the *second*, intermediate question is, At what period should these converts begin to act for themselves in this matter?

I. The *relations between different Missionary Societies* constitute a problem which may be difficult in theory, but which very seldom, comparatively speaking, has been found difficult in practice. It does not, of course, necessarily follow, that because there has been very little difficulty in the past, there will be none in the future. One cause of the hitherto prevailing absence of friction has been the fact that, at least until a somewhat recent period, almost all non-Roman Missionaries have held very firmly and definitely those particular doctrines known as *Evangelical*, and recognised under that name such organisations as the Evangelical Alliance, the Religious Tract Society, and the London City Mission. Of late years there has been an increasing number of zealous Missionaries from the Church of England, who do not come within the category just referred to. And there is also, I believe, less of rigid doctrinal uniformity among those sent out by the British Congregationalist bodies. One at least of these conceivable causes of differences is to be found in East Africa. There, however, amicable feelings seem to prevail, and little or nothing has been heard of dispute or contention. For my own part I rather expect that in the Mission-field generally, such mutual amicableness will continue, even though there should be a large increase in the number of Missionaries belonging respectively to the schools of Dr. Pusey and Dr. Arnold.

Unity in the faith the basis of uniform work.

I believe that the great majority of Missionaries will always be men who truly love the Saviour, and who therefore in their hearts will love all those who love Him. Missionaries animated by this spirit will, I think, be guided by the two following principles: First, they will rejoice heartily when any heathen man has been brought to give his heart to the living Christ set forth in the four Gospels, whether his teacher has been a Baptist or a High Churchman, or has belonged to any other Protestant body; secondly, they will feel that the persons for whose good they are labouring, the persons whom they have gone out to convert, are not Plymouth Brethren on the one hand, or Ritualists on the other, but the heathen and Mohammedans. True hearted Missionaries, who differ widely one from another on ecclesiastical or even doctrinal questions, will say: "We rejoice that there are supremely important points in which we agree; and as for our differences our work is too engrossing to give us much time for thinking about them, much less for talking and disputing about them."

The natural result of the principle just referred to will be the continuance of the course of action that has on the whole been adopted hitherto, which may be described thus: In choosing a field of action, every Society will seek for those localities where it will come in contact with persons not reached by the agencies of other Societies. This, of course, will not prevent two Societies from working side by side in large towns, though it would tend to prevent them from occupying the same village. Each Society will abstain from all efforts to draw away converts belonging to another Society, or in dealing with the heathen to prove its superiority over another Society. But, thirdly, the mental and spiritual freedom of the individual will be so far respected, that if any native Christian from intelligent conviction desires to transfer himself to another denomination, no hindrance beyond that of temperate persuasion will be placed in his way.

Their course of action.

I pass on to my second question: *How soon should the native Christians of a newly evangelised country be encouraged to decide for themselves as to their own ecclesiastical organisation?* On this question also I wish to be brief. All practical Missionaries would give the same answer to it, up to a certain point,—all, that is to say, would reply, " Self-management, by the converts, of their own religious externalities, must proceed gradually. Nearly all, I hope, would also say, " *It must begin from the first.*" And all, I believe,

Self-government should mean self-support. would say, " It must be accompanied from the first by pecuniary self-support." That is to say, a part at least of the united external religious action of the new converts must be of a kind that requires no pecuniary subvention from the Foreign Society. In other words either pecuniary contributions or voluntary service or both combined must be supplied by the native Christians themselves, from the time that they first attach themselves to the visible Christian Church. It is also almost universally admitted that the Foreign Missionary cannot, as a rule, be a part of the pastoral organisation which the native Christians support. It is, however, at the same time certain that the Missionary and the Missionary Society ought, wherever possible, to aid the infant Christian congregations by advice and instruction. It is also certain that as a matter of fact the Foreign Societies do in most cases exercise control and government over these congregations. Now our question is *not*, " How long should advice and counsel be given?" or " How long shall instruction be given by the agents of the Missionary Society in higher schools and in theological colleges?" *but*, " How long shall the Missionary Society exercise government or coercive control over the newly-formed Christian bodies.

One part of the reply which would be given to this question by most Missionary Societies is, I believe, as follows : " Our control must be continued, so long as we give pecuniary subvention." This answer can scarcely be avoided. The pecuniary supplies of Missionary Societies come from

Committee responsible to subscribers. voluntary contributions ; and the contributors will, in this nineteenth century, quite rightly I think, insist upon appointing the persons, the Committees by whom these funds are to be disbursed. But, *delegatus non potest delegare.* The Committees to whom this duty is delegated, cannot in their turn delegate it to others. It is only with careful reserve that they can make grants of money to other persons, or other bodies of persons. They must retain in their own hands the power of controlling and even ultimately directing the expenditure. There may doubtless be exceptions to this rule, but they are the exceptions by which the rule is proved. And indeed there is a practical advantage in the adoption and statement of this principle. It enables us to say with perfect frankness and sincerity and truth to the foreign Christian brethren who ask our help, " If you have our pecuniary help, you must also be under our rule, and your being under our rule is the very thing we must as far as possible decline. We are not Societies to rule over Christians but to evangelise heathens." This is just as *true* as saying, " Our money is not raised in order to help Christians ;" and while equally true it is more pleasant for us to say and for them to hear.

If it is asked why we should not make ourselves responsible both for the pecuniary support and for the government of the converts, the answer is plain, that the burden thus imposed on us would indefinitely increase as the number of converts increased, and would thus more and more tend to clog our efforts for the propagation of the Gospel—for the very work, that is to say, which is itself the reason of our existence. But further than this, the result would be, nay, rather, has been—for the plan has been far too widely adopted already—that the converts and their children, where the system has prevailed for more than one generation, more and more lose their self-reliance, their direct trust in God, and so become, just in proportion as this system is carried out, more and more feeble for all Church purposes as years roll on.

Reasons against home direction of Foreign Church.

It must be borne in mind that habituation to dependence by no means prepares men for independence. Christian communities who are living in complete dependence upon a Foreign Society, are not at all ripening for direct dependence on divinely imparted strength. The progress is rather in the opposite direction. Every year of the continuance of such a system renders them in many respects less and less fit for self-government, and so far makes its introduction more and more difficult.

Reliance on Committees weakens reliance on themselves.

The proper mode, I venture to assert, is to introduce from the first a tolerably complete though very simple system of self-support; to accompany this at first with a considerable amount of advice and help from without; but to keep the two factors—the internal and the external—as distinct as possible from the very first, and steadily to go on diminishing the external aid until they gradually learn not to feel the need of it.

It remains to consider the *third* question. *When the native Christians in newly evangelised countries are sufficiently numerous and sufficiently strong to feel themselves able to decide on their own ecclesiastical organisation, what is the result which may be wished for and expected?*

I say, "*When they feel themselves able.*" For it is a question which they will decide for themselves. They will do it *when* they choose, and *as* they choose. I say also "*wished for*," and "*expected.*" It is of course possible in this matter, as in any other, that we may wish for that which we do not expect. But I believe that in this case the issue which present appearances would lead us to anticipate, is one in the prospect of which we may on the whole very cordially rejoice.

I would deal then with the probabilities of the case.

It seems quite certain to begin with that *those sectional differences among Protestant Christians, which are purely owing to historical causes or to local causes,* will disappear among converts gathered in by bodies so divided, if the converts act for themselves in countries where those historical or local causes are inoperative. This principle would apply to Christians in foreign countries who have been brought into Christendom by the labours of Scotch Presbyterians, belonging respectively to the Established and non-established Churches. The same principle would be extended without difficulty to American Presbyterians and to American and British Congregationalists, and

I presume also to American and German Lutherans—as soon, I mean, as the question is really taken in hand by the native Christians themselves. Where there are two or more bodies of Christians, not differing appreciably in their modes of government, discipline, ritual, and doctrinal statement, but differing only in the fact that they owe their Christianity, humanly speaking, ultimately to Christian bodies kept apart one from another by causes which have no existence in the infant Churches themselves, I do not believe that any power on earth will prevent these Churches from being re-united and merged into one body. And who could wish that they should be so prevented?

Neither does it seem to me likely that this amalgamation will be prevented by differences of ritual,—such differences of ritual, I mean, of course, as are found among those Mission congregations which are not ashamed to call themselves Protestant. I can only say Differences from personal knowledge that these differences are, of ritual. comparatively speaking, little thought of among, for instance, the Tamil Christians of South India and Ceylon. Not a few Tamil Christians in Ceylon, who have come from non-liturgical bodies, and find themselves in places where the only Tamil Christian congregation is one connected with the Church Missionary Society, join themselves heartily to it without the smallest scruple or difficulty. They would therefore, I imagine, see no difficulty whatever in there being in the same Church some congregations habitually adopting liturgical services, and some where the prayers were always extemporaneous. The use or non-use of a liturgy in different congregations would not of itself, so it seems to me, prevent union in some larger body.

Church government, however, may seem, at least at first sight, to present a more serious obstacle. Yet even in this matter the obstacle may not seem so serious to the native Christians in the Mission-field as it does to us. Take, for instance, the case of the Tamil Christians in Congregational Nagercoil and Episcopalian Tinnevelly respectively. The unity that exists among the Nagercoil Christians might be manifested by an annual or half-yearly gathering Of Church of ministers and lay delegates in a Congregational Union, government. presided over by a president chosen at each occasion. The corresponding body in Tinnevelly might be a Central Church Council, presided over by a bishop. But the two central representative bodies might each regard the other as representing a part of the visible Church; and the constituents of the two bodies might have similar reciprocal feelings. They might act together by means of joint committees for such purposes as revision of Bible translation, preparation of Christian literature, and mutual strengthening and consultation in respect of Church discipline.

Suppose, therefore, that in one of two contiguous districts in India all Protestant Christians were under Episcopal government, and that in the other all were under Presbyterian government, my belief is that these two bodies of native Christians, if animated by the feelings at present prevailing among the Indian Protestant Christians, would have no difficulty in fully recognising each other as belonging to one and the same visible Church, and that if the question were left to their own decision, there would be full and unrestricted intercommunion between them. The difference in Church government would not really break or even obscure their visible and evident union.

This certainly seems to me probable, almost certain, if the native Christians act for themselves. But it will be asked, "Supposing it be probable, is it desirable ?" Well, let me pass for a moment from the question of probability to the question of advisability. And first *Is such union* let me say that such a state of things would be just that which *advisable?* many high authorities believe to have existed in the early part of the second century of the Christian era. I quote from one of the most recent of these authorities. I find the following words in Bishop Lightfoot's "Apostolic Fathers," published in 1885 :—

"In the epistles of Ignatius there is no indication that he is upholding the Episcopal against any other form of Church government, *Lightfoot on* as, for instance the Presbyterial. The alternative which he *"Church* contemplates is lawless isolation and self-will. No definite *government."* theory is propounded as to the principle on which the Episcopate claims allegiance. It is as the recognised authority of the Churches which the writer addresses that he maintains it. Almost simultaneously with Ignatius, Polycarp addresses the Philippian Church, which appears not yet to have had a bishop, requiring its submission ' to the presbyters and deacons.' If Ignatius had been writing to this Church he would doubtless have done the same. As it is, he is dealing with communities where Episcopacy had been already matured, and therefore he demands obedience to their bishops."

It will be said perhaps, Even if this was the case for two or more decades of years after the passing away of the Apostles, yet does not the fact of the universal adoption of the Episcopal government before the close of the second century, and its continuance from that time until the sixteenth century, prove that the government of the Church ought to be Episcopal ?

Speaking now as a member of an Episcopally-governed Church, I would say that the discontinuance of the Presbyterial form of government seemed certainly at the time to be advisable. I believe that it was ; but that that advisability may have been owing to change of circumstances. And if so, a subsequent change of circumstances, might render advisable, or at least permissible, *Social and poli-* another change in the mode of government. The change *tical conditions* that took place in the second century was when, what are *forms of* commonly called the miraculous exercises of divine power *government.* in the Church seemed to pass away, and to be succeeded by the not less blessed, but more quiet and (so called) ordinary operations of the Spirit of God. Instead of gifts coming from above unexpectedly and with seeming suddenness, and thus fixing for each individual the work in which he should be engaged, it was rather that God in His Providence, and by the inward movement of the Holy Spirit, first led the individual to a certain kind of work, and then bestowed on him the gifts needed. Obviously, this latter state of things more resembles the Divine action in civil and political government. The

political government of the time being always monarchical, it became
natural to introduce the same system into ecclesiastical affairs.

But in the present day, the state of the case is altogether different. Among the more progressive Christian countries of the world,
the non-monarchic element of civil government seems, on the whole,
at the present moment, to be growing stronger and stronger. And,
therefore, it would almost seem as if the self-same cause which at
one time led to the introduction of Episcopacy, might now have a
tendency in the exact opposite direction. Yet one must speak
doubtfully, remembering for instance the remarkable fact, that in
the country which is popularly regarded as the very embodiment of
democracy, the most powerful Church is one governed by Bishops
though it has not the historical succession,—I mean, of course, the
Methodist Episcopal Church of America.

But it is time to draw this Paper to a close. In conclusion, then,
I will only say, speaking altogether as an individual, and regarding
it as highly probable that many members of my own Society may
strenuously differ from me—that the eventuality to which I look
forward to is somewhat of the following kind :—

That there will be, in India, for instance, a great Indian
Probability of an Church, from which the Roman Catholics and some
Indian Church. smaller bodies will stand aloof, but to which, notwith-
standing, the great mass of Indian Christians will belong.

That the earnest and active members of this Church will hold
fast to such great facts, and truths, and beliefs as the following:
If possible,   The Triunity of God ; the Incarnation ; the Propitiation
its tenets.   through Christ's death ; the Resurrection of Christ, involving in itself the ultimate resurrection of all believers; the present
and eternal spiritual union of all believers with Christ, and so with
one another, and the indwelling in them of the Holy Spirit;
" Eternal life and eternal punishment " (Matt. xxv. 46) ; the Bible
as the sole and unerring rule of faith ; the reality, the necessity,
duty, and efficacy of prayer, especially of united prayer. (I say
such truths as these, because I do not mean the list to be in any
way exhaustive.)

That in this Church there will be a very wide variety of ritual,
Ritual and   including also a very large degree of liberty as to the
government. mode and the time of the administration of the sacraments.

That great varieties of Church government will co-exist in the
Indian Church, some congregations being under Episcopal rule,
others under Presbyterian, while others again will be more independent, but that all these will recognise each other as belonging to
the same outward visible Church, the union being manifested by
some corporate and representative action, and by very free intercommunion ; and that this variety will be found not unfrequently,
even in the same localities, especially, for instance, in the large
cities.

In saying that I look forward to this, I do not mean positively to *predict* it ; I think that it is the issue to which the existing currents of thoughts, and feelings, and events, seem to me to point. New currents may, of course, arise which are at present invisible. It is also a consummation which I, individually, so far as I can at present judge, would hail with satisfaction.

There are many learned and spiritually-minded members of the Church of England, who regard what they term "Apostolical succession," as essential to the well-being, if not *Apostolic succession.* the being, of the Church. There are such at this time in India ; and probably there always will be some such. Those Indian Anglicans who hold this view very strongly, will, of course, be unable to join the body thus described if it should be formed. They will constitute a separate Church. But, I believe, they will be comparatively few in number. I believe the great majority of lay Anglicans, whether in the British Isles, or the Colonies, or India, attach comparatively little importance to the fact or the theory of the so-called Apostolical succession, and that in India, they will at once set it aside, if it should assume such a shape as to be an obstacle to the larger comprehension.

One word more. True union between Christians is vital, springing from vital union with Christ. It can, and it does, over-leap ecclesiastical barriers. But it dislikes them. And *Vital union.* this dislike will, I believe, grow more and more powerful until at length it will sweep those barriers away ; and in India and throughout the world, there will be "One flock, One Shepherd."

DISCUSSION.

Rev. Leonard W. Kip (Reformed Church in America, from Amoy): Three minutes is not much to tell about what has happened during the last twenty-seven years in Amoy ; but I can say, with reference to that United Church of which Dr. Taylor has read, that another gentleman on the platform as well as myself was there and saw its beginning. It was a growth by the blessing of God. It began with five Churches without any native pastor. Two years later there were two native *Spontaneous growth.* pastors. Now the Presbytery is composed of sixteen Churches, and twelve native pastors are connected with it. And to show that this Presbytery is able to attend to its own business, I may say it has a Board of Foreign Missions with the same import as the American Board, and its work has been managed by the natives alone,—they raised the funds and they have sent the preachers.

There is unfortunately in the south part of China a great number of dialects, and so these Christian brethren on sending their preachers only one hundred miles, put them in a place where, like ourselves, first going to China, they must learn a Chinese dialect, and therefore that distance of only ninety or one hundred miles in a land where there are no railroad accidents because there are no rail-roads, means a distance perhaps from here to Vienna or to Italy. So that to these Amoy Christians this Mission has all the effect *Native Mission Board.* of a Foreign Mission ; and, as I say, this Chinese Presbytery has established this Board of Foreign Missions, itself commissions the men, provides their support, and gives all the directions without any assistance from us. Now I think we see in this the hand of God. I am sure that in all these years God has been with His Church there, and He has granted this spirit of co-operation, this great desire that the Church growing up in that place should not contain two denominations where one was possible, that it should not be an American Church in China or an English Church in China, but in all respects a Chinese Church.

Mr. Reginald Radcliffe (Liverpool): I will just take the last question, "Is it possible or desirable to map out the whole heathen world among different Missionary Societies or Churches, so as to ensure its more rapid evangelisation?" I think not, dear friends. If we take Africa, there all the Societies represent about five millions of Africa. The population is two hundred millions: there is one hundred and ninety-five millions not represented by any of the Protestant Missionary Societies of the world. I think this brings on at once the question that has been thought of by some of you during this Conference whether we should not, if possible, before we had separated, contemplate once more the enormous amount of the heathen population of the world that is utterly untouched by any of our Evangelisation Societies. Well, then, in regard to that, dear friends, we cannot withdraw our beloved Missionaries, honoured servants who are amongst us, and those that have lived in the field, God bless them! but we can at once get from America and Britain and Germany, we can get spies,—not such as the twelve spies, but such as the two spies, Caleb and Joshua,—laymen if you will, who will go out at once and spy out the one hundred and ninety-five millions of Africa, and a similar quantity perhaps of China and of other countries in the world, and these men, though they cannot talk the languages, if they go to survey for railways or anything of that kind they go with the English tongue, and they can find their way, and they can get an interpreter. There are such men in London and England, in New York and America, and there are such men, I am sure, in Germany who will be ready to go. I have one minute more and that will be time enough to fasten this thought on the whole world. We must not separate and think we have got one hundred and twenty Missionary Societies represented here, and we are doing a great thing—we are reaching five millions out of two hundred millions in Africa, and perhaps similar numbers in other parts of the world. Now we must have a new departure,—a departure right from God, a departure right from the Holy Ghost,—we must lift up the Jews and let them take their glorious position to evangelise the world; and we must lift up men and women that will deny themselves, and give up their positions, whether they are merchants, or lawyers, or doctors, and go into the utmost parts of the world. And we will not wait for a decade of ten years and then start, but let them go out if possible at this Conference, and let them bring back word within twelve months.

Rev. Wilson Phraner (Presbyterian Board of Foreign Missions, U.S.A.): The reader of the second Paper said this matter of union was a matter which was vital,—it touched our hearts. I have noticed in our gatherings here from day to day, and in other assemblies for years that no sentiment could be uttered, so popular, or that so touched the popular heart, as this sentiment of unity among the people of God. Now, cannot the Church of Christ find out in some way a method of carrying

Present forces unable to evangelise the world.

Faithful spies.

How to meet the difficulty.

The longing for unity.

into execution that which she so evidently longs for, loves and desires. May this Conference contribute something towards the solution of that great problem. Dear brethren, I would not have spoken to-day for myself. I come to bear you a message. When in Shanghai in January last, I attended a conference of Missionary brethren in that city. This question among others was alluded to.

The next morning, as I was about to sail, the venerable Dr. Muirhead, of the London Missionary Society, known by many in this assembly, who has been in China more than forty years, said to me: "My dear brother, you are going to London. You are to attend that Conference. Will you not lift up your voice, and say a word in behalf of larger union and co-operation among the various Missionary organisations of this land?" I am fulfilling the promise I made. I can, in the brief time given me, simply allude to this fact of his earnest desire, representing other brethren there, that after all that is attained in the way of Christian co-operation and unity more is desirable. *A message from China.*

Let me say only one word with regard to Japan. I want to remind the brethren here that this call for union, and this union which has become a fact, so far as seven different denominations are concerned, and will be for eight I hope soon, originated not with the Missionaries, but was demanded by the natives, and the Missionaries could not resist the demand. The same will be true elsewhere when the Gospel of the Lord Jesus Christ takes hold upon the hearts of the people.

Rev. W. S. Swanson (English Presbyterian Mission, Amoy): I shall only occupy your attention two minutes. Every one who has been in the Mission-field knows that separation there means mischief. There is no mistake about it, we are exposed to influences there that make friction very much more easy than friction is at home. And I do sometimes think that we who are in a foreign field are those that are most ready for union. I am afraid the want of readiness is not when you get to 120° East Longitude, but a very considerable distance *west* of that. If there is one thing more than another that has struck me, in connection with these meetings, it is this—I cannot get away from it—here we are united hand in hand and heart to heart for the biggest work that the Christian Church has to do, and the biggest question that the Christian Church has to face, and I ask you what is here to hinder us, not merely from co-operation, but from union? As one means of settling this question, I hold in my hand a letter which I have been requested to read, a letter from one of the oldest, and let me say the most influential Missionary Society in this country to one of the youngest Missionary Societies in this country; a letter from the Church Missionary Society to the China Inland Mission, and I think its terms should sink very deep into the hearts of every one of us. "The Committee are desirous of taking up work either in Kiang-si or Si-chuen, by preference the former. Can you kindly inform me how it can enter into these provinces without coming into collision with your work, or rather so as to preach the Gospel where Christ has not been named? Can you also give me any other advice or information that may be useful to us in carrying out one or both of these plans?" Let Missionary Societies take this method, and then the question will very soon be settled. *Longitude and union.* *A good example. The C.M.S. and C.I.M.*

Rev. Professor T. Smith, D.D. (Free Church of Scotland): I shall confine myself to one of the questions on the programme,—"At what stage of

Missionary work should Independent National Churches be encouraged ? "
I suppose this is one of the questions that one of the readers of the very
excellent Papers we had relegated to the consideration of "wise men
from the East." It is in that character that I venture to appear before you
now, and to say that I suspect that my wisdom when I was
Experience in the East. in the East was at fault. I believe we all were too timid with
regard to our native Christians. When I was on my way to
India, within a few months of fifty years ago, I met at the Mauritius a
number of native Christians expelled from Madagascar. They were expelled
thence, as all the Church knows, and were without Missionaries for a very long
time,—I think eighteen years,—and it was supposed the Church must simply
have become extinct. The Missionaries would certainly have predicted that
it must of necessity have become extinct, yet when, by God's
Example of Madagascar. providence, the Missionaries were enabled to return to Madagascar, they found. the Church not only subsisted, but that it had
grown and flourished.

I know very well that there is a temptation to all Missionaries to keep their
converts somewhat longer in leading strings than perhaps is desirable. I know
very well when I was in Calcutta, we had such an affection for our converts that
we would have been very sorry that the link between us should have been in any
way weakened, and I think I may say that they have had that same kind of
affection towards Dr. Duff, Dr. Ewart, and myself, that it would have been to
them a matter of great regret if there had been any severance
Converts too long dependent. between them and us. But, at the same time, I do not know
whether it was particularly good for them that they were so long
associated with such men as Dr. Duff, to whom they naturally looked up, and
upon whom they felt themselves properly dependent. It is very generally a
desirable thing that men should be taught to swim by being pitched into the water;
and I suspect we all have too much the tendency to mistrust our converts. That
rule that the excellent secretary of the Church Missionary Society laid down as
to self-support going along with self-management is no doubt substantially true,
yet I think it might be modified, or, at all events, both self-support and self-
government should be introduced gradually. I would give what we call in
Scotland diminishing grants for a time, giving them partial self-government
with the certainty that the grants of the foreign government were to cease at a
stated time, and to make them feel that they were growing towards a higher
state and a higher privilege.

Rev. Dr. Kalopothakes (Athens) : I was very much gratified to hear
the unanimous expressions with regard to Church Government and the
union and co-operation among native Christians. It is a question which
must be left with the natives. But, dear friends, if you want
Precept and practice. the natives to unite and co-operate with each other, you, the
Missionaries, must show the example. When the natives hear
one Missionary say that one cannot be a complete Christian unless he is
re-baptised, or he cannot be a true preacher unless he is re-ordained,
you cannot expect them to co-operate or to unite. These differences must
cease to exist in the Mission-field, and then the natives will unite and co-
operate one with each other.

Rev. H. Williams (C.M.S. from Bengal) : I wish to speak about
union among Christians, and in representing Bengal, I think I speak
for all the brethren there when I say it is the deepest longing and yearning
of our hearts to arrive at something like unity in the Missions in that part

of the world, and I think I can emphasise this by bringing before you how the matter must appear to an inquirer into Christianity on visiting Calcutta. I am reminded of it as often as I go to Calcutta, for on leaving Sealdah station I go down an important street called Bow Bazaar. The first building I see is a large Roman Catholic Church; and **The effect of our divisions on native inquirers.** if the inquirer goes there, what is he told? That he will find salvation there, but if he goes any further down the street he certainly will be damned, more certainly than if he remain in Hinduism or Mohammedanism. That will be the message given to him by the Roman Catholics. He goes a little further down, and comes to the Oxford Mission House (or might have come two years ago), and there he would have been told he might receive salvation in the Church he had just left, but he would be more secure with them, and be even less secure than with the Roman Catholics if he goes a little further down the street. He goes a little further, and then he will come to the Presbyterians. I am glad to say we do work well together there, but a stout Presbyterian would congratulate him upon having escaped Popery and Prelacy. He goes a little further down, and then comes to the Baptist Church, and is there congratulated on escaping Popery, and Prelacy, and Presbyterianism, and coming to be properly baptised. He goes a little further down, and then he comes to the Plymouth Brethren who congratulate him upon escaping from them all and arriving where he will find true unity. Now I say that is how it must strike a native inquirer in India; and can you wonder at this remark made by a man in a bazaar to one of our preachers when he said, " First of all settle your differences between Church and Chapel, and then come and try to convert us"?

Rev. Henry Stout (Reformed Church in America, from Japan): I rise merely to speak in regard to the desirability of concentrating upon special fields for work, and I have a proposition of a very definite nature to make to you. I believe, in the good providence of God, that the two hundred and fifty Foreign Missionaries now at work in Japan, together with the twenty thousand Christians who are already gathered into that Church, are a power sufficient for the salvation of that land. But it seems to me—and it does not only seem to me, but to the whole body of Foreign Missionaries in that land—that it is not a question which should be **Japan cannot wait.** relegated to the future. The question of the conversion of Japan is one *that is imminent,* and now is the supreme moment for that land.

When I first went to Japan about twenty years ago I think I could have counted upon the fingers of one hand all those who had been baptised in the name of our Saviour, and these men were baptised in secret because of the laws of that land; but to-day there are more than twenty thousand who acknowledge Christ as their Saviour. When I tell you that in those days it was worth more than a man's life to dare to speak of Christ, and that it was impossible for me to get two of my pupils together to study the Scriptures, but that now men everywhere are glad to hear the tidings of salvation, and that a spirit of inquiry is abroad among the people,—when I tell you these things, and many other indications of the providence of God at the present time, I ask you, What do these things mean? There is a change already among the people, the men in high places desire Christians to come and save their land **The soil ready for the seeds of union.** for Christ. Now what shall we consider as the conclusion of this whole matter? It seems to me that this is not only the supreme moment for Japan, but it is the supreme moment for the Church of Christ to

ιook to and to go to Japan, and to send not merely two hundred and fifty men
there, but perhaps a thousand men and women ; not to raise a few thousand
pounds for Japan, but to raise many tens of thousands of pounds, and so to
labour that perhaps within the present generation Japan shall be won for Christ.
If this be done, what will be the result upon that people themselves? I cannot
speak of what will be the result upon the world. Men speak of the failure
of Missions. Let us who are living to-day so labour that we shall be able
to point to Japan as a land won for Christ, and say, "That is what the
Church can do for Christ." What will be the effect upon the Church? I very
well remember the impression produced when it was announced that the
American Board had succeeded in evangelising the Sandwich Islands—what
will be the effect when the Church can point to Japan in the near future won
for Christ? A wave of enthusiasm will sweep over the Church which will
prepare it to go into those great Empires like China and India, and conquer
them for Christ.

Rev. J. L. Potter (Presbyterian Board of Foreign Missions [U.S.A.],
from Persia): Mr. Chairman, and Christian friends,—It is my privilege to
represent before you a little body of workers in Eastern Persia—the division
of Eastern is with respect to our Western Mission. With regard to the
whole of the country it might more properly be designated the
Comity in Persia. north-east. The fraternal co-operation and counsel which have
existed in our Mission may be worthy of note. A leaf or a few lines from
our experience may be of interest. First in Hamadan, about two hundred
miles from Teheran ; a Missionary from another Society came there.
Fraternal relations were entered into between our Mission and the new
Missionary. He was himself convinced that it was not necessary for him
to remain there, that the work was being done by a Society already there.
He made such representations to his own Society that they withdrew, and
a successor has not been appointed. With regard to Teheran, the capital
of Persia, our fraternal relations with our good brethren at Ispahan have
been most friendly and cordial, and it seems to me that these fraternal
relations may extend at least to a correspondence on subjects of mutual
interest and occasional personal intercourse. At Teheran our situation is
fortunate. Our brethren of the Church Missionary Society in going to and
from their field naturally pass through Teheran. We have had the pleasure
and privilege of greeting them and talking over the Lord's work. We have
had the pleasure, also, of hearing them speak in our chapel. As we
maintain a service in English, and for the foreigners resident, it has been our
privilege to have them not only speak in Persian but in English also. A
venerable father in Christ this morning suggested the desirability of double
ordination. Perhaps I may be permitted to say the Presbyterian ministers
at Teheran, at the request of the foreigners resident, use the English morning service with slight alterations,—prayer for the Shah and for the President
of the United States, and some minor additions besides. This has worked
favourably and prosperously ; it has met the desire of the foreigners
resident without a second ordination.

Rev. John McLaurin (Canadian Baptist Mission): There seems to be
union in the air that we breathe here, and I have only just one practical
question to ask upon that subject, and it is this, Suppose your Missionaries
out in the field set about carrying all this good advice into practice, will
you sustain them ? If I begin baptising infants, and my brother next door

begins immersing adults, shall we be left alone? Shall we not be recalled? Now, brethren, it seems to me, with all due deference to a great deal that has been said here to-day, that we have com- *Will Home Boards encourage practical union?* menced at the wrong end of this. As long as we are dependent upon Boards at home, as long as we are dependent upon the contributions of the Churches that lie at the basis of these Boards, so long will the present state of things exist on the foreign field.

There is one other matter I wish to refer to. Concentration has been spoken of, and I would fain see the efforts of God's people concentrated upon this map of the world; but I think there is one thing that has been overlooked in the past—I hope it will not in the future,—and that is, Why should not our great Societies concentrate more than they do? Why should a Society put down a man in a large city here, and leave him alone, and then put another man down five hundred miles distant in another city, and leave him alone, and why should anybody be allowed to come in between these two men and occupy the territory? That has been done, that is being done, in fact, at the present day. There is another thing that puzzles me here this afternoon, and it is this, Why should all the Societies of Great Britain and America, for instance, concen- trate among the eight hundred thousand people of Calcutta, and *Co-operation in large towns, not in country.* for reasons best known to themselves, agree to work together there, when half the same number may not concentrate over half a million of people spread out in the country? Why? If we can do it in Calcutta, brethren and sisters, we can do it anywhere, and live peaceably and amicably with the blessing of God resting upon us.

Professor R. B. Welch, LL.D. (Auburn, New York): Students come to us from abroad to our seminaries; what is their feeling with regard to this question? So far as I have noticed from experience in teaching in a theological seminary, universally it is in favour of Mission Comity, of co-operation. I know that such young men generally, indeed desire, to go back not under the restriction of a denomination *Native students favour Comity.* in this country, but to give themselves to the work of Christ. This, I think, indicates the feeling of the young Christians thee that are hopeful for the progress of Christianity. Now what is the feeling in our Home Churches? I think evidently growing everywhere, this desire for Mission Comity, for co-operation,—not necessarily union, certainly not uniformity, but Comity and co-operation. A year ago I was in the great Assembly of Presbyterian Churches representing seven hundred thousand Christians at Omaha. This subject of co-operation had been prepared for the year before. A Committee had been appointed to consider the question and report to the Assembly. The report was not long; it was full of resolutions on specific details; every resolution was carefully considered, thoroughly discussed, and then the final vote came upon the whole body of resolutions for more Mission Comity and co-operation, and it was the supreme moment of that great General Assembly,—it was one great unani- mous consent; and I am sure this indicates the feeling that is growing at home. Now how is it among the native Christians where they are? I believe it is increasing mightily. I believe it is the current feeling there. How is it among the Missionaries? That is the great question, I believe, of this hour. Here are Missionaries, this is a Missionary Convention,—what will the Missionaries say in view of this feeling at home, in view of this feeling of the young men abroad, in view of this feeling *Call for courage in Missionaries.* among the native Christians? What will they say? Will they be bold enough, and brave enough, and true enough to the spirit of unity and Christ to go home and cultivate this feeling anywhere, and everywhere? If they will, then there is one great accord in this rising current, and it must then increase. I believe we have reached the supreme moment in this Conference,—I believe this is a crowning question; I believe this comprehends, and intertwines, and interfuses all; and if we go home across the seas, and out to the Mission-fields, and feel that we have not settled in this Conference that this is the high demand, yea the unanimous demand, I think we have made a crowning mistake. God save us from such a mistake!

Rev. A. D. Gring (Reformed Church in the United States, from Japan): I want to witness to-day as a member of the Union Church of Christ in Japan what an intense pleasure it is, and how much of the sacrifice and trouble of a Foreign Missionary is taken away in the united movement for the establishment of the Church of Christ abroad. I can witness that my life in Japan in this Union Church has been of the most pleasant sort. It

Experience in Union Church, Japan. has come from this source largely that the brethren there of different names have united as one man that all the results of our work shall go into one native Japanese Church. We have not lost our individuality by so doing. Our individual Missions may be working in certain quarters, yet all the fruit of our work shall go into this native Union Church of Christ which aims to be self-supporting, self-propagating, and self-governing.

A most delightful work it is. The Japanese have demanded it, and for what reason? They say they are too poor to have denominationalism in Japan.

Too poor to be denominational. Denominationalism is a luxury which can only be enjoyed on your home soil. The Japanese are a poor people, and they say, "Give us one united Church. We are now united under one common ruler, the Emperor. Heretofore we were cut up into little districts under the feudal system, but as we have one ruler so we would like one Church." You were speaking this morning of boundary lines. What would be the result if we were all to set off to get alone? Why, we Presbyterians would become so strong we would not look at anybody else,—so the Baptists, and so the rest. It is the greatest blessing of God that we are all thrown together, so that the rough edges are worn off, and we all come into a larger union. You can see the effects of this great union in Japan. It does away with all these many schools, these theological seminaries, and these different ordinary schools, we are there combining into large schools, but each Mission is putting its strength into its work. Work in this way, and the conversion of Japan for Christ by this union will be hastened by ten or twenty years.

Dr. Erik Nyström (Swedish Missionary, from Algiers): What is the reason of ecclesiastical differences? The reason is only this, that forms of expression and forms of devotion are regarded as the chief end, and not as the means. And where this is the case, where people seek unity in outward uniformity hearts are separated. But let it be changed, so that

Uniformity will destroy unity. what is the chief thing may be the chief thing, and what is the means be the means; that is to say, let love of God, and love of our neighbour, be the chief end, and let forms of expression and forms of devotion be means subordinated unto the chief end, and then love will be burning, and hearts will be united. It has been said at this meeting that we need a new departure. I should like to say we have had too much of departure, we have gone away from something, we need turning back. And what is the departure? and what is the turning back? I would refer to

the first verse of the second chapter of Revelations. "Unto the angel of
the Church at Ephesus,"—so orthodox and zealous,—"I have somewhat
against thee, because thou hast left thy first love. Remember, therefore,
from whence thou art fallen and repent, and do the first works." Oh, let
us unite for the chief end, and let us remember that the forms and
expressions are only means and not the end.

Rev. Washington Gladden, D.D. (Ohio): I shall address myself to the
question which is upon the programme,—"How far may fraternal counsel
and co-operation be maintained between Missions on the same fields, though
not organically connected?" I think the answer to that question is simply
this: fraternal counsel and co-operation may be maintained
abroad to about the same dregree that it is maintained at As at home
so abroad.
home, and not to any very much greater degree. Now we
heard this morning from the Missionaries who spoke to us, reports from the
foreign field, showing that there is certainly in some fields a great lack of
this fraternal counsel and co-operation, that there are intrusions and confusions and divisions, which are very unhappy indeed. These facts are mostly
covered up as one said in the Missionary reports, but they exist. But, do
any of you wonder at it? Is it not just the same sort of thing that we are
seeing at home all the while? Is it not true in all our cities, and in
America? I speak for America, because I do not know anything about
England or Germany; but, on the frontiers of the West, is it not
true that such confusions and intrusions are all the while occurring?
Now, if this is true at home, it will be true abroad. Brethren, you cannot
export an article that you do not produce at home. If you have division
and confusion at home you will have it abroad, and the place to begin the
reformation of this evil is at Jerusalem. You have to begin at home.

Rev. W. McGregor (English Presbyterian Mission, Amoy): The first
question to-day is: "How far has union among native Christians in heathen
lands been found practicable or desirable?" I have no hesitation in saying
that union among the native Christians in heathen lands is far more
practicable than union among the Missions and the Boards representing them
at home. If, in any case, such union does not take place it is Native
Christians unite
naturally.
not due to the native Christians. When a man is rescued from
heathenism, the central truths of Christianity are brought
before him, and he cannot realise what the differences are between the
various Evangelical denominations working alongside of each other. You
have already learned, from Dr. Taylor's Paper, that the Amoy Church is the
first in which organic union in the Mission work, representing two different
Missions, has really and actually taken place. Missionaries came from the
English Presbyterian Church and from the Reformed Churches of North
America, worked alongside each other, visited and preached at each other's
stations, and the native Church was never separated; it was from the
beginning one Church. It never entered the minds of the native Christians
that there should be a separation, but it did enter the mind of the Church in
America. When at first it was explained to them that this was one native
Church, and that there was no reason for separation, they decided that separation must take place, and it was only when their Missionaries in the field
sent home their resignations that the Church in America realised the gravity
of the situation.

Now Missionaries may not always be prepared to take that step, and the Board at home might not perhaps take the action that the American Church did; it decided that this Union should continue, and the Union has continued and prospered unto this day. Just one word about the money. I believe the money sent from home should always be under the management of the Missionaries sent from home. It should not be in the hands of the native Church. I mention this because I know in some cases there has been money sent from home that really has fallen under the management of the native Church. I believe this is to be deprecated, and in every case avoided.

The difficulties are at home.

Lord Radstock: I cannot help feeling that perhaps we have been in danger during this afternoon's meeting of forgetting the very source and direction of the whole of this movement. There seems to me a danger of our limiting our expectations by the experience of the past. Thank God, we not only believe, but we have had an experience that there is one Body and there is one Spirit. Thank God these difficulties which have come to light during this Conference have been very few and may be simply met. Supposing we had all had to face these difficulties eighteen hundred years ago, when the Blessed One was upon earth, what would we have done? We should have said, "We will just go and ask the Lord about it." He would have put it all right, do not you think? If there were one hundred or two hundred disciples would not He have instructed them? Is He less in our midst to-day? Have we not been looking to our organisations and our plans, and have forgotten Him? We have forgotten that He is really in each place, in each place the Head of the little Church, and that when the little Church recognises Him as the Head He will, according to the very constitution of that Church, not merely guide it, but manifest Himself as the Head of the Body. Now one single word more. When I was in India I had the great privilege of visiting many Mission stations. In nearly all the larger stations there were monthly Conferences of Missionaries of different denominations. Those seemed to me to be the germ of the formation of the Church in each place, and my earnest desire is that true servants of God who work in the Committees at home may realise that there are Churches existing, and they should hesitate very much about interfering with decisions which these Churches may come to under the guidance of the Head of the Church. Meanwhile let us trust Him. Let us know that it is going to be manifested as one Church in the glory without spot or wrinkle or any such thing, and that meanwhile in each place, whatever the difficulties are, they are not to be met by fresh resolutions or methods, but rather simply waiting for Him and waiting upon Him we shall renew our strength.

A present Christ and unity.

Home Committees and native Churches.

Mr. J. Bevan Braithwaite: I have very great diffidence in coming forward amongst so many excellent friends, but I have just a word or two to say, having thought very much upon this great subject. I think we shall all agree that unity is not to be found in an insisting upon an outward uniformity. We must not hope, looking to the constitution of the human mind, for an absolute uniformity in worship or an outward observancy; but each, whilst faithful to our own convictions as to these things, should seek to dwell, as Lord Radstock has just said, in the very bosom of the Lord Jesus Christ, abiding in His love, and endeavouring to keep the unity of the Spirit in the bond of peace.

Unity in Christ the true Comity.

There will ever be the true living Church of that Redeemer who is still our one Lord, our one Head. It is a continual looking unto Jesus and abiding in His love.

Rev. C. H. Bell, D.D. (Cumberland Presbyterian Church Board of Missions, U.S.A.): Since coming to the Conference I have received news from our General Assembly in America, stating that it was felt desirable on the part of our highest Church Court that our Board should unite with the Union Church in Japan in the work, if proper and desirable arrangements could be made. I would state that our Church, I believe, is the only one there that bears the name Presbyterian in Japan, the others having united under another name. Now we do not love Presbyterians less, but I think we will love Christ more.

The Chairman: A letter has just come from Lord Harrowby, expressing deep regret that he was unable to leave the Royal Commission on Education, so that he was deprived of the pleasure of being present at this meeting. I have just one solitary remark to make with reference to this new departure and Missionaries denying themselves. I do not see one word in this Book of God *Self-abnegation* that calls upon a Missionary to deny himself more than *must begin* it calls upon every one of us. There is a great deal *at home.* talked about heroic Missionaries. I want to talk about heroic committee men at home. They must go together. As the life of the Church is at home, so will be the life of the Church in the foreign field; they are both one and indivisible. I dare not minimise the difficulties in the way, but the one solution of them is the power of the Holy Ghost right in our midst, and no other power that I know of will accomplish the end in view. The human heart is subdued by His power in the first instance, and all difficulties are removed out of the way, and I believe the Church on her knees before God, will accomplish more than all the organisations of all the Committees, and all the Societies together, not that I have anything but praise to say for all of them. If that spirit of self-denial is poured out upon the whole Church at home we shall have a grand march onward, and God will be more and more glorified.

Dr. Murray Mitchell pronounced the Benediction.

MEETINGS OF MEMBERS IN SECTION.

HOME WORK FOR MISSIONS.

(1) *SPIRITUAL AGENCIES.*

(*a*) How to raise the Churches to the degree of consecration required for the evangelisation of the world.

(*b*) Increased observance of the monthly concert, and a larger place for Foreign Missions in the schedules for the Week of Prayer.

(*c*) The value of simultaneous meetings, Missionary conventions, and other special services.

(*d*) The responsibilities of wealth.

(*Monday morning, June 18th, in the Lower Hall.*)

Rev. Cavalière de Prochet in the chair.
Acting Secretary, Mr. B. Broomhall.

Rev. George Wilson offered prayer.

The Chairman: Ladies and gentlemen,—In Italy, when we do not want to hear the voice of a man in the Church we put him in the chair, and I shall act on that principle, although I am in London. Allow me only to say one word to express all the deep satisfaction I have felt in attending these Conferences. My work is not a work to the heathen; it is a work to Roman Catholics. And let me say, by way of parenthesis, that I have been exceedingly struck by the great similarity between the work of Missions to the heathen and the work of evangelisation among the Roman Catholics. While listening with attention to the speakers who, one after another, have instructed us, I have found that the difficulties are the same, that the objections are the same, and many other things into the details of which I need not enter. You see, then, that although I came prepared to sympathise, my sympathies have been greatly increased by what I have heard. You know that we

Italians are rather talkers than listeners ; and when I go back to my friends and tell them that for three days (unfortunately I could not be here the first two days) I have actually been listening, attending three meetings each day, and that I have survived it, it would be the best compliment I could pay ; for were I to expatiate on the subject in Italy for two hours it would not tell so much upon my people as saying to them that I have been listening for three days, and am ready for three days more.

But I am afraid that I am giving you an illustration of the talkativeness of Italians, and I must therefore check myself. We have to-day to address ourselves to what is certainly a most important subject. I am reminded of the noblest words that I ever read, as coming from the lips of an Admiral. (I have been a soldier myself, and everything that is soldier-like comes home to me.) I refer to the words of Nelson, at Trafalgar, when he said, "England expects every man to do his duty." Well, what The duty of all Christians. is it that we have to do to-day ? If I understand your English, and if I grasp the subject, we have only to consider this : How shall we ministers and all Christians who have at heart the cause of our Master, make every man in our congregations hear, not Nelson, but the Captain of our salvation, saying, "Your Father expects every one of His children to do his or her duty." That is, according to my understanding, what we have to do to-day ; and we may well, from the bottom of our hearts, ask for wisdom from above. May He Himself preside over our meetings, and give to the speakers a word in season, and to all of us those feelings of receptiveness of truth which will enable us afterwards in our own sphere to spread abroad what we have heard here. I will now call upon the readers of the Papers that are to be brought before the Conference.

The Acting Secretary: Before Dr. Pierson reads his Paper, I may mention that our friend is the Editor of a Missionary publication, entitled *The Missionary Review of the World*. It was started by the late Rev. George Wilder, and conducted by him for ten years. It differs from other publications in this respect, that it gives a survey of the entire Mission-field. I know no publication that equals it in the information which it gives in regard to the operations of all the Missionary agencies.

PAPER.

1. By THE REV. ARTHUR T. PIERSON, D.D. (Philadelphia, U.S.A.).

Home Work for Missions. (1) *Spiritual Agencies.*

What the *source* is to the *supply*, the motor to the machine, the Home Church is to the Foreign field. The vigour of the heart's beat determines the pulse beat at the extremities. It is of first importance that, at home, work for Missions abroad be continuous and constant, healthy in tone and spiritual in type.

How shall the Churches be raised to the degree of consecration required for the evangelisation of the world ? Sheldon Dibble used to say, that two conversions are needful: first, to Christ as Two conversions a Saviour from sin ; and then to Missions as the correc- needed. tive and antidote to selfishness. A century ago William Carey felt the thrust of the keen lance of Sydney Smith, who by his unsanctified wit proposed to rout out that nest of consecrated cobblers; and Carey had to fight for fifteen years the apathy even of his own Baptist brethren. Dr. Judson's hand was nearly shaken off, and his hair shorn off, by those who, in the crises which can be met only by self-sacrifice, would, to save themselves, willingly have let Missions die.

Foremost among the means by which deeper devotion to the work of evangelisation is to be secured, I would put *the education of* **Teach the prin-** *the Church* in the very *principle of Missions.* Where **ciple of Missions.** the hearty acceptance of this is lacking, the impulse and impetus of Missions are wanting. The Church of God exists not only as a *rallying* but as a *radiating* centre. It is indeed a home, but also a school ; a place for worship, but not less for work. For a society of disciples to be engrossed even in self-culture is fatal to service and even to true sanctity. The Church is no gymnasium, where exercise is the law and self-development the end. The field is the world, and the sower and reaper, while at work for a harvest, each gets in his exertion the very exercise which is needful to growth.

So important and so fundamental is this principle of Missions, that any Church which denies or practically neglects it deserves to be served with a writ of " *quo warranto.*" This law of Church life must be constantly kept before believers, enforced and emphasised by repetition, that upon every believer is laid the duty of personal labour for the lost. This conviction must be beaten in and burned in, till it becomes a part of the very consciousness of every disciple—until the goal is seen to be, not salvation or even sanctification, but service to God and man in saving souls.

In the education of a Church in Foreign Missions, nothing is more essential than that the Missionary spirit burn in the *pastor.* **The pastor's** A stream rises no higher than its source ; and ordinarily **example.** the measure of the pastor's interest in the world field determines the level of his people's earnestness and enthusiasm. He ought to be a student of Missions, an authority on Missions, and a leader in Missions. He is not the driver of a herd, but the leader of a flock ; he must therefore go *before.* His contagious enthusiasm and example must inspire in others the spirit of consecration. The personal character of the man gives tone to his preaching, and is perhaps itself the best kind of preaching. That must be a frozen Church in which a man, alive with intelligence and zeal for the work of God, cannot warm into life and action, under such a pastor as. the Rev. W. Fleming Stevenson.

The rudiments of a true education being laid, we must go on **Feed with** unto perfection ; and among all the means of this higher **knowledge** training we put first and foremost a *knowledge of the* **of Missions.** *facts* of Missionary history and biography. Information is a necessary part of all university training in Missions—not a partial, superficial impression, but information—a knowledge of Missions complete enough and thorough enough to crystallise into symmetrical form in the mind and heart. Facts are the fingers of God. To a devout student of His will they become signs of the times and signals of His march through the ages. Like the gnomon of a sundial, even their shadow may mark the hour in God's day. Prince Albert used to say to the young men of Britain: "Find out God's plan in your generation, and never cross it, but fall into your own place in it." There is a pillar of Providence, the perpetual pillar of cloud and fire, whereby we may be led. That pillar is built up of facts, oftentimes mysterious and dark, like a cloud, yet hiding the presence and power of Him who dwelt in the cloud, and made it luminous.

To a true disciple Missions need no *argument*, since the Church has, what the Iron Duke called, her "*marching orders.*" But duty becomes delight, and responsibility is transfigured into privilege, when it Some significant facts. is clearly seen that to move with the Missionary band is to take up march with God. The apathy and lethargy prevailing among believers upon the subject of Missions is to me unaccountable in view of the multitude and magnificence of the facts which justify the statement that in the movements of Modern Missions more than in any other of the ages there has been a demonstration and a revelation of God.

We are observing the Centenary of Modern Missions. But the most amazing results of this century have been wrought during its *last third*, or the lifetime of the generation now living. This World's Conference is simply the Church coming together at the Antioch of the Occident, to hear those whom the Holy Ghost has chosen and the Church The Church awakening. has separated unto this work, rehearse all that God has done with them, and how He has opened the door of faith unto the Gentiles. Who dares to say, in the light of Modern Missions, that the days of supernatural working are passed? So far as in primitive days the disciples have gone forth and preached everywhere, it has still been true that the Lord has wrought with and confirmed the Word with signs following—signs unmistakable and unmistakably supernatural. Doors have been opened within fifty years that no human power could have unbarred. The mighty moving of God can be traced back through the centuries, long since giving Protestant England a foothold in the very *critical* centre, the *pivotal* centre of oriental empires and religions. The necessity of protecting her Indian possessions, of keeping open the line of communication between London and Calcutta, determined the attitude of every nation along the water highway. Then from beyond the Pacific another mighty, puissant people, the offspring of Protestant Britain, moved forward thirty years ago to turn the extreme Eastern wing of the enemy, while Britain was piercing and holding the centre. Commodore Perry knocked at the sea gates of Japan, and in the name of a Christian republic demanded entrance. Rusty bolts that had not been drawn for more than two centuries were flung back, and the two-leaved doors of brass were opened to the commerce of the world. Rapid has been the progress of the march of God. Japan unsealed her gates in 1854. From that time not a year has passed The world opened. without some mighty onward movement or stupendous development. The year 1856, saw signed and sealed the Hatti Sherif in Turkey, by which the Sultan, at least in form, announced the era of toleration. The next year the Mutiny in India changed the whole attitude of the East India

Company toward Missions, and prepared the way for the surrender of its charter to the Crown of England. In 1858, the great breach was made in the Chinese wall, and by the treaty of Tien-tsin one-third of the human race were made accessible to Christian nations; and, as Dr. Gracey says, that wide door was opened, not by the vermilion pencil of the Emperor, but by the decree of the Eternal.

Let us leap the chasm of twenty years, and note the progress of events on the dark continent. In 1871 Stanley pierced the jungles to find the heroic Livingstone, who in 1873 died near Lake Bangweolo; Recent progress in Missions. in 1874 Stanley undertook to explore Equatorial Africa; in 1877, after a thousand days, he emerged at the mouth of the Congo. At once England took up the work of following the steps of the explorer with the march of the Missionary, and now, ten years later, the Missions of the great lakes in the East, and those of the Congo Basin at the West, are stretching hands to link East and West together; give us ten years more and Krapf's prophecy will be fulfilled,—a chain of Missions will cross the continent. In 1884 fifteen nations, called together by King Leopold, and presided over by Bismarck, met in Berlin to lay the basis of the Congo Free State; and in that Council, not only Protestant, but Greek, Papal and Moslem powers, joined !

Such are some of the great *Providential* signs of a supernatural Presence and Power. What shall be said of the *gracious* transformations that have displaced cannibal ovens by a thousand Christian churches in Providential signs. Polynesia; that reared Metlakahtla in British Columbia; that made Madagascar the crown of the London Missionary Society; that turned Sierra Leone into a Christian state; that wrought mightily with Hans Egede in Greenland, Morrison and Burns in China, Perkins and Grant in Persia, Carey and Wilson and Duff in India, and McCall in Belleville !

If disciples are *indifferent* to Missions, it is because they are *ignorant* of Missions. A fire needs first of all to be kindled, then to be fed, then to have vent. The only power that can kindle the flame of Provide fuel of information. Missionary zeal is the Holy Spirit. The coal must be a live coal from God's altar. But, having the coal and a breath from above, all that is needed is *fuel to feed* the flame, and that fuel is supplied by a knowledge of *facts*. Too much care cannot be taken to supply these facts in an attractive, available form, at the lowest cost. The Women's Boards and Societies have done no greater service than in providing and distributing a cheap *literature* of Missions. The printed facts that are to do this work of education must be put in the briefest and most Statements clear and brief. pointed form. This is an age of steam and telegraph. While Methuselah turned round we have gone around the globe. Men need now what they can catch at a glance. Ponderous volumes may do for ponderous men, who have leisure for prolonged study and research. But the bulk of people must get their knowledge of facts in a condensed form. Our bulletins must be bullet-ins. Some of us must skim the great pan and serve up the cream in a little pitcher, rich and sweet; we must boil down the great roots and give others the sweet liquorice in the stick, so that a bite will give a taste and make the mouth water for more. Students of Missions will read with avidity the " Ely Volume," and the " Middle Kingdom," and kindred books that are the authorities on Missions; but students of Missions are not *made* by this process. We must feed first with milk and not with strong meat, and by the spoonful, until both capacity and appetite are formed.

The value of simultaneous meetings, Missionary conventions, and other special services consists perhaps *mainly* in the wide, rapid, attractive, and effective *dissemination of intelligence.* Truths and facts are brought before the mind with all the help of the enthusiasm of a public assembly. The eye helps the ear in producing and fastening impression. The hearer confronts the living men or women who have come from the field, perhaps with the very idols of the heathen in their hands, or the relics of their superstitious practices; sometimes the native convert, or preacher, himself pleads for his benighted fellow-countrymen. And so the most apathetic soul, in whom grace has kindled the fire of love, finds the fire burning, spreading, consuming selfishness, and demanding a proper vent in Christian effort. This is the way that Missionaries are made. *Simultaneous meetings.*

In 1885, there assembled at Mr. Moody's boys' school at Mount Hermon, in Massachusetts, about three hundred students from the various colleges for a few weeks of study of the Word of God. A few who had in view the foreign field greatly desired a Missionary meeting, and all the students were invited. There was not even a Missionary map to assist in impressing the facts; the speaker drew on the black board a rude outline of the continents, and then proceeded to trace the great facts of Missions, and so deep was the interest awakened that meeting after meeting followed; from about a score, the number who chose the Mission-field rose to a hundred. Then certain chosen men resolved to go and visit the colleges, and carry the sacred fire; they went, met their fellow-students and brought out the leading facts of Missions. And to-day, in America and in England, a band of probably not less than three thousand young men and women stand *ready* to go to the foreign field if the door shall open before them. If disciples do not wish to flame with Missionary zeal, they must avoid contact and converse with the facts, and with the heroic souls who are the living factors of Missions. It is dangerous business to trifle with combustible material, unless you are quite sure there is not even a spark of life or love in your soul. *Moody's convention.*

Among these means of education we mention last what, in the order of time and of importance, belongs first: the *influence of Christian women in the home life.* If God has shut out the ordinary woman from much participation in public life, and shut her in the home, it is because her sphere makes up in quality what it lacks in quantity. Here are life's arcana, veiled from the common eye,—the home is the matrix of character. The faith of the grandmother Lois and mother Eunice still descends to Timothy. Anthusa and Monica still give the Church her golden-mouthed Johns and her giant Augustines. To one woman may be traced the rise of the seven kingdoms of the Saxon Heptarchy. At every stream there is a point where a human hand might turn its current; and at that point in human lives the wife and mother presides. The heathen rhetorician Libanius exclaimed, "What women these Christians have!" And, if the secret things were brought to light, it might be found that many, beside Morrison and Burns, and Lindley, and Patteson, have owed their saintly character and Missionary career to the sanctity of a mother. Even before birth maternal character leaves its impress upon *Woman's influence.*

the unborn, and at the mother's breast and knee the earliest lessons are learned in piety and prayer and personal consecration.

The nursery may be the garden where the precious germs are first nourished, from which develop pillars of cedar and olive for the temple of God. The Earl of Shaftesbury learned of humble Maria Millis the first lessons in living which made his influence capable of being measured only by parallels of latitude and meridians of longitude, and its results only to be computed by the æons of eternity ! My sisters in Christ, do not hesitate to break on your Master's feet your alabaster flask ; though it may seem but as waste to some, the house shall be filled with the odour of your consecration, and you shall at least create in the home a mighty mould of character from which shall go both men and women whose words and deeds shall shake the world !

The nursery training.

Here, in the home, if prevailing selfishness and extravagant self-indulgence are to be corrected, must be taught first lessons in giving, the Divine doctrine of stewardship, and the responsibilities both of wealth and poverty. Munificent legacies cannot atone for parsimonious gifts. It is not God or His poor that need our gifts, so much as we ourselves need to give. Giving is the sovereign secret of serving, but also of getting and growing. To deny self and help others is God's antidote to that monstrous sin of selfishness which is the root of all others ; and so it is more blessed to give than to receive. And if there ever was an altar that sanctified, magnified, glorified, the gift, it is the altar of Missions. Let the ethics, the economics, the æsthetics of giving be taught at the mother's knee, and we shall have a new generation of givers.

Train to self-denial.

Too much emphasis cannot be laid on placing at the centre of the family a consecrated woman. She is like Goëthe's mythical lamp which, set in the humblest hut of the fisherman, changed all within it to silver. She pours on the root of the cocoanut tree the water which comes back, by-and-bye, sweetened and enriched in the milk of the cocoanut which falls from the top. A selfish, sordid woman, presiding at the home, perverts child life ; in such a household there is a malign influence which, like the mirrors in the temples of Smyrna, represents the fairest images distorted and deformed, and makes even piety seem repellant. The more I see of woman's influence on the whole structure of society the more I feel the stress of the Apostolic injunction that the believer should *marry only in the Lord.*

The responsibilities of wealth are to be discussed by another in a separate Paper. But I must add, to complete my own thought, that among other necessary reforms in our Church life we must cease to *depend upon the donations of the rich.* It is alike harmful to them and to the Church. God never meant that with such wealth of Divine promises we should appeal to the rich, and especially the worldly wealthy, for money for the kingdom. Such appeals discount our faith, dishonour our Lord, and humiliate the Church ; while they inflate the rich with self-righteous conceit and complacence as patrons of the cause of God. Let there be a Bible type of systematic and proportionate giving by every disciple, and the treasures of the Church would overflow with the voluntary gifts of disciples.

Systematic and proportionate giving.

Above all other spiritual agencies affecting Missions from the home side we place *earnest and habitual prayer.* This is a supernatural Gospel, and demands a supernatural power, for conversion is a supernatural work. Not even a knowledge of facts can make a Missionary or inspire a Missionary spirit. The coal must be there and the breath of God, beforeeven the best fuel will take fire. A thermometer Prayer, earnest and habitual. may be held in the direct line of the sun's rays and show but little rise in the temperature, because the radiant heat is reflected from the bright glassy bulb, like light from a mirror. Heat rays from the sun may pass through a lens of ice, and be concentrated to a sufficient degree to ignite, at the focus, combustible material, and yet those rays not melt the ice of which the lens is formed. It is only when knowledge is sanctified by prayer that it becomes a power.

For one, I regard the increased, or rather the *revived* observance, of the *monthly concert* as a necessity to true Home work for Missions. It is now comparatively a thing of the past. Once it was a regular observance of the first Monday of each month; then merged into the first Sunday evening; then the first mid-week service; and in many cases divided between Home and Foreign Missions; and so it lost its original The monthly concert. special character, and has now only a name to live and is practically dead. I know a Church member who thought the monthly concert meant a musical entertainment. To allow so valuable a help to the culture of intelligent interest in Missions to be dropped from our Church economy and become an archæological curiosity, is a fundamental mistake. It may be made both interesting and stimulating. I have found the most successful way of conducting it, to be, to divide the world field among the Church membership, so that every man and woman willing to help may have a special field from which to report from time to time, changing the fields once a year in order to broaden both intelligence and interest. Then have *maps*, and, best of all, maps made by the Church members themselves. A man or woman who draws a map of any Mission-field will never lose the image of that field from the mind's eye. I have had a full set of fine maps made for me without a penny's cost, by members of my own congregation.

The lack of earnest, believing, united *prayer* for Missions is both lamentable and fatal to success. Prayer has always marked and turned the crises of the kingdom. No sooner do devout souls begin to unite in definite supplication than stupendous results begin to develop. Fifty years ago the burden of prayer was for the opening of doors, and one after another the iron gates opened as of their own accord. Then New lessons in prayer. the plea went up for larger gifts of *money*; and at a critical period, when the whole onward march of Missions was threatened, God gave a spirit of liberality; in 1878, that *annus mirabilis*, some twenty persons gave about four millions of dollars. Woman came to the front and showed how, by gathering the mites systematically, the aggregate of gifts may grow steadily year by year and rapidly. Then devout disciples were led to pray for more labourers, and especially for the consecration of our foremost youth; and now, from the universities of Britain and America, a host of three thousand young men and women are knocking at the doors of the Church, saying, " Here we are, send us; " and even the Church that has been praying for this very result can scarce believe that they stand before the gate !

Brethren, we shall have learned little at this great Conference if we shall not have learned new lessons of the power of prayer. Themistocles delayed the naval engagement at Salamis until the land breeze blew, which swept his vessels toward the foe and left every oarsman free to use the bow and the spear.   How much wasted time and strength might be saved if the Church of God but waited for the breath of the Holy Spirit to provide the impulse and momentum which we vainly seek to supply by our own energy and endeavour !   When He breathes and blows upon us, how they who have toiled in rowing are left free to wield the weapon of the Lord's warfare, to exchange secular anxieties for spiritual successes !

Zoroaster bade his followers let the fires go out periodically upon their hearthstones, that they might be compelled to rekindle them at the sacred altars of the sun.   What mean the smouldering embers on *our* Re-kindle hearths and altars, but that we have forgotten whence come the live coals, and the Breath which alone can fan them into an undying flame !

PAPER.

2. By the Rev. Forrest F. Emerson (Newport, Rhode Island, U.S.A.).

The Responsibility of Wealth for the Success of Christian Missions.

We have heard much in the meetings of the Conference concerning the kind of men needed, the methods that are most Christianity and expedient, and the agencies that are necessary in carry-self-sacrifice. ing Christian Missions to successful issue.   Men and methods, however, are of slight value, without money ; and to learn what are the true relations of money to Missionary enterprise, we must go back to the Fountain-head of Missionary inspiration,—the teachings of Christ,—and learn what He taught concerning the uses of money.   As the essence of evil is selfishness, and the essence of Christianity is self-sacrifice, and as selfishness is most easily fostered by our material possessions, we find Christ applying the precepts of the new life directly to the duties involved in the ownership of Teachings property.   The Master had behind Him the teachings of of Christ the Mosaic law, not only in the tithe, and the sacrifice, and Moses. and the temple gifts, but in the fundamental moral law itself, for it contained three laws (out of ten) aimed at evils growing out of the love of money ;—theft, coveting, and labour on the Sabbath for worldly gain.

My task at this time is to point out some of those things which Christ said about the use and misuse of money.

And in the first place, our attention may be called to the fact Christ's many that He had very many things to say on this theme.   It references to is surprising to find how many things, if, with special money. reference to this subject, we study carefully His teachings. From the opening of the first general discourse reported in the

Gospels, to the end of His last general discourse to the people, His teachings abound in comments, injunctions, and commands, relating to property, and to that intimate relation which our ways of regarding it and gaining it, of holding it and using it, bear to the moral character and the spiritual life.

The general principle is laid down in the Sermon on the Mount. The breadth and depth of the Master's wisdom concerning property, and the large place He gave to this theme in His instruction, are accounted for in the keynote of this sublime discourse. Covetousness is here treated as a general principle of selfishness, and money when supremely loved is personified as a being worshipped in the place of God. The whole passage in Matthew vi. from the nineteenth verse, beginning with the words, " Lay not up for yourselves treasures on the earth," down to the close of the chapter, turns on one idea, that the love and the service of God stand for all that is right and good in human conduct, while the inordinate love of possessions stands as a kind of symbol of evil representing the whole spirit of selfishness. Riches are personified under the name of Mammon, and we are warned that we cannot serve God and Mammon at the same time. The whole discussion turns on the heart's allegiance and supreme love. To love and worship that which is above ourselves, ennobles ; to love and worship that which is beneath us, degrades. We may be assured that when, among all the forms of evil spoken of in the Sermon on the Mount, money was the only one selected and personified as a being whose worship was antagonistic to the worship of God, it was no thoughtless choice on the part of Christ.

Out of this general principle grew all those striking sayings of His which have embedded themselves in the literature of the world,—" Lay not up for yourselves treasures on the earth ; " " Give unto him that asketh of thee ; " "How hardly shall a rich man enter into the kingdom of Heaven ; " "Beware of covetousness, for a man's life consisteth not of the abundance of the things which he possesseth ; "—sentiments which were afterwards woven into all the writings of the Apostles with a beautiful simplicity, and in most weighty and powerful forms of statement.

Still more striking are the *parables* of Christ. Notice that almost all of these are stories which represent the relations of men to earthly possessions. In all parables we look for two things :—the primary statement, and the spiritual interpretation. I am not speaking of the spiritual or theological interpretation which may be put upon the parables, but of their framework as primary statements,—that is, the story by itself, and standing on its own merits ; and it is surprising that when thus considered they show in manifold forms how closely the thought of Christ judged the Christian's conduct and the Christian's heart by a criterion based on his relation to property and his relation to money.

Some illustrations may be given. In the parable of "The Sower," peculiar emphasis is laid on the third failure, where the good seed, escaping the perils of the birds by the wayside, and of the thin soil overlying the granite ledge, grows up, but comes to nothing, the maturity of Christian character being finally prevented by the "cares of the world and the deceit-fulness of riches." The parable of "The Tares," portrays the **Examples of parables.** sin of injuring another man's property and business; there are other ways of doing it than the literal one of sowing tares in his field of wheat. The parable of "The Hid Treasure,"—a man finding which goes and buys the field,—shows how he may injure another by concealing from him the true value of that which we purchase of him. The parable of "The Unmerciful Servant" turns on the hard-heartedness of a creditor, who having just been forgiven a debt he owed to his lord, went forth and took *his* debtor by the throat, saying: "Pay me what thou owest me." The parable of "The Labourers in the Vineyard" teaches a merciful discrimination in the payment of wages. The parable of "The Two Sons" intimates how largely children are indebted to their parents in labour and service. "The Wicked Husbandmen," "The Unjust Steward," and the "Talents," teach the great lesson of the accountability of all who hold property in trust, and that needed sense of honour, the lack of which is such a prolific source of crime and disgrace in our day. "The Friend at Midnight,"—the story of the person coming to buy bread,—shows the close relationship of men to each other as to material things, their dependence on each other for help and kindness, and the obligation to give and lend. The story of the "Good Samaritan" turns on the obligation to give alms to those who are in need, and we instinctively couple it with Christ's pathetic words: "The poor ye have always with you." The story of "The Rich Fool" who congratulated himself that he had much goods laid up for many years, is an exhibition of the folly of making the whole of life to consist of the abundance of things to eat and drink and wear; and while the parable of "The Rich Man and Lazarus" teaches us how we may sin in the hoarding of money, the parable of "The Prodigal Son" teaches us how we may sin in spending it.

Remarkable, is it not, that in the long list of parables spoken by our Lord, the ownership of property, the use and misuse of money, are never for once lost sight of, and are put before us in every imaginable phase of forcible and beautiful statement?

Take the parable of the "Prodigal Son." It illustrates one of the ways in which covetousness operates, or rather it shows how property may become **The Prodigal Son.** the instrument of evil. Covetousness sometimes wastes money upon ignoble pleasures. A man covets wealth, not to hoard it, but to spend it upon his lusts. When we are warned against covetousness in Scripture, and books, and sermons, we usually think of the hoarding miser; but all the covetous people are not misers. The prodigal coveted his patrimony that he might spend it; and he did spend it in riotous excess and with reckless waste. This was his sin; he wanted property to use in sensual self-indulgence. And it is a striking illustration of the breadth of Christ's teaching, and that no aspects of truth are left untouched in the rounded fulness of his instruction, that the wasting of money is set forth as an evil as well as the hoarding of it; and it ought not to be forgotten that the parable out of which so much spiritual truth has been drawn, and rightly so, and from which so many religious and even theological doctrines have been deduced is, at bottom, the story of a man who squandered his fortune. Christ chose the spendthrift as the form of character by which to represent one of the lowest forms of degradation to which human nature can descend,— a sinner in spending money as other men are sinners in hoarding it; that we who profess to be His disciples may learn from the prodigal's lavish expenditure upon his animal pleasures, that we are to have a care how we spend as well as how we save.

In the parable of "Dives and Lazarus," the thrilling story that the world will never forget, nor can forget if it would, we find outlined in startling incident and colour another phase of the abuse of money. Very little is said about the character of the rich man in other respects; he is not said to be sensual, nor dishonest, nor cruel; *Dives and Lazarus.* he is neither a prodigal, nor a robber of other men's goods. He lived a respectable life. No overt act of transgression is mentioned against him. His purple and fine linen and daily sumptuous fare marked him as one of those conservative and respectable gentlemen who would be admitted into the most select circles of ancient or modern society. His sins were passive and not active. He took little notice of Lazarus the beggar. That is about all; till, all at once the curtain falls, the scene is shifted, and when we look again the rich man is in Hades, lifting his eyes in the midst of torment to behold the beggar in that state of joy and felicity which the Rabbins described as being "in Abraham's bosom." The parable is a magnificent work of literary art. You forget the language in which the story is told because you do not need to remember it. You see the picture. It is burnt into the brain as with the vivid colours of the painters' art. Here is the table of the rich man sumptuously spread; there the beggar at the gate, full of sores. Here is Dives in the place of misery; there the beggar resting amid the peace and splendour of Paradise. All is remembered, not as you remember reflections and reasonings, but as you remember a great painting. But underlying it all, and running through it all, this is to be remembered; that a parable which has been unfolded and interpreted with scholarly ingenuity and gorgeous phrase by Chrysostom, and Augustine, and Massilon, and by every eloquent orator of the pulpit from the earliest days of the Church until now, turns on the relation of a man to his money. For while we are not to infer that all rich people are bad and all poor people good, we may infer that this reversal and change after death was on account of some subtle relation, which in this particular instance did exist between these men and their outward fortune. We must infer that the rich man, while not necessarily guilty for being rich, became guilty through that supreme regard for money and the things that money can purchase which made him heartless and indifferent towards his neighbour's need; and it is sufficient to point out that this parable is one of the many ways in which our Saviour turns and turns again this great theme of the uses of money, with what patience He does it, with what endless forms of memorable and thrilling speech, and in its every imaginable phase.

And then, there is a beautiful incident related in the Gospels, wherein Christ improved the occasion for showing that there may be times when the religious zeal of a generous heart may be forgiven for passing by ordinary philanthropic claims to pour out its all upon the altar of a loving Christian devotion. A woman who had been a sinner, her heart all warm with gratitude to Him who had renewed her life and character, *The box of spikenard.* comes and pours upon His feet the contents of a box of costly spikenard; and on another occasion Mary offers the same gift in the anointing cf His head; and when the disciples complain of the extravagance, and declare that this expensive offering might have been given to the poor, Christ said: "Why trouble ye the woman? Verily I say unto you, Wherever this

Gospel shall be preached in the whole world, there shall also this, which this woman hath done, be told as a memorial of her."

And lest any person assume that this theme does not apply to them on the score that they are not rich, we may cite Christ's words concerning the gift of the widow who in her two mites gave, as He declared, more than all rich men and princes. Riches are relative, not absolute. There *The widow's mite.* is no standard or fixed figure which when a man reaches he may be called a rich man. He is rich who has ought that he can impart to his fellow-men. It is required of a man according to what he hath, and not according to what he hath not; and "whoever giveth but a cup of cold water only, in the name of a disciple, shall not lose his reward."

One more specimen of the many forms of our Saviour's teaching on this theme. It occurs in the last discourse of Christ to the people. The general theme is the judgment of the nations. Even here He does not forget that *The final judgment.* selfishness is the essence of evil, and that it takes strongest root in our love for material possessions. The panorama is unrolled. Men are separated before the Judge as sheep from goats in the herdsman's pastures. And what is the point on which the decision turns? What is the index of moral distinctions and of the estimates to be put upon character? Not professed belief in God, though Christ laid strong emphasis upon that; not ecclesiastical connections, though they are important; not acceptance of a formulated creed, though that is desirable; but this was it: Ye did not feed the hungry, nor give drink to the thirsty, nor visit those who were sick and in prison. And in not doing these things to them, ye did not do them unto Christ Himself. For every one in need, He says, is My representative on earth, and wherever the sons and daughters of want are found, there I am, and if ye had possessed a gentle heart, and had exercised kindness towards them, ye would have done a service unto Me.

Thus the Founder of Christianity has kept before us through all His teachings down to the very close of His ministry, the spiritual perils that are involved in our relations to the property which we possess, and has enforced the importance of our ways of using it as a criterion for the judgment of character. It is safe to say that there is no other application of religion to practical life in His teachings that occupies anything like so large a place.

The very facts of His life are in this direction significant. It was in a journey made to be enrolled for the Roman taxation that His mother *The facts of Christ's life and money.* found the stable of the inn far from the Nazarene home; it was in His forerunner's preaching that we find the message to the citizens, "He that hath two coats let him give to him that hath none;" to the publicans, "Exact no more than that which was appointed you;" and to the soldiers, "Be content with your wages." It was one of His converts who exclaimed, as the first evidence of his conversion, "One half my goods I give to the poor, and if I have defrauded any I will restore unto him fourfold;" it was to pay a just tax as a citizen of the Jewish state that He performed a miracle to obtain a coin; it was in His disavowal of the ownership of property, declaring that He had not where to lay His head, that we discern His low estimate of riches; it was His warnings against covetousness that were so strangely confirmed in the ignoble bargain that delivered Him to death for thirty pieces of silver; while the only saying of Jesus quoted in the Epistles, which is not found in the

Gospels, is the sentence preserved by St. Paul: "It is more blessed to give than to receive."

And, whatever a man's theory may be concerning Christ and Christianity, he cannot refuse to give sober attention to the fact that one whose life and influence have had such a prodigious effect upon mankind, should have said so many things concerning the one item of money and its spiritual perils, and that those sayings were among the most emphatic and memorable of His instructions.

The application of these teachings of Christ to the problem of the world's conversion is so obvious that it scarcely requires mention on an occasion like this. Missions cannot be carried forward without money; and when it is remembered that this is not only true as an abstract statement, but that all our Societies are in need of money to man properly the fields already opened,—when from many new quarters comes the cry, "Come over and help us," but the Societies are unable to move their forces into new fields for lack of funds; and when, too, our great wealth in England and America is taken into account, it will be seen that the consideration of Christ's teachings as to money and the implied necessity of the consecration of wealth are of the utmost importance in our Churches. As an American delegate I offer some figures showing what we have done in the way of giving to Missions, and also what we might do. The Americans will soon be, if not already so, the wealthiest nation on the globe; and the leading question with us as Christian men, is, How will American wealth respond to the call for Missionary money for the next twenty-five years? *The bearing on Missions.*

Let us look at the record. Notwithstanding the hundreds of thousands now given for charitable and Missionary work, the question may be asked, How much per Christian member, taking the country through, is being given to the cause of Christ outside the support of the local church? Dr. Daniel Dorchester has lately made an elaborate estimate based on the gifts of the Evangelical Churches of the United States, to Home and Foreign Missions, for the thirty years between 1850 and 1880. The total amount given for Home and Foreign Missions in 1850, was $1,250,000, and in 1880, $5,900,000, so that the increase in thirty years for Foreign Missions was about fourfold, and for Home Missions sixfold, and for the average of both fivefold; but when we compare these figures with the increase of membership, and the increase of wealth there is no occasion for boasting. The membership test is as follows. Counting all the Evangelical Churches, the donations to Home and Foreign Missions amounted in 1850 to only thirty-five cents per member, or about 1s. 6d.; in 1860 forty-eight cents, or about 2s. per member; in 1870 sixty-three cents per member; in 1880 fifty-nine and a half cents per member; in 1886 fifty-seven cents per member. The benevolence per member for 1886 fell below that of 1880 and 1870, though the field for Missionary work has been larger and more urgent, and the means more ample. So much for the membership test. *The contributions for Missions.*

The wealth test is based on the officially reported wealth of the United States. It is based also on the supposition that the Evangelical Churches may be regarded as having their *pro rata* share of wealth numerically. For instance, if the communicants of these Churches, in 1880, were one-fifth of the population, which is very nearly the correct estimate, then the wealth of those communicants may be safely estimated as one-fifth of the total wealth of the country. Thus in 1850 the communicants of Evangelical Churches were worth over a billion of dollars, or £200,000,000; in 1880 they were worth nearly nine billions, or £1,800,000,000. Now then, the Evangelical Christians of the United States in 1850 gave for Home and Foreign Missions $1\frac{1}{10}$ million on every dollar of their aggregate wealth, that is, about one-fifth of a farthing on every 4s.; in 1860 nine-tenths of a million; in 1870 eight-tenths of a million; in 1880 six-tenths of a million. So that while the total sums raised for these purposes have increased fivefold, it does not keep pace with the immense increase of the wealth of the Churches, which increased more than eightfold, nor with the style and luxury of living which have increased much more than eightfold. How infinitesimal do the offerings for Home and Foreign Missions appear! How lavish the outlay on our tastes and pleasures!

I do not bring forward these figures to find fault with the American Churches. The seven millions of dollars raised last year for Home and Foreign Missions constitute a gift not to be despised. But I aim to show what might be done if only a slightly larger percentage of our wealth was consecrated to the work of Christ. The call was never so urgent as now, and the opportunity for wise expenditure never so great. The number of young men now offering to go to the foreign field is unprecedented in the history of Modern Missions. There are now two thousand young men and women in the colleges and seminaries of the United States ready to go into the foreign service, if the money can be found to send them. When we remember the vast sums of money that Christian men expend upon their pleasures, the question arises: What might not this money be the means of accomplishing, if it were spent in the education and conversion of the heathen nations?

What might be done.

I think it must be admitted that the gifts of the Church are small when contrasted with its numbers, with its wealth, and with our lavish expenditure upon pleasures, not all of them very ennobling or very pure. Is it not true that with many of those who enter the race for wealth, the social reforms of the day, however needed and however promising, the uplifting of the poor and degraded, the call for religious work, sink into insignificance beside that feverish aim and purpose of life, the getting of money? I call to mind a noble lord of England, Shaftesbury by name, whose voice was often heard in these halls,—noble by legitimate title, noble in character for virtue and lofty sense of duty, noble in the love of Christ that was in him, who gave of his money, of his time, of his immense influence to bless the poor; he did not think it unfitting work for his hands to improve the condition of shoeblacks and newsboys; he did not think it beneath him to address words of kind advice to an assembly of thieves in the slums of London; and he was the man who, by persistent effort in behalf of the children of operatives, revolutionised the factory system of England. When you contrast such a life as Shaftesbury's with that of a man who wastes money on his pleasures, or hoards it for the satisfaction of gain, or corrupts with it the voters at the polls, or abuses it and misuses it as thousands do in a thousand ways, you see how it is that a man is not converted till his money is converted; that Christ touched the weakest spot in human nature in dwelling so persistently on the relation of men to money; and that it is not till we find men who are Christian in their holding, in their regarding, and in their using of money, that we strike the higher ranges of human character.

The love of money.

Christ touched man's weak spot.

It is not impossible that Tennyson had Shaftesbury in mind when he wrote :—

> " How e'er it be, it seems to me,
> 'Tis only noble to be good ;
> Kind hearts are more than coronets,
> And simple faith than Norman blood."

DISCUSSION.

Rev. F. A. Noble, D.D. (Chicago) : Mr. Chairman,—I am not certain that I shall succeed in speaking in a consecutive way, for I still feel a little dizzy. I tried to listen, and I think I did listen, from beginning to end, to the remarkable Paper of Dr. Pierson. He spoke in the Paper of Methuselah. Now while Methuselah was turning round in his age, we in this can travel round the world. As Dr. Pierson was going on from page to page with a kind of speed that would put lightning to shame, I was wishing that dear old Methuselah could come back and read just a page of it, so as to give us a little relief. I am exceedingly thankful for the illustration which the Paper affords of what I wanted to suggest. The question with me all through these days has been, How shall we utilise the results of these magnificent meetings ? There are only a few hundreds of us here, and we *How to utilise results of meetings.* come from large bodies of Christian people in this and other lands, and it would not be strange if it took a long time for the information given here to get sifted through the religious newspapers, and to reach the apprehension of these people. Now it seems to me that we ought to contrive some method by which we can communicate the results of this Conference far and near, and put them before the Churches ; and I rise for the purpose of making the simple suggestion, that those of us who have anything to do with religious newspapers, or who have any influence in the religious bodies with which we are associated, shall urge with all our power that our own programmes in all the Protestant Churches for the next year shall be constructed on the basis of the programme of this Conference and of the published report of its proceedings. The volume will appear, I apprehend, just in time for us to begin in January next. I trust that it will be laid before the Protestant Christian Churches before that time.

It seems to me that we could not have a completer scheme for getting before our people the wealth of information that has been poured in upon us. That is my suggestion, and it seems to me to be entirely practicable, that ministers and editors who can exert influence on others should let it be known that that volume is to be the basis of our study in the work of *Monthly concert* Missions for the next twelve months, of course keeping our eyes *for prayer.* open to the items of interest that may arise in the current months. Let me say a word, before my time expires, about the monthly concert. My brother Pierson has spoken of the necessity of ministers being alive to this work. Amen to that. He has spoken also of the necessity of creating an interest in Missionary operations in the home. Amen to that. But there is a place where it seems to me we do not put so much emphasis upon the work as we might—that is in the regular monthly concert in the Churches. I speak from a pretty long experience when I say that it is possible to make these monthly concerts in our Churches the most interesting meetings we have during the year. For almost ten years in my church in Chicago we have had the monthly concert. For a large part of the time I have arranged the pro-gramme, and at the beginning of the year it has been distributed *Method of* *arranging it.* in a little pamphlet to all the members of the church and congre-gation. Persons are appointed to read papers, and items of interest are set down ; and on the Wednesday evening after the first Sabbath in the month the people are there (I do not think that in ten years there have been six failures) with their papers and their statements and their items of information. That is the largest meeting we have, and the interest to-day is greater than it was when we began nine years ago. I hold in my hand our latest manual, containing the particulars of these meetings ; and I may utilise my few remaining seconds by indicating the topics brought forward. In January we have prayer for all Christian Missions. In February the meeting is in charge of the Young Ladies' Missionary Society. In March we study Paul's Missionary methods, with items from the field where he ministered. In April we have the present outlook of Missions among the Jews. In May we consider what can be done to stimulate the cause of Missions in Churches. That paper fell to me, and on the last Wednesday evening before coming here I gave them the best paper I knew how to give on the life of that magnificent Missionary, Dr. Schauffler, whose sons are working as Missionaries, one in New York in the slums, and the other in Cleveland among his Bohemian brethren and other foreign nationalities. And so on throughout the year.

Rev. William H. Belden (Chairman, Committee of Synod of New Jersey, U.S.A., on Simultaneous Meetings) : Mr. Chairman,—In common with many others I have hoped that beside the advances abroad, there might result from this Conference some definite, well-planned, resolute, practical action at home on behalf of the Missionary spirit. My own experience and that of my associates, in using the device of Simultaneous Meetings, included in this "Simultaneous morning's programme, seems to me to justify its mention and meetings," and commendation here. "Simultaneous meetings" is a term used their origin. to describe a multitude of public mass meetings held in many towns within a given region and under one general direction, on any or all of the days of a single week. We are indebted to the Church Missionary Society for its inception. Their "F. S. M." (February Simultaneous Meetings), held in 1886 and 1887, are too well known here for me to say much about them ; but their main features may be named. These were (1) to present Missionary work as the glorification of Christ the Great Head of the Church, and as the obedience to His commands ; (2) to plead the cause of Missions rather than the claims of a Society ; and (3) the question of funds was to be kept in the background.

A modification of the "F. S. M.," including, however, the features just named, was conducted last November by my own Synod in all its churches in the State of New Jersey, under the similar name, "November Simultaneous Meetings." This undertaking commended itself so far Their adoption to the denomination, that our General Assembly just adjourned in New Jersey. has called the attention of other Synods to it, and repeated its own last year's counsel that such meetings be widely appointed. The peculiar features of the "N. S. M." were : (1) The intent to reach, chiefly, persons and communities not reached by other methods ; instead of striving to bring them to great meetings, to carry the spirit and matter of such meetings to them in their own places of assembly ; (2) the effort to develop Missionary study and speech among the Ministry, by enlisting them all as the orators of the week, furnishing them (and to some extent, to leading laymen also) special material ; and (3) the accomplishment of these ends by the direct action of the ecclesiastical authority within whose bounds the undertaking was made. It is said that we depend for our Missionary successes altogether on the Holy Spirit. Yes, we cannot too greatly emphasise this. I think that this device of Simultaneous Meetings puts us in this attitude. The Holy Spirit requires zeal; and the only objection I have ever heard made to Simultaneous Meetings is that "it is too hard work." The Holy Spirit acts upon the intellect through the Scriptures; and this undertaking of ours surpasses other familiar ones in its mingling of carefully-prepared addresses, with praying assemblies. The Holy Spirit requires the unity of the Church of Christ; Simultaneous Meetings greatly assist towards this. How have we beheld it illustrated in this very Conference, that the only union thus far accomplished in the Church is in and through Missions!

I would that one great simultaneous week could be arranged for all Churches and Societies; at least in America, if it might not yet be on a wider scale. There are many who would favour it. But I would say that this device for stirring up the Missionary spirit in Christians ought not to be undertaken without thorough- *Should be adopted universally.* ness in detail, for it is a delicate instrument, worthless if too roughly handled. Rightly used, it has a singular adaptedness to this age of general peace, and of wide intercourse, favoured by the press, by the facilities for travel and the prevalence of our English tongue, and Divinely aided with God's threefold help for us all.

Rev. George Wilson (Edinburgh): Mr. Chairman, dear friends,—I wish to refer to one fragment of the question, How to raise the Churches to the degree of consecration required for the evangelisation of the world. I agree that we must have on the part of our people the study of Missionary principles, Missionary methods, Missionary history, very specially Missionary biography. But there is another aspect of the question which I think we need to have studied. I am speaking in the interest of the people at home. I am thinking of the six hundred thousand members of my own Church whom I am exceedingly anxious to see educated in Missions. And it seems to me that what we specially need is *Education of Christian congregations.* that the condition of the heathen world, not through statistics and vague general statements, but through accurate photographs, should be brought home to the people. We must bring home these heathens of the world to the people; we must be able to let them see them, and to see them from a standpoint that will lead, by the working of the Holy Spirit in their hearts, to the outflow of practical effort. And how is this to be done? In the first place,—and here I am glad to have the opportunity of saying a word to our beloved brethren the Missionaries,—it must be done very largely by your realistic descriptions. Believe me, you do a great work for the Church by sitting down and trying to get the standpoint of Christ, looking at what you see, and listening to what you hear in the life that environs you in these heathen lands, and sending it all home to us as a living picture—a call from the Lord.

I often wish, in reading the works of that great countryman of mine, Thomas Carlyle, that he had been a Missionary. What an eye he has! He sees everything, and he knows how to tell us what he sees. That is what we want on the part of our Missionary brethren. Then, I think, we must do more in the visitation of the Mission-field on the part of our brethren at home. Some of you rich men, who have money to spend in your *Visitation of the Mission-field.* holidays, have also ears and eyes, and you want to go sight-seeing. I say to you, pack up, and be off to the Mission-field. There you have a grand sight awaiting you. Tell us about them when you come home; do not keep it all to yourselves; tell us what you see and hear; bring home these heathen lands with you. If you do not like to go yourselves, send me, and I will try and go, and do what I can to look and listen, and tell—in the name of the Lord—what I have seen and heard. Then the last thing, I think, we need, is to utilise the artist's pencil and brush. I long to see a splendid Missionary panorama, something that will attract the thousands. It would be the best amusement they could have to let them see the heathen world pass before them,—that Macedonian, that Turk, that black brother from Africa. In this way, I believe, there would be a ready response from the Church, if it only knew the great necessities of the work abroad. All that they know now is that the Missions are "to **Ignorance on** foreign pairts," as my Scottish friends would say, somewhere **subject of** across the seas; they know very little more about it than that. Let **Missions.** me say for myself that one of the things that have gone most home to my heart here—indeed, it was a kind of inspiration to me—was the address of Dr. Post on Medical Missions. How was it that it was so powerful and telling? It consisted of pictures. As he spoke I seemed to see the people as Christ saw them, and there came a response from my own poor heart that I would try and re-draw these pictures of the Missionary needs throughout the world. This is but a fragment, I allow, but it seems to me a very important fragment in the education of the Church at home.

Professor R. B. Welch, LL.D. (Auburn, New York): Mr. Chairman, and Christian brethren,—We are reaching a crisis in the onward march of Christianity. Such crises have been reached in other days, and the way out of the crisis, or through the crisis, has been shown, but shown from God **A crisis coming.** on high, who has led the Church onwards. We may learn from those occasions, and so adapt ourselves to the present. In the great crisis after Christ ascended, which was a marvellous crisis indeed, the disciples went back to Jerusalem, and in continuous prayer and supplication reached the source of Divine power, and the power came upon them, and then the wondrous works. When the people of Israel were moving out toward the promised land they reached a crisis; and the cry went up from Moses to God, as he bade the people stand still and see the salvation of God. And God said to Moses: "Speak unto the people that they go forward, and lift thou up thy rod over the sea;" and then they moved forward. So, by communion with God, receiving the power and the wisdom which we cannot have unless God gives them, we are prepared to go on in the crisis. Now it seems to me that this occasion is an accumulating crisis, because we are here from all parts of the world as friends of Missions. Are we to go back with increased power and increased wisdom? If we get it we must get it from concentrated communion with the source of power. So in this crisis we make a new departure toward the very beginning at the Red Sea, and **Works will** after Pentecost. Then, after this communion with God by **follow on** prayer, the next thing is the works that shall follow. If we do **communion.** not forget the source of power and wisdom, if we go back filled with these ourselves, we may be assured that God will reveal the works, and that they will come in ways that we have now perhaps no idea of. At Pentecost they came in wondrous ways, and lo! the crisis was met, and the way opened. At the Red Sea the wondrous power came, and the sea opened before the Israelites, and they moved on. Shall we by God's grace get this power and take it back with us, so that the sea shall open, so that the tongue shall be on fire, so that God's influence shall work through us in all the lands towards which we go.

Then there is another thing we should impress more and more upon our Christian Churches and Christians everywhere, that they are to continue in prayer, and that they are to worship God also in giving. In America, which is securing such vast amounts of wealth, we must impress upon our Christian people the absolute duty of giving as a service, which God shall bless. From one end of the land to the other we must make this to be felt, that great riches are to be held in trust for God ; that men are to give, *Prayer and liberality.* not to patronise, but as a duty ; that in prayer, in the demonstration of works, and in giving everywhere, they may be armed with power. With regard to literature, it must come when the works are done. It must record the wondrous workings of God through us. When we have the prayer and the worship and the works and the service, men will be raised up to flood the world with literature. We want present day tracts. We want the facts that are coming all over the world to be brought to the front, and we want to show Christians cause and effect, that the Almighty Cause, Christ, the great Leader, is leading us on to a glorious victory.

Rev. W. J. R. Taylor, D.D. (Reformed Church in America) : Many years ago, in my youthful ministry, I heard that veteran Secretary of Missions, the Rev. Dr. Anderson, of the American Board, say *An emergency turned to account.* that an emergency was always worth a hundred thousand dollars to the American Board of Commissioners for Foreign Missions. Well, the emergency of Foreign Missions has become chronic ; it is perpetual, and God will never take the pressure off the Church until the dawn of the millennial morning streaks the East. Let me give you a single illustration— a very recent occurrence in the Church which I represent, perhaps one of the smallest of all the tribes—you may call it the tribe of Benjamin.

On the 1st of April this year our Board of Foreign Missionaries was more than fifty thousand dollars in debt. Young men and women had been standing at the doors of the Board, knocking for admission, begging to be sent to India, China, Japan, anywhere where we had Missions ; but we were obliged simply to say, " We cannot send you, we have not *A conscience awakened.* the funds ; we have exhausted the liberality of the Church, we dare not go a step further." One day there appeared in the organ of the Church, our weekly newspaper, an anonymous article entitled " *In extremis*," which, as I have since learned, was written by one of the most retiring of all our ministers. It was a plea for the raising of the amount of that debt, and a suggestion as to the way in which it should be done. One morning one of the younger ministers went to the office of the Corresponding Secretary of the Board of Foreign Missions, and said, " I have read that article : there are some things that I do not approve, but there is one thing that I do approve, and it seems to come home to me, saying, ' Thou art the man.' I have now come to offer my services to the Board to raise this debt, and I believe I can do it. I have some facilities for it. I want to go to rich people and poor people ; I want to go specially to those who have been accustomed to giving, because people who have been giving are the people who will give when they know the facts." Well, we accepted his services ; and what has been the result ? When I left home on the 26th of May, nearly the whole of that debt of more than fifty thousand dollars had been raised ; and I have no doubt that when the General Synod assembled in Catskill during this last week, the debt was reported as paid, and that in addition to having raised sixty-five thousand dollars for the theological seminary in India. The contributions to the Board of Missions this year, although we never raised a hundred thousand dollars before, have amounted to a hundred and sixty-five thousand dollars. It only shows that the water is in the rock, and that when the rock is smitten the water will flow.

Rev. W. F. Armstrong (American Baptist Mission, Telugu) : Mr. Chairman, brethren, and friends,—I have listened with very great interest and joy to the discussions that we have had upon Missionary methods, but it seems to me that we are now coming to a great crisis in our work. I do not wish to introduce anything of controversy here with reference to the coming of our Lord; but He Himself says, "Behold, I come quickly;" and it will not be introducing controversy to say that in all our deliberations we ought to let this enter in as one of the factors—the possibility that our Lord may come soon.

"The time is short."

Many of our plannings and deliberations have been conducted along the lines of supposing that we have almost the eternal ages in which to evangelise the world. Brethren, I am profoundly impressed with the thought that we need to be up and doing. Before the bell rings I want to utter a thought which has been in my mind, but which I have not yet mentioned to any person. I want to see a Missionary crusade preached throughout all Christendom by men whom God has filled with His spirit, and on whose hearts He has laid the evangelisation of the world.

Rev. John McLaurin (Canadian Baptist Mission): Mr. Chairman,—I have only a few words to say to this Conference. I should like every one to look at the words on this map, "Go ye into all the world, and preach the Gospel to every creature." It is the Lord Jesus Christ, your Lord and mine, who says that. Now what does He mean? Does He mean that we shall do it? Perhaps my question might be put in this way: Does the Lord Jesus Christ mean that the world shall be evangelised by us in this generation? Does He mean that, or does He mean that we shall wait until the next generation? He lays the obligation upon us who are living upon the face of the earth now. That is my idea.

Is the command to be obeyed?

Well, if that be so, what do we need? It seems to me that we have come to the grand crisis in Missionary work, and I believe that the Lord has prepared this Conference for that crisis. I sincerely hope so. We have the regenerated hearts that are needed to carry out this work and evangelise the world inside the next fifteen or twenty years. We have all the money, as we have been told this morning, and all the means at our disposal. And the eternal God has placed Himself with all these gifts at our disposal, and He has given us the key with which to unlock all the treasures of wisdom and knowledge. Jesus said, "All power is given unto Me in heaven and on earth. Lo, I am with you; I am side by side with you in this great work." We have all this at our disposal. Oh! let us pray every heart and every soul, and work for it too, that God would pour out His spirit in rich abundance upon His own people all the world over; and then God, even our God will bless us."

Rapid evangelisation of the world.

Rev. N. Summerbell, D.D. (American Christian Convention): Dear friends,—This meeting has been to me the joy of my life. I have never attended a convention where we have had so much of the Spirit of Christ. I regard Christ our Lord as the first great Missionary sent from the Home Society up in heaven. I regard His commission to His disciples to "go into all the world, and preach the Gospel," as a commission to Missionaries; and I regard the Missionaries whom we have greeted here during the meetings as these best representatives of these early Missionaries. May God still bless them in their field of labour!

Christ, His disciples, and Missionaries.

I went myself as a Missionary to the early settlers in our own country, and to the wild savages, and for four years I laboured there. It now gives me joy to think of those labours, but they were very little—nothing. Here I am after fifty years in the ministry, instead of talking about sorrow for the lack of Missionary spirit, I am in a great jubilee—a great jubilee meeting of Missionaries from various parts of the world. So that I thank God and take courage. God bless you ! Let us pray and labour for the success of this effort ; and may there be scores and hundreds of Missionaries in the coming decade where there were only units fifty years ago before. This is evangelical religion.

Rev. Professor T. Smith, D.D. (Free Church College, Edinburgh): I wish to touch upon what may appear a very insignificant, but what I think a very important corner of this subject. The point to which I wish to refer has reference to method rather than principle. I trust by God's grace that we have the principle ; but we require to be wise in our methods, and I wish to say a word in regard to a method of giving, which I am sure would benefit all Christian causes, and benefit our Christian peoples' hearts. I refer to what has been called systematic, or, more correctly, proportionate giving. *Method in giving.*

I believe a great number of people deceive themselves by the belief that they are giving a great deal more than they actually do give. They say they are constantly giving and giving, but without any method ; and they seem to think that they are giving a great deal, whereas, perhaps if they kept a correct account, they would find that the amount was very small. One passage in one of the Papers read to-day struck me as being very important in regard to the magnitude of a gift depending, as it does, simply and exclusively upon proportion. The widow gave a hundred per cent. of her living, while the rich man, who gave probably a larger sum, a sum which, perhaps, he thought was very large, gave a much smaller percentage. I believe that if all our people, rich and poor alike, were to bind themselves to give a certain proportion, it would be much better for themselves and much better for the Church and all Christian objects. It is a Divine institution which, I think, has not been repealed, that a tenth is to be the minimum proportion. *Proportionate value of gifts.*

Rev. J. A. Taylor (Baptist Foreign Missionary Convention of U.S.A.): Mr. Chairman,—Second in importance with me among all the questions that have been before this Conference since it has been in session, is the question, How to raise the Churches at home to the degree of consecration required for the evangelisation of the world ?

We have gone forward and tried to raise up men and women. There are now in the seminaries all over the country men of African extraction who are fitting themselves and are saying to us, " When we shall have completed our instructions we are ready to go forward and do this work." Then we want to know how we can raise the Churches to the degree of consecration required to assist the cause, because these men must go forth supported by the Christians at home. That is the difficulty that we find, and therefore we have organised our Churches into districts, each having an agent whose duty it is to travel over his portion of the territory and keep before the Churches and ministers the importance of the grand work of spreading the Gospel of Jesus Christ, bringing in such information as can be gathered through the records from the various Missionary fields. We want to know from the Missionaries labouring in Africa something about that large continent. We want it drawn out before us, so that when we talk to the people we can bring before them a panorama of the scenery, and paint the condition of the heathen world ; and wherever we have gone in this way we have found that the people out of their scanty means are prepared to give, as far as it lies in their power, to help to send out the Gospel of Jesus Christ. *Supply and support.*

Rev. G. Appia (Paris Missionary Society): Dear brethren,—We come here to learn. There is one great power. which alone is sufficient for us in France as here, and that is the Holy Spirit ; and we are here to pray to that

Holy Spirit and to be endued with power. But there is a secondary consideration, and that is obtaining information. Dr. Pierson *Information the* spoke about the monthly concert. I am astonished that pastors *Church's need.* do so little in awakening a Missionary interest. I had my monthly concert in the Waldensian valley; I have had one in Naples and also in Paris. I have always had it for eighteen years, and God has always blessed it. I would say, do not be afraid if you have only two persons. At my last monthly concert at Naples, I had five persons; but our collection was £5 in pocket, and the result was so good that they said that the monthly concert must be kept up.

Then there is one point for which I appeal to the Missionaries. How many Missionaries go through Paris? A great many; but the greatest part of them never call at our Missionary House, 102, Boulevard Arago. We had Robert Moffat, we have had some others. Next year will be the year of the Exhibition. Come if you can to Paris, and come to our Missionary House. In comparison with the strong Anglo-Saxon, we are a feeble body and want *Personal work.* brotherly aid. Be assured that the work is to be done by individuals. A previous speaker spoke about systematic giving. Twenty years ago we had a committee formed at Paris with reference to this very subject. The president was a physician. Two years after he had lost his wife he came to us with a box, and said, "There is a box for you. I have written on it 'Mission House,' and there is £5,000 to begin with." We told him afterwards that we were not able to carry out the project and build the house; but he said, "Go on with it;" and then he went with his book to one lady, asking for 20,000 francs, and to another lady for 15,000 francs, to another asking for 5,000; and so the Missionary House was finished and paid for. Lastly, I would say that we should try and get our young men as Missionary auxiliaries.

Rev. J. McMurtrie (Church of Scotland Foreign Missions Committee): The question before us is how we are to raise our Churches to a higher level of spiritual life, and thereby get increased support for Missions. I think I can make a very short answer that has a good deal in it. Christians must *Christians to* go to the front. How is it that a captain leads his company *the front.* into the battle? He steps out before them, he runs more risk than they do, and they follow him. How is it, my dear friend Cavalière Prochet, that your grand old Waldensian Church has been such a blessing to the Christian world, and is now evangelising Italy? It is because the Lord called you to suffer for His name's sake.

I think that we who are enjoying the blessings of this Conference ought to go back and try to do some great things for Christ. I have a great deal to do in the Church of Scotland with getting contributions for our Foreign Missions, and I tell you, that the most splendid offerings that we have got have by no means *The power* been always from the rich people, but often from the poor; they *of the poor.* have been from hearts that were full of faith and the Holy Ghost. We have gifts of £2,000 and £3,000 at a time; but we have had small gifts that have given us quite as much pleasure. I have had a poor servant come and give me £1, when I knew that she could not very well afford it. You may ask why I took the pound from that poor woman. Well, it was because I had had the privilege of helping her in a crisis of her life, and I knew it was a thank-offering; I knew it was a precious ointment, and I therefore took her money and told her that God's blessing would rest upon it. Why should there not be more of our people who go to our Mission-field without asking anything at all from the Church? I know that some rich men have done it; all honour to them for it! Let me tell you the story of a poor person who did it the other day. I knew in Edinburgh three sisters who had a great desire to go to Africa, but they knew that we were in difficulties with regard to money, and they would not ask a penny from the Church. They were not rich. One of them was teaching at a school in the old town of Edinburgh; another was in a millinery establishment, and the other was doing something else; and they simply said, "We will make a bargain that two of us will stay at home and keep the third who shall be a Missionary in Africa." She is now out in that Mission about which you heard the other day, and is working in the joy of the Lord.

Three noble sisters.

Rev. F. E. Wigram (Hon. Sec., C.M.S.): How will God raise the Churches to a due degree of consecration? I want to answer that question by referring to the responsibility of wealth in a particular direction. Have we not now a wealth of sons and daughters yearning for high deeds of goodness? Are we going to hold them back? I fear there is a disposition to do so. As I have been about the country, since I went round the world, telling my tale I have had again and again to plead, knowing that sometimes there has been a reason for the plea, with fathers and mothers not to dare to hold back their best son or their best daughter whom the Lord is honouring by calling to the work. I am certain that as we give of our best so God will be giving back to us a hundredfold.

Responsibility of parents.

I have seen many illustrations of it. Here is one brother who tells us that the best thing his parish ever did for the work of Missions was when it gave our Society the ablest curate they ever had, a man exercising a wondrous influence in his parish, second only to the influence he is now exercising in that same parish from his far-off Mission-field. Our Society has accepted an earnest, devoted labourer, one of a band of clergy working in an enormous parish; and the mere fact of his coming has seemed to give a lift to the whole of the staff in regard to Missionary work in the parish,—a further consecration to labour on the part of those who remain at home, simply from the fact that one of their number is going forth. I press this upon you. Let us realise what our wealth is in this direction, for I believe that God is pouring out His Spirit upon our sons and daughters. Then in regard to wealth in the other point of view. Surely everybody is responsible to a large extent for having wealth. A man who, having £100 a year, lives on £50, is a wealthy man; while the man with £10,000, who lives upon £10,100, is a poor man. We must really look to the adjusting of our mode of life, and learn what the necessaries of life are, in such a way as to have the gold and the silver to give to the Lord's service. With regard to what Dr. Wilson said about people going round the world, I am sure that he is right if only they will educate themselves a little beforehand, so as to know what they have to look for. I met our noble President and his lady at Agra, and I know they went to see all they could about Mission work, and it has helped them very much indeed. We have seen here as he has presided over this Conference how hearty his Missionary zeal is. Our Society has had the privilege this last winter of having a number of Mission preachers going forth to India, and in connection with them, three ladies went out at the same time; they have all come back with a keen interest in the work, and they have excited an interest in others who have heard what they saw.

Reflex influence of Missionaries.

Must re-adjust personal expenditure.

Rev. C. G. Moore (China Inland Mission): I have three suggestions to make bearing on the matters discussed this morning. We have heard much about a monthly concert for prayer. As a pastor I want to give my testimony to the large blessing that God has given to a weekly concert for prayer. To me as a Missionary it has seemed most inconsistent and unfair that only once a month God's work in the great world should be remembered. In my own work as a pastor we

Constant prayer and reference to Missions.

made all our weekly prayer meetings Missionary prayer meetings. We had
on the wall a map of the world, and no part of our Church work was more
abundantly blessed of God. Souls were saved at those meetings, and we
had no difficulty in sustaining the interest for an hour and a half. If the
work of Christ in the world is to be made the great and absorbing interest of
the Church, how can it be done by merely bringing it before the people once
a month?

Secondly, as to the bearing of our home life on this increase of Missionary
interest. I have found it, and others have found it, a great advantage to keep
Missionary work constantly before us at the family altar. We have had a plan
in our own home for taking the whole world once a week at the family altar in
prayer before God. In our children's nursery we have had put up a map of the
world, and they have been taught that that is their parish; they have been
taught from the very first to think of that as an object of their prayers. Thirdly,
I would suggest as a help in this work that we should lay ourselves out to
make our Missionary meetings times of spiritual power, that we definitely seek
from God that He would give spiritual power and spiritual results in our Missionary meetings. And as we speak loudly for Christ, Christ will speak loudly
to the hearts of His stewards for the work He has committed to us.

Rev. H. M. Parsons, D.D. (Toronto): Mr. Chairman, and friends,—The
remarks of the last brother are in the line that I wish to follow for a
moment; I mean with reference to the increase of power, consecration and
devotion to this Foreign Missionary work in our Churches. I believe the
monthly concert is the centre through which this power is to be developed,
and that for the preparation in the monthly concert of prayer
Public and
private prayer. once a month, there must be private prayer over it, the remembrance of it in the closet, at the family altar, in the weekly
prayer meetings, then culminating in the monthly meeting. And besides
the imparting of information and knowledge with regard to the work in the
field, I will put even before that the prophecies of God in the Old Testament,
in respect to this very age in which we are living, with regard to what God
has given to His Son, the distinction between the Jewish and the Christian
Church and so on, the marching orders given to both Jew and Gentile.
We have not prayed enough for the Jew.

I believe that God is waking up the Jew, and that if we had prayed according to the directions of the Holy Ghost we should have seen a baptism of power
far more than we have done. Nobody can pray and have the
Prayer
promotes giving. baptism of the Holy Ghost without giving. There must always be
a collection, and this collection should be according to the principles laid down by the Holy Ghost—proportionate giving, systematic giving,
giving in prayer, and personal consecration. It is through these channels that
God pours out His blessing. There are in the country from which I come
small churches where they feel, "We are poor and can do nothing." Now that
is the ground to be tilled. If we get baptism from above, we shall bring an
offering for Foreign Missions from every single church in the world. As soon
as the Lord's command is obeyed in this particular, we shall receive the fulness
of the promise that comes with it, "Lo, I am with you," which is the presence
of the Holy Ghost to baptise.

What we want is increased devotedness and consecration, and the bringing
out of offerings of money and men to go into the field to fill up the waste
places. The baptism of souls that I have seen in a ministry of twenty-five or
thirty years has often arisen at these meetings, when young men and women
would come and say, "I want to go into the field; can I go to the Foreign
Missions?" It has often happened that very small and apparently insignificant

Churches have given us men who have done noble work, and have been honoured of God in that work.

Rev. J. S. Balmer (President, United Methodist Free Churches Home and Foreign Missionary Society): One of our City Missionaries had just closed his address to some poor people in a back yard in the City where he laboured, when an aged woman went to him, and said, "Now, sir, you have *told* us how to do it; will you come and live in our yard and *show* us how it is to be done?" I am thankful to *Precept and example.* recognise that the Missionaries are going all over the world, not only to tell the story of the Cross, but to show the people how to love Christ; how to live a Christlike life. But what to me is more important still, is that Christ Himself came into our world to tell us how to do it, and to show us how to do it. He gave Himself. Let a man be personally consecrated to God, and there will be no difficulty about the money. The essential question is personal consecration to God.

I feel that a man who has money is as much bound to give his money for the work of the Church as I, a Minister of the Gospel, am bound to preach Christ to the people. If my preaching power is my talent, his power to give constitutes at least one of his talents, and he is as much bound *Our talents different.* to give as I am to preach. I believe the time is coming when we must insist more and more upon that. We have often been reminded to-day (by the ringing of the five-minutes' bell) of the shortness of time, and I will, therefore, close with the words of Bonar:—

> "Death worketh,
> Let me work too;
> Death undoeth,
> Let me do.
> Busy as death my work I ply,
> Till I rest in the rest of eternity.
>
> Time worketh,
> Let me work too;
> Time undoeth,
> Let me do.
> Busy as time my work I ply,
> Till I rest in the rest of eternity.
>
> Sin worketh,
> Let me work too;
> Sin undoeth,
> Let me do.
> Busy as sin my work I ply,
> Till I rest in the rest of eternity."

Rev. A. W. Frater (Utrecht Missionary Society): Christian friends,—I rise to give expression to a thought which has taken a deep hold of me for the last year or so, which, if carried out, would, I think, add to the practical value of our meeting here. As I am one of the last speakers, I should like to recall to your minds the principle of our Missions: the *The foundation* foundation of all is oneness-with Christ. It is a Divine work *of all oneness* which we have before us, a work which man alone cannot do. *with Christ.* Our strength and our consolation lie—in what? Is it not in this, that we are one with Him? He was the great Missionary who went about continually doing good, who came to seek and to save that which was lost. Now what do I mean by oneness? It is, as the Apostle so beautifully expressed it, "I live, yet not I, but Christ liveth in me." We must become dead; we are already dead; what then is our hope for the evangelisation of the world? It is Christ. Let us not forget that truth; let us take it with us to our different fields. It is not that we have Christ at our side in our difficulties and troubles, and so on; no, that is nothing: we have something more; we have Christ living *in* us, not at our side.

Bishop Suter, D.D. (of Nelson, N.Z.): One point I think has not been touched upon in connection with the raising of money: the danger of estimating money according to its ordinary value. Here is a penny and here is a pound; in commerce one will get so much, and the other will get so much more. In our work it is different, and we are in danger of forgetting that. My belief is that according to the way in which the penny is given it may do a thousandfold more work for God than the pound; therefore do not let us make too much of statistics, percentages, and arithmetic. We move in a different sphere. Where our work is purely commercial, we must do it on commercial principles; but we must not forget that we have other powers and influences which modify our position. Then it seems to me we do not—I speak for myself, and I offer the remark to you— dwell sufficiently upon what is contained in John xiv. 12. I seldom hear it referred to: "Verily, verily I say unto you, he that believeth on Me" (not said only to Ministers, Pastors, or Bishops), "the works that I do shall he do also, and greater works." Greater works than raising the dead; greater works than giving sight to the blind? Why is that? Because God's greatest work is the conversion of souls. There can be no greater work than that. "Greater works shall he do, because I go to the Father."

True value of gifts.

A promise to all believers.

The Chairman offered prayer.

MEETINGS OF MEMBERS
IN SECTION.

Twenty-first Session.

HOME WORK FOR MISSIONS.

(2) *MATERIAL AGENCIES.*

(a) Comparative methods of securing Missionary contributions from Churches and Sabbath schools.

(b) The need of supplementing the contributions of the Churches with gifts and legacies from those who have been made the stewards of large possessions.

(c) How to deal with the question of special objects, and gifts of limited application.

(d) Statistical tables.

(e) Financial statements.

(Monday afternoon, June 18th, in the Annexe.)

Rev. F. M. Ellis, D.D. (Baltimore, U.S.A.), in the chair.
Acting Secretary, Mr. B. Broomhall.

Rev. B. La Trobe offered prayer.

The Chairman: I have been asked by the Committee to take the chair this afternoon. You will observe from the programme we are to continue the consideration of the questions before us at the meeting in the Lower Hall, this morning, on Home Work for Foreign Missions. At that meeting we had under our consideration the Spiritual Agencies; at this we come to the practical aspect of Material Agencies. These are succinctly and comprehensively divided under three general heads. I do not propose to detain the Conference long, but there are one or two things which I think might properly be said by way of introducing the subject. In the first place, before we shall ever reach any commensurate measure of charity there must _{The source} come into Christian lives and hearts a profound conviction _{of charity.} of personal responsibility in this matter of giving. We have dissociated giving from worship. "Thy prayers and thine alms are come

up before God as a memorial." There are many questions which
come up at once when you use the word systematic giving or benevolence. How are these questions to be answered? We have been
attempting to answer them for a long while.

I do not think we require any new expedients. I do not think we need
trouble ourselves about the originating of new schemes so much
The Scriptural plan. as honestly facing the practical question, How shall we return
to the old plan which inspiration has given us so clearly and
simply in the Word of God? The Apostle Paul devotes no less than two
chapters in his Letter to the Corinthians to the discussion of the question of
the subject of Christian benevolence; and I do not hesitate to make the
assertion that until we come to understand the meaning of the Apostle in
these and other portions of Scripture we shall fail of the rudimentary idea of
Christian benevolence. We have been influenced heretofore by the thought
of the importance of Missions to the heathen. I would not abate one jot or
tittle from that. We have placed before us the marvellous works of Societies;
they are all valuable in their place. But when we come to face a great practical question such as that before us this afternoon, and when we come to
feel we are stewards of the property we possess; and that God
The principle of benevolence. expects us to administer that first of all in His interests, we
shall fail to understand the duty He has laid upon us. What is
the supreme motive of Christian benevolence? Is it the perils of the heathen?
Is it the obligations of consistency? It seems to me that when we come to
understand that the ultimate aim of Missions or benevolence is the glory of
God and the honour of Jesus Christ His Son, we shall fail to apprehend the
supreme motive of Christian benevolence. It is an essential part of worship.

We hear of times past when people, moved by thrilling descriptions of
the state of the heathen, fell into one another's arms, and contribution boxes
came back laden with jewels of women and men who had given them in the
cause of Christ. It is not to be wondered at. This motive has largely had
its day. I am not saying one word against it; but it seems to me we want
to get back to the simple rule of God's Word. The principles are there, the
motives are there; and it seems to me the methods are just as distinctly
revealed to us. It is sometimes asked, "Why was the amount of each
Christian's contribution not distinctly named?" In the first place, we are
not under law, but under grace. The only law which can be
God's requirement. given is, "Thou shalt love the Lord thy God with all thy heart
and mind and strength." So when it comes to this matter of
giving, shall we give less than to our utmost ability? Reference was made
this morning to the tenth of the Jew. That was the minimum of his giving.
He probably gave nearer one-fifth than one-tenth. Now the question I want
to raise for you this afternoon—a question which comes to us with the
greatest force when we feel we are nearest God in communion—is, Do you
think the Lord Jesus will require less in this matter of giving from you than
He required from the Jew? The Jews' religion was stationary; our religion is
world-wide and world-conquering. A tenth is not all the Christian is to give.
I believe the Christian ought to begin with that. I believe that is the minimum of our giving. But the rule that inspiration gives in advance of that
is, that every Christian shall give as God prospers him; he shall not withhold that which the Lord calls His own.

We are here this afternoon to consider some very practical aspects of the question. No one method possibly will comprehend every condition everywhere. I suppose the conditions on the Foreign field are somewhat peculiar, as compared with the Home field; but one **Methods and conditions.** of the most inspiring conditions of the Foreign field is, that they are holding closer fellowship with the Apostolic methods than we are at home, and for this, I suppose, God blesses them, because one of the best ends to be attained is the revelation of the consistency and power of the Divine methods given us in the Word of God. I take very great pleasure in introducing to you as the reader of the first Paper, the Rev. B. Romig.

PAPER.

· 1. BY THE REV. B. ROMIG, of Herrnhut, Germany (Moravian Missions).

Mr. Chairman, and Christian friends,—I find myself placed in a rather awkward position this morning. When I was requested to prepare a Paper for this Conference the programme had not been published, and no particular subject was assigned to me. I was therefore requested to select a theme for myself. That which presented itself to my mind as the most suitable was the claims of the Missionary upon the Home Churches, viz., claims on their sympathies, their prayers, and their financial support. **An explanation.** As my Paper therefore is not relevant to the subject in hand this afternoon, I shall beg leave to omit the reading of it, and substitute instead a few thoughts roughly thrown together on the topic before us.

Before doing so, however, permit me to say that I esteem it one of the greatest privileges of my life to be present at this great Convocation of the disciples and servants of our Lord Jesus Christ, and to learn of the great things being accomplished, being undertaken, and being forecast by men strong in faith and in the power of the Holy Ghost.

It appears to me that the Executive Committee of this Conference has already done an incalculable amount of good Home work for Missions, by gathering together so many Missionaries and those interested in Missions from all parts of the world, to discuss the important and difficult problems that have been brought before us, most of them being questions of the day, in one field or the other. Surely, as we return to our various homes and work in different and distant places, we shall carry with us the blessed influences of this Conference, to help us in ever working, praying, and planning for that glorious time, when the kingdoms of this world shall become the kingdoms of our Lord Jesus Christ, and all the ends of the earth shall see the salvation of our God.

As the first topic in the schedule for this morning is *comparative methods of securing Missionary contributions* from churches and Sabbath schools, it will naturally lead each speaker to refer to the methods pursued in his own Communion. I have therefore briefly sketched the plan pursued in the denomination of which I am a member.

The Moravian Church, to which I have the honour to belong, Our methods of although but a small body, has, as is well known, very raising funds. extensive Missions. They stretch from "Greenland's icy mountains to Afric's burning sands," and from the snowy summits of the Himalayas to the desolate shores of Alaska. We have one hundred and seven Mission stations, served by three hundred and thirty-five Missionaries, and one thousand five hundred and ninety-eight native assistants.

I would add that while this may well be called the Centenary of Missions our own work stretches back half a century more, having been begun in 1732.

The income for the support of these Missions is raised in the following manner. In the Church itself *every* member is expected to take a lively interest in the Mission cause. Her whole history is bound up with Mission work. Her memorial days bring the subject continually before her sons and daughters. They are trained from their childhood to recognise the support of Mission work as a sacred duty. Every one is therefore *expected* to contribute of his or her substance for this purpose.

(1) Annual Missionary festivals are held to excite deeper interest in, and to supply information upon, the needs of the various Mission-fields. At these festivals contributions are taken up.

(2) Sermons in behalf of the cause are regularly preached, and stated collections received from the members and friends of the Church.

(3) Missionary Associations are formed in each congregation, called in England Mite Societies, and in Germany "Fünf pfennig Verein," which gather small weekly or monthly contributions. We find these Associations very helpful. The collectors who give their services voluntarily for the purpose, usually seek out the subscribers at their homes, and at such times when they are best able to give. The amount asked for is so small in itself that it can be easily and cheerfully paid even by the poorer members of the congregation. There is an old Scotch proverb that says, "Many a mickle maks a muckle;" and so we have found that these small gatherings, coming in from various quarters regularly, amount eventually to a very respectable sum. In nearly all our Sunday schools similar associations are formed.

I may add here that the same method is pursued in our Mission congregations, and our converts are taught, as soon as possible, that Converts in addition to their contributions for sustaining the work trained to give. among themselves, they must also help to spread the Gospel abroad by giving of their earnings for this cause.

The sums raised at the various Mission stations for this purpose help very materially to lighten the burdens resting on the Home Board.

At the same time it is but right to say that we would never be able to carry on this work as it is now done, were it not for the liberal and generous help received from members of other Churches, both in England and on the continent of Europe. We gratefully acknowledge the help received from ministers and members of the Anglican, Presbyterian, Lutheran, and other Churches. The London Association, and the "Society for the Furtherance of the Gospel," in England relieve us of many cares; and in Australia, while we furnish the men for *Extraneous aid.* carrying on a blessed work among the Papuans, our Presbyterian brethren there supply the necessary funds. We have in this way been enabled to do much more than would have been possible, if left to our own unaided resources.

In connection with the second point raised on this topic, I may add that, notwithstanding all that is raised in these ways, we yet find ourselves often unable to meet the demands and requirements of the work. We very often have the year's accounts closing with a deficiency, and, as one of our brethren quaintly said, "we have to open our mouths very wide and cry out for help," a cry which is usually warmly responded to by members and friends. But there is another aspect of the subject which strongly emphasises *the need of supplementing the contributions of the Churches, with gifts and legacies from those who have been made the stewards of large possessions.* I refer to the fact that new fields of work are continually opening before us, which we are not able to enter for lack of means. It is well known that the work of the Moravian Church is chiefly among the lowest and most degraded tribes of the children of men, such as the Eskimos of Greenland and Labrador, the Hottentots and Bushmen of South Africa, and the Papuans of Australia; and therefore to begin a new work in such circumstances requires a substantial financial basis to start with. Within the last twelve months three or four such opportunities to commence new work have been offered, but they had to be declined, not for lack of men, but for lack of means.

The Mission work of the Moravian Church is carried on in eleven different provinces, with one hundred and fifteen stations and out-stations. There are twenty-nine thousand eight hundred communicants, and a total membership of eighty-three thousand.

The actual expenditure for carrying on this work amounts annually to about £50,000, of which £25,000 is raised in the Mission-fields themselves by contributors, and by trades *Sources of* carried on in some places. There have been employed *revenue.* in this work since its commencement in 1732, about two thousand three hundred brethren and sisters, most of whom are now at rest in everlasting bliss, rejoicing in the presence of Him who redeemed us out of all nations, kindreds, tribes, and tongues, and hath made us kings and priests unto God.

PAPER.

2. BY THE HON. JOHN MACDONALD (Member of the Canadian Senate).
Read by the Rev. A. SUTHERLAND, D.D. (Toronto, Canada).

*Christian liberality and its place in connection with the conversion
of the world.*

Notwithstanding all that has been achieved in the Mission-field
during the " Century of Protestant Missions," closing with the
Increase   year 1886, the fact remains that, with all the money
of heathen. which has been expended, with all the prayers that have
been offered, the tears that have been shed, the labours bestowed,
and the lives which have been spent in the service, " the heathen and
Mohammedan population of the world is more to-day by two hundred
millions than it was a hundred years ago, while the converts and their
families do not amount to three millions." * So that " those who
calculate on Christian Missions converting the world at the present
rate of increase strangely overlook the annual increase of the
heathen population of 1,047,000,000 by birth rate." *

The contemplation of this at first sight is bewildering if not
overwhelming, so that one is tempted to inquire, what will the end
be ? Infinitely beyond the wisdom or ability of any one would
it be to satisfactorily answer this question but for the light which
is thrown upon the subject in God's Word. But with the many and
precious promises which are found there, all pointing to the general
diffusion of the knowledge of the Lord throughout the earth ; to the
ultimate and complete triumph of the Gospel of our Lord Jesus
The promises Christ over every system of superstition and error ; the
ensure success. answer is not plain only, but conclusive ; and that
despite every discouraging and disheartening circumstance ; despite
all that may appear irreconcilable in the conversion of the world, in
the face of this increase of the heathen population. The child of
God may and does confidently rely upon the fulfilment of God's
precious promise in the coming of that time, when " they shall not
hurt nor destroy in all My holy mountain : for the earth shall be full .
of the knowledge of the Lord, as the waters cover the sea "
(Isa. xi. 9).

While fully realising how helpless man is in his best efforts;
while realising all that is implied in the words, " Not by might nor
by power, but by My Spirit, saith the Lord of hosts " (Zec. iv. 6) ;
Human   realising also that in the conversion of the world, as in the
instrumentality.change of the individual human heart, this also is the gift
of God, " Not of works, lest any man should boast " (Eph. iii. 8, 9).
Still, the fact remains that God works through instrumentalities,
and that He has so ordered it, that the world is to be brought to the
knowledge of Him by the preaching of His Word, and for this the

* " A Century of Missions."

consecrated lives of men, called of God and qualified, and the means of God's people consecrated to the carrying out of this work, are the agencies which He sees fit to use, and that when the Church awakens to an enlightened sense of its responsibility in connection with its duty to God and the heathen, then will there be such a consecration of men and means as the world has never witnessed, and then will results follow such as the Church (judged by its past action) has never yet dared confidently to expect. How concisely the Apostle puts the whole case : " How then shall they call on Him in whom they have not believed? and how shall they believe in Him of whom they have not heard? and how shall they hear without a preacher ? and how shall they preach, except they be sent ? As it is written, How beautiful are the feet of them that preach the Gospel of peace, and bring glad tidings of good things ! " (Rom. x. 14, 15). None but those sent in the truest sense, that is those who are called and fitted by the Holy Spirit ; those who are sent forth, not with the consent only, but with the full approval of the Church, are fit messengers to declare the Gospel of the Son of God to A new call for money. the perishing heathen. But in order that this may be accomplished the wealth of the Church must be poured out to an extent which has never yet been attempted, and with a cheerfulness expressive of its obligation and its duty.

This leads us to inquire what part is the wealth of the Church to play in the conversion of the world? Are the givings of Christ's people commensurate with the needs of the heathen or with their own financial ability ? To these questions let us address ourselves.

Let us first inquire as to the sources from which means are supplied for the carrying on of this most important work. Many Churches have their own peculiar methods, and it is not likely Means and sources of revenue. that we will be able to give anything like an accurate account of the various agencies employed by each for this purpose, nor is it necessary. The following are, however, common to all :—

1. Sunday school Missionary organisations.
2. Sabbath collections (quarterly or annually).
3. Congregational Missionary anniversary services.
4. Missionary contributions annually obtained by collectors.
5. Special donations.
6. Legacies.

Does the Church from all these sources secure one tithe of what it needs, or what from these sources it ought to receive ? We think not. In confirmation of this view, witness the debts which press upon Missionary Societies. The fields from which calls are presented, but to which the reply is sent,—too often the only one possible,—We are unable to take up the work ; the fields which lie open to the Church, but which the Church finds itself unable to occupy, and yet the cry goes on ceaselessly, imploringly, " Come over and help us.'" It is in the power of the Church to raise double the amount which has been raised in any previous year for the spread of the Gospel in heathen lands. and that without any sacrifice to any one, or without having other effect, so far as the contribution is concerned, than making the giver the possessor of a joy which he had never experienced before.   Will the Church do it?

The writer of this Paper undertook, when a fraternal delegate from a sister Church, to call the attention of the General Conference An encouraging of the Methodist Episcopal Church at Baltimore in 1875, example.   to the need that existed and to the ability of that great Church to raise $2,000,000 annually for Christian Missions, the Missionary contributions that year being some $580,000 or $600,000, and ventured to say that such a result would have the effect of awakening a new interest in all the Churches in the cause of Missions throughout the world.   Who that has watched the progress of events in that Church has not rejoiced in the splendid results which have been accomplished in its Missionary department under the earnest and indefatigable labours of Chaplain McCabe in seeing its Missionary contributions reach for the present year nearly one million and a quarter of dollars?   And who is there who does not look forward confidently to the period, and that very soon, when the contributions of that Church will amount to double that sum, say two millions and a half?   Will the Church generally determine to raise this year for its Missionary work 50 per cent. more than has ever been raised in any one year?   And if so, how is this to be secured?   To some one abler must be left the work of presenting the best methods to secure this end.   But the following may be noted as having a bearing on the subject which may not be without significance.

1. Let new interest be awakened in every Sabbath school among the officers, teachers, and scholars, even where the interest at Methods for   present is deep, by the circulation of Missionary literature, increasing funds appropriately illustrated (cuts and paper being of excellent quality), and of a character which will attract attention in the home, and be there preserved, in connection with every Sunday school.   By having, where the custom does not already exist, a Missionary Sunday, or Missionary Sundays, and by aiming at the best methods of securing enlarged contributions.

2. By having in the congregations Missionary prayer meetings, say once a month, and by giving prominence to Missionary intelligence ; by the preaching of Missionary sermons at least once a year in every congregation throughout the world, and by the taking of collections at such services for the cause of Missions.

3. By having platform Missionary meetings, and securing the best talent of the Church, lay and clerical, at such meetings for the advocacy of Christian Missions, and by observing this in every Christian congregation everywhere, and in taking up a collection at every such meeting for Missionary purposes.   The writer was present at such a meeting in the wilds of North America,

the audience being Ojibeway Indians. The interest was intense. About thirty Indians, heads of families, were present, and the amount subscribed was £36. If such a meeting with such results was possible among such a people and in such a place, where is the place where such a meeting might not be held, and where correspondingly greater results might not be realised?

We come now to consider the matter of annual subscriptions for Missionary purposes. Here it is where the great revolution is to take place. Here it is where one has the opportunity of dealing plainly with the individual Christian. Here it is where one has the power of influencing others. Amid the thousands of Israel, how few are there who, if they were to submit to the tribunal of their conscience the question, "Is this a meet offering *Personal responsibility to God.* from me for such a cause?" would receive an affirmative reply? How many are there who never inquire what are the wants or what are the triumphs of the Mission-field? How many are there who allow themselves to remain in comparative ignorance of the work and the workers, who yet have means so abundant as to enable them to meet the pressing needs of committees, without denying themselves of one of the comforts which they are accustomed to enjoy? How many are there who, although they give statedly, yet give amounts so small that when viewed in connection with what God has done for them their contributions can only be looked at in the light of an insult to Him to whom they owe their all? To speak more plainly, are there not thousands of professing Christians who give for Missions one pound per annum, or at most five pounds, who could with the same ease give annually one hundred or *Not conventional contributions.* two hundred pounds? And so in the ascending scale, are there not those who give their one hundred or two hundred pounds who could with just as much ease give their five hundred or even one thousand pounds, and do this every year? To some these figures may appear extravagant, but any one who has studied and realised the vast stores of wealth that are in the hands of Christian people, and the vast additions that are steadily being made to that wealth, will have no difficulty in realising the reasonableness of the statement.

Again, there are many who, by the public character of their givings, often embarrass where they had supposed they were helping. For example, many become impressed with the need *Embarrassing gifts.* that exists in some new field, and they invite the Church to engage in its development; they give a subscription which they describe as being "special for China" or "special for Africa" or some other field, while the amount which they so give for this object, in which they are for the moment engaged, they withdraw from the amount hitherto given for the support of the general work, and to that extent embarrass the Missionary Committee with which they are connected. Every Missionary giver who studies the subject cannot fail to realise that, however much he may be impressed with the opening of new fields, and however desirable it is that they should be occupied, his first duty should be the efficient maintenance of the work to which the Church is committed in each of its departments, and the support of the men then employed in the Mission-field who have left home and friends, confidently relying upon the fidelity of the Church in sustaining its work.

In whose hands is the wealth of the world to-day? Firmly do we believe that it is largely in the hands of God's people. How

The wealth in the Church. can it be otherwise if God's Word be true? Religion makes a man thrifty; saves him from extravagance; brightens his ideas; makes him cheerful; gives him character, which to every business man is a fortune, so that even the world has confidence in him. These, as well as the many other qualities which religion brings to a man, but confirm the truth of the Apostle's saying: "Godliness is profitable unto all things, having promise of the life that now is, and of that which is to come" (1 Tim. iv. 8). The words are as true to-day as when they were first uttered. "There is that scattereth, and yet increaseth; and there is that with-holdeth more than is meet, and it tendeth to poverty." God has so ordered it that the very exercise of beneficence tends to the increase of one's means. So that he who honours the Lord with his substance and with the firstfruits of all his increase, his barns shall be filled with plenty, and his presses shall burst out with new wine (Prov. iii. 9, 10).

Then we come to consider the sums secured from legacies. Better is it that men should do something for God's cause by will than that they should not do anything. But better still would it be, yea infinitely better, if they would while living give to His cause the sum, or part of it, which they had determined should be available

Rather give during life than at death. only after their death. When money was dearer than it is to-day many a well-established and well-managed business doubled its capital every eight years. The same principle might be applied in a greatly intensified form to amounts given by Christians during their lives in preference to leaving amounts by will. Thus a man leaves by will, say to the cause of Missions, twenty thousand pounds. He lives, after making his will for twenty years, and at his death the Missionary Society so benefited becomes possessed of that sum; but if twenty years before he had given four thousand pounds even, the financial benefits to the Missionary Society would have been vastly greater. Interests would have been strengthened which may have been allowed to drop. The benefit of the example would have had such an effect as could not be estimated by any method of calculation. The man himself would have been the witness of the energies which had been awakened by his own act, and would have been the partaker of a joy which is only felt by those who in a spirit of thankfulness bring their offerings into the Lord's treasury.

The Divine Being, as we have said, works by means. Never

before was there such an opportunity for work as that which now presents itself. " Between six and seven thousand agents are now in the field, composed of Missionaries, laymen, and women," * preaching in the languages of the people among whom they are labouring; ministering to their wants as Medical Missionaries, finding their way to the ills which overwhelm the soul by healing those which pertain to the body ; steadily making inroads upon the strongholds of paganism, and calling imploringly for help. Shall it be denied? The outlook, despite the *The cry for help.* increase of the heathen world to which we have alluded, is full of encouragement. The work hitherto has been preparatory only. It has been like the work of establishing some immense business, where, for a time, the outlay has seemed out of all proportion to the results ; where the advertising, the organisation, the establishment of agencies absorbed large sums, and yet appeared to yield but little return. But watch the results when the arrangements have been perfected ; watch the marvellous success which crowns the patient, trustful policy which could wait and hope. See the fame of such an enterprise, filling not a continent only but the world ; and see the accumulation of means, surpassing in extent the wealth of the greatest monarch on earth : and all this achieved in the lifetime of one man. Shall such results as these be possible in the things of this world, and shall matters relating to God's work be matters of doubt or uncertainty?

How long ere the labour of those who are working at the foundations of some great pile of buildings is manifest! How poor the conception, then, which one can form of the beauty and grace of the superstructure! But the time comes when the foundations are completed ; when the style and character of the elevation are apparent; when the " headstone is brought forth *The sowing time.* with shoutings." Then, and not till then, is the harmony of the whole realised. Then, and not till then, does it appear how well was the time employed in laying the foundations, and how essential the work was to the safety and beauty of the whole. But in the Mission-field results have been achieved vastly greater than any which appear on the surface. Natives in heathen lands (notably in India) who have themselves been brought to the knowledge of the truth, have in their journeyings far beyond where any Missionaries are found, brought the tidings of the new religion, and awakened an interest in those to whom they have spoken to listen themselves to some teacher, so that to an extent which very few are ready to believe, the words of the Saviour apply to the entire heathen world to-day : " Behold, I say unto you, Lift up your eyes, and look on the fields, for they are white already to harvest" (John iv. 35). But vastly more than could possibly be noted in a Paper of this nature is included in what we understand by the preparatory work in the Mission-field. The mastery of languages ; the removal of prejudices;

* " A Century of Missions."

the toleration of governments leading to the positive invitation to *Encouragements* labour, in some countries at least, where Christianity by *and calls.* law was proscribed. Speaking of the removal of prejudice alone as compared with former years, let us ask what, in China for example, would have been the result if the Christian people of Great Britain and America had, in the recent visitation caused by the overflow of the Yellow River, by which so many people lost their lives, and by which from one to two millions were rendered homeless, sent fifty or one hundred thousand pounds for the relief of the sufferers, which they could so easily have done? Would it not have afforded the grandest commentary upon the excellence of that religion whose principles are, " Glory to God in the highest, and on earth peace and goodwill towards men" (Luke ii. 14)? Would it not, to an extent that nothing has ever done, have created a widespread interest in a religion which cannot behold suffering without alleviating it, and which cares for the "bodies as well as the souls of men"? God has said, " Bring ye all the tithes into the storehouse, that there may be meat in My house; and prove Me now herewith, saith the Lord of hosts, if I will not open you the windows of heaven and pour you out a blessing, that there shall not be room enough to receive it" (Mal. iii. 10). Will the Church respond? Will the Church rely upon God's promises? Will the Church rise to a sense of its obligations? Will it furnish the men who are urgently needed in so many fields to-day? Will the Church bring of its great wealth and lay it at the Master's feet? Assuredly if each individual member did but realise how much he owed, there would be no difficulty.

As we have already asked, Is it not possible then, that, as the *To increased* result of this Conference, the contributions towards the *liberality.* spread of the Gospel, towards the great Missionary enterprise carried on by all the Churches, should for the year 1888-9 be 50 per cent. more than it ever has been in any one year during the Century of Protestant Missions? The want exists. The means are there. It needs but the will to secure the results. " Let the people praise Thee, O God ; let all the people praise Thee. Then shall the earth yield her increase; and God, even our own God, shall bless us. God shall bless us; and all the ends of the earth shall fear Him" (Psalm lxvii. 5-7).

DISCUSSION.

Rev. Dr. Grundemann: I think Missionary periodical papers are the very best medium for furthering in the Home Churches the interest in Foreign Missions. I am now referring to the distinction between general Missionary *On increasing* papers and the periodicals giving information only about the *information.* work of one of the Missionary Societies. Such papers ought to be read by supporters of any Missionary Society. I should be glad if this meeting would lay before all our friends the importance of this question. I am sorry that even ministers of Churches do not read their Missionary papers. There cannot be a sound interest in the progress of Missions in the Foreign field without reading such papers. You cannot do without a certain measure of knowledge of facts, and I am afraid that Missionary periodicals are not so well used as they ought to be. There are some excellent ones,—for instance, the *Church Missionary Intelligencer*, which I may point out as the very best journal of its kind; but it is strange that it should not be more largely sold; it ought to be circulated at least to the number of twenty thousand amongst the members of the Church Missionary Society, and it should not only be circulated but read. I must say a word or two about another class of papers. I am sorry to say many of them do not give full, accurate information about the proceedings in the field. Time does not allow me to dwell more extensively upon this subject.

All I wanted to say about it has been said this morning in the Lower Hall by the Rev. Mr. Wilson of Edinburgh, and better than I could say it. But let me point out another fact illustrating a great lack in our Missionary literature. One of the greatest triumphs of Modern Missions over the darkness of heathenism is the work in the Fiji Islands. Now all of us should watch the work for the development of Christianity in those islands, but in all England there is no report to be obtained giving information about that Mission. Formerly it was given in the *Wesleyan Missionary Journal*, but since the separation of the Australasian Conference from the English Wesleyan Church complete silence is kept about it. I have written two or three times to Sydney about it, but have not succeeded in my object. Let us get full and correct Missionary information, and I am sure you will stir up the Churches to contribute largely. *A lack in Missionary literature.*

Rev. A. D. Gring (Reformed Church in the United States, from Japan): I think that one of the most interesting facts concerning this great Conference is not so much the interest that we ourselves take in it, as that there are thousands of Foreign Missionaries abroad who are looking to this Conference with a great deal of expectation. To these Missionaries the great significance of this Conference is that the managers of Societies are waking up at home. There is no doubt about it at all that every Missionary on the field is quite awake to the great demands of the work abroad, but they have always lamented that the Church at home has not felt as they have felt, and has not been as zealous in the work as they themselves have been. Now this Conference shows to them that there is a waking up. I want to refer to one matter here—the way of interesting the Churches at home. I have only, of course, to speak of that Union Church in Japan, which I have the honour to belong to. It is now the largest church in Japan. I have only to refer to the way we take in trying to interest the Japanese in their own work there. *Missionaries and the Conference.*

When we preach to the Japanese, and when we examine them for baptism, we say, " Will you now from henceforth do all that lies in your power to lead those of your family, your father and mother, your brothers and sisters to Christ ? " That means not only by Missions but by personal effort as well, and we are bringing home this great point—personal responsibility for their neighbours' salvation. · This is the great point that must come home to every true Christian Church in the Home field. We have proposed to the Native Church that if they would raise one dollar we would raise three dollars. This has been a great encouragement to the Church in Japan, and they have come forward nobly to pay their part. This independence of character in the Churches in Japan has helped the Boards at home wonderfully. *Personal responsibility.*

One other point.   It seems to me the great thing for the Home Churches is for them to realise just what we realise.   I have often thought it would pay our Boards at home if they were to select some good men, gifted with **A new way to increase enthusiasm.** the ability to speak, and to appeal, and to transfer their enthusiasm to others, and send them out to the field with this idea,—that they go there and live among the people, and work with their Mission for five or six or more years, and then they might be brought home again with the idea of keeping them at home three or four or five years going about among the Churches.   In this way you will create at home such enthusiasm as you can never do by written letters.   We feel how infinitely poor are the descriptions we write.   One other thing.   The end will not be accomplished until every Christian feels his own responsibility.   Here, it seems to me, is where we ought to bring in the subject of special objects.   Every Church ought to have her Missionaries ; every individual, as far as he can, ought to have his Missionaries abroad ; every Presbytery, every Society, ought to have two or three Missionaries abroad ; so with every Church, and every rich man ; and then the Missionaries could send home their letters to the Presbyteries, the Churches, or the individuals, and there would be a personal responsibility awakened. Responsibility is too much generalised.   People drop their pennies in the little collection box, and they do not know what they are giving to.   Let every man say, "My Missionary is in Japan, at Tokio, and unless I support him from week to week he must come home."   But it is not so now.   When I put my penny in the box it is distributed all over the world.   The same responsibility that a Church has in engaging a pastor, in supporting and sustaining him, has in the case of Missions to be brought home to every member of the Church.   Give everybody something to do,—every man, woman, and child.   I am convined from my little experience in the Churches at home that special work is the great thing by which the Boards can call out the liberality of the Churches.

Rev. John Pagan, D.D. (Church of Scotland Foreign Missions Committee): As a minister ordained thirty years ago, I venture to speak of Sunday schools giving support to Missions.   The system that prevailed **Support from Sunday schools.** at that time was to have one Mission-box put down once a month.   After I had tried that for a little time, and endeavoured to supplement it by collecting cards, I found the system did not draw out the Missionary sympathies of the children.   The great object is to secure intelligent and interested giving.

My own experience is not to support a child here, and an orphan there, but to get the children interested in two or three departments of the Church's work,—the work in India, the work in Africa, the work in China, a part of the year given to one, and another part to another.   I find in this way they get acquaintance with the whole field with which our **How to interest the young.** Church has to do.   The children should all know how much is given by their class by opening the box every two or three months.   In this way the interest is much better sustained.   They are easily interested. Give them information, and they will give a support proportionate to the interest they feel.   We do not get support from the children of the well-to-do classes nearly as large as from the children of the poor.   We all wish systematic support for Missions, and we can have no better support than the childen of the poor, bringing their halfpenny or penny a week.

We found we were not getting the young men of the Church to be interested as they ought to be in Missions.   We have an organisation of Young Men's Associations, called guilds, in connection with the Church.   They were invited to take up a special field for themselves ; one of our most important stations in India was selected, and we resolved to put ourselves into communication with each member of the guild, and ask what they were willing to give.   We have got an exceedingly good response.   We have got one of the ablest and most devoted young men at our Divinity Hall to go out at the head of the Mission, and, so far as we can see, this promises to be a carrying forward of the interest from the Sunday school through the young men of the Church.

Mr. David Maclaren, J.P.: I think what is to be said on this subject might be summed up in two words, principle and plan. The only principle that will carry us through is that of stewardship, and we should recognise that, not only as regards our money, but as regards everything else, we are stewards for God. I hear somebody say, "How can a man be interested in the conversion of the heathen when he is living in such and such a house, and driving about in a carriage?" Why, if he recognises that he is God's steward he should spend his money upon his support and upon his recreation *as* a steward of God. The certain proportion ought to be laid aside for God's work. I have heard people object to that plan of laying aside one portion. "Why," they say, "we should give the whole;" just as I have heard objections to keeping the Lord's Day, because every day should be sacred to the Lord! In connection with this a passage is quoted over and over again with a totally perverted meaning, "Prove me herewith, and see if I will not pour you out a blessing?" Wherewith? With what? "Bring ye all the tithes into the storehouse, that there may be meat in Mine house." I venture to say there is a good proportion of the people in this room at this moment who do not know that that promise is given to those who bring their tithes into the storehouse. I should like very much to know to what extent the higher life has influenced the purses of those who hope they have entered on it.

Principle and plan of giving.

Miss Annie R. Butler (Medical Missionary Association, London): One of the questions before the Conference is, How shall money be got from the children of our Sabbath schools? As an answer to that I would suggest another question: How shall they believe in that of which they have not heard, or which, if they have heard it, has not been presented to them in a form that they can assimilate? I remember when I was a little child I was expected to give money for a child in a school in India. Every now and then a few dull sentences were read out to me about the child, and it was of no interest to me at all; but by-and-by a cousin came who had personal interests in the Mission-field, and she talked, and then wrote me letters about them. That touched my heart, and I felt that I, too, had a hold on the Mission-field. I remember reading in "Children's Work for Children," how the little Siamese children were taught to kiss. From that time I felt that little Siamese children had become a reality to me, and any child would feel the same. Tell our children then that which will touch their sympathies.

The importance of Mission literature for children has not been dwelt upon yet, I think, in this Conference. I wish that people, when they read a Mission book that takes hold of their hearts, would try to write some simple account of it, and pass it about among the children of their acquaintance. Or, if they are happy enough to find a publisher, they might publish it. Abundance of literature has been written to interest our children about the little ones in the East End of London. Would not the same kind of literature enlist their sympathies for the children in foreign lands? A lady whom I know was sent to the foreign field through reading, as a young girl, a book which one would have thought would have disheartened a girl,—"The Finished Course"—accounts of Missionaries who died soon after arrival in Africa. It touched her heart. She thought "That which is worth

Mission literature for children.

dying for is worth living for;" and she is at the present moment doing Medical Mission work in Cashmere. When going back from one of these meetings of Conference one evening, in a third-class carriage, 1 fell in with a very pleasant-looking lady who had also been here; and she said, "I began to be interested in Medical Missions through reading a story called 'The Crown of Glory.'" I do not myself care much about fiction, but if fiction must be written let it be utilised to bring in Missionary facts, and so let it take the place of literature which too often injures the hearts and minds of children.

Fiction with Missionary facts.

Mrs. Mary C. Nind (Woman's Foreign Missionary Society of the Methodist Episcopal Church, U.S.A.): It is from a mother's standpoint I want to speak. First, then, I am indebted to God for the great deal of Missionary enthusiasm I have, so that I am sometimes called a Missionary cylone. It began with the instructions of my mother and father in this land, for I was born in this country, though I am really now an American. First, then, with regard to the instruction received. Early led to Christ. That is the great bottom, basal thought. Then the great truth taught that I must be all the Lord's, not a half Christian, but entirely His. Then instruction on great Missionary themes in the home and around the family altar. Then I was taken to Missionary meetings when I was very little, and sat on my mother's lap and listened to great Missionary speeches, which I have not forgotten to this day. Then Missionary literature was put in my hands. I never read a novel, except Harriet Beecher Stowe's "Uncle Tom's Cabin;" but before I was twelve years old I had read some religious books, such as Doddridge's "Rise and Progress of Religion in the Soul," Baxter's "Saints' Rest," and all Angell James' works. My first pastor was an exiled Missionary from Madagascar, John Joseph Freeman. My mother used to invite to her home very often the six Malagasy refugees, at whose feet I almost adoringly sat, and listened to their recitals of their persecutions.

Early instruction.

Then we were early taught to save our money from candies and superfluities of naughtiness, in order to put it into the Missionary box. We saved the rags, we picked up the pins, for which we were paid, and we faithfully saved the old bones so that we could sell them for Missionary purposes. We dressed plainly and lived plainly, and the house was furnished plainly, in order that we might give more to the cause of Christ. That is good bringing up. I recommend it to all you mothers and all you fathers. Teach your children that they ought to save to give. Our immortal Wesley said, "Get all you can;"—of course he meant honestly and righteously,—"save all you can; give all you can." That is good doctrine.

Saving to give.

The next thought is, teach your children that the great aim in life is to glorify God and to enjoy Him for ever, and make the last, the enjoying Him for ever, only the blessed end of gloriously living here. I do not care, I think, much about "the hereafter," but I taught my children as my mother taught me, to live for God and for souls, and to find a niche in the great spiritual temple. We should be earnest, consecrated Christians, and go anywhere the Lord sends us. Some mothers teach their daughters that the great end of life is to marry a man with lots of money. That is a miserable doctrine. I am glad I was brought up on the Westminster Catechism, and that I am a Methodist. I do not believe in predestination, mind. I want to impress this upon you. First, get the children to Christ early. I was converted before I was five, and all my children before they were twelve.

Teach children consecration to God.

Secondly, get them to realise that the consecration must be complete. Thirdly, attend to the Divine call, whatever it is, and wherever it calls them. Then, let us feel that all our money is his. I desire to be known as a walking, living collection, gathering money for Christ, and I have brought up all my children to feel that at least one-tenth of every dollar they have belongs to the Lord, and if He should ever give them abundance,—I do not know He ever will,—one-fifth. If we begin with enthusiasm, pray it at the family altar, live it every day, we shall not have so many stingy Christians as we have.

Rev. Dr. Schreiber (Rhenish Missionary Society): You will allow me to make a few remarks, because I have been for a long time busy on the kind of work that we are speaking about this afternoon. I have found out that the less we speak about money when addressing *Interest people in the work.* Christian people, the better. The best way is to get them deeply interested in the work before us, and then the money comes of itself. But, on the other hand, I say you cannot by any means lay down a rule which will hold good everywhere. The only way is at the end of the year to tell the people, "The Lord has given us all we have need of."

One other remark. A previous speaker told me his Society had got three or four calls for extending their work last year, but they did not do it because they were short of money. Now I do not think that is a *Societies going forward in faith.* right way. I have found at least twice in our own Society that as soon as you begin a new work you will be sure to get a lot of money. The best way is not to stop short because of money, but to trust in the Lord, and we may be sure that He will not let any of His work fail for want of money. A very experienced man said to me the other day, "If they are really doing the Lord's work, and in earnest, the Lord will not let the money be missing for that work."

In Germany we have a great many poor rich men, because they do not possess the money but the money possesses them. In former times I was always of opinion that there was a difference between England and Germany. We in Germany get a great amount of money *Gifts of the poor in Germany.* from poor people, and there are people there who can make many others ashamed. I have seen a poor needlewoman, who gave one-fourth of all she earned to the Mission. I have a letter from a poor man who sent me sixty marks; they said it was too much, but he said, "It is not too much." I have learned that in England it is just the same,—that a great part of the money comes from poor people,—and I was very glad when I heard it. If the rich will come and help us, God bless them, but we will rely on the poor; and we are very glad that so many of the poor are rich in Christ.

Rev. William B. Derrick, D.D. (African Methodist Episcopal Church Missionary Society, U.S.A.): Mr. President, ladies, and gentlemen,—It affords me supreme pleasure to be present on such an occasion as this. It is true I am among those who were not allowed to be present at the opening of the Conference. My cause of not coming earlier is to be attributed to the fact of my attending our General Conference, which did not adjourn before the 30th of May, after which I had to travel four thousand miles to reach London. I come as the representative of an organisation known as the African Methodist Episcopal Church in the United States, Africa, and West Indies, numbering four hundred thousand communicants and three thousand ministers. We come with the greetings of this branch of Christ's Church, praying that the blessing of our most merciful Creator may rest upon all your deliberations, likewise assuring you that this Convention has its hearty sympathy and earnest prayers.

I am pleased to say that the Papers to which I have listened I heartily approve, especially that of the Rev. Mr. Romig, for whom I am here to certify as to

On adaptation of Missionaries.

the correctness of his statements, as the Church, of which he is the honoured head, has been, and is, doing much good in my island home. But may I be allowed to call attention to two very important thoughts which should not be lost sight of by this Convention. First, the kind of material which is selected as Missionaries in foreign lands. I am strongly of the opinion that they should be individuals who are thoroughly adapted for the great work. I am conscious that this Convention is aware of the great fact that adaptability is an indispensable requisite to success in all branches of our busy life, be it secular or spiritual.

The only standard by which individuals ought to be measured should be mental and moral culture, backed with Divine grace. This, and this alone, should be the gauge, and not that of colour, without which the prayer, which is continually going up, "Let Thy kingdom come," will never be answered. All natives are invited to rally beneath the folds of salvation's banner as equals in Christ Jesus. All are united as children of one common Parent, as is laid down in the writings of the holy Apostles, "Of one blood God made all nations to dwell upon the face of the earth."

Rev. R. H. Warden (Foreign Missionary Society of the Canadian Presbyterian Church): One point has been so very strongly emphasised by Mrs. Nind that I shall not refer to it. I believe there is no school in this world like a Christian home. I believe it is desirable to have in every home a Missionary box, and that the children should be encouraged to contribute, from time to time, for the kingdom of Christ. I believe the living voice is infinitely better than the periodicals. I like the plan of weekly

His method in the congregation.

Sabbath-giving for Christian work. In the congregation with which I am identified the plan is this: last year we had one envelope weekly, in which we put our contributions for Missionary and congregational purposes combined. Now we use two envelopes, into one of which we put the contribution for congregational purposes, and into the other the contribution for Missionary purposes; and the experience in Canada East is that far more money is contributed for the Lord's work, by means of this system, than by any other plan.

I think each congregational Society should publish annually the names of the donors, with the amounts they contribute. I know there is a difference

Names and amounts should be published.

of opinion with regard to this. I believe the text applicable to this matter, as well as to others, is this: "Let your light so shine before men, that they may see your good works, and glorify your Father which is in heaven." Example is better than precept, and one of the most liberal men in the City of Montreal learned to give simply by the knowledge he had of a man, who was supposed to be less wealthy than himself, giving more than he did, as published in the annual register. I believe the publication has its advantages, and that it is desirable, on the part of those identified with Christian Churches and Missionary Societies, to publish the names, with the amounts contributed from year to year. I believe every method good in itself must be well worked; because, humanly speaking, the success of any system will depend very largely on those who administer it, and however theoretically good a system may be yet people get into a rut after five or ten years. No matter how wisely planned any system of Christian finance may be, its success will be found to depend on the Church's own efficiency in cultivating the spiritual life of its members. Overflowing grace will produce overflowing liberality.

Rev. W. F. T. Hamilton (British Syrian Schools and Bible Mission): I have two practical suggestions to make to this meeting on the subject of Material Agencies. The first is this, which I would venture to address to those who, like myself, at the present moment, are presiding over parishes, either in England or elsewhere. For every deputation or Missionary, whom you ask to come and speak to your people, give two addresses yourself. *Practical interest by home clergy.* I believe we cost our Societies a very large sum in sending to us Missionaries and deputations, and our people will never believe in our earnestness till they have practical proof that we take the trouble to study Missions, and can give them interesting accounts from the platform or pulpit. In the large parish which, at present, is under my charge, I believe that, although I spoke very feebly, yet a lecture I gave on Japan convinced the people more of my interest in Missions than all I had done in getting deputations to address them before.

I have had some slight experience of juvenile associations, and I wish to commend a plan which has been adopted with great success in more than one place, and that is to have for young women, and for children of the upper class and also of the lower class, working parties, to be presided over by one or more ladies, who will undertake to prepare the work for the children (who work for the benefit *Missionary working parties.* of Missions), and to give them interesting Missionary information while they are at work. I could mention one or two cases to you where great interest in Missions has been excited by gathering the children together, weekly or fortnightly, for working purposes.

Rev. George Wilson (Edinburgh): I have to apologise for letting my voice be heard this afternoon. I speak simply because I cannot help it. I have waited to the very end to hear reference made to what I believe to be a very material agency. I believe the day has come when we may make large and most blessed use of the industrial gifts of artisans in the great work of evangelising the world, and sending abroad men of God who have all the qualifications of a Missionary, but *Missionary artisans.* who have the additional gift of some handicraft, so that they may go and live a Christian life and illustrate before the heathen the Christian family, and show the heathen how to use their hands as well as to teach them the way to God. I believe that is one of the mighty forces of the Missions of the future.

I know this moment of a boy being trained in Mr. Grattan Guinness's college. I knew his gift and his sterling Christian character. When that boy came to me, he said, "I want to go to the Mission-field, but I have been reading the parable of the talents, and I read there that if a *A blacksmith's Missionary consecration.* man does not use his whole talents for God, God will not bless any other talent. I am a blacksmith, I am a good blacksmith, and I want to consecrate my gift for the Lord; I will go anywhere in the world provided I may teach the uncivilised savage to use the forge." I said, "I will take the responsibility of your training." I believe this is one of the mighty Missionary forces of the future. We know that Missionaries going as brethren among the heathen are necessary, and that great preachers are very useful, but they are not so much needed in the Mission-field as holy men, men who will show the heathen all the sides of a Christian life, the home life, social life,

Sunday life, daily life. Now an artisan who is a man of God can do that as well as I can, and I do believe that for the transplanting of a Christian community into these Mission lands, and the raising up of a native Christian community, we have in this Industrial Mission one of the great forces of the future. I do trust, therefore, the Church will realise that there is a great power in this. There are thousands of artisans ready to go forth to-day, and it will cost little money.

Mrs. Brissell (United States): Within the last few weeks it has come to my knowledge, not from rich Boston, the city of merchant princes, but from a Southern State ravaged most terribly by the late war, and from a man of Scotch descent, though a Virginian by birth, that many of his fellow-members have adopted the one-tenth system, with the result that there has been an increase of contributions of 2,000 per cent. from his poor Church.

The Chairman: Allow me to say that the American Christians last year raised between four-and-a-half and five millions of money for Missions, while at the same time the Evangelical Christians of the United States hold in their hands eleven billions. We pay nine hundred millions a year for the liquor traffic, six hundred millions a year for the tobacco traffic, five hundred and sixty-eight millions for jewellery, and five millions for ostrich plumes. It is time we began to consider whether the property put in trust for Christians to use is being used as wisely for God's kingdom as it ought to be.

Missions and national expenditure.

The Chairman pronounced the Benediction.

MEETINGS OF MEMBERS
IN SECTION.

TWENTY-SECOND SESSION.

THE RELATIONS OF COMMERCE AND DIPLOMACY TO MISSIONS.

(*a*) What commerce is, and what commerce on Christian principles might be in relation to Missions.

(*b*) The Missionary bearings of the liquor traffic and trade in guns and powder in Africa and elsewhere.

(*c*) The relation of the Missionary to commercial men in heathen countries.

(*d*) The effects of the opium trade on China and on India.

(*e*) How shall the united influence of Missionary Societies and of all Churches be brought to bear upon this evil?

(*f*) How far should the friendly co-operation of European and American residents on the Mission-fields be invited?

(*Tuesday morning, June 19th, in the Annexe.*)

Duncan McLaren, Esq., in the chair.
Acting Secretary, Mr. Reginald Radcliffe.

Prayer was offered by the **Rev. A. J. Gordon, D.D.**

The Chairman: The topic sent down for our consideration this morning differs somewhat from those that have occupied our attention during the previous meetings of this Conference. Hitherto we have looked at the agencies at work and at the methods employed in our Mission-fields, and considered how these may be rendered *New class* more efficient, and what helps we can give. To-day we *of topic.* are asked to look rather at the other side of the picture and to see some of the hindrances that stand in the way of Mission work, and to take counsel together how what are but hindrances can be turned into helps, and how what is essentially evil can be altogether removed out of the way.

Two of the greatest evils with which our Missions have to contend are specially mentioned in the topic set down for discussion; the one, " The Missionary bearings of the liquor traffic and trade in guns and powder in Africa and elsewhere." That trade, we know, is working deadly evil in all parts of Africa, and some of those who are well entitled to speak tell us that the evils resulting from it are almost as great as the evils resulting from the open sore of slavery itself. Another of these evils which are mentioned is, " The effects of the opium trade with China and with India," and from *Opium and liquor.* what we know of the opium trade in those countries, there is very little doubt that the effect of it is as injurious to Mission work in the Eastern continent, as the liquor traffic is to the great Southern continent ; with this aggravation to those of us who are British subjects, that we have a direct responsibility in what is done in connection with it—that unlike the liquor trade, it is not the act of individuals or of corporations for the purpose of trading, but it is the act of the Indian Government, and as British subjects we have a direct responsibility in it. Another great evil not mentioned there, but which immediately occurs to us along with this, and which Government sets as an obstacle in the way of Mission work both in India and some other of the Crown Colonies, is those Acts for the regulation of vice which are working incalculable mischief in those lands, and which, though condemned by the House of Commons a fortnight ago, and for the moment suspended by the Indian Government, are not yet altogether repealed in some places. It becomes us to remember that unless we co-operate with others who are likeminded, and insist on their total repeal, we cannot be sure that these Acts will be altogether cancelled.

Looking at these questions from a Missionary point of view, we find they are a very great evil standing in the way of all Mission work. They are a standing reproach to Christianity and tend *A reproach to Christianity.* to associate in the natives' mind immorality and Christianity; for they ask, " Why should we forsake the faith of our fathers for a religion which permits its professors to do such things ? " While it is against our rules to submit any memorial for presentation to Government, or to pass any resolutions at the Conference itself, we rejoice to know that in addition to the meetings mentioned in our syllabus, there is to be a meeting in the large hall to-morrow night, when resolutions will be submitted condemnatory of those evils to which I have just alluded, and it is to be hoped the result of that meeting will be to influence our Government, and the Indian Government as well, on these subjects. We have also to consider this morning the relations of commerce to Missions. All must admit that Missions have been very beneficial to commerce. Wherever the Missionary has made an entrance, commerce has followed through the open door. I am sorry to say the benefits are not altogether reciprocal, for though we have much to rejoice at in having so many Christian merchants going forth both from Britain and America, who do a great deal to help Mission work in those places where Missionaries are labouring, we also know that in many instances the influence of those who conduct the commerce of our country, and that of America and other nations, in those heathen countries, is far from beneficial to Mission work.

PAPER.

1. By the Rev. F. F. Ellinwood, D.D. (Secretary, Presbyterian Board of Foreign Missions, U.S.A.).

The Relations of Commerce and Diplomacy to Missions.

Mr. Chairman,—I ought to say that the Paper which I was to read on this occasion was presented on Tuesday evening last, in order to fill a vacancy, and for the reason that it seemed to belong to the discussion of that hour.

In that Paper I spoke at length on the liquor traffic in the Congo, and shall not therefore add anything on that subject now. But the topic presented by the programme for this morning, viz., the "Relation of Missions to Commerce and Diplomacy," is a much broader one. Commerce in its complete sense is the synonym of intercourse, and it properly covers all the relations of Missionaries to their fellow-countrymen who live in heathen lands. I find in the list of sub-topics the question, "How far should Missionaries seek the co-operation of foreign residents in the Mission-fields?" And it is a very important and timely question. *[Commerce synonymous with intercourse.]*

It seems probable that in the next quarter of a century some new exigencies may appear in the work of Missions, and that some changes may be required. In the first place, the new impulse of the European powers towards colonisation, and the probability that large portions of Africa and the unoccupied islands of the sea will be taken under European protectorates may affect our Mission-fields seriously.

For example, the Board which I have the honour to represent, the Presbyterian Board of Foreign Missions of New York, has received notice that in its Mission schools on the Gaboon and the Ogovie rivers in West Africa the English language must give place to the French—that even the local vernacular must be laid aside and only French employed. As a result of these requirements we have been compelled to employ French teachers in our schools instead of Americans. In Tahiti, under similar circumstances, the London Society Mission has been transferred to the "Société des Missions Evangéliques." *[Effect of European colonisation and Missions.]*

For like reasons I understand that the English Baptist Mission at Cameroons has been transferred to the Basle Missionary Society, that field having come under a protectorate of the German Government.

I am also informed that the French Missionaries under the

British rule in Basutoland are obliged to employ the English language in all schools above the lowest grade; not, however, in this case from any law enforcing it, but from the advantages to be derived from a knowledge of English.

Is this rule to become general under the different Powers? As the lines of political geography are extended to all parts of Africa and to the islands of the sea, and as transfers may be made from one government to another by treaty or otherwise, must the *personnel* of our Missions be changed accordingly, and our whole policy be made to suit the various political and diplomatic differences of the various nations?

A division of Mission-fields according to nationalities would have some advantages, but there are weighty considerations against it.

One thing seems to me specially desirable in this new outlook, viz., that the different Protestant Missionary Societies shall strengthen the bonds of a common fellowship. It may be that the policy of employing agents of other and various nationalities in our Missions will tend to obliterate national distinctions, and make us all one. God has doubtless some wise plan in this thing, and will turn it to His glory.

One feature in the new colonial development demands particular attention. An agreement has been entered into between the Vatican and the President of the German Commercial Company, which has been established over the large German territory lying between Zanzibar and the African lakes, to the effect that Catholic Missions only shall be admitted to that field. The German Government has not given its sanction to this arrangement, but Roman Catholic papers in America have not been slow to exult over it as an accomplished fact.

Attempt to exclude Protestant Missions.

This new proof that the Papal hierarchy is resorting to diplomacy to exclude Protestant Missionaries from great Mission-fields on the pretext of colonial boundaries, is one which demands attention. It may, at no distant day, demand united action.

A *second* exigency which seems likely to arise, is one growing out of our successes.

While we have been tolerated, and in some countries have received encouragement and aid from the native governments, it is not improbable that a greater and more threatening development of our influence may excite jealousy and alarm. That stage in our history has already come in the Turkish Empire; but for the British rule it would have come in India. It was stated by a Mohammedan paper in Lahore a year ago, that unless measures should be adopted to counteract the Zenana work of Missionaries the Mohammedan women would all be led astray from Islam, and could not be kept in proper subordination.

Missionary success may rouse opposition.

That was only a frank expression of an alarm which is sure to be felt sooner or later in many lands. Quite recently the Government of Corea has ordered a suspension of religious instruction. This restriction will, we trust, be temporary. Japan seems little likely to be disturbed by reactionary measures, as the religions of the country have but slight favour with the Government ; it rather accepts the spread of Christianity as a foregone conclusion. But it might be far otherwise with Siam if Christianity were to grow into a great power. Persia, as well as Turkey, is sure to place restrictions on all possible inroads of the Gospel upon Islam, and in the latter country all educational institutions would be liable to total suspension at any time but for fear of diplomatic complications.

Doubtless in their future growth Missions must necessarily become more intimately connected with, and dependent upon, diplomacy; and a diplomacy which shall defend Missions can only be inspired by a strong and general home sentiment.

Whatever else may be done to prepare for possible embarrassments to Missionary work, it is particularly important to develop the strength and constancy of the native Church.

The history of Missions in Madagascar is one which may possibly be repeated ; and if so, we could wish that the native Church might always endure the ordeal as nobly as did the Malagasy Christians when all their Missionaries had been banished, and the terrors of persecution were upon them.

Let us then seek for our Missionary work and for the native Churches such a spirit of earnestness and consecration, so complete and deep a baptism by the grace of God and the power of His Spirit, that even if we were all banished from our Mission-fields, Christian institutions would not only live but even gather strength from persecution. And, Mr. Chairman, we find *Need for grace and organisation.* just here a new argument for organic union of our Missions, so far as practicable. If the trials which I have named should come let not our work be found divided and scattered in mere driblets—each, possibly, at variance with the other. Union is strength against a common foe, and never is this principle of greater importance than in the maintenance of truth in the day of small things.

Third,—In the coming years we shall find a much larger foreign population engaged in secular pursuits in all the Mission-fields. The spirit of enterprise is rife, and its extension is world-wide. The nations emulate each other in the development of their commerce. Our work will everywhere encounter evil-minded men, but we shall also meet many who have named the name of Christ, *Foreign residents* whose influence ought to be helpful, with whom it were *will multipy.* wise to cultivate fellowship, and to enlist and subsidise in the service of the Master. Two extremes are possible in the practical treatment of the question by Missionaries : one is to so cultivate the friendship of foreign residents as to become conformed to their ways, and lose the Missionary spirit ; the other is to stand aloof from them, and not only lose the good influence which they might be led to exert, but

even to antagonise them and make them enemies of the whole Mis-
Let us seek to sionary work. Between these extremes there is a happy
influence them. medium, and many have found it. There are now great
numbers of Christian men and women in the great marts of the
East, and their number is increasing. Many young men from our
Home Churches are finding employment there, and not only the
Missionaries in the fields but the pastors whose churches they have
left behind, should seek to conserve their Christian influence. What
a grand example have we in Paul's Epistle to the Romans! He was
writing to a Mission-field—to a great heathen city. There were
Christians there, some of whom were noted for their zeal at home.
They were to be sought out, and greeted with Christian salutations.
Their friendship was to be cultivated and their influence utilised.

If every modern pastor would follow his Church members to the
ends of the earth, with Epistles like the last chapter of Paul's
Epistle to the Romans, the Missionary would find many helpers.

The children of this world are frequently wiser than the children
of light. And the sowers of tares are often more diligent than the
true husbandmen. I am informed by a member of this Conference
that a certain magazine article by the sceptic Ingersoll was
re-published and widely circulated in India within three months of
its issue.

I believe that a great work may be done by our Young Men's
Christian Associations in extending their branches and their general
influence, not only to the young men who go on business errands to
the commercial centres of heathendom, but to the native Christians
Use young men, who already number thousands. It is said that in India
native and there are now not less than three thousand native Chris-
foreign. tian young men who have been educated in English-
speaking institutions. To guard and organise and utilise these
forces that they shall help forward the great cause of Missions is
certainly an end to be carefully considered.

The needs of the times demand that all Christians everywhere
shall be recognised and employed as Christians and Christian
All Christians workers. Whether traders, or consular agents, or
must be workers. physicians, or teachers, all must be made Missionaries,
all soldiers of one aggressive army of spiritual conquest. In the
early Church not merely those who were specially set apart were
Missionaries, but all those who were " scattered abroad," whether by
persecution or for purposes of trade. And it is only by a little
employment of all our forces that we can win our generation to the
truth.

PAPER.

2. By MR. WILLIAM WALKER (Glasgow and Ceylon).

Christianised Commerce: Consecrated Wealth.

The subject entrusted to me is Christianised Commerce, and it is a large subject. If choice of terms were left to me, I should prefer to say Christianised Business. Commerce proper is the interchange of products between nations or individuals, but the term is frequently restricted to foreign trade. " Business " takes in all honourable occupations by which a man can maintain himself and contribute to the wealth of the community. But whichever term I use, I shall use it in this general sense, making it a net large enough to catch the big fish of foreign commerce, and fine enough to include the smaller sorts of all honest workers.

What, then, are the conditions necessary to Christianise commerce? For the present I name three:—

First—That we be satisfied that the business we engage in is in itself right;

Second—That we so conduct it as to bring no dishonour to our Christian profession ; and

Third—That our business and all that it gives us,—it may be wealth, or social position, or influence over either our own country-men or people of other lands, or whatever else it may give us,—we hold as a trust from God, to be used, not for our own aggrandisement, but for the advancement of His kingdom in the world.

[Mr. Walker then goes on very fully to discuss these three conditions. The paper is being published separately in full ; but we give the following passages.—ED.]

Although we are all stewards, we are yet all freemen. It is God's grand and generous way of dealing with us. Sovereign Stewards, but as He is, He leaves us free. He *gives* us everything, but freemen. He lets us do as we please with His gifts. He gives us " talents," and "pounds," and everything else, and His word with whatever He gives is, " Trade with it until I come ; " do with it what seems best to you, until I come. The coming is taken for granted. Whatever may be the result of the trading, the coming is certain.

Stewards, but trusted and free ! I wish I could get all wealthy people to take in both sides of the truth. It is truth for all men, rich and poor, and it means that God will have willing service, and willing service alone. " God," says Richard Baxter, " takes men's hearty desires and will instead of the deed, where they have not power to fulfil it ; but He never took the bare deed instead of the will." The heart must go with the hand in any service we render to God. To the poor it must ever be a comfort to know that great wealth is not a condition of acceptable service ; but, on the other hand, where there is great wealth, great service is possible, and, when rendered, it will be acceptable service "if there be first a willing mind."

It is a beautiful picture of the working of Old Testament willinghood that we have in the twenty-ninth chapter of the first Book of Chronicles, and it is one upon which New Testament Christians may look with delight. It was the occasion of the offering of all the stores that had been prepared by King David and his people for the building of the Temple—stores of gold, and silver, and brass, and iron, and precious stones, to an extent sufficient to startle even Mr. Goschen, if he ever looks into the statistics of the Book of Chronicles.

A Jewish free-will offering.

"Who is willing," said David, "to consecrate his service this day unto the Lord?" and the response was almost overwhelming. "The chief of the fathers and princes of the tribes of Israel, and the captains of thousands and of hundreds, and the captains of the king's work, offered willingly; and they gave,"—gave to such an amount that one shrinks from making even a guess at what it meant in pounds sterling; but the amounts named are, "of gold five thousand talents and ten thousand darics, and of silver ten thousand talents, and of brass eighteen thousand talents, and of iron one hundred thousand talents;" and all this was in addition to the immense stores already laid up by King David himself. Passing by some very extravagant estimates of the total offering made at this time, I simply note here that Dr. Kitto, after going into the matter most fully, easily brings down the amount to one hundred and twenty millions sterling, a sum which he thought "comparatively reasonable, and not absolutely impossible;" but he gives reasons for thinking that the whole amount of GOLD used in the decorations of the Temple itself, and for its furniture and utensils, "might not much exceed ten millions sterling." As for the large quantity of SILVER, he easily accounts for its disposal. "It was used to pay the workmen, and to purchase materials." At all events, "the people rejoiced because they offered willingly; for with perfect heart they offered willingly to the Lord; and David the king also rejoiced with great joy . . ."

The incident.

The Rev. William Arthur, in discussing the question of proportionate giving, puts this question—"Is it lawful for a Christian to be more selfish than it was lawful for a Jew to be?" Lawful or unlawful, the answer is clear. If we except the great outburst of unselfishness at the pentecostal baptism—and that took place among Christian Jews—the givings of Christians will not at any time compare with the givings of the Jews in their best days. Dr. Giffen told us, in 1886, that the total yearly income of the United Kingdom had now reached the enormous amount of 1270 millions sterling. Mr. Mulhall, in 1885, estimated it at 1240 millions. Let us not push accounts too closely, and let us take the smaller amount, 1240 millions. And then see what we should have to give if we gave to God what He claimed for His service

Jewish and Christian giving.

under the Jewish law. The tenth of 1240 millions is 124 millions; and can we believe that all the gifts and contributions of all the Christians in the United Kingdom, for the support of Christian ordinances, for the propagation of the Gospel at home and abroad, and for every sort of charitable and benevolent work—can we believe that all this will in one year amount to 124 millions sterling? No; but—shall I say it?—we all know where a certain sum of 124 millions goes. It is just the amount that goes to the great god of the Distillery, the Brewery, and the Public-house. The total amount of our National Drink Bill for 1887 was just £124,953,630 ! The figures require no comment from me : they speak for themselves.

God has lavished upon this country wealth and other advantages combined, to an extent unknown, I believe, in any other country. Let us look for a few minutes at some of these special advantages. I shall not trouble you with great rows of figures, but I should like to give a few. And it will save separate references if I at once say that I take them from Dr. Giffen, Mr. Mulhall, and the *Statesman's Year Book*. It is not with the idea that they are new that I give them, but because I wish to make them speak.

And first, as regards our WEALTH. The Income Tax is a good indication of the wealth of the country.

In 1855 the amount assessed was . . . . . . 308 millions.
In 1885 the amount had risen to . . . . . . 631 millions.

So that in thirty years the amount assessed for Income Tax was more than doubled.

In 80 years the property of the United Kingdom more than quadrupled.

In 1801 the value of landed property was . . . 990 millions.
In 1882 „ „ „ . . . 1,880 „
In 1801 the value of house property was . . . 306 „
In 1882 „ „ „ . . . 2,280 „
In 1801 the value of all other sorts of property was 734 „
In 1882 „ „ „ . . . 4,560 „
Total values in 1801 . . . 2,030 millions.
„ „ 1882 . . . 8,720 „

So that the accumulated property of the United Kingdom increased during these years 4¼ times.

One hundred years ago the TOTAL YEARLY INCOME of the United Kingdom was less than one-sixth of what it has lately been.

One hundred years ago the total income was about 200 millions.
Fifty years ago the total income was about . . 500 „
In 1886, according to Dr. Giffen, it was . . . 1,270 „

And let it be noted that this large increase has not all gone to make the rich richer. It is away from my immediate object, but it is nevertheless an interesting fact to note, that the earnings of the working classes have immensely increased during these fifty years.

Fifty years ago the working classes of the United Kingdom earned . . . . 171 millions.
In 1886 the amount earned by them was . . . . 550 „
Fifty years ago the amount earned per head was £19
In 1886 it had risen to £42

That is to say, the total amount earned fifty years ago was less than a third of the amount earned in 1886 ; and the amount per head fifty years ago was less than a half of the amount for 1886.

But not only the gross income of all classes has grown to the immense amount already stated. The annual SAVINGS from that income now make up a very large amount. Mr. Johnston in his " Century of Missions," a work
Annual savings. for which we are all greatly indebted to him, reminds us that Mr. Giffen's estimate is that nearly one-fourth of the entire national income is saved annually, so that the savings alone of the country must now amount to about three hundred millions per annum. I lately saw that Archdeacon Farrar stated that the working classes saved annually one hundred millions. Upon what grounds this statement was made I cannot say, but Dr. Giffen assures us that *all classes* save, and this is confirmed by the fact that there are now over five millions of depositors in the savings' banks, with a total amount deposited of about one hundred millions.

That is perhaps enough as to the WEALTH that God has given us ; but I have referred also to special opportunities and advantages, and I wish to give a few figures illustrative of these. They are scarcely needed, but I may as well give them.

Some other Advantages.

In SHIPPING, the increase, as indicated by clearances only, has been from ten millions of tons in 1855, to thirty-two millions of tons in 1885 ; that is to say, the total shipping engaged in foreign trade has been during these years MORE THAN TREBLED.

For 1886, the total shipping belonging to the United Kingdom, including both sailing and steamships, and in home and foreign trade, is given thus :—

Total number of vessels	17,917
Tonnage	7,144,097
Number of men employed	204,470

In 1886 there passed through the Suez Canal a total of 3,100 steamers, of gross tonnage 8,183,313 tons ; and without going into all the nationalities included in that tonnage, I give these particulars :—

Total British tonnage	6,254,417
French, German, and Dutch	1,326,873
All others	602,023
Grand total	8,183,313

That is to say, more than three-fourths of the entire shipping that passed through the Canal was British. And this, I suppose, would pretty fairly represent the position of our country in relation to the entire ocean shipping of the world.

Think, next, of the foothold which as a nation we have got all over the world. It may be that we do not care to name some of the points occupied by us in the Mediterranean ; but there we are, and it is probable that we may stay for some time. Of Egypt I do not speak ; but leaving it for the East, we come upon Perim in the Red Sea, and then on to Aden, the half-way house between Suez and Bombay. That brings us to
British influence universal. India, Burmah, and Ceylon, and there we are in a marvellous position. Our countrymen in British India are barely as 1 to 2,500 of the native populations ; in Ceylon they are as 1 to 600. And yet

we are the rulers, and our sons are there "as princes in all the earth." Going still farther east, we come to the Straits, then on to the Treaty Ports of China, and thence to Yokohama; for even in Japan our countrymen manage to get a footing. In the Southern Hemisphere, with our seven or eight different colonies, we are building up a new world; in Southern and Western Africa we are settled and growing; and, passing across the wide Atlantic, we are there in the West Indies, and in North America struggling to fill up a territory two-thirds the area of the continent of Europe. It is a wonderful spectacle that is thus presented to us; our country's flag flying in all parts of the globe; our language everywhere being taught and spoken.

Think of all this that I have here very rapidly and imperfectly outlined to you,—of our accumulated wealth; of our commanding position on the chief lines of communication throughout the world; of the vast and varied realms over which our Queen holds sway, and the great area—America included—over which our language is spoken; and thinking of it, can we get ourselves to believe that an over-ruling Providence has no hand and no purpose in it all?

"THOU SHALT REMEMBER THE LORD THY GOD; FOR IT IS HE WHO GIVETH THEE POWER TO GET WEALTH."

"AND WHO KNOWETH WHETHER THOU ART COME TO THE KINGDOM FOR SUCH A TIME AS THIS?"

It *is* a great stewardship, and He has given it to us in a grand and handsome way; giving us ample means for the work, and trusting us fully. The money is *there*, for certain: Dr. Giffen tells us it is there; the national records tell us it is there; the long prevailing low rate of interest for money tells us it is there; the very comforts and elegancies of our homes tell us it is there; but the work is not done. The work of making known Christ to men—His own last charge to His followers—is not being done. How can it be done while we hoard so much, and give so little?　　The work not done.

The Christian conscience has been quickened in regard to many social duties in our day, and it may be that it has yet to be quickened a good deal in regard to stewardship. Here is a weighty word from Canon Liddon:—"Perhaps the deepest of all differences between man and man is that which divides the man who does in his secret heart believe that he is a steward who has an account to give, from the man who does not. With the one man there is the very prevalent motive of an almost incalculable power, entering into the secrets and recesses of life; he is constantly asking himself, 'How will this look at the day of judgment; what is the Eternal Judge thinking of it now?'" And of this I feel assured, that if we could get into the hearts of the wealthy men and women of our country, this "motive of an almost incalculable power," we should soon see the sluices of many banking accounts uplifted; we should soon see many hidden and unused stores brought to light; we should soon see the balances of many Missionary Societies adjusted, and the hearts of many secretaries and treasurers made light. We should, perhaps, even see the beginning of that happy time of which we get a little glimpse in Tennyson's "Golden Year":——　　The Christian conscience and giving.

When wealth no more shall rest in mounded heaps,
But smit with freer light shall slowly melt
In many streams to fatten lower lands,
And light shall spread, and man be liker man
Through all the season of the golden year.

DISCUSSION.

Rev. G. Piercy (Wesleyan Missionary Society, from Canton) : I have been thirty years in China, and the last five years in London, as a Missionary to 'the Chinese, and day by day almost I see more of the vices of Chinese people, that is from opium dens and smoking, than any other man in London. Now I speak to one point only. The Indian traffic in opium has risen from 200 chests, 12 tons, in 1767, to 85,000 chests, or 5,312 tons, in 1887. Opium smoking has spread over all China. Those who use it number from eight to ten millions ; some of these are women. The Indian trade is an evil in itself of great magnitude, and also the parent of a still greater evil, for it has forced on and resulted in the home growth and production of this drug in China. For, whereas, thirty or forty years ago, there may have been a few acres of the poppy grown in the Empire, now it is grown on a large acreage in every province, probably already double the quantity now sent from India, this growth increasing year by year. Now what is the result ? This opium is smoked by from eight to ten millions of Chinese, of all classes from the highest to the lowest. It has destroyed innumerable lives, and spread a baleful shadow over many more. Politically, it has lowered the high principle of former rulers, who refused to receive revenue from the vices of the people ; commercially, it drains the country of its wealth, and it effectually bars the enlargement of legitimate traffic with other lands, and most of all with our own; socially and in regard to the race, it saps the virility and productiveness of those addicted to it. To other countries, it sends men with viler habits and steeped in deeper vices, to become a curse there. It is only evil, and that at all times and in all places. Our opium trade with the Chinese has been a curse and not a blessing, it has cursed their blessings. Its history in the past is a roll written within and without, a record of " lamentation, mourning, and woe." It has doomed to death, directly and indirectly, as many men and women and children, as would re-people London, if all its four millions were to vacate their homes, and the dead in China could live again—and they will. But what a huge aceldama, what a field of blood ! The outlook in regard to the opium and drink traffic of a so-called Christian country, is such as to lead one to question whether on the whole Britain is not a greater curse than a blessing to the world.

Statistics of opium traffic.

Unmixed evil.

Moreover, China has not done with the evils of opium, even if our hands were washed of this traffic to-day. China in her desperation has invoked Satan to cast out Satan. She now grows her own opium, vainly dreaming that if the Indian supply lapse, she can then deal with this rapidly growing evil. But Satan is not divided against himself ; he means his kingdom to stand. Opium growing will not destroy opium smoking. Larger quantities and freer opportunities to use it will only rivet the fetters now on that noble land till she is utterly helpless, led captive by the devil at his will. This is the present outlook, though I do not despair, only let Britain do its duty, aided by the Christian sentiment and Christian principle of all her sons.

Dr. Robert Pringle (Bengal Army) : We are all so apt to be charged with intemperance when we speak on the subject of temperance, that I have brought official documents about the liquor traffic in India. Here is what the Government says: " That no consideration of revenue can be allowed to outweigh the paramount duty of Government to prevent the spread of intemperance." We may indeed thank God for the Christian man, Sir Rivers Thompson, who in the face of a diminishing revenue placed that on record, and behind that we can fight a splendid battle. Let us see what the Commission itself has said: " The Commission consider that there has been a very serious increase of drunken- **A Government** ness in many parts of Bengal and Behar; but they think this **report on Indian** to have been relatively less than the increase in consumption, **liquor traffic.** and they also hold that, as a rule, the increase in habitual drinking and in drunkenness has been greater in urban than in rural tracts." Let us see how that has been brought about. " The excessive number of shops as compared with the number of actual consumers in some parts of the province, especially in Bengal proper, has undoubtedly had a tendency to encourage consumption, and the Commission have felt bound to urge strongly the danger of looking merely to total population and area in fixing excise shops. The consideration which should be mainly regarded is the probable number of actual consumers. It also appears to the Commission that the increase of drinking has been in some measure due to the selection of improper sites for shops, especially in the neighbourhood of villages, of aborigines, and of factories and other places where large bodies of the wage-earning classes are congregated together." I need add nothing to this.

What about opium? Here is the Government report of Sir Charles Aitchison. He says: " The replies which have been received disclose a state of things which urgently calls for the serious **Sir C. Aitchison** attention of the Government." This is with reference to the **on " Opium."** Government's own service so that we can fancy what the condition in China must be. " It is no debatable question of the effect of opium on the human frame that is here raised. Under some conditions the moderate use of opium may be beneficial." I have been thirty years in India and I can honestly say I never saw a single case in which I would prescribe or recommend the regular taking of opium, so I state that that is not true, as far as my experience of the most malarious districts of Bengal and the North-West Provinces enable me to offer an opinion. It is not founded on a vestige of fact, and I am prepared to defend my statement before any body of medical men in Europe. " The Chinese population in British Burmah, and to some extent also the immigrants from India, especially Chitta-gonians and Bengalis, habitually consume opium without any apparent bad effects." I fail to see that myself. " Those of them who have acquired the habit do not regularly indulge to excess. With the Burmese and other indigenous races the case is different. The Burmese seem quite incapable of using the drug in moderation. A Burman who takes to opium smokes habitually to excess, and this infirmity of temperament is pandered to by the dealers in opium, who tempt young and respectable men to their ruin by giving them opium for nothing, well knowing that the taste once acquired will be habitually indulged." These are not my words, they are the words of the Government. " The papers now submitted for consideration present a painful picture of the demoralisation, misery, and ruin produced among the Burmese by opium smoking. Responsible officers in all divisions and districts of the province and natives everywhere bear testimony to it. To facilitate examination of the evidence on this point, I have thrown some extracts from the reports into an appendix to this memorandum. These show that, among the Burmese, the habitual use of the drug saps the physical and mental energies, destroys the nerves, emaciates the body, predisposes to disease, induces indolent and filthy habits of life, destroys self-respect; is one of the most fertile sources of misery, destitution, and crime; fills the jails with men of relaxed frame predisposed to dysentery and cholera; prevents the due extension of cultivation and the development of the land revenue, checks the natural growth of the population, and enfeebles the constitution of succeeding generations."

Mr. David McLaren, J.P.: This question has engaged my attention for many a day. My first effort in that direction was a letter to the *Times*, which I wrote in 1840. I am very hopeless about it. There is one thing that is certain, that there is a great deal of ignorance about what the actual facts of the case are. You have heard about the opium trade from the last speaker, but I will just say, in indication of what goes on, that that paper from which he read was one which I had the privilege of getting into this country. I requested Sir Joseph Pease to ask for its production in the House of Commons. Sir Joseph Pease was told by Lord Hartington that such papers were kept in India, and not sent here until they were asked for.

What were the successive steps of this trade? First of all the East India Government made opium from the poppy; secondly, they sold it to **History of opium trade.** the Chinese; thirdly, when the Chinese declared that to be smuggling they withdrew from the shipping of opium to China and left that in the hands of private merchants. Next, when the Chinese resisted, the Opium War took place, and the Chinese were obliged to pay for the expenses of that war. A second war followed, which Lord Elgin, our plenipotentiary, said was a war on most frivolous pretences. That resulted in the legalisation by China of the importation of opium, which formerly had been prohibited. The next step was the Chinese growing opium for themselves. The next step was that the English Government took over the management of India, and at this moment, the Viceroy of India is the largest manufacturer of opium in the world. The last step was when the Chinese themselves began to draw revenue from opium, not only opium imported, but opium grown in their own country. I have gone through the successive stages. The last step has been the debauching of the Chinese Government—the Government which once said, "I will never consent to draw revenue from the misery of my people." We are responsible in the sight of God for this culminating wickedness.

The next question on the Paper is, "How are the united influences of Missionary Societies and of all the Churches to be brought to bear upon this **Leave government of China free.** evil?" Well, I do not know what we can do. In this country we can say to the Government that when the Treaty expires, the Chinese Government shall be left with as much liberty to make a Treaty as the Government of France is. We must give the Government of China perfect liberty to say what terms it will insert in any renewal of that Treaty. The Indian Government are themselves still the makers and producers of the article. Samples from China are brought to India and are chemically examined in order that they may produce the exact flavour which the Chinese like. Our revenues are to a large extent supported by opium. What are we to do? Bankruptcy seems to be almost staring in the face of the Indian Government; and yet if we are to be true to our principles we must say to these men, "This trade must be abandoned." I frankly confess to you that I gave up the hope some years ago that we should ever be able to arrest this evil. I believe what we have to do now is to teach the Government and the people of this country : that when God's judgment falls upon us we may be prepared to recognise our sin. I candidly confess I do not see what is to be done. At the same time I would say to the Government, "Give it up." They say, "I must live." That is what the poor outcast of the street says of herself. Do we admit the validity of the plea in her case? Is it any more valid because it is made by a Government? I tell you frankly over again I do not see my way out of the difficulty in which we are; unless it be by our Government very much curtailing their expenditure in India, and not engaging in wars as they have done. The last thing I shall say is just this. When the first Opium War took place they secured a revenue, but the first Afghan War immediately followed and the entire army, with the exception of one man who came back to tell the tale, was massacred. When the second Opium War was commenced the Indian Mutiny broke out, and the troops that were sent to carry on the Chinese War were diverted in the providence of God to save India. Shall we connect these two things together? We only say this, that He who saw the one event permitted the other.

Mr. B. Broomhall (Secretary, China Inland Mission): It is quite right that in a meeting such as this in connection with this great Missionary Conference, the things that hinder the progress of Mission work should be distinctly recognised. I had no thought of speak- *American liquor traffic.* ing this morning, but I heard a word that there might be something said on this question in defence of things as they are, so far as China is concerned. I almost wish it had been so, for what can we say? We can but have one opinion about some of these questions. In regard to the liquor traffic, one fact came before us a few days ago, a most important fact, that our friends connected with Missionary work should know. It appears that from Boston alone in five years there were sent to Africa 8,800,000 gallons of rum. Now our friends on the other side are stirred about this question very deeply. I rejoice that they are, and one of the advantages of the meeting to-morrow night will be that we shall have strong deliverances from our American brethren on the question of this liquor traffic on the Congo.

I quite share in the feeling of despair which our dear friend Mr. McLaren has just given expression to. For years I have studied this opium ques- tion. I do marvel at the indifference of Christian people about *Indifference of* it. It has been to me perplexing and distressing beyond mea- *Christians in-* sure. I cannot understand it. There is some knowledge, but *comprehensible.* the question is not grasped. The people of England do not realise the sin that is being committed in their name or they would rise as one man, and insist upon the Government putting a stop to England's connection with this traffic. But why is it there is such ignorance? Attention has been publicly called to it, in one form or another, by representatives of all Christian bodies in the land, but with criminal neglect our Christian people have failed to inform themselves of the mischief done by this deadly poison.

We raise a revenue of five or six or seven millions a year for the Indian Government from the manufacture and sale of opium. Can any of us estimate the results of the use of so much opium? Mr. Piercy has referred to the use of it by ten millions of people in China. I am afraid he has very greatly under- stated the number of people who are using it. But if you take eight or ten millions, what a number of people these figures represent, to be debased and ruined for the profit of any government. I referred to the fact that we have not done with opium. No, if we were able to cleanse our hands from complicity in this terrible crime to-morrow, we could not stop the stream of sorrow which we

have started. We have lifted the floodgates of suffering and death, and we
cannot stop the torrent. We have set in motion forces of evil
Injury to posterity. which we cannot arrest, and for generations to come China will be
the worse for what we have done. It is impossible to consider
the condition of China, through our action in this matter, without feeling
that one has not words to express our sorrow that the land we love should have
any connection with a business so fearful. And shall it continue? May it not
be hoped that from this Conference, through God's mercy, there shall be aroused
such a feeling of interest in this question, such a determination to deal with it,
that something shall be done to bring about a different state of things? As far
as we are concerned, I look upon this question as a question of national sin, more
as a question to be dealt with on the ground of righteousness than on grounds
of benevolence merely to the Chinese. It is true, as Mr. McLaren said, that we
have to reckon—I firmly believe it—with Divine judgment if we neglect this
matter. How much we have suffered already I know not, but I do believe
that we have never been a shilling the richer for our wrong-doing in China.
I cannot believe that He who rules the world in righteousness will allow us to
profit from our wrong-doing. We have wronged China as I believe no nation
ever wronged another. But what shall be done? Shall we go on? Shall we
continue for the sake of revenue? No. I feel that if you cannot reduce
Indian expenditure within a reasonable compass, for a time we must be prepared
to bear the burden ourselves, till the thing can be dealt with; but as soon as
the Government of India has resolved it shall be dealt with, as soon as the
Government of this country says it must be dealt with, it will be done, and we
shall have no difficulty about revenue. Let this curse be swept out of the way,
and let us say, if need be, "We will take our share of the burden till the sin is
put away."

Mrs. Mary C. Nind (Woman's Foreign Missionary Society of the
Methodist Episcopal Church, U.S.A.): I have nothing to do with the opium
traffic in the few words that I shall address to you. America has never had
anything to do with that, thank God. I am sorry that she has had so much
to do with the liquor traffic. I am glad to be connected with the great army
of White Ribbon women of the United States, dealing as well as it can with
this great question of the liquor traffic. Our beloved President sent me a
few days ago this memorial. I want to read it, that it may sound in your
ears and hearts, and I trust it will be signed by a great many of our noble
Comparative international responsibility. women here. "It is a fully authenticated fact, that through the
operation of a few merchants and trading companies in
America, Germany, Holland, England, France, and Portugal, a
flood of deadly intoxicating liquor is being poured into the Congo Free
State and the basin of the Niger. During the year 1885 more than ten
million gallons of the cheapest and vilest spirits ever manufactured were
sent from those six Christian countries to the ignorant savages of Africa."
Oh, how we need to hide our heads in shame! "The quantity contributed
by these countries was as follows: England, 311,884 gallons; Germany,
7,823,042; the Netherlands, 1,096,146; the United States, 787,650;
France, of pure alcohol, 405,944; Portugal, 91,525; the awful total being
10,468,640 gallons. It is to be remembered that in Article VI. of the
General Act of the Berlin Conference, the so-called Great Powers there
recited bound themselves to watch over the preservation of native tribes,
and to care for the improvement of the conditions of their moral and material
well-being. In view, therefore, of this declaration, and the awful condition
of things in West Africa to-day, we your memorialists do most humbly and
earnestly entreat that immediate and decisive steps may be taken to bring

about such a revision of the General Act of the Berlin West African Conference as shall prohibit the sale or giving to the natives within the Congo Free State, and in the basin of the Lower Niger, any alcoholic drink of any sort whatever, and to prohibit further the importation or manufacture of alcohol therein in any form. Second, to suppress the exportation of spirits from America or any other country into any part of Africa : To afford your memorialists the support of your honourable body in their efforts with other governments, looking to the accomplishment of the end herein set forth."

Now, beloved, this is the only way to get at these people. We have been trying to keep the Atlantic back with a broom too many years. We want to get at the great basal truth, prohibition, so that the liquor does not go to these parts. This is sent out by the Women's Christian Temperance Union of the world. They have nothing to do with any other parish than the **Prohibition the remedy.** world. I wish this Conference would put itself on record in this matter. I believe there ought to be a clear round clarion note that the world shall hear that this Missionary Conference puts itself on record with regard to this liquor traffic. Nothing else than this will satisfy us ; nothing else than this will satisfy the Lord. I have just one minute. I want to say whether you are Episcopalians, or Methodists, or Baptists, or Presbyterians, we are all one in Christ Jesus, and it seems to me that from this great Conference there ought to go out a round " Amen," the vibrations of which shall touch the uttermost ends of the earth. Beloved, it is too late in the day for us to do anything else than sound the note of prohibition. And as to your matter of revenue, God forbid I should mention it. It is a burning shame to our Christian nations to talk about a revenue that comes from the blood, and tears, and cries, and groans, and moans, and the damnation of thousands of precious souls.

Rev. J. A. Taylor (Baptist Foreign Missionary Convention of U.S.A.) : Among all the very important questions that have been before this Conference, one of the points of the subject before us this morning has the most interest to me : that is the Missionary bearing of the liquor traffic on the coast of Africa. If there is any one thing more than another that prompted the Society that I have the honour to represent in this body, the coloured Baptist Foreign Missions Convention of the United States, to send me here as a delegate, it was the fact that they have learned that one of the main questions to be discussed and considered in this Conference was how best to combine the influence of Christians all over the **Worst form of slavery.** world to stop the importation of liquor to the coast of Africa. We have had some experience of the effect of this traffic in the United States. Bound in the chains of slavery, and cut off almost from the association with Christian nations, we struggled for years, till God in His wise providence struck from the limbs of four millions of human beings that accursed chain of slavery, and trusting in our God and looking up to catch the first gleam of the sunlight of liberty, we started out. But as we moved out on the threshold, we found ourselves confronted with a worse slavery than ever we had before. That was the intoxicating liquor that had been instilled into us by men who called themselves Christians. It has been the work of twenty odd years, with the aid of eminent Christian friends and our own endeavours to rid ourselves of this slavery, and to be able to reach across the broad Atlantic to help our people in that dark continent of Africa.

I was asked to entreat you Christian men and women to unite in prayer to God in appealing to the heads of governments, in appealing to Parliament and to the Congress of the United States, that there may be one united effort to stop, if possible, the pouring in of this stuff that is cursing the body, corrupting the brain, and damning the souls of the people. We are with you. We are going to do all we can in America. God help us to move up and onward. Assisted by the grace of God; aided by your prayers, and your strong arm, and your money; we expect to move on and on until all the corrupting and immoral influences in the train of commerce shall be banished from the world, and our God shall reign all the civilised world over; and Africa, that has been shut up in darkness, shall come forth, bathed in the sunlight of the glory of God; every soul washed clean in the blood of Jesus; and then we shall take our place amid the nations of the earth, waving the banner of Jesus as King of kings and Lord of lords.

Rev. Wilson Phraner (Presbyterian Board of Foreign Missions, U.S.A.): I have just been visiting the various countries of the world, and have been surprised to find how far there was a lack of interest and sympathy between the residents from Christian nations and the Missionaries in their work. I have been astonished to find, when I asked

Merchants and Missionaries. mercantile men, for example in the cities of Yokohama or Shanghai or elsewhere, about Missionary work that they knew nothing about it. I had one intimate friend living in the city of Shanghai for thirty-six years, and he did not know what Missionary work had been going on in that city. The fact is he cared nothing about it; he had been indifferent to it. There is a certain reason for this. First, I will speak of what I saw of putting obstacles in the way of Missionary work. The spirit of the commercial man is different from the spirit of a Missionary. They are in these countries for a different purpose. The object of the commercial man is to make a fortune, and to make it quickly, and he is not always scrupulous as to the terms and conditions on which he makes it. He is very often the advocate of principles that our Missionary brethren have to condemn and speak against, and that causes a lack of sympathy between the two; and, indeed, they sometimes come to feel that the Missionaries are almost their enemies because they have to speak out on the part of the natives, and to take the part of the natives against the commercial men because of their violation of principle in dealing with them.

In Tien-tsin, when I was there, there were some American sailors in port, and they had committed an offence against certain regulations, and were to be tried by a jury of American citizens. They could not get enough to make a jury, and so they called in two Missionaries to make the number. I thought, of course, the sailors would be very glad about that, and said, " Oh, but you need not be troubled about the Missionaries being on, you will get justice done." " Yes, that is just what we are afraid of; we do not want justice done." They knew the Missionaries would simply go for the right, whether against or in favour of American citizens. That actually occurred while I was there.

Japan has put under a ban the matter of lottery business, but in the city of Yokohama you will see in the Concession that lotteries are to be re-

Vice protected by foreign traders. cognised; and that is the way in which a commercial Government avails itself of its liberty in violating the law of the land. Go to Nagasaki. There you will find a block made up entirely of saloons and brothels, and there is more drunkenness and riot and wickedness in that block and coming out of it than there is altogether in the rest of the city of Nagasaki put together. And yet the Government of Japan cannot touch it. This commerce, this money-making in the sale of liquor and of wickedness is the whole secret of this matter. We do not condemn all these men, for we find some noble specimens of Christian men who do sympathise with Missionaries and their work, and do help them in it. I am glad to bear such testimony; but, alas! there are too many of the other sort, and this puts an obstacle directly in the way of Missionary work. The dealings of these men excite the prejudices of the heathen, and they do not discriminate. An Englishman is an Englishman, whether he is a Christian man or something else, and your work as a nation is greatly embarrassed in China and will be embarrassed in China from the very fact of the connection with this traffic in opium. It excites prejudice in the minds of the Chinese. The Chinese are going to raise opium themselves. Why? They are not going to let you have the profit. But I believe if the Indian Government would stop the traffic to-morrow, the Chinese Government would stop the raising of opium in the land of China. The King of Siam recently said to our Missionaries, " You are the only people that come here that do not come to squeeze my people." That is the impression throughout the East; it is a system of squeezing. There are Germans, Frenchmen, and Portuguese there, and a few Englishmen in Bankok where this occurred ; and they try to make money fast, but they do it by squeezing the people. The Missionaries are there for other purposes, and act upon different principles, and the king of that country is intelligent enough to discriminate and mark the difference. But, alas ! great multitudes do not have intelligence enough to discriminate in such matters.

Native opinion of Englishmen.

Rev. J. F. B. Tinling : I wish just to say a word with respect to the opium trade, about which I have thought and written a good deal. It is not a wonder to me that most people shrink from the question because of its vast and varied character. I wish specially to make this suggestion. There is a question agitated just now between the two sections of those who support the anti-opium movement, and that question ought to be settled immediately. The fact is the agitators are paralysed by a certain doubt and difference of opinion respecting the present position of China, respecting the amount of coercion or the presence of any coercion exercised by our Government over the Chinese. I think this ought to be a matter of Conference; that a meeting should be held of all persons who are interested in the question, and some *modus vivendi*, some mode of common operation, should in the interests of this great moral cause be immediately found. But I wish more particularly to say that while we have, and while I am very glad that we have, an anti-opium movement—two anti-opium movements—and I am connected with both of them ; while I think the present movement of Mr. Mabbs for stirring up an increasing interest in this cause deserves a great deal more support than it is getting, and that it will get support as it becomes known ; still I believe the true Anti-Opium Society is, or ought to be, the union of all the Missionary Societies. I believe we are making a great mistake in leaving a cause of this kind as a speciality in the hands of certain persons outside the organisation of our Missionary Societies.

United action needed.

Mr. Moir B. Duncan, M.A. (B.M.S., from China) : The last speaker has largely anticipated what I wished distinctly to lay before the Conference, namely, the desirability of having accurate statements with regard to the opium traffic. I have been particularly interested in this question, and have attended the Conference all through. I was perplexed to find that many seemed to support the views given in defence of Dr. Cust. So far as I could follow that gentleman's position, it is briefly this: that in point of policy it cannot be opposed. Is policy, therefore, to be the regulative idea, either in regard to this or any other problem ? Certainly not. And, again, the whole lesson of history has been to show that what is morally wrong never can be politically right. Another point is that it is contrary to the principles of

Christian commerce; for, applying the canons laid down so eloquently by Dr. Cairns, what Divine idea is realised by this opium trade? The second point was that in commerce, international as well as individual, there ought to be a principle of righteousness recognised. Where is that principle displayed in this desolating trade of the opium traffic? Surely we can believe that the same God of truth who hitherto has guided us will yet help us soon to efface also this awful blot upon our Christian honour and name to-day.

Rev. Henry Duncan (Church of Scotland Foreign Missions): I venture to express the view that no more important question has come before this Conference than that which we are called upon to deal with at our meeting here. We are constantly asked why it is that our Missionary work is not progressing. Why, when I look at the facts in the Mission-field, when I look at the vices of Europeans in heathen lands, when I look at the liquor traffic carried on by professing Christians, I think it is a marvel that we are making any impression on the ranks of heathenism. I would just like to quote a few words that appeared last year in *The Times*, which I think express a great truth, which ought to find an echo in such a Conference as this. "It is almost inconceivable that Christians and civilised men should disregard every argument of equity and right and adopt a policy which is tantamount to the destruction of the souls and bodies of innocent savages. For savages, whether in Africa or elsewhere, alcohol in its European forms is ever harmful. Its mischief is without alloy and without compensation." Now let me ask the attention of the Conference to these words, "Against it Missionaries and schools and laws fight to no purpose." Here are what we might call the resources of civilisation and Christianity frustrated by the liquor traffic, and therefore I say there is no subject to which the attention of the members of this Conference may be more properly directed than the consequences of this evil traffic.

Testimony of the "Times."

And now I would just like to appeal to Missionaries present, and if possible to Missionaries absent, to give us who are at home some information on this subject. I am the convener of a very large and important Committee of the Church of Scotland which the General Assembly of our Church ordered to take special cognisance of this matter, and I have preached frequently, and spoken on platforms frequently, on the subject. But what I feel is that we who are at home and who are trying to influence public opinion on the subject must be supplied with facts from those who are in the Mission-field. An intimate friend of mine in the Lower Room yesterday appealed to Missionaries for information on general Mission work as the best means of stimulating the zeal of the Churches in this and other countries. I would appeal to the Missionaries to send us information on this subject, for if we who go to platforms can only speak in general terms, we will not speak with power or effect. But if we can bring before those to whom we speak facts attested by earnest Missionaries on the spot, I feel sure that we shall do something, at any rate, to rouse the conscience of this country and to everthrow a system which is bringing such disgrace on civilised nations and upon Christianity.

More information needed.

Rev. G. Smith (English Presbyterian Mission, Swatow, China): I did not intend to take any part in this meeting, but owing to some remarks that fell from one of the speakers I was led to hand in my card, and I would remark in regard to the opium traffic, from my connection with Missions in China, that it is not only a fearful evil to the Chinese, but it is a fearful evil to our own country. In five minutes it is impossible to speak of all the evil that it does to the Chinese. I commend to your attention the remarks of my friend Mr. Piercy, so terse, so true, and so comprehensive; every one of them might be a text for a long commentary. But with regard to our own countrymen, what evil it does to them! Young men from Christian families go out to China, they get into firms connected with the opium traffic; they gradually become partners and take part in this traffic. Their consciences become defiled and debased; gradually they separate themselves from Christian Missionaries, and at length there is an antagonism between the mercantile community and the Missionary community; and it is almost impossible that there can be a true understanding between two parties so long as one is committed to a traffic that is immoral, on which the blessing of God cannot be asked, while the others preach and practise the doctrines of Christianity. Hence the evil that is being done to the sons and daughters of those who go out and become connected with the opium traffic is incalculable. Not only is their own spiritual character affected by it, but their moral character is affected.

Reflex evils of opium trade.

Another feature of the trade is this. So far as I know there is no Missionary Society, no Church in China that would receive into its membership an opium smoker. Then there is another aspect, namely, this: If people in our country have any doubts about the righteousness of the traffic, other nations have none whatever. Those interested in any business can hardly look upon it with a disinterested eye. France looks down upon us with contempt in all our pretensions to Christianity, and sneers at us for partaking in the opium traffic. We drug the Chinaman in order to get his money to maintain our Government in India. Germany looks down upon us; America looks down upon us; there is not a country in the world in which public opinion is not against our country in this matter. Then there is another view of it which it is important to bear in mind. We have heard it stated here,—and this is what led me to hand in my card—that it seems to be a hopeless thing. I think we should never go away with such an idea from a Conference like this. If anything is anti-Christian, we must remember that we have the Almighty power of Christ on our side against it, and we must lay hold upon that power, and use that power, in order to overthrow it.

Opinion of other nations.

Rev. James Thomas (B.F.B.S., formerly of Shanghai): I should not have risen but for the remark of a previous speaker, a remark which I fear will be very widely misinterpreted, and which, if misinterpreted, will be very damaging indeed. It is not that we do not know something of the opium traffic, and sorrow over it. It is michievous, and mischievous only. I should like to have said something about its evils, physical, moral, and commercial, but time will not allow me. May I recommend, those who do not know much about the traffic, for the traffic itself deserves to be known, to refer to the Blue Book and compare these two items, the value of tea exported from China, and the value of the imports into China. The very startling fact will be found, for the last decade China has given us tea,—I am referring to the United Kingdom,—receiving in exchange opium, with a balance of trade against her. Now supposing it were even a luxury, without any harmful propensity whatever, there is bankruptcy alone upon a national scale. The great difficulty in dealing with this, as far as the Englishmen is concerned, is the Indian revenue. Who could have thought of what has passed within the last month in this country without feeling the great force of what one gentleman stated as to the revival of a Christian conscience? And if the Christian conscience of

Bad trading.

this country can be but touched by the immorality of this traffic, and pressure bo brought to bear upon the Government, whether it be a Conservative or a Liberal Government, I venture to believe that Government will yield.

My work in China was the work of a Christian Minister in Shanghai, to the mercantile community there. I should be ashamed of myself if I kept silence after what has been said, if I did not say one word to show that the merchants in our treaty ports in heathen lands, if other Mission lands bo like China, will help Christian Missionaries anywhere, everywhere, if you will give them the opportunity. I was the first Minister of the Union Church in Shanghai; I could not stay there without helping in Mission work, and the merchants on the spot supported through that Church two European Missionaries, paying their salaries. They supported a great many schools, and worked them, and they have borne the entire cost of the largest hospital devoted to the Chinese work in the whole of China; and during the ten years of my work there they have given to me—they have passed through my hands, as charitable gifts, over £50,000. If Christian Missionaries will show merchants on the spot how they can help them in their work, I will undertake to say for the merchants that they will help largely and with all their hearts.

A word for the merchants.

Rev. Goodeve Mabbs: What I want to say especially is this, that so far from this time being a time for intense discouragement, it seems to me that it is a time for encouragement. Perhaps there never was so much attention drawn to the question in various ways as at the present time. And I think the influence of this Conference will tend powerfully in that direction. We have facts fighting for us. Within the last two or three years there has been a falling off of a million sterling in the opium revenue derived by the Indian Government from China. Have we not encouragement there? The tendency is for the Indian Government to lose its opium revenue, and that must go on from bad to worse, so far as we can see. Is there not in this every reason why we should take courage and put forth our utmost efforts in order that we may make an end of this great evil. Then India is depending for its revenue upon something that comes from a foreign source, and which is under foreign control; and as the influences are such as lessen it from year to year, surely there is every reason why our Indian Government should put its finances in order, otherwise there will be bankruptcy. Hence we have this necessity again fighting in our favour. Then let us do what we can in every way. One direction in which we could do more is prayer. There is an Anti-Opium Prayer Union, I do not know whether it is known to all in this room. Members may affiliate themselves with it and join in the work.

Reasons for encouragement.

Rev. W. Stevenson (Secretary, Free Church of Scotland Ladies' Society for Female Education, formerly of Madras): One or two words. First with reference to this opium traffic I will say this, that our influence with Government and with the general public may be expected to be in proportion to the certainty of the ground which we take up, and we ought to make perfectly sure that every statement we make is backed up by facts. We must approach the whole question in a spirit of utter fairness and real love of truth, so that we may not merely make general statements and broad condemnations. It is a complicated question. I know Christian men, very earnest supporters of Missions, who defend the course the Indian Government now takes in the matter. Now I do not say whether they are right or wrong. I know quite well how far the atmo-

Care in approaching subject.

sphere of Indian officialism influences even good men, but I say if we are to make sure of influencing the public, and influencing the Government we must take care that the ground we take up can be sustained through and through.

I wish therefore further that some one who really is conversant with the subject could put before the public the question with full knowledge of all its details and with reference to all its bearings, so that the general public who cannot be expected to have full information on the matter may be informed; and if there is such a book already written I wish it were brought to the notice of the Conference, so that we might know where to look for the information that we really need.

Another point in regard to Missions and wealth, Dr. Warneck's book on "Culture and Missions" brings out this fact, that it would pay merchants, it would pay commerce to treat our Missions as a great investment. Missions have such a wonderful influence in developing trade that **Missions a good investment.** any Company who would go in and found a Mission for the mere purpose of developing trade in a great savage or barbarous land would find it pay as a mere matter of commerce. It is well worth while reading the facts of this question as given in that book of Dr. Warneck's. We are met in God's Providence with two tremendous facts in the present day in which we see the connection between commerce and Missions; we see a wonderful opening up of all lands to the Gospel, and we see in connection with that also a most wonderful development of trade, a vast increase in the wealth of the country, so striking that we really may question whether we are proportionately doing so much for Missions as was done fifty or sixty years ago. Is there as large a proportion of the private income of the nation given to Missions as there used to be? Have we not these two great facts standing opposite to each other in God's Providence? God has opened the world to the Gospel; God has given us wealth. If we could only consecrate our wealth and devote it to the spread of the Gospel, we should find a most wonderful harvest to the honour of our Lord and Saviour Jesus Christ.

Mr. David McLaren: May I give a word of explanation as I have been referred to? I do not despair of the triumph of the cause of righteousness. I intend doing all in my power, as I have done for forty-eight years. But I read in history that God gives nations a *locus* **An explanation.** *penitentiæ,* a place for repentance, and if that is not availed of, He then takes it into His own hands. I would not despair of the cause of righteousness in any part of the contest going on between God and the enemy. How was the slave trade abolished? Wilberforce persevered; he enlightened the conscience of this country, and he secured eventually its abolition. His work was taken up by Buxton, and others, and slavery itself in the West Indies was abolished. The conscience of the country was informed. Let us go on trying to inform the conscience of this country. How shall we thank God if so be we succeed? But my fear is this. We know that is not the only mode in which the cause of righteousness triumphs. Will any one tell me how slavery was abolished in the United States? We in this country endeavoured to influence their conscience; men in the North endeavoured to influence the conscience of America; they refused to listen, and by such judgments as the world never saw was that great blot effaced. My fear has been of late, that whilst it is our duty to labour on constantly, it may be by the latter means that God will awaken us. But, as I said, it is our duty to enlighten the conscience of Christians in this country so that when the judgment comes they may discern what it has come for.

Dr. Maxwell closed the meeting with prayer.

APPENDIX.

What are we to expect from German colonisation for German and other Mission work?

BY THE REV. DR. SCHREIBER (Rhenish Missionary Society).

As it is a well-known, and from all sides acknowledged, fact that our whole modern Mission work has a very intimate relation to modern colonisation, the entering of the German Empire amongst the colonising powers could not but arouse the keen interest of all who care for Mission work and its extension. But it seems to me as if the feelings and forebodings thus created differ very widely indeed, especially so between English and German Christians. If my judgment is right, I would venture to say that, generally speaking, in England people have expected too little, and in Germany too much, good for Mission work from this newly and so unexpectedly begun German colonisation. It was this observation that induced me to bring the question before the General Missionary Conference, hoping that it might be given to me to take away at least some misunderstandings, and by doing so to further and foster, at least, to some extent, the mutual sympathy and cordial co-operation between English and German Missions. In order that we may come to a right and unbiassed judgment about the question : What is to be expected from German colonisation for German and other Mission work ? it seems to be the best and safest way to try to understand rightly the forces now at work, and especially to notice carefully the effects produced already by this noteworthy movement.

Let me begin, then, with some dark forebodings that have been aroused by the German colonisation, especially amongst English people. The fear was expressed, at least some time ago, lest the political and mercantile antagonism, naturally enough elicited and strengthened by the German power becoming a competitor in colonial enterprises, might extend itself also to the sphere of Mission work, and disturb the sympathy and happy concord that hitherto has reigned almost uninterruptedly in those regions between German and English Christians.

I can fully understand how such fears must have been engendered by certain articles in German newspapers and periodicals, but anyone who knows how very little connection there is between our German Mission people and the general daily press, would not be very prone to foster such fears, and anyone who has read our German Missionary publications, during these last years, and has taken notice of the verdict of the united secretaries of almost all the German Missionary Societies gathered at Bremen, two years ago, about the thoroughly international character of Evangelical Mission work, will be quite ready to agree with me, that we have no reason whatever to forbode such a disastrous effect of German colonisation upon Missionary enterprise. But there were other apprehensions for which there seemed to be much more reason, and which have found utterance, even in many English Missionary periodicals. No doubt the Germans, and even the German authorities in the new-born German colonies, were going to adopt the French system of political narrow-mindedness, so that only German, and no other Missionaries, should be allowed to live and work within the borders of those colonies. Was not this clearly proclaimed in many a leading article of German newspapers; was not this brought forward as a matter that needed no production of any reasons being a necessary condition of the prosperity of our young colonial enterprises ? And, what must be considered as of still greater weight, was not the Government really acting according to this rule ? Were not the English Baptist Missionaries of the Cameroons induced, or even compelled, to leave that region in order to be supplanted by German Missionaries ?

Now, as for this last named fact, I have never been able to see the matter right through ; and really, up to this day, I do not at all feel certain that the English Baptists were in fact driven away, and that they did not choose of their own accord, for one or other reason, to leave this Mission-field. But even if this deplorable fact could not be denied, and likewise the existence of this wrong tendency in the German colonial quarters must be admitted, I, nevertheless, am prepared to assert that we have not to expect any such thing, for the future, from German colonisation. It has been clearly and emphatically stated, by all German Missionary Societies, that this theory, if adopted by Germany, would be almost a death blow to the whole German Mission work, two-thirds of our Foreign Missionaries being at work in English and Dutch colonies. And therefore, and for the sake of justice and gratitude, we have protested against it with all our might, and have asked for any Foreign Missionaries within the borders of our colonies the same freedom and protection, as our own Missionaries are enjoying in English and Dutch colonies, as we *Anticipations unfounded.* have gratefully acknowledged at every opportunity. I am assured our colonial movement has already overcome this children's disease ; and every thoughtful German will be quite as unwilling to take the French for his pattern in this as in any other respect.

But you will ask me what reasons I have for such hopeful expectations. Let me refer you to East Africa, where till now nothing has been heard about removing the English Missionaries or to the Bismarck Archipelago, where the Australian Missionaries are allowed to go on with their work without any molestation ; or to the Marshall Islands, where the American Missionaries, after some little transient trouble in the beginning, even hail the German Government as promoting their work.

But here it does not seem to me to be out of place to remind you of the fact, that the greater part of our German colonies are not under the immediate direction of the German Imperial Government, but under that of private companies, which have obtained a royal charter very much in the same way as the old English East Indian Company. It is obvious that the German Government or the German people in general cannot be made responsible for *German nation not responsible.* any wrong tendencies that may be found in some of those companies. That would be quite as unjust as if I were to blame the whole English people for the well-known enmity of the old English East India Company against Missionaries. But I think we have every reason to expect that by dint of the supreme direction of the German Government and owing to the influence of German Missionaries and Missionary Societies, those wrong tendencies will be counterbalanced and overcome by-and-by.

This is also my opinion about one other very dangerous tendency, which has been shown in the German colonial movement, in a very alarming degree,—I mean the tendency of confounding colonial interests with those of the Gospel. I am sure many English Christians must have been very much alarmed, perhaps even shocked, by numerous articles in our German newspapers, in which the Missionaries were declared to be the best pioneers for colonisation, and were even admonished not any longer to be so foolish and unpatriotic as only to think of furthering the interests of Christ's kingdom, but *Another danger.* to remember also their duty of furthering the interests of the German Empire. I should say it is on account of such expectations that the coming of German Missionaries into the German colonies has been hailed and even asked for by those who do not care a bit for the spread of the Gospel.

There was no doubt a great danger of the German Mission being led astray by those tendencies especially as they were accompanied by many alluring promises on the one hand and menaces on the other. We have every reason for thanking God that this danger has been avoided. Very fortunate it was, that German Mission work has not sprung up simultaneously with German colonisation, but is of much older standing. It had, therefore, already acquired firmness enough to withstand those temptations ; there were real Missionary spirit and Christian understanding enough in our leading Missionary bodies to feel at once that it was quite out of place to appeal to our German patriotism as far as Missionary enterprises are concerned. The same Conference of Bremen that so strongly emphasised the international character of Evangelical Mission work, at the same time declared it to be improper and inconsistent with the principles of the Gospel, to make the Missionaries subservient to any colonial interests, although, of course, all of us agree that their work is of the utmost importance for the healthy development of any European colony or possession.

But there were not only those dark forebodings roused by the German colonial movement, some of which I have just tried to refute, or at least to reduce to their proper value : with us in Germany especially, many bright hopes were also raised, which I am afraid will never be fulfilled. There were many amongst us who thought that now we had got our own colonies with a numerous heathen population, the Missionary duty would become so obvious The bright side. and urgent, that Mission work would at once cease to be the concern of some small minority of the nation, as had been the case till then, but would become by degrees an enterprise supported and fostered by the whole German nation. Those persons were not aware that only thoroughly believing Christians will ever show a lasting interest for the spread of the Gospel, and make sacrifices for it. There have been made numerous appeals upon our German merchants and upon our educated classes in general for a larger and more liberal participation in Mission work, but those who had expected any considerable result from it have been sorely disappointed. No; with us in Germany as everywhere else Mission work has been confined, as it must be, to the little flock of real believers. But, as regards all real Christians in Germany, we may assuredly expect that they will be more earnest for Missions than they have been hitherto. They have got a new impulse by the German colonisation, the heathen have been brought nearer to their heart by becoming their fellow subjects, and the duty of making the way of salvation known to them is dawning more and more upon the minds of all who wish to do God's will and to be led by His guidance. Germany has been providentially prepared for the fulfilment of its Missionary duty resulting from the acquirement of colonies ; it has plenty of Missionary Societies and organisations, and even of Missionary experience, the only thing wanting till recently was a more general and especially a more generous love and interest for Mission work. This want I expect to be supplied, at least to a large extent, by-and-by in consequence of this impulse given by the Colonial movement. In order to prove the good reason we have Three new for such hopes, I need only point to the three new Missionary Societies. Societies that have sprung into existence within the last few years, and to the fact that at the same time the older Societies have not at all been crippled in their means, but on the contrary have been able even to enlarge considerably their spheres of working. But we must not shut our eyes to the fact that a similar impulse has been given to the Roman Catholic Mission in Germany also, and we must be prepared to see the German Roman Catholics take a much livelier interest in Foreign Mission work than they have done hitherto. Already some new seminaries for training the Missionaries have been erected, and especially in our German Colonies the Roman Catholics will prove very keen competitors of the Evangelical Missionaries. This seems to be the more dangerous as the German Government, like some other Governments, that of the United States for instance, has shown some signs of preferring Roman Catholic to Protestant Missions. The reason for this very obvious and remarkable tendency I cannot explain just now.

However, our Evangelical Missionary Societies have no reason to complain as yet. On the contrary, they have met with very friendly treatment, and even Government with many valuable encouragements from the side of the German encouragement. Imperial Government, as well as of the leaders of the Colonial Companies. The Basle Missionary Society will gladly confirm this, concerning their newly-begun work in the Cameroons, and our Rhenish Society can only do the same regarding the reception and assistance our Missionaries find in German New Guinea.

But I think not German Missionary Societies alone, but all Evangelical Missions, will derive at least some benefit from German colonisation. The extension of colonies belonging to Evangelical powers, as caused partly by the rise of German colonies, partly by the impulse given through it to the English possessions for further expansion, especially in Africa, must be hailed by all Mission friends as identical with an extension of those regions, where Evangelical Missionaries will be allowed to work without molestation.

There is left one rather delicate and critical point to be mentioned here,—I mean the influence German colonisation must have upon the dreadful rum trade,—this very lamentable and shameful hindrance of all Mission work. No doubt our colonies have given and will give a mighty *The liquor traffic.* stimulus to German trade; and as, alas! the rum trade forms a very considerable part of our trade, especially with Africa, and as brandy is produced in enormous quantities in Germany, I am afraid this scandalous trade will go on and even increase until either the Christian conscience will be sufficiently aroused to enforce the extinction of this shocking stain upon the Christian name, or until prudence will teach the traders that by means of the rum trade they saw off the branch upon which they are sitting. Meanwhile, I am afraid we have no reason to blame one another, as there is no great difference in this respect between German and English or Dutch and American trade, and any increase of the trade in general would produce the same obnoxious effect.

But I am very glad I have to say one thing more concerning this topic. German colonisation is by no means everywhere an agency for promoting the rum trade. On the contrary, in all the possessions of the German New Guinea Company all selling of rum or brandy to the natives has *Prohibited in New Guinea.* been strictly interdicted. Perhaps we may hope that this excellent pattern will be followed also in other German colonies.

I shall be content if I have succeeded in convincing you that we are by no means to expect nothing but bad results from German colonisation for Foreign Missions, but that this, like almost all important movements in the world's history, has a twofold aspect,—on the one side producing new hindrances to, on the other new furtherances for the growth of God's kingdom. But if in this case the furtherances are of greater consequences than the hindrances (as is my own opinion), or the reverse, I leave to everyone to decide as he likes ; but I hope all of us will unite in trusting to our Lord, that He by His overruling power and wisdom will make this, like all other things, subservient to His thoughts of mercy and compassion towards mankind.

APPENDIX.

LIST OF CONTENTS.

I. MEMORIAL FROM THE NETHERLANDS MISSIONARY SOCIETY.

II. PAPER BY THE REV. J. T. GRACEY, D.D. (U.S.A.).

III. LETTER FROM DR. HAPPER (CANTON).

IV. LIST OF SOCIETIES SENDING DELEGATES AND REPRESENTATIVES TO THE CONFERENCE.
   (1) GREAT BRITAIN AND IRELAND.
   (2) UNITED STATES OF AMERICA.
   (3) CANADA.
   (4) CONTINENT OF EUROPE.
   (5) COLONIAL.

V. ALPHABETICAL LIST OF THE MEMBERS OF CONFERENCE.
   (1) GREAT BRITAIN AND IRELAND.
   (2) UNITED STATES OF AMERICA.
   (3) CANADA.
   (4) CONTINENT OF EUROPE.
   (5) COLONIAL.

APPENDIX.

I.

MEMORIAL PRESENTED TO THE CENTENARY CONFERENCE ON FOREIGN MISSIONS BY THE NETHERLANDS MISSIONARY SOCIETY.[*]

The experience of the Netherlands Missionary Society in regard to some of the topics moved in the Programme of the Committee for the London General Conference of Foreign Missions.

IN the Mildmay Conference of 1878 the Deputy of the Netherlands Missionary Society had the honour to deliver a report in reference to the state of that Society and to some questions in connection with the subject, to which it may be allowed to refer as introduction to the present Memoir. (See "Proceedings of the General Conference on Foreign Missions," etc. London : John F. Shaw & Co., 1879, p. 155, etc.).

The topics mentioned in the programme of the Committee for the present Conference had, since long in high degree, the attention of the Directors of our Society, and we shall be happy to learn from the experience of other brethren. The following may be considered as a survey of what we learned from the history of our own Society during almost a century.

We shall follow the order proposed by the Committee.

I. MODES OF OPERATION IN THE FOREIGN FIELD.

1. *Self-support and self-government in native Churches.*

(1) As for *self-support* in native Churches much depends on the social condition of the natives. Our Society experienced, that in general the native churches could not contribute but a small share in the support of their church and school buildings, salaries, and further expenses for public service and education.

In reference to *self-government* we observe that our native preachers, though well trained and in many respects equal to their task, still want the supervision of European Missionaries, if to be kept in constancy and soundness of preaching. Being raised by Christianity from very primitive conditions, they have not reached that degree of consistency which can make them fully answerable for their conduct. There are gratifying exceptions, no doubt, but in general the Missionary must be on the alert. For this reason the ministration of the sacraments cannot be trusted to native ministers.

The preachers are assisted by *elders,* by which means we succeeded in interesting the Church members in the concerns of public worship. In consistorial meetings the interests of the congregation are discussed, and as these

[*] The following document, coming with the official sanction of the Committee of the Netherlands Missionary Society, is entitled to a place in the Report. We regret that no other place could be found for it.—ED.

are generally presided over by the Missionary, he partakes in every concern, finds opportunities to advise and to instruct, etc.·

Some of the members have their private religious meetings, which they call *compoolans*, in which they read the Scriptures, pray, and sing.

The female members have their *special meetings*, and gather contributions for the schools.

2. (a) *How to educate native evangelists and pastors, and* (b) *to stimulate the higher life and enthusiasm of converts for the conversion of the heathen.*

(a) With a view to educating native evangelists and pastors, our Society has a *training institution* in the Minahassa, where, besides some of the secular branches, Biblical instruction and practical exercises in teaching and preaching form the principal materials.

In Java every Missionary has a number of young men, partaking of his instruction, and being in that way educated for their task.

A distinction is made between schoolmasters and evangelists or catechists, depending entirely on the propensities and fitness of each individual for either task, although the schoolmasters partake of the same instruction, and must be able to catechise young people, where this is required.

(b) As for stimulating the enthusiasm of our converts for the conversion of the heathen, we experience that in our Missions this is a very difficult task, on account of the low standard of civilisation of the natives. There are among them some instances of real interest in the propagation of the Gospel ; but in general we experience that such a spirit is not alive among our neophytes, although our Missionaries endeavour to raise it.

The Javanese are under certain conditions fit and ready to propagate the Christian religion. We had our Paulus Jossari and his fellows, men full of the spirit of Christ, who contributed greatly to the spread of the Gospel among their relations and friends. But the opposition of Mohammedan priests and Hadjis is there a real stumbling block, and has a great influence upon natives, who, though true Christians, yet by a certain natural apathy abstain from regular preaching, only now and then testifying of Jesus Christ and their faith in private conversation.

Yet the European Missionary draws great advantage from his native helpers, teachers, and preachers, who open ways of access to the natives, and contribute greatly to confidential intercourse. The helpers, etc., form the line between the Missionaries and the population.

3. *How to adapt Missionary methods to the different states of civilisation or barbarism among heathen nations :* (a) *Education ;* (b) *Woman's work ;* (c) *Medical Missions, etc.*

In general our Missionaries endeavour to gain a firm position in the Mission-field. They are, by their studies in Europe tolerably acquainted with the Malay, and, being destined for Java, likewise with the Javanese language, before entering the field. They improve their linguistic knowledge by continued study and by conversation with the natives.

As long as they are considered as strangers their influence is scant. By medical and surgical aid they attract some of the natives, so at least it is in Java, and though the effect in regard to Christianisation may not directly be visible, yet a spirit of good will is raised, which leads to familiar intercourse with the Missionary and his native assistants.

Those assistants are generally young men, living with the Missionary and his family, and partaking of his instruction and family worship, having on their side to render household services, for which they are fed and dressed. In the Minahassa those young men are called Moorids. The lady of the house has her anak-piaras (adopted children, however, in a sense that they continue to be members of their own native families, whom they visit regularly), girls, who partake of the same advantages as the boys, and render services in the female line, being instructed in all sorts of household business.

All this and more may be considered as introduction to the labours, and has proved to lay a reliable foundation.

4. *How to adapt Missionary methods to the different forms of religion among non-Christian peoples ; especially those having sacred books.*

We must begin to observe that sacred books are in the Netherland East Indies out of the question. The Mohammedans there cannot be said to have their Koran. Although the priests and santris read it, they do not understand it, and will hardly be able to quote passages in Arabic. In their controversies they will rarely allude to the Koran, sometimes to the Moslem legends, but then generally in a form, which in Java is known as gnelmoo or ilmoo (mysterious science).

In Java Islam is corrupted by Hinduism, of which as well as of nature-culture considerable remnants are alive. The religion of the Javanese stands in consequence as near to heathendom as to Islam. Only the heathen is rarely a fanatic, whereas the Moslem under every form is easily roused to fanaticism. It is on this account that the Dutch Government is obliged to be very prudent in regard to religious matters. Public speeches, bazaar-preaching, and the like, would not be allowed, but would besides this prove of no effect ; on the contrary, they would be encountered by the priests and their adherents in a manner that would for a long time exclude or neutralise all evangelical work.

Our experience is that the Gospel must be preached more by individual influence and the example of a Christian life, than by speeches, sermons, and controversy. Our method is that of the sower, who, after having sown his seed in the proper way, waits for the precious fruit of the earth, being patient over it, until it receive the early and latter rain. Indeed, patience, by regular and constant labour, sustained by faith, is the first requisite in our labours.

6. *The proper treatment of such questions as Polygamy, Slavery, Caste, the Marriage of Infants and of Widows, etc.*

.Of these topics only polygamy and marriage are of moment in our Missions, and as for these we may testify that polygamy has almost no occurrence but among the Mohammedans. The heathen generally are monogamists, although the ties of marriage among them are very loose. Among the native Christians marriage bears a different character. Husband and wife live, in general, in full harmony, and where dissolution of the matrimonial ties becomes necessary it does not take place but in the formal manner prescribed by Church institution. It is of rare occurrence, and it is remarkable how family life has obtained a Christian character.

II. METHODS OF MANAGEMENT AT HOME.

1. *Comity of Missions, or their relation to one another and to their respective spheres of labour ; and the apportioning unoccupied fields to different Societies.*

If we understand well what is meant by a "Comity of Missions," it must be a comity composed of deputies of several Societies as temporal or constant members, all interested in the same great cause, and, though ardently labouring in the sphere of their own Society, ready to promote by main force all that relates to the common and mutual interests of the respective Missions.

Our opinion is that such a plan is to be considered of the highest interest. And we may add that the Missionary Societies in the Netherlands, with a single exception, have begun to operate in that way. Since last year, 1887, such a comity is constituted, and has begun to operate on the following principles :—

(a) Co-operation without entering into one another's private business.

(b) Co-operation, as far as possible, with an eye upon the times and circumstances.

(c) Co-operation in furthering mutual interests and concerns.

(d) Co-operation, with due estimation and appreciation of the principles and methods of the respective Societies.

It may be sufficient for the present to have mentioned this point, as we cannot yet speak of our experience.

The plan, however, involves obviously what is intended in the rest of the point, and it would greatly heighten the significance of this general Conference if co-operation on the same or similar footing could be attained. As champions in the cause of our Lord and Saviour we ought to sustain each other, to stand firm against all sorts of opposition, to advise and comfort each other, that, having taken up the whole armour of God, we may be able to withstand in the evil day.

This would also be the best way where there is question of apportioning unoccupied fields to different Societies, a matter of special delicacy, as it requires a sound knowledge of many circumstances and relations.

2. *The choice and training of Missionaries with reference to different spheres of labour.*

With a view of what has been mentioned above, about the character of the Missions of our Society, we state that we trained for many years our Missionaries as young men in our Mission-house, where they form, with the director and his family, one household ; that the branches of instruction are of a nature to educate them to be intelligent, well informed, pious men ; that we do not aim at scientific distinction, but at practical usefulness. So they study, besides the principles of theology, the Malay and Javanese languages, together with ethnology, more especially in reference to the nations and races among whom their lot will be cast. As we possess several very good translations of the Scriptures, and it is not required that our Missionaries devote themselves to this branch, they do not study Greek or Hebrew ; in general, they do not partake of classical or erudite instruction. And, by experience, we know that in our way this is the most practical plan, confirmed by valuable results.

3. *The nature and extent of the control to be exercised by Committees or Churches at home.*

By long experience, we have the conviction that the control to be exercised by a Committee must bear the most liberal character. The young Missionary receives on his departure for the field special instructions. Does he appear not equal to his task, which has rarely occurred, measures are taken according to his person and circumstances.

But does the Missionary after some time prove to be the right man in the right place, he is left free in his methods and ways, and is sustained as much as possible by means, under approbation in special cases of the Committee.

We always try to improve the advice of our Missionaries, reflecting that they are better than we acquainted with local circumstances.

In possible cases of dissension we are following the way of appeasing, and generally with good success.

Our correspondence with our Missionaries always bears a brotherly character, and often enters into particulars, submitting even our advice to the opinion of our brethren.

In financial matters alone our correspondence is more official. We lament to state that finances are generally the crux of our Committee, they being, almost without exception, straitened in their means.

4. *Support of Missions and finance.*

As we just observed, our Committee is generally straitened in financial matters. Our receipts are not equal to the necessary expenses for our Missions. Too often it occurs that considerable legacies must restore the balance ; but, even then, we could do much more if our income was not so scant.

What shall we say under circumstances as these of finance ? We do what we can to stimulate liberality on the side of our friends, and with more stress, when our finances are ebbing.

The topics mentioned in the Programme under III.—V. lie too far beyond the sphere of our experience to be touched in this memorial.

May what we yielded prove a tolerable contribution to the interests of this Conference ! May the Lord grant His blessing upon all our labours, and may He by this Conference open a new era in our Missionary exertions, to His own glory and to the salvation of mankind !

For the Directors of the Netherlands Missionary Society,

J. C. NEURDENBURG, Secretary.

CHRISTIAN EVIDENCES AND CHRISTIAN EXPERIENCE OF MISSION CONVERTS.*

BY REV. J. T. GRACEY, D.D. (President of the International Missionary Union, U.S.A.).

IN presenting the evidences of Christian revelation on Foreign Mission-fields, there is need for judicious discrimination as to the state of progress and ethnic appetencies of the people.

There are large portions of the Moslem population of the world, among whom the historico-critical faculty is sufficiently developed and exercised to demand the most thorough acquaintance with the latest critical knowledge of Christian evidence and of Christian theories of inspiration and exegesis. Japan, too, is so far lacquered with knowledge of modern methods of thought as to require, so far as Missionaries come in contact with it, a wise use of the same class of thought ; and even young Bengal has acquired sufficient familiarity with Western criticism to make it necessary to be thoroughly careful in the presentation of Christianity. An illustration or two will, perhaps, best emphasise the need specified.

In a conversation which I once had with a Moslem Moulvie, the Christian doctrine of the Trinity was objected to as implying the divisibility of the Godhead. "Either," said he, "the entire Trinity became incarnate and died on Calvary, or the Trinity is a Triad and not Tri-unity." I modestly ventured to suggest that, as the Koran asserts the Christian Scriptures to be an inspired revelation, the difficulty or mystery that was implied in their teaching was no more mine than it was his, and we were both obliged to take the New Testament statement of facts as we found them. His reply was that Mohammedans hold the theory of "gradual revelation" ; and lay down as a law of interpretation that when two passages of Divine revelation are seemingly contradictory, the earlier revelation must be expounded in the light of the later one ; the later abrogates the earlier.

Now as the Koran is the latest revelation, such passages in the Jewish and Christian Scriptures as teach the Trinity, either were interpolated or have been falsely interpreted. "Even Christian commentators," he continued, "acknowledge ' various readings ' ; and ' councils ' have been called to determine the teachings of the Scriptures. The Mohammedan's thought is, that God has made a later revelation by Mohammed to save the world from these errors of false interpretation, interpolation, etc."

On another occasion a Moslem government official asked, "What is the ground on which one should conclude that any Scripture is a Divine revelation? If it is intrinsic goodness, then, as portions of the Hindu Shastas are excellent, must it not be admitted that those parts at least of Hinduism A Moslem on "Revelation." are of Divine origin ? If the antiquity of the record is an evidence of a revelation, the Hindus will set up the claim of their ancient sacred books. If miracles are the evidence of inspiration, then Mohammed worked miracles." I asked him how he interpreted those passages of the Koran, in which Mohammed disclaimed his ability or purpose to work miracles. He said that meant no more

---

* It was impossible to find a place for this Paper in the programme to vol. II. We are under the necessity of transferring it to the Appendix.—ED.

than the writer of the Gospel meant when he said Christ could do no mighty works
under given circumstances and places because of the unbelief of the people.
In a long discussion which followed on the credibility of Moslem historians in
general, between the Hegira and the days of Othman, I suggested the lack of
contemporary evidence to Mohammed's miracles. His reply I translate literally.
He said, "First, contemporary evidence is not always, nor necessarily, true.
Second. later evidence is not always, nor necessarily, false. Third, when Abu
Becr collected the Suras and collated the Koran, he had it proclaimed through
all the country, and no one arose to challenge its accuracy. Fourth, much of the
Gospels and of the Old Testament history could not, from the necessity of the
case, have been written *without some interval* between the occurrence of the event
and the record, and it seems to be a question what interval will invalidate the
testimony.'

As to the objection to Mohammed splitting the moon because there was no
reference to such an occurrence in the literature of the Bactrian and other
neighbouring nations, he thought that of no greater force than the
objection against the miracle of Joshua stopping the sun, as lacking
any contemporaneous evidence in the literature of the Hindus and
Chinese. That man was not a Christian "inquirer," but he was sincere, yet
unsettled in his faith in Islam, and regretted having trained his children as
Mohammedans. He represents a class of Moslem controversialists daily to be
met with by the Missionaries in the bazaar and village itineraries. Is it not providential, that simultaneously with the geographical extension of Christianity
through the Modern Mission, to the ends of the earth, that the modern "critics"
have compelled Christian scholarship to re-examine and re-expound our noble
Scriptures ready for presentation to all classes of minds that are to be met with
in all the world; and amidst our splendid later resources for research, to forge
in the fires of controversy the very weapons needed by Missionaries of the
Protestant propaganda in Moslem and heathen lands. The defence of herself
against the "reviewers" has made the Church, unwittingly, furnish herself with
burnished weapons for aggressive warfare in the ends of the earth.

But the vast Brahmanic, Buddhistic, and nature-worshipping communities
of the world do not have this historico-critical element in them; nor are they
likely to have, till, farther on, Christianity shall create it. Miracles are to these
communities only wonder-works, matched any day by the traditional stories of
their gods, or by their new and current exploits. No man who understands
ethnic appetencies would approach these peoples on this side. The
internal evidence which Christianity furnishes is what is forceful
to them; combined, perhaps, with that which is always impressive
to an Asiatic, the material development of the Christian world,
alleged to be the immediate result or product of the Christian religion. He
has firm faith that your religion is good for you, but of no avail for him, because
he believes in ethnic revelations. But when, coming to the Christian Scriptures,
he finds a *prophetic description of himself*, his pains and problems, and unrest;
and having longings for a future life unlike anything hitherto known to him,
he catches a glimpse of something which is to give him soul-rest, and tells him
whither he goes; and when, so far as he tests the word, he finds it to fit as key
to lock, to all the exercises of his soul, he is drawn to it, and convinced by it,
without knowing, or caring to know, anything about its external evidences.
Now, the great bulk of the heathen world is in just this case, from philosophic
Brahman and meditative Buddhist to Indian spirit-worshipper and African and
Oceanic fetish-devotee. The great bulk of the men of heathendom are, therefore,
to be reached at present on this plan.

As with Christian evidence, so with Christian experience. Each nation must
get its own line of Christian evidence, and each ethnic class must be allowed to
develop its own type of Christian life and character. It must be encouraged to
cherish its *own* spiritual experiences and not those of some other nation.

Our Western Christian life and thought, have been largely moulded by Roman
ideas of government and jurisprudence. Our Western anthropology is in its

rhetoric Roman. It may be, that it expresses views of man's relations to God, and the eternal principles of rightness, in a way which will ultimately commend it to all men, ultimately appeal to a universal consciousness which is innate, or which Christianity develops; but it is scarcely to be doubted that it thrusts into large if not disproportionate prominence one phase of Christian thought. "Justification by faith" is worthy of all the hold it has obtained, but the commentary on Paul's Epistle to the Romans has been found in Roman jurisprudence.

It is not, however, the only possible *first view* of spiritual life, and may not be always the best with which to begin. Even if it be held that these views are inherent in human nature and must, on knowledge, come to be apprehended and received by all nations, there is still a question of precedence and adaptation in the order of presenting truths and Christian experience.

A Hindu seeks, first, last, and all the time, religious *rest*. He is weary and heavy-laden with poverty, and injustice, and oppression, and over-reaching, and usurpation, and false-witnessing; with sorrows and bereavements, and spiritual darkness and nightmare; and with religious ceremonialism that taxes his time, his fortune, and his faith, but affords him no solace but transmigration possibly to heavier woes and deeper despair, no ultimate hope but *Nirvana*, which he does not comprehend.

It is not so much the command "Repent" that will arouse him, but "Come unto Me, all ye that labour and are heavy laden." His great normal, first Christian experience is, that in accepting Christ he finds soul-rest, mental quiet, and heart solace. Do not quarrel with him because he is not overwhelmed with conviction of sin, and does not apprehend your ideas of judicial pardon. All that will take care of itself. Meanwhile he may develop a Church that will teach the west some lessons in leaning on the bosom of the great All-Father. *More than one view of truth.* If you think of God as a Governor, do not quarrel with him for thinking of Him as a Father. If you think of the *principles* on which God can pardon as a Governor and Judge, do not be distressed because he thinks of the *pleasure* with which the Father accepts those who seek Him.

If you study the equity of God's law, do not interrupt him if in unquestioning surrender he submits to the eternal sovereignty of God. It is just possible that, in the mighty up-building of the temple of God, his thought is essential to the placing of the cap-stone; that his contribution to Christian experience is necessary to the total mosaic of Christian life; that his strain lacking the symphony of the Redeemed would-be marred. The heathen world redeemed to Christ may furnish the complement of all that now is, and so tend to the "perfecting of the saints."

III.

LETTER FROM DR. HAPPER, PRESBYTERIAN BOARD OF MISSIONS (U.S.A.), CANTON.

[Dr. Happer, who has for more than forty years laboured in Canton, was one of the first fixed on by the Committee for a Paper. The request seems not to have reached him ; but we are favoured with the following letter, accompanied by pamphlets and articles which we could not reprint. As the letter touches on many topics, it could not be read out at any of our sectional meetings, but the experience of such a distinguished Missionary is well worthy of a place in our records.—ED.]

CANTON, CHINA, *April* 24th, 1888.

REV. JAMES JOHNSTON,—

Rev. and Dear Brother,—I have noticed the list of topics to be considered at the Conference as given in the March number of the *World's Missionary Review*, of New York, at page 221. I send by mail addressed to you since then, pamphlets containing Papers on subjects to be considered :—

I. The number of *Buddhists* in the world. II. What shall be done with converts who have two or more wives at the time of conversion ? III. On the need and benefit of a professorship in theological seminaries to give special instruction to introducing " Foreign Missionaries."

I. It appears to me the Conference ought to express an opinion on this point. Mr. Arnold, in his "Light of Asia," places the number of Buddhists at 470,000,000, or greater than any other religion. Others have stated the number at 400,000,000 or 300,000,000. Professor Monier-Williams somewhere has expressed the opinion that 100,000,000 is a large estimate. The large number has been given with the view to disparage Christianity. I give my reasons for stating the number to be 72,000,000. If a Committee of Conference had time to examine the subject and report confirming the opinion of Professor Williams, that 100,000,000 was a large estimate, it would put a stop to this false statement. For many Christian writers, in their ignorance of the matter, accept and publish these statements of the enemies of Christ our Lord.

II. On the matter of what shall be done with those who have two wives, I urge that they should be received without putting away the second wife. This view has been confirmed more and more the longer I am in China. See the review of the subject in the *Andover Review* for September 1887, or the epitome of Mr. Lawrence's article in *World's Missionary Review* for January 1888, p. 16 ; also Rev. Mr. Lucas's article in *Indian Evangelical Review* for April 1886. You will see there is a departure from the views adopted by different Missionary Societies forty years ago. They acted in view of the almost promiscuous intercourse and temporary engagement of savage tribes in Oceania and Africa, and not in view of the settled and legal relation in their old civilisations and lands of China and India. I am free to say that I hope the Conference will come to the opinion that in these old lands the relationship should only terminate by death, but in the uncivilised tribes where the relation is loose they should adhere to the first formed connection.

III. As to the professorship for giving special instruction, my opinion is more confirmed by every succeeding year's observation and experience in the need of them. Many young men come out with the most crude idea of what work they are to engage in or how to do it. The loss of time and the salaries paid to many of those who come out without any instruction as to the kind of work to be done—while they are learning by experiment how to do something, or what work they can do—would pay the salaries of these professors many times over, and save the expense for the passages out and home again of those who are found incapable of Missionary work, for various reasons, which incapability would have been discovered by any professor giving Missionary instruction. I hope the Conference will see the way to giving a very decided opinion in this matter of Missionary instruction to intending Missionaries. This is all the more necessary now than it was forty years ago, because of the greater number intending ; and there is little self-denial or self-sacrifice in going to most of the large Missionary fields.

I heard the wife of a Missionary, who went home at the end of two years, say in reference to the matter, that when they were considering the question of coming as Missionaries, " she did not know whether she could be a Missionary, but she thought if they did not stay as Missionaries they would get the trip to China and across the American Continent." And they went home after two years' uselessness on the field, and having expended for passages, and outfit, and salaries, say $3,500, with as little compunction of conscience for such an expenditure of Missionary money as possible. Forty years ago the discomfort of the voyage, the little facilities for intercourse, and the other great trials of Missionary life, deterred all persons except most resolute and zealous men and women. Now the passages are in well-appointed steamers, and there is great *éclat* in going as Missionaries.

There are other points in the topics suggested in the Paper in the *World's Missionary Review*, in which I would like to make remarks, but I have no written Papers on any of them. Taking the list as given on page 221 of the *Review*, second column, I would say, in regard to (e) a common scale of salaries, that the thing is *desirable* and *practicable*.

Under the second head, Education, on the point (d) " How far is the concert or co-partnership of different Societies in college education practicable?" I would say to a large *extent*, and refer to the Christian College at Madras, India, under the charge of Rev. Mr. Miller.

Under the third head, Training and support of native workers,—in answer to (b) I say very decidedly not to send any to Europe or America for education. In answer to (d) it would ordinarily be very undesirable to send such a one to a Mission work in another country, as his salary would be then the same as a European or American,—he would not be *nearly as efficient* as the American or European.

In answer to (e) I would say yes, for that is done in all Western lands. On page 222, under head IV., in answer to (a) I would say by all means, keep the expenses at such a scale that the native church can take them over at an early day.

In reference to Missionary literature, in answer to (d), by all means. Missionaries of different Societies should co-operate in the preparation of a Christian literature. I also send a copy of a "Paper on the number of opium smokers in China." The Conference will, no doubt, take up the matter of the supply of drink to the people in Africa, and the stills in India. I hope that it will also take up the matter of opium in China. The evil is now greater than when this Paper was written—and increasing every year. The members of the Inland Mission at home in England can give their testimony.

I pray that the spirit of wisdom and of a sound mind may be given to the Conference in the consideration of all the questions that may come before it.

With much esteem and regard, yours in Christian work,

A. P. HAPPER.

IV.

*LIST OF SOCEITIES SENDING DELEGATES AND REPRE-
SENTATIVES TO THE CONFERENCE.*

GREAT BRITAIN AND IRELAND.

1. Baptist Missionary Society, 19, *Furnival Street, Holborn, E.C.*   **B M S**
2. Baptist Missionary Society (Ladies' Association)   .   . **B M S L A**
   The College, Regent's Park, N.W.
3. Bible Christian Missionary Society, 26, *Paternoster Row, E.C.*   **B C M S**
4. British and Foreign Bible Society   .   .   .   . **B F B S**
   146, *Queen Victoria Street, E.C.*
5. British Society for the Propagation of the Gospel among the
   Jews, 96, *Great Russell Street, W.C.*   .   .   . **B S P G J**
6. British Syrian Schools and Bible Mission   .   .   .   . **B S S**
   18, *Homefield Road, Wimbledon.*
7. China Inland Mission, 6, *Pyrland Road, N.*   .   .   .   . **C I M**
8. Christian Vernacular Education Society for India   .   . **C V E S**
   7, *Adam Street, Adelphi, W.C.*
9. Church Missionary Society, 16, *Salisbury Square, E.C.* . **C M S**
10. Church of England Women's Missionary Association   . **C E W M A**
    143, *Clapham Road, S.W.*
11. Church of England Zenana Missionary Society   .   . **C E Z M S**
    9, *Salisbury Square, E.C.*
12. Church of Scotland Foreign Missions Committee   .   . **C S F M**
    6, *North St. David Street, Edinburgh*
13. Church of Scotland Ladies' Association for Foreign Missions
    22, *Queen Street, Edinburgh*   .   .   .   . **C S L A F M**
14. Edinburgh Medical Missionary Society .   .   .   . **E M M S**
    56, *George Square, Edinburgh.*
15. Evangelical Continental Society, 18, *Blomfield Street, E.C.*   **E C S**
16. Foreign Aid Society, *Christ Church Vicarage, Barnet, N.*   . **F A S**
17. Free Church of Scotland Foreign Missions Committee   . **F C S F M**
    Free Church Offices, The Mound, Edinburgh
18. Free Church of Scotland Ladies' Society for Female Education
    in India and South Africa   .   .   .   . **F C S L S**
    Free Church Offices, The Mound, Edinburgh.

19. Friends' Foreign Mission Association, *Leominster* . . FFMA
20. General Baptist Missionary Society . . . . GBMS
  60, *Wilson Street, Derby.*
21. Indian Female Normal School and Instruction Society, or
  Zenana Bible and Medical Mission . . . . IFNS
  2, *Adelphi Terrace, Strand, W.C.*
22. Indian Home Mission to the Santhals . . . . IHMS
  1, *Chamberlain Road, Edinburgh.*
23. Ladies' Kaffrarian Society . . . . LKS
  Polmont Park, Linlithgow, N.B.
24. London Association in aid of the Moravian Missions . LAMM
  29, *Ely Place, Holborn, E.C.*
25. London Bible and Domestic Female Mission (Foreign Department)
  2, *Adelphi Terrace, Strand, W.C.* . . . . LBDFM
26. London Missionary Society . . . . LMS
  14, *Blomfield Street, E.C.*
27. London Missionary Society (Ladies' Committee for Female Missions)
  22, *Cavendish Square, W.* . . . . . LMSLC
28. London Society for Promoting Christianity amongst the Jews LSPCJ
  16, *Lincoln's Inn Fields, W.C.*
29. Medical Missionary Association, London . . . . MMA
  104, *Petherton Road, N.*
30. Methodist New Connexion Missionary Society . . MNCMS
  Richmond Hill, Ashton-under-Lyne.
31. Mildmay Missions, *Conference Hall, Mildmay, N.* . . My M
32. Missionary Leaves Association . . . . . . MLA
  20, *Compton Terrace, Upper Street, Islington, N.*
33. Missionary Training Home, 33, *Drayton Park, N.* . . MTH
34. Mission to Lepers in India, 17, *Glengyle Terrace, Edinburgh* . MLI
35. National Bible Society of Scotland . . . . NBSS
  5, *St. Andrew Square, Edinburgh;* 224, *West George Street, Glasgow.*
36. North Africa Mission, 21, *Linton Road, Barking, E.* . . NAM
37. Presbyterian Church in Ireland, Foreign Missions . . IPCFM
  Fortwilliam Park, Belfast.
38. Presbyterian Church in Ireland, Female Association . IPCFA
  Fortwilliam Park, Belfast.
39. Presbyterian Church of England Foreign Missions . . EPC
  7, *East India Avenue, E.C.*
40. Presbyterian Church of England Women's Missionary Association
  The Ferns, Frognal, Hampstead, N.W. . . EPCWMA
41. Primitive Methodist Missionary Society . . . PMMS
  71, *Freegrove Road, Holloway, N.*
42. Religious Tract Society, 56, *Paternoster Row, E.C.* . . RTS
43. Society for Promoting Female Education in the East . . FES
  267, *Vauxhall Bridge Road, S.W.*

44. South American Missionary Society .   .   .   .   **S A M S**
    1, *Clifford's Inn, Fleet Street, E.C.*
45. Turkish Missions' Aid Society .   .   .   .   .   **T M A S**
    32, *The Avenue, Bedford Park, Chiswick.*
46. United Methodist Free Churches Missionary Society . **U M F C M**
    443, *Glossop Street, Sheffield.*
47. United Presbyterian Church of Scotland Foreign Missions **U P C S F M**
    College Buildings, Castle Terrace, Edinburgh.
48. United Presbyterian Church of Scotland Zenana Mission . **U P C S Z M**
    College Buildings, Castle Terrace, Edinburgh.
49. Waldensian Church Missions, 120, *Queen's Gate, S.W.* .   . **W C M**
50. Welsh Calvinistic Methodist Foreign Missionary Society **W C M F M S**
    28, *Breckfield Road South, Liverpool.*
51. Wesleyan Methodist Missionary Society .   .   . **W M M S**
    17, *Bishopsgate Street Within, E.C.*
52. Wesleyan Methodist Missionary Society (Ladies' Auxiliary) **W M M S L A**
    2, *Belitha Villas, Barnsbury, N.*
53. Zenana Medical College .   .   .   .   .   . **· Z M C**
    58, *St. George's Road, S.W.*

Members invited by the Executive Committee .   .   .   . **M I**

UNITED STATES OF AMERICA.

American Advent Mission Society, 144, *Hanover St., Boston, Mass.* . **I**
American Baptist Missionary Union, *Tremont Temple, Boston, Mass.* . **II**
American Baptist Publication Society .   .   .   .   . **III**
    1,420, *Chestnut Street, Philadelphia, Pa.*   .
American Bible Society, *Bible House, Astor Place, New York* .   **IV**
American Board of Commissioners for Foreign Missions .   . **V**
    1, *Somerset Street, Boston, Mass.*
American Christian Convention of the United States and Canada . **VI**
American Church Missionary Society, 80, *Bible House, New York* . **VII**
American Missionary Association, 56, *Reade Street, New York* . **VIII**
Baptist Foreign Mission Convention of the U. S. of America .   . **IX**
    520, *St. James Street, Richmond, Va.*
Board of Foreign Missions of the General Synod of the Reformed
    Presbyterian Church of North America .   .   .   .   . **X**
    2,102, *Spring Garden Street, Philadelphia, Pa.*
Board of Foreign Missions of the Presbyterian Church of the
    U. S. of America, 53, *Fifth Avenue, New York* .   .   . **XI**
Board of Foreign Missions of the Reformed Church in America .   . **XII**
    26, *Reade Street, New York.*
Board of Foreign Missions of the Reformed Presbyterian Church
    of North America, 126, *West 45th Street, New York* .   . **XIII**

Woman's African Methodist Episcopal Mite Missionary Society
921, *Bainbridge Street, Philadelphia, Pa.* XXXIX

Woman's Baptist Foreign Missionary Society XL
84, *Waterman Street, Providence, R. I.*

Woman's Baptist Foreign Missionary Society of the West . . XLI
8,112, *Forest Avenue, Chicago, Illn.*

Woman's Board of Foreign Missions, Cumberland Presbyterian
Church, 826, *Chestnut Street, Evansville, Ind.* . . . XLII

Woman's Board of Foreign Missions of Presbyterian Church . XLIII
53, *Fifth Avenue, New York.*

Woman's Board of Foreign Missions of the Reformed Church in
America, 762, *High Street, Newark, N.J.* XLIV

Woman's Board of Missions A. B. C. F. M. XLV
1, *Congregational House, Boston, Mass.*

Woman's Board of Missions of the Interior XLVI
53, *Dearborn Street, Chicago, Illn.*

Woman's Board of Missions of the Methodist Episcopal Church
South, 421, *Sands Street, Covington, Ky.* XLVII

Woman's Board of the Seventh Day Baptist Church . . . XLVIII
Milton, Wis.

Woman's Foreign Missionary Society, Iowa Meeting of Friends XLIX
415, *Dearborn Street, Chicago, Illn.*

Woman's Foreign Missionary Society of the Methodist Episcopal
Church, 280, *West 59th Street, New York.* L

Woman's Foreign Missionary Society of the Methodist Protestant
Episcopal Church, *Allegheny City, Pa.* LI

Woman's Foreign Missionary Society of the Presbyterian Church LII
1,334, *Chestnut Street, Philadelphia, Pa.*

Woman's Missionary Association of the United Brethren in Christ LIII
Cor. of Main and Fourth Streets, Dayton, O.

Woman's Missionary Society of the Evangelical Association . LIV
Oakdale, Cor. Steinway Avenue, Cleveland, O.

Woman's National Indian Association LV
412, *South Broad Street, Philadelphia, Pa.*

Woman's Presbyterian Board of Missions of the North-West . LVI
Room 48, McCormick Block, Chicago, Illn.

Woman's Union Missionary Society LVII
41, *Bible House, New York.*

Delegates at large appointed by the New York Committee. LVIII

CANADA.

Baptist Foreign Missionary Society, Ontario and Quebec . . LIX
Hamilton, Ont. Maritime Provinces, *St. John, N.B.*

Congregational Union of Nova Scotia and New Brunswick . . . LX
Sheffield, N.B.

Foreign Missionary Society of the Presbyterian Church . : **LXI**
  Eastern Section, *Hopewell, N.S.*; Western Section, *Toronto, Ont.*
Missionary Society of the Methodist Church in Canada . . **LXII**
  Toronto, Ont.
Protestant Ministerial Association of Montreal, *Montreal* . . **LXIII**
Toronto Association of Congregational Churches, *Toronto, Ont.* . **LXIV**
Woman's Baptist Missionary Union of the Maritime Provinces . **LXV**
  St. John, N.B.
Woman's Foreign Missionary Society of the Presbyterian Church. **LXVI**
  Eastern Section, 41, *Victoria Road, Halifax*; Western Section,
  248, *Sherbourne Street, Toronto, Ont.*
Woman's Missionary Society of the Methodist Church in Canada **LXVII**
  118, *Hughson Street, Hamilton, Ont*

CONTINENT OF EUROPE.

Basle Evangelical Missionary Society, *Basle, Switzerland* . . **LXVIII**
Berlin Evangelical Missionary Society, *Georgenkirchstr.* 70, *Berlin* **LXIX**
Christian Reformed Church's Mission, *Leyden, Holland* . . **LXX**
Danish Evangelical Missionary Society, *Gladsaxe, near Copenhagen* **LXXI**
Dutch Reformed Missionary Society, *Rotterdam, Holland* . . **LXXII**
French Evangelical Missionary Society . . . . . **LXXIII**
  Boulevard Arago, No. 102, *Paris.*
Java Comité, *Amsterdam, Holland* . . . . : : **LXXIV**
Mission of the Free Churches of French Switzerland . . . **LXXV**
  Lausanne, Switzerland.
Moravian Missions, *Herrnhut, Saxony* . . . : : **LXXVI**
Netherlands Missionary Society, *Rotterdam, Holland* . . . **LXXVII**
Netherlands Missionary Union, *Rotterdam, Holland* . . . **LXXVIII**
Neukirchen Mission Institution . . . . . . **LXXIX**
  Neukirchen, Moers, Rhenish Prussia.
North German Missionary Society, *Bremen, Germany* . . . **LXXX**
Norwegian Missionary Society, *Stavanger, Norway* . . . **LXXXI**
Rhenish Missionary Society, *Barmen, Germany* . . . . **LXXXII**
St. Chrischona Missionary Society . . . . . **LXXXIII**
  Karthausgasse, 42, *Basle, Switzerland.*
Swedish Missionary Association, *Stockholm, Sweden* . : . **LXXXIV**
Utrecht Missionary Society, *Utrecht, Holland* . . . . **LXXXV**

COLONIAL.

Board of Church Missions, *Melbourne* . . : : : . **LXXXVI**
Dutch Reformed Church of South Africa . . . . **LXXXVII**

V.

ALPHABETICAL LIST

OF THE

MEMBERS OF CONFERENCE.*

GREAT BRITAIN AND IRELAND

Aberdeen, Right Hon. the Earl of Pres.	Anson, Mrs. . . . . I F N S
Abraham, Mr. W., M.P. W C M F M S	Arbuthnot, Mr. G. . . . C M S
Achonry, Very Rev. Dean of . C M S	Arbuthnot, Mr. H. R. . . C M S
Adam, Miss '. . . U P C S Z M	Archibald, Mr. John . . . N B S S
Adamson, Rev. Dr. . ! . L M S	Archibald, Mr. W. F. A. . . L A M M
Adamson, Rev. W. . . . C M S	Arden, Rev A. H. . . . C M S
Adcock, Rev. John . . U M F C M	Armitage, Mr. Robert . . M I
Adler, Mr. James A. . . . My M	Arnold, Mr. A. J. . . . M I
Aldis, Rev. J. . '. . . B M S	Arthington, Mr. Robert . . M I
Alexander, Rev. W. B. . . E P C	Arthur, Rev. W., M.A. . . W M M S
Alexander, Lady '. ! . F E S	Ashburton, Louisa Lady . . M I
Alexander, Mr. J. . . . E P C	Ashton, Rev. J. P., M.A. . . L M S
Alford, Right Rev. Bishop, D.D. C M S	Ashton, Rev. R. S., B.A. . . E C S
Allan, Rev. W., M.A. . . . C M S	Askwith, Miss . . ' . C E Z M S
Allan, Mrs. . . C S L A F M	Aston-Binns, Rev. T. . . E C S
Allen, Rev. R. W. . . W M M S	Atkinson, Rev. John . . P M M S
Allen, Rev. W. H. . . P M M S	Atkinson, Mr. H. J., M.P. . . W M M S
Allen, Mr. Alexander . . L M S	Avis, Mr. H. . . . . W M M S
Amos, Mrs. Sheldon . . W M M S L A	
Anderson, Lieut.-Gen. . . E P C	Bacon, Mr. J. P. . . . B M S
Anderson, Major-Gen. . . E P C	Badenoch, Mr. P. S. . . . M I
Anderson, Mr. George . . L M S	Baedeker, Dr. . . . . M I
Anderson, Mr. John A. . . M I	Baedeker, Mrs. . . . . M I
Anderson, Mrs. W. D. . E P C W M A	Bagster, Mr. S. S. . . . M I
Anderson, Miss . . . M I	Bailey, Rev. J., B.A. . . B M S
Anderson, Miss . . C S L A F M	Bailey, Mr. Wellesley C. . . M L I
Anderson, Miss L. H. . U P C S Z M	Baillie, Rev. J. . . . . B M S
Andrews, Rev. W. . . ' C M S	Bain, Rev. J. Alexander, M.A. F C S F M
Andrews, Miss . . . F E S	Bain, Miss . . . C S L A F M
Angus, Rev. J., D.D. . . . B M S	Ballantyne, Rev. W., M.A. . R T S
Angus, Mrs. . . . B M S L A	Ballard, Miss . . . I F N S
Angus, Miss A. G. . . B M S L A	Baller, Rev. F. W. . . . C I M

* No names except those of regularly deputed or elected members are entered on these lists ; but a few will be found of persons who were unable to be present, and, notwithstanding the utmost care, we fear some actually present are not recorded.

Baller, Mrs. . . . C I M	Bird, Mr. Robert, J.P. . U M F C M
Balmer, Rev. J. S. . . U M F C M	Bishop, Rev. J. H. . . . C M S
Bambridge, Rev. J. J. . . C M S	Bishop, Mrs. . . . . M I
Bangert, Miss . . . C I M	Black, Rev. Jno. . . . E P C
Barclay, Mr. J. Gurney . . B F B S	Black, Colonel G. R. S. . C E Z M S
Barclay, Mr. Robert . . B F B S	Blackett, Rev. W. R. . . M I
Barclay, Mr. W. L. . . F F M A	Blackwood, Sir S. A., K.C.B. . M I
Barclay, Miss Ellen . . F F M A	Blaikie, Rev. Prof., D.D., LL.D. F C S F M
Bardsley, Mrs. . . C E Z M S	Blandford, Rev. T. . . M I
Barfield, Mr. John, M.A. . C I M	Bliss, Mr. H. S. . . . M I
Baring-Gould, Rev. A. . . C M S	Blomfield, Mr. W. . . . B F B S
Baring-Gould, Rev. B. . . C M S	Blomfield, Mrs. W. . . L M S L C
Baring-Gould, Mrs. . . C M S	Blomfield, Miss Emilie . L M S L C
Barker, Mrs. Frederick . B S S	Boileau, Mrs. . . . M I
Barlow, Rev. W. H., B.D. . C M S	Bompas, Mr. H. M., Q.C. . . B M S
Barlow, Mrs. W. H. . . C M S	Bond, Rev J . . . W M M S
Barnaby, Sir N., K.C.B. . B F B S	Booth, Rev. S. H., D.D. . B M S
Barnard, Mrs. . . B M S L A	Boswell, Mr. H. Bruce . C M S
Barnes, Lieut.-Col. J. R. . L M S	Bott, Rev. Sydney . . C M S
Barnett, Rev. T. H. . . B M S	Bottomley Rev. Henry E. . L M S
Barnett, Mr. Henry . . My M	Boulter, Mrs. . . W M M S L A
Baron, Mr. David . . My M	Bounsall, Miss L. M. . L M S L C
Baron, Rev. Richard . L M S	Bourne, Rev. F. W. : . : B C M S
Baron, Mrs. Richard . L M S L C	Bourne, Mr. Jas. Johnsten . C M S
Barrett, Rev. G. S., B.A. . L M S	Bousfield, Mr. Charles H. . . C M S
Barton, Rev. J., M.A. . C M S	Bow, Mrs. . . C S L A F M
Batt, Rev. J. H. . . B C M S	Bowser, Mr. A. T. . . B M S
Baxter, Mrs. M. E. . . M T H	Bowser, Mr. Howard . . B M S
Bayley, Mr. W. H. . . M I	Bowser, Mrs. A. T. . . B M S L A
Baylis-Thompson, Mrs. L M S L C	Boyd, Rev. Jno. . . I P C F M
Baynes, Mr. A. H., F.S.S. . B M S	Brackenbury, Miss . . My M
Baynes, Mr. Carleton . M I	Brackett, Mr. William . L M S
Baynes, Mr. W. W., J.P., D.L. B M S	Braithwaite, Mr. J. B. . . B F B S
Baynes, Mrs. A. H. . . B M S	Braithwaite, Mr. W. C. . . B F B S
Beattie, Mr. Alexander, J.P. . C M S	Braithwaite, Miss A. . . M I
Beet, Rev. J. A. . . W M M S	Brander, Mr. William . B S P G J
Bell, Rev. R. R. . . C M S	Brasher, Mr. A. . . I F N S
Bell, Mr. John . . E P C	Brasher, Mrs. . . I F N S
Bell, Mr. Thomas . . E P C	Bridgford, Mr. J. H. . . N A M
Bell, Mrs. R. R. . . C M S	Briggs, Mr. Isaac . . L M S
Bembridge, Mr. W. B. . G B M S	Broadley Rev B. . . W M M S
Bennett, Sir J. Risdon, F.R.S., M.D. R T S	Brock, Rev. W. . . B M S
Bennett, Miss Risdon . L M S L C	Brodie, Rev. David . . B F B S
Bernard, Miss . . M T H	Brodie, Mr. David, M.D. . . M M A
Bevan, Mr. F. A. . . M I	Broen, Miss de . . . M I
Bevan, Mr. R. C. L. . . M I	Bromley, Miss . . C M S
Bewes, Mrs. . . I F N S	Brooke, Col. Wilmot . . M I
Beynon, General . . I F N S	Brooke, Mrs. Wilmot . . M I
Beynon, Mrs. . . I F N S	Broomhall, Mr. B. . . C I M
Billing, Rev. Prebendary . M L A	Brown, Rev. Jas. . . F C S F M
Binns, Rev. H. K. . . C M S	Brown, Rev. James, D.D. U P C S F M
Bird, Rev. Benwell . . B M S	Brown, Rev. J. J. . . B M S
Bird, Mr. E. W. . . M I	Brown, Rev. John, D.D. . L M S

Brown, Rev. J. T. . . .	B M S
Brown, Rev. Principal, D.D.	F C S F M
Brown, Rev. T. W., D.D. .	T M A S
Brown, Rev. W. W. . .	I P C F M
Brown, Mr. Jno. A. .	U P C S F M
Browne, Rev. H. Joy, M.A.	F A S
Bruce, Rev. Robert, D.D. .	B F B S
Bruce, Rev. R., D.D. .	L M S
Bruce, General . . .	C V E S
Brunygate, Mrs. .	W M M S L A
Bryden, Miss . . .	B S S
Buchanan, Rev. James .	U P C S F M
Buckland, Rev. A. R. .	C M S
Budgett, Mr. J. S. .	W M M S
Bullinger, Rev. E. W., D.D. .	Z M C
Bumsted, Mr. J. C. . .	E C S
Bunting, Mrs. P. W. .	W M M S L A
Burgess, Rev. Wm. .	W M M S
Burgess, Mrs. . .	W M M S L A
Burnett, Rev. R. W. .	P M M S
Burnett, Miss . . .	C E W M A
Burns, Rev. Dawson, D.D. .	G B M S
Burnside, Rev. H. .	C M S
Burnside, Mrs. . .	C M S
Burton, Mr. C. M. . .	L M S
Burton, Mr. W. Schoocroft	B F B S
Bush, Rev. J. . . .	W M M S
Butler, Miss A. R. . .	M M A
Buxton, Mr. A. F. . .	B S S
Buxton, Lady Victoria .	C M S
Buxton, Sir T. Fowell, Bart. .	C M S
Buxton, Miss . . .	M I
Byles, Rev. A. Holden .	L M S
Byles, Rev. John . .	L M S
Cadman, Rev. Canon . .	C M S
Caine, Mrs. W. S. .	B M S L A
Cairns, Rev. Prof., D.D. .	U P C S F M
Caldwell, Right Rev. Bishop, D.D.	M I
Caldwell, Mr. R. . .	C I M
Calthrop, Rev. Gordon .	C M S
Calvert, Rev. James .	W M M S
Cameron, Rev. A. B. .	U P C S F M
Cameron, Rev. G. . .	B M S
Campbell, Rev. W. . .	E P C
Campbell, Mr. James A., M.P., LL.D.	M I
Candler, Mr. G. . .	W M M S
Canning, Hon. Miss .	L B D F M
Carmichael, Rev. P. . .	E P C
Carruthers, Mr. Wm., F.R.S., F.L.S.	B S P G J
Carruthers, Mrs. Wm. .	E P C W M A
Carstairs, Rev. George L.	U P C S F M
Carter, Rev. A. M., B.A. .	L M S

Cavalier, Rev. A. R. . . .	I F N S
Cave, Rev. Principal Alfred, B.A.	L M S
Cavendish, Miss . .	C E W M A
Cayford, Mr. E. . .	G B M S
Channer, Colonel George .	S A M S
Chaplin, Dr. T. . .	L S P C J
Chapman, Rev. W. Hay .	C M S
Chapman, Mr. C. E. .	C M S
Charteris, Rev. Professor, D.D. .	C S F M
Charters, Rev. D. . .	B M S
Chatterton, Rev. F. W. .	M I
Chitty, General W. T. .	C M S
Chubb, Mr. Hammond .	L A M M
Chubb, Mrs. .	W M M S L A
Chubb, Sir G. H., Kt. .	W M M S
Clapham, Rev. J. E. .	W M M S
Clark, Rev. T. H. .	L M S
Clark, Rev. Wm. .	U P C S F M
Clark, Mr. Hy. E. .	F F M A
Clark, Mr. Wm., M.B., C.M.	U P C S F M
Clark, Mrs. R. . .	C M S
Clarke, Rev. G. W. .	C I M
Clarke, Mr. S. R. .	C I M
Clarke, Mrs. Fairlie .	M I
Clarke, Mrs. G. W. .	C I M
Clarke, Mrs. S. R. .	C I M
Clayton, Rev. Walter .	C M S
Cleeve, Mr. F., C.B., R.N. .	B F B S
Cleghorn, Mr. Hugh, M.D. .	E M M S
Clifford, Rev. J., LL.B., D.D. .	G B M S
Clifford, Mr. E. . .	C M S
Clowes, Rev. J. H. .	C M S
Cobain, Mr. E. S. W. de, M.P.	Z M C
Cobban, Rev. G. Mackenzie	W M M S
Cockell, Brigade-Surgeon .	M I
Cocker, Rev. W., D.D. .	M N C M S
Cockin, Miss M. A. .	L M S L C
Cockin, Mrs. . .	L M S L C
Cockle, Miss . .	C E Z M S
Collett, Rev. W. Lloyd .	B S S
Collett, Miss F. M. .	B S S
Comber, Rev. P. E. .	B M S
Cook, Rev. J. A. B. .	E P C
Cook, Rev. R. P. .	G B M S
Cook, Miss Jessie .	U P C S Z M
Cook, Miss Mary E. .	U P C S Z M
Cooke, Rev. J. . .	W M M S
Cooke, Mrs. J. .	W M M S L A
Cooling, Rev. Jas., B.A. .	W M M S
Cooling, Mrs. .	W M M S L A
Cooper, Rev. T. T. .	L M S
Cooper, Rev. Wm. .	C I M
Cooper, Mrs. . .	C I M

Coote, Mr. A. C. P.	.	.	.	N A M
Copp, Mr. Alfred	.	.	.	M I
Corbold, Mrs.	.	.	.	L M S L C
Corderoy, Mrs. G.	.	.	W M M S L A
Corderoy, Miss	.	.	W M M S L A
Corfield, Mrs.	.	.	.	M I
Cornford, Rev. J.	.	.	.	M I
Cornford, Mrs.	.	.	.	C M S
Corry, Sir James P., Bart., M.P.	I P C F M
Corsar, Mr. David	.	U P C S F M
Cousins, Rev. G.	.	.	.	L M S
Cousins, Rev. W. E.	.	.	.	L M S
Cousins, Mrs. W. E.	.	L M S L C
Couvè, Mr. J. B.	.	.	.	M I
Coventry, Miss	.	.	.	My M
Cowan, Rev. Henry, D.D.	.	C S F M
Cowan, Mr. J.	.	.	F C S F M
Cox, Rev. W. J.	.	.	.	L M S
Cox, Rev. W. Wetton	.	L A M M
Cox, Mr. W. F.	.	.	L A M M
Crabb, Dr.	.	.	.	M I
Craig, Rev. James, D.D., PH.D.	.	R T S
Craig, Rev. Robert, M.A.	.	L M S
Cribb, Rev. Arthur W.	.	C M S
Critchley, Rev. George, B.A.	.	L M S
Crittall, Miss	.	.	I F N S
Crofton, Lieut.-General, R.E.	L S P C J
Crosfield, Mr. A. J.	.	.	F F M A
Cross, Miss	.	.	F C S F M
Crossley, Mr. Edward, M.P.	.	M I
Crowther, Right Rev. Bishop, D.D.	C M S
Crozier, Mr. F. H.	.	.	M I
Cuff, Rev. W.	.	.	.	B M S
Culross, Rev. J., D.D.	.	.	B M S
Cumming, Rev. J. Elder, D.D.	.	N B S S
Cunningham, Miss	.	U P C S Z M
Cunningham, Miss M. B.	.	U P C S Z M
Curwen, Mr. T. Cecil	.	.	L M S
Curwen, Mrs.	.	.	.	L M S L C
Curwen, Miss	.	.	L M S L C
Cust, Mr. R. N., LL.D.	.	.	B F B S
Dale, Rev. W.	.	.	.	E P C
Dalgleish, Mrs.	.	.	L M S L C
Dashwood, Mr. Thos.	.	L A M M
Davies, Rev. David	.	.	B M S
Davies, Rev. Gethen, B.A.	.	B M S
Davies, Rev. J. E., M.A.	.	W C M F M S
Davies, Rev. T., D.D.	.	.	B M S
Davies, Rev. W. Ryle	.	W C M F M S
Davis, Rev. C. A.	.	.	B M S
Davison, Rev. M.	.	.	E P C
Davison, Rev. W. T., M.A.	.	W M M S
Dawson, Rev. R., B.A.	.	.	M I
Dawson, Mrs. R.	.	.	L M S L C
Dawson, Miss	.	.	.	F E S
Dawson, Miss	.	.	L M S L C
Dawson, Miss S.	.	.	L M S L C
Deacon, Miss	.	.	.	F E S
Denny, Mr. E. M.	.	.	M I
Denny, Mr. T. A.	.	.	M I
Dibdin, Mr. Charles	.	.	R T S
Dibdin, Miss Emily	.	.	C M S
Dick, Mrs.	.	.	U P C S Z M
Dickson, Mrs. David	.	F C S L S
Dilmas, Mrs. F.	.	.	M I
Dixon, Dr. John	.	.	F F M A
Dobson, Rev. N.	.	.	B M S
Dobson, Mr. J.	.	.	W M M S
Dobson, Mr. J. D.	.	.	P M M S
Dowsley, Rev. Andrew, B.A.	.	C S F M
Drummond, Rev. Geo.	.	L M S
Drummond, Rev. Prof.	.	F C S F M
Drury, Rev. T. W.	.	.	C M S
Duka, Mr. Theo., M.D.	.	B F B S
Dunbar, Mr.	.	.	I F N S
Dunbar, Mrs.	.	.	I F N S
Duncan, Rev. Henry	.	C S F M
Duncan, Mr. G.	.	.	E P C
Duncan, Mr. Moir B., M.A.	.	B M S
Duncan, Mrs.	.	.	I F N S
Dunlop, Rev. J.	.	.	B S P G J
Durham, Mrs. Maxwell	.	C S L A F M
Durran, Rev. J.	.	.	E P C
Durrant, Rev. G. B.	.	C M S
Durrant, Mrs.	.	.	C M S
Dyer, Rev. J. A., L.R.C.S., P.ED.	E M M S
Dykes, Rev. J. O., D.D.	.	E P C
Dykes, Mrs. Oswald	.	E P C W M A
Dymond, Rev. J.	.	.	B C M S
Dyson, Rev. Dr.	.	.	C M S
Earguvine, Rev. T., B.A.	.	L M S
Eason, Mr. A.	.	.	C I M
Eason, Mrs.	.	.	C I M
East, Rev. D. J.	.	.	M I
Eastman, Mr. W. T.	.	W M M S
Eccles, Dr. W. S.	.	.	N A M
Edgar, Mr. J.	.	.	W M M S
Edge, Mrs.	.	.	L M S L C
Edmond, Rev. J., D.D.	.	E P C
Edmond, Mrs.	.	E P C W M A
Edmonds, Rev. Prebendary, B.D.	B F B S
Edwards, Rev. A. T., M.A.	.	Z M C
Edwards, Rev. E.	.	.	B M S
Edwards, Rev. W., B.A.	.	B M S

Edwards, Mr. W. E., Junr.	L M S
Eglinton, Mr. R. L.	B F B S
Ekins, Rev. G. R.	C M S
Elkington, Miss	C E Z M S
Elliott, Rev. R., B.A., L.R.C.S.E.	C M S
Elliott, Miss E. S.	M I
Ellis, Rev. James	L M S
Ellis, Mr. T. E., M.P.	W C M F M S
Ellis, Mrs.	F E B
Elphinston, Mr. J.	C V E S
Ensor, Rev. G.	C M S
Eppstein, Rev. J. M.	L S P C J
Evans, Rev. G. D.	M I
Evans, Rev. W. Justin	L M S
Evans, Mrs.	B S S
Ewen, Rev. T.	B M S
Exeter, Right Rev. Bishop of, D.D.	M I
Fallon, Miss	I F N S
Farrar, Miss M. M.	W M M S L A
Fenn, Rev. Ch. C.	M I
Fenn, Mr. Robert	L M S
Fennell, Miss	M I
Ferguson, Mr. Wm.	F C S F M
Field, General, C.B.	I H M S
Fishe, Mr. Charles T.	C I M
Fleming, Rev. A. G.	U P C S F M
Fleming, Rev. Canon, B.D.	R T S
Fleming, Rev. J. R.	N B S S
Fleming, Rev. W., LL.B	L S P C J
Fleming, Miss	I P C F A
Fleming, Miss H. D.	I P C F A
Fletcher, Rev. Joseph	G B M S
Fordyce, Rev. John	M I
Fordyce, Mrs.	M I
Fortescue, Mr. J. F.	L A M M
Fowler, Right Hon. H. H., M.P.	W M M S
Fowler, Sir Robert N., Bart., M.P.	M I
Fox, Sir Douglas	C M S
Fox, Lady	C M S
Fox, Rev. H. E.	C M S
Fox, Dr. J. T.	F F M A
Fraser, Rev. D., D.D.	E P C
Fraser, Mrs. Donald	E P C W M A
Fraser, Miss	E P C W M A
Frean, Mr. G. H.	L M S
Freeman, Mr. Frederick	M I
Freeman, Miss E.	I F N S
Freese, Mr. F. W.	L A M M
Frere, Mrs. J. A.	C M S
Frost, Miss Emily	C I M
Fry, Mrs. R.	C M S
Fry, Miss E. C.	C M S

Fryer, Mr. John	M I
Fuller, Rev. A. R.	C M S
Fuller, Rev. J. J.	B M S
Fyson, Rev. P. K.	B F B S
Gard, Mr. William S.	L M S
Gardner, Rev. James F., B.D.	F C S F M
Gardner, Rev. William, M.A.	F C S F M
Gardner, Mr. Thomas	L M S
Gardner, Mrs.	L M S L C
Garnett, Mr. Thomas	S A M S
Gauld, Mr. William, M.D.	M M A
Gauld, Mrs.	M I
Gault, Miss	I F N S
Gedge, Mr. Sydney, M.P.	C M S
Gedge, Miss Mary R.	C M S
Gedye, Mr. Fras. W.	W M M S
George, Mrs.	B M S L A
Gibbon, Rev. Canon	C M S
Gibson, Rev. J. Monro, D.D.	E P C
Gibson, Mrs.	E P C W M A
Gilfillan, Rev. T.	L M S
Gilkes, Mr. A. H.	M I
Gill, Rev. W. Wyatt, B.A.	L M S
Gillespie, Rev. R.	I P C F M
Gillies, Rev. J. R.	E P C
Gilmore, Mrs.	I F N S
Gilpin, Miss	F F M A
Girdlestone, Canon	M I
Girdlestone, Rev. A. G.	C M S
Gladstone, Rev. George	L M S
Glenny, Mr. E. H.	N A M
Glover, Rev. R.	B M S
Glyn, Rev. Carr J.	B F B S
Goddard, Mr. D. Ford	L M S
Godfrey, Mr. W.	Z M C
Gollmer, Rev. C. H. V.	C M S
Goold, Rev. W. H., D.D.	N B S S
Gore, Miss	C E Z M S
Gotch, Rev. F. W., LL D.	B M S
Gough, Rev. Mr.	M I
Grant, Rev. Charles M.	C S F M
Grant, Dr.	E P C
Grant, Major-General]	F C S F M
Graves, Mrs.	I F N S
Gray, Rev. J. H., M.A.	C M S
Gray, Rev. W.	C M S
Gray, Mrs. W.	C M S
Greaves, Miss	C E Z M S
Green, Rev. S. G., D.D.	R T S
Green, Rev. W.	W M M S
Green, Mr. G. J.	Z M C
Green, Mrs. Henry	M I

Green, Mrs. S. G.	B M S L A	Hawkesley, Rev. Canon	M L A
Green, Miss S.	M I	Hay, Miss	W M M S L A
Greenhough, Rev. J. G., M.A.	B M S	Hayward, Mr. J. N.	C I M
Greeves, Rev. Dr.	W M M S	Head, Rev. G. F.	C M S
Greeves, Rev. J. W.	W M M S	Head, Mr. Albert	M I
Gregory, Rev. Dr.	W M M S	Healey, Miss	I F N S
Greig, Mrs.	U P C S Z M	Henderson, Lord Provost (Aber-	
Gresham, Mr. J. H.	L A M M	deen)	F C S F M
Griffin, Colonel	B M S	Henderson, Rev. W. J., B.A.	B M S
Griffith, Dr. G. de G.	Z M C	Herschell, Rev. Abraham	M I
Griffith, Mrs. W.	W M M S L A	Hetherwick, Rev. Alex., M.A.	C S F M
Gritton, Rev. John, D.D.	O M S	Hewitt, Mr. A. S.	L A M M
Grubb, Rev. G. C.	C M S	Hewitt, Miss	C M S
Grubb, Rev. H. P.	C M S	Hewlett, Rev. John, M.A.	L M S
Guinness, Mr. Grattan, F.R.G.S.	N A M	Hewlett Mrs. John	L M S L C
Guinness Dr. H. Grattan	M I	Highton, Miss E.	C E Z M S
Guinness, Mrs. Grattan	N A M	Hilditch, Mr. George	B S P G J
Guinness, Mrs. H. Grattan	M I	Hill, Rev. G., M.A.	B M S
Gunn, Surgeon-General	M I	Hill, Rev. William	G B M S
Gurney, Mr. J. J.	B M S	Hill, Mr. R. H.	C I M
Gurney, Mr. Richard H. J.	M I	Hill, Mr. T. Rowley, J.P.	L M S
Gurney, Mrs.	B M S	Hill, Mr. W. Byron, M.R.C.S.	Z M C
Gurney, Miss E. M.	W M M S L A	Hindsley, Rev. T.	L M S
Guttery Rev. T.	P M M S	Hiss, Madame	B S S
Guyton, Rev. R. F.	B M S	Hitchens, Rev. Dr.	Z M C
Gwanamutther, Mr.	W M M S	Hoare, Rev. Canon	C M S
		Hoare, Rev. J. C.	M I
Habershon Mr. W. G.	B S P G J	Hoare, Rev. J. G.	C M S
Hacker, Rev. I. H.	L M S	Hoare, Mr. S., M.P.	B S S
Hacker, Mrs. I. H.	L M S L C	Hoare, Mrs. S.	B S S
Haegert, Pastor A.	M I	Hobbles, Mr. R. G., F.R.S.L.	L S P C J
Haig, Major-General F. T., R.E.	N A M	Hobson, Rev. J. P.	C M S
Haig, Mrs. F. T.	N A M	Hodgkin, Mr. J. B.	F F M A
Hall, Mr. W.	C I M	Hogg, Mrs.	F E S
Halliday, Lieut.-General	C V E S	Hope, Miss Louisa	F E S
Hamilton, Ven. Archdeacon	O M S	Horder, Rev. W. G.	M I
Hamilton, Rev. R. W.	I P C F M	Houghton, Rev. W. S.	L M S
Hamilton, Rev. Thomas, D.D.	I P C F M	Houston, Miss	C S L A F M
Hamilton, Rev. W. F. T.	B S S	Howard, Mr. D.	L A M M
Hamilton, Mr. J. C.	Z M C	Howard, Mr. Elliot	C M S
Hamilton, Miss	I F N S	Howard, Mr. Theodore	C I M
Hanbury, Miss	M I	Howieson, Rev. W.	B M S
Haukin, General G. C., C B.	L S P C J	Hubbard, Mr. A.	B F B S
Hannay, Rev. Alexander, D.D.	L M S	Huggins, Dr.	M M A
Hannington, Mrs.	C M S	Hughes, Rev. H. P.	W M M S
Harris Mr. W. H.	B F B S	Hughes, Rev. J. Elias, M.A.	W C M F M S
Harrison, Rev. J.	C M S	Hughes, Rev. J. G.	L M S
Harrison, Mr. T. H.	G B M S	Hunt, Mr. Edward	C I M
Harrowby, The Rt. Hon. the Earl of	M I	Hunter, Sir William W., K.C.S.I., etc.	M I
Hart, Rev. T. Baron	E C S	Huron, Rt. Rev. Bishop of, D.D.	M I
Hartley, Mr. Fountain J.	M I	Hurry, Rev. N.	E C S
Harvey, Mr. T. M.	W M M S	Hurry, Mrs.	L M S L C
Hatton, Lieut.-Col. V. la Touche	Z M C	Hutcheon, Rev. John, M.A.	W M M S

Hutchins, Mr. A. R.	.	CVES
Hutchinson, Major-General	.	CMS
Hutchison, Mr. J., L.R.C.P. & S.E.		CSFM
Ingram, Rev. George S.	.	LMS
Iron, Mr. O. S.	.	LAMM
Jackson, Mr. Robert.	.	IHMS
Jacob, Mrs.	.	IPCFA
James, Rev. D. B.	.	LMS
James, Rev. F. H.	.	BMS
James, Rev. Lewis	.	LMS
James, Rev. W. B.	.	BMS
Janson, Mr. D.	.	LAMM
Jeffrey, Rev. Robert.		IPCFM
Jenkins, Rev. E. E., M.A.		WMMS
Jennings, Rev. Nathaniel	.	MI
Jepps, Mr. J. W.	.	WMMS
Jerrons, Miss	.	FES
Jewson, Rev. A.	.	BMS
Jobson, Mrs.		WMMSLA
Johnson, Mr. Lindsay, M.D.		BSS
Johnson, Mr. W.	.	WMMS
Johnson, Mrs. Lindsay		BSS
Johnston, Rev. R. E.	.	CMS
Johnstone, Miss	.	FES
Jones, Rev. Edward H.	.	LMS
Jones, Rev. J. Ireland	.	CMS
Jones, Rev. John	.	LMS
Jones, Rev. John		WCMFMS
Jones, Rev. W. Monk	.	LMS
Jones, Mr. E.	.	MI
Jones, Mr. H. Cadman	.	RTS
Jones, Mr. Joseph Harrison		WCMFMS
Jones, Mr. J. W.		WCMFMS
Jones, Mrs.	.	LMSLC
Jones, Mrs. J. Ireland	.	CMS
Jones, Mrs. John	.	LMSLC
Jones, Mrs. W. Monk	.	LMSLC
Joyce, Mrs. S. A.	.	LMSLC
Jukes, Dr. A.	.	CMS
Jukes, Rev. W.	.	CMS
Kalopothakes, Rev. Dr.	.	BFBS
Karney, Rev. Gilbert, M.A.		CEZMS
Kearns, Mrs.	.	CEZMS
Keen, Rev. J. O., D.D	.	BCMS
Kelly, Rev. C. H.	.	WMMS
Kelly, Rev. John	.	RTS
Kemp, Mr. Caleb R.	.	FFMA
Kennaway, Sir John H., Bart., M.P.		MI
Kennaway, Lady	.	CMS
Kennedy, Rev. J., M.A.	.	LMS

Kennedy, Rev. John, D.D.	.	LMS
Kenyon, Rev. G.	.	WMMS
Kilner, Rev. J.	.	WMMS
Kilner, Mr. W.	.	WMMS
King, Rev. W. H.	.	BSPGJ
Kinnaird, The Right Hon. Lord.		TMAS
Kinnaird, Rt. Hon. Dowager Lady		IFNS
Kinnaird, Hon. G.	.	IFNS
Knagga, Rev. James	.	LMS
Knight, Mrs.	.	BMSLA
Knowles, Rev. Frederick	.	LMS
Lachlan, Mr. H. N., B.A.	.	CIM
Laidlaw, Mr. Robert, M.D.	.	MMA
Laird, Dr.	.	MI
Lamb, Mrs.	.	CMS
Lambert, Rev. J. A.	.	LMS
Lambert, Mr. Charles W.	.	CIM
Lambert, Mrs. J. A.	.	LMSLC
Lamont, Mr. J.	.	EPC
Landale, Mr. R. J., M.A.	.	CIM
Landels, Rev. W., D.D.	.	BMS
Lang, Rev. R.	.	CMS
Lang, Mrs. R.	.	CMS
Lark, Rev. W. B.	.	BCMS
Lash, Rev. A. H.	.	IFNS
Lawder, General	.	CMS
Lawrence, Mr. Thomas	.	PMMS
Lea, Rev. George H.	.	LMS
Lee, Rev. W.	.	LMS
Lee, Mr. Henry, J.P.	.	LMS
Lee, Mr. Henry	.	LMS
Legg, Mr. D. J.	.	RTS
Leitch, Miss	.	MI
Leitch, Miss M. W.	.	MI
Lemon, Mrs.	.	IPCFA
Leonard, Mrs. H. Selfe		LBDFM
Lewis, Rev. C. B.	.	BMS
Lewis, Rev. W. S., M.A.	.	RTS
Lewis, Mr. Thomas, M.P.		WCMFMS
Liesching, Mr. Louis	.	MI
Lillingston, Rev. F. A. C.	.	CMS
Lindsay, Rev. Prof. T., D.D.		FCSFM
Lindsay, Mrs.	.	FCSLS
Ling, Miss	.	CEZMS
Linney, Mr. Charles	.	FFMA
Litchfield, Miss	.	CMS
Littleboy, Mr. Richard	.	FFMA
Lloyd, Miss	.	CEWMA
Lockhart, Mr. William	.	LMS
Lockhart, Miss R. E.		FCSLS
Logan, Miss	.	MI
Lombe, Rev. Edward	.	CMS

Lombe, Mrs. Edward	. .	C M S
Lones, Rev. Ezekiel .	. .	W M M S
Lord, Mrs. . .	. .	M I
Lovett, Rev. Richard, M.A.	.	R T S
Lowe, Rev. John, F.R.C.S.E.	.	E M M S
Lowe, Mrs. . .	. .	M I
Lundie, Rev. R. H. .	. .	E P C
Lyall, Mrs. David	.	U P C S Z M
Lynd, Rev. R. J. .	.	I P C F M
Mabbs, Rev. Goodeve	. .	M I
Macalister, Professor, F.R.S.	.	M I
Macaulay, Mr. James, M.D.	.	R T S
Macdonald, Rev. Finlay R.	.	C S F M
Macdonald, Rev. James	.	F C S F M
Macdonald, Mrs. .	. .	M I
MacEwan, Rev. David, D.D.	.	L M S
Macfarlane, Rev. S., LL.D. .	.	L M S
Macfarlane, Mrs.	. .	I F N S
Macfarlane, Mrs. S.	.	L M S L C
Macfie, Mr. R. A.	. .	M I
Macfie, Mrs. R. A.	. .	M I
Macgowan, Rev. J.	. .	M I
MacGregor, Mr. J.	. .	B F B S
MacGregor, Miss Ina .	.	C M S
MacInnes, Miss .	. .	C M S
MacInnes, Miss Agnes	.	U P C S Z M
Mackay, Rev. Patrick R.	.	F C S F M
Mackenzie, Rev. John	.	L M S
Mackenzie, Rev. W. D., M.A.	.	M I
Mackenzie, Mrs. John	.	L M S L C
Mackenzie, Miss	.	C S L A F M
Mackincoll, Mr. A. N.	.	B S P G J
MacKinnon, Mr. Peter	.	M I
MacKinnon, Mr. William .	.	M I
Maclagan, General, R.E.	.	L S P C J
Maclaren, Rev. A., D.D.	.	B M S
MacLean, Mr. J.	.	L M S
MacLean, Miss M. S.	.	L M S L C
MacLeod, Rev. A., D.D.	.	E P C
MacMillan, Rev. John	.	I P C F M
MacPhail, Rev. W. M.	.	E P C
MacPherson, Rev. D. P., D.D.	.	B M S
Macpherson, Mrs.	. .	F E S
MacPherson, Miss Annie .	.	M I
Mahaffy, Rev. Gilbert, M.A.	.	M L I
Malaher, Rev. W. E.	.	M L A
Malaher, Mr. Hubert G.	.	M L A
Malcolm, Mr. A. J. .	.	L M S
Mann, Rev. T. .	.	L M S
Mann, Miss .	.	E P C W M A
Mantle, Mr. Edward .	.	C M S
Marnham, Mr. J., J.P.	.	B M S
Marshall, Rev. J. W. .	. :	C M S
Marston, Dr. Henry .	.	M I
Marston, Miss A. K., L.K.Q.C.P.I.		I F N S
Martin, Miss .	.	U P C S Z M
Martyn, Mr. S. Symons	.	M I
Matheson, Mr. Donald	.	W C M
Matheson, Mr. H. M.	.	E P C
Matheson, Mr. T. .	.	E P C
Matheson, Mrs. H. M.	.	E P C W M A
Mathieson, Mr. J. E.	.	MyM
Mathieson, Mrs. J. E.	.	E P C W M A
Maughan, Mr. W. C.	.	N B S S
Maxwell, Mr. James L., M.D.	.	M M A
Maxwell, Mr. Richard	.	M I
Maxwell, Mrs. James L.	.	M I
Maylott, Rev. D. F.	.	P M M S
McArthur, Mr. A., M.P., F.R.G.S.		B F B S
McCalmont, Mrs.	.	F E S
McCree, Rev. G. W.	.	G B M S
McCullagh, Rev. T.	.	W M M S
McDowall, Miss M. H.	.	U P C S Z M
McFarland, Rev. George	.	I P C F M
McGregor, Rev. W.	.	E P C
McIlwraith, Mr. J.	.	L M S
McKenna, Rev. A.	.	B M S
McKenny, Rev. J.	.	W M M S
McKenzie, Miss H.	.	C I M
McLaren, Mr. David, J.P.	.	M I
McLaren, Mr. Duncan	.	U P C S F M
McLaren, Mr. James	.	L M S
McLaren, Mrs. Duncan	.	U P C S Z M
McLean, Dr.	. .	M I
McLean, Mrs.	.	C S L A F M
McLeod, Rev. J.	.	M I
McLeod, Mrs.	.	M I
McMaster, Mr. J. S.	.	B M S
McMurtrie, Rev. John, M.A.	.	C S F M
McMurtrie, Mrs. John	.	M I
McNair, Mr. M.	.	C I M
McNeill, Lady Emma	.	F C S L S
McNeill, Rev. George	.	U P C S F M
Meade, General Sir Richard	.	I F N S
Meade, Lady .	.	I F N S
Meadows, Rev. R. Rust	.	M I
Medley, Rev. E., B.A.	.	B M S
Melliss, Mr. J. C.	.	B S P G J
Melvill, Mr. P. S.	.	C M S
Melville, Miss .	.	U P C S Z M
Mennasseh, Dr. Bishara	.	F F M A
Menzies, Rev. James	.	L M S
Meredith, Mrs.	.	C E W M A
Meyer, Rev. F. B., B.A.	.	B M S
Meyer, Rev. Horace .	.	M I

Meyer, Rev. Theodore	M I
Middleton, Mrs.	L K S
Middleton, Miss	U P C S Z M
Midwinter, Mr. Henry F.	L M S
Miller, Rev. Prin., C.I.E., LL.D.	F C S F M
Mills, Mr. Arthur	C M S
Milne, Dr.	M M A
Milum, Rev. John	W M M S
Mitchell, Sir H.	W M M S
Mitchell, Rev. J. Murray, LL.D.	M I
Mitchell, Mrs. Murray	M I
Moffatt, Mrs.	F C S L S
Moinet, Mrs.	E P C W M A
Moncrieff, Mr. R. Scott	I H M S
Monier-Williams, Sir M., K.C.I.E., LL.D.	M I
Moore, Rev. C. G.	C I M
Moore, Rev. W. Kennedy, D.D.	M I
Moore, Mr. Joseph	B F B S
Moreton, Rev. W T.	L M S
Morgan, Mr. R. C.	N A M
Morley, Mr. William	M I
Morley, Miss	I F N S
Morris, Rev. R. E., B.A.	W C M F M S
Morris, Rev. T. M.	B M S
Morris, Rev. W.	B M S
Morris, Mr. Henry	C V E S
Morris, Mrs. Henry	C M S
Morton, Mr. J. T.	M I
Moule, Rev. H C. G.	C M S
Muir, Sir William, K.C.S.I., D.C.L.	I F N S
Muir, Lady	I F N S
Mulvany, Miss J.	C E Z M S
Mulvany, Miss S.	C E Z M S
Murdoch, Mr. John, LL.D.	M I
Murrell, Mrs. Charles	B M S L A
Myers, Rev. J. B.	B M S
Myers, Rev. M. T.	U M F C M
Nairn, Mr. William	U P C S F M
Nairn, Mrs. William	U P C S Z M
Nelson (N. Z.), Right Rev. Bishop of	M I
Nettleton, Rev. Joseph	W M M S
Now, Rev. Chas.	L M S
Newman, Mr J. E.	B S P G J
Newman, Miss H. M.	F F M A
Newth, Rev Samuel, D.D.	L M S
Newton, Rev. H.	C M S
Newton, Rev. Horace	M I
Nicol, Rev. Thomas	C S F M
Nicoll, Rev. W. Robertson	M I
Nicoll, Mr. George	C I M
Nicoll, Mrs.	C I M
Nicoll, Mrs. W. R.	M I

Nisbet, Rev. J. S.	N B S S
Noel, Hon. Henry	M I
Norris, Rev. Alfred	L M S
Northbrook, The Right Hon. the Earl of, G.C.S.I., D.C.L.	M I
Nugent, Mr. Richard	B S S
Nugent, Miss S. M.	C M S
Nuttall, Miss	C E W M A
Oldham, Colonel	C M S
Olver Rev. G. W., B.A.	W M M S
Ordish, Rev George S.	L M S
Ord-Mackenzie, Inspector-General W., M.D.	L S P C J
Orton, Mr. J. S.	L A M M
Osborn, Rev. Dr.	W M M S
Osborn, Rev. M. C.	W M M S
Ostle, Rev. W.	F A S
Owen, Rev. George	L M S
Owen, Rev. James	B M S
Owen, Mrs. George	L M S L C
Oxlad, Miss	F E S
Padfield, Rev. J. E., B.D.	C M S
Pagan, Rev. John, D.D.	C S F M
Pantin, Miss E.	C E Z M S
Park, Rev. William	I P C F M
Park, Mrs. William	I P C F A
Parker, Rev. E., D.D.	B M S
Parrott, Mr. A. G.	M I
Parry, Mr. J. C.	B M S
Parsons, Miss Emma	L M S L C
Paterson, Rev. H. Sinclair, M.D.	Z M C
Paterson, Mr. C. A., M.A., LL.B.	C S F M
Paton, Mr. Robert	R T S
Paton, Mr. W.	E P C
Paton, Mr. W. J.	I F N S
Paton, Miss	I F N S
Pattison, Mr. S. R., F.G.S.	R T S
Paul, Mr. G. B.	W M M S
Paul, Mr. T. D.	B M S
Paull, Rev. W. Major	B F B S
Payne, Mr. G. W.	L A M M
Payne, Mrs.	L M S L C
Pennefather, Mr. A. R.	C M S
Penrose, Miss	C E W M A
Perkins, Rev. James P.	L M S
Perks, Mr. R. W.	W M M S
Perry, Right Rev. Bishop, D.D.	B F B S
Perry, Mrs.	M I
Peto, Sir S. Morton	B M S
Peto, Lady	B M S L A
Petrie, Miss M. L. G., B.A.	M I

Sawyer, Mr. George D.	L M S
Scales, Mr. G. J.	W M M S
Scaramanga, Mrs.	F E S
Schaeffer, Mr. F.	B F B S
Schroder, Miss	My M
Sclater, Rev. J.	E P C
Scott, Rev. Archibald, D.D.	C S F M
Scott, Rev. Harry	L M S
Scott, Rev. James	F C S F M
Scott, Rev. J. Grierson	U P C S F M
Scott, Mrs.	L M S L C
Scott, Mrs. H.	L M S L C
Scowley, Rev. T.	M N C M S
Seaber, Mr. T.	W M M S
Seaman, Mr. W. M.	B F B S
Seaver, Rev. J.	M I
Seaver, Mrs. M. E.	C M S
Selby, Rev. T. G.	W M M S
Selincourt, Mr. C. D.	B F B S
Selincourt, Mrs. de	L M S L C
Selkirk, Mr. Thos.	C I M
Sell, Rev. E.	C M S
Sessions, Mr. Frederick	F F M A
Sewell, Mr. Joseph S.	F F M A
Shackell, Mrs.	C M S
Shakespeare, Rev. J. H., M.A.	B M S
Sharp, Rev. J., M.A.	B F B S
Sharp, Mr. Wm.	C I M
Sharpe, Rev. Henry	C M S
Shaw, Rev. A. D.	C M S
Shaw, Rev. George	I P C F M
Shaw, Rev. J. Hall	C M S
Shaw, Rev. W. W.	I P C F M
Shaw, Miss Marion	I P C F A
Sheppard, Mr. S. G.	I F N S
Sherbrooke, Rev. H. N.	C M S
Sherring, Mrs.	L M S L C
Shillidy, Rev. J.	L P C F M
Shillington, Miss E. C.	W M M S L A
Shirreff, Rev. F. A. P.	C M S
Shoolbred, Rev. W., D.D.	U P C S F M
Short, Rev. G., B.A.	B M S
Sidgett, Mrs. J. J.	W M M S L A
Sierra Leone, Rt. Rev. Bp. of, D.D.	C M S
Silver, Mr. S. W.	B F B S
Simester, Mr. J.	B S P G J
Simpson, Rev. R. J.	S A M S
Sinclair, Mr. Thomas, J.P.	I P C F M
Sinclair, Mrs.	U P C S Z M
Skilbeck, Mr. J.	M I
Sleigh, Rev. James	L M S
Sleigh, Mrs. James	L M S L C
Slight, Mr. John	U P C S F M
Slowan, Mr. Wm. J.	N B S S
Small, Mr. D. H.	T M A S
Smith, Rev. F., M.A.	L S P C J
Smith, Rev. G.	E P C
Smith, Rev. G. Furness	C M S
Smith, Rev. James	L M S
Smith, Rev. John, M.A.	U P C S F M
Smith, Rev. John	P M M S
Smith, Rev. Prof. T., D.D.	F C S F M
Smith, Rev. W. Joseph, M.A., F.R.G.S.	C M S
Smith, Rev. W. M.	E P C
Smith, Mr. Abel, M.P.	C M S
Smith, Mr. B. Woodd, J.P.	B F B S
Smith, Mr. C.	W M M S
Smith, Mr. George, C.I.E., LL.D.	F C S F M
Smith, Mr. J. J.	B M S
Smith, Mr. P. V.	C M S
Smith, Mr. Samuel	I H M S
Smith, Mrs. J. T.	B M S L A
Smith, Miss	B M S L A
Smith, Miss	F E S
Snape, Mr. Thomas	U M F C M
Solomon, Mr. S. R. B.	M I
Soltau, Mr. Henry	C I M
Soltau, Mrs.	C I M
Spensley, Rev. W.	L M S
Spicer, Mr. A., J.P.	L M S
Spicer, Mr. Edward	M I
Spicer, Mr. George	B F B S
Spicer, Mrs. Edward	M I
Spicer, Mrs. Evan	L M S L C
Spong, Rev. Ambrose D.	L M S
Spurgeon, Rev. C. H.	B M S
Spurgeon, Rev. J. A.	B M S
Spurrier, Rev. E.	B M S
Squires, Rev. R. H.	C M S
Starkey, Mr. S. F.	L M S
Steane, Mrs. Eliza	B M S L A
Stephen, Mr. J.	F C S F M
Stephen, Miss	F C S L S
Stephens, Rev. James, M.A.	N A M
Stephens, Rev. J. M., B.A.	B M S
Stephens, Mr. Horatio	L M S
Stephenson, Rev. Dr.	W M M S
Stephenson, Rev. Jabez B.	M I
Stephenson, Rev. Robert, B.A.	W M M S
Stevens, Mr. William	R T S
Stevenson, Rev. William	F C S L S
Stevenson, Mr. James	M I
Stevenson, Mrs.	C I M
Stevenson, Mrs.	E P C W M A
Stevenson, Mrs. James	M I
Stevenson, Mrs. W. Fleming	I P C F A

Stewart, Rev. Canon, D.D.	C M S	Thornton, Rev. R. M.	E P C
Stewart, Rev. James, M.D.	M I	Thornton, Mrs.	E P C W M A
Stirling, Miss A.	F E S	Tilly, Rev. A.	B M S
Stock, Mr. Eugene	C M S	Tindall, Rev. R. A.	M I
Stock, Miss	M I	Tinling, Rev. J. F. B.	M I
Stoker, Dr.	Z M C	Todd, Miss C. R.	C I M
Stone, Mr. Thomas	I H M S	Torrance, Rev. Arch., B.D.	U P C S F M
Stone, Miss F.	M I	Touch, Lieut.-Gen. J. G.	C M S
Storrow, Rev. Edward	L M S	Townsend, Rev. Thomas	L M S
Stott, Mr. George	C I M	Townsend, Rev. W. J.	M N C M S
Stott, Mrs.	C I M	Toy, Mrs.	L M S L C
Stoughton, Rev. John, D.D.	R T S	Trafford, Rev. J., M.A.	B M S
Stoughton, Mrs.	M I	Trafford, Mrs.	B M S L A
Stoughton, Miss	L M S L C	Traill, Rev. John	U P C S F M
Stuart, Mr. James	C E Z M S	Travancore, Rt. Rev. Bp. of, D.D.	C M S
Stubb, Rev. S. D.	C M S	Trench. Mr. Frank	C I M
Summers, Rev. E. S., B.A.	B M S	Tresidder, Mrs.	B M S L A
Sutcliffe, Mr. J. S., J.P.	W M M S	Trestrail, Rev. F., D.D.	B M S
Sutherland, Mr. H. H.	I H M S	Treugove, Rev. A.	B C M S
Sutton, Rev. H.	C M S	Tristram, Miss	C E Z M S
Sutton, Mr. Alfred	M I	Tritton, Mr. J. Herbert	M I
Swanson, Rev. W. S.	E P C	Tritton, Mrs. J. Herbert	F E S
Swanston, Mr. J. A.	E P C	Tugwell, Rev. Canon	C M S
Sylvester, Mr. H. T., M.D., V.C.	Z M C	Turnbull, Mr. R. T.	E P C
		Turner, Rev. F. Storrs	M I
Tait, Mr. G. Martin	C M S	Turner, Rev. G., LL.D.	M I
Tait, Miss	F E S	Turner, Rev. T.	C M S
Tarn, Rev. T. G.	B M S	Turner, Miss	C I M
Tasker, Rev. J. G.	W M M S	Tweddle, Rev. W. J.	W M M S
Taylor, Rev. Edward	L M S	Tyler, Rev. Wm., D.D.	L M S
Taylor, Rev. J. Hudson	C I M	Tyler, Mr. Charles	B F B S
Taylor, Rev. Robert	M I		
Taylor, Mrs. J. Hudson	C I M	Underhill, Mr. E. B., LL.D.	B M S
Tebb, Rev. Robert	W M M S	Upton, Rev. W. C.	B M S
Telford, Rev. J., B.A.	W M M S	Urmston, Mrs.	C M S
Temple, Sir Richard, Bart., M.P.	Z M C	Urwick, Miss	F E S
Thomas, Rev. H. Arnold, M.A.	L M S		
Thomas, Rev. James	B F B S	Vanner, Mr. W.	W M M S
Thomas, Rev. John, B.A.	W C M F M S	Vanstone, Rev. J. B.	B C M S
Thomas, Rev. Josiah, M.A.	W C M F M S	Vaughan, Rev. John	G B M S
Thomas, Rev. J. W.	B M S	Vidal, Miss	M I
Thomas, Rev. N.	B M S	Vincent, Rev. S.	B M S
Thomas, Rev. Urijah R.	L M S	Viney, Rev. Josiah	L M S
Thompson, Sir Rivers, K.C.S.L.	C M S	Viney, Mr. Arthur E.	M I
Thompson, Rev. R. Wardlaw	L M S		
Thompson, Mrs.	L M S L C	Wade, Rev. T. Russell	C M S
Thompson, Miss E. Wharton	C M S	Waiapu, Right Rev. Bishop of, D.D.	C M S
Thomson, Rev. Alex., D.D.	B F B S	Waite, Mr. H. W.	E P C
Thomson, Rev. J. H.	E P C	Wakefield, Rev. Thomas	U M F C M
Thomson, Mr. W. Burns, F.R.S.E.	M M A	Waldock, Rev. F. D.	B M S
Thomson, Mrs.	L M S	Walker, Mr. G.	W M M S
Thomson, Mrs. W. Burns	M I	Walker, Mr. Theodore	N A M
Thorp, Miss	B M S L A	Walker, Mr. William	M I

Wallbridge, Mrs. . .	L M S L C
Waller, Rev. D. J. . .	. W M M S
Wallinger, Miss . .	C E Z M S
Wallis, Mr. Charles T. .	. L M S
Walser, Mr. E. .	. B F B S
Walton, Rev. J., M.A. .	. W M M S
Walton, Rev. J. H. .	. L M S
Walton, Mr. W. Spencer .	. M I
Wanton, Miss . .	C E Z M S
Ward, Rev. A. . .	. W M M S
Ward, Mr. F. Peterson .	. C M S
Wardlaw, Mrs. John .	. F E S
Ware, Mr. Martin .	. B F B S
Wareham, Rev. E. A. .	. L M S
Warren, Rev. Charles .	. M I
Waterston, Miss M. D. .	F C S L S
Watson, Rev. J. George .	. M I
Watson, Mr. W. L. . .	. I H M S
Watson, Mrs. Jas. .	. E P C W M A
Watts, Rev. J. C., D.D. .	M N C M S
Weakley, Rev. R. H. .	. B F B S
Weatherley, Mr. James .	. M I
Weatherley, Mrs. . .	. F E S
Webb, Miss . . .	. F E S
Webb-Peploe, Rev. H. .	. C M S
Webb-Peploe, Mrs. H. .	. C M S
Webster, Miss . .	W M M S L A
Weir, Rev. R. W . .	C S F M
Weitbrecht, Rev. Dr. .	. M I
Welby, Mrs. . . .	. I F N S
Werner, Mr. L P. . .	. B F B S
West, Rev. J. M. . .	. C M S
West, Mr. W. N. . .	L S P C J
Whately, Ven. Archdeacon	. S A M S
Whately, Miss Mary .	. M I
Wheeler, Rev. T. A. . .	. B M S
Wheeler, Mr. H. S. . .	. L M S
White, Rev. Edward .	. L M S
White, Rev. L. B., D.D. .	. R T S
White, Mr. G. F. . .	. B F B S
White, Mr. J. C. . .	F C S F M
White, Mr. R. Holms .	. R T S
White, Mrs. Edward .	B M S L A
White, Miss A. L. . .	. C M S
Whitehead, Rev. Silvester	W M M S
Whitehead, Rev. Thomas .	. P M M S
Whiting, Rev. J. B. . .	. C M S
Whitwell, Mr. Edward .	. L M S
Whitworth, Mr. J. . .	. M N C M S
Whyte, Mr. R., Junr. .	L A M M
Wickson, Rev. A., LL.D. .	B S P G J
Wigram, Rev. F. E. . .	. C M S
Wigram, Mr. E. F. E. .	. C M S

Wigram, Mrs. . . .	. C M S
Wilkin, Rev. S. R. . .	W M M S
Wilkin, Mrs. . .	W M M S L A
Wilkins, Rev. H. . .	. B M S
Wilkins, Rev. W. J. . .	. L M S
Wilkins, Mr. W. G. . .	. L M S
Wilkinson, Rev. John .	My M
Wilkinson, Mrs. F. W. A. .	. C M S
Williams, Rev. C. .	. B M S
Williams, Rev. E. O. .	. C I M
Williams, Rev. H. .	. C M S
Williams, Rev. H. C. .	. B M S
Williams, Mr. George .	. B F B S
Williams, Mr. H. R. .	. R T S
Williams, Mr. John H. .	. F F M S
Williams, Mr. R., Junr. .	. C M S
Williams, Mrs. .	. C I M
Williams, Mrs. R. .	. M I
Williams, Miss . .	. M I
Williamson, Rev. A. W., LL.D. .	M I
Williamson, Mrs. . .	F C S L S
Wilson, Rev. C., M.A. .	. L M S
Wilson, Rev. George .	C S F M
Wilson, Rev. George, M.A. .	B F B S
Wilson, Dr. . .	. C I M
Wilson, Mr. John E. .	. F F M A
Wilson, Mrs. . . .	. C I M
Wiltshire, Rev. D. . .	. M I
Windle, Rev. W. . .	. S A M S
Wingate, Rev. William .	B S P G J
Wiseman, Mrs. .	W M M S L A
Wood, Rev. D. . .	. C M S
Wood, Rev. John . .	. L M S
Wood, Rev. J. R. . .	. B M S
Wood, Mr. F. J., LL.D. .	. B F B S
Wood, Mr. P. F. . .	. B F B S
Woods, Rev. W. J., B.A. .	. L M S
Woolmer, Rev. T. . .	W M M S
Workman, Rev. R. . .	I P C F M
Workman, Mr. John, J.P. .	I P C F M
Wotherspoon, Miss Alice J. .	M I
Wright, Rev. E. . .	M N C M S
Wright, Rev. Morley .	. L M S
Wright, Rev. William, D.D. .	B F B S
Wright, Mrs. . . .	. C M S
Wright, Mrs. H. . .	. C M S
Young, Rev. Dr. . .	W M M S
Young, Rev. D. D. . .	F C S F M
Young, Rev. John, M.A. .	U P C S F M
Young, Colonel Arch. G. .	F C S F M
Young, Colonel S. Denholm .	M I
Young, Mr. Jasper . .	. E P Q

Young, Mr. Robert . . .	E P C	Young, Mrs. . . .	F C S L S
Young, Mr. William, J.P. .	I P C F M	Young, Miss . . .	I P C F A
Young, Mrs. William .	I P C F A		

UNITED STATES OF AMERICA.

Adam, Mrs. J. N. . . .	XLIII	Davis, Miss Gettie . .	LI
Aiken, Rev. Charles A., D.D. .	LVIII	Deovies, Mr. Christian . .	XXIII
Alexander, Mr. A. . .	XIII	Derrick, Rev. W. B., D.D. . .	XXXV
Allen, Rev. Young J., D.D. .	XV	Dobbins, Rev. Frank S. .	LVIII
Anderson, Rev. G. W., D.D. .	III	Dowkontt, Mr. G. D., M.D. .	XXX
Anthony, Rev. Alfred W. .	XXV	Dugdale, Mrs. William .	LII
Armitage, Rev. Thomas, D.D. .	LVIII		
Armstrong, Rev..W. F. . .	II	Ellinwood, Rev. F. F., D.D. .	XI
Armstrong, Mrs. W. F. . .	II	Ellinwood, Mrs. F. F. .	XLIII
Arnold, Rev. T. B. . . .	XXVIII	Ellis, Rev. F. M., D.D. .	III
		Emerson, Rev. F. F. .	LVIII
Babcock, Mr. G. H. . .	XXXVI	Emerson, Mrs. Ralph .	LVII
Babcock, Mrs. G. H. .	XLVIII	Esher, Bishop J. J. . . .	XXXIII
Bacon, Rev. H. M., D.D. .	LVIII		
Bailey, Miss Mary F. .	XLVIII	Fisk, General Clinton B. . .	LVIII
Barboza, Mrs. M. H. Garnet	XXXIV	Fitch, Miss Jessie C. . .	——
Beard, Rev. A. F., D.D. . .	VIII	Fitz, Hon. Eustace C. . .	II
Belden, Rev. W. H. . .	XXXI	Fitzgerald, Rev. J. N., D.D. .	XXXII
Belden, Mrs. W. H. . .	XXXI	Forsythe, Mrs. Henry .	LVI
Bell, Rev. C. H., D.D. . .	XIV	Fowler, Mr. Anderson .	XXXVII
Blackstone, Mr. W. E.	XVIII & XXIX	Fowler, Mrs. Anderson .	XXXVII
Bliss, Mr. Howard S. .	LVIII		
Boardman, Rev. G. D., D.D. .	LVIII	Gilman, Rev. Ed. W., D.D. .	IV
Boardman, Mrs. G. D. .	LV & LVII	Gilman, Miss E. S. . .	XLV
Bonney, Miss Mary L. .	LV	Gladden. Rev. Washington, D.D.	LVIII
Borden, Miss Carrie . .	XLV	Gordon, Rev. A. J., D.D. . .	II
Braislin, Rev. Edward, D.D. .	LVIII	Gordon, Mrs. A. J. . .	XL
Brewster, Mrs. M. M. .	XXVI	Gracey, Rev. J. T., D.D. .	XXXI
Briggs, Rev. C. H., D.D. .	LVIII	Grant, Rev. Miles . .	I
Brounell, Mrs. C. G. .	LVI	Graves, Hon. N. F. . .	LVIII
Brown, Mr. Harold . .	LVIII	Gring, Rev. A. D. . .	XVII
		Gulick, Rev. J. F. . . .	V
Camp, Mr. I. N. . .	LVIII		
Camp, Mrs. I. N. . .	XLVI	Hall, Dr. John . .	LVIII
Case, Mr. C. H. . .	LVIII	Hart, Miss Isabel . .	L
Case, Mrs. C. H. . .	XLVI	Hatcher, Rev. William E., D.D. .	III
Chambers, Rev. R. . .	V	Hayes, Mrs. Juliana . .	XLVII
Chambers, Rev. T. W., D.D. .	XII	Horn, Rev. D. Van, D.D. .	XVII
Chase, Mrs. M. J. . .	XL	Houston, Rev. M. H., D.D. .	XXIII
Child, Miss Abbie B. .	XLV	Hoyt, Rev. Wayland, D.D. .	LVIII
Clark, Rev. N. G., D.D. . .	V	Hutchinson, Mrs. Elizabeth C. .	XLIX
Clarke, Miss Ella, M.D. .	XLVIII		
Coburn, Mrs. G. W. . .	XLV	Jackson, Rev. S. M. .	LVIII
Cole, Rev. David, D.D. .	LVIII	Jay, Hon. John . .	LVIII
Coppin, Mrs. Fanny M. J. .	XXXIX	Jones, Rev. W. M., D.D. .	XXXVI
Cowen, Mrs. B. R. . .	L	Judson, Rev. Edward, D.D. .	LVIII

Keister, Mrs. L. R.	LIII
Kip, Rev. Leonard W.	XII
Kneeland, Rev. Martin, D.D.	LVIII
Langford, Rev. William S., D.D.	XIX
Lefevre, Rev. J. A., D.D.	XXIII
Lewis, Rev. A. H., D.D.	XXXVI
Lombard, Miss M. I.	XLIII
Lowe, Mrs. J. E.	XLI
Mabie, Rev. H. C., D.D.	LVIII
MacArthur, Rev. R. S., D.D.	III
Main, Rev. A. E., D.D.	XXXVI
Mallalieu, Bishop W. F.	XXXII
McAllister, Rev. D., LL.D.	XIII
McClurkin, Rev. J. K., D.D.	XIII
McCorkle, Rev. E. W., D.D.	XXIII
McFalls, Rev. D.	XIII
McLean, Rev. A.	XX
McLeod, Rev. J.	LVIII
Miles, Rev. Charles	LVIII
Miller, Mrs. L. K.	LIII
Miller, Mrs. Mary A.	LI
Mitchell, Rev. J. B., D.D.	XIV
Moore, Rev. Halsey, D.D.	LVIII
Morgan, Mr. James L.	XXII
Murdock, Rev. John N., D.D.	II
Murkland, Rev. W. M., D.D.	XXIII
Newman, Rev. S. M., D.D.	LVIII
Nind, Mrs. Mary C.	L
Noble, Rev. F. A., D.D.	LVIII
Noble, Miss M. P.	XLVI
Orden, Rev. Emmanuel Van	LVIII
Outland, Professor Philander	XXXV
Parke, Rev. N. G., D.D.	LVIII
Pateon, Rev. Samuel	X
Pattison, Rev. T. H., D.D.	LVIII
Peet, Mr. W. W.	V
Phillips, Mr. John M.	XXXII
Phraner, Rev. W.	XI
Pierson, Rev. A. T., D.D.	LVIII
Pierson, Mrs. A. T.	LII
Pitzer, Rev. A. W., D.D.	XXXVIII
Post, Rev. George E., M.A., M.D.	LVIII
Potter, Rev. J. L.	XI
Potter, Mr. Charles	XXXVI
Pritchard, Rev. T. H., D.D.	III
Pullan, Rev. F. B.	LVIII
Quinton, Mrs. Amelia S.	LV

Rambaut, Rev. Thomas, D.D., LL.D.	LVIII
Reid, Rev. J. M., D.D.	XXXII
Roberts, Rev. B. T.	XXVIII
Roberts, Rev. D. P., M.D.	XXXV
Roberts, Prof. B. H., A.M.	XXVIII
Robinson, Rev. Thomas H., D.D.	LVIII
Rood, Rev. D.	LVIII
Rust, Mr. G. H.	LVIII
Sabine, Rev. W. T.	XXII
Schaff, Rev. Philip, D.D., LL.D.	LVIII
Scovel, Mrs. Sylvester F.	XLIII
Severance, Mrs. S. L.	XLIII
Sewall, Rev. John S., D.D.	LVIII
Shaffer, Rev. C. T.	XXXV
Skidmore, Mrs. H. B.	L
Smith, Rev. Judson, D.D.	V
Smith, Dr. J. R.	LVIII
Smith, Mrs. Moses	XLVI
Stephens, Mrs. A. H.	XLII
Stevenson, Rev. Samuel Brown	X
Stewart, Mr. George	XII
Stout, Rev. Henry	XII
Strieby, Rev. M. E., D.D.	VIII
Strong, Rev. Josiah, D.D.	LVIII
Strong, Mr. Theodore	LVIII
Summerbell, Rev. N., D.D.	VI
Syle, Rev. Edward W., D.D.	VII
Tagg, Rev. F. T.	XVI
Taylor, Rev. J. A.	IX
Taylor, Rev. W. J. R., D.D.	XII
Taylor, Rev. William M., D.D.	LVIII
Taylor, Mrs. W. J. R.	XLIV
Thomas, Mrs. E. C.	XXI
Thompson, Rev. A. C., D.D.	V
Thompson, Mr. William	XXVII
Thompson, Mrs. A. C.	XLV
Thompson, Mrs. Susan	XXVII
Thurston, Rev. John R.	V
Torrey, Mr. Elbridge	V
Tupper, Rev. H. A., D.D.	XXIV
Vanderbilt, Mr. Cornelius	LVIII
Velthuysen, Rev. G.	XXXVI
Wagner, Rev. S. G., D.D.	XVII
Weiser, Rev. C. L., D.D.	XVII
Welch, Professor R. B., LL.D.	LVIII
Wells, Rev. C. L., D.D.	XII
Weston, Rev. H. G., D.D.	LVIII
Whitford, Rev. O. U.	XXXVI
Whitford, Mrs. O. U.	XLVIII

Williams, Rev. Leighton . . LVIII
Williams, Col. and Hon. G. W., LL.D. LVIII
Williamson, Mr. Cornelius T. . XII
Wilson, Bishop A. W., D.D. . XV

Wishard, Mr. Luther D. . . LVIII
Woodside, Mrs. T. W. . . LIV
Wyckoff, Mrs. J. N. . . . XL
Wylie, Mrs. R. M. . . . XLIII

CANADA.

Blackstock, Mrs. W. S. . . LXVII
Burson, Rev. George . . . LXI
Burton, Rev. John, D.D. . . LXIV

Cruikshank, Rev. W. R. . . LXI

Duff, Rev. Charles, M.A. . . LXIV
Everett, Rev. Thomas . . LXIII

Fleck, Rev. James, B.A. . . LXI

Grant, Rev. James . . . LIX

Hay, Mr. George, J.P. . . LXI

Jordan, Rev. L. H. . . . LXI
Junor, Rev. Kenneth F., M.D. . LXI

Macdonald, Hon. John . . LXII
Macdonald, Mr. J. D., M.D. . LXI

Maclaren, Rev. Professor, D.D. . LXI
Maclaren, Mrs. LXVI
MacVicar, Rev. D. H., D.D., LL.D. LXI
MacVicar, Mr. J. H., B.A. . . LXI
Mathews, Rev. G. D., D.D. . LXI
McLaurin, Rev. John . . . LIX
McMurrich, Mr. W. B. . . LXI
Milligan, Rev. G. M., A.M. . LXI

Parsons, Rev. H. M., D.D. . LXI

Saer, Rev. John B., B.D. . . LX
Shenston, Mr. T. S. . . . LIX
Skinner, Mrs. LXVII
Stewart, Rev. W. J. . . . LIX
Stewart, Mrs. W. J. . . . LXV
Sutherland, Rev. Alexander, D.D. LXII

Warden, Rev. R. H., D.D. . . LXI
Watson, Mrs. James . . LXVI

CONTINENT OF EUROPE.

Appia, Rev. G. . . . LXXIII

Bertrand, Professor . . . —
Boegner, Rev. Alfred . . LXXIII
Bruyn, Herr Van Oosterwijk . LXXIV

Cachet, Rev. F. Lion . . LXXII
Creux, Rev. Ernest . . . LXXV

Dahle, Rev. L. . . . LXXXI
Descœudres, Rev. Paul . . LXXV
Drost, Rev. Dr. A. . . . LXXVII
Drury, Mr. Wm. V., M.D. . LXXVI
Dumas, Rev. Frederick . . LXXIII

Engvall, Mr. Carl . . . LXXXIV

Feldmann, Mr. C. H. . . LXXVI
Frater, Rev. A. W., M.A. . . LXXXV

Grundemann, Rev. Dr. (Germany) —

Hanna, Rev. G. H. . . . LXXVI
Hesse, Rev. J. . . . LXXVI
Hines, Rev. T. H. . . . LXXVI
Holm, Rev. W. . . . LXXI
Hoorn, Rev. B. Van den . LXX
Hoorn, Rev. S. A. Van den . LXX

Kammerer, Rev. Paulus . . LXVIII
Knüsli, Rev. John . . . LXXX

Merensky, Rev. A. . . . LXIX

Nyström, Dr. Erik . . . LXXXIV

Pemsel, Mr. J. F. . . . LXXVI
Pfleiderer, Herr G. . . . LXVIII
Porter, Rev. J. A. . . . LXXVI

Rappard, Rev. C. H. . . LXXXIII
Reesse, Rev. J. C. LXXVIII & LXXXV
Robbins, Rev. W. . . . LXXVI

Romig, Rev. B. . . . LXXVI

Schreiber, Dr. A. . . . LXXXII
Stirum, Count Van Limburg . LXXVII
Stursberg, Herr Julius . . LXXIX

Taylor, Rev. W. . . . LXXVI

Trobe, Rev. B. La . . . LXXVI

Vahl, Dean LXXI
Viehe, Rev. F. W. . . . LXXXII

Warneck, Rev. G., D.D. (Germany) ——

Ziegler, Rev. Fr. . . . LXVIII

COLONIAL.

Murray, Rev. A. M . LXXXVII | Reyneke, Rev. J. C. . LXXXVII

Veal, Mr. J. W. . . .LXXXVI

PROGRAMME

OF

CONFERENCE ON MISSIONS.

From June 9th to 19th, 1888.

WEDNESDAY, JUNE 13th.

THURSDAY, JUNE 14th.

TUESDAY, JUNE 19th.

The following gentlemen formed a Committee, having charge of the meetings during the sittings of the Conference:—

INDEX.

tion to literature, 317; English literature in India, 325.
Motto of the Missionary model, St. Paul, 82.
Multiplying Missionary agencies, danger of, *Warneck*, 434.
Murdoch, John, LL.D., his literary services in India, *Northbrook*, 273.
His work in China, *L. B. White*, 338.
Abstract of his work in connection with the C.V.E.S., 340.
Paper on the Missionary in relation to literature (read by Mr. Henry Morris), 317—323.
Murdock, Rev. J. N., D.D. Paper on Women's Work in the Foreign Field, 160—168; the training of native workers, 377; difficulty between American Baptist and Lutheran Missionary Societies, 447.
Mutual relations of Missionary Societies. *See* **Missionary Comity.**
National Bible Society of Scotland, extent of its work, *Sloman*, 297.
Native Agent. *See* **Native Workers.**
Native Churches. A united Church in India impossible, *Stuart*, 342.
Organisation and results of the Basle Mission in China, *Kammerer*, 344—350.
Formation of an evangelistic association in Tinnevelly, *Caldwell*, 353.
Means for self-support and government (India), *Caldwell*, 356.
Church organisation in Amoy, *McGregor*, 357.
Organising evangelistic work, *Haegert*, 358.
The union of Churches in Japan, 359; self-government, 360, *Warren*.
Wesleyan organisation in Ceylon, *Tebb*, 360.
Organisation in Madagascar, *H. E. Clark*, 361.
Missions should lead to self-government, *T. Smith*, 362.
Development of, *Gulick*, 363.
A limit to independence, 364; Presbyterianism in Java; must support evangelists, 365, *Cachet*.
Self-government not to be given prematurely, *Hanna*, 366.
Experience of the C.M.S. in India, *Gray*, 366.
The training of native workers, *Stephenson*, 369; *Hewlett*, 373—376.
Importance of a trained native agency, *Murdock*, 377.
The object of Missions to establish, *Swanson*, 379.
Presbyterianism in Japan, *Gring*, 385.
Organisation in the West Indies, *East*, 395.

Native Churches. Church architecture, *Wigram*, 401; *Mrs. Bishop*, 416; *Sleigh*, 420; *Macfie*, 422.
Self-support, *Wigram*, 401.
Experience of self-support in Athens, *Kalopothakes*, 421.
Zulu church building, *Rood*, 423.
Organisation in New Guinea, 424.
Self-support, *Baldwin*, 427.
A Chinese church for China, *Williamson*, 461.
Independence a natural growth, . *J. R. Taylor*, 467.
Self-government should mean self-support, 472; reasons against home direction of a foreign Church; ecclesiastical organisation by natives, 473; differences of ritual and Church government, 474; Lightfoot on "Church government"; conditions which affect forms of government, 475; probability of an Indian Church, 476; Apostolic succession, 477, *Fenn*.
Growth of a Church in Amoy, *Kip*, 477.
Independence often withheld too long, *T. Smith*, 480.
Example of unity must be shown by Missionaries, *Kalopothakes*, 480.
United Church of Japan, *Taylor*, 466; *Gring*, 484.
Native Converts. *See* **Converts.**
—— customs to be retained by children in schools, *Morris*, 221.
To be considered by Missionaries, *Mrs. Bishop*, 416.
—— **Female Agency, a,** *Miss Mann*, 178; *Mrs. Nind*, 180.
—— **helpers** to be respected, *Hesse*, 37.
—— **itinerant Missionaries** in China, *Ross*, 43.
—— **labour,** success from, *Murdock*, 377.
—— **opinion** of Englishmen, *Phraner*, 553.
—— **pastors.** *See* **Native Workers.**
Native workers, the training of, 373—376; individual training; the establishment of central institutions, 374; training in the vernacular or English; educating agents in Europe and America, 375; Western methods objected to, 376, *Hewlett*.
In connection with the Basle Mission in China, *Kammerer*, 346.
The training of, *Stephenson*, 369.
Importance of their work, *Murdock*, 377.
To take the place of Missionaries, *Aiken*, 378.
Objections to educating them in the West, *Swanson*, 379.
Reasons against an English education; high education and high pay, 380, *Owen*.

Lightning Source UK Ltd.
Milton Keynes UK
UKHW020258310119
336487UK00011B/782/P